Canon Law Society of America

Proceedings of the Eighty-Fifth Annual Convention

Milwaukee, Wisconsin
October 9-12, 2023

Canon Law Society of America

ISBN 978-1-932208-68-9
ISSN 0277-9889
SAN 237-6296

Unless otherwise noted, all canons quoted are from the *Code of Canon Law, Latin-English Edition* (Washington, DC: Canon Law Society of America, 2023) and the *Code of Canons of the Eastern Churches, Latin-English Edition* (Washington, DC: Canon Law Society of America, 2001).

Printed in the United States of America.

Canon Law Society of America
415 Michigan Avenue NE, Suite 101
Washington, DC 20017-4502

TABLE OF CONTENTS

FOREWORD

The Canon Law Society of America is pleased to publish the *Proceedings of the Eighty-Fifth Annual Convention*. This year's convention was held in Milwaukee, Wisconsin, from October 9 through 12, 2023.

The events of the 2023 convention are recorded here in these *Proceedings*, and they join eighty-four years of previous publications from our annual gatherings. The theme for this year's convention was "Role of Law in the Life of the Church: Is It Relevant Now?"

We are grateful to all of the presenters who expertly delivered their presentations and, in a special way, to those who submitted their written texts for this publication. Their contributions have been edited in conformity with the most recent CLSA style and publication guidelines and with previous editions of *Proceedings*. Our annual business meeting was held on Wednesday, October 11, and the minutes from that meeting are included herein with the varia.

We are grateful to all of those who stood for election, and we look forward to working with all those who were elected to serve the Society. We were very happy to welcome more than 400 attendees to the three-day convention. A list of participants is included at the end of this volume.

Special thanks go to Ms. Kathleen Butler (General Secretary) and Mr. Mark Francisco (Membership Coordinator) for their indispensable help in preparing this volume of *Proceedings* for publication.

The CLSA, established as a professional association on November 12, 1939, presently has more than 1200 members who serve the People of God in more than thirty countries. Interested persons may apply for membership via the CLSA website (clsa.org) or by contacting the administrative office. We offer Active, Associate, and Student memberships to qualified persons. A new member type—the Morrisey Membership—was approved in 2020. Details can be found on the CLSA's website.

Additional copies of this issue of *Proceedings* may be purchased at clsa.org.

Donna Miller, JD, JCL
Executive Coordinator/Editor of *Proceedings*
Canon Law Society of America
415 Michigan Avenue NE, Suite 101
Washington, DC 20017-4502
(202) 832-2350
ExecutiveCoordinator@clsa.org

FOREWORD

CLSA PROCEEDINGS 85 (2023) 1-16

MAJOR ADDRESS

THE ROLE OF LAW IN THE CHURCH: WHAT IS ITS RELEVANCE TODAY?

Most Reverend Juan Ignacio Arrieta, JCD

1. General Approach

The ephemeris of historical events or facts usually provide an opportunity to reflect retrospectively on the social impact they had in time, and to appreciate with some perspective what were their successes and failures, trying to draw from them some lessons that can be used to project our future.

I think that this may have been the purpose of those who, in designing the present congress, which is being held 40 years after the promulgation of the 1983 Code of Canon Law, wanted to include a general report on the role of law in the Church, and more generally still, on its relevance at the present time.

This is what I will try to do here, from the perspective in which I find myself, after years of working in the current Dicastery for Legislative Texts. I will try to reflect, firstly, on the role played by the Code of Canon Law, the codicial system, in the life of the Church, as the central axis of her normative system. From there I will also try to reflect, in even more general terms, and without philosophical pretensions, on the role of canon law and the canonist in the life of the Church today.

2. Standard and Law in Universal Perspective

To begin with, I would like to note the difference that I attribute to these two arguments: one thing is to speak of the code and the canonical normative system, the canonical order, which is the work of the legislator, and a different thing, at least in my viewpoint, is to deal with law in general, and canon law in our particular case, which is the task of the canonist who has to make law.

When we reflect on the code and on the system of norms that gravitate around it, we should consider the series of general norms produced by the canonical legislator, whether universal or particular, with the intention of guiding ecclesial society toward the fulfillment of its ends. The ecclesial norms are human initiatives that are charged with hierarchical authority and that are obligatory for all the faithful. Like any human work, they can have greater or lesser success. Moreover, they are subject to technical parameters of foundation, coherence, opportunity, etc. In effect, ecclesial norms in the Church are subject to the interpretation and hermeneutical use of those who must operate with them, that is, of the canonist who cultivates the law in the Church.[1]

The law, in fact, does not coincide with the norm, especially in canon law. The law—at least in the sense in which I will speak here—is the elaboration of the norms made by the jurist, in this case, by the canonist, who is the jurist of the Church. And it is the task of the canonist to use the entire normative system of canon law to provide an answer and to establish justice in each concrete situation that arises. The law that the canonist thus elaborates, using the set of elements provided by the juridical order, must serve to establish justice in the real situation that arises.

Norm and law are two different concepts that do not necessarily run parallel.[2]

As history shows, there can be times of great flourishing and production of technically adequate norms, and at the same time a lack of jurists at that time in the ecclesial society. And there have also been times of scarcity and normative confusion, which have produced excellent canonists who, despite the limits of the legal system, without departing from the legal system or claiming to replace the legislator, have been able to find solutions that respond with criteria of justice to real situations.[3]

The canonical order has, moreover, a characteristic that is proper and totally exclusive with respect to other juridical systems that influences the law, and that we must never forget. The ecclesiastical society is a universal society, and its law is in force all over the planet. For this reason, and because of the organization proper to the Church, canon law must maintain overall unity, allowing at the same

---

1 See G. Capograssi, Preface in F. López Oñate, *La certeza del diritto* (Roma: n.p., 1950); S. Berlingò, *L'ultimo diritto. Tensioni escatologiche nell'ordine dei sistemi* (Torino: Giappichelli, 1998); C.J. Errazuriz, *Il diritto e la giustizia nella Chiesa. Per una teoria fondamentale del diritto canonico* (Milano: Giuffrè, 2000); G. Lo Castro, Il *mistero del diritto. I. Del diritto e della sua conoscenza* (Torino: Giappichelli, 1997).

2 See G. Lo Castro, "L'uomo e la norma," in *Ius Ecclesiae* 5 (1993) 159-194; E. Baura, "Norma canonica," in J. Otaduy and A. Viana-J. Sedano, eds., *Diccionario General de Derecho Canonico* (*DGDC*) (Pamplona: Universidad de Navarra, 2012) V:570-575.

3 See F. Calasso, *Medioevo del Diritto. I. Le fonti* (Milano: Giuffrè, 1954); N. Álvarez de las Asturias and J. Sedano, *Derecho canónico en perspectiva histórica: fuentes, ciencia, Instituciones* (Pamplona: Ediciones Universidad de Navarra, SA, 2022); G. Boni and I. Samoré, *Il diritto nella storia della Chiesa* (Brescia: Morcelliana, 2023).

time adequate responses to the different situations that the cultures and history of the five continents present. This is a peculiarity that canon law, despite the inevitable limits, has been able to face over twenty centuries of history, precisely thanks to the peculiar technical institutions of elasticity and adaptation that have been configured in it over time and that every canonist must know how to use.

3. The Adoption of the Codicial System in 1917: Advantages and Limitations

The event we are commemorating, the promulgation by St. John Paul II of the Code of Canon Law 40 years ago, replaced, with new criteria, a juridical system adopted since work began on the Pio-Benedictine Code, promulgated in 1917: a codicial system, which had already been adopted by various countries.[4]

Despite the objections that, even then, emerged from the perspective of the Church's legislative tradition, the choice of the codicial system in 1917 was made mainly for the sake of the unity of the ecclesial structure and the clarity and certainty of the norms to be observed in very diverse cultural contexts in the Church. The code arose, moreover, in the context of the conciliar reflection of Vatican I, which favored the centralizing impulse and the Pontifical initiative as universal legislator.

Already during the Council there were many voices expressing the difficulty of continuing to apply the complex *Corpus iuris canonici*, but then the idea was shelved because of the problems following the loss of the Papal States. Some years later, in 1904, St. Pius X took up again the initiative to simplify the canonical order with the motu proprio *Arduum sane munus.*[5] With this, the criteria of the modern codifications that had been imposed during the previous century were immediately adopted.

A codicial system was adopted, centralizing, yes, but aimed at preserving unity, and strongly balanced also with elements coming from the canonical

---

4 See P. Gasparri, "Storia della codificazione del diritto canonico per la Chiesa latina," in *Acta Congressus iuridici internationalis VII saeculo a Decretalibus Gregorii IX et XIV a Codice Iustiniano, promulgatis, IV* (Romae: Pontifical Institutum Utriusque Iuris, 1937) 1-10; C. Fantappiè, "Dal paradigma canonistico classico al paradigma codificatorio," in E. Baura, N. Alvarez de las Asturias, and T. Sol, eds., *La codificazione e il diritto nella Chiesa,* (Milano: Giuffré Editore, 2017) 3-34.

5 See Pius X, m.p. A*rduum sane Munus*, March 19, 1904: *ASS* (1903-1904) n. 36, 549-551; C. Fantappiè, "Alle origini della codificazione pio-benedettina. Nuovi sviluppi delle teorie canonistiche sotto il pontificato di Leone XIII," in *Quaderni fiorentini* 25 (1996) 347-407.

tradition that gave elasticity to the positive system, such as the dispensation, the custom against the law, the canonical equity, etc.[6]

In the end, there emerged what we could call an "open codicial system," which left wide margins of evaluation and adaptation to those who had to apply the law, allowing to decline its precepts according to the specific circumstances of each situation. It was a system that, as the doctrine has not failed to point out, was halfway between the "closed codicial system" and the "common law" system, of Anglo-Saxon and Roman tradition, which gives greater prominence to the judge.[7]

In any case, the 1917 code was presented as an instrument to guarantee, above all, the disciplinary unity of the Church. And probably this stark disciplinary approach, devoid of sufficient doctrinal foundations to support it, would later *provoke an understandable reaction of disaffection towards the law of the Church, which we still suffer today.*

From the outset, a strongly positive approach was adopted to ensure the application of the code and to restrict the canonical order, as far as possible, only to the norms of the code, both those promulgated in 1917 and those that were successively added to the code as necessary.

Although it was never put into practice, the initial idea was that the dicasteries that judged it necessary to issue new laws would provide the text to the Code Commission, so that it could draft new canons to be incorporated into the body of law or to replace canons that had become obsolete.[8] Although it was never observed, this criterion gives an idea of the strongly positivist situation of the time, centered on the code, seen as a panacea for the disciplinary problems of the Church.

The teaching of canon law itself, in seminaries and in programs of higher studies, was to be limited to the exegesis of the norms of the code, as indicated by

---

6 See G. Feliciani, "Codex Iuris Canonici" (1917), in *DGDC* II, 167-172; C. Fantappié, "Gli inizi della codificazione pio-benedettina alla luce dei nuovi documenti," in *Il diritto ecclesiastico* 113 (2002) 16-83.

7 See J. Martínez-Torrón, *Anglo-american law and canon law: Canonical roots of the common law tradition* (Berlin: Duncker & Humblot, 1998); R.H. Helmholz, *Canon law and the Law of England* (London: Hambledon Press,1987).

8 See Benedetto XV, m.p. *Cum iuris canonici*, September 15, 1917: *AAS* 9 (1917) 483-484.

the Congregation for Seminaries and Universities,[9] which generated a type of teaching of limited quality and with few doctrinal foundations: based excessively on the authority that emanated the norms, and less attentive to show their reasonableness and coherence with the doctrinal pillars that support the ecclesial society.

As I say, it is quite understandable that in this situation the science of canon law had few intellectual influences and provoked disaffection and contrary attitudes within the Church.

In the end, canon law was a discipline that could not be explained in priestly formation and so many pastors, who are still at the head of Christian communities, were formed in such circumstances, with a reduced knowledge or with a mistaken idea of the role of canon law in the life of the Church. For this reason, as the years went by, the distancing of those positive thesis that the codicial text brought with it from pastoral action and from the evolution and needs of the Church society became more evident. For all these reasons, many of its provisions simply ceased to be applied.[10]

4. A Farsighted Choice: To Revise the Code at the End of the Ecumenical Council.

For this reason, the decision that the Holy Pope John XXIII announced on January 25, 1959, in the Basilica of St. Paul Outside the Walls, to convoke the Second Vatican Council and also to review the 1917 Code of Canon Law, was far-sighted. The code was barely forty-two years old since its promulgation but, because of its approach, it had quickly become obsolete.

In considering the preparation of a new code, the utility of the codicial system was not in question: what was being questioned were the criteria with which the text had been elaborated at the beginning of the century.

The new code that was being planned was obviously to be nourished by the contributions of the council, and so, although the commission in charge met for the first time almost immediately—*L'Osservatore Romano* announced its creation on March 30, 1963—it was decided to postpone the beginning of the work to the time after the conclusion of Vatican II.[11]

---

9 See Congregatio de Seminariis et Universitatibus, Instruction of August 7, 1917: *AAS* 9 (1917) 439; Congregatio de Seminariis et Universitatibus, del 31 ottobre 1918: *AAS* 10 (1918) 19; V. Gómez-Iglesias C., "La ricezione del Codice del 1917 nella dottrina e nell'insegnamento," in *La codificazione e il diritto nella Chiesa*, cit., 71-119.

10 See J. Herranz, *Codex Iuris Canonici* (1983), in *DGDC* II, 172-186.

11 See B. Bertagna, *Commissio Codicis Iuris Canonici Recognoscendo*, in *DGDC* II, 256-260.

The new norm was to be nourished by the theological doctrine emanating from the council, and on the basis of its theology it was to provide the basis and reason for the new juridical system: in short, this codicial legislation will only have utility and sense if it succeeds in expressing well the nature of the Church's being.

Moreover, this new norm had to also take into account the concrete juridical experience, the ecclesial praxis, and for this reason, in the years that followed the conclusion of Vatican II, the Code Commission in charge of the application of the decrees that the council was producing, maintained a close relationship with the other commission that was beginning to prepare the reform of the code. A good part of the people who were part of one commission were also members of the other.[12]

For this reason, the experiences produced after the council, the large number of provisional norms or *ad experimentum* that were promulgated at that time were to give the right measure of the norm that would eventually become the code. In fact, some sectors of the codification discipline, such as penal law, in which important novelties had been introduced with respect to the previous codification and that could not enjoy that experimental period before the promulgation of the code in 1983, would be strongly affected by the lack of connection with the social reality of the Church.

5. The 1983 Code

Thanks to the doctrinal support of the Second Vatican Council, the new code promulgated in 1983 is today rooted in the essential foundations of the Church: as St. John Paul II would say, it is the expression in juridical language of the theology of the council.[13]

Naturally, although it is the result of eighteen long years of authentically synodal and collegial work, it has all the limits of a human work. Moreover, it has the limits proper to juridical science, which is incapable of adequately expressing a spiritual reality of communion as represented by the Church of Christ.[14] The

---

12 See J. Herranz, "Génesis del nuevo cuerpo legislativo de la Iglesia (del Codigo de 1917 al Codigo de 1983," in *Ius canonicum* 46 (1983) 491-526; W. Onclin, "Le nouveau Code de Droit Canonique," in *Ephemerides theologicae lovanienses* 60 (1984) 235-245.

13 See e.g., John Paul II, *Speech for the Official Presentation of the New Code of Canon Law*, February 3, 1983; Eng. trans. available on pages 31-39 at https://www.canonlaw.info/PDF-Promulgation.pdf (accessed on 12 Mar, 2024).

14 See *Codex Iuris Canonici*, 1983, *Preface*. See P. Lombardia, "Codificación y ordenamiento canónico," in *Escritos de derecho canónico y ecclesiástico del Estado*, V (Pamplona, 1991) 187-221.

juridical methodology, which tries to give to each his own, cannot embrace a reality such as the Church which, ecclesiologically speaking, expresses itself in terms of immanence and communion.[15]

In spite of all this, the 1983 code is an adequate expression of the being of the Church: many of its expressions—above all the basic canons governing the most important institutions—are taken directly from the conciliar texts, and from the successive elaboration that took place during the preparation of the *Lex Ecclesiae Fundamentalis* which, although it was never promulgated, undoubtedly represents the greatest juridical effort to translate the theological concepts that structure the Church. In fact, its main canons passed directly into the various parts of the code.

The code defined, for the first time, the fundamental rights of the faithful,[16] based on baptism, as well as the rights and duties of clerics[17] and religious, based on the theological reflection of their relative positions in the Church. The code coherently developed the jurisdictional bond of power that binds the faithful to hierarchical authority, based on the doctrine of the episcopate and apostolic succession. In the same way the code defined the consultative and co-responsible bodies which, the council configured at various levels on the basis of the theological reflection carried out in each sector: then the canons only completed the normative profile.

In short, if we now look at the 1983 code, we see that all its institutions—with some exceptions that we will see later—have their corresponding foundation in the novel doctrinal syntheses that Vatican II made, and also in the traditional principles of the Church that the council itself ratified. Apart from that, especially in Book I and Book VII, we find, modernized, the canonical institutions that throughout history have shaped the canonical doctrine and that, in some cases, have been exported by the general juridical culture.

The juridical norm, that of the code and any other arising from it, has thus been logically connected with Catholic theology and with divine law, which inevitably forms part of the canonical juridical system of the Church. All this has increased the possibilities of doctrinal elaboration of canon law, detaching, with

---

15 See *Sinodus episcoporum, Principia quae Codicis Iuris Canonici recognitionem dirigant* in *Communicationes* 1 (1969) 77-85; See J. Canosa, ed., *I principi per la revisione del Codice di Diritto Canonico. La ricezione giuridica del Concilio Vaticano II*, (Milano: Giuffré, 2000).

16 See cc. 208-223 *CIC*: cf. Second Vatican Council, dogmatic constitution *Lumen gentium* 37, November 21, 1964: *AAS* 57 (1965) 42-43.

17 See cc. 273-289 *CIC*.

new vigor, the canonist from the mere literalness of the normative text. And I say "with new vigor" because the canonist, as the only exception in the modern juridical world, has always enjoyed the necessary freedom from the positive statement of the written norm, being bound above all, with much greater force, to the natural and divine law, and to the obligation to know how to read from it the positive dictation of the human legislator.

Norm and law are two notions that are not identified. The norm is inevitably linked to the authority of the one who holds the juridical power, while the right is committed only to the truth. Normally, in the Church, the norm is based on criteria of truth, but in any case, the interpreter, in this case, the canonist, in trying to establish justice in the concrete case, must always know how to govern himself according to an order of hierarchical gradation of norms, in such a way that he never sacrifices truth—real justice—to the literal dictation of the human norm.[18]

In wanting to adjust the code to the theological foundations of Vatican II, the legislator adopted criteria derived from the reflection on the episcopate, which corrected at its root the approaches of the 1917 code. In particular, I will refer to two, which are reflected in the entire body of the code and are particularly important in the subject we are dealing with now.

On the one hand, canons 381 and 86 of the new code, following the dictates of numbers 23 and 27 of *Lumen gentium* and number 8 of *Christus Dominus*, modified the previous system of granting habitual faculties by the Holy See, replacing it with that of the ordinary power of bishops. The bishops now have ordinary power in all that is not expressly reserved to the Holy See and can even dispense from universal norms when they believe that the spiritual good of the faithful requires it. In this way, the council expanded considerably the juridical power of the bishops in their dioceses.

On the other hand, in consonance with what we are saying, the code also adopted a general criterion of normative decentralization. It reduced the number of canons to those that define the essential nucleus of juridical institutions, that is, to those most closely linked to doctrinal formulations, which for reasons of unity must be common to the whole Church, with the intention—unsuccessful, as we shall see—that the rest of the normative framework would be defined by the particular law legislated by the bishops themselves and, in some matters, by the episcopal conferences, according to the diverse cultures and pastoral needs of each place.

---

18 Compare P. Fedele, *Lo spirito del diritto canonico* (Padova: Cedam, 1962); P. Fedele, *Discorsi sul diritto canonico* (Roma: Officium Libri Cattolici, 1973).

For example, on November 8, 1983, the Secretariat of State issued a list of matters on which the national episcopal conferences had to legislate, and another list of matters on which they were free to legislate.[19] Similarly, the Congregations for Bishops and for the Evangelization of Peoples, in the annex to the Instruction on Diocesan Synods, which was jointly promulgated on March 19, 1997,[20] included, by way of example, a long list of matters which, according to the provisions of the code, could be legislated by the bishops at the particular level.

6. The Normative Development of the 1983 Code

As regards the normative development of all the norms of the Church, in the years following the promulgation of the code of 1983, during the pontificate of John Paul II, in conformity with the provisions of the code and in the framework of the theology that integrates it, the entire juridical order of the Church and of the universal, national and local institutions regulated by the code was renewed: statutes of episcopal conferences or presbyteral councils, of associations or foundations or religious congregations, etc.

At the universal level, successive documents have also replaced those that still were gravitating around the 1917 code, in matters of universities, sacraments, discipline of the clergy, and so on. All these new norms now make up a body of universal norms that is substantially coherent in general terms, leaving aside some less successful solutions, on which I will not comment here.

On the other hand, the evaluation of the evolution of the canonical normative system at the level of particular law, in which the legislator of 1983 had placed so much hope, in line with the council's doctrine on the episcopate, has turned out to be an almost complete failure.

The episcopal conferences have promulgated the legislative decrees that the code asked of them, although there are still some, in mission territory, that have not succeeded in doing so.[21] In most cases, however, the conferences have limited themselves to copying directly the provisions issued by other conferences, renouncing an analysis of the pastoral reality of their own country. Moreover, only a small number of episcopal conferences have legislated on other matters in which it was not obligatory but only advisable to legislate by means of general decrees.

---

19 See Segreteria di Stato, Lettera ai Presidenti delle Conferenze Episcopali circa i decreti generali complementari al CIC, November 8, 1983, in *Communicationes* 15 (1983) 135-139.

20 See Congregation for Bishops and Congregation for the Evangelization of People, Instruction on Diocesan Synods, March 19, 1997: *AAS* 89 (1997) 706-721.

21 See J. Marti de Agar and L. Navarro, *Legislazione delle Conferenze Episcopali Complementare al CIC*, 2nd ed. (Rome: Pontifical University Santa Croce, 2009).

In many cases, the conference assembly has left it up to each bishop to legislate on specific matters for his diocese, thus avoiding the adoption of a norm of a collegial nature.

Something similar can be said at the particular diocesan level. The diocesan synods, in their practical majority, have abstained from establishing truly normative dispositions, preferring programmatic declarations of a pastoral nature, which—in most cases—have turned out to be of limited effective value. Apart from that, the bishops themselves, only in very specific cases, normally of a disciplinary nature, have promulgated their own norms on associations, administration of the sacraments, etc.

In general terms and as a whole, it seems inevitable to conclude that the episcopate has renounced to practice the demands of collegiality at the national level in the legislative field; it has preferred to avoid reasons for confrontation and situations in which each of its members would be forced to renounce the singular exercise of its own power and to seek common ground with the other bishops in order to develop programs at the national level. This is not without its problems, given the high rate of mobility of the population in today's society. The habitual exercise of episcopal collegiality in the governance of the particular Churches is still a pending matter in the Church.

I think that this point—on which, as I say, the conception of the legislative system of the 1983 code was based—is also linked to the insufficient juridical sensitivity—I am aware of having used a rather benign expression—of so many pastors who are today at the head of Christian communities. I believe that it is the fruit of the disappointment produced at the time by the excessively "disciplinary" experience of the code of 1917. Without wanting erring on the side of excess, I believe that having ignored the requirement contained in canon 331 §5 of the 1917 code, demanding that candidates for the episcopate have a sufficient theological and canonical formation, has also weakened the institutional perception required for the pastoral government of Christian communities. This institutional sense provided by law includes respect for the rights of the faithful, the use of the institutional means provided for the governance of the community, and also the submission to the law in the pastoral activity of governance, which presupposes a high appreciation of the role that the general norm, that is, the law, plays in the governance of the Church. In a system of law, the law is also an instrument of coherence and a limit to arbitrary exercise of the power.

In short, there has been no development of particular canon law as was intended by the 1983 code.

What there has been, instead, is a deployment of autarchy in local government, that is, a regular and widespread use of the decentralized powers granted to local bishops by canon 381, as well as of the faculties of dispensation from universal law granted to them by the cited canon 87.

In other words, the decentralization postulated by the theology of the episcopate has been practiced in the exercise of executive power and very scarcely in that of legislative power. It is easier to resolve individual cases rather than to establish general parameters of conduct, especially if they have to be in agreement with one's own peers. Certainly, this avoids overloading the ecclesial society with rules and juridical norms, but it also avoids, in many cases, the need for clear directives in sectors that would have prevented further conflicts.

7. Subsequent Modifications of the Canons of the Code of Canon Law

The doctrinal-theological *substratum* that the canons of the Code of Canon Law received in 1983 has meant that an important part of the modifications made in the following years to the canons of the code has been motivated by new specifications or changes from the doctrinal perspective of the magisterium of the Church.

New definitions have made it necessary to introduce changes in the canons. The first was brought about by the modification of the Profession of Faith made in 1989, followed by the motu proprio *Ad tuendam fidem*,[22] which made it necessary to change the text of canon 750, introducing a §2 that determines the assent of faith required also by the doctrines proposed by the Church as definitive, and consequently expanding the crime against the faith defined in the current canon 1365. Later, reflection on the formal abandonment of the Church led to the correction, with the motu proprio *Omnium in mentem*,[23] of canons 1086 §1 and 1124, requiring canonical form for the validity of marriages of baptized Catholics. In truth, I would not know if in this case the problem regarding marriage was adequately resolved. It seems to me that the problem originally posed responded more to the discipline followed in some episcopal conferences regarding the religious tax, mainly in Germany, Austria, and Switzerland. Unfortunately, a chance was missed to explain the real problem of canonical marriage law and to

---

22 See John Paul II, m.p. *Ad tuendam fidem*, May 18, 1998: *AAS* 90 (1998) 457-461. See Congregation for the Doctrine of the Faith, *Nota doctrinalis Professionis fidei formulam extremam enucleans*, June 29, 1998: *AAS* 90 (1998) 544-551.

23 See Benedict XVI, m.p. *Omnium in mentem*, October 26, 2009: *AAS* 102 (2010) 8-10.

limit the requirement of form only to the canonical "liceity" of consent that is potentially sufficient from the sacramental point of view.[24]

Similarly, the distinction introduced in the definitive edition of the *Catechism of the Catholic Church* on the different "*munera*" conferred by the diaconate and the presbyterate led to the correction of canons 1008 and 1009, in the same motu proprio *Omnium in mentem* that I have just mentioned. Even more recently, the change of perspective that took place in 2021 with the motu proprio *Spiritus Domini* regarding the content of the "lay ministries,"[25] not only as propaedeutic for the reception of sacred orders, as it was before, but as a concrete expression of the baptismal "*munera*" common to all the faithful, led to the correction of canon 230 §1, allowing also women to receive such ministries in a liturgical function.

Other changes have arisen to homogenize the Latin discipline with the Eastern one in pastoral matters, as well as to adapt some initiatives of the council to the new law of the curia, or to resolve specific dispositions in the law of religious.

In any case, the 1983 code succeeded in developing decentralization in the Church, as far as it is possible in order to ensure the unity of the Church, as Vatican II had requested. Proof of this is the very little practical impact of the motu proprio *Competentias quasdam,* which,[26] despite long years of decentralizing efforts by the Commission of Cardinals created by Pope Francis to support reforms, succeeded in identifying only a few transfers, mainly in the field of the law of religious.

Other areas of the code that have had to be completely reworked, mainly concerning the matrimonial process and penal discipline, deserve a very different evaluation.

In my opinion, it is likely that the marriage discipline reformed in 1983 focused too much on developing the juridical consequences of the "*ius connubii*," now defined as a fundamental right in canon 219, reflecting less on the social reality of the Church and on the objective limits of its administrative organization.

---

24 See Pontifical Council for Legislative Texts, Circular Letter to the Presidents of the Bishops' Conferences, March 13, 2006 in *Communicationes* 38 (2006) 170-172.

25 See Francis, m.p. *Spiritus Domini*, January 10, 2021: *AAS* 113 (2021) 169-170. On this topic see "Letter of his Holiness Pope Francis to the Prefect of the Congregation for the Doctrine of the Faith regarding Access of Women to the Ministries of Lector and Acolyte," January 10, 2021: *AAS* 113 (2021) 177-181.

26 See Francis, m.p. *Competentias quasdam decernere,* February 11, 2022: *AAS* 114 (2022) 290-295.

Consequently, in 2015, the motu proprio *Mitis Iudex Dominus Iesus*[27] carried out a profound revision of the declarative process of matrimonial nullity, rethinking also the configuration of the judicial instances, with the idea of bringing them closer to the faithful and submitting their creation to the discernment of the diocesan bishops themselves.

Similarly, the almost complete disregard for the penal system of Book VI, after the well-known centralizing interventions in matters of abuse of minors and indiscipline of the clergy, led in 2021 to the promulgation of a new Book VI of the code, with the apostolic constitution *Pascite gregem Dei.*[28] The praxis of the previous years had also shown that the principle of decentralization with which the canonical penal system was approached in 1983—which resulted in the criminal sphere in the indetermination of criminal types and penal sanctions—had injured at its source fundamental principles of penal law, namely the principle of legality and the obligatory character of penal action, above all, with the consequent inoperability of the canonical penal system as a whole, which had been left to the discretion of individual bishops.

Recently, a non-normative explanatory guide has also been published to help ordinaries, with less juridical experience, to use the penal system and to avoid the need for further centralization, as was the case in the past.

All these modifications to the code, and others that would have to be made, as I will say in a moment, do not alter, however, the validity of the codicial system as the central legislative instrument of the Church's juridical order. The changes I have mentioned prove that it is possible to update the normative provisions of specific sectors, without bringing into crisis the code as a whole, because—unlike its predecessor of 1917—it is based on the necessarily stable principles provided by the council. On the other hand, the general norms of Book I, and the general framework of procedural law in Book VII, have a general usefulness as a whole, also for dialogue with state legal systems, which do not require substantial changes and are, on the other hand, a guarantee of unity in ecclesial society. The same is true of the basic rules that regulate the subjective positions of the faithful, the organs of government and participation, the sacraments and the ministry of the word, in its various expressions.

---

27 See Francis, m.p. *Mitis Iudex Dominus Iesus*, August 15, 2015: *AAS* 107 (2015) 958-967; Francis, *Ratio procedendi in causis ad matrimonii nullitatem declarandam*, August 15, 2015: *AAS* 107 (2015) 967-970.

28 See Francis, apostolic constitution *Pascite gregem Dei*, May 23, 2021: *AAS* 113 (2021) 534-555.

From time to time we hear proposals for a general revision of the 1983 code. I think that these ideas are not in harmony with ecclesial reality, that they are not at all necessary, and that it would be risky to proceed in this way in these times in which canonical science is no better prepared than that which formed the generation of our masters of the 1960s and 1970s when they drew up the code currently in force. This would run the risk of repeating the experience of the General Part of the recent Apostolic Constitution *Praedicate evangelium*[29] on the Roman Curia, which reproduces substantially the same norms contained in *Pastor bonus*, but with language and juridical rigor of lesser quality.

On the other hand, it is clear that the occasional substitution of certain provisions of the code, including their eventual increase, if necessary, with canons of duplicate numbering—as was proposed when the code of 1917 was promulgated—helps to maintain the doctrinal foundation of the council, to preserve the unity of the Church and to adapt the norms to the real demands of the evolution of ecclesial society.

On the other hand, as the experience of all these decades has also shown, the pretension—sometimes made—of replacing the universal norms of the code with norms of particular law that are adapted to the different regional situations, given by the episcopal conferences, lacks realism.

Along these lines, however, I think that it will still be necessary to work on further modifications to the code on some points. 1) It will be necessary to elaborate administrative procedures for the formation of the acts of government, if we wish to make effective the much proclaimed synodality and allow it to be translated into real participation of those who were called to intervene.[30] 2) The basic approach of Book V of the code, too attentive to the protection of the state property of the Church in the code of 1917, should also be revised if it is to be adapted to the demands of the present patrimonial management, which also calls for the participation of professional experts in the decisions, and to relieve the hierarchical authority of responsibility. Specifically, the patrimonial development will have to be mainly of particular law, if we wish to respect the diversity of the state systems in the matter.[31] 3) It will also be necessary to redevelop the systems of mediation that were planned in the initial phases of the work of revising the code and then abandoned, in order to limit procedural disputes and resolve them

29 See Francis, apostolic constitution *Praedicate evangelium*, March 19, 2022: *AAS* 114 (2022) 375-455.

30 See J.I. Arrieta, "Presentazione," in M. del Pozzo, J. Llobell, and J. Minambres, *Norme Procedurali Canoniche Commentate* (Roma, Coletti a San Pietro, 2013) 23-27.

31 See J. Miñambres and J.-P. Schouppe, *Diritto patrimoniale canonico* (Rome: Pontifical University Santa Croce, 2022).

with forms that are probably much more ecclesial.[32] 4) Finally, the formulation of canon 129 on the exercise of power by the lay faithful will have to be reconsidered if it is to be consistent with the evolution of the magisterium that we have indicated above in relation to the specific *munera Christi* of the deacons and that which all lay faithful receive with baptism, which should not be redirected only to the field of the liturgy.[33]

I would like to stop here because I want to dedicate the final part of this intervention no longer to the canonical normative system, but specifically to the law and to the task of reconstructing the law, which is the task of the canonist at the present time.

8. The Role of Canon Law at the Present Time

Up to this point, I have referred to the normative system of the Church, whose center is the code of 1983; it is a system that can give a certain impression of chaos from time to time, at least in some instances. It should not be forgotten, however, that the decentralization advocated by the council necessarily entailed a broadening of the Church's normative sources, at the universal, regional, and local levels, and while many of these instances have remained inactive, the presence of this set of elements contributes to complicating their overall treatment.

In this context, what is the relevance of canon law, understood not as a norm but as the hermeneutic elaboration that the legal professional in the Church must carry out, each time he is confronted with new cases that are presented to him? What is the role that this function must occupy today?[34]

It seems to me that today, more than ever, the canonist is called upon to introduce himself with expertise, using all the instruments of the canonical order in the whole normative system of the Church—which, as I say, can sometimes be

---

32 Cf. J.I. Arrieta, "I metodi alternativi di risoluzione di controversie nell'ordinamento canonico: le possibilità offerte dalla normativa vigente," in P. Szabó and T. Franko, eds., *Sacrorum canonum scientia. Radici, tradizioni, prospettive. Studi in onore del Cardinale Péter Erdo per il suo 70° compleanno* (Budapest: Szent István Társulat, 2022) 19-33.

33 See J.I. Arrieta, "Sulla partecipazione dei fedeli laici nell'organizzazione della Chiesa. Esercizio dei diritti e della potestà di governo," in A.P. Bosso and E.B.O. Okonkwo, *Quis custodiet ipsos custodes? Studi in onore di Giacomo Incitti* (Roma: Urbaniana Univesity Press, 2021) 149-164.

34 Cf. J. Hervada, *Pensieri di un canonista nell'ora presente* (Venezia: Marcianum Press, 2004) 27-65; J. Hervada, *Coloquios propedeuticos sobre el derecho canónico*, 2nd ed. (Pamplona: University of Navarre, 2002); J.I. Arrieta, "Ius divinum e ruolo della canonistica," in *Ius divinum,* Consociatio Internationalis Studio Iuris Canonici Promovendo, Atti del XIII Congresso Internazionale di Diritto Canonico, Venezia 17-21 settembre 2008 (Venezia: Consociatio Internationalis, 2010) 1391-1406.

chaotic—in defense of the truth, that is, in defense of justice in each concrete case that is presented to us.

However great, the normative confusion that can result from the set of canonical sources, canon law includes, first and foremost, norms of natural law, which must always prevail in the resolution of cases.

The canonical discipline established by the 1983 code, unlike its predecessor of 1917, has its roots, as we have said, in the doctrine of the Second Vatican Council, and it is from this doctrine and from divine law that every positive norm elaborated by the human legislator must be read. This is an operation that the canonist must perform in order to protect the rights of the person, and to defend the essential nature of the Church's institutions in every field: from ecclesiastical organization to the sacramental sphere, or the exercise of the *munus docendi*, or the rights of the faithful.

More than before, if the norms do not serve or are insufficient, the canonist must strive to illuminate the truth of the situations—truth and justice appear to be the same thing—acting with the full freedom of one who does not yield to the literal dictation of the norms, but seeks in them the reason for justice, which they must necessarily include.

The task of the canonist, then, is to carry out a hermeneutic work, which, starting from the foundations of the concrete juridical interest, that each norm or each canonical institution seeks to protect, uses with mastery, all the instruments of elasticity and equity that canonical science has accumulated over the centuries, so that always prevails the justice and truth that each concrete situation requires.

He must never be a blind enforcer of the law, but an attentive observer of the reality of each situation, in such a way that he can then use those precise canonical norms that will do justice and re-establish social order. And all this must be done without substituting himself for the legislator and without ceding to the temptation of transgressing the law.

No other legal system gives the operator the freedom that canon law gives to the canonist who, over and above the text of the norm, is bound by his own conscience to a superior law.

This is an art that those who teach in seminaries or at the higher education level must transmit to those who study canon law, so that canonists may truly emerge, relatively free from the positive text of the laws and effectively bound by the truth and justice on which interpersonal relationships in the Church are based.

Thank you very much for your attention.

CLSA PROCEEDINGS 85 (2023) 17-29

MAJOR ADDRESS

UPDATE FROM THE DICASTERY FOR THE DOCTRINE OF THE FAITH

Reverend Monsignor John J. Kennedy, JCD

Introduction

Working in a Dicastery is an education in many things, not least in world geography but most importantly it is an opportunity to focus on respect for the human person and on justice. Each day, when I see cases sent from the four corners of the globe, I think of the women and men canonists, and various other persons whose dedicated hard work lies behind the material that we receive, the names and faces not mentioned in the correspondence. I think too of those who are the subject of an accusation. Being among you at the convention for the second time affords me another priceless opportunity to meet you again face-to-face and to forge new links.

So, perhaps some of you are wondering what happens to your work once it crosses the Atlantic and arrives in the Vatican? What are the mechanisms that are set in place to motivate the replies that you receive? Is it just one person who decides everything?

For this reason, I thought it appropriate today to give you, in as much as time allows, a first-hand account and an inside look at the workings of the dicastery so that our common bonds of friendship and cooperation might be strengthened for a better service of the Holy Father and for the ordinaries whom we strive to accompany in their ministry.

First of all, the dicastery, which for many years was called a congregation, is situated to the left of Saint Peter's Square in Piazza del Sant'Uffizio. From our terrace we can see the Pontifical North American College perched on the Janiculum Hill. The office is an extraterritorial property of Vatican City and is home to the offices, mainly on the ground and second floors, and to several apartments inhabited by cardinals, archbishops and other curial officials. It was first built in 1514 for Cardinal Lorenzo Pucci and was initially called Palazzo Pucci. Ten years later the façade was rebuilt and one of the architects employed was Michelangelo. In 1542—and this is where our story begins—Pope Paul III created a group of six cardinals to watch over all matters pertaining to the Catholic faith, creating a tribunal structure and giving the group of six juridical powers. The building was purchased for 9,000 *scudi*, the currency in circulation at the time and up until 1866 in the Papal States. Interestingly, the word *scudo* also means a shield and has a connection to our work of protecting minors and the holiness of the sacraments.

Once the material leaves your office, it usually is sent to us through the Papal Nunciature. Up until recently, the diplomatic pouch leaving the Vatican departed on a weekly basis. In order to reduce costs, this is now less frequent, and I understand that this is now fortnightly. We know that some things are urgent and, for this reason, if you feel that something falls into this category and needs immediate attention, please do not hesitate to use e-mail and attach the documentation as a PDF. The most commonly used address is that of the *Capo Ufficio*, or office manager, of the Discipline Section which is: disciplinaryoffice@cfaith.va. He will ensure that the matter is given attention.

In a similar vein, we are also aware that some decisions are eagerly awaited at the local level and so we recently began the practice of sending, for example, PDF copies of our letters by e-mail to ordinaries in cases granting the remission of an excommunication, with the originals following through the usual channels. If you feel that the case requires this type of attention, please indicate your wish to receive an e-mail reply and we will gladly accommodate this request.

Most of what we receive is delivered by diplomatic mail, but we also get material, often delivered by hand, by the various procurators general of religious orders. Equally, some diocesan ordinaries, knowing that they have other appointments in Rome, prefer to bring the material with them and hand deliver it. From our point of view, this is perfectly fine though we would suggest that at least a note be sent to the Apostolic Nuncio informing him of this. The Apostolic Nuncio is a key figure and, in his role, he can often provide invaluable assistance as a case develops.

When we speak about the Dicastery for the Doctrine of the Faith, it should be noted that the full reality involves more than just those who work here on a daily basis. If you open the *Annuario Pontificio*, that red book with all the ecclesiastical details and contacts, you will notice the names of the members of the dicastery. Many of them are cardinals, others are archbishops and bishops. Many of them are resident in Rome while others are local ordinaries. These members, this group, essentially forms something akin to the senate of the dicastery and are usually convoked every two years when there is the *Plenaria* or

Plenary Session in January. They are also invited to be present at the *Feria IV*, which is the Wednesday meeting called approximately once a month to discuss matters of great importance. The day-to-day work, on the other hand, is done by the staff, the officials, who are present each day in the office. Currently there are eleven cardinals listed as members as well as five archbishops and one bishop. The total number of superiors is six and there are sixty officials and other employees.

It is opportune at this point to mention those who have been named as members of the Pontifical Theological Commission and the Pontifical Biblical Commission who each assist the dicastery with their study and reflection during the period of the mandate that they receive.

Before moving forward, if you will permit me to pause for a moment and share with you a word about Cardinal Ratzinger, who was the first Prefect under whom I served, and which still serves as a guiding principle for how we work. His episcopal motto was *cooperatores veritatis*, co-workers of the truth. Our current prefect has chosen the words, "In the midst of your people." I feel that these combined expressions reflect the overarching approach of the dicastery in terms of our *modus operandi* both internally and externally. The "all eyes on" approach that we adopt is an expression of our collegial approach in serving the Holy Father, as if we were standing among you.

For the rest of this presentation, I wish to illustrate how everything we do is founded on our long experience and deep conviction that by working for the truth and discerning together in a collegial way with the ordinary and canonical advisors worldwide, as if we were among them, we can strive together for truth and justice that make the difference at the local level.

Whenever something arrives, a case, a letter, an e-mail, the first thing is that it is seen by all the superiors. Who are these persons? The Cardinal Prefect is Victor Manuel Fernández, an Argentinian. There are two secretaries, one for the Doctrinal Section—Monsignor Armando Matteo, from Calabria—and I am the other, with responsibility for the Discipline Section. There is also an Adjunct Secretary, Archbishop Charles J. Scicluna, who is Archbishop of Malta and who travels regularly to offer invaluable assistance to the dicastery when cases are presented as recourses to the college established by Pope Francis. The remaining superiors are Under-Secretary Monsignor Philippe Curbelié, from Toulouse in France, and Promoter of Justice Father Robert J. Geisinger, SJ, who, in this gathering, needs no introduction. As you will see, it is a balance of religious and diocesan clerics. Might I just add by way of a personal comment that we are so grateful to Bob Geisinger who in the overall fulfilment of the office brings one facet that is of particular utility, namely his experience of fifteen years as Procurator General of the Society of Jesus. As a diocesan priest, there are aspects of religious law that I do not have at my fingertips and so Bob's insights and experience are invaluable and critical to the proper functioning of the section.

Each of the superiors will read the letter of presentation, often containing the ordinary's *votum*, and sometimes some of the acts before then putting their initials on the cover letter of the document. The material is seen by the Protocol Office where it is identified (if it is an existing case) and then registered for the first time if it is a new case. Everything that enters the building is then registered in a postal database, as is everything that leaves the building. When a case is new, the *Capo ufficio*, or office manager, of the Discipline Section identifies the nature of the accusation or accusations, and assigns the case to an official, either based on the geographical location or on language.

If it happens that material is sent to us but upon examination it turns out that it is not of our competence, we sometimes forward the material directly to the appropriate dicastery or in other cases write back to the ordinary, suggesting that he perhaps re-package and re-present the material according to the requirements of the competent dicastery.

In terms of copies, the dicastery wishes to receive one copy of doctrinal and disciplinary material. Traditionally three copies of the acts in a matrimonial case were required, but, from 1 January 2024, it will only be necessary to send one copy.

In terms of the registration of the case, specifically under the name of the accused, we sometimes find it helpful to have some form of official identification so that the case can be registered properly. From time to time there can be incomplete names found in the acts and sometimes names and surnames are misspelled. In Haiti, for instance, we have discovered the cultural phenomenon whereby names and surnames are often interchangeable—such as in the name Pierre Bernard which can often appear as Bernard Pierre—and this creates the possibility of a duplication in terms of registration. There are countries where the accused has a fairly common name and where he may be known locally, for instance, as José Hernández. We have sometimes found that the first letter communicating the case gives us the name José Hernández while subsequent documents, often with material from the civil forum, reveal that the person is really José Luís Santos Hernández. The danger with only partial information on the initial arrival of the case is that the same case could end up being registered under two separate numbers and as a consequence followed by two distinct officials.

We live in a world where information is key and where ordinaries are often subject to the gaze of public opinion in terms of how quickly they respond to and handle cases under our competence. For this reason, we are aware that sending an acknowledgement quickly can be of enormous benefit. The Matrimonial Office also does this upon receipt of a case by way of e-mail. In the Doctrinal Section too, as a first step in a new case, the official will also write to the bishop and inform him that the case has been assigned a protocol number and requests that all future correspondence could utilize this indication.

In terms of the next step, both in matrimonial and disciplinary cases, the official reads through the *Tabella* which forms part of the acts and, if this has not been prepared, will then fill it himself or herself out using the tabular model which is available on the Vatican website. To avoid duplication and to speed up the case a little, it is rather helpful if the *Tabella* could be sent by e-mail to the Dicastery. It is perhaps interesting to know that the *Tabella* forms part of the presentation to the Holy Father in an audience.

If at a first glance, it appears that the material is not sufficient to allow the dicastery to move forward in a substantive way, a letter outlining the elements to be furnished is prepared. This is a form of initial quality control and ensures that the ordinary is best placed to know what to do in a timely fashion. The dicastery is also active in replying to an ordinary who communicates allegations made against a cleric who is deceased. We have a special file for these cases and our reply will outline why no canonical action may be taken in this situation.

Otherwise, if everything is in order then, having read the entire acts, as well as the ordinary's *votum*, the official will draw up a report at the end of which he will outline the various aspects of the case, perhaps with some questions and observations, and will then make a proposal or two for discussion for how to move forward procedurally. The case is then often scheduled to be discussed in what we call an internal commission which is composed of three persons: the promoter of justice, the office manager, and the official who examined the material. Other possibilities and times for a for discussion also exist. Traditionally the internal commission meets a number of times per week, usually on Tuesday and Thursday afternoons, or additionally as required.

In this commission, the official will present the findings in the case, like a *ponens*, and a discussion will follow. Deliberations are not always quick as cases are sometimes complicated. There is a most interesting dynamic at play when three persons who are not connected to the case in any way focus their attention on seeking truth and justice. I was at those discussions for five years and I can testify that the momentum and mental energy which guide us to the outcome have always been a moment both of discernment and of learning. When there is consensus in terms of the next procedural step to be taken, a decree (a draft of which has often been prepared in advanced) is signed. Any modifications to the proposal in the decree are made by hand then the three members of the commission sign the decree. It is then stamped with the seal of the dicastery. The decree is then given to the official who places it in the acts of the case. It remains an internal document.

The decree is essentially a proposal outlining the findings of the internal commission to be approved by the superiors. In practical terms, the content of decree is then transformed into a letter, sometimes with very specific details and instructions, to be sent to the ordinary. As part of the process of preparing any letter, the draft of the response to the ordinary is prepared by the official and viewed and approved by the office manager, the promoter of justice, the under-secretary, the relevant secretary and, in some cases, the prefect. Modifications are a standard part of the evolutionary process of a letter and sometimes the proposed content gives rise to a need to have a discussion about the response. Perhaps a recent meeting will have raised an element that is not strictly part of the case but which forms an important part of the context. The final version of the letter is then prepared and a copy, with an indication of proof of the date of postage, is then given to the official to be inserted into the file.

Already you can see that the case is not the exclusive domain of the official but is a matter that is under examination before the entire dicastery. This is the culture of the dicastery and facilitates a great sense of teamwork. This is key to how the office operates, with transparency and collaboration at every step of the process. People don't take offence if someone corrects a letter, makes a suggestion, or rejects a proposal. It truly is a situation in which we all seek the best outcome.

The Matrimonial Section continues to operate in a similar collegial manner with the assistance of its external experts who are divided into two groups: commissioners and defenders of the bond. As soon as the dissolution of the marriage bond is granted by the Holy Father, the office sends a notification to the ordinary by e-mail and then the rescript follows through the usual channels. One of our concerns is to have the correct e-mail address and so a diocese is asked to inform us, perhaps in the letter of presentation of the case, of the most appropriate electronic address to use. If your diocese is not receiving the rescript by e-mail, please inform us and we will rectify this. Equally, if your diocese is not availing of the dissolution in favour of the faith in cases where it can be applied, perhaps this might be an opportunity to revisit the norms and make contact with the

Matrimonial Section. Additionally, the norms governing the granting of the dissolution as well as several articles and the tabular presentation are available on the Vatican website. The Matrimonial Section has its own e-mail address where enquiries and any other correspondence may be sent: infavoremfidei@cfaith.va

One of the questions that people often have is how does the dicastery make a determination as to which penal canonical process is authorized. What are the thought processes behind it? As you know, traditionally the judicial process is the one preferred in the Code of Canon Law. That said, such a process requires a number of canonists, and ordinaries do not always have the trained personnel. I recently spoke to an ordinary with reduced clergy numbers who told me quite openly, and with considerable regret, that undertaking a judicial process would simply be out of the question for him. He is not alone in the world, and we see this in many places.

In answering the question, I would say that our decision-making process is collegial and done in strict dialogue with the ordinary. When an ordinary makes a request to undertake a certain type of canonical process, serious consideration is given to this. If the decision is not to accept the ordinary's proposal, the letter will explain the reasons and often invite a response before the case then moves forward. Equal deliberation is given when an ordinary presents a case and asks for guidance in terms of which path should be chosen. We are acutely aware that the ordinary is clearly in possession of the most accurate local knowledge regarding the case and in order to respect the principle of subsidiarity.

Let us take the example of the authorization of an administrative penal process. This is not a real case, but it gives you a clear idea.

Case A

The Bishop of *Pine Lake*, a far-flung, geographically vast and uninhabited rural diocese, has few Catholics, no vocations, and consequently limited diocesan personnel with a canon law qualification. The bishop himself is a philosophy graduate with a keen interest in psychology. His aging judicial vicar is pastor of two thriving parishes and has been appointed a member of multiple diocesan boards and committees.

An accusation of downloading and distributing child pornography against a priest is brought to the attention of the child protection office. The accused cleric is contacted by the local police who had been monitoring the electronic exchanges in an undercover operation, and, under examination, admits to the offence without hesitation. A court date has been set and the cleric has been released on bail. In presenting the scenario to the dicastery, the bishop was careful not to begin the preliminary investigation until the civil process had been completed though he has imposed precautionary measures on the cleric.

In referring the case to the dicastery, along with copies of the civil documentation that he had obtained, the bishop requested early authorization to undertake an administrative penal process. His motivations were the following: the superfluous nature of the preliminary investigation, the cleric's admission of guilt, the considerable scandal, the vociferous demands for justice and the fact that there was little to be gained by doing a judicial process. The case was effectively cut and dried, and it was expected that the cleric would spent at least ten years in prison after which he did not foresee a return to ministry.

The case was presented and discussed at the internal commission. The matter of prescription was not relevant in this case since the alleged delicts dated from 2022. However, in other cases this does form part of the deliberation, even if no mention of this is made in the initial presentation of the case. It is important to note that just because derogation is requested does not automatically mean that it will be granted in every case. I will pause for a moment in the consideration of the case at hand for an observation. It is important to note that a request for derogation from prescription is considered seriously, but it must be supported by substantive, even perhaps exceptional, reasons. For instance, the United States continues to see accusations arise from decades ago in which the likelihood of finding sustainable proofs is quite low, let alone getting to moral certitude that can withstand the scrutiny of recourse. With the significant passage of time, it may also be the case that the accused cannot defend himself for reasons of health, particularly dementia. If it serves no sustainable purpose, prescription is not lifted, as some of you may have experienced in cases with which you are familiar. The dicastery, however, does not hesitate to derogate from canonical prescription when warranted in those cases in which the pursuit of the truth and the justice that follows demands it, and when a potential process shows promise that such an end can be reached.

Returning the case being discussed, the proposal of the Internal Commission was to authorize a canon 1720 process as requested by the bishop. In addition, although not requested, a mandate was granted in advance to impose a perpetual expiatory penalty, not excluding dismissal from the clerical state.

Perhaps you have come across cases like this which can be handled by a canon 1720 process. In terms of personnel, this approach facilitates the involvement of members of the lay faithful. For example, as per canon 1424 of the Latin code, there is no requirement that the named Assessors be in the clerical state. The norms of *Sacramentorum Sanctitatis Tutela* also provide for the possibility of dispensations from the requirements of priesthood and academic degrees, as needed (cf. *SST* art. 21). The ordinary can undertake the process himself or delegate it. Another advantage is speed. Civil cases can often take time and so, pending a final decision, cases like this continue to attract attention and are a source of scandal. A timely decision in the canonical forum brings justice and can allow healing to begin. It also facilitates the canonical reality to reflect the lived reality more promptly.

Although there is a possibility for making *remonstratio* or subsequent hierarchical recourse, the time limits involved in an extrajudicial process are clearly determined by law. The same applies to a recourse to the College for Recourses which accepts cases only if recourses arrive at the dicastery within 60 days.

Let us look at another case, this time one that involves a potential judicial penal process.

Case B

The Archbishop of *Blue Springs* has none of the challenges of his brother in the episcopal conference. He has lots of clergy and religious, and an unusual number of his pastors have a licentiate in canon law or even doctorates. The tribunal is well run and efficient. It was recently reorganized. A priest from another country, who has been ministering in the diocese while he is pursuing further studies as a favour to a bishop in a developing country, has been accused of the sexual abuse of a 17-year old minor over a two-year period, solicitation in confession of three adult women, indirect violation of the sacramental seal, and absolution of a female accomplice in a sin against the sixth commandment of the Decalogue. Although unrelated to the accusations, it turns out that the accused cleric has a history of requesting money from individuals in order to support, he claims, his elderly parents in their village. The cleric denies the accusations and claims by way of rebuttal to be the victim of racial intolerance. Text-message exchanges captured by a forensic investigation also indicate that attempts were made to have the victims withdraw or at least modify their testimony.

In civil law, sexual activity at age 17 in that particular jurisdiction was not considered a crime, so the police were not involved in terms of taking the case forward. Therefore, no documents of any substance were forthcoming to assist in a canonical process. After a preliminary investigation, it was determined that the other accusations were well-founded and consequently the archbishop wrote to the Dicastery for the Doctrine of the Faith requesting to undertake a process for the delicts mentioned in *Sacramentorum Sanctitatis Tutela*.

The Internal Commission concurred with the archbishop's request and authorized him to undertake a judicial penal process. One aspect of this case which prompted the decision was the adamant denial of the accusations on the part of the cleric and claims that he was ready to sue the ordinary in civil court. Thus, it was evaluated that the judicial process was well suited to adjudicate a matter that was clearly contentious.

Although it was not necessary in this case because of the abundance of canonists locally, in regard to the judicial penal process, *ex* canon 1721 of the Latin code, the case may be entrusted to another tribunal, again keeping in mind the norm of canon 1717 §3, or the ordinary may even name a priest or priests from outside the diocese/religious institute to serve as collegiate judges, promoter of justice *ad casum*, or notary as needed. Given the fact that this is a tribunal of first instance, should there be a need to appoint qualified lay canonists to serve in the trial, a dispensation should be sought from the dicastery. During this penal trial at first instance, care should be taken that the accused is fully aware of the allegations and proofs and that he receive, *via* his canonical procurator/advocate either freely chosen or appointed *ex officio* (cf. c. 1481 §2), a proper defense.

You may be aware in some cases that clerics faced with accusations sometimes request a dispensation either on presentation of the case or at some other point. How does the dicastery consider these requests?

It has been the praxis of the Dicastery for the Doctrine of the Faith to consider a request for a dispensation in the spirit in which the Code of Canon Law governs such requests. In this regard, we do not wish to confuse a dispensation with a solution in these cases. In fact, we are dealing here with a personal request by a cleric to the Holy Father, a grace he is permitted to seek at any time following ordination, and a grace which remains within the Holy Father's purview to grant or not to grant. Prior to the presentation of the request in an audience, the dicastery will make a determination as to where this is opportune, all the while leaving the decision to the Supreme Authority. Of course, once a dispensation is granted and the rescript is signed, the canonical proceedings are concluded and the case is placed in the archives of the dicastery. If, for instance, the cleric refuses to sign the rescript, the canonical process may of course resume. You may have noticed that sometimes the dicastery makes mention of the possibility of seeking a dispensation, often as a reminder of what is established in the Code of Canon Law and in a desire to present the full range of canonical possibilities in a case but in no way as a means of circumventing a process.

Allow me to add some more details about requesting a dispensation. Sometimes a cleric may feel unwilling to go into a lot of detail. This is not necessary. In a petition, which need not be lengthy, but must be precise, the cleric should: 1) address a letter directly to the Holy Father; 2) request that he be dispensed from the obligations of the clerical state, including the obligation of celibacy, with the resultant loss of the clerical state; 3) sign the document in his own hand; 4) date the letter. This document should be forwarded to this dicastery; coupled with a favorable *votum* from the ordinary, the petition would then be presented to the Holy Father for his consideration (cf. art. 27 *SST*). If, on the other hand, the ordinary were not in favour of granting the dispensation, this would be considered in the dicastery prior to or and/or at the time of presenting the request.

There is another category of case which prompts the ordinary to have recourse to article 26 of the norms (*SST*). The accusations in cases like this are so grave and the facts so glaring that often nothing less than a direct presentation of the case without a canonical process for dismissal would appear sufficient. To illustrate what this might look like, here is the scenario.

Case C

The recently-appointed superior general of the *Disciples of the Servant Shepherd*, a relatively newly-founded community of clerics and lay male religious presented the case against its founder, a highly charismatic yet austere priest accused of the delicts of the sexual abuse of eighteen minors. Many were aged between thirteen and fourteen years, although some who later became novices alleged that the abuse began when they were seventeen, upon entry into the community. All were male, as most of the victims in our cases tend to be. His *modus operandi* demonstrated a clear pattern. As a talented artist and musician, he often gave private music classes after school in his private quarters and is alleged to have visited the pupils' dormitory on a weekly basis over the course of five years to offer follow-up lessons on music theory. The older male victims report receiving gifts of money and other privileges in return for sleeping naked in the cleric's bed. Other reports concerning the nature of the abuse vary but sixteen of the victims suffered abuse which, according to the new superior general, was the worst he had ever heard about.

Prior to founding the community, the cleric had been chaplain to a college for the deaf in an isolated woody district where his actions displayed similar patterns. The subsequent closure of the college due to bankruptcy and the suppression of the institute prompted the cleric to find his own community without any apparent suspicions. In the light of the new allegations, reports emerged that five of the first group of victims had committed suicide, others had received payments in return for not testifying, and the parents of three others had been threatened with being fired from their posts as school caretakers and cleaning staff should they say anything against the cleric. A subsequent deeper delve into the cleric's formation demonstrated that he had been expelled from three seminaries on two different continents prior to his ordination. Some of the formation records were missing or incomplete. A fire in an administration office was supposedly the cause.

In forwarding the material, the superior general noted the egregious nature of the accusations, as well as the cleric's partial admission of some of the abuse. Thus the internal commission proposed that the case be deferred to the *Congresso* of the Dicastery for the Doctrine of the Faith with the recommendation that the case not be subject to a canonical process but rather, by way of exception, be presented to the Holy Father *ex* article 26 (*SST*), for his decision. The dicastery wrote to the superior general requesting that the cleric submit his defense, with the assistance of an advocate, in the likelihood that the dicastery was considering presenting his case for a possible dismissal from the clerical state, *ex officio et in poenam*. No defense was received within the time limit established even though proof of delivery of two requests had been obtained.

The case was the discussed again in congress and soon thereafter was presented to the Holy Father, who dismissed the accused from the clerical state, granting him a dispensation from the obligations of the clerical state, including celibacy, along with a dispensation from his religious vows.

Since the arrival of our new prefect on 11 September 2023, there has been a modification in terms of how decisions are made at the *congresso*. In a derogation to the General Regulation of the Roman Curia granted by Pope Francis on 11 September 2023, which has been published on the Vatican website, the *congresso* at which cases of the abuse of minors is now presided over by the Secretary for the Discipline Section. All other cases under the competence of the dicastery, i.e. cases involving crimes against the Eucharist, penance and orders, are discussed in *congresso* once a month under the presidency of the prefect. This decision is an application of *Praedicate evangelium*, by which a secretary was appointed to each of the two sections of the dicastery.

Conclusion

These are just some of the types of cases that illustrate the background and methodology adopted in terms of considering how to resolve cases. Once the process has been authorized, the matter lies with the ordinary. The dicastery, as part of its *praxis*, will usually monitor the situation and will usually write after six months to request an update.

I wish to conclude as I began. The work of safeguarding children and of upholding truth and justice is a work of collaboration of the whole Church. We are part of this. We are aware from our daily interactions that canonists, whether in Rome or worldwide, strive to make these goals a reality every day. It is a hidden but essential work of the Church. If these thoughts have been of any benefit to this endeavor, I am grateful for the opportunity to have shared them with you and I look forward to a deeper level of exchange and collaboration in the future as we strive to serve the Holy Father in this most delicate mission. I leave you with contact details of the dicastery, which can be found in the back of the convention papers.

Please feel free to contact us via Zoom, by telephone, by e-mail, or by letter. We often say that it is better to get the case off on the right footing from the very start, and if some form of initial contact can ensure that this is achieved, then we welcome this. If your ordinary happens to be in Rome, or wishes that you visit in his name, do not hesitate to make contact and arrange an appointment. Various groups and organizations take advantage of this possibility, including the Presidency of the United States Conference of Catholic Bishops (USCCB), Conference of Major Superiors of Men (CMSM), Conference of Major Superiors of Women Religious (CMSWR), and the Canon Law Society of America (CLSA) itself. Various groups of students from canon law faculties worldwide also visit and have an opportunity to learn at first-hand what our mission entails, as well as being able to ask questions and discuss our role in the Church.

Our *Vademecum*, now in its second version, is also available on-line[1] and we are committed to updating it as circumstances require.

On a personal note, it is refreshing to come to work each day knowing that there is no competition between officials, no striving to look better than anyone else but rather a shared desire to do the best we can as an entire body, and all in what you might call a hidden and humble way. I say this because most of the officials will never sign a letter on the dicastery's headed paper during their time. This responsibility is left to the superiors, who are keenly aware of the work that lies behind each case.

I conclude with a word of thanks to the ordinaries and to the priests from the United States of America who have served in our dicastery over the years and who continue to assist us so generously with their time and expertise.

---

1 See https://www.vatican.va/roman_curia/congregations/cfaith/ddf/rc_ddf_doc_20220605_vademecum-casi-abuso-2.0_en.html (accessed on 14 Nov. 2023).

CLSA PROCEEDINGS 85 (2023) 30-45

SEMINAR

SACRED STORIES AND THOSE WHO TELL THEM: TRAUMA-INFORMED MINISTERIAL PRINCIPLES FOR RESPONDING TO SURVIVORS OF CLERGY SEXUAL ABUSE AND OTHER FORMS OF TRAUMA

Dr. Heather T. Banis, PhD[1]

Premises

This paper is based on three important premises. First, as canonists you will encounter trauma survivors in various contexts in the normal course of your ministry. Second, as canonists you are exposed vicariously to trauma. Third, as canonists who are also clergy, you may well have experienced the impact of stigma, suspicion, and/or the fear of, if not an actual, accusation of sexual misconduct by virtue of your status as clergy.

This paper strives to present "best principles" rather than "best practices" as the latter are continuously evolving whereas the principles relevant to being trauma-informed in all areas of ministry are longstanding. Thus, this paper will discuss how to be trauma-informed (or trauma-sensitive) in ministry in general, with specific development of concepts as they apply in matters of clergy or church perpetrated abuse, in particular.

Additionally, this paper will present practical steps that can be taken relative to preventing re-traumatization, creating a safe space for those being served in various ministries (who may be trauma survivors), conducting communications, interviews, and generally interacting with trauma survivors, including supporting them during the fact-gathering phase of a canonical process and sensitively conveying the findings and outcome of said process, and finally, understanding triggered behavior and how it relates to perceived credibility.

---

1 Dr. Heather Banis is the Victims Assistance Coordinator for the Archdiocese of Los Angeles.

Finally, this paper is offered to this audience based on the understanding that as canonists, you are uniquely positioned to serve as ministers of mercy, justice, and compassion.

Pausing to Reflect

As a starting point, it is encouraged that you pause for a moment to reflect on the following questions as you engage with this topic and the material presented herein:

- How is your heart?
- What's stirring in you?
- What is it about this topic that speaks to you?
- What did you bring (in terms of history, personal experience, sensitivity, bias, etc.) with you?

Additionally, these questions are posed as you think specifically about interactions with people who are in a state of vulnerability:

- Knowing that one out of four people with significant mental health challenges will first present to their faith leader, not a mental health practitioner (e.g., psychologist, social worker), how prepared are you to respond in a compassionate and impactful manner?
- How is that person framing their mental health within the context of their faith?
- Are you able to expand their perspective, de-stigmatize, receive, and refer as appropriate?
- What about your own mental health needs?

Research indicates faith leaders often struggle with their own mental health challenges and can feel shame, guilt and even doubts in their own faith when facing such struggles themselves or when overwhelmed by the needs of those to whom they minister (Ansberry, 2021). The chronic strain of the past few years of pandemic, coupled with the specific stressors the clergy abuse phenomenon, has made many faithful feel as if all clergy are under attack. Envisioning a path of healing amid such pain and distress can be difficult and, ironically, can lead to a blaming response towards those who bring forward such issues. Thus, attention to the mental health of both those being ministered to and those ministering is important. Being trauma-informed speaks to both these concerns.

Roles and Needs

Mindful of the statistic reported above, it is also important to clearly identify what the roles of a canonist and/or clergy are in response to a trauma survivor, and equally importantly, what roles said minister does not have. Knowing that most men who answered the call to become priests and deacons did so with a sincere desire to help others, it is important to recognize that such a calling can result in one feeling compelled or responsible for fixing something they simply cannot fix. Clergy can be ministers of mercy, justice, and compassion, but they are not the savior, rescuer, therapist, victim (at least in that moment, in that context), nor perpetrator. Clergy, mental health practitioners, and many others in various helping professions share a common desire to serve others. Many of us, in responding to this call, harbor what are called "rescue fantasies" where we believe, or at least hope, we can rescue someone from the dire circumstances in which they are living. While not inherently bad, such fantasies are often unconscious and serve as a source of further motivation to persist in efforts that may lead to the crossing of boundaries set for the protection of all. Self-recrimination, feelings that one has failed in one's vocation to serve, or save, can lead to feelings of compassion-fatigue, depression, and failure. Hence, a solid grounding in what one's role is and the scope of competence within which one functions is essential to the well-being of both the person served and the minister serving.

Canonists and clergy will encounter "need" in a huge variety of settings and contexts while engaging in ministry—in some instances, the need will be the defining feature of that context (e.g., someone who requests pastoral counseling), while in others it will emerge, often camouflaged by emotional tensions arising out of happy events (e.g., a wedding rehearsal). A partial list of possible settings wherein such an encounter might occur follows and is intended to give some indication of the breadth of settings and circumstances described above:

- Couples and families in crisis, seeking support
- Tribunal proceedings
- Staff and workplace tensions
- Amongst fellow clergy and religious
- Addictions, compulsions
- Suicide, attempted suicide, self-harm
- College dormitories
- Schools and teams
- Weddings, funerals, graduations, sacramental celebrations

- Community violence or trauma
- Health care facilities, sudden illness or injury
- Bullying
- Immigrant communities, communities under duress
- Congregations, changes in ministerial leadership, conflict within a ministry group
- Holiday visitors
- Current and past abuse survivors
- Confessional
- Trafficking, current and past
- Pornography/sexual abuse materials

Trauma-Informed Principles

It is important to remember that trauma survivors, including clergy- or church-perpetrated abuse survivors, can be encountered and experienced as healthy, successful, accomplished persons living lives that are productive and rewarding, in addition to those who are struggling profoundly and living in desperate circumstances, and everywhere along the spectrum in between. Evidence of just how "common" trauma is in life can be seen in the findings of the Adverse Childhood Experiences research conducted by the Centers for Disease Control in partnership with Kaiser Permanente Health Care. In the original study, 17,000 patients in the Kaiser system were asked about potentially traumatic events that occur in childhood. Findings from the original and subsequent studies have identified a powerful connection between the toxic stress generated by the Adverse Childhood Experiences and the health and well-being of those exposed to said stressors, leading the researchers to conclude there is a significant link between Adverse Childhood Experiences and chronic health problems, mental illness, and substance misuse in adulthood. With one in six adults experiencing four or more Adverse Childhood Experiences (e.g., child abuse or neglect, domestic violence, substance abuse in family, incarceration of a parent or caregiver, suicide or attempted suicide of a family member, or parental separation or divorce) Adverse Childhood Experiences are common, not rare. In fact, almost two-thirds of participants reported at least one Adverse Childhood Experience in their childhood. Furthermore, statistics suggest that one in four women and one in six men have experienced child sexual abuse, further underscoring the reality that Adverse Childhood Experiences are more common that one would like to think. Note, clergy, mental health practitioners, and others in helping professions are not immune to these experiences in their own lives and in fact, in many instances, lived experience serves as the inspiration for pursuing a vocation to serve. Hence, the wise, timeless words of Henri Nouwen in his book *The Wounded Healer* are so relevant and important for us to understand as he challenges us to imagine how we might put our own woundedness into the service of others:

> We are all wounded people, whether physically, emotionally, mentally, or spiritually. The main question is not, "how can we hide our wounds?" so we don't have to be embarrassed, but "how can we put our wounds in the service of others?" When our wounds cease to be a source of shame, and become a source of healing, we have become wounded healers.[2]

Mindful of the findings of the Adverse Childhood Experiences research and related scientific studies, we now understand how the developing brain is literally "wiring up" in response to experiences; when that brain is immersed in trauma, it is forging connections and organizing in response to that trauma. In an ideal world, children (and their developing brains) are growing up, wiring up, in a loving, safe, nurturing, enriched context such that their brains are foundational to a mind that is characterized by coherence, integration, and a capacity for imagination. A child whose brain is percolating in trauma is establishing and refining neural systems focused on vigilance, threat detection, and, quite literally, survival. Fortunately, while there is an intense and profoundly important period of brain development in childhood, the brain remains responsive to experience, throughout the lifespan such that the most traumatized person can, with repeated experiences that embody safety, acknowledgement, and compassion, begin to trust—risk more intimacy in relationships with the hope and understanding that not everyone is dangerous or threatening. This is a sacred space into which canonists, by virtue of what brings them in contact with others, and clergy overall, by virtue of their position, can exemplify right relationship and in doing so, perhaps, allow a trauma survivor to experience a safe and healthy relationship. Dr. Eboni Webb, an expert in dialectal behavior therapy (commonly used in trauma work), considers the parts of the brain that perceive abandonment to be the most neuroplastic, able to rebound as there is consistency in attachment and connection and a felt sense of safety.[3]

---

2 Henri Nouwen, *The Wounded Healer* (Garden City, NY: Doubleday Image Books, 1979).

3 See Eboni Webb, "Finding the Wounded Child Inside the Monster: Applying a DBT-Focused Lens to Trauma and Addiction" digital seminar Oct 07, 2022, available for purchase at https://catalog.psychotherapynetworker.org/item/finding-wounded-child-monster-applying-dbtfocused-lens-trauma-addiction-117546 (accessed on 15 Mar. 2024).

Paul Tillich, 20th-century theologian, famously stated, "The first duty of love is to listen."[4] As ministers of mercy, justice, and compassion, as you listen, it is paramount that you understand how and where you may encounter trauma-survivors. Trauma may be central to the matter at hand; it may be a risk factor that has created vulnerabilities; it may be unrelated to the matter at hand but relevant to the individual's situation at present and the outcome sought. Understand, too, that the trauma may have happened a very long time ago, but it is being triggered in or by the present situation. Creating a space in which that trauma can be "held" is a powerful gift to the person who has survived the trauma as it creates a sense of witness and connection when by its very nature, trauma tends to isolate. The words of psychologist, Robert Stolorow, speak to this:

> Trauma is constituted in an intersubjective context in which severe emotional pain cannot find a relational home in which it can be held. In such a context, painful affect states become unendurable.[5]

Definitions

Defining what is meant by *trauma* and *trauma-informed* helps focus understanding and efforts to serve those traumatized. The United States Substance Abuse and Mental Health Services Administration (SAMHSA) offers the following definition:

> Individual trauma results from an *event* [what happened and in what circumstances], series of events, or set of circumstances that is *experienced* [individual's interpretation, understanding, assigned meaning of event], by an individual as physically or emotionally harmful or life threatening and that has lasting adverse *effects* [can be immediate, delayed, long-lasting, pervasive] on the individual's functioning and mental, physical, social, emotional, or spiritual well-being.[6]

Having identified the 3 Es of trauma, the administration offers the 4 Rs to establish the parameters of trauma-informed work such that a program, organization, or system that is trauma-informed realizes the widespread impact of trauma and understands potential paths for recovery; recognizes the signs and symptoms of trauma in clients, families, staff, and others involved with the system; and

---

4 Paul Tillich, *Love, Power, and Justice* (Oxford: Oxford University Press, 1960).

5 Robert Stolorow, *Trauma and Human Existence: Autobiographical, Psychoanalytic, and Philosophical Reflections* (Oxfordshire, Eng.: Routledge, 2007) 10.

6 SAMHSA, "Trauma-Informed Care in Behavioral Health Services Treatment Improvement Protocol (TIP)," Series #57, Part 3: A Review of the Literature, 1-1, at https://store.samhsa.gov/sites/default/files/sma14-4816_litreview.pdf (accessed on 12 Feb. 2024).

responds by fully integrating knowledge about trauma into policies, procedures, and practices, and seeks to actively resist re-traumatization.

By its very nature, trauma experience is embedded in a power differential in which one person, institution, entity, has power over another. Recognizing this power structure is essential to understanding how the trauma survivor can be mired in the essential question, "why me?" To answer that question, the survivor often assumes or accepts some responsibility for the trauma eliciting profound feelings of shame, blame, and guilt, particularly when the trauma was perpetrated by a trusted person, institution, or entity. This process is further compounded by any threats or manipulations by the perpetrating person, institution, or entity, whether actual or implied. Further still, the lived experience of the trauma is embedded in cultural, historical, and gender- and race-based realities, which may amplify the impact and influence or even dictate the response to the trauma, both by the survivor and by those in relationship with the survivor.

The impact of trauma, particularly sexual abuse by a trusted person, can be immediate, delayed, long-lasting, and pervasive. The pattern of exposure to trauma, particularly in a young child, can result in the neurological organization and structuring previously described such that vigilance and constant arousal, threat detection, numbing, or avoidance responses are "hard-wired" and become the default mode for the survivor. Such exposure to a betrayal trauma like sexual abuse, can impact the survivor's capacity to function in some, many, or all aspects of life—personal relationships, school, and work settings, in relation to authority, in one to one or group settings, regardless of the "objective" safety of any of these contexts. Safety, in service of survival, becomes the priority, and its pursuit can eclipse all other aspects of human functioning. Hence, to be trauma-informed is to understand the following six principles as essential if the survivor(s) are to fulfill their potential:

1. Safety – physical, emotional, psychological, spiritual
2. Trustworthiness and Transparency
3. Peer Support
4. Collaboration and Mutuality
5. Empowerment, Voice, and Choice
6. Cultural, Historical, and Gender Issues

Hence, to cultivate a ministry culture that is trauma-informed, those engaged in ministry leadership must operate in a manner that conveys understanding and prioritizing of these survivor needs, with the knowledge that trauma-survivors may not "look" or "act" the way you would expect them to and with the assumption that at any given time there are unidentified trauma survivors in the midst of the ministry. Dr. Bruce Perry and Dr. Thema Bryant Davis, both esteemed mental health practitioners, advocate a shift from the "what's wrong with you?" response often elicited when a trauma survivor's self-protective mechanisms manifest, to a "what happened to you?" framework such that the survivor's behavior can be understood as a plausible means of increasing one's chance of survival in circumstances that are perceived by the survivor to be potentially threatening.

Sexual Abuse, Clergy-Perpetrated Sexual Abuse, Abuse of Power

Sexual abuse, which is far more likely to be perpetrated by a known and trusted person, is considered a betrayal trauma based in an abuse of power. The very beliefs by which we operate—that the world is (should be) a safe place, that the people I trust will not harm me, that God is good—are all threatened by a betrayal trauma such that the survivor of such a trauma learns to anticipate threat, harm and abandonment, even as they live in a state of disbelief that such an act could have been perpetrated. This is anxiety-inducing, to say the least, and can give rise to a way of being that is rooted in self-protection even if not productively so. Hypervigilance, all-or-none thinking, substance abuse, history of broken and conflicted relationships, inability to sustain employment vis a vis problems with authority figures, aggression, social isolation, criminal activity, and even abuse of others can all result from trauma exposure.

Clergy-perpetrated sexual abuse seems often to have been committed against children for whom some pre-existing vulnerability was exploitable—children from dysfunctional or broken homes, single-parent homes, dual-parent homes with both parents working and less able to supervise their children, children from families with language barriers and/or immigration status concerns, and similar were often targeted. It is important to recognize these factors particularly as they relate to questions as to why the abuse was not disclosed at the time is was happening, or at least, shortly thereafter. According to the Center for Disease Control, the average age at first disclosure for sexual abuse survivors is somewhere in their early 50s. Barriers to disclosure include a significant fear of being disbelieved, judged, shamed, and held culpable for the abuse—a fear many predators further exploited and a fear that often resulted in a survivor recanting their disclosure. Notably, researchers have found that the first disclosure has a 95% chance of being truthful and that intentionally false allegations by children are quite rare. Disclosure may also be hampered by the survivor's desire to protect their parents from any knowledge of or feeling of responsibility for the child's abuse. Additionally, many clergy-abuse survivors love, or loved, their church and their faith; they do not, or did not, want to do anything, such as disclosure or seeking justice, because it could hurt their church. Others are disconnected from the church, their faith practices, and God because of the abuse; this is an important feature that distinguishes clergy-sexual-abuse survivors from other trauma survivors, as spirituality is an important factor in trauma recovery that may be unavailable to the clergy-abuse survivor. Abuse experienced in the church challenges, and for some obliterates, foundational beliefs about the church, including its benevolence and trustworthiness, and about God, with profound impact on the survivor's sense of worth.

Given the interconnection between clergy-perpetrated abuse and its impact on the survivor's faith, as stated so eloquently by theologian Deborah van Deusen Hunsinger:

> [P]astoral leaders need to recognize the power inherent in their position to frame and interpret any traumatic event that has occurred. In doing so, they can either inflame the situation by escalating anxiety or decrease anxiety and facilitate healing by opening channels of communications . . . as they offer a secure holding environment to strengthen frayed bonds of trust, and as they call upon God to minister to the community in its pain, they offer space to the hurting to tell their story.[7]

With more than twenty years of reckoning with the clergy abuse phenomenon, the church has made significant strides in understanding the impact of and supporting those impacted by this trauma. Learning from survivors, listening with an open heart to what they have experienced, both at the hands of their perpetrator and in the responses they received when they did disclose, has been pivotal in the church's ability to implement impactful prevention policies and provide the resources necessary to foster genuine healing. Regardless of the circumstances of the trauma, encountering a trauma survivor presents an opportunity for the church to impact the way in which a survivor experiences the church—a chance for that person to feel what it is like to be seen through eyes of God, not the eyes of their perpetrator. Seek to awaken in them an awareness of their original grace—that part of them that remains God's, untouched—beyond the reach of the perpetrator. Seek to awaken in them an awareness of and respect for their resiliency, their strength, and their capacity to survive.

---

7 Deborah van Deusen Hunsinger, "Bearing the Unbearable: Trauma, Gospel and Pastoral Care," *Theology Today*, vol. 68, no. 1 (2011) 8-25.

Practical Suggestions

In the spirit of listening to and learning from survivors, Teresa Pitt Green, survivor and co-founder of Spirit Fire, created a list of "Do's and Don'ts." As per their website:

> Spirit Fire is a fellowship of survivors of abuse within the Church who share, as part of our ongoing recovery, a spiritual practice which permits us to offer our wisdom, experience, and faith to all others who seek healing, growth, and reconciliation in the wake of the abuse of children and vulnerable adults in a faith setting—in particular in the Catholic Church.[8]

Created within a restorative justice framework, Spirit Fire seeks the many paths to reconciliation and accompanies survivors and clergy. The list of "Do's and Don'ts" can be applied at a very practical level and is shared with permission.

DON'T	DO
Don't talk.	Listen.
Don't know.	Learn.
Don't defend.	Acknowledge guilt of abusers/enablers.
Don't minimize.	Recognize the burden.
Don't intellectualize.	Permit strong feelings.
Don't launch a pep talk.	If it were possible, we'd be over it.
Don't be impatient.	Remember healing is on God's time.
Don't be directive.	Follow our lead and pace.
Don't be linear.	Appreciate healing as circular, repetitive.
Don't wing it.	Be knowledgeable and prepared.
Don't be goal oriented.	Be God-oriented. His presence is enough.
Don't judge or shame.	Offer radical respect to a humiliated person.
Don't talk to a diagnosis.	Talk to us about the diagnosis.
Don't own.	Respect boundaries on a person's burdens.
Don't fix.	Accept healing as a process.
Don't assume this is past.	Care for the here and now.
Don't push.	Pace, go slowly.
Don't expect efficiency.	Simplify, repeat, confirm.

8 "Spirit Fire: Christian Restorative Justice," https://spiritfirelive.wordpress.com/ (accessed on 15 Mar. 2024).

Don't expect reliability.	Expect no-shows, late arrivals.
Don't personalize.	Depersonalize errors and rough edges.
Don't take responsibility.	Set firm boundaries, softly.
Don't analyze.	Affirm mystery and grace in this life.
Don't shift into therapy.	Know how to refer for professional help.
Don't go it alone.	Let the Holy Spirit do the heavy lifting.
Don't hesitate.	Pastor.[9]

In addition to this list from Spirit Fire, I offer the following suggestions:

Don't control unnecessarily.	Offer and respect choices.
Don't offer platitudes.	Offer genuine expressions of concern, hope.
Don't offer scriptural references carelessly.	Cultivate a vocabulary for trauma.
Don't ignore or minimize disclosure.	Acknowledge disclosure.
Don't lead with distrust.	Acknowledge the courage it took to come forward.
Don't underestimate fear of being disbelieved.	Strive to create a safe space.
Don't rush healing or spur forgiveness.	Trust the healing process: the need to forgive will emerge, in some form, in some time.

Understanding How Trauma Manifests in Survivors and What Survivors Need

All too often, survivors report that they were rushed to forgive, encouraged to do so by someone in the church who is well-meaning but insensitive to how this is received by someone harmed in the church. Inadequate preparation for such a conversation leads too often to a sense that the survivor is responsible for "ending this" and that if only the survivor could "forgive and forget" all would be well, and everyone could "move on." In some cases, survivors have been told to pray for their perpetrators and to stop attacking the church. The sacred moment when a survivor of clergy perpetrated abuse discloses and seeks the presence and understanding of someone in the very institution where the harm took place is a precious opportunity to provide an experience that contradicts the abuse, is respectful of what has been experienced and the burden that has been imposed on

9 The list of "Do's and Don'ts in Survivor Ministry" is no longer available on the Spirit Fire website. See https://thehealingvoicesnewsletter.wordpress.com/2017/02/17/dos-and-donts -in-survivor-ministry/ (accessed on 15 Mar. 2024).

that survivor – it is an opportunity to be church to that person, or as Saint Teresa of Avila said, "Yours are the hands with which Christ is to bless all people now." At the very least, seek to do no harm. At the most, strive to see the face of Christ in the survivor and respond with compassion, seeking the ways in which you can be a minister of mercy and justice.

According to Diane Langberg, PhD, Christian trauma psychologist, because trauma silences those traumatized, recovery from trauma requires the "reversal of trauma dynamics" such that survivors are encouraged to and are supported when they speak up and speak out, shedding light on what was contained in darkness and isolation. She also speaks of the healing power of hope—instilling a sense of hope rooted in the future and its possibilities. That said, it is important to recognize that surviving and healing from trauma is rooted not just in these emotional shifts, but it is a neurological process as well. In the midst of trauma, the person experiencing the traumatic event may also experience, through no action or intention of their own, the following survival reflexes:

- Alterations in perceptions of time and time sequencing.
- Dissociation (an alternation in attention and awareness such that the person feels spaced out, a sense of disappearing, leaving one's body)—this is more common than a fight or flight response.
- Memory alterations with some details retained with vividness and others vague, inconsistently recalled, or even missing.
- Fight, flight, or freeze response, the latter of which can create immobility, impaired rational thinking processes, and an overreliance on habitual behaviors regardless of the circumstances.

Considering these survival reflexes, which can be readily triggered long after the traumatizing event, a number of practical concerns are important to understand. First, a felt sense of safety—felt in the body—is critical to enable someone with a trauma history to stay present in the moment and engaged in the task at hand. Creating a safe space includes attention to the physical attributes of the space (location, size, ease of access and egress, items and images in the space, clerical garb, lighting, and more). Some of this can be anticipated; some of it will be idiosyncratic and require gentle inquiry of the person invited to the space. Sensitivity in communications, both what is communicated and how it is communicated, is also important. Before and during any interviews, be prepared to repeat, be concrete, and when possible, put things in writing to support survivors whose capacity to remember when emotionally stressed may be compromised. Allow time for information to be processed, understood, and responded to, and follow-up and affirm what was understood or not. Provide updates throughout the process as a lack of communication while the process is ongoing can be misinterpreted in many ways. Use clear and simple language, avoiding jargon and terminology when possible, defining terms as needed and as often as necessary. Be mindful of the aforementioned "Do's and Don'ts" as you strive to convey acknowledgement and concern. Be mindful of what message the body is conveying nonverbally via facial expressions, posture, proximity, restlessness, impatience, distraction, eye contact, touch, comfort with silence and state of tension. Finally, recognize that a personal experience of trauma will also impact how you listen to another survivor—self-monitor for triggering or vicarious trauma exposure and be intentional about self-care before and after such exposure.

Both for your well-being and for that of the other person, it may be helpful to think about interactions with trauma survivors as an opportunity to concretely demonstrate trustworthiness, thereby, hopefully, enabling the survivor to experience that felt sense of safety that is paramount to their ability to participate in the process before you.

Demonstrating trustworthiness is necessary but may not be sufficient to prevent re-traumatization—good intentions and efforts may not be enough, and the behavior triggered by emerging fear may disrupt and derail the process at hand. Triggers (e.g., clerical garb or smells such as incense that are reminiscent of the trauma) are directly connected to the survivor's perceived sense of safety—they serve as beacons to a survivor whose experience of threat, in that moment, is eliciting behaviors that may seem disproportionate, irrational, and even disconnected from the event to observers. Understanding that the perception of these triggers is rooted in the traumatized brain seeking to ensure survival and, in that sense, the triggered behaviors are purposeful and may be lifesaving. As Dr. Langberg has said, trauma survivors often experience life as persistently terrifying; possible threats to safety are encountered in new circumstances and said perceived threats have the power to transport the survivor "back" to the time and place of the original trauma instantaneously.

In a moment such as this, the survivor may be re-experiencing the terror felt at the time of the traumatic event, which can compromise their ability to recall and/or connect the experience to the present. Dissociation, in the past and in the present, can result in a survivor who is unable to convey historical information and/or maintain engagement with whatever the current process is in such a way that an uninformed observer may misperceive the survivor as having less credibility when they are unable to provide a cohesive narrative describing what happened. Fear of not being believed is one of the key factors delaying and even precluding disclosure of such traumatic experiences as child sexual abuse; it is also a factor that many perpetrators will exploit to further silence a victim. When dissociation is combined with a fear of not being believed, the resulting portrayal of the trauma can appear so compromised as to call into question the credibility of the reporting person. Hence, the importance of fostering a felt and genuine sense of safety is critical not only for the ease and comfort of the survivor engaged in a canonical process but also to maximize the survivor's ability to provide as complete and accurate an account of the relevant matter(s) as possible.

Fostering a Sense of Safety and, Hopefully, Hope

As ministers of mercy, justice, and compassion, canonists are uniquely positioned to spark what Fr. Ron Rolheiser, OMI, and others call the Paschal Imagination: to inspire in a survivor a renewed capacity to see themselves through the eyes of God and not through the perpetrator's eyes. As Rolheiser states:

> We lack imagination when we stand before our own experience petrified, frozen and unable to accept or cope with what is there; or when we stand before it stunned, benignly unaware that forces are about to destroy us. We have healthy imaginations when we can stand before any reality and have a sense of what God is asking of us. A healthy imagination is the opposite of resignation, abdication, naïve optimism or despair. It is the foundation of hope.[10]

Hope is also sparked by positive experiences, and such experiences can serve as powerful antidotes to trauma. Dr. Bruce Perry, Dr. Marty Seligman, and Dr. Robert Sege, among many others, all affirm that neurological reorganization—literally the re-wiring of the brain—can begin with key positive experiences that affirm our inherent worth and significance, leading to healthier outcome. Church, as one powerful and impactful manifestation of community, can thus be essential in this process, fostering healing in its very basic functions—welcoming and holding space for those who seek God. An unnamed author speaks to this in his or her statement on social media: "My story is filled with broken pieces, terrible choices, and ugly truths. It's also filled with a major comeback, peace in my soul, and a grace that saved my life."[11]

Such grace opens the door to healing—healing that is constituted of integration, resilience, agency, spontaneity, wonder, joy, personal wellness, healthy relationships, freedom from the tyranny of triggers, release from grief and

---

10 Ron Rohlheiser, "Paschal Imagination," February 18, 1991, https://ronrolheiser.com/paschal-imagination/ (accessed on 12 Feb. 2024).

11 As quoted by Kathy Browne, *The Minds Journal*, https://themindsjournal.com/quotes/my-story-is-filled-with-broken-pieces/ (accessed on 12 Feb. 2024).

haunting memories, and engagement. Such a life is lived in the moment, or as Dr. Bessel Van der Kolk, an international expert on trauma, has stated, "[W]hen you're healed, you're here and not there . . . you don't get distracted by your fears or your terror or your rage."[12]

In closing, whether you are dealing specifically in the realm of clergy sexual abuse or more broadly drawn into the traumatic history of a petitioner in a canonical process, I offer you the borrowed wisdom of a bishop, a mystic, and a saint:

> Remedies cannot be confined to psychology and structural reforms. They are needful but not sufficient. Over and above them, we need contrition, the rekindling of faith, a new heart. We must relearn what it means to live and die in Christ.[13]

****

May you be blessed with a wise and compassionate guide,
Who can accompany you through the fear and grief,
Until your heart has wept its way to your true self.[14]

****

Christ has no body now on earth but yours,
no hands but yours, no feet but yours.
Yours are the eyes through which Christ's compassion
is to look out to the world.
Yours are the feet with which Christ
is to go about doing good.
Yours are the hands with which Christ
Is to bless all people now.[15]

---

12 Bessel van der Kolk, "How to Help Traumatized Patients Restore their Vitality," National Institute for the Clinical Adaptation of Behavioral Medicine (see transcript), at https://www.nicabm.com/aliveness-and-vitality/ (accessed on 12 Feb. 2024).

13 Erik Varden, Bishop of Trondheim, Norway, Interview, "From Grace to Blasphemy," *The Tablet*, 5 January 2022, https://www.thetablet.co.uk/features/2/21244/victims-in-the-cloisters-from-grace-to-blasphemy (accessed on 12 Feb. 2024).

14 John O'Donohue, excerpt from poem: "For Someone Awakening to the Trauma of His or Her Past," in *To Bless the Space Between Us: A Book of Blessings* (New York: Doubleday, 2008).

15 Adapted from prayer of St. Teresa of Avila, "Christ Has No Body but Yours," https://catholic-link.org/quotes/st-teresa-of-avila-quote-christ-has-no-body-but-yours/ (accessed on 12 Feb. 2024).

ADDITIONAL RESOURCES

Ansberry, Clare, "The Religious Leaders on the Front Lines of Mental Health," *Wall Street Journal*, July 22, 2021.

Adverse Childhood Events Research, https://www.cdc.gov/violenceprevention/aces/about.html.

Davis, Thema Bryant, President of American Psychological Association, https://www.apa.org/monitor/2023/01/thema-bryant.

Green, Teresa Pitt, https://spiritfirelive.wordpress.com/who-we-are/teresapittgreen/ and https://endersisland.org/people/teresa-pit-green.

Langberg, Diane, https://www.dianelangberg.com/.

Perry, Bruce and Oprah Winfrey, *What Happened to You? Conversations on Trauma, Resilience, and Healing* (Chicago: Flatiron Books: An Oprah Book, 2021).

Catholic Bishops Conference, *The Isaiah Journey*, https://www.cbcew.org.uk/.

John N. Sheveland, ed., *Theology in a Post-traumatic Church* (Maryknoll, NY: Orbis Books, 2023).
Fr. Hans Zollner, S.J., Foreword.
Dr. Heather Banis, Chapter 1.

CLSA PROCEEDINGS 85 (2023) 46-67

SEMINAR

RATIO FUNDAMENTALIS INSTITUTIONIS SACERDOTALIS, *PPF6*, AND THE CODE OF CANON LAW

Reverend Phillip Brown, PSS, JCD

I. Introduction.

Thank you for attending this workshop on the new *Ratio fundamentalis institutionis sacerdotalis*, the Program of Priestly Formation Sixth Edition for the United States, and canon law. I would like to outline the kinds of questions seminary rectors and other administrators, bishops, and vocation directors may ask you as canonists in the course of their efforts to implement the Program of Priestly Formation. I would also like to offer some hermeneutical, that is interpretative, principles for addressing the issues they raise. In doing so I will point out some ambiguities and even conflicts in some of the documents and canon law texts applicable to the administration of seminaries and implementation of the new Program of Priestly Formation. I will be aiming at a critical analysis of the provisions of these texts from a canon law perspective. Some questions have already been arising regarding their interpretation. It is not unlikely that seminary and diocesan personnel will resort to canonists for assistance in understanding and applying the provisions of these texts. It is no secret that seminary administrators, bishops, and vocation directors in the United States have been puzzling over how to implement that *Ratio* and Program of Priestly Formation 6 as approved by the Dicastery for Clergy in the context of the pastoral situation and culture in the United States, in particular in relation to what seem to be some of the inflexible requirements of the *Ratio* written into the Program of Priestly Formation in order to obtain the dicastery's approval.

Canonists analyzing the texts of the applicable documents may recognize, however, that from a canonical point of view there may be more flexibility available to implement the norms contained therein than would be obvious to those who have not been trained as canonists. Bishops, seminary administrators, and vocation directors may well turn to canonists to help them interpret the relevant documents when faced with what appear to them to be ambiguous norms or conflicting norms, all of which they feel responsible for implementing. It is in this service to bishops, seminary administrators, and vocation directors that canonists may be able to be of the greatest assistance relying on their canonical training, calling to mind Archbishop Arrieta's comment at the end of his presentation to the general assembly of the Society this morning that:

> The task of the canonist, then, is to carry out a hermeneutic work, which, starting from the foundations of the concrete juridical interest that each norm or each canonical institution seeks to protect, and use with mastery, all the instruments of elasticity and equity that canonical science has accumulated over the centuries, so that what always prevails is the justice and truth that each concrete situation requires.[1]

Canonists also are reminded that when interpreting the 1983 Code of Canon Law it must always be interpreted in the light of the teaching of the Second Vatican Council.

While I am approaching these topics as a canonist, I have also been a seminary rector for twelve years, first at Theological College at the Catholic University of America, then at St. Mary's Seminary and University in Baltimore for the past seven years. Before delving into our topic, I want to thank the Canon Law Society of America for inviting me to present this workshop, and I express my gratitude to the Society of St. Sulpice for my formation as a priest and the opportunities it has afforded me to serve as a seminary formator and administrator. Also, thanks to the Pontifical Gregorian University where I received my training as a canonist, and the School of Canon Law at the Catholic University of America where I was a member of the faculty for several years.

II. Paramount Canonical Issues

1) What is the canonical status of the *Ratio*?
2) What is the canonical status of the Program of Priestly Formation?
3) Who is the competent authority for resolving the canonical issues that have arisen or are likely to arise regarding the implementation of the *Ratio* and Program of Priestly Formation 6; and
4) What canonical means are available for addressing and resolving those questions?

As will become evident, various provisions of the *Ratio*, the Program of Priestly Formation 6, and the Code of Canon Law are not completely in accord with one another. In some instances, ambiguities may need to be resolved with the

---

1 Juan Ignacio Arrieta, "The Role Of Law In The Church: What Is Its Relevance Today?" *CLSA Proceedings 85* (2023) 16.

assistance of a canonist. In other instances, there may appear to be conflicts between different provisions that need to be resolved. That is why there are canonists: written texts almost always contain ambiguities and need to be interpreted. Sometimes there are apparent or real conflicts between different norms or directives. As new regimes come into power and new documents issue, they begin to pile up. Periodically someone has to try to bring them into accord. That was Tribonian's project on behalf of the Emperor Justinian resulting in the *Corpus Iuris Civilis*. That was Gratian's project resulting in his *Concordia discordantium canonum*, the famous *Decretum* of Gratian. That is what jurists and canonists do, among other things.

III. Canonical Status of the *Ratio*.

To begin with, then, what is the *Ratio fundamentalis institutionis sacerdotalis*? What is its canonical status? It states in a couple of places that it is a "general executory decree." It also says in footnote 6:

> The document is a general executory decree, *ex* can. 31 §1 C.I.C. which, in applying the canonical norms regarding formation, replaces the *Ratio Fundamentalis Insitutionis Sacerdotalis* of 6 January 1970, and its revised edition of 19 March 1985; cf. Second Vatican Council, Decree on the Formation of Priests, *Optatam totius* (28 October 1966), n. 1: *AAS* 58 (1966), 713.[2]

Two clarifications to avoid any confusion regarding competence. Before 2013 the Congregation for Catholic Education and Seminaries was responsible for matters pertaining to seminaries. In 2013 Pope Benedict XVI transferred this jurisdiction to the Congregation for Clergy. In 2022 Pope Francis changed the designation "congregation" to "dicastery" in *Praedicate evangelium*.[3] What was the Congregation for Catholic Education and Seminaries is now the Dicastery for Culture and Education; the Congregation for Clergy is now the Dicastery for Clergy. But the Dicastery for Culture and Education still has competence in the accreditation of seminary academic programs granting pontifical degrees, such as St. Mary's in Baltimore. We have many masters at St. Mary's: the Dicastery for Clergy; the Dicastery for Culture and Education; the United States Conference of

---

2 Congregation for the Clergy, *Ratio fundamentalis institutionis sacerdotalis,* December 8, 2016: https://www.vatican.va/roman_curia/congregations/cclergy/documents/rc_con_cclergy_doc_20161208_ratio-fundamentalis-institutionis-sacerdotalis_it.pdf (accessed on 5 Feb. 2024); Eng. trans. at https://www.sdb.org/en/ Council_Resources/Formation/Documents/ratio_fundamentalis_institutionis_sacerdotalis_8_dicembre_2016 (accessed on 5 Feb. 2024) (hereafter "*Ratio* 2016").

3 Francis, apostolic constitution *Praedicate evangelium,* March 19, 2022: *AAS* 114 (2022) 375-455.

Catholic Bishops; and secular accrediting agencies (Association of Theological Schools [ATS] and Middle States). As for St. Mary's and our sister seminaries, we have the Society of St. Sulpice. And of course, we fall under the jurisdiction of the Archbishop of Baltimore over seminaries in his territory, and we need to respond to the bishops who send men to St. Mary's, many of whom are on our civil Board of Trustees, to which we also answer.

The 2016 *Ratio* is a general executory decree. What is a general executory decree? It is not the same as a general decree. Canon 31 §1 states that "Those who possess executive power are able to issue, within the limits of their competence, general executory decrees, namely, those which more precisely determine the methods to be observed in applying the law or which urge the observance of laws."[4] Canon 33 §1 goes on to say that "General executory decrees, even if they are issued in directories or in documents of another name, do not derogate [in Latin *derogo, derogare*] from laws, and their prescripts which are contrary to laws lack all force."[5] Latin dictionaries tell us that *derogo, derogare* means "to propose to repeal [a law] in part; to restrict, modify [a law]."[6] We will see as we go along, therefore, if there appear to be any such provisions in the *Ratio*. Whether or not a provision derogates from applicable law will be a key issue for canonists to consider when they are sought out for advice and counsel.

The laws the *Ratio* and its predecessors were promulgated to give guidance on the implementation of the decree *Optatam totius* of the Second Vatican Council and the provisions of the Code of Canon Law. It may not be apparent to non-canonists whether a provision of the *Ratio* does or does not derogate from these laws, but uncertainty over some provisions already exists when trying to apply various provisions together. Canonists are likely to be asked for advice on such points, therefore.

IV. Canonical Status of the *PPF*

The Program of Priestly Formation is what the code and the *Ratio fundamentalis* refer to as a "*Ratio nationalis*." Canon 242 §1 provides that:

> §1. Each nation is to have a program of priestly formation that is to be established by the conference of bishops, attentive to the norms issued

---

4 *Codex Iuris Canonici auctoritate Ioannis Pauli PP. II promulgatus* (Vatican City: Libreria Editrice Vaticana, 1983) c. 31 §1; Eng. trans. from *Code of Canon Law: Latin–English Edition. New English Translation* (Washington, DC: CLSA, 2023). All English translations from this code will be taken from this source unless otherwise indicated.

5 Ibid.

6 See, e.g., John C. Traupman, *The New College Latin & English Dictionary* (New York: Bantam Books, 1966) 80.

by the supreme authority of the Church, and which is to be approved by the Holy See. This program is to be adapted to new circumstances, also with the confirmation of the Holy See, and is to define the main principles of the instruction to be given in the seminary and general norms adapted to the pastoral needs of each region or province.

§2. All seminaries, both diocesan and inter-diocesan, are to observe the norms of the program mentioned in §1.[7]

What is the canonical status of the Program of Priestly Formation, then? Canon 242 is obviously a law. But is the Program of Priestly Formation, which it mandates, law? It is a little hard to say. Is the *Ratio nationalis*, as a "*ratio,*" also a general executory decree that may not derogate from the laws it concerns, but not a law itself as in the case of the *Ratio Fundamentalis*? Or does the *Ratio nationalis* have greater canonical force than the *Ratio fundamentalis*? If it is a general executory decree, it must not derogate from true laws. If it is truly a law, then it has the canonical force of a law. What then if its provisions derogate from other applicable laws, or even contradict them? Canonists may be called on to assist in resolving such questions.

V. Underlying Law

It is clear that the laws that underlie the *Ratio* and *PPF* are:

- The Code of Canon Law
- *Optatam totius*[8]
- *Presbyterorum ordinis*[9]

Regarding *Optatam totius* and *Presbyterorum ordinis:*

- Both are decrees.
- *Optatam totius* (the Decree on Priestly Training of the Second Vatican Council) was approved and promulgated by Pope Paul VI on October 28, 1965.
- *Presbytorum ordinis* (the Decree on the Ministry and Life of Priests) was promulgated by Pope Paul VI on December 7, 1965.
- Both contain provisions relating to the education and formation of priests.

---

7 Canon 242 §1.

8 Paul VI, Decree on Priestly Training *Optatam totius*, October 28, 1965: *AAS* 58 (1966) 713-727.

9 Paul VI, Decree on the Ministry and Life of Priests *Presbyterorum ordinis*. December 7, 1965: *AAS* 58 (1966) 991-1024.

The Code of Canon Law consists of laws, of course, and a decree of an ecumenical council is a true law.

- Canon 29 states: "General decrees, by which a competent legislator issues common prescripts for a community capable of receiving law, are laws properly speaking and are governed by the prescripts of the canons on laws."
- Canon 30 states: "A person who possesses only executive power is not able to issue the general decree mentioned in can. 29 unless, in particular cases, it has been expressly granted to that person by a competent legislator according to the norm of law and the conditions stated in the act of the grant have been observed."

By its own terms, however, the *Ratio* is a general executory decree, not a general decree.

Pope St. John Paul II's 1992 post-synodal apostolic exhortation *Pastores dabo vobis*[10] also set forth provisions for the conduct of seminary formation, but it was neither a decree nor a general executory decree, but an apostolic exhortation, following a meeting of the Synod of Bishops: exhortative, not prescriptive, however closely it may have been followed by seminaries.

VI. Ethos of the 2016 *Ratio*

The 2016 *Ratio* expresses a different ethos than that expressed by the 1970 and 1985 *Rationes* which it replaces. The Preface to the 1985 *Ratio* stated regarding The Basic Norms for Priestly Formation (1970 *Ratio*):

> [S]uch a document contained only the general themes of ecclesiastical pedagogy, from which [the] mind of the Second Vatican Council shone forth, and the limits within which the life of seminaries could safely progress. . . . [T]he document not only did not inhibit the work and initiative of each country, but helped and stimulated it as much as possible.[11]

> In its introduction, it states:

> By the decree . . . *Optatam totius* the Second Vatican Council provided the principal and more general rules for today's efforts towards seminary reform. . . . Certain further determinations are needed *in order*

10 John Paul II, post-synodal apostolic exhortation *Pastores dabo vobis*, March 25, 1992: *AAS* 84 (1992) 657-804.

11 John Paul II, *Ratio fundamentalis institutionis sacerdotalis*, March 19, 1985, Preface, at https://www.vatican.va/roman_curia/congregations/ccatheduc/documents/rc_con_ccatheduc_doc_19850319_ratio-fundamentalis_it.html (accessed on 5 Feb. 2024).

> *that the reforms may be adapted in the best possible way to the special needs of individual nations*, and for the preservation of that unity and that image of the Catholic priesthood which it demands of its very nature . . . .[12]

The 2016 *Ratio* seems to value uniformity of seminary programs over adaptation to local cultures and circumstances and a centralizing ethos. The 1970 and 1985 *Rationes* contained only very general guidelines for the development of individual *Rationes Nationalis*. With its detailed prescriptions for seminary programs the 2016 *Ratio* requires that the *Rationes Nationalis* be developed in close conformity with those detailed prescriptions, and that all seminaries in the territory of the episcopal conference be in strict compliance with it.

In describing its "sphere of application," the general norms section of the *Ratio* states in relevant part: "This *Ratio Fundamentalis Institutiones Sacerdotalis* is to be applied in its entirety in those countries which fall within the competence of the Congregation for the Clergy . . . ."[13]

Footnote 6 does acknowledge that the *Ratio* is a general executory decree, citing *Optatam totius* as the undergirding law. The main text goes on to say:

> 1. Each conference of Bishops is required to prepare its own *Ratio Nationalis* on the basis of this *Ratio Fundamentalis Insitutionis Sacerdotalis*, which, in accordance with no. 1 of the Conciliar Decree *Optatam totius* and can. 242 §1 of the Code of Canon Law, must be approved by this same Congregation, after having heard the opinion of the Congregation for Catholic Education on matters within its competence. This is to ensure the necessary harmonization and coordination of the Program of Studies and its consistency with the Program of Studies of individual countries.[14]

Whenever it may prove necessary to make changes to a previously approved *Ratio Nationalis*, due to new or unexpected developments, the text may be amended by seeking the further approval of the Dicastery for the Clergy.

The norms of such a *Ratio* must be observed in all diocesan and interdiocesan seminaries in the country, while their particular application must be given effect in the statutes, the rule of life and the program of formation of each institution.

---

12 Ibid., Introduction.
13 *Ratio* 2016, I.a.1.
14 *Ratio* 2016, I.b.3.

I think we can presume that the norms are also to be observed by seminaries operated by religious communities and societies of apostolic life that train diocesan priests.

Canon 242 §1 states that each nation is to have a program of priestly formation established by the conference of bishops, attentive to the norms issued by the supreme authority of the Church and approved by the Holy See. Canonically speaking, therefore, the norms to be applied in formation programs are to be promulgated by the bishops' conference for its own territory, attentive to the norms issued by the supreme authority and approved by the Holy See. This juridic structure reflects the ethos of *Optatam totius* and the 1970 and 1985 *Rationes* in relation to general guidance by the supreme authority with local bishops' conferences developing appropriate norms for their own territory, placing the emphasis on each bishops' conference's knowledge of its own culture, needs and educational systems.

VII. Overview of the *Ratio fundamentalis* and the New Vision of Priestly Formation in the Program of Priestly Formation 6

The 2016 *Ratio* seeks to rethink formation in terms of "stages" as opposed to the standard academic divisions of minor seminary/major seminary, philosophy/ theology. It speaks, therefore, of: 1) the Propaedeutic Stage; 2) the Discipleship Stage; 3) the Configuration Stage; and 4) the Vocational Synthesis Stage. The Discipleship Stage corresponds to the time of philosophy studies, the Configuration Stage the study of theology. The corresponding stages in the earlier system can be a bit confusing because of realignments in the formation system that took place in the twentieth century, but the current pattern is familiar to all: college seminary (four years), or pre-theology for those without prior seminary experience who have an undergraduate degree, during which philosophy is studied along with spiritual formation; followed by major seminary (four years).

The Propaedeutic and Vocational Synthesis Stages are something new. The *Ratio* requires at least one and not more than two years of a propaedeutic stage prior to philosophy studies, or at any time prior to starting the study of theology; dedicated to spiritual formation, an introduction to cultivating a prayer life, and basic Catholic beliefs. There is to be little academic coursework, and the study of philosophy is forbidden during this stage. It originally was to take place in a location physically separated from the seminary, directed by priests not a part of a seminary faculty. Something like a novitiate, or a solitude year in religious institutes and societies of apostolic life, or the kind of "spirituality year" some seminaries already offer. The dicastery now allows it in a seminary, however, if separate and distinct from the seminary community.

The Vocational Synthesis Stage is to take place in the candidate's diocese after the seminary program has been completed. The *Ratio* explicitly indicates that ordination to the diaconate is to occur after the seminary program has been completed; ordination to the priesthood, at least six months after returning to one's diocese. The Vocational Synthesis Stage is to involve primarily diaconal ministry, with the parish pastor the deacon's principal mentor and formator. It aims at "integration" into the life of the diocese, priesthood, and the presbyterate. The *Ratio* presumes the Configuration Stage will last for four full years in the seminary, as prescribed by canons 235 §1 and 250. The Program of Priestly Formation 6, however, suggests that the time in the seminary may be shortened to three and a half or three and a quarter years. Although approved by the dicastery in the Program of Priestly Formation, this raises questions about compliance with the Code of Canon Law.

The *Ratio* continues to refer to the "four dimensions" (or "four pillars") of *Pastores dabo vobis*, and the degree program requirements for philosophy and theology, but rebrackets them within concept of the four "stages" of formation. The expressed intent of the *Ratio* is to stop conceiving of priestly formation as primarily an academic exercise leading to degrees, in favor of "stages" on the pathway to priesthood, an integrated process of human, intellectual, spiritual, and pastoral formation, each equally important.

Why did the Dicastery for Clergy undertake this radical restructuring of priestly formation? At a conference in Rome in 2017 representatives of the (then) Congregation for Clergy noted how disturbed they had been by the number of petitions for laicization in recent decades. They concluded that something must have gone seriously wrong in the process of priestly formation for this to occur. The *Ratio* represents the dicastery's attempt to affect this:

1. It is convinced too many men enter seminary inadequately prepared to be formed humanly, spiritually, and theologically; and
2. Candidates for the priesthood have not been forming deeply enough with secure enough relationships with their own dioceses and diocesan presbyterates to provide the personal support needed to live out their vocations successfully and in a satisfying manner.

The propaedeutic year seems designed to provide candidates with a sufficient introduction to prayer and basic Catholic beliefs to prepare them for seminary formation and a deep commitment to the priesthood (or to lead to a determination that they are not called).

The Vocational Synthesis Stage seems designed to strengthen candidates' ties to their own dioceses and integration into a life of fidelity and service in the diocese of incardination; a period of time for one's vocation and formation to "gel" before advancing to the priesthood. This stage is not viewed as a final evaluation of suitability, since ordination to the diaconate presumes suitability for the priesthood. Rather, the emphasis is on a gradual but intensive integration into life in one's diocese and its presbyterate after formation in the seminary has been completed.

This is an overview. Consideration of the challenges the new system presents for transitioning from the current model to this new and different way of looking at formation will be left to workshops on seminary formation. I will now concentrate on strictly canonical issues that may come up during the process of making this transition.

VIII. Ambiguities and Possible Conflicts

I would like to identify what I believe will be specific issues that bishops, vocation directors, and seminary officials may bring to canonists for advice.

Contrasting Ethos: *Optatum totius* to 2016 *Ratio*

First is the contrast between *Optatam totius*, the 1970 and 1985 *Rationes*, and the 2016 *Ratio* which may raise questions of interpretation. The 1970 and 1985 *Rationes* have been replaced by the 2016 *Ratio*, so they currently have no force or effect. They do, however, provide a lens for interpreting *Optatam totius*, which does remain in full force and effect.

As previously noted, *Optatam totius* acknowledges that "only general laws can be made where there exists a wide variety of nations and regions" and that "a special 'program of priestly training' needs to be undertaken by each country or rite," such that universal laws may be adapted to the particular circumstances of the times and localities, and so that priestly training will always be in tune with the pastoral needs of those regions in which the ministry is to be exercised. The 2016 *Ratio* contains many more specific prescriptions to be followed in all seminaries throughout the world than the general provisions of the earlier *Rationes*. This change in ethos has already led to many questions, both by seminary administrators and by representatives of the bishops' conference in the United States as to how the *Ratio* and the Program of Priestly Formation 6 are to be applied in the light of local conditions and the educational system and traditions of seminary formation in the United States. For instance, challenges are evident in the three "possible" models of implementation of the Configuration Stage suggested in the Program of Priestly Formation 6 without specifying which model seminaries should adopt or setting forth any specific curriculum in the program as required by the *Ratio*.

If one were to survey the different seminary programs that have already been adopted in response to Program of Priestly Formation 6, you would find a hodgepodge of widely varying programs, and a great deal of uncertainty whether they fully comply with the program or not, and whether they are likely to prove workable in the cultural and educational context of the United States. You may be called on for assistance to bring greater stability to seminary formation in the United States, therefore, in the coming years. Ironically, while the *Ratio* appears to attempt to bring uniformity and stability to seminary formation programs, its result in the United States seems to have been to create a wide variety of programs—that is a lack of uniformity—and a sense of instability likely to continue for a number of years as seminaries, and also dioceses with respect to the Propaedeutic and Vocational Synthesis Stages, struggle to understand how to come into compliance with the promulgated norms without challenging the quality of programs already in place being disrupted by implementation efforts.

Role of Bishops versus Role of the Dicastery for Clergy

Optatam totius states that "In order that the spiritual training rest upon a more solid basis and that the students embrace their vocation with a fully deliberate choice, it will be the *prerogative of the bishops* to establish a fitting period of time for a more intense introduction to the spiritual life."[15] The imposition by the Dicastery for Clergy of a mandatory propaedeutic year prior to entering the seminary would appear to disregard that *Optatam totius* states this is the prerogative of the bishops. Given that the *Ratio* is a general executory decree, rather than a law, that must be in accord with the law and not derogate from it, the *Ratio*'s imposition of a mandatory propaedeutic year not required by *Optatam totius* or mentioned in the Code of Canon Law may be seen as derogating from the law in light of canon 33 §1. However advisable a full propaedeutic year may be with respect to at least some candidates for seminary formation, arbitrarily setting it at one full year may be, with no allowances for adjustments or waiving it in the case of candidates who in the judgment of the bishop are ready to go directly into seminary formation, does seem to co-opt a determination that *Optatam totius* leaves to the bishops, and for that reason can be seen as derogating from the norm of *Optatam totius*. *Optatam totius* considers each bishops conference better suited to making this determination, and each individual bishop better capable of determining whether or not it would be advisable and what the period it should be in individual cases.

Apropos to this issue, our colleague Monsignor Fredrik Hansen will be giving a paper at the "Leuven Encounters in Systematic Theology SIV—60 Years

15 *Optatam totius* 12.

Vatican II: The End of the Western Church?" conference at the Catholic University, Leuven, in November on the relationship between local ordinaries, bishops conferences, the Bishop of Rome, and dicasteries of the Holy See. He notes in his paper, which I have been able to review in advance, that Cardinal Avery Dulles and others expressed in their evaluation of Vatican II that chapter III of *Lumen gentium* regarding the relationship between the bishops and the Bishop of Rome and the Roman Curia is destined to be the teaching of Vatican II that will be recognized as having had the greatest historical significance.

Dispensations

Canonists may wish to consider whether a bishop has the power to dispense requirements of the *Ratio* or the Program of Priestly Formation, such as the mandatory one-year propaedeutic experience: "[T]he relaxation of a merely ecclesiastical law in a particular case, can be granted by those who possess executive power within the limits of their competence" (c. 85). Arriving at an opinion would require keen analysis around several points: the *Ratio* is not a law, but a general executory decree. Would dispensing the propaedeutic stage and other aspects of the *Ratio* and the Program of Priestly Formation be within the limits of the bishop's competence? Are the norms of the *Ratio* and the Program of Priestly Formation "merely ecclesiastical laws," and are they laws at all? If the bishop can dispense a merely ecclesiastical law, does he have the power to dispense the norms of a general executory decree given for the interpretation and application of a law, in the face of the prescription of canon 242 that the Program of Priestly Formation is "to be attentive to the norms issued by the supreme authority of the Church" (c. 242 §1). Are the provisions of the Program of Priestly Formation and *Ratio* laws that can or cannot be dispensed, or merely "decrees which more precisely determine the methods to be observed in applying the law or which urge the observance of laws" (c. 31) which, however, may not derogate from laws? Do the norms of the *Ratio* and the Program of Priestly Formation "define things which are essentially constitutive of juridic institutes or acts," or are they disciplinary laws issued by the Supreme Authority of the Church (c. 87 §1)? I am not taking a position on whether the dispensing power is available to bishops with respect to the *Ratio* and the Program of Priestly Formation, but rather wish to identify specific issues that should be taken into consideration if a bishop would like to do so and seeks your advice. A considerable amount of discussion has taken place among bishops, vocation directors, and seminary formators regarding the propaedeutic stage and whether it should really be considered necessary in all cases, or for the full time period mandated by the dicastery. Efforts have been made to explore whether other pre-seminary experiences could not be accumulated as equivalent to the propaedeutic year, or at least a part of it, but to no avail. The dicastery has insisted that it be one full year for all prospective seminarians. Due to wide variety of opinions about this outside of the dicastery, the mandated propaedeutic year may be an element of the *Ratio* that warrants being revisited if experience demonstrates it is not as effective as its proponents believe it will be.

Time Spent in Formation in the Seminary

The Code of Canon Law is clear regarding the amount of time to be spent in formation in a major seminary. First of all, regarding the studies to be undertaken, canon 250 clearly states that philosophical studies and theological studies are to encompass at least *six full years*, such that the time dedicated to philosophical disciplines equals two full years, and theological studies four full years.

Alternative "c" of the three suggested Configuration Stages set forth in paragraph 147 of Program of Priestly Formation 6 states that the Configuration Stage could consist of three and a half years and "the equivalent of four years of theological studies," a format that many seminaries have already put in place (whether exclusively, or as available for dioceses which choose it). It is hard to see how this does not derogate from the norm of canon 250 (and the *Ratio* itself) which states "four full years," not "the equivalent of four full years of theological studies." The norm of canon 250 quite clearly is using "four full years" in a temporal sense, signifying "four full years," not an academic sense of the number of credit hours that add up to four full years of study, even if completed in three and a half years, or two years, or one year. The norm of canon 235 is that those intending to enter the priesthood are to be provided with suitable spiritual formation and otherwise prepared throughout the entire time of formation *in a major seminary*. Paragraph 74 of the *Ratio* states that the Vocational Synthesis Stage is the time *from leaving the seminary until subsequent priestly ordination*, which it says "obviously is brought about by conferral of the diaconate" (perhaps a bit ambiguous: is it priestly ordination that is brought about by ordination to the diaconate or the Vocational Synthesis Stage?). Paragraph 145 of the Program of Priestly Formation 6 states that the Vocational Synthesis Stage "always takes place after the completion of the configuration stage (i.e., the stages are never concurrent)."

There is even greater inconsistency with respect to alternative "b" of the proposed Configuration Stage in the Program of Priestly Formation 6, which posits that the Configuration Stage last three and three quarters years with diaconal ordination at the end of the Configuration Stage and vocational synthesis lasting one to three months *in the seminary* to complete theological studies and then six months in a parish after leaving the seminary. This is confusing and inconsistent. Proposal "b" seems to have the Configuration and Vocational Synthesis Stages running concurrently (one to three months in *the seminary* to complete theological studies, which is part of the Configuration Stage, while the Vocational Synthesis Stage is initiated in the seminary!). The *Ratio* and the Program of Priestly Formation 6 itself insist that the Vocational Synthesis Stage may only begin after the seminarian has completed the Configuration Stage and after he has left the seminary and returned to his diocese. I do not know of any seminary planning to implement option "b," which may already be a dead letter. But many are implementing option "c," and that is where the conflict between the norms of the Code of Canon Law and the Ratio and the Program of Priestly Formation 6 become evident.

Canon 250 requires that the study of philosophy and theology, along with suitable spiritual formation, encompass *six full years in a major seminary*, at least two years of philosophy and four full years of theology. By truncating the Configuration Stage, the six full years in a major seminary mandated by canon 250 and canon 235 is reduced to five and a half years at most. It is hard to see how this does not derogate from the applicable law, lacking therefore all force, with potential consequences for the validity of orders, certainly its liceity, for those candidates who have not completed the six full years in a major seminary required by canon 250 and canon 235.

A non-canonical consequence of efforts to truncate the Vocational Synthesis Stage, that bodes ill for formation and the wellbeing of seminarians, concerns the idea of completing four years of theological studies in three and a half years. Without detailing how the calculations are arrived at, a normal course load during theological studies is considered twelve credit hours per semester. Currently, when pastoral field placement requirements are included, as they should be, most seminaries are requiring fifteen to eighteen credit hours per semester. Jamming four years of theology courses into a three-and-a-half-year program is going to result in seminarians in reality being required to take eighteen to twenty-one credit hours per semester, a seven to ten credit hour overload from the ideal of twelve hours. We have already seen the impact on stress levels and negative impacts on the community and human formation of requiring seminarians to take these kinds of course loads during seminary.

One of the greater concerns in seminary formation today is the quality and effectiveness of human formation, the greatest impediment to sound human formation we have found being the excessive demands of the program, and the stress and dysfunction this causes in the lives of seminarians. Requiring seminarians to complete four years of formation and study in three and a half years is not going to ameliorate that stress; the resulting dysfunction in human formation will only exacerbate it. But that is a human, not a canonical consideration, and as we all know, the consequences for real human beings is not always the first concern of canon law, or any legal system, so let us return to canonical considerations.

The Code of Canon Law makes no mention of "the equivalent" of two full years, four full years, or six full years. Rather, it states quite clearly: "at least six full years;"[16] two full years studying philosophy, and four full years studying theology. Canon 235 further stating quite clearly that "[M]en who intend to enter the priesthood 'are to be provided with a suitable spiritual formation and prepared for their proper duties *in a major seminary throughout the entire time of formation*.'"[17]

The *Ratio* does not really disrupt this schema, retaining the same time requirements: two full years devoted to the study of philosophy and four full years devoted to the study of theology. Program of Priestly Formation 6, however, does suggest that this schema can be disrupted if a seminary decides to provide a program for the Configuration Stage that can ostensibly be completed in three and a half years (or three and three quarters years). The *Ratio* states in paragraph 154:

> The study of propaedeutic materials should last at least a year. The study of philosophy must be for a minimum duration of two years, *or a corresponding number of semester hours*, according to the academic system followed in some countries. The study of theology must last for at least four years (*or a corresponding number of semester hours*). In this way, the study of philosophy and theology must last for at least six years in total [citing canon 250] (*or, according to other programs of study, which should include the quantity of academic material that ordinarily would be covered in six years*).[18]

While the *Ratio* does make an accommodation for considering semester hours as the measure of a year, canon 250 of the code does not qualify the number of years of spiritual formation and study with the phrase "or a corresponding number of semester hours," or "according to other programs of study, which should include the quantity of academic material that ordinarily would be covered in six years." It states, rather, that "the philosophical and theological studies . . . are to encompass at least six full years in such a way that the time dedicated to philosophical disciplines equals two full years and to theological studies four full

---

16 Canon 250.

17 Canon 235 §1 (emphasis added).

18 *Ratio* 2016, 154 (emphasis added).

years."[19] That is the law. A general decree may not derogate from the law, but only gives guidance as to how it is to be implemented in accordance with the underlying law itself. A law cannot be amended, repealed, or abrogated by a general executory decree, nor by a program of priestly formation that is dependent on such a decree, but only by a law. The suggestion of Program of Priestly Formation 6 that the Configuration Stage in the seminary may be shortened to three and a half or three and three quarters years appears to be *contra legem* and, therefore, of no force or effect (c. 33 §1).

Gearing the time spent in a major seminary to the number of credit hours earned seems contrary to the spirit and the express provisions of the *Ratio*, which highlights that:

> The entire journey of formation must never be reduced to a single aspect to the detriment of others, but it must always be an integrated journey of the disciple called to priesthood. . . . Moreover, it should be emphasized that the intellectual dimension, with the prescribed study of philosophy and theology, is not the only factor to be considered when evaluating the journey completed by the seminarian in each stage.[20]

Later in paragraph 118, the *Ratio* states that "[W]hile it is necessary, on the one hand, not to neglect a solid and adequate intellectual formation, on the other hand, one needs to remember that the successful completion of the requirements of study cannot be the only criterion for determining the length of the formative *iter* of the candidate for priesthood."[21]

It may be noted that the *Ratio* speaks of the *Ratio Nationalis* (Program of Priestly Formation) expanding the essential elements of intellectual formation, but nowhere does it speak of it "contracting" those requirements. In advising bishops, vocation directors, and seminary administrators regarding compliance with the *Ratio* and the Program of Priestly Formation 6, and fulfillment of the requirements of the Code of Canon Law and *Optatam totius*, canonists should be alert to whether or not the seminary is proposing to contract or even eliminate required features of the program as set forth in the *Ratio* and the Program of Priestly Formation 6 in order to try to fit their programs into a timeframe considered more desirable than the law requires.

---

19 Canon 250.

20 *Ratio* 2016, 3: *Characteristic Elements and Fundamental Content.*

21 *Ratio* 2016, 118.

Ordo Studiorum

Apropos to these concerns, the introduction to the *Ratio* admonishes in section 3:

> A further integral part of this *Ratio Fundamentalis*, as of the 1970 edition, is the *Ordo Studiorum*. This provides a descriptive list of materials that must be included in the course of studies for seminarians, during the various phases, within the wider intellectual formation. It must be applied in its entirety in Seminaries and in those houses of formation that offer the prescribed six years of philosophy and theology courses internally.[22]

Relevant to this prescription is paragraph 154 of the *Ratio,* which states:

> The *Ratio Nationalis must* contain an overall presentation of the subjects to be covered in intellectual formation at each stage of formation. It *must* briefly indicate the objectives of each discipline, its place within the context of the entire course of *studies, the syllabus, as well as the arrangement of years and semesters, including the number of credits for each course.*"[23]

Paragraph 9 of the Preface to the Program of Priestly Formation 6 lays down an interpretive principle that may be relevant here, stating that "The word 'must' means that an action is required. Authorization from the competent authority is required for an exception from following the required course or action."[24] Does this principle apply with equal force to the *Ratio*? In stating that the *Ratio Nationalis* must include the syllabus, arrangement of years and semesters, and number of credits for each course, does it mean that it must, that this action is required? If so, seminary administrators are still waiting for an overall presentation of the subjects to be covered in their intellectual formation programs, with sequence, syllabus, number of credit hours and syllabi for each course, which is not presently in the published version of the Program of Priestly Formation 6. This has made implementation of the Program of Priestly Formation 6 quite difficult since the coordinators of intellectual formation do not have this essential information at their disposal for planning and implementing their academic programs. Canonists might therefore be able to be of service to seminary administrators, as well as bishops and vocation directors, by helping them to bring this *lacuna* to the attention of the Committee on Clergy, Consecrated Life and

---

22 *Ratio* 2016, 3.

23 *Ratio* 2016, 154 (emphasis added).

24 Committee on Clergy, Consecrated Life and Vocations of the United States Conference of Catholic Bishops, *Program of Priestly Formation*, sixth edition (Washington, DC: USCCB, 2022) (hereafter "PPF 6") 9.

Vocations of the United States Conference of Catholic Bishops, which is responsible for the Program of Priestly Formation, and ask when seminaries may be able to expect to receive this critical information and direction for their formation programs and implementation of Program of Priestly Formation 6.

For seminaries that offer pontifical degrees, the degree requirements must also comply with the accrediting standards of the Dicastery for Culture and Education. All of which are the same, as far as the academic degree programs are concerned, as they were prior to promulgation of the *Ratio* and Program of Priestly Formation 6. For those programs that have opted for a three-and-a-half-year Configuration Stage, this means that all of the course requirements of a four-year academic and formation program will now have to be completed in three and a half years as previously noted.

Ordination to the Diaconate

The only norms of the law respecting when a candidate for the priesthood may be ordained to the transitional diaconate are found in canon 1025 which states:

> Can. 1025 §1. To confer the presbyteral or diaconal orders licitly, it is required that the candidate, *having completed the period of probation according to the norm of law*, is endowed *in the judgment of his own bishop* or of the competent major superior with the necessary qualities, is prevented by no irregularity and no impediment, and has fulfilled the prerequisites according to the norm of canons 1033-1039. Moreover, the documents mentioned in canon 1050 are to be obtained and the investigation in canon 1051 is to be completed.
>
> §2. Furthermore, it is required that he is considered in the judgment of the same legitimate superior as useful for the ministry of the Church.[25]

The essentials of these norms for valid and licit ordination are that the candidate: 1) has completed the period of probation according to the norm of law; 2) is endowed with the necessary qualities; 3) is prevented by no irregularity or impediment; and 4) has fulfilled the prerequisites outlined in canons 1033-1039 *in the judgment of his own bishop*; and that the documents in canon 1050 have been obtained and the investigation of canon 1051 completed. Suitability for ordination is *according to the judgment of the candidate's own bishop*, not any other authority.

The relevant norms of canons 1033-1039 to our discussion of ordination to the transitional diaconate are: 1) that he has been enrolled as a candidate through

---

25 Canon 1025 (emphasis added).

the liturgical rite of admission by his proper bishop or of the diocese to which he intends to devote himself; 2) he has received the ministries of lector and acolyte; 3) at least six months have passed since conferral of the ministry of acolyte; 4) he has presented a petition in his own hand attesting that he is receiving the order of his own accord and will devote himself perpetually to ecclesiastical ministry; 5) and has made the required five day retreat. The documents required are: 1) that his studies have been completed according to the norm of canon 1032; and 2) a testimonial that baptism, confirmation and lector and acolyte have been received, as well as his petition declaring his freedom and intention to devote himself to ecclesiastical ministry. Canon 1051 further requires that the investigation referred to include a testimonial of the rector of the seminary or house of formation about the required qualities for ordination and a properly executed inquiry about the candidate's physical and psychic health.

Canon 1032 §1 states the norm of law regarding the studies to have been completed by those being ordained to the diaconate: "Those aspiring to the presbyterate can be promoted to the diaconate only after they have completed the fifth year of the curriculum of philosophical and theological studies." This is the key norm of law in relation to the *Ratio* and Program of Priestly Formation 6 with respect to when a candidate may be ordained to the diaconate: ". . . only after he has completed the fifth year of the curriculum of philosophical and theological studies." Conversely, once a candidate has completed the fifth year of philosophical and theological studies he may be ordained to the transitional diaconate if the other requirements outlined in the Code of Canon Law have been met.

Paragraph 73 of the *Ratio* states "At the conclusion of this stage [the Configuration Stage], or during the following one, if he has been judged suitable by the Bishop, after having heard the formators, the seminarian will petition to receive diaconate ordination." Paragraph 74 goes on to say that "The pastoral stage, or vocational synthesis, ["the following one" as referred to in paragraph 73] is the time from leaving the Seminary until the subsequent priestly ordination, which obviously is brought about by conferral of the diaconate."

This paragraph of the *Ratio* is stating that seminarians petition to receive diaconate ordination after completing the Configuration Stage, although it is possible to understand it to imply "if it has not already been received." To reiterate, the *Ratio* does repeat the norm of canon 250 that this means *at least four years* of theological studies and spiritual, human, and pastoral formation *in a major seminary*. The Program of Priestly Formation 6, however, as approved by the dicastery, suggests that the Configuration Stage could be completed in three and a half or three and three quarters years. In either case, however, the *Ratio* and the Program of Priestly Formation 6 suggest that ordination to the diaconate occurs after the Configuration Stage has been completed, thereby extending the minimum period of studies and formation before diaconate ordination, if this is an obligatory norm, from five years, to five and a half or even six years (that is, to the end of the four or three and a half years of the Configuration Stage posited by these documents, added to the minimum of two years of the Discipleship Stage, which includes the minimum time of philosophical studies).

The question for canonists to address is: Do these provisions of the *Ratio* and the Program of Priestly Formation 6 derogate from the law of the cited canons in the Code of Canon Law regarding ordination to the diaconate? And do they, therefore, lack all force (c. 33)? Or, if the Program of Priestly Formation 6 is considered law, which the *Ratio* as a general executory decree clearly is not, and if the "suggestions" of the Program of Priestly Formation are somehow considered norms of law, do those suggestions, as particular law, derogate from the norms of the universal law set forth in the code? Furthermore, does the proper competent authority (the diocesan bishop of a candidate for holy orders) have the same power to dispense from the "suggestions" of the Program of Priestly Formation that he has to dispense from laws?

It is worth noting that paragraph 73 of the *Ratio*, regarding when a candidate petitions for ordination to the diaconate, is by its terms descriptive not prescriptive. One must ask, therefore, if it is a norm at all. Or is it merely a description of what the issuing authority wishes or would prefer to be the case? It gives no clear command that men may be ordained to the diaconate *only* after they have completed the Configuration Stage, and that they may not be ordained sooner than that. Canon 1032, an indisputable norm of law, however, states that while candidates may be promoted to the diaconate only after they have completed the fifth year of the mandated six-year curriculum of philosophy and theology, in the positive sense it implies and does not prohibit that they may be promoted to the diaconate any time after they have completed the fifth year.

This is a question canonists may very well be asked to weigh in on by bishops, vocation directors, and seminary administrators. I have tried to outline the canonical considerations they may wish to reflect on before offering their advice.

The impact that prohibiting ordination to the diaconate prior to completing the Configuration Stage will have on seminary programs is beyond the scope of this presentation, but I can share that it will be very significant and quite disruptive to existing programs. As just one example, seminarians as part of their homiletics courses will no longer be able to preach, or even proclaim the Gospel in seminary liturgies, something that is currently standard practice once a man has been ordained to the diaconate. You can imagine all of the other consequences, especially with respect to pastoral placements, if seminarians are no longer able to be ordained to the diaconate at the end of their third year or during their fourth year of seminary formation. Where the Configuration State is truncated to three and a half years, it will inevitably have a significant impact on fourth-year pastoral formation programs and fourth-year placements in parishes, where supervising pastors will no longer be able to rely on seminarians for preaching, other diaconal ministry, or a full year of teaching, Rite of Christian Initiation of Adults, or sacramental preparation ministries.

One Final Apparent Inconsistency

Paragraph 454 of the Program of Priestly Formation requires that the Coordinator of Intellectual Formation be a priest, but canon 254 of the code does not (although other canons specific that other administrators must be priests). Does the Program of Priestly Formation derogate from the code, therefore, by imposing a more restrictive norm than that which is contained in the Code of Canon Law?

IX. Proposed Interpretative (Hermeneutical) Principles.

My presentation has already suggested certain hermeneutical, that is interpretive, principles for reading the *Ratio* and the Program of Priestly Formation 6 in light of the norms of the Code of Canon Law and *Optatam totius*, the underlying law. I will attempt to to identify those principles in a succinct way now, and then open the floor for questions and discussion.

1. The most important canonical norms for resolving apparent ambiguities or conflicting norms in the *Ratio* and Program of Priestly Formation 6 are those found in the Code of Canon Law and applicable decrees of the Second Vatican Council. Everything stated as normative in the *Ratio* or the Program of Priestly Formation 6 has to be measured against those legal norms.
2. The *Ratio* is not law, it is a general executory decree. Anything in it that derogates from the norms of law found in the code and applicable decrees lacks all force (c. 33 §1).
3. It is uncertain whether the Program of Priestly Formation 6 should be considered law or in the nature of a general executory decree, since it depends on the *Ratio*. If it is law, it is particular law for the United States, not universal law, which presumptively must accord with universal law. The actual force of provisions that derogate from the universal law may be open to question, which requires careful analysis by canonists.

4. Neither the *Ratio* nor Program of Priestly Formation 6 abrogate the dispensing power of a diocesan bishop, which may be able to be applied to some of the normative provisions contained in those documents that the bishop determines may prudently be dispensed in order to serve the pastoral needs and formation tradition of the seminaries he entrusts his seminarians to. *Optatam totius*, the *Ratio*, and Program of Priestly Formation 6 all acknowledge that the general provisions of universal law must be adapted to local conditions, the pastoral context of local Churches, and the pastoral needs of the local Church.

5. Provisions of the *Ratio* and Program of Priestly Formation 6, even if they are referred to as "norms" cannot be considered norms unless they are stated in a prescriptive manner, that is mandatory.

6. When a provision says "must" it presumptively means the action must be taken if those it is directed to are bound by the provision. This is as true of the *Ratio* as it is of Program of Priestly Formation 6. However, the nature of the provisions as normative or obligatory has also to be taken into consideration in relation to the nature of the documents in which they appear as containing obligatory legal norms, or only guidance and suggestions.

7. Suggested ways of proceeding do not overrule, nor do they grant the authority to disregard, positively stated, obligatory prescriptions of law.

8. Who is the competent authority whose prerogative it is to make the determination under consideration? For instance, it is the prerogative of the diocesan bishop to determine suitability for ordination in accordance with the norms of the Code of Canon Law. It is the competence of the Dicastery for Clergy to approve the Program of Priestly Formation and amendments to it. Who has the competence to make a given determination may not always be readily apparent? Canonists should be attentive, therefore, to ascertaining accurately and with certainty who the competent authority is in a given instance.

CLSA PROCEEDINGS 85 (2023) 68-85

SEMINAR

RESTRUCTURING CANONICAL GOVERNANCE IN FIDELITY TO THE JOURNEY[1]

Sister Sharon Euart, RSM, JCD

Thank you very much for the opportunity to be part of the 2023 Convention here in Milwaukee. I am grateful to the Convention Planning Committee for the invitation to share with you some observations on canonical governance and some options for restructuring governance in religious institutes. This morning, I hope to describe a theological framework for restructuring, the demographic reality of religious today especially in the United States, the life cycle of a religious institute or society, and to address the notion of canonical governance, options for governance that are found in the Code of Canon Law as well other possibilities with special attention to the option of a canonical commissary in the context of the synodal path moving forward.

Introduction

In 1965 the Fathers of Vatican Council II issued the Decree on the Renewal of Religious Life (*Perfectae caritatis*), a momentous document that called religious and the entire Church to an adaptation and renewal of religious life.[2] This renewal was to be based on a return to the sources of all Christian life, especially the Gospel, as well as the original spirit of the founders and its adaptation to the changed conditions of our time (*PC* 2). Women and men religious throughout the world responded with enthusiasm to take a fresh look at their charism, spirit, purpose, and traditions and to adapt their proper law to new circumstances in the Church and the world.

Thirty-one years after *Perfectae caritatis*, Pope John Paul II published the apostolic exhortation on Consecrated Life (*Vita consecrata*), in which he invited

---

1 This paper is an updated and expanded version of an article by Sr. Sharon Euart, RSM, published in Thomas P. Gaunt and Thu T. Do, eds., *New Faces, New Possibilities, Cultural Diversity and Structural Change in Institutes of Women Religious* (Collegeville, MN: Liturgical Press, 2022).

2 See Second Vatican Council, decree *Perfectae caritatis*. October 28, 1965: *AAS* 58 (1966) 702-712.

religious to view the future with hope, urging consecrated women and men to "look to the future, where the Spirit is sending you to do even greater things."[3] Pope Francis insists that personal conversion is not enough; religious institutes[4] are called to align their structures to the mission of the Church today. He urges religious in *New Wine, New Wineskins* "not to have fear of making changes according to the law of the Gospel. . . Leave aside fleeting structures—they are not necessary. . . and get new wineskins, those of the Gospel."[5] Today, religious institutes continue to respond to this call for renewal in ways and in light of signs perhaps not anticipated or even imagined in 1965.

Demographic Reality

Since the mid-1960s, the overall change in the demographics on *women* religious in the United States and Europe has been one of significant and persistent decline. In the U.S., from its peak of 178,954 in 1965 to 36,321 in 2022, this change represents a 79.8 percent decline.[6] In the U.S., while the decline in the number of *men* religious (priests and brothers) is not as steep, the decrease from 1965 with 34,978 to 13,750 in 2022 is 60.6%.[7] Particularly noteworthy is the 2023 age distribution data from the National Religious Retirement Office (NRRO) representing 380 women's religious institutes indicates that 20,303 of 24,965 members (81%) are age seventy or above.[8] NRRO's 2023 Age Distribution data for 126 institutes of men religious indicate that 3702 of the 7270 members (51%) are 70 or above.[9]

In February 2023, the Vatican's Statistical Yearbook of the Church reported an overall decrease in the number of sisters in the world for a total at the end of 2021 of 608,958 down from 801,185 in 2000. The 2021 figures represent increases in Africa (+835) and Asia (+599) while decreases were reported in

---

3 John Paul II, apostolic exhortation *Vita consecrata* 110, March 25, 1996: *AAS* 88 (1996) 484; Eng. trans. at https://www.vatican.va/content/john-paul-ii/en/apost_exhortations/documents/hf_jp-ii_exh_25031996_vita-consecrata.html (accessed on 7 Nov. 2023).

4 The word "institute" will be used in this paper as the umbrella term for different types of institutes of consecrated life and societies of apostolic life described in canon law.

5 Dicastery for Institutes of Consecrated Life and Societies of Apostolic Life, *New Wine, New Wineskins: The Consecrated Life and Its Ongoing Challenges since Vatican II* (Rome: Libreria Editrice Vaticana, 2017) no. 10.

6 CARA, "Frequently Requested Statistics in the Church in the United States," *The CARA Report*, 29:2 (Fall 2023) 6.

7 Ibid.

8 See "Age Distribution of Religious as of 12/31/2022," p. 4 in *National Religious Retirement Office*, "Statistical Report—August 2023," https://www.usccb.org/resources/Statistical%20Report.pdf (accessed on 6 Nov. 2023).

9 Ibid. [Editor's Note: This report is updated annually and uses the same URL, so the quoted figures are available only until the report is replaced.]

Europe (-7,400), the Americas (-5,315) and Oceania (-281).[10] It is important to keep in mind that women religious in North America (Canada and the U.S.) represent only 8% of the women religious throughout the world.[11]

Life Cycle of a Religious Institute

But these statistics do not tell the full story. Reflecting on a sociological model of the life cycle of a religious institute can help inform the larger picture of what is happening in religious life today. The work of Marianists Lawrence Cada, SM, and Raymond Fitz, SM, in *Shaping the Coming Age of Religious Life,* though published in 1979, can be very helpful in understanding today's reality.[12] This model for the life cycle of an individual religious institute organizes the important components of the development of the institute. It divides the life cycle of a religious institute into five periods: foundation, expansion, stabilization, breakdown, and critical.[13] The model can be depicted in the shape of bell curve representing the vitality of the institute as it passes from one period to another.

---

10 See Thomas Dobbins, "Vatican – Statistics of the Catholic Church – 2021," *Just Catholic*, Oct. 22, 2021, https://justcatholic.org/vatican-statistics-of-the-catholic-church-2021/ (accessed on 6 Nov. 2023).

11 Carol Glatz, "Vatican statistics show decline in clergy, religious women, worldwide," Catholic News Service, at Catholic Review, March 6, 2023, at https://catholicreview.org/vatican-statistics-show-decline-in-clergy-religious-women-worldwide (accessed on 6 Nov. 2023). See also CARA, "Religious Sisters by World Region by Percent," available at p. 3 in Anne Munley, "Learnings from the Collaborative Leadership Hubs," presented at the 2022 Assembly of the Leadership Conference of Women Religious, https://www.lcwr.org/files/pdf/2022_lcwr_assembly_-_learnings_from_the_collaborative_leadership_hubs.pdf (accessed on 6 Nov. 2023).

12 See Lawrence Cada, Raymond Fitz, et al., *Shaping the Coming Age of Religious Life* (New York: Seabury Press, 1979). For similar studies, see Amy Hereford, *Navigating Change: The Role of Law in the Life-Cycle of a Religious Institute* (St. Louis, MO: Religious Life Project, 2014), 17-21, 99–103, and Amy Hereford, *Religious Life at the Crossroads* (Maryknoll, NY: Orbis Books, 2013), xiv–xvi. For another perspective, see Gerald Arbuckle, *Out of Chaos: Refounding Religious Congregations* (New York: Paulist Press, 1988). See also David Nygren and Miriam Ukeritis, *The Future of Religious Orders in the United States: Transformation and Commitment* ("FORUS") (Westport, CT: Praeger, 1993); Ad Leys, "Structuring "Completion" of a Religious Institute: Some Canonical Provisions," *The Jurist* 76 (2016) 447-487.

13 Cada and Fitz, *Shaping the Coming Age of Religious Life*, 53.

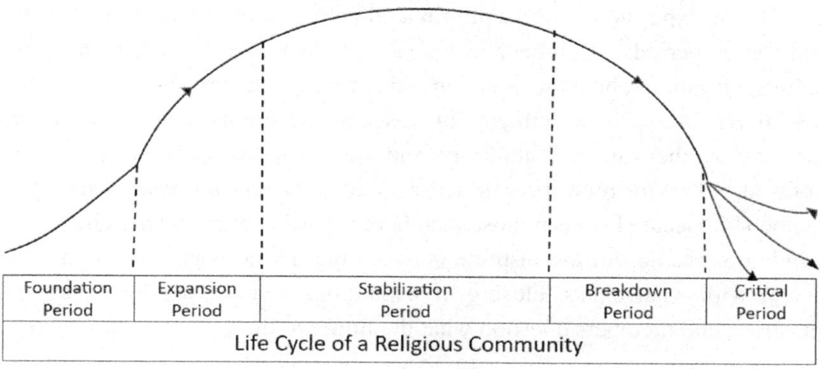

The first period centers around the founder and his or her vision of religious life, usually lasting ten, twenty years or longer with a structural organization taking shape and authority emanating from the wisdom of the founder.

During the second period the institute undergoes a significant period of expansion when the founding charism is institutionalized. This includes a belief system, norms and customs, institute direction, rituals and symbols, procedures for decision-making and communication. Large numbers of new members enter the institute, new apostolates/ministries are established, spiritual manuals of direction are developed. Organizational crises also occur during this period—particularly around how authority is delegated; how to integrate membership and new apostolic works; and how to maintain the founding vision.[14]

The third period is one of stabilization—a long period extending to two or three generations in which a sense of success characterizes the members, the institute is accomplishing its purpose, and it is self-evident.[15] Over time, this period reflects the belief that "religious life has always been the way it is now and that it will always remain so in the future."[16] Formation emphasizes conformity to standard patterns of behavior. Crises develop especially allowing satisfactions and successes in the apostolate to replace centeredness in Christ. The institute has become highly institutionalized. The institute is not open to change or adaptation and those promoting change are often silenced.[17]

The fourth period is a time of breakdown; in some instances, gradual lasting 50-100 years and, in others, lasting only a few decades. This period is characterized by "dismantling of institutional structures and belief systems" that

14 Cada and Fitz, *Shaping the Coming Age of Religious Life*, 54.
15 Ibid., 56.
16 Ibid., 56-57.
17 Ibid., 57.

began in the expansion period and provided guidance for the institute during the stabilization period.[18] Members become dissatisfied with the current state of the institute. Questions about the direction and purpose of the institute arise. Solutions look to renewal of commitment, to mission and charism. A sense of crisis increases as the roles of authority and decision-making structures become confused.[19] The institute loses it sense of identity and purpose; a net loss of membership occurs between those members departing and new members. Crises include polarization in the institute between those who want change and those content with what exists; closing of institutions and leaving long-established ministries; and members question what the future of the institute will be like.

Finally, the fifth period, the critical period, presents three possible outcomes: extinction, minimal survival, or revitalization.[20] Today, many religious institutes in North America, Europe, and Australia, though not all, are in or approaching the fourth period when the signs of organizational decline or breakdown occur.[21] What are some of these signs in institutes of men and more so institutes of women religious in the United States?

With a rising median age and a smaller number of new members, there are fewer members available for institute leadership and governance roles as well as for compensated ministry or external service. These signs correspond closely to the indicators of decline listed in the apostolic letter *Ecclesiae sanctae*, that is, "the small number of Religious in proportion to the age of the institute or the monastery, the lack of candidates over a period of several years, the advanced age of the majority of its members."[22]

In *Vita consecrata*, Pope John Paul II also addresses the decrease in numbers of religious. He states, "While individual institutes have no claim to permanence, the consecrated life itself will continue to sustain among the faithful the response of love towards God and neighbor" (*VC* 63). He noted, however, that "it is necessary to distinguish the *historical destiny* of a specific institute or form of

---

18 Cada and Fitz, *Shaping the Coming Age of Religious Life*, 58.

19 Ibid.

20 Ibid., 59.

21 See, for example, Liz Murphy, "Is Religious Life in Ireland Moving Toward Closure," in *Doctrine & Life* reprinted in https://www.mercyworld.org/f/45074/x/30135a027f/is-religious-life-in-ireland-moving-towards-closure-final.pdf (accessed on 18 Mar. 2024); Cees van Dam, Theo Sponselee, and Ad Leys, "Explorations on the 'Completion' of Religious Institutes," in *RCRI Bulletin* 8 (2012) 9-22.

22 Paul VI, mp *Ecclesiae sanctae* II/41, August 6, 1966: *AAS* 58 (1966) 782; Eng. trans. at https://www.vatican.va/content/paul-vi/en/motu_proprio/documents/hf_p-vi_motu-proprio_19660806_ecclesiae-sanctae.html (accessed on 7 Nov. 2023).

consecrated life from the *ecclesial mission* of the consecrated life as such" (*VC* 63).

Today, religious life is in transition. Rather than a dramatic change, transitions usually manifest themselves gradually. Pope Francis referred to transitions during a Mass celebrated in Casa Santa Marta on October 23, 2015, "Times are changing, and we Christians must change continuously . . . while remaining steadfast in our faith in Jesus Christ, in the truth of the Gospel, but moving forward according to the signs of the times."[23] Addressing challenges and transitions in changing times in the *Joy of the Gospel*, Pope Francis urges consecrated persons to "be realists, but without losing our joy, our boldness and our hope-filled commitment."[24]

This involves continued discernment to move into a future created in response to the Gospel and its mission. It is in this context of faith and the truth of the Gospel that I want to describe canonical options for restructuring the canonical governance of religious institutes that are in transition and planning for a future of hope in fidelity to the journey.

Canonical Governance of Religious Institutes

When a religious institute is established, its constitutions, which describe the institute's identity, founding charism, purpose, and traditions, are approved by an ecclesiastical authority to ensure that the institute will "flourish according to the spirit of the founder and sound traditions" (c. 576). With this approval, the institute is given just autonomy in governing its internal life (c. 586 §1) and in exercising the apostolate (c. 677 §1).

Primary responsibility for sustaining the life and mission of the institute and protecting its identity rests with the superior general and the general chapter in accord with the institute's proper law (cc. 587 §1, 622, 631). If the general government is unable to provide for the institute's life and the needs of its members as described in its proper law, the leadership of the institute must seek assistance in carrying out its responsibility to preserve the nature, spirit, and

---

23 Francis, morning homily, Santa Marta, October 23, 2015, quoted in James Schall, "Pope Francis and the Changing Times," *The Catholic World Report*, November 13, 2015, https://www.catholicworldreport.com/2015/11/13/pope-francis-and-the-changing-times/ (accessed on 6 Nov. 2023).

24 Francis, apostolic exhortation *Evangelii gaudium* 109, November 24, 2013: *AAS* 105 (2013) 1065; Eng. trans. https://www.vatican.va/content/francesco/en/apost_exhortations/documents/papa-francesco_esortazione-ap_20131124_evangelii-gaudium.html (accessed on 19 Dec. 2023).

character of the institute according to the constitutions (c. 578) and the signs of the times.[25]

The response of institutes in the United States and elsewhere to the signs of the times has been and continues to be multifaceted. Some institutes have merged; others have combined provinces to create fewer and larger provinces or regions; still others suppressed provinces for a return to a centralized government as a single institute. Major superiors have been "recycled," serving first in the 1980s or 1990s and again in the 2000s and the 2020s; other major superiors are in third and fourth terms with indults from competent ecclesiastical authority. Some small institutes have formed "covenant relationships" with a larger institute to oversee administrative and management issues or look to other institutes to provide their canonical governance. And some institutes have not yet accepted the reality of their future and the need to plan accordingly.

While the 1983 *Code of Canon Law* did not directly address the sharp decline in the number of vocations and the demographic shifts evident in the United States and other parts of the world, the law does contain provisions for mergers and unions of institutes, though these options are rarely used today and are no longer the preferred or ideal solutions. Today, institutes look for new options that will address canonical governance, the care of members, the institute's patrimony (c. 578), its mission, ministries[26] and its legacy. So, what are some of these options for canonical restructuring?

Options for Restructuring in the Code of Canon Law

The Code of Canon Law contains several models for restructuring governance in religious institutes that do not require permission from the Holy See for pontifical institutes or the diocesan bishop, in the case of a diocesan institute. There are, however, some forms of restructuring that require changes in the constitutions of the institute and, therefore, subsequent approval by the Holy See or the diocesan bishop.

---

25 See Lynn Jarrell, "The Roles of the Religious Institute and the Diocesan Bishop When the Institute Is Facing the Reality of Decline," *CLSA Proceedings* 80 (2018): 174–94, for a detailed description of the responsibilities of the institute and the diocesan bishop.

26 For more on transitioning sponsorship or ministries, see, for example, Amy Hereford, "Transitioning Sponsorship," *RCRI Bulletin* 17 (2017) 5-18; Sharon Holland, "Vatican Expert Unpacks Canonical PJP Process," *Health Progress* 90:5 (September 2011) 50-62; Sharon Euart, "Ministerial Public Juridic Persons: Model for Canonical Governance," *Studia Canonica* 55 (2021) 319-339.

Division into Parts and Establishing New Parts

For example, canon 581 acknowledges the principle of subsidiarity in recognizing the proper authority of an institute (i.e., general chapter, superior general, etc.) over the institute's internal structure. The canon describes the following actions: *Division into parts* occurs when a single institute is divided into provinces or regions, and *establishing new parts* is the creation of new units such as provinces, regions, or canonical houses.

An example of an institute's division into parts occurs within an international institute when the sustainability of a province or region is no longer possible, for example, due to the availability of members for leadership, number of members, etc. In some of these situations, the superior general transitions the province or region to a canonical house with an appointed local coordinator/superior of the house (c. 608), who is accountable to the superior general. This is the situation with the U.S. Province of the Sisters of Mercy of the Holy Cross whose status recently has been changed from province to a canonical house. In this governance structure, there is also representation at the General Chapter.[27]

An example of institutes *establishing new parts* or creating new units is occurring in the United States when international religious institutes mission small groups of members to establish a new community in the United States for a particular ministry.[28] Canonically, the group might be designated as a region, though more frequently its canonical status is as a single community with a local superior accountable to the general superior in the home country. Prior to the arrival of the new community, the superior general has sought and received the written permission of the diocesan bishop where the community will reside. With this permission the members may exercise their ministry in accord with their mission and diocesan policy (c. 678 §1).[29]

---

27 See Pat Cormack, "Choosing Our Future," in *RCRI Bulletin* 26 (Winter 2021) 10, in which the author describes how the structure of U.S. Province of the Sisters of Mercy of the Holy Cross changed from a province to a canonical house.

28 See *CARA Special Report on International Women Religious in the United States*, for the results of a study on the experience of international women religious in the United States; at https://tinyurl.com/ya3cdhn3 (accessed on 6 Nov. 2023).

29 There are, however, occasions when a leader of an institute does not realize she/he should contact the diocesan bishop prior to moving into the diocese. There are also instances when a pastors might invite into the country a community that is willing to work in his parish without authorization from the diocesan bishop.

Mergers, Unions, and Federations

Canon 582 refers to mergers, unions, and federations of institutes of consecrated life and states that authorization for these forms of restructuring is reserved to the Holy See. A merger (sometimes called a "fusion") of established parts of the same institute happens when an institute combines several units by modifying their composition, such as several regions becoming a province, the merger of several provinces into a single province, or the consolidation of several provinces into a single institute.

An example of a merger of several provinces occurred not long ago when the Society of Jesus in the United States created the second largest Jesuit province: United States East. Regarding this reconfiguration, Reverend Arturo Sosa, SJ, superior general, commented, "We are learning that Province reconfiguration helps us to recover our deepest identity as Jesuits. . . [It] widens apostolic horizons . . . facilitating a more effective distribution of workers in the vineyard of the Lord."[30]

Other restructuring options are often referred to as a *merger* even though the structures and procedures for establishing them differ. A common example of a merger occurs when a small institute is absorbed into a larger institute. The effect of such a merger is that the smaller institute loses its proper identity and assumes the identity of the larger institute.

Canon 582 also refers to a *union* which occurs when several—two, three, or twenty—different institutes come together to form a new institute that is different from any of the individual institutes. An example of this occurred when the Sisters of Mercy of the Americas was created in 1991. After ten years of planning, sixteen independent Mercy congregations and one union composed of nine provinces, created a single institute with twenty-five provinces, and in 2008 it merged the twenty-five provinces into six provinces.[31] In 2019, the institute suppressed the provinces becoming a single institute. Referring to this experience as the "Journey to Oneness," the institute articulated a vision for the process in two questions: "Who do we desire to be for one another as Sisters of Mercy? Who do we desire to be for our suffering world?" Sister Patricia McDermott, RSM, president of the

30 See Communications Office, "Birth of the Second Largest Jesuit Province: United States East (UEA)," Jesuits USA East, July 27, 2020, https://www.jesuits.global/2020/07/27/birth-of-the-second-largest-jesuit-province-united-states-east-uea/ (accessed on 6 Nov. 2023).

31 See Pat McDermott, "Canonical Governance Options and Opportunities for Collaboration," *RCRI Bulletin* 24 (Winter 2020–2021) 8.

Sisters of Mercy of the Americas at the time, said, "Vision is a must . . . and that vision must be about mission and life."[32]

The conciliar and post-conciliar documents *Perfectae caritatis* and *Ecclesiae Sanctae* encouraged the merger of institutes and monasteries that, left alone, offered no reasonable hope for growth and development (*PC* 21–22; *ES* 39–41). If possible, such institutes were to be merged with institutes possessing a similar character, purpose, and spirituality and whose future looked more promising. The same was true for unions among institutes if, according to *Perfectae caritatis* 22, "their constitutions and customs were practically the same and a kindred spirit animates them . . . especially when of themselves they are very small."[33] An important canonical requirement at the end of *Ecclesiae Sanctae* states that, prior to proceeding to a merger or union, every religious is to be heard and all is to be done in charity (*ES* 41).

Today, despite the availability of mergers and unions for restructuring religious institutes, they are not often considered to be practical options given the demographic realities of many institutes. The merging of two small institutes with few members and a high median age or a merger of several aging institutes only creates larger non-viable institutes. A primary concern of members of institutes regarding mergers and unions is a desire to maintain their identity and live their remaining years as members of the institute they entered and to which they devoted their lives as religious.

Even though new unions are rare, recently, in July of this year, the Holy See formed a union of seven independent institutes of Sisters of the Incarnate Word and Blessed Sacrament, called the new institute the Order of the Incarnate Word and Blessed Sacrament, with central offices in the Archdiocese of Madrid and the United States headquarters in Corpus Christi, Texas. The decree included the appointment of the new superior general and five general councilors for a three-year term as well as new constitutions, *ad experimentum*, to be modified and approved at the first general chapter in 2026. Regional superiors will be appointed in mid-November. The eleven regions of the United States institutes, currently under the authority of a delegate of the superior general, are in the very early stages of implementing the new regional structure which will include

32 McDermott, "Canonical Governance Options," 9.

33 Sharon Holland, *Procedural Handbook for Institutes for Consecrated Life and Societies of Apostolic Life* (Washington, DC: CLSA, 2001) 41–42; see ibid. for procedures and options for individual members, at 43; Rose McDermott, "Institutes of Consecrated Life and Societies of Apostolic Life," in *New Commentary on the Code of Canon Law* (Mahwah, NJ: Paulist Press, 2000) 750–751.

communities in Mexico and the southwest United States. So, unions, though rare, are still being erected.

An option often utilized by institutes as they begin to discern that they may not be able to meet their governance requirements for the future is to request permission from Rome or the diocesan bishop for changes in their constitutions regarding the number of council members, the term of office for elected leadership, and/or the criteria for chapter participation. All these options require canonical consultation and approval by the appropriate ecclesiastical authority.

What Are Other Options for Canonical Governance for Institutes Transitioning to Historical Completion?

Although most institutes in transition have been able to retain their canonical leadership, there is an increasing number of institutes that are moving toward fulfillment of their historical life cycle, are in their final era of general government (namely, celebration of a general chapter and election of superior general and council), and no longer have members capable of exercising leadership roles. This can be a very painful time for an institute and its members. It also can be a time of peace and acceptance in which members are sustained by the realization that they have responded faithfully to God's call and fulfilled the mission entrusted to them.

Though the process of moving toward historical completion is not regulated in the Code of Canon Law, many of the following actions and procedures are guided by canonical principles. There are three structures that I would like to address: the Covenant Relationship, Collaborative Governance Models, and the Canonical Commissary.

Covenant Relationship

Canon 580 describes a relationship of accompaniment, a walking together, between religious institutes that respect the autonomy of each institute. It may exist within charism groups or across charisms. It may be inspired by a historical relationship dating back decades or even centuries. [34] The non-juridical relationship does not result in a merger of the institutes; rather, this relationship between the institutes has been described as a covenant or partnership to assist an institute coming to fulfillment on its journey. The covenant relationship is often described in an agreement or a memorandum of understanding detailing what

---

34 An example of this type of covenant relationship is the one between the Sisters of St. Casimir (Chicago) and the Sisters of the Immaculate Heart of Mary (Scranton). Currently, the Sisters of St. Casimir have petitioned the Holy See for a commissary from the IHM Sisters.

services might be rendered to the completing institute from the accompanying institute in the covenant. In this relationship, each institute retains its identity. The services provided are contingent on the needs of the smaller institute and the resources of an accompanying institute to meet those needs. Not all covenant relationships will be alike. Some may include providing oversight for financial administration, personnel services and property, provision for retirement and health care of members, administration of any remaining sponsored ministries, divesting of property, and legacy planning.[35]

The covenant relationship may be short-term or long-term, depending on the needs of the smaller, more fragile, institute. When the smaller institute is no longer able to provide its own canonical governance, it might request leadership from outside the institute. This would require petitioning the Holy See or the diocesan bishop for a suspension of its governance and a request for a commissary, canonical trustee or administrator to provide canonical leadership during the last phase of the institute's journey. A covenant relationship is often a first step leading to the petition for a commissary.

Collaborative Governance Models

For some institutes moving toward historical completion, the covenant relationship is not the best option since it would only temporarily address the governance issues. It could also mean that the smaller, more fragile institute might be subsumed into the other, even though they are juridically separate institutes. Currently, there are two different models for collaborative governance implemented by some U.S. institutes. These models are shared services models with civil law status, but no ecclesial status, with a focus on sharing certain management services.

In one model, the Sisters of the Most Precious Blood and the Franciscan Sisters of Mary began a conversation in 2013 and, after six years of intense planning, created a third civil corporation named Collaborative Governance (CG), which manages and oversees human resources, property management, legal issues, and management tasks for the institutes' remaining sponsored ministries. Each institute retains its own identity and charism and its canonical governance

---

35 See Resource Center for Religious Institutes, *Fidelity to the Journey: New Paths of Hope* (Silver Spring, MD: Resource Center for Religious Institutes, 2021) 22-25. See also Dan Ward, "Covenant Relationship," in *RCRI Bulletin* 8 (Fall 2012) 4-8; Amy Hereford, "Canon 580: Aggregation and Covenants," in Sharon Euart, John Alesandro, and Thomas Green, eds., *Roman Replies and CLSA Advisory Opinions 2012* (Washington, DC: CLSA, 2012) 83-86; "Planning for the Future: The Covenant Relationship," *RCRI News in Brief* vol. 3, no. 4 (Fall 2011) 2–3.

for as long as possible. When either institute can no longer provide canonical leadership for its members, the institute will petition the Holy See for appointment of a canonical commissary.

The commissary could be selected from among members of the board of the new civil corporation, thereby providing a relationship between the two institutes that respects their heritage while providing the support necessary to live out their vocation. Sister Janice Bader, President of the Sisters of the Most Precious Blood, described a significant advantage of this model as allowing the sisters "to maintain their identity as Sisters of the Most Precious Blood."[36] She also noted that openness and honesty are essential in collaborative ventures. "It is the only way to move from 'we/they' to 'us.'"[37]

A second type of collaborative governance model involving several religious institutes within a single geographic area is the Wisconsin Religious Collaborative (WRC), a small nonprofit corporation established in 2018. The collaborative is designed to serve member institutes of women religious "to enable greater stewardship of resources, facilitate collaboration in programs and activities, and support for personnel."[38] The leaders of nine religious institutes in Wisconsin and northern Illinois created mission and vision statements to focus the work of the collaborative. The members of the collaborative have different needs, and the institutes are at different stages of transition. An important step in the genesis of the collaborative was to connect with others experiencing similar challenges while sharing learnings that can be helpful to other institutes through its website at www.wrcollab.org. They hope that "developing a structure to foster collaboration in internal governance and management functions will allow leaders and members to give energy, time, and attention to mission."[39]

Canonical Commissary

When an institute is moving toward historical fulfillment of its mission and is no longer able to provide for its canonical governance, the superior general may petition the competent ecclesiastical authority for a canonical administrator, steward or trustee, generally referred to as a commissary, who will be entrusted

---

36 Dan Stockman, "Collaborative Governance Model Helps Congregations Carry on with Limited Resources," *Global Sisters Report*, February 12, 2018; https://tinyurl.com/muxexxx8 (accessed on 6 Nov. 2023). See Janice Bader, "Canonical Governance Options and Opportunities for Collaboration," *RCRI Bulletin* (Winter 2020–2021) 11.

37 Bader, "Canonical Governance Options," 11.

38 See Lyn Korte, "Canonical Governance Options and Opportunities for Collaboration," *RCRI Bulletin* 24 (Winter 2020–2021) 13.

39 Vision Statement, Wisconsin Religious Collaborative, www.wrcollab.org .

with the canonical governance of the institute.[40] The process may begin when an institute is still able to elect a general superior/president but lacks members capable of serving as councilors. In this case, it is possible to seek dispensation from the institute's constitutions to permit fewer councilors or for the appointment of a religious from another institute to serve as a member of the council.

The appointment of a canonical commissary is an alternative for an institute in which the regular or ordinary governance has been suspended. Though this option for governance does not appear in the Code of Canon Law, it is not new. The notion is that one person is sent to provide oversight for others. Canonically, the petition for a commissary involves a change in the constitutions and proper law of the institute (c. 623). Petitioning for a commissary calls for serious prayer and discernment on the part of the requesting institute.

A commissary is appointed by the competent ecclesiastical authority, either by the Holy See for pontifical institutes or by the diocesan bishop for diocesan institutes, with the canonical authority to act as the superior general for governance of the institute according to the constitutions and proper law of the institute the commissary is serving, as well as the decree of appointment.[41] In monastic congregations where all the monasteries collectively constitute the monastic congregation, the federation, or association, the president may have the authority to appoint a commissary for a member monastery according to the monastic congregation's constitutions.[42]

Generally, a commissary for a women's institute is a woman religious with a similar experience of living religious life, though often not a member of the requesting institute's charism group. Clerics may also be appointed to serve in this role for women's institutes. Currently a layperson cannot be appointed a commissary for a religious institute. The requesting institute is encouraged to recommend a suitable person who is known to the institute to be appointed as commissary; however, the appointment of the commissary is made by the Holy See or the diocesan bishop.

Some institutes have requested another institute or a conference of religious to serve as a commissary. In response to one such request from a conference of religious, the Dicastery of Institutes of Consecrated Life and Societies of

---

40 See van Dam, Leys, and Sponselee, "Explorations on the 'Completion' of Religious Institutes," 20.

41 See canons 312 and 318 for an analogous situation for moderators of public associations of the faithful. See also Hereford, *Navigating Change*, 229.

42 See M. Weisenbeck, "Sooner Rather Than Later: Preparing for the Institute's Journey to Fulfillment," *RCRI Bulletin* 26 (Winter 2021) 20.

Apostolic Life responded in the negative indicating that the proposal was not consistent with the nature of a conference of religious and that the proposal did not provide for a *person* responsible to assume the role of commissary. The dicastery stated that the principle of personal authority with the assistance of a council should be respected in situations for which a commissary is requested. Other options proposed by the dicastery in its response include the covenant relationship (referred to as an "extended aggregation") or the appointment by the dicastery or diocesan bishop of the superior of another institute as superior general of a small institute.[43]

As with every major superior, the commissary should have a council (c. 627), or advisors, referred to in the decrees as "a competent person or persons of her choice."[44] If possible, all or at least some of the advisors should be members of the institute she is serving. She can, however, ask assistance from members of her own institute. Decrees or letters of appointment of some commissaries imply that the *election* of councilors or advisors is not required. Consultation with the members prior to appointment of the advisors is sufficient.[45] The advisors provide the collective wisdom needed for the regular life of the institute as well as for important decisions. In many cases, the commissary does not have a specific term, though a commissary could request one. The appointment of pontifical commissaries is usually *ad nutum Sanctae Sedis,* at the will of the Holy See. The appointment may last several years, even throughout the lifetime of the last member of the institute.[46] Other details regarding the role of the commissary, such as compensation, vacation, residence, etc. are incorporated into a contract or memorandum of understanding.

Together with the members of the institute, the commissary does what is necessary to plan for the closure of the institute when that time arrives. This would include first and foremost the care and well-being of the members, disposition of

---

43 Letter from Dicastery for Institutes of Consecrated Life and Societies of Apostolic Life to President of CRA, September 14, 2020. Private letter made available to this author.

44 Dicastery for Institutes of Consecrated Life and Societies of Apostolic Life, Decree of Appointment of the Congregational Leader of the Marianites of the Holy Cross as Commissary for the Sisters of the Most Blessed Sacrament, January 13, 2015.

45 Weisenbeck, "Sooner Rather Than Later," 20.

46 See "25 Q&As: Commissary for Religious Institutes," RCRI website at www.trcri.org, https://cdn.ymaws.com/www.trcri.org/resource/resmgr/2019_updates/commissary_q_and_a_2019_upda.pdf (accessed on 6 Nov. 2023). See also S. Euart, "Canonical Governance: Commissary of a Religious Institute," in Canon Law Society of America, *Roman Replies and CLSA Advisory Opinions 2018*, ed. S. Euart and J. Alesandro (Washington, DC: CLSA, 2018) 157–59.

assets, ministries, properties (if any remain), and dissolution in accord with canon and civil law.

I would like to offer observations from several decrees of appointment. Recently, an institute seeking a commissary interviewed three congregations discerning which one was a suitable fit for the institute. The institute petitioned the Holy See for one of the three institutes to serve in this role, and the Holy See appointed the superior general of that institute as the commissary for the requesting institute. She, as well as her successors, were appointed *ad nutum Sanctae Sedes* with all the "rights and obligations of universal law and the proper law of the institute attributed to the general superior and the council to be assumed by the pontifical commissary."[47] In this case, the superior general then appointed a member of her institute to serve in the role of commissary with delegated authority. The commissary in this situation is accountable to her superior general, and the superior general to the Holy See.

In another case, a 2018 decree from the archbishop of a U.S. archdiocese appointing a woman religious as a commissary for a diocesan institute authorized her to exercise all the responsibilities required of a major superior of a diocesan institute."[48] The decree included a term of three years which was renewed once. The commissary is currently completing her second term and will not be accepting a third term. In preparation for the appointment of a new commissary, the current commissary and her superior general met with the archbishop to discuss the possibility of his appointing the superior general of the commissary's institute as the commissary moving forward with the superior general then delegating the authority of a commissary to a member of her institute. This arrangement was well received by the archbishop and members of the small community since they have a close relationship with the commissary's institute.

Some final comments on commissary and canonical governance. A superior general of an institute in transition while also serving as a commissary for another institute describes fidelity to the journey this way: "Gratitude and Hope are sisters and we who journey to completion are challenged to bring Hope: To look forward

---

47 Decree of appointment of the General Superior of the Sisters of Providence of St. Mary of the Woods as Pontifical Commissary for the Missionary Sisters of Our Lady of Victory, July 14, 2022.

48 Decree of Most Reverend Allen H. Vigneron, appointing Sister Paul Cooney, IHM Commissary for the Servants of Jesus for three years, March 5, 2018.

with active hope; acknowledging our pain; letting go of what hinders us; viewing life with new eyes; moving forward to all God calls us to be."[49]

Conclusion

Today, leaders and members of religious institutes are all seeking the best way to move forward. Not everyone is prepared to face the realities of today and tomorrow. Those who have begun the work of restructuring for the future, as well as the latest research, urge others not to wait.[50] Now is the time. Members of institutes that are assessing options for restructuring canonical governance or moving toward fulfillment of their mission exude a spirit of faith, joy and hope that continues to guide their mission and their lives. While this is a time filled with unanticipated challenges including grief, it is also a time of spiritual growth and renewal as well as an occasion for strengthening communion through cooperation, joint efforts, and looking at how together we are being Church going forward under the guidance of the Holy Spirit. Such communion is an experience of synodality.

During the 2022 Annual Conference of the Resource Center for Religious Institutes, Cardinal Wilton Gregory, in his keynote address, described the witness of women and men religious to the love of Christ as having "an immeasurable impact in serving the most vulnerable, transforming our communities, and strengthening our Church."[51] He then related this witness of religious communities to the Synodal process, saying that the witness of religious "has the potential to once again transform and strengthen our Church." Religious communities, having maintained synodal structures throughout their histories, "have much to teach the rest of us—both laity and clergy, including bishops in the Church—about how to be synodal."

In his homily on the World Day of Consecrated Life in 2022, Pope Francis encouraged religious to be hopeful in the midst of crises. He stated:

> [T]he Lord never fails to give us signs that invite us to cultivate *a renewed vision* of consecrated life. . . . We cannot pretend not to see these signs and go on as usual, doing the same old things, drifting back through inertia to the forms of the past, paralyzed by fear of change.... Let us open our eyes: the Spirit is inviting us amid our crises—and

---

49 Ann Lacour, "Canonical Governance Options and Opportunities for Collaboration," *RCRI Bulletin* (Winter 2020–2021) 7.

50 See Sharon Euart, "Canonical Governance Options and Opportunities for Collaboration," *RCRI Bulletin* 24 (Winter 2020–2021) 5-6. See also CARA 2019 Report to LCWR, August 2020.

51 Wilton Gregory, "Together as a Synodal Church," *RCRI Bulletin* 28 (Winter 2022) 6.

> crises there are . . . to renew our lives and our communities. And how do we do this? He will show us the way. Let us open our hearts, with courage and without fear. . . . Let us not waste today by looking back at yesterday or dreaming of a tomorrow that will never come; instead, let us place ourselves before the Lord . . . and ask for eyes to see goodness and to discern the ways of God. The Lord will give them to us if we ask him.[52]

As an increasing number of religious institutes cultivate *a renewed vision* of consecrated life, may they move forward with joy, with courage, and without fear in fidelity to the journey.

52 Pope Francis, 26th World Day of Consecrated life, accessed at https://www.vatican.va/content/francesco/en/messages/consecrated_life/documents/20220202_omelia-vitaconsacrata.html (accessed on 12 Feb. 2024).

CLSA PROCEEDINGS 85 (2023) 86-107

SEMINAR

THE EASTERN CATHOLIC EXPERIENCE OF SYNODALITY

Chorbishop John D. Faris

Introduction

Synodality has been a constant theme throughout the papacy of Francis, whose goal has been to create a trajectory that will make the Catholic Church a *synodal Church.* Expectations are high—perhaps excessively so—for the synod on synodality (2021-2024) that is currently in session in Rome. The theological and ecclesiological literature on synodality is beyond the scope of this brief study. Instead, we shall focus on the institutional facet of the Roman Synod of Bishops (terminology in this paper adopted for the sake of clarity). Eastern Catholics and Orthodox view this assembly, compare it with their own experience of the synod, and raise questions. Metropolitan Job of Pisidia made these comments at the 2023 Roman Synod of Bishops:

> It is through this practice of synodality, as described by the Apostolic Canons and the canons of the First Ecumenical Council, that the Orthodox Church has been administered over the centuries until the present day, although the frequency and constitution of the synods may vary from one local autocephalous Church to another.
>
> In light of this, we could say that the understanding of synodality in the Orthodox Church differs greatly from the definition of synodality given by your present assembly of the Synod of Bishops.[1]

Admittedly, the nature and role of the Roman Synod of Bishops is currently not the most important aspect of synodality, but it cannot be ignored as the institution evolves. Failure to do so will result in a series of sentimental, ineffective gestures and a lack of definition and parameters. It should be recalled that the recent significant news regarding participation with a deliberative vote in

---

1 Job (Getcha) of Pisidia at the Roman Synod of Bishops, "Synod: Testimony of Metropolitan of Job (Getcha) of Pisidia," Vatican News, 9 October 2023, https://www.vaticannews.va/en/vatican-city/news/2023-10/intervention-of-his-eminence-metropolitan-of-pisidia-job-getcha.html (accessed on 2 Nov. 2023).

the synod is an institutional matter that greatly changed the dynamics of the October synod.[2].

While the Synod of Bishops is at the level of the supreme authority of the Church, it is operationally an institution of the Latin Church—and there is nothing wrong with that. The Code of Canons of the Eastern Churches[3] treats the institution only concerning the participation of Eastern Catholic hierarchs (c. 46 §2). It is no surprise that the Catholic Church is struggling since a synod is an *avis rara* in the Latin Church. The 1983 Code of Canon Law[4] has provisions for a plenary council (*CIC* c. 439 §1) and provincial council (*CIC* c. 439 §2), episcopal assemblies with legislative power (*CIC* c. 445), but such assemblies are rarely convoked. On the other hand, synodal institutions (even if called something other than a "synod") are a familiar reality for the Eastern Churches, both Catholic and Orthodox.

The purpose of this brief study is to offer insights into the experience of synodality in the Eastern Catholic Churches. Perhaps the role and function of the synods of the Eastern Catholic Churches—*which are already a component of Catholic ecclesial governance*—can help canonists as they articulate institutions and procedures that will facilitate the appropriation of synodality in the Latin Catholic Church.

Patriarchal/synodal governance is the traditional form of governance in Eastern Churches and finds many expressions.[5] We shall examine three institutions of the Eastern Catholic patriarchal Churches that might serve as models for the Latin Church: (1) the Synod of Bishops of the patriarchal Church; (2) the permanent synod; and 3) the patriarchal assembly. We shall also look at

---

2 "It is therefore in the role/function of memory that the presence of non-bishops is included, and not in that of representation. In this way, the specifically episcopal nature of the Synodal Assembly is not affected, but rather is confirmed." Synod 2021-2024, "Some news for the October 2023 Assembly," 26 April 2023, https://www.synod.va/en/news/some-news-for-the-october-2023-assembly.html (accessed on 2 Nov. 2023).

3 *Codex Canonum Ecclesiarum Orientalium auctoritate Ioannis Pauli PP. II promulgatus* (Vatican City: Libreria Editrice Vaticana, 1990) (hereafter "Eastern code" or "*CCEO*"). All canonical references are to this code unless indicated otherwise.

4 *Codex Iuris Canonici auctoritate Ioannis Pauli PP. II promulgatus* (Vatican City: Libreria Editrice Vaticana, 1983) (hereafter "Latin code" or "*CIC*").

5 Second Vatican Council, decree *Orientalium Ecclesiarum*, November 21, 1964: *AAS* 57 (1965) 76-85 (hereafter *OE*), no. 9 and 11; Second Vatican Council, dogmatic constitution *Lumen gentium*, November 21, 1964: *AAS* 57 (1965) 5-67 (hereafter *LG*), n. 23; Second Vatican Council, decree *Unitatis redintegratio,* November 21, 1964: *AAS* 57 (1965) 90-107 (hereafter *UR*).

the council of hierarchs of the metropolitan Church *sui iuris*, a more restricted form of self-governance.

An understanding of these bodies will facilitate a *communicatio disciplinarum* or sharing of disciplines[6] between East and West as the Latin Catholic Church seeks to institutionalize synodality in its governance structures. After the expository section treating Eastern Catholic institutions, we shall examine certain aspects of the Synod of Bishops in Rome from an Eastern Catholic perspective.

Some preliminary ecclesiological and canonical issues need to be addressed to provide a context for this reflection.

Communion of Churches *Sui Iuris*

The Catholic Church, as a *communio Ecclesiarum*, comprises 23 Eastern Catholic Churches (with a total membership of 15 million faithful) and the Latin Church (with a membership of 1.2 billion). An Eastern Catholic Church is an ecclesial grouping, a *coetus fidelium*.[7] *Lumen gentium* describes the coalescence of churches into such a *coetus*.

> [I]t has come about that various churches, established in various places by the apostles and their successors, have in the course of time coalesced into several groups, organically united, which, preserving the unity of faith and the unique divine constitution of the universal Church, enjoy their own discipline, their own liturgical usage, and their own theological and spiritual heritage.[8]

In its articulation of the unity and variety of the Churches,[9] this passage affirms the unity of the faith and the unique divine constitution of the Church,

---

6 "In virtue of this catholicity each individual part contributes through its special gifts to the good of the other parts and of the whole Church. Through the common sharing of gifts and through the common effort to attain fullness in unity, the whole and each of the parts receive increase." *LG* 13; Eng. trans. at https://www.vatican.va/archive/hist_councils/ii_vatican_council/documents/vat-ii_const_19641121_lumen-gentium_en.html (accessed on 2 Nov. 2023). All subsequent English translations from this document are found at this location unless otherwise noted.

7 Some of the Eastern Catholic Churches are quite small, perhaps constituting a sole exarchate. Others lack a bishop, which means that they are a community, but not a church.

8 *LG* 23d.

9 See also *LG* 13c: "Moreover, within the Church particular Churches hold a rightful place; these Churches retain their own traditions, without in any way opposing the primacy of the Chair of Peter, which presides over the whole assembly of charity and protects legitimate differences, while at the same time assuring that such differences do not hinder unity but rather contribute toward it."

along with the various expressions of discipline, liturgical usage, and theological and spiritual heritage, identified as a "rite" in canon 28 §1 of the Eastern code.[10]

The Second Vatican Council asserted that the Catholic Eastern Churches have the full right to govern themselves according to their disciplines which find the sources in antiquity, and which are more harmonious and better suited to promote the good of the souls of their faithful.[11] The basic self-governing structure is the *Ecclesia sui iuris*, a Church "of its own right" or an "autonomous Church." While the term is often left partially untranslated as "Church *sui iuris,*" it will suit our purposes to use the term "self-governing Church."

Eastern code canon 27 defines the self-governing Church:

> A community of the Christian faithful, which is joined together by a hierarchy according to the norm of law and which is expressly or tacitly recognized as *sui iuris* by the supreme authority of the Church, is called in this Code a Church *sui iuris*.

The Church *sui iuris,* a community of the Christian faithful (*coetus Christifidelium*) is an intermediate ecclesial body between the universal Church and the eparchy/diocese. The governance arrangements are "expressly or tacitly recognized as *sui iuris* by the supreme authority of the Church." Note that it is not the rite (cf. c. 28 §2) of the Church *sui iuris* but the self-governing hierarchy ("joined together by a hierarchy") that individuates each Church *sui iuris*, that is, distinguishes one community of faithful from another.

Source of Patriarchal/Synodal Authority

In the case of the patriarchal Church, the patriarch and Synod of Bishops of the patriarchal Church exercise power over all the Christian faithful of their respective Church, including the bishops and the metropolitans (c. 55). The Synod

---

10 See *CCEO* c. 28 §1: "A rite is a liturgical, theological, spiritual, and disciplinary heritage, differentiated by the culture and the circumstances of the history of peoples, which is expressed by each Church *sui iuris* in its own manner of living the faith." Eng. trans. in *Code of Canons of the Eastern Churches: Latin-English Edition: New English Translation* (Washington, DC: Canon Law Society of America, 2001); all subsequent English translations of this code are from this source unless otherwise indicated.

11 ". . . the Churches of the East, as much as those of the West, have a full right and are in duty bound to rule themselves, each in accordance with its own established disciplines, since all these are praiseworthy by reason of their venerable antiquity, more harmonious with the character of their faithful and more suited to the promotion of the good of souls." *OE* 5. Eng. trans. at https://www.vatican.va/archive/hist_councils/ii_vatican_council/documents/vat-ii_decree_19641121_orientalium-ecclesiarum_en.html (accessed on 2 Nov. 2023). All subsequent English translations from this document are from this source unless otherwise noted. The Council made a similar declaration regarding the governance of the Orthodox Churches in *Unitatis redintegratio* 16.

of Bishops, comprising all and solely the ordained bishops of a Church *sui iuris* (c. 102), exercises legislative and judicial authority over that Church *sui iuris* (c. 110 §§1 and 2). The patriarch generally exercises executive authority (c. 110 §4). Often these intermediate authorities are misconstrued as encroaching on the power of the bishop in his eparchy/diocese or interloping on the primatial power of the Roman Pontiff. Its rightful place in the ecclesial and hierarchical structure of the Church must be articulated. To begin, from where do the patriarch and Synod of Bishops derive their power?

Since the decretalists,[12] traditional ecclesiology and canon law have held *ex iure divino* there exist two "poles" of power: primatial and episcopal. According to this approach, any intermediate, i.e., supra-episcopal, exercise of power could exist only *ex iure canonico* and participate in the primatial power.[13] In this ecclesiological model, the Roman Pontiff possesses all the power of governance, which can be shared with other subordinate entities. This is reflected in the structures of the 1917 *Codex Iuris Canonici* and the 1957 motu proprio *Cleri Sanctitati,* which presents a bilevel hierarchical infrastructure comprising the Roman Pontiff and the bishops. Intermediate entities, such as the cardinals, the

12 Peter Szabó offers several examples of from decretal law that envision that Roman Pontiff as the source of all power in the Church. See "The Local Origin of Supra-Episcopal Power. A Further Step towards Catholic-Orthodox Ecclesiological Convergence?" in Peter Szabó and Tamás Frankó (eds.) *Sacrorum canonum scientia: radici, tradizioni, prospettive: Studi in onore del cardinale Péter Erdő per il suo 70° compleanno* (Budapest Hungary: Szent István Társulat az Apostoli Szentszék Könyvkiadója, 2022) (hereafter Szabó, "Origin of Supra-Episcopal Power"] 649, fn. 10. See also Péter Szabó, "Approfondimenti sull'origine e sulla natura della potestà sovraepiscopale in prospettiva ecumenica," *Eastern Canon Law* 6 (2017) (hereafter Szabó, "Approfondimenti") 77-112.

13 These assertions are consonant with the approach of the 1917 *Codex Iuris Canonici* which portrayed the hierarchical structure of the Church as:

> *Tit. VII. De suprema potestate deque iis qui eiusdem sunt ecclesiastico iure participes.*
>
> *Title VIII. De postestate episcopale deque iis qui in eadem participant.*

The 1957 motu proprio *Cleri sanctitati* followed the same pattern:

> *Pars I. De suprema potestate deque iis qui eiusdem sunt canonico iure participes.*
>
> *Pars II. De potestate episcopali deque iis qui eam participant.*

The motu proprio, which treated the hierarchical structures of the Eastern Catholic Churches, treated patriarchs after cardinals, the Roman Curia, and papal legates.

The 1962 draft of *Orientalium Ecclesiarum* included an argument set forth by Cardinal Amleto Cicognani that patriarchal power is "*quaedam Pontificae potestatis primatialis participatio.*" Cicognani claimed that the Nicene Fathers considered the patriarchal sees to be connected to participation in the authority of the Apostolic See. Nedungatt indicated that this position was not acceptable to some of the Council Fathers. George Nedungatt, "The Patriarchal Ministry of the Church of the Third Millennium," *The Jurist* 61 (2001) 33.

Roman Curia, papal legates, and patriarchs participate in the authority of the Roman Pontiff.[14]

Father Ivan Žužek, SJ, secretary of the Commission for the Revision of the Eastern Code, is regarded as a proponent of this approach and is presumed responsible for the inclusion of the phrase "the patriarchs and synods are sharers in the supreme authority of the Church by canon law"[15] in the apostolic constitution, *Sacri Canones*, the promulgatory instrument of the *Codex Canonum Ecclesiarum Orientalium.*[16]

This approach is inadequate because it does not appreciate the role of the intermediate ecclesial and hierarchical structures, which include the ancient institute of the patriarch (see Nicea I, c. 6). Another approach is possible, considering the two agents of supreme power in the Church—the Roman Pontiff and the college of bishops (c. 49).

The primary role of the Roman Pontiff, as the individual successor of Peter, is to maintain the unity of the Church. The Roman Pontiff, who continues the Petrine office, is the head of the college of bishops, Vicar of Christ, and pastor of the entire Church on Earth (c. 43). This power is not only over the Church as a whole but is "also the primacy of ordinary power over all the eparchies and their groupings. Moreover, this primacy strengthens and protects the proper, ordinary, and immediate power which bishops possess in the eparchy entrusted to them" (c. 45 §1).

The college of bishops, many individuals and successors of the apostolic body, expresses the variety and universality of the People of God. *Lumen gentium* states:

> This college, insofar as it is composed of many, expresses the variety and universality of the People of God, but insofar as it is assembled under one head, it expresses the unity of the flock of Christ. In it, the

---

14 "Participation" should not be construed as "delegation." The Second Vatican Council (see *LG* 23 and *OE* 9) is clear that the patriarch does not govern his patriarchal Church as a vicar of the Roman Pontiff. Canon 78 §1 describes the power of the patriarch as ordinary and proper. To fashion the patriarch and the Synod of Bishops as exercising delegated power contradicts traditional doctrine and is ecumenically lethal.

15 ". . . patriarchae et synodi iure canonico supremae ecclesiae auctoritatis participes sunt . . ." John Paul II, apostolic constitution *Sacri canones*, October 18, 1990: *AAS* (82 (1990) 1037.

16 At a symposium on the occasion of the tenth anniversary of the acquisition of the force of law of the *CCEO*, Cardinal Angelo Sodano made the same assertion: "nullam concipi posse partem ecclesiasticae potestatis qua non comprehenderetur in eius suprema potestae," November 24, 2001 in *Ius Ecclesiae* 13 (2001) 886.

> bishops, faithfully recognizing the primacy and pre-eminence of their head, exercise their own authority for the good of their own faithful, and indeed of the whole Church, *the Holy Spirit supporting its organic structure and harmony with moderation.*[17]

This conciliar passage speaks of supporting the *organic structure* of the Church. Most conceive of the organic structure of the Church with two levels of ecclesial communions governed by a hierarchy in virtue of divine law: (1) the universal Church (governed by the Roman Pontiff and the college of bishops); and (2) the eparchy/diocese (governed by an individual bishop). Such a model is inadequate because it does not include the intermediate ecclesial and hierarchical structures as described in *Lumen gentium*:

> By divine Providence, it has come about that various churches, established in various places by the apostles and their successors, have in the course of time coalesced into several groups, organically united, which, preserving the unity of faith and the unique divine constitution of the universal Church, enjoy their own discipline, their own liturgical usage, and their own theological and spiritual heritage. Some of these churches, notably the ancient patriarchal churches, as parent-stocks of the faith, so to speak, have begotten others as daughter churches, with which they are connected down to our own time by a close bond of charity in their sacramental life and their mutual respect for rights and duties.[18]

The patriarchal churches described in the dogmatic constitution[19] are one form of an intermediate ecclesial/hierarchical structure: the Church *sui iuris* as defined in canon 27.

This phenomenon of the coalescence of ecclesial and hierarchical structures is an example of the episcopate crafting itself to meet the needs of the faithful. Ecclesial communions are not exclusively found at the level of universal and particular but can also arise as *some* Churches served by *some* members of the college of bishops.

This manner of exercising collegial power is treated in chapter III of *Christus Dominus*, "The Cooperation of Bishops for the Common Good of a Number of Churches:"

> From the very first centuries of the Church bishops, as rulers of individual churches, were deeply moved by the communion of

---

17 *LG* 22 (emphasis added).
18 *LG* 23.
19 See also *OE* 9.

> fraternal charity and zeal for the universal mission entrusted to the Apostles. And so they pooled their abilities and their wills for the common good and the welfare of the individual churches. Thus came into being synods, provincial councils, and plenary councils in which bishops established for various churches the way to be followed in teaching the truths of faith and ordering ecclesiastical discipline.[20]

This governance by a patriarch and Synod of Bishops is a distinct and canonically sanctioned form of the solicitude that the college of bishops has for a determined *coetus Ecclesiarum.*

> "[T]he Synodal element in the sphere of the particular Churches is not a participation in the supreme power, but only a special form of the cooperation of the bishops for the common good of several Churches even though the competence and thus the authority of the synods is not the sum of the authority of the bishops participating but an authority *sui generis*. . . . Thus, the synodal element appears clearly as derived from the episcopal power and is not to be misunderstood as deriving from the primatial power.[21]

Nor is the group of bishops acting with the delegated authority of its members because bishops cannot transfer their authority to another individual (e.g., the patriarch) or a group (e.g., the synod). Even in his diocese/eparchy, a bishop delegates segments of his authority to certain individuals, while the legislative power cannot be delegated.

The status of an episcopal ministry of some bishops exercising authority over a group of Churches is also of divine right because it is one more expression of the solicitude of the episcopal body for an ecclesial communion.[22] In the case

---

20 Second Vatican Council, decree *Christus Dominus* 36, October 28, 1965: *AAS* 58 (1966) 673-696 (hereafter *CD*); Eng. trans. at https://www.vatican.va/archive/hist_councils/ii_vatican_council/documents/vat-ii_decree_19651028_christus-dominus_en.html (accessed on 2 Nov. 2023). All subsequent English translations from this document are from this source unless otherwise noted.

21 Klaus Mörsdorf, "Decree on the Bishops' Pastoral Office in the Church," in Herbert Vorgimler, ed., *Commentary on the Documents of Vatican II* (New York: Herder and Herder, 1968) 2:281. The assertion that the synodal element is not a participation in the supreme power could perhaps have been more precise and referred to the primatial supreme power.

22 "[T]he gradations of the episcopal ministry flow from the Church's power to organize itself, but the content of the concrete ministries that are to be exercised remains of divine right because the episcopate is of divine origin." Klaus Mörsdorf, "Bishop IV (Canon Law)," in Karl Rahner, ed., *Encyclopedia of Theology. A Concise* Sacramentum Mundi, (Freiburg-im-Breisgau: Herders, 1975) 153.

of the Eastern Catholic Churches, a group of bishops cooperate in the governance of a Church *sui iuris.*

This ecclesiological principle is also reflected in the canonical norm that the patriarch or a member of the Synod of Bishops of the patriarchal Church must be an ordained bishop, i.e., a member of the college of bishops. In the former legislation of *Cleri sanctitati,*[23] one could participate in the Synod of Bishops, but not yet be an ordained bishop.[24] It is through the sacramental bond of ordination and membership in the College of bishops that an individual bishop can participate in the Synod of Bishops and thereby exercise authority over all the faithful of a Church *sui iuris.*[25]

Gradations of Self-Governing Authority

There is a cynical declaration in George Orwell's *Animal Farm* that, "All animals are equal, but some animals are more equal than others." Absent the negative nuance, this dictum is true of the definition of a Church *sui iuris* in canon 27: All the Churches *sui iuris* are self-governing, but some have greater self-governing authority than others. The Eastern code delineates four categories of Churches *sui iuris* designated according to their hierarchical heads: the patriarchal Church (cc. 55-150) which has the highest degree of autonomy whose head exercises supra-metropolitan power; the major archiepiscopal Church (cc. 151-154) whose powers are almost identical to the patriarchal Church (see c. 152) and can accurately be construed as "quasi-patriarchal;" the metropolitan Church (cc. 155-173) with much less autonomy whose head exercises supra-episcopal power and is assisted by a council of hierarchs (see c. 155 §1); the "other" Churches (cc. 174-176) which lacks either a synod or council and whose head acts with power delegated by the Apostolic See (see c. 175).

23 Pius XII, m.p. *Cleri sanctiati,* June 2, 1967: *AAS* 49 (1957) 433-603 (hereafter *CS*).

24 "In electione Patriarchae voce activa fruuntur omnes et soli eiusdem patriarchatus Episcopi, edam titulares, legitime electi atque confirmati, etsi episcopali charactere non aucti . . ." (*CS* c. 224 §1).

25 "By virtue of sacramental consecration and hierarchical communion with the head and members of the college, bishops are constituted as members of the episcopal body" (*CD* 4).

We must keep in mind that the Latin Church is also a Church *sui iuris*,[26] though *sui iuris* because does not conform to the juridical structures of the Eastern Catholic Churches *sui iuris.*[27]

Eastern Catholic Synodal Structures

The Eastern code provides several synodal structures at the level of Church *sui iuris* even though not all of them bear the title of "synod." There is the Synod of Bishops of the patriarchal Church (cc. 102-113); the permanent synod (cc. 115-121); the patriarchal assembly (cc. 140-145); the metropolitan provincial synod (c. 133 §1, 2°); the council of hierarchs of the metropolitan Church (cc. 155 §1; 164-169);[28] the assembly of hierarchs of several Churches *sui iuris* (c. 322).[29] For the sake of our discussion, we shall confine ourselves to certain synodal structures of the patriarchal Church, which can offer the Synod of Bishops a variety of structures to serve as models for the Synod of Bishops in Rome.

Synod of Bishops of the Patriarchal Church[30]

All and only the ordained bishops of the patriarchal Church are members of the Synod of Bishops of the patriarchal Church. Except for those lacking physical and mental capacity (c. 953 §1) or punished by canonical penalties (cc. 1433-1434), all the bishops must be convoked (c. 102 §1). Except for those who are retired, the bishops have a serious obligation to attend (c. 104 §1) and cannot send a proxy (c. 105). The voting power can be restricted in consideration of age, office, or territorial limits (cc. 78; 102; 146 and 147).

---

26 See Pontifical Council for Legislative Texts, "Explanatory Note," 8 December 2011: *Communicationes* 43 (2011) 316.

27 Ivan Žužek states, "It is worth observing here, as regards the Latin Church, which is also an *Ecclesia ritualis sui iuris*, as is clear from Canons 111 and 112 of the 1983 Code of Canon Law, that is nature is such that it cannot be fitted into any of the juridical forms listed, even though the titles of the Roman Pontiff include that of 'patriarch.'" "The Ecclesia *Sui Iuris* in the Revision of Canon Law," in René Latourelle, ed., *Vatican II Assessment and Perspectives. Twenty-Five Years After (1962-1987)* (New York: Paulist Press, 1989) 2:298. See also John D. Faris, "The Latin Church *Sui Iuris*," *The Jurist* 62 (2002) 280-293.

28 The predecessor of this institution is the Synod of Bishops and hierarchs of several provinces (*CS* cc. 340 §2; 342-343).

29 *Cleri sancti* c. 340 §4 treats the predecessor of this assembly, but calls it a synod: "Bishops and other hierarchs of several rites can convene in a synod after they obtained the permission of the Roman Pontiff, who designates the place where the synod shall meet, and appoints his legate who is to call together and preside over the synod."

30 *Cleri sancti* delineated various synods; the synod for the election of patriarchs (*CS* cc. 221-239), which is the predecessor of the current Synod of Bishops of the patriarchal Church. Canon 247 of *CS* called the patriarch to convoke annually all or some of the bishops of his Church, a requirement that is consonant with c. 106, 5°.

Orientalium Ecclesiarum 9 describes the patriarch and the Synod of Bishops in sharing the responsibility of governing the patriarchal Church. The three powers of governance (c. 985 §1) are generally allocated as follows: the Synod of Bishops of the patriarchal Church exercises legislative and judicial power and the patriarch exercises executive power. In the patriarchal Churches, an exercise of legislative and executive power is required to establish law (see c. 1488). The Synod of Bishops is exclusively competent to make laws for the patriarchal Church (c. 110 §1) and the patriarch is competent to promulgate the law (c. 112 §1)

All three powers of governance, i.e., legislative, executive, and judicial, extend over the patriarchal territory, i.e., those regions in which the rite of the Church *sui iuris* is observed and the patriarch as the right to erect ecclesiastical jurisdictions for his Church (c. 146).

Patriarchal Assembly

The Eastern code developed[31] a synodal institution unique to the Eastern Catholic Churches, the patriarchal assembly (cc. 140-145). Although it lacks the title of "synod" (a term reserved for episcopal bodies), it is an institutional expression of synodality as called for by Pope Francis.[32]

The patriarchal assembly (*conventus patriarchalis*) is a consultative body of the entire patriarchal Church which is presided over by the patriarch. The purpose of this body is to assist the patriarch and the Synod of Bishops of the patriarchal Church in dealing with matters of major importance to harmonize the apostolate and ecclesiastical discipline (c. 140). The patriarchal assembly is to be convoked every five years and whenever the patriarch with the consent of the Synod of Bishops considers it beneficial to do so (c. 141). It is for the patriarch to convoke and preside over the synod (c. 142 §1). If the patriarchal see becomes vacant (c. 142 §2), the synod is suspended until the new patriarch decides on the matter.

The following are to be convoked to the patriarchal assembly: eparchial bishops and other local hierarchs; titular bishops; presidents of monastic confederations, superiors general of institutes of consecrated life and superiors of monasteries *sui iuris*; rectors of Catholic universities and ecclesiastical universities as well as deans of faculties of theology and canon law in the patriarchal territory; rectors of major seminaries; from each eparchy at least one

31 The *CCEO* provides no *fontes* for this institution.

32 For various reasons, the patriarchal assembly has not fully realized its benefits in the lives of the Eastern Churches. The Eastern Catholic Churches need to explore ways to increase the effectiveness of this institution.

of the presbyters, especially pastors, one of the religious or members of societies of common life according to the manner of religious, as well as two lay persons, unless the statutes determine a greater number, all of whom are designated in a manner determined by the eparchial bishop and indeed, if it is a case of a member of a religious institute or a member of a society of the common life according to the manner of religious, with the consent of the competent superior (c. 143 §1). Persons of another Church *sui iuris* can be invited to participate according to the norm of the statutes (c. 143 §3). Non-Catholics can be invited as observers (c. 143 §4).

The long list of participants in the patriarchal assembly indicates that it is to be a body representational of the entire patriarchal Church. The term "representational" is intended to indicate that the participants are not representatives of a certain constituency. The diversity of participants in terms of roles in the Church is intended to provide for a diversity of perspectives not to create a forum for various special interest groups.

The preparation of the agenda pertains to the patriarch of the Synod of Bishops of the patriarchal Church (c. 144 §1).

The code does not speak of promulgation of the acts since the assembly is a consultative body.

Permanent Synod

Since it is ordinarily impractical to convene all the bishops every time a matter of importance arises, a permanent synod is constituted to cooperate with the patriarch as an "executive committee" in these matters. (The counterpart of this institution in the Orthodox Church is the *endemousa* or *permanent synod.*[33]) The permanent synod is comprised of the patriarch and four bishops (c. 115 §1). One of the bishops is to be appointed by the patriarch and the other three are elected (two of whom must be eparchial bishops) by the Synod of Bishops (c. 115 §2), all for a five-year term.

The patriarch is solely competent to convoke and preside over the permanent synod. He can convoke the synod whenever he deems it necessary but must convoke it at least twice a year and whenever a matter requires the counsel or consent of the synod (c. 120).

One of the purposes of the permanent synod is to maintain "guardrails" in the actions of the patriarch. In various matters, the patriarch is obliged to consult

---

33 Aristeides Papadakis, "Endemousa Synodos," in Alexander Kazhdan, ed., *The Oxford Dictionary of Byzantium*, (Oxford and New York: Oxford University Press) 697.

with or obtain the consent of some bishops before performing certain acts, e.g., interpretation of laws enacted by the Synod of Bishops of the patriarchal Church (c. 112 §2) and suppression of juridic persons established by the patriarch (c. 928, 1°). The patriarch is obliged to have the consent of the permanent synod to erect, modify, or suppress an exarchy (c. 85 §3) or exempt a juridic person or place from the power of the eparchial bishop (c. 90). In addition to the role of giving counsel or consent, the permanent synod also has other responsibilities, e.g., regarding the budget and financial reports (c. 122 §3).

The permanent synod retains its competency even if the Synod of Bishops is in session (c. 119).

Council of Hierarchs

The governance structures of the metropolitan Church *sui iuris* reveal the reduction in autonomy of these Churches. The metropolitan, assisted by the council of hierarchs, is appointed by the Roman Pontiff (c. 155 §1). Concerning the appointment of the metropolitan and the bishops, the council of hierarchs compiles a list of three candidates for each office and submits it to the Apostolic See (c. 168). The legislative authority of the Council of Hierarchs is restricted to those matters which common law remits to the particular law of the Church *sui iuris* (c. 167 §1). Furthermore, laws enacted by the council cannot be validly promulgated until the metropolitan has received written notification from the Apostolic See (c. 167 §2).

We have now examined a few of the synodal structures articulated in the Eastern code. Let us now examine the . . .

Roman Synod of Bishops

When Pope Paul VI announced on 14 September 1965 that he intended to establish the Synod of Bishops of the Universal Church, the Orthodox presumed this to be the introduction of elements of a genuine Eastern synodal governance system into the Latin Church. Even before the Council, there had been proposals for a permanent body of bishops who would serve in a consultative or a legislative role in union with the pope. During the second period of the Council, Melkite patriarch Maximos IV Sayegh proposed that there be a permanent body of relatively few bishops who would always be in session to assist the pope. The Synod of Bishops, established with the apostolic constitution *Apostolica sollicitudo* on 15 September 1965,[34] evokes the Church's ancient synodal tradition

34 Paul VI, m.p. *Apostolica sollicitudo*, September 15, 1965: *AAS* 57 (1965) 775-780 (hereafter *AS*).

but would normally exercise only a consultative role, offering insights and counsel to the Roman Pontiff on various ecclesial questions. For more than fifty years, numerous synods have been celebrated with varying degrees of satisfaction. Some critics felt that the procedures did not provide for a free exchange of opinion or a definitive expression of the synod.

On 15 September 2018, Pope Francis promulgated the apostolic constitution *Episcopalis communio*.[35] The constitution provides for the Synod of Bishops to be a "privileged instance of listening to the people of God" (n. 6). The Synod of Bishops, which is "in some manner the image" of an Ecumenical Council and reflects its "spirit and method," is configured as an episcopal body, but others who are not bishops can be invited to participate in roles determined by the Roman Pontiff (n. 8). The Synod of Bishops generally functions as a consultative body, but this does not diminish its importance.

> "[T]he fact that the Synod ordinarily has only a consultative role does not diminish its importance. In the Church the purpose of any collegial body, whether consultative or deliberative, is always the search for truth or the good of the Church. When it is therefore a question involving the faith itself, the *consensus ecclesiae* is not determined by the tallying of votes, but is the outcome of the working of the Spirit, the soul of the one Church of Christ". Therefore the vote of the Synod Fathers, "if morally unanimous, has a qualitative ecclesial weight which surpasses the merely formal aspect of the consultative vote".[36]

Let us now examine at least briefly some aspects of the Roman Synod of Bishops as an institution.

Nature

It is an institution of the supreme authority of the Church. But is it an exercise of the primatial power of the Roman Pontiff or the collegial power of the college of bishops? This issue is of great ecumenical import. After a reintegration of the Orthodox and the Catholic Churches, would Orthodox hierarchs be amenable to participating in a Synod of Bishops that functioned as an instrument of the exercise of primacy?

The Synod of Bishops of Rome, comprising bishops chosen from various parts of the world, is: a) a central ecclesiastical institution; b) representing the

---

35 Francis, apostolic constitution *Episcopalis communio*, September 15, 2018: *AAS* 110 (2018) 1359-1378; Eng. trans. at https://www.vatican.va/content/francesco/en/apost_constitutions/documents/papa-francesco_costituzione-ap_20180915_episcopalis-communio.html (hereafter *EC*).

36 EC 7 (internal citations omitted).

whole Catholic episcopate; c) of its nature perpetual; d) as for structure, carrying out its function for a time and when called upon (*AS* I).

There are a few points regarding the nature of the Synod of Bishops of Rome that draw our attention.

As a central ecclesiastical institution, the Roman Synod of Bishops is treated in the Code of Canon Law under the Supreme Authority of the Church immediately after the college of bishops and before the cardinals, the Roman Curia, and legates of the Roman Pontiff. Appropriately, the Roman Synod of Bishops in Rome is not part of the Roman Curia, but it does bear many similarities to a curial dicastery.

It is asserted that the presence of non-bishops in the synod does not reduce the ability of the episcopal members to represent the entire episcopate (*EC* 4). Perhaps the participants in the Roman Synod of Bishops can be characterized as *representational* rather than *representative*: a body representing the Catholic episcopate.

Synods in the Eastern Churches are not representative episcopal bodies, that is, a group of bishops representing or legislating as a parliament, but rather a group of bishops in their name on behalf of the college of bishops. It is by their membership in the college of bishops that they have a right to be convoked to the Synod of Bishops of the patriarchal Church (c. 102 §1).[37] Participation in the synod is personal and cannot be entrusted to a proxy, nor can one bishop have several votes (c. 105). Except in the case of elections (c. 66 §2), non-bishops can be invited as guests according to particular law or with the consent of the permanent synod (c. 102 §3).

Purpose

The general purposes of the synod are: (a) to promote a closer union and greater cooperation between the Supreme Pontiff and the bishops of the whole world; (b) to see to it that accurate and direct information is supplied on matters and situations that bear upon the internal life of the Church and upon the kind of action that should be carrying on in today's world; (c) to facilitate agreement, at least on essential matters of doctrine and on the course of action to be taken in the life of the Church (*AS* II, 1).

---

37 The voting rights of bishops not entrusted with an eparchy can be restricted except in the case of elections (c. 102 §2).

The synod also has special and immediate purposes: (a) to provide mutually useful information and (b) to discuss the specific business for which the synod is called into session on any given occasion (*AS* II, 2).

Composition

Ordinarily, the Roman Synod of Bishops is what its name implies: it is a synod comprised of bishops. The expansion of participation to non-bishops (priests, deacons, consecrated men and women, laity) was declared not to be a modification of the episcopal nature of the body and that the arrangement whereby non-bishops can participate with a deliberative vote does not detract from the episcopal nature of the body but rather enhances the function of the synod.[38] It is not clear how the episcopal character of the Roman Synod of Bishops is to be retained if non-episcopal members constitute such a significant proportion and have a deliberative vote.

Function

The Synod of Bishops is directly and immediately subject to the authority of the Roman Pontiff, whose competency it is: (a) to convoke the synod and determine the time and place; (b) to ratify the elected members; (c) to set the agenda and send appropriate materials to the members; (c) to preside at the synod either personally or through a delegate (*AS* III).

The function of the Synod of Bishops of Rome is to provide information and offer advice. It can also enjoy the power of making decisions when such power is conferred upon it by the Roman Pontiff; in this case, it belongs to him to ratify the decisions of the synod.

Episcopalis communio 18 states that if a final document is expressly approved, it participates in the ordinary magisterium of the Successor of Peter. The same article provides that the Roman Pontiff can give the Synod of Bishops deliberative power and that, after ratification and promulgation, the final

---

38 "The synod of bishops is a group of bishops who have been chosen from different regions of the world . . ." (*CIC* c. 342); "It is in this perspective that one must understand the Holy Father's decision to maintain the specifically episcopal nature of the Assembly convened in Rome, while at the same time not limiting its composition to bishops alone by admitting a certain number of non-bishops as full Members." *Announcement* by the Synod Press Office, 26 April 2023, regarding the expanded participation of non-bishops; Eng. trans. at https://www.synod.va/content/dam/synod/news/2023-04-26_punto_stampa/2024.04.26_EN_FAQ_Partecipanti_Assemblea.pdf (p. 4) (accessed on 3 Nov. 2023). Non-episcopal participants do not *per se* alter the episcopal character of an ecumenical council. However, proportionality needs to be taken into consideration in the case of the Roman Synod of Bishops.

document participates in the ordinary magisterium of the Successor of Peter. The distinction between the two procedures is that the first is a consultative act with subsequent approval while the second is a deliberative vote with subsequent ratification and promulgation, a distinction ultimately without a difference since in both cases the Roman Pontiff has the final word.[39]

Essentially, the synod is acting with power delegated by the Roman Pontiff—another exercise of primacy. Further, Orthodox perceive the arrangements to be a representational group of bishops (and possibly those who lack episcopal character) exercising deliberative power over the entire Church; they find this to be problematic. As praiseworthy as the injection of a spirit of synodality in the Catholic Church is, it must be admitted that, except for the ecumenical synod, synodal institutions in the ancient, Eastern understanding of the term do not exist at the universal level of ecclesial governance or for that matter at the level of the governance of the Latin Church.

An Evolving Model

During the past half century, the Synod of Bishops has evolved. At the discourse opening the final session of the Second Vatican Council on 14 September 1965, Pope Paul VI announced his intention to establish a Synod of Bishops. This synod would be a regular form of consultation and collaboration of the episcopate with the Roman Pontiff and would "serve a useful purpose in the daily work of the Roman Curia."[40] It was to be composed of "bishops nominated for the most part" with papal approval by the conferences of bishops and would be convened when the Roman Pontiff considered it "opportune."[41] The next day

---

39 Ironically, if the Roman Synod of Bishops were to function with a deliberative vote, it might be most problematic for the Eastern Orthodox.

40 The advanced information that We Ourselves are happy to share with you is that We intend to give you some institution, called for by this Council, a 'Synod of Bishops,' which will be made up of bishops nominated for the most part by the Episcopal Conferences with our approval and called by the Pope according to the needs of the Church, for his consultation and collaboration, when for the well-being of the Church it might seem to him opportune. It goes without saying that this collaboration of the episcopate ought to bring the greatest joy to the Holy See and to the whole Church. In a particular way it will serve a useful purpose in the daily work of the Roman Curia, to which We owe so much recognition for its most valuable help, and for which, as bishops in their diocese, We also have permanent need in Our apostolic concerns.

Holy See Press Office, "The Synod of Bishops: An Introduction," Jan. 1, 1995 (quoting Pope Paul VI); original text in English by the General Secretariate of the Synod of Bishops, at https://www.vatican.va/roman_curia/synod/documents/rc_synod_01011995_profile_en.html (accessed on 3 Nov. 2023).

41 Holy See Press Office, "The Synod of Bishops: An Introduction."

the pope established the Synod of Bishops,[42] an institution that is not part of the Roman Curia and is subject to the Roman Pontiff.

> The principal characteristic of the Synod of Bishops is service to the communion and collegiality of the world's bishops with the Holy Father. It is not a particular organism with limited competence as that of the curial dicasteries. Instead, it has full competence to deal with any subject by the procedure established by the Holy Father in the letter of convocation. The Synod of Bishops with its permanent General Secretariat is not part of the Roman Curia and does not depend on it; it is subject directly and solely to the Holy Father, with whom it is united in the universal government of the Church.[43]

Christus Dominus, the conciliar decree on the pastoral office of bishops promulgated after the establishment of the Synod of Bishops, takes a different approach regarding the nature of the Synod of bishops. It describes the synod as "acting in the name of the entire Catholic episcopate, it will at the same time show that all the bishops in hierarchical communion partake of the solicitude for the universal Church."[44]

Eastern Catholics and Orthodox might construe this synod as similar to the permanent *(endemousa)* synod of the patriarchal Churches, a small group of bishops who would be readily accessible to the patriarch for consultation or consent. However, it would not be appropriate for the Roman Pontiff to have a permanent synod similar to those in the Eastern Churches since the purpose of the permanent synod is to counsel and exercise restraints on the actions of the patriarch.

Time does not permit a descriptive history of the vicissitudes of the synod, but we now have an assembly representational of the entire Church. The comments that follow are not intended to be critical. For whatever it is worth, I enthusiastically support the efforts of Pope Francis to instill synodality in the life of the Church. I realize that he is using the Synod of Bishops in Rome as a tool to carry out this work. It is "the only tool in his belt!"

But we need clarity regarding the institutional evolution that is taking place. Pope Francis, with the expansion of the membership and their deliberative role, has moved the Synod of Bishops from an episcopal collegial model to something else. The insistence that the synod with lay persons, clerics, and religious is still

---

42 Paul VI, m.p. *Apostolica sollicitudo,* September 15, 1965: *AAS* 57 (1965) 775-780.
43 Holy See Press Office, "The Synod of Bishops: An Introduction."
44 *CD* 5.

an episcopal body, with all due respect, is a challenge to appreciate. A new model for the Synod of Bishops has evolved. Again, the Eastern code might be of service.

The *patriarchal assembly* described above provides a governance model that can offer the Roman Pontiff an institution that might be useful. While it does not contain the term "synodal" in its title, it can still facilitate the adoption of a synodal model in the life of the Church. It may be that the modifications being introduced are morphing the Synod of Bishops in Rome into a kind of patriarchal assembly without an explicit intention to do so.

From the perspective of the East, this Synod of Bishops should not be an attempt to be at the service of the universal Church but could serve the Roman Pontiff as he addresses the needs of the Latin Church. This is not intended to curtail the role of the Roman Synod of Bishops, but rather to avoid any pretensions to create a parliamentary structure as a substitute for an ecumenical council, which is historically the expression of the solicitude of the college of bishops for the universal Church.

From the perspective of the East, one more change might be beneficial. Perhaps the institutionalization of synodal life can begin with providing the Latin Church with a synod, at the service of the Latin Church and not construed in service to the universal Church—as is the present synod. The assembly could be a *Synodus Ecclesiae Latinae.*[45] Send the Eastern Catholics home![46]

Such a modification does not preclude the creation of a council of bishops at the service of the universal Church as called for in *Christus Dominus.*

Churches *Sui Iuris* from the Latin Church

There are 4500 bishops in the Latin Church. How can there be a synod in which they all effectively participate? A "parliamentary" model of episcopal representatives is not consonant with Catholic canonical tradition since personal participation of the members of the college of bishops is the norm. The Eastern code is opposed to the possibility of a proxy (cc. 950-951). Consideration might be given to the establishment of Churches *sui iuris* which have their origins in the Latin Church. For example, the supreme authority of the Church could establish Churches *sui iuris* for a region or nation. For example, all the Latin dioceses in Brazil could be established as Church *sui iuris* and govern itself accordingly.

45 The Latin Church can use the term synod according to its needs and purposes.
46 Forty Eastern Catholic hierarchs and faithful are participants. One might say that the Eastern Churches are over-represented in this body because there are only 15 million Eastern Catholics in a Church of approximately 1.2 billion.

Clinging to centralization is unrealistic and likely futile. Neither the Roman Pontiff nor the Synod of Bishops has a monopoly on the interpretation of social realities or the proposal of solutions to contemporary problems. It would be futile for the Synod of Bishops to attempt to provide a uniform answer for the entire Church.

> In the face of such widely varying situations, it is difficult for us to utter a unified message and put forward a solution that has universal validity. This is not our ambition, nor is it our mission. It is up to the Christian communities to analyze with objectivity the situation which is proper to their own country.[47]

Pope Francis is clear that neither the pope nor the Roman Curia can offer a definitive or complete word on every question affecting the Church and the world. There is no "one size fits all" for the governance of the Church.

> Nor do I believe that the papal magisterium should be expected to offer a definitive or complete word on every question that affects the Church and the world. The Pope should not take the place of local Bishops in the discernment of every issue that arises in their territory. In this sense, I am conscious of the need to promote a sound "decentralization."[48]

Such an approach will likely result in a variety of disciplines among the Churches. This is not necessarily problematic; recall the notions of unity and diversity in *Lumen gentium* 13 and 23. But we must not be naïve. One need only look at the disparate positions taken by the German and American hierarchies to realize that we will all be challenged as to what diversity is tolerable in the one Church.

The Catholic Church—with its 1.2 billion faithful spread throughout the world—needs an institution that can empower the local Churches to allow for diversity, while retaining the unity of communion. The structure already exists: the Church *sui iuris* defined in canon 27 of the Eastern code cited above.

Supra-metropolitan and supra-episcopal governance is one of the most ancient institutions in the Church. The First Council of Nicaea (325) recognized the extension of the authority of the bishops of Rome, Alexandria, and Antioch

---

47 Paul VI, apostolic letter *Octogesima Adveniens* 4, May 14, 1971: *AAS* 63 (1971) 403.
48 Francis, apostolic exhortation *Evangelii gaudium* 16, November 24, 2013: *AAS* (2013) 1026-1027; Eng. trans. at https://www.vatican.va/content/francesco/en/apost_exhortations/documents/papa-francesco_esortazione-ap_20131124_evangelii-gaudium.html (accessed on 3 Nov. 2023).

over the surrounding region[49] according to the dynamic described in *Lumen gentium* 23 (quoted above). The passage of time resulted in the establishment of other churches that have their origins in these three sees. These churches are instances of intermediate hierarchical authority and are the predecessors of the 23 Eastern Catholic Churches *sui iuris* and the Latin Church *sui iuris.*[50]

One further comment about this Nicaean canon is appropriate. It is important to note that the Council was not innovating, but rather recognizing that the custom of the bishops of Rome, Alexandria, and Antioch exercising authority over bishops and metropolitans has the force of law. Interestingly, this action is precisely the action of the Holy Spirit described in canon 1506 §1 of the Eastern code: "A custom of the Christian community, insofar as it corresponds to the action of the Holy Spirit in the ecclesial body, can obtain the force of law."[51] It is interesting that canon 27 states that the supreme authority "recognizes" (*agnoscit*)—rather than "establishes"—a Church *sui iuris.* Perhaps there is a coalescence within the Latin Church that can be recognized.

The response to such a proposal is usually—to use an archaic term—an *alarum* of danger ahead. It is not a call for splintering or disintegration. The Second Vatican Council in *Orientalium Ecclesiarum* 11 envisioned the possible establishment of new patriarchates for Churches that have attained a certain degree of maturity. *Lumen gentium*, in its treatment of the patriarchal Churches, alludes to the possibility of episcopal conferences carrying out a similar function: "In like manner the Episcopal bodies of today are in a position to render a manifold and fruitful assistance, so that this collegiate feeling may be put into practical application" (*LG* 23).

This proposal is not advocating an increase of autonomy to the episcopal conferences but rather the adoption of either the model of the metropolitan Church *sui iuris* (cc. 155-173) or the major archiepiscopal Church *sui iuris* (cc. 55-150) for use in the Churches *sui iuris* originating in the Latin Church.

---

49 "Let the ancient customs in Egypt, Libya, and Pentapolis prevail, that the Bishop of Alexandria have jurisdiction in all these since the like is customary for the Bishop of Rome also. Likewise in Antioch and the other provinces, let the Churches retain their privileges." First Council of Nicea (A.D. 325) c. 6; Eng. trans. at https://www.newadvent.org/fathers/3801.htm (accessed on 3 Nov. 2023).

50 Since 2006, there has been no official term to identify the role of the Bishop of Rome when he acts as *Caput Ecclesiae Latinae.* The title "Patriarch of the West" was inappropriate but requires a replacement.

51 For more on the role of custom in the recognition of intermediate ecclesial structures, see Szabó, "Approfondimenti,"103-105.

In the case of the metropolitan Church *sui iuris*, the metropolitan is a bishop of a determined see who is appointed by the Roman Pontiff (c. 155 §1). The metropolitan Church *sui iuris* would have a council of hierarchs comprising all and only the ordained bishops of that Church (c. 164 §1). The appointment of the metropolitan and council of hierarchs would comprise a list of at least three candidates for each office and the Roman Pontiff makes the appointment (c. 168). The legislative authority would be exercised by the council of hierarchs with the provision that laws cannot be promulgated without the prior written notification of reception by the Apostolic See (c. 167 §2).

In the case of the major archiepiscopal Church, the major archbishop would be the bishop of a determined see who is elected by the bishops and confirmed by the Roman Pontiffs (c. 153). Bishops would be elected with a prior assent from the Roman Pontiff. (c. 110 §3) and would comprise a Synod of Bishops (c. 102 §1). The Synod of Bishops would exercise legislative and judicial authority (c. 110 §§1 and 2). The major archbishop would exercise executive authority (c. 110 §4). This proposal should not be characterized as a decentralization because a portion of the college of bishops will be carrying out that responsibility for a portion of the people of God. *Alarums* need not be raised. The proposed arrangements are already operative in the Catholic Church and sanctioned by the supreme authority.

***

With confidence, let us trust in the Holy Spirit who will provide us with the tools we need to govern our Churches.

CLSA PROCEEDINGS 85 (2023) 108-122

SEMINAR

TRADITIONIS CUSTODES: PART I

Dr. Chad J. Glendinning, JCD

Introduction[1]

On July 16, 2021, Pope Francis issued new ecclesiastical legislation on use of the Roman Liturgy prior to the reforms of Pope Paul VI, by means of the apostolic letter motu proprio *Traditionis custodes.*[2] This motu proprio significantly revised the existing legislation of the motu proprio *Summorum Pontificum*, issued by Pope Benedict XVI in 2007. The legislation was issued following a consultation of the episcopacy by the Congregation for the Doctrine of the Faith in 2020. Although the results of the survey have not been published, Pope Francis presents the provisions of *Traditionis custodes* as responding to "the wishes expressed by the episcopate." In his accompanying letter, Pope Francis explains his motivation more clearly, and underscores the need to preserve ecclesial communion.

> With the passage of thirteen years, I instructed the Congregation for the Doctrine of the Faith to circulate a questionnaire to the Bishops regarding the implementation of the *Motu proprio Summorum Pontificum*. The responses reveal a situation that preoccupies and saddens me and persuades me of the need to intervene. Regrettably, the pastoral objective of my Predecessors, who had intended "to do everything possible to ensure that all those who truly possessed the desire for unity would find it possible to remain in this unity or to rediscover it anew," has often been seriously disregarded. An opportunity offered by St. John Paul II and, with even greater magnanimity, by Benedict XVI, intended to recover the unity of an ecclesial body with diverse liturgical sensibilities, was exploited to widen the gaps, reinforce the divergences, and encourage

---

1 The author and Reverend Peter Mottola presented this seminar together. Reverend Mottola's text follows this article.

2 Francis, m.p. *Traditiones custodes* On the Use of the Roman Liturgy Prior to the Reform of 1970, July 16, 2021: *AAS* 113 (2021) 793-796, Eng. trans. at https://www.vatican.va/content/francesco/en/motu_proprio/documents/20210716-motu-proprio-traditionis-custodes.html (accessed on 20 Dec. 2023).

> disagreements that injure the Church, block her path, and expose her to the peril of division.
>
> At the same time, I am saddened by abuses in the celebration of the liturgy on all sides. In common with Benedict XVI, I deplore the fact that "in many places the prescriptions of the new Missal are not observed in celebration, but indeed come to be interpreted as an authorization for or even a requirement of creativity, which leads to almost unbearable distortions." But I am nonetheless saddened that the instrumental use of *Missale Romanum* of 1962 is often characterized by a rejection not only of the liturgical reform, but of the Vatican Council II itself, claiming, with unfounded and unsustainable assertions, that it betrayed the Tradition and the "true Church." The path of the Church must be seen within the dynamic of Tradition "which originates from the Apostles and progresses in the Church with the assistance of the Holy Spirit" (*DV* 8). A recent stage of this dynamic was constituted by Vatican Council II where the Catholic episcopate came together to listen and to discern the path for the Church indicated by the Holy Spirit. To doubt the Council is to doubt the intentions of those very Fathers who exercised their collegial power in a solemn manner *cum Petro et sub Petro* in an ecumenical council, and, in the final analysis, to doubt the Holy Spirit himself who guides the Church.[3]

In presenting the new legislation to the bishops, Pope Francis urges them to be motivated by two overarching principles:

> Indications about how to proceed in your dioceses are chiefly dictated by two principles: on the one hand, to provide for the good of those who are rooted in the previous form of celebration and need to return in due time to the Roman Rite promulgated by Saints Paul VI and John Paul II, and, on the other hand, to discontinue the erection of new personal parishes tied more to the desire and wishes of individual priests than to the real need of the "holy People of God." At the same time, I ask you to be vigilant in ensuring that every liturgy be celebrated with decorum and fidelity to the liturgical books promulgated after Vatican Council II, without the eccentricities that can easily degenerate into abuses. Seminarians and new priests should be formed in the faithful observance of the prescriptions of the Missal and liturgical books, in which is reflected the liturgical reform willed by Vatican Council II.[4]

---

3 Francis, accompanying letter to *Traditionis custodes*, July 16, 2021: *AAS* 113 (2021) 804-805; Eng. trans. at https://www.vatican.va/content/francesco/en/letters/2021/documents/20210716-lettera-vescovi-liturgia.html (accessed on 20 Dec. 2023).

4 Ibid.

While pastoral solicitude is to be extended to those who adhere to earlier liturgical forms, the intent of the new legislation is "to provide for the good of those who are rooted in the previous form of celebration and need to return in due time to the Roman Rite promulgated by Saints Paul VI and John Paul II." Unlike the earlier provisions of *Summorum Pontificum*, the present legislation has as its goal "to discontinue the erection of new personal parishes tied more to the desire and wishes of individual priests than to the real need of the 'holy People of God.'"[5]

The approach adopted in *Traditionis custodes* and the current praxis of the Holy See could not stand in starker contrast to the earlier provisions and praxis of *Summorum Pontificum.* Indeed, this is a remarkable turnabout, in a rather short period of time. It has understandably generated strong reactions, particularly from those adherents to the older liturgical reforms. By means of our presentation, we hope to contribute to a better understanding of these existing provisions and the pastoral challenges they present in many particular churches.

Our presentation will be organized into two principal sections. First, I will begin with an overview of the earlier provisions for use of the 1962 *Missale Romanum*, following the introduction of the liturgical reforms of the Second Vatican Council. Second, Father Peter Mottola, will provide an overview of *Traditionis custodes*, highlighting the more difficult points of interpretation. Finally, we will offer some concluding remarks, as a means of generating questions and dialogue with those present.

PART I: PROVISIONS FOR USE OF THE 1962 ROMAN MISSAL[6]

By the apostolic constitution *Missale Romanum*, Pope Paul VI approved the revised Roman Missal. Recalling the memory of his predecessor, Pope St. Pius V, who promulgated the *Missale Romanum* of 1570 in execution of the decree of the Council of Trent,[7] Pope Paul VI provides his own motivation and expectation for the revised Missal:

> After what we have presented concerning the new Roman Missal, we wish in conclusion to insist on one point in particular and to make it

---

5 Francis, accompanying letter to *Traditionis custodes*.

6 Portions of this section have been adapted from Chad J. Glendinning, *Summorum Pontificum and the Use of the Extraordinary Form of the Roman Rite: A Canonical Analysis in Light of the Current Liturgical Law*, JCD dissertation (Ottawa, ON: Faculty of Canon Law, Saint Paul University, 2010) 192-217.

7 Council of Trent, Session XXV, Concerning the index of books and the catechism, breviary and missal, December 4, 1563. Eng. trans. in N. Tanner, ed., *Decrees of the Ecumenical Councils*, vol. 2 (Washington, DC: Georgetown University Press, 1990).

> have its effect. When he promulgated the *editio princeps* of the Roman Missal, our predecessor St. Pius V offered to the people of Christ as the instrument of liturgical unity and the expression of a pure and reverent worship in the Church. Even though, in virtue of the decree of the Second Vatican Council, we have accepted into the new Roman Missal lawful variations and adaptations, our own expectation in no way differs from that of our predecessor. It is that the faithful will receive the new Missal as a help toward witnessing and strengthening their unity with one another; that through the new Missal one and the same prayer in a great diversity of languages will ascend, more fragrant than any incense, to our heavenly Father, through our High Priest, Jesus Christ, in the Holy Spirit.[8]

Consequently, the Sacred Congregation of Rites, with an express mandate from Pope Paul VI, promulgated the *editio typica* of the revised *Ordo Missae.*[9] As the entire *Missale Romanum* was not yet complete, a small book was published containing the General Instruction of the Roman Missal, the Order of Mass, the prefaces, and four Eucharistic Prayers, in addition to the Sacred Congregation of Rites' decree of promulgation and Pope Paul VI's apostolic constitution *Missale Romanum.*[10]

1. Exceptions for Elderly and Infirm Priests

By October 20, 1969, the revision of the *Missale Romanum* was incomplete. Three parts of the Missal had appeared, namely, (1) the *Institutio generalis Missalis Romani*; (2) the *Ordo Missae*; and (3) the *Ordo lectionum Missae*. An instruction issued by the Sacred Congregation for Divine Worship proposed a gradual implementation, depending upon the availability of liturgical texts.[11] Once vernacular translations of the *Missale Romanum* were completed, the conferences of bishops were to set a date when the texts of the new Roman Missal would become obligatory (n. 14), except in the following situation:

> Elderly priests who celebrate Mass without a congregation and who might encounter serious difficulty in taking up the new Order of Mass

8 Paul VI, apostolic constitution on the Roman Missal *Missale Romanum*, April 3, 1969: *AAS* 61 (1969) 217-222; Eng. trans. in *DOL*, n. 202, 458-461.

9 Sacred Congregation of Rites, Decree promulgating the *editio typica* of the *Ordo Missae, Ordine Missae*, April 6, 1969; Eng. trans. in *CLD* 7:620-621.

10 *Ordo Missae*, April 6, 1969 (Vatican City: Typis Polyglottis Vaticanis, 1969).

11 Sacred Congregation for Divine Worship, Instruction on the gradual carrying out of the Apostolic Constitution *Missale Romanum*, October 20, 1969: *AAS* 61 (1969) 749-753.

and the new texts of the Roman Missal and Lectionary for Mass, may, with the consent of their Ordinary, keep to the rites and texts now in use.[12]

A notification from the Sacred Congregation for Divine Worship, following the promulgation of the *Missale Romanum*,[13] provided further clarification on the exception specified above:

> Continued use, in whole or in part, of the *Missale Romanum* in the 1962 *editio typica,* as amended by the 1965 and 1967 decrees and of the *Breviarium Romanum* formally in use is allowed, with the consent of the Ordinary and only in celebrations without a congregation, for all those who because of their advanced years or illness find serious difficulties in using the new Order of Mass in the Roman Missal, the Lectionary for Mass, or the book of the liturgy of the hours (n. 3).[14]

The exception refers to amendments which occurred to correspond with the directives of *Sacrasanctum Concilium.* The amendments followed upon two instructions issued by the Sacred Congregation for Rites for the implementation of Constitution on the Liturgy.[15] It was possible for Ordinaries, therefore, to grant permission for continued use of the 1962 *editio typica* of the *Missale Romanum* for elderly and ill priests, provided that the amendments lawfully introduced in 1965[16] and 1967[17] were observed. Likewise, permission could only be granted for celebrations without a congregation. To remove any source of confusion, a notification from the Sacred Congregation for Worship specified that once a conference of bishops decrees that a translation of the Roman Missal, or any part of it, is obligatory in a territory, Mass—whether in Latin or in the vernacular—

---

12 Instruction on the *Missale Romanum* 19; Eng. trans. in *DOL,* n. 209, 534-537.

13 Sacred Congregation for Divine Worship, Decree promulgating the first *editio typica* of the *Missale Romanum, Celebrationes eucharisticae*, March 26, 1970: *AAS* 62 (1970) 554; Eng. trans. in *DOL*, n. 213, 543.

14 Sacred Congregation for Divine Worship, Notification on the Roman Missal, the book of the Liturgy of the Hours, and the Calendar *Instructione de Constitutione,* June 14, 1971: *AAS* 63 (1971) 712-715; Eng. trans. in *DOL*, n. 216, 545, par. 1772.

15 Sacred Congregation for Rites, First instruction on the orderly carrying out of the sacred liturgy *Inter Ecumenici*, September 26, 1964: *AAS* 56 (1964) 877-900; Eng. trans. in *CLD* 6: 73-99; Sacred Congregation for Rites, Second instruction on the orderly carrying out of the Constitution on the Liturgy *Tres abhinc annos*, May 4, 1967: *AAS* 59 (1967) 442-448; Eng. trans. in *CLD* 6: 131-137.

16 Three notable changes were introduced in 1965: (1) *Ordo Missae, Ritus servandus in celebratione Missae et De defectibus in celebratione Missae occurrentibus*, January 27, 1965 (Vatican City: Typis Polyglottis Vaticanis, 1965); (2) *Ritus servandus in concelebratione Missae et Ritus Communionis sub ultraque specie,* March 7, 1965 (Vatican City: Typis Polyglottis Vaticanis, 1965); (3) *Variationes in ordinem hebdomadae sanctae inducendae*, March 7, 1965 (Vatican City: Typis Polyglottis Vaticanis, 1965).

17 *Variationes in Ordinem Missae inducendae ad normam Instructionis S.R.C., die 4 Maii 1967*, May 18, 1967 (Vatican City: Typis Polyglottis Vaticanis, 1967).

may be celebrated lawfully only according to the rite of the Roman Missal promulgated by Pope Paul VI on April 3, 1969. The notification refers directly to the exception for elderly and ill priests noted above, yet specifies that ordinaries cannot grant permission for use of the 1962 *Missale Romanum*, as amended in 1965 and 1967 to correspond to the directives of *Sacrosancum Concilium*, for the celebration of Mass with a congregation.[18]

2. Provision for Use of the 1962 Missal in England and Wales

As a result of the direct intervention of Cardinal Heenan, the then-Archbishop of Westminster and chairman of the Episcopal Conference of England and Wales, Pope Paul VI was made aware of the petitions from groups of converts and elderly people requesting use of the former Roman Missal on special occasions. Archbishop Bugnini, former secretary of the *Consilium*, recalls that Pope Paul VI himself, in a handwritten letter, requested that the Sacred Congregation for Divine Worship provide a favourable response to Cardinal Heenan's request.[19]

The rescript, in virtue of special faculties granted to the Sacred Congregation for Divine Worship by Pope Paul VI on October 30, 1971, granted the following provision:

> [I]t is permitted to the local Ordinaries of England and Wales to grant that certain groups of the faithful may on special occasions be allowed to participate in the Mass celebrated according to the rites and texts of the former Roman Missal. The edition of the Missal to be used on these occasions should be that published again by the decree of the Sacred Congregation of Rites (27 January 1965), and with the modifications indicated in the *Instructio altera* (4 May 1967). . . .[20]

The rescript continued by specifying that permission may be granted "provided that groups make the request for reasons of genuine devotion, and provided that the permission does not disturb or damage the general community of the faithful." The permission, therefore, is limited to certain groups and on special occasions. The rescript warned that the use of the Order of Mass of the 1962 *Missale Romanum* should not be "a sign or cause of disunity" in the community. For this

---

18 Sacred Congregation for Divine Worship, Notification on the obligatory nature of the Roman Missal of Paul VI *Conferentiarum Episcopalium*, October 28, 1974: *Notitiae* 10 (1974) 353; Eng. trans. in *DOL*, n. 219, 549.

19 Annibale Bugnini, *The Reform of the Liturgy, 1948-1975*, trans. Matthew O'Connell (Collegeville, MN: Liturgical Press, 1990) 297-298.

20 Sacred Congregation for Divine Worship, Rescript permitting the use of the 1962 Missal in England and Wales, November 5, 1971: *CLD* 10:147-148.

reason, the rescript admonishes bishops to adopt a uniform policy to be applied equally throughout the entire episcopal conference.

In addition to the provision above for well-intentioned groups of the faithful requesting use of the former rite, the rescript contains an additional provision for priests. The rescript indicates: "Priests who on occasion wish to celebrate Mass according to the above-mentioned edition of the Roman Missal may do so by consent of their ordinary and in accordance with the norms given by the same." By the rescript of the Sacred Congregation for Divine Worship, therefore, an ordinary in England and Wales could permit a priest to celebrate Mass according to the 1962 *Missale Romanum*, as revised in 1965 and 1967. Furthermore, local ordinaries could permit groups of the faithful, on special occasions, to attend Mass celebrated according to the same rite. In all other situations, the *Missale Romanum* approved by Pope Paul VI remained the normative expression of the Church's Eucharistic liturgy in England and Wales. Interestingly, a similar request to use the *Missale Romanum* of 1962 from Monsignor Plourde, then-Archbishop of Ottawa, received an unfavourable response from the same congregation. Instead, Monsignor Plourde was encouraged to remind the faithful of their grave obligation of obedience to faithfully accept the directives of the Church.[21]

3. *Quattuor abhinc annos*

A survey, conducted by the Sacred Congregation for the Sacraments and Divine Worship, occurred in 1980.[22] The survey concerned the use of Latin in the Mass and requests for its use, in addition to questions concerning the implementation of the liturgical reform and opposition experienced as a result. Overwhelmingly, ninety-eight percent of the bishops surveyed were strongly opposed to any eventual concession permitting the use of the former missal. Despite this clear response from the bishops consulted, Pope John Paul II elected to provide an additional faculty to bishops, whereby all diocesan bishops were permitted to allow those who are explicitly named in a petition submitted to him to celebrate Mass according to the 1962 *editio typica* of the Roman Missal.[23] The following norms were to be observed:

---

21 Sacred Congregation for Divine Worship, Private response to Archbishop Plourde's request for permission to allow use of the 1962 Missal within the Archdiocese of Ottawa, May 24, 1974, *La Documentation catholique* 73 (1976) 242.

22 Sacred Congregation for the Sacraments and Divine Worship, Investigation of the use of the Latin language in the Roman liturgy and the 'Tridentine' Mass, June 19, 1980: *Notitiae* 17 (1981) 589-611; partial Eng. trans. in *Origins* 11 (1981-1982) 556-559.

23 Congregation for Divine Worship, circular letter On the use of the 1962 Roman Missal *Quattuor abhinc annos,* October 3, 1984: *Communicationes* 17 (1985) 3-4; Eng. trans. in *CLD* 11:3-4.

a. There must be unequivocal, even public evidence that the priest and people petitioning have no ties with those who call into doubt the lawful force and doctrinal soundness of the Roman Missal promulgated in 1970 by Pope Paul VI.

b. The celebration of Mass in question must take place exclusively for the benefit of those who petition it; the celebration must be in a church or oratory designated by the diocesan bishop (but not in parish churches, unless, in extraordinary instances, the bishop allows this); the celebration may take place only on those days in those circumstances approved by the bishop, whether for an individual instance or as a regular occurrence.

c. Their celebration is to follow the Roman Missal of 1962 and must be in Latin.

d. In the celebration there is to be no intermingling of the rites or texts of the 1962 Roman Missal with those of the Missal of Paul VI.

e. Each bishop is to inform this Congregation of the concessions he grants and, one year from the date of the present indult, of the outcome of its use.[24]

Quattuor abhinc annos, unlike the exceptions for elderly and ill priests and the provisions of the 1971 English indult noted above, permited the use of the 1962 *editio typica* of the *Missale Romanum* without observing the lawful adaptations introduced in 1965 and 1967. Furthermore, the faculty was granted to diocesan bishops, rather than to ordinaries who had also been granted the habitual faculty according to the 1971 English indult.

The new provisions of *Quattuor abhinc annos* were not universally accepted. Representatives of the English-speaking episcopal conferences, under the presidency of Archbishop Denis Hurley of Durban, expressed "grave concern, regret and dismay" at news of the new indult.[25] The resolution argues that the indult seems to support those who have resisted the liturgical renewal, and demonstrates a lack of concern for those who wholeheartedly embraced the desires of the council—often at great personal cost and with great difficulty. The

---

24 Congregation for Divine Worship, circular letter, 3-14.

25 Denis Hurley, Letter from representatives of English-speaking episcopal conferences concerning the provisions of *Quattuor abhinc annos*, October 28, 1984: *Origins* 14 (1984-1985) 334-335. It should be noted that the division of the congregation on 2 August 1984 was seen as a source of the problem: "It was resolved that the recent division of the Congregation of the Sacraments and Divine Worship posed a potential threat to the ongoing work of liturgical renewal because of a seeming return to a preconciliar understanding of the sacraments."

resolution asserts further that *Quattuor abhinc annos* violated the collegial sense of the worldwide episcopate, ninety-eight percent of whom did not consider the "problem of the Tridentine Mass" a matter requiring further concessions from the Holy See, a clear allusion to the extensive survey conducted by the Sacred Congregation for the Sacraments and Divine Worship in 1980.

4. Motu proprio *Ecclesia Dei*

Despite a formal canonical warning, Monsignor Marcel Lefebvre, founder of the Priestly Society of St. Pius X, proceeded to ordain four bishops without a pontifical mandate in 1988. In virtue of canon 1382 (now c. 1387),[26] both the consecrating bishop and those receiving consecration from him incurred a *latae sententiae* excommunication reserved to the Apostolic See. The Congregation for Bishops subsequently declared that Monsignor Lefebvre and the four he consecrated incurred this excommunication (cf. c. 1331, §2).[27]

On July 2, 1988, John Paul II, through his apostolic letter motu proprio, manifested his will to facilitate ecclesial communion with those faithful attached to an earlier liturgical and disciplinary form of the Latin tradition.[28] Although the motu proprio *Ecclesia Dei* provides no new provision for the use of the 1962 *Missale Romanum*, "it is necessary that all the pastors and the other faithful have a new awareness, not only of the lawfulness but also the richness for the church of a diversity of charism, traditions of spirituality and apostolate, which also constitutes the beauty of unity in variety" (n. 5, a). The motu proprio encouraged bishops to respect the feelings of all those who are attached to the Latin liturgical tradition, through "a wide and generous application" of the provisions in *Quattuor abhinc annos* (n. 6, c). To facilitate ecclesial communion with the former adherents of Monsignor Lefebvre, and "to guarantee respect for their rightful aspirations" (n. 5, c), Pope John Paul II established the Pontifical Commission *Ecclesia Dei*. To achieve these ends, the pontifical commission was granted special faculties,[29] and issued guidelines to assist bishops with the implementation

26 Francis, Apostolic constitution reforming Book VI of the Code of Canon Law *Pascite gregem Dei*, May 23, 2021: https://www.vatican.va/content/francesco/en/apost_constitutions/documents/papa-francesco_costituzione-ap_20210523_pascite-gregem-dei.html (accessed on 20 Dec. 2023).

27 Congregation for Bishops, Decree declaring the excommunication *latae sententiae* of Mgr. Lefebvre and those he consecrated bishop, July 1, 1988; Eng. trans. in *CLD* 12: 804-805.

28 John Paul II, m.p. *Ecclesia Dei*, July 2, 1988: *AAS* 80 (1988) 1495-1498; Eng. trans. in *CLD* 12:805-808.

29 Pontifical Commission *Ecclesia Dei*, *Rescriptum ex audientia Sanctissimi* concerning faculties entrusted to the Pontifical Commission, October 18, 1988: *AAS* 82 (1990) 533-534; Eng. trans. in *CLSGBI Newsletter* 77 (1989) 19-20.

of the motu proprio and ensure a "wide and generous" application of the existing provisions.[30] These guidelines derogated from a number of the restrictions of *Quattuor abhinc annos*.[31]

5. *Summorum Pontificum*

On July 7, 2007, Pope Benedict XVI promulgated the apostolic letter motu proprio *Summorum Pontificum*, which allowed general use of the 1962 *Missale Romanum* (art. 1) in addition to the pre-conciliar liturgical rites for the administration of the sacraments of baptism, marriage, penance, the anointing of the sick (art. 9 §1), and confirmation (art. 9 §2).[32] Use of pre-conciliar liturgical rites, other than that of the *Missale Romanum* of 1962, was a provision unique to *Summorum Pontificum*, which had previously been granted only in extraordinary circumstances.[33] *Summorum Pontificum* distinguished between the ordinary and extraordinary forms of the Roman Rite. The ordinary form consisted of the current liturgical rites revised after the Second Vatican Council. The "extraordinary expression" of the Roman rite utilized the liturgical books prior to this liturgical reform. The motu proprio asserted that "these two expressions of the church's *lex orandi* will in no way lead to a division in the church's *lex credendi*. They are in fact two usages of the one Roman rite" (art. 1).

Summorum Pontificum explicitly revoked the provisions of both *Quattuor abhinc annos* and *Ecclesia Dei* (art. 1). In Masses celebrated without the people, use of either the Missal promulgated in 1962 or 1970 could be used by all priests, except during the Triduum, with no need for permission from the Apostolic See or the local ordinary (art. 2). These celebrations could also be attended by those members of the faithful who, on their own free will, requested to be admitted (art. 4). When requested, use of the former Missal could be used for special occasions such as marriages, funerals, and other occasional celebrations (art. 5 §3). For Masses with the people, the readings could be given in the vernacular, using translations approved by the Apostolic See (art. 6). Institutes of consecrated life

---

30 Pontifical Commission *Ecclesia Dei*, Guidelines for implementing the Apostolic Letter *Ecclesia Dei*, April 19, 1991; Eng. trans. in *Origins* 21 (1991-1992) 144-145.

31 See William H. Woestman, "*Ecclesia Dei* and Ecclesial Communion," *The Jurist* 53 (1993) 206, fn. 22.

32 Benedict XVI, Apostolic letter motu proprio *Summorum Pontificum*, July 7, 2007: *AAS* 99 (2007) 777-781; Eng. trans. in *Origins* 37 (2007-2008) 129-132.

33 See Pontifical Commission *Ecclesia Dei*, Decree erecting the Priestly Fraternity of St. Peter as a clerical society of apostolic life of pontifical right. October 18, 1988. Eng. trans. in *CLSGBI Newsletter* 77 (1989) 27-28. The decree specifically notes: "The use of the liturgical books in force in 1962 is granted to members of the Priestly Fraternity of St. Peter, and also other priests who may be guests in houses of the Fraternity, or exercising the sacred ministry in its churches."

and societies of apostolic life that wished to utilize the 1962 *Missale Romanum* could do so. If a community or the entire institute wishes to do so habitually, the decision must be taken by the supreme moderator, in accordance with the law and the statutes of the institute (art. 3).

Where a group of the faithful adhering to the earlier liturgical tradition stably exists (*stabiliter exsistit*) in parishes, the pastor should willing accommodate their requests (art. 5 §1). If requests for such celebrations were not satisfied, the faithful were to inform the bishop, who was strongly requested to satisfy their wishes. If the bishop did not want (*non vult*) to provide for such celebrations, the matter was to be referred to the Pontifical Commission *Ecclesia Dei* (art. 7). The same pontifical commission was to provide counsel and assistance to bishops desiring to satisfy the requests of the faithful (art. 8). The local ordinary, if he deemed it necessary, could erect personal parishes in accordance with c. 518, or appoint a chaplain, for celebrations according to the extraordinary form of the Roman Rite. The Pontifical Commission *Ecclesia Dei* continued to exercise the authority of the Holy See in these matters and was to supervise the observance and application of the provisions of *Summorum Pontificum*, which became effective on 14 September 2007 (art. 12).[34] A comprehensive instruction was issued in 2011 by the Pontifical Commission *Ecclesia Dei*, to address ancillary questions arising from the provisions of *Summorum Pontificum*.[35]

6. *Traditionis Custodes*

On July 16, 2021, Pope Francis promulgated *Traditionis custodes*, whicexplicitly abrogated the earlier provisions of *Summorum Pontificum*. Although a detailed review of these provisions will follow in the second part of the presentation, it is worth recalling that there have been several interventions to clarify the intent and extent of the new legislation.[36] These consist of the *Responsa ad dubia* issued by the Congregation for the Divine Worship and the Discipline of

---

34 The Pontifical Commission *Ecclesia Dei* was suppressed in 2019, and its competencies were assigned to the Congregation for the Doctrine of the Faith. See Francis, m.p. on the Pontifical Commission *Ecclesia Dei*, January 17, 2019: https://www.vatican.va/content/francesco/en/motu_proprio/documents/papa-fran cesco-motu-proprio-20190117_ecclesia-dei.html (accessed on 20 Dec. 2023). For an overview of the PCED, see Dawid Pietras, *The Pontifical Commission* Ecclesia Dei *(1988-2019): Competences, Structure, and Activity* (Krakow: Wydawnictwo scriptum, 2023).

35 See Chad J. Glendinning, "*Universae Ecclesiae*: Text and Commentary," *Studia canonica* 45 (2011) 355-409.

36 For a juridical analysis of the provisions of *Traditionis custodes*, see John G. Lessard-Thibodeau, *Mutual Liturgical Enrichment: Juridical Consideration of 20th and 21st Century Conciliar, Papal, and Curial Documents*, JCD dissertation (Ottawa, ON: Saint Paul University, 2022) 71-75; 331-338.

the Sacraments in 2021; the decree of Pope Francis concerning the Priestly Fraternity of St. Peter (FSSP) in 2022; and the rescript *ex audientia Sanctissimi* in 2023.

6.1. *Responsa ad dubia*

The Congregation for Divine Worship and the Discipline of the Sacraments responded to several questions concerning the new legislation by means of the *Responsa ad dubia*, December 4, 2021. In presenting the responses, the dicastery notes that the provisions of *Traditionis custodes* aim to preserve ecclesial communion:

> The text of the Motu Proprio and the accompanying Letter to the Bishops of the whole world clearly express the reasons for the decisions taken by Pope Francis. The first aim is to continue "in the constant search for ecclesial communion" (*Traditionis custodes*, Preamble) which is expressed by recognising in the liturgical books promulgated by the Popes Saint Paul VI and Saint John Paul II, in conformity with the decrees of the Second Vatican Council, the unique expression of the *lex orandi* of the Roman Rite (cf. *Traditionis custodes*, n. 1). This is the direction in which we wish to move, and this is the meaning of the responses we publish here. Every prescribed norm has always the sole purpose of preserving the gift of ecclesial communion by walking together, with conviction of mind and heart, in the direction indicated by the Holy Father.[37]

These responses deal with such matters as the use of parish churches for celebrations of the Eucharist using the 1962 *Missale Romanum*, the continued use of the older *Rituale Romanum* and *Pontificale Romanum* for the celebration of other sacraments and sacramentals, permission for priests ordained after the promulgation of *Traditionis custodes* to use the 1962 *Missale Romanum*, and authorization for deacons and other instituted ministers to participate in these celebrations.

6.2. Decree Concerning the Fraternity of Saint Peter following *Traditionis Custodes*

---

37 Congregation for Divine Worship and the Discipline of the Sacraments, *Responsa ad dubia* on certain provisions of the Apostolic Letter *Traditionis custodes,* December 4, 2021: *AAS* 114 (2022) 139-149; Eng. trans. at https://www.vatican.va/roman_curia/congregations/ccdds/documents/rc_con_ccdds_doc_20211204_responsa-ad-dubia-tradizionis-custodes_en.html (accessed on 20 Dec. 2023).

Following *Traditionis custodes*, questions were raised about the status of various religious institutes erected by *Ecclesia Dei* and who made use of the earlier liturgical books exclusively. Pope Francis confirmed that each and every member of the Fraternity of Saint Peter (FSSP), a society of apostolic life of pontifical right erected in 1988, may "carry out the sacraments and other sacred rites, as well as to fulfill the Divine Office, according to the typical editions of the liturgical books, namely the Missal, the Ritual, the Pontifical, and the Roman Breviary, in force in the year 1962." Members may use this faculty "in their own churches or oratories; otherwise it may only be used with the consent of the Ordinary of the place, except for the celebration of private Masses." Nevertheless, the provisions of *Traditionis custodes* are recalled: "Without prejudice to what has been said above, the Holy Father suggests that, as far as possible, the provisions of the motu proprio *Traditionis Custodes* be taken into account as well."[38]

6.3 Rescript *ex audientia SS.mi*

Questions remained regarding the ability of diocesan bishops to dispense from provisions of *Traditionis custodes* by means of canon 87 of the Code of Canon Law, particularly following the *responsa ad dubia*, which reinforced the competencies of the Congregation for Divine Worship and the Discipline of the Sacrament in a variety of these matters. By way of a rescript *ex audientia Sanctissimi* of February 20, 2023, Pope Francis confirmed that dispensations are reserved in a special way to the Dicastery for Divine Worship and the Discipline of the Sacraments in the following cases:

- the use of a parish church or the erection of a personal parish for the celebration of the Eucharist using the *Missale Romanum* of 1962 (cf. *Traditionis custodes* art. 3 §2);

- the granting of permission to priests ordained after the publication of Motu proprio *Traditionis custodes* to celebrate with the *Missale Romanum* of 1962 (cf. *Traditionis custodes* art. 4).[39]

---

38 Francis, Decree confirming the use of the 1962 liturgical books for the FSSP, February 11, 2022. A copy of the decree, in the original Latin and Spanish, can be found here: https://www.fssp.org/en/decree-of-pope-francis-confirming-the-use-of-the-1962-liturgical-books/ (accessed on 20 Dec. 2023).

39 Dicastery for Divine Worship and the Discipline of the Sacraments, Rescript *ex audientia SS.mi*, February 20, 2023: https://www.vatican.va/roman_curia/congregations/ccdds/documents/rc_con_ccdds_doc_20230220_rescriptum-traditioniscustodes_en.html (accessed on 20 Dec. 2023).

If a diocesan bishop had granted a dispensation regarding these matters, "he is obliged to inform the Dicastery for Divine Worship and the Discipline of the Sacraments, which will assess the individual cases."[40]

Conclusion

Pope Benedict XVI, in his accompanying letter to *Summorum Pontificum*, expressed a desire that his new provisions would promote an "interior reconciliation in the heart of the Church."[41] Pope Francis, likewise, in his accompanying letter to *Traditionis custodes* laments that these earlier provisions have been "exploited to widen the gaps, reinforce the divergences, and encourage disagreements that injure the Church, block her path, and expose her to the peril of division."[42] The provisions of *Traditionis custodes*, he argues, are intended to thwart these divisions by restoring a single expression of the Roman Rite, as a means of preserving ecclesial communion. Elsewhere, in *Desiderio desideravi*, number 31, Pope Francis identifies the tensions around the celebration of the Eucharist as primarily ecclesiological in nature:

> It would be trivial to read the tensions, unfortunately present around the celebration, as a simple divergence between different tastes concerning a particular ritual form. The problematic is primarily ecclesiological. I do not see how it is possible to say that one recognizes the validity of the Council— though it amazes me that a Catholic might presume not to do so—and at the same time not accept the liturgical reform born out of *Sacrosanctum Concilium*, a document that expresses the reality of the Liturgy intimately joined to the vision of Church so admirably described in *Lumen gentium*. For this reason, as I already expressed in my letter to all the bishops, I have felt it my duty to affirm that "The liturgical books promulgated by Saint Paul VI and Saint John Paul II, in conformity with the decrees of Vatican Council II, are the unique expression of the *lex orandi* of the Roman Rite." (Motu Proprio *Traditionis custodes*, art 1).[43]

With the same objective of preserving and fostering ecclesial communion, Benedict XVI and Francis have responded in rather divergent ways, responding to the needs of the Church in new times and places. The provisions of *Traditionis*

---

40 Rescript, February 20, 2023.

41 Benedict XVI, Letter on the Use of Roman Liturgy Prior to 1970, July 7, 2007: https://www.vatican.va/content/benedict-xvi/en/letters/2007/documents/hf_ben-xvi_let_20070707_lettera-vescovi.html (accessed on 20 Dec. 2023).

42 Francis, accompanying letter to *Traditionis custodes*.

43 Francis, apostolic letter on Liturgical Formation of the People of God *Desiderio desideravi*, June 29, 2022: https://www.vatican.va/content/francesco/en/apost_letters/documents/20220629-lettera-ap-desiderio-desideravi.html (accessed on 20 Dec. 2023).

custodes may appear to be rather restrictive when compared to *Summorum Pontificum*, but this is only so when examined in isolation. The survey of earlier provisions for use of the 1962 *Missale Romanum* reveals, in fact, a considerable level of continuity between *Traditionis custodes* and the Holy See's approach since the promulgation of the new liturgical books following the Second Vatican Council.

CLSA PROCEEDINGS 85 (2023) 123-133

SEMINAR

TRADITIONIS CUSTODES: PART 2

Reverend Peter B. Mottola, JCL

Introduction: Overview of the Document's Provisions

Article 2 of *Traditionis custodes* states that "it is the exclusive competence [of the diocesan bishop] to authorize the use of the 1962 Roman Missal in his diocese, according to the guidelines of the Apostolic See."[1] Therefore, if the 1962 Roman Missal is being used in a diocese, the diocesan bishop should have made some canonical intervention to confirm or authorize its use. This article, rather than going sequentially through the articles of *Traditionis custodes*, will examine the provisions of the document under three headings: Buildings, People, and Sacraments, concluding with some pastoral considerations.

Buildings

> The bishop of the diocese in which until now there exist one or more groups that celebrate according to the Missal antecedent to the reform of 1970: [...] §2. is to designate *one or more locations* where the faithful adherents of these groups may gather for the eucharistic celebration (*not however in the parochial churches* and *without the erection of new personal parishes*).[2]

This provision against the use of the parish church is a restatement of the earlier norm of *Quattuor abhinc annos* of 1984,[3] as discussed in the first part of this article.

Shrines, chapels, and oratories are examples of places that would meet this description of a non-parish church location. The 2020 Instruction of the Congregation for the Clergy entitled "The pastoral conversion of the parish

---

1 Francis, m.p. "*Traditionis custodes*" On the Use of the Roman Liturgy Prior to the Reform of 1970, July 16, 2021: *AAS* 113 (2021) 793-796 (hereafter *TC*).

2 *TC* art. 3 §2 (emphasis added); Eng. trans. at https://www.vatican.va/content/francesco/en/motu_proprio/documents/20210716-motu-proprio-traditionis-custodes.html (accessed on 20 Dec. 2023).

3 Congregation for Divine Worship, circular letter On the use of the 1962 Roman Missal *Quattuor abhinc annos*, October 3, 1984: *Communicationes* 17 (1985) 3-4.

community in the service of the evangelizing mission of the Church" foresees extinctive unions of several formerly distinct parishes into one parish.[4] If there are former parish churches in such amalgamations, those buildings, if not now being used as the parish church, would possibly be suitable places.

The *Responsa ad dubia* published by the Congregation for Divine Worship on 4 December 2021,[5] and the *Rescriptum ex audientiae SS.mi* of 21 February 2023,[6] make clear that the dispensation from this prohibition on the use of a parish church is now reserved to the dicastery, as is the erection of new personal parishes. Although any dispensations from the universal law given by diocesan bishops in the months immediately following the publication of *Traditionis custodes* were valid applications of canon 87, such dispensations are no longer possible without a rescript from the dicastery. The 2023 *rescriptum* also notes: "Should a diocesan bishop have granted dispensations . . . , he is obliged to inform the Dicastery for Divine Worship and the Discipline of the Sacraments, which will assess the individual cases."[7]

Anecdotally, the author of this article has been made aware of rescripts received in the United States granting permission for the continued use of parish churches that have been given for a period lasting two years, after which time the bishop is asked to send a *relatio* to the Dicastery. The *taxa* for the rescript is 250 Euro.

Traditionis custodes further states that the bishop is to "establish at the designated locations the *days* on which eucharistic celebrations are permitted using the Roman Missal promulgated by Saint John XXIII in 1962."[8] For example, in a shrine where there was a custom of having a monthly First Friday

---

4 See Congregation for the Clergy, instruction "The pastoral conversion of the Parish community in the service of the evangelising mission of the Church" 48, July 20, 2020: *AAS* 112 (2020) 751-752; Eng. trans. at https://press.vatican.vacontent/salastampa/en/bollettino/pubblico/2020/07/20/200720a.html (accessed on 20 Dec. 2023).

5 Congregation for Divine Worship and the Discipline of the Sacraments, "*Responsa ad dubia* on Certain Provisions of the Apostolic Letter *Traditionis custodes* issued *motu proprio* by the Supreme Pontiff Francis," November 18, 2021: *AAS* 114 (2022) 139-149; Eng. trans. at https://www.vatican.va/roman_curia/congregations/ccdds/documents/rc_con_ccdds_doc_20211204_responsa-ad-dubia-tradizionis-custodes_en.html (accessed on 20 Dec. 2023).

6 *Rescriptum ex audientia SS.mi*, February 20, 2023, *L'Osservatore Romano* (February 21, 2023) 8; Eng. trans. at https://press.vatican.va/content/salastampa/enbollettino/pubblico/2023/02/21/230221a.html (accessed on 20 Dec. 2023).

7 Ibid.

8 *TC* art. 3 §3 (emphasis added).

Mass according to that Missal, the bishop might have confirmed the continued monthly celebration.

Additionally, the bishop is "to verify that the parishes canonically erected for the benefit of these faithful are effective for their spiritual growth, and to determine whether or not to retain them."[9] This can be accomplished through his regular visitation of the diocese per canon 396, and through dialogue with the priests assigned to the spiritual care of these members of the faithful.

People

"The bishop of the diocese . . . is to determine that these groups do not deny the validity and the legitimacy of the liturgical reform, dictated by Vatican Council II and the Magisterium of the Supreme Pontiffs."[10] This was also a concern of Pope Benedict XVI. In the letter to bishops accompanying *Summorum Pontificum*, Benedict wrote:

> It behooves all of us to preserve the riches which have developed in the Church's faith and prayer, and to give them their proper place. Needless to say, in order to experience full communion, the *priests of the communities adhering to the former usage cannot, as a matter of principle, exclude celebrating according to the new books.* The total exclusion of the new rite would not in fact be consistent with the recognition of its value and holiness.[11]

In order to understand and assess the attitude of the faithful toward the Church's liturgical expressions and the magisterium, a great deal of pastoral closeness will be necessary. Accordingly, the bishop is to

> appoint a priest who, as delegate of the bishop, is entrusted with these celebrations and with the pastoral care of these groups of the faithful. This priest should be [both *liturgically*] suited for this responsibility, ... *and* be animated by a lively pastoral *charity* and by a *sense of ecclesial communion.* This priest should have at heart not only the correct celebration of the liturgy, but also the pastoral and spiritual care of the faithful.[12]

---

9 *TC* art. 3 §5.

10 *TC* art. 3 §1.

11 Benedict XVI, "Letter to the bishops on the occasion of the publication of the apostolic letter *motu proprio Summorum Pontificum* on the use of the Roman liturgy prior to the reform of 1970," July 7, 2007: *AAS* 99 (2007) 795-799 (emphasis added); Eng. trans. at https://www.vatican.va/content/benedict-xvi/en/letters/2007/documents/hf_ben-xvi_let_20070707_lettera-vescovi.html (accessed on 20 Dec. 2023).

12 *TC* art. 3 §4 (emphasis added).

Each bishop must identify a priest who loves the people attached to this traditional liturgical expression and who, at the same time, possess the firmest attachment to the communion of the Church. Any priest who would allow the members of lay faithful under his pastoral care to adopt an attitude of "total exclusion of the new rite," which Pope Benedict had warned against, would be unsuitable for this role.

Besides the priest or priests whom the bishop assigns to care of these faithful, article 5 of *Traditionis custodes* states: "Priests who already celebrate according to the *Missale Romanum* of 1962 should request from the diocesan Bishop the authorization to continue to enjoy this faculty."[13] If priests have not already done so spontaneously, a bishop might invite members of the presbyterate to submit such a letter seeking this authorization. It seems fitting that this authorization should be noted in a priest's clergy file in the diocesan curia.[14]

However, article 4 notes: "Priests ordained after the publication of the present Motu Proprio, who wish to celebrate using the *Missale Romanum* of 1962, should submit a formal request to the diocesan Bishop who shall consult the Apostolic See before granting this authorization."[15] As with the permission to use parish churches, this dispensation was reserved to the Apostolic See, per the *responsa* of December 2021 and the *rescriptum* of February 2023. Anecdotally, the author of this article is aware of negative responses to requests for this authorization but is aware of none granting this authorization to priests ordained after July 2021.

Sacraments

What about the other sacraments besides the Mass? While *Traditionis custodes* itself does not speak to this important question, the *responsa ad dubia* says:

> The diocesan Bishop is authorized to grant permission to use only the *Rituale Romanum* (last *editio typica* 1952) and not the *Pontificale Romanum* which predate the liturgical reform of the Second Vatican Council. He may grant this permission only to those canonically erected personal parishes which, according to the provisions of the Motu Proprio Traditionis custodes, celebrate using the Missale Romanum of 1962.[16]

---

13 *TC* art. 5.

14 See c. 486.

15 *TC* art. 4.

16 CDWDS, "*Responsa ad dubia,*" Question 2.

It is, therefore, not foreseen that, for example, baptisms or the anointing of the sick would be celebrated according to the 1952 *rituale* outside of those personal parishes.

One other liturgical question treated in *Traditionis custodes* notes that: "In these celebrations the readings are proclaimed in the vernacular language, using translations of the Sacred Scripture approved for liturgical use by the respective Episcopal Conferences."[17] What Scripture translation should be used?

A word of caution from the 1984 *Quattor abhinc annos*: "In the celebration there is to be no intermingling of the rites or texts of the 1962 Roman Missal with those of the Missal of Paul VI."[18] It would be a fool's errand to try to square the 1969 lectionary with the pericopes of the older lectionary. The December 2021 *responsa* responds to the question: "Is it possible to use the full text of the Bible for the readings, choosing the pericopes indicated in the Missal?" in the affirmative.

While the *responsa* goes on to recommend in its accompanying explanatory notes the "translation of the Bible approved by the individual Bishops' Conferences for liturgical use," this is not an option for Americans, since, as Richard John Neuhaus lamented as far back as 2001, "you cannot buy an ARNAB [Amended Revised New American] Bible, since only the pericopes (liturgical readings) exist . . . . So Catholics do not have a Bible for personal or group reading that uses the same text that they hear at Mass."[19] Accordingly, the author of this article suggests that the priest-celebrants familiar with the ancient liturgy be given a wide latitude in choosing from among translations previously approved by the episcopal conference, including that which was published in the Missal of 1965. In any case, communities in the United States have always had the custom of hearing the Sunday Mass readings in English.[20]

---

17 *TC* art. 3 §3.

18 "Nulla habeatur commixtio inter ritus et textus alterutrius Missalis." This document could not be located on the Vatican website. An unofficial copy of the original Latin text and an English translation are available at Corpus Christi Watershed, https://archive.ccwater shed.org/media/pdfs/19/10/24/19-52-37_0.pdf (accessed on 16 Jan. 2023).

19 Richard John Neuhaus, "Bible Babel," *First Things*, May 2001, https://www.firstthings.com/article/2001/05/bible-babel (accessed on 20 Dec. 2023)

20 See Nico Fassino, "The Epistles & Gospels in English: A history of vernacular scripture from the pulpit," February 27, 2023, *Hand Missal History*, https://handmissalhistory.com/feature-epistles (accessed on 20 Dec. 2023).

On November 3, 2022, Vatican Secretary of State Cardinal Pietro Parolin delivered a message from Pope Francis to the bishops of France gathered for their plenary meeting in Lourdes. He said:

> Pope Francis . . . invites you to the greatest solicitude and paternity for those people—especially young people, priests and laity—who are disoriented by the motu proprio *Traditionis custodes*, which you will be working to implement. They are often wounded sheep who need to be accompanied, listened to, and given time.[21]

In a liturgical conference held at Fontgombault in July of 2001, Joseph Ratzinger gave a paper on the "Future Prospects" of the 1962 Missal in which he explored the question "how are we to regulate the use of the two rites?", seeing that although "there are no liturgical arguments against the plurality of rites, . . . there is a difficulty with the canonical criteria."[22] He said that the case was "very simple in the case of abbeys . . . and likewise religious communities," because these "seem to offer an objective criterion," as opposed to people simply choosing a missal based on nothing more than their own proclivities.[23] His paper admits frankly, however, that this does not answer the canonical difficulty of what to do with the lay faithful attached to the older rite.[24]

---

21 Pietro Parolin, "Assemblée plénière de novembre 2022: message du Cardinal Pietro Parolin aux évêques français," October 27, 2022, https://eglise.catholique.fr/conference-des-eveques-de-france/cef/assemblees-plenieres/assemblee-pleniere-de-novembre-2022/531520-assemblee-pleniere-de-novembre-2022-message-du-cardinal-pietro-parolin/ (accessed on 20 Dec. 2023); Eng. trans. at Luke Coppen, "Pope to French bishops: Care for people 'disoriented' by '*Traditionis custodes,*'" *The Pillar*, November 4, 2022, https://www.pillarcatholic.com/p/pope-to-french-bishops-care-for-people-disoriented-by-traditionis-custodes (accessed on 20 Dec. 2023).

22 Alcuin Reid, ed., *Looking Again at the Question of the Liturgy with Cardinal Ratzinger: Proceedings of the July 2001 Fontgombault Liturgical Conference* (Farnborough, Hampshire: St. Michael's Abbey Press, 2003) 148.

23 Ibid., 150.

24 The reader's indulgence is asked for the inclusion in this footnote of an interesting historical precedent. Francisco Ximénez de Cisneros, Archbishop of Toledo from 1495 to 1517, established a chapel for the celebration of the Mozarabic rite: "A bull of Pope Julius II (1508) approved the use of the rite in this chapel; Julius issued another bull in 1512 to confirm the foundation's endowments." Susan Boynton, "Restoration or Invention? Archbishop Cisneros and the Mozarabic Rite in Toledo," *Yale Journal of Music & Religion,* vol. 1, no. 1, art. 3 (2015) 5-30, 6. Footnote 11 in this article furnishes further reading on the subject: "For a detailed account of the foundation with supporting documents, see Juan Meseguer Fernández, 'El Cardenal Jiménez de Cisneros, fundador de la Capilla Mozárabe,' in *Historia mozárabe: Ponencias y comunicaciones presentadas al I Congreso Internacional de Estudios Mozárabes* (Toledo: Instituto de Estudios Visigótico-Mozárabes de San Eugenio, 1975) 149–245."

Pope Francis seems to think along similar lines. In September 2022, Pope Francis responded to a question about *Traditionis custodes* from Geoffrey Kemlin, Abbot of the Abbaye Saint-Pierre de Solesmes, France, by saying: "I don't say 'yes' or 'no' to you, but I let you discern and make your decision."[25] On 11 February 2022, the Holy Father issued a decree to the Priestly Fraternity of Saint Peter (FSSP), a society of apostolic life. According to the press release from the fraternity: "[T]he Pope made it clear that institutes such as the Fraternity of St. Peter are not affected by the general provisions of the Motu Proprio *Traditionis Custodes*, since the use of the ancient liturgical books was at the origin of their existence and is provided for in their constitutions."[26]

If the *praxis curiae* in the coming decades should continue to deny to diocesan priests ordained after 2021 the authorization for celebrations according to the older missal, it seems prudent for bishops to plan to invite into their dioceses those institutes of consecrated life or societies of apostolic life dedicated to the celebration of this liturgical patrimony (attentive to the provision of *Traditionis custodes* that he should "take care not to authorize the establishment of new groups"[27]). One recent example: it was announced on 21 September 2023 in the Diocese of Worchester that "Bishop [Robert] McManus has decreed that St. Paul Church in Warren is now an oratory in which the extraordinary form of the Mass will be celebrated. . . . Bishop McManus has invited the Institute of Christ the King Sovereign Priest to be responsible for the pastoral care and administration of St. Paul Oratory."[28]

Above all, we must keep in mind the chief underlying intention in publishing the *motu proprio*: unity in the Church. Pope Francis wrote on this theme of unity in his letter to bishops accompanying *Traditionis custodes*: "St. John Paul II and, with even greater magnanimity, . . . Benedict XVI, intended to *recover the unity*

---

25 I.Media, "*Traditionis custodes*: «Je te laisse discerner», confie François à l'abbé de Solesmes," *Aleteia*, September 8, 2022; https://fr.aleteia.org/2022/09/08/traditionis-custodes-je-te-laisse-discerner-confie-francois-a-labbe-de-solesmes/ (accessed on 20 Dec. 2023); Eng. trans. at CWN Editor, "Pope trusts Solesmes Congregation to make its own decisions about extraordinary form, abbot says," *Catholic Culture*, September 9, 2022, https://www.catholicculture.org/news/headlines/index.cfm?storyid=56080 (accessed on 20 Dec. 2023).

26 Priestly Fraternity of St. Peter, "Official Communiqué," February 21, 2022, at https://fssp.com/decree/ (accessed on 20 Dec. 2023).

27 *TC* art. 3 §6.

28 Raymond L. Delisle and Tanya Connor, "Changes in Warren parishes: St. Paul Church now an oratory for Latin Mass," in *The Catholic Free Press*, September 21, 2023, https://catholicfreepress.org/news/changes-in-warren-parishes-st-paul-church-now-an-oratory-for-latin-mass (accessed on 20 Dec. 2023).

of an ecclesial body with diverse liturgical sensibilities."[29] Pope Francis has explained his intention in *Desiderio desideravi*:

> I ask all bishops, priests, and deacons, formators in seminaries, instructors in theological faculties and schools of theology, and all catechists to help the holy people of God to draw from what is the first wellspring of Christian spirituality. We are called continually to *rediscover the richness* of the general principles exposed in [*SC*]. For this reason we cannot go back to that ritual form which the Council fathers, *cum Petro et sub Petro*, felt the need to reform, approving, under the guidance of the Holy Spirit and following their conscience as pastors, the principles from which was born the reform. . . . For this reason I wrote *Traditionis custodes*, so that the Church may lift up, in the variety of so many languages, one and the same prayer capable of expressing her unity. As I have already written, *I intend that this unity be re-established in the whole Church of the Roman Rite.*[30]

Does "unity" in the Church mean total "uniformity," as it did for the 19th-century American bishops whose treatment of Eastern Catholics drove large numbers of them into the Orthodox Churches?[31] Let us remember that on 3 July 2022, and again on 1 February 2023, Pope Francis presided at the celebration of Mass in the Congolese Rite or the Zaire Use of the Roman Rite.[32] Diverse uses within the Roman Rite have always existed historically, for example in the particular feast days as well as rubrics unique to religious congregations, and this diversity poses no threat to unity.

Helpful reference points to the thinking of Pope Francis on the meaning of unity versus uniformity can be found in Massimo Borghesi's *The Mind of Pope*

---

29 Francis, Letter of the Holy Father Francis to the Bishops of the Whole World, That Accompanies the apostolic letter motu proprio *Traditionis Custodes*, July 16, 2021: *AAS* 113 (2021) 802-808 (emphasis added); Eng. trans. at https://www.vatican.va/content/francesco/en/letters/2021/documents/20210716-lettera-vescovi-liturgia.html (accessed on 20 Dec. 2023).

30 Francis, apostolic letter On the liturgical formation of the people of God *Desiderio desideravi* 61, June 29, 2022: *L'Osservatore Romano* (June 30, 2022); Eng. trans. at https://www.vatican.va/content/francesco/en/apost_letters/documents/20220629-lettera-ap-desiderio-desideravi.html (accessed on 20 Dec. 2023).

31 See, e.g., John Faris, *The Communion of Catholic Churches: Terminology and Ecclesiology* (Brooklyn, Saint Maron Publications, 1985) 55: "In the past, diversity was seen as a threat to unity, which was identified with uniformity. As far as spiritual life, liturgical practices, theology, and ecclesiology, the Catholic Church was virtually identified with the Latin Church."

32 Stanislas Kambashi, "Catholic and African - The Zaire Rite", *Vatican News*, February 1, 2023, at https://www.vaticannews.va/en/church/news/2023-02/zaire-rite-use-catholicity-africanness-congo-drc-libambu.html (accessed on 20 Dec. 2023).

Francis: Jorge Mario Bergoglio's Intellectual Journey.[33] From among the documents Borghesi cites, see, first, Pope Francis' Address to the European Parliament: "It is no secret that a conception of unity seen as uniformity . . . leads to the risk of living in a world of ideas, of mere words, of images, of sophistry."[34] And again, *Evangelii gaudium* 236:

> *[O]ur model is not the sphere*, which is no greater than its parts, *where every point is equidistant* from the centre, *and there are no differences between them. Instead, it is the polyhedron*, which reflects the convergence of all its parts, *each* of which *preserves its distinctiveness*. Pastoral and political activity alike seek to gather in this polyhedron the best of each. There is a place for the poor and their culture, their aspirations and their potential. Even people who can be considered dubious on account of their errors have something to offer which must not be overlooked. It is the convergence of peoples who, within the universal order, maintain their own individuality; it is the sum total of persons within a society which pursues the common good, which truly has a place for everyone.[35]

See also *Evangelii gaudium* 228:

> [C]onflicts, tensions and oppositions can achieve a diversified and life-giving unity. This is not to opt for a kind of syncretism, or for the absorption of one into the other, but rather for a resolution which takes place on a higher plane and preserves what is valid and useful on both sides.[36]

One final example of this theme, Pope Francis' 2017 homily for Pentecost:

> [T]he same Spirit creates *diversity and unity*, and in this way forms a new, diverse and unified people: the *universal* Church. First, in a way both creative and unexpected, he generates diversity, for in every age

---

33 Massimo Borghesi, *The Mind of Pope Francis: Jorge Mario Bergoglio's Intellectual Journey* (Collegeville, MN: Liturgical Press, 2018). The citations that follow can be found in Borghesi's text at: p xxv for discussion of the Pentecost homily of 2017, p 115 for citations *EG*, and pp 199–200 for the citation of the address to the European Parliament.

34 Francis, *Address upon Visit to the European Parliament*, Strasbourg, November 25, 2014: *AAS* 106 (2014) 1001; Eng. trans. at https://www.vatican.va/content/francesco/en/speeches/2014/november/documents/papa-francesco_20141125_strasburgo-parlamento-europeo.html (accessed on 20 Dec. 2023).

35 Francis, apostolic exhortation On the proclamation of the gospel in today's world *Evangelii gaudium* 236, November 24, 2013: *AAS* 105 (2013) 1115 (emphasis added); Eng. trans. at https://www.vatican.va/content/francesco/en/apost_exhortations/documents/papa-francesco_esortazione-ap_20131124_evangelii-gaudium.html (accessed on 20 Dec. 2023).

36 *EG* 228.

> he causes new and varied charisms to blossom. Then he brings about unity: he joins together, gathers and restores harmony: "By his presence and his activity, the Spirit draws into unity spirits that are distinct and separate among themselves" (CYRIL OF ALEXANDRIA, *Commentary on the Gospel of John*, XI, 11). He does so in a way that effects true union, according to God's will, a union that is not uniformity, but *unity in difference.*
>
> For this to happen, we need to avoid *two* recurrent *temptations*. The first temptation seeks *diversity without unity*. This happens when we want to separate, when we take sides and form parties, when we adopt rigid and airtight positions, when we become locked into our own ideas and ways of doing things, perhaps even thinking that we are better than others, or always in the right, when we become so-called "guardians of the truth." When this happens, we choose the part over the whole, belonging to this or that group before belonging to the Church. We become avid supporters for one side, rather than brothers and sisters in the one Spirit. We become Christians of the "right" or the "left," before being on the side of Jesus, unbending guardians of the past or the avant-garde of the future before being humble and grateful children of the Church. The result is diversity without unity. The opposite temptation is that of seeking *unity without diversity*. Here, unity becomes uniformity, where everyone has to do everything together and in the same way, always thinking alike. Unity ends up being homogeneity and no longer freedom. But, as Saint Paul says, "where the Spirit of the Lord is, there is freedom" (2 Cor 3:17).[37]

It is possible to hold the position that Pope Francis is correct in saying that "we cannot go back to that ritual form which the Council fathers, *cum Petro et sub Petro*, felt the need to reform"[38] in speaking of the vast majority of Latin Catholics, while at the same time acknowledging that there exist (relatively small but still) numerous persons in the Latin Church who have no affection for the reformed rites, but whose spiritual proclivities attract them to the older tradition in a way that does not constitute a moral or doctrinal failure. This acknowledgement of unity in diversity allows us to cease the acrimonious cross-ritual proselytizing that has characterized the Liturgy Wars.

---

37 Francis, Homily for the Solemnity of Pentecost, 4 June 2017: *AAS* 109 (2017) 710-711; Eng. trans. at https://www.vatican.va/content/francesco/en/homilies/2017/documents/papa-francesco_20170604_omelia-pentecoste.html (accessed on 20 Dec. 2023) (some emphasis in italics in original; additional underlined emphasis added by author).

38 *Desiderio desideravi*, 61.

I will conclude with the closing words of Pope Francis' *Desiderio desideravi*:

> *Let us abandon our polemics* to listen together to what the Spirit is saying to the Church. Let us safeguard our communion. Let us continue to be astonished at the beauty of the Liturgy. The Paschal Mystery has been given to us. Let us allow ourselves to be embraced by the desire that the Lord continues to have to eat His Passover with us. All this under the gaze of Mary, Mother of the Church.[39]

39 *Desiderio desideravi,* 65 (emphasis added).

CLSA PROCEEDINGS 85 (2023) 134-154

SEMINAR

POPE FRANCIS EMPOWERS INSTITUTES AND SOCIETIES: TEN YEARS OF REVISED CANONS

Dr. Eileen Jaramillo, DMin, JCL

The Vision of Pope Francis

The key to understanding Pope Francis' revision of canon law for institutes and societies centers on his apostolic vision. Therefore, this seminar begins by looking very closely at how he envisions the mission of institutes and societies.

On the eve of the conclave, Cardinal Jorge Bergoglio begins designing the blueprint for his pontificate. In a four-minute speech with only handwritten notes in front of him, he speaks to the College of Cardinals about the cries being heard in every corner of the earth. He says:

> The Church is called to come out of itself and go to the peripheries, not only geographic, but also the existential: those of the mystery of sin, of suffering, of injustice, those of ignorance and of the absence of faith, those of thought, those of every form of misery.[1]

Once he is elected, our Holy Father continues along this same path in his apostolic exhortation *Evangelii gaudium.*[2] He sets the plan for its implementation in motion when he sees the need for an urgent revitalization of the contemporary Church. He desires a "path of pastoral and missionary conversion which cannot leave things as they presently are" (*EG* 25*)*. In a very important statement for canonists, he says that "even good structures are only helpful when there is a life

---

1 Jorge Bergoglio, *Address to the College of Cardinals*, March 9, 2013. While this speech is not usually shared with others, Cardinal Jaime Ortega, the then-Archbishop of Havana, Cuba, eventually received permission to make it known to the public; available at https://www.foxnews.com/world/popes-2013-stump-speech-to-cardinals-a-blueprint-for-papacy, translated by Matthew Sherry in "The Last Words of Bergoglio Before the Conclave" by Sandro Magister, http://chiesa.espresso.repubblica.it/articolo/1350484bdc4.html?eng=y (accessed on 7 Nov. 2023).

2 Francis, apostolic exhortation *Evangelii gaudium,* November 24, 2013: *AAS* 105 (2013) 1019-1137 [*EG*]; Eng. trans. at https://www.vatican.va/content/francesco/en/apost_exhortations/documents/papa-francesco_esortazione-1p_20131124_evangelii-gaudium.html (accessed on 7 Nov. 2023).

constantly driving, sustaining, and assessing them" (*EG* 26). Therefore, the call in this exhortation is dynamic and forward looking. It is a movement from maintenance to mission because its focus centers on missionary outreach and conversion.

A few years after making such important statements in *Evangelii gaudium,* Francis specified how its contents apply to all consecrated people in his apostolic letter proclaiming the Year of Consecrated Life.[3] He referred to the variety of forms that are named in the 1983 Code of Canon Law.[4] The two individual forms are hermits (c. 603)[5] and consecrated virgins (c. 604 §1).[6] Professing private vows is also possible.[7] The two corporate forms are religious institutes (c. 607 §2) and secular institutes (c. 710).[8] The code then states that societies of apostolic life, the other corporate form, "resemble institutes of consecrated life" (c. 731 §1).[9] Additionally, the code recognizes the possibility of new forms of consecrated life in canon 605.[10] Therefore, it leaves room for the Holy Spirit to create a configuration of consecrated life that is not currently recognized in ecclesiastical law. Ecclesial families are in this process.[11]

---

3 Francis, apostolic letter To All Consecrated People on the Occasion of the Year of Consecrated Life, November 21, 2014: *AAS* 106 (2014) 935-947 [ALCP].

4 *Codex Iuris Canonici auctoritate Ioannis Pauli PP. II promulgatus* (Vatican City: Libreria Editrice Vaticana, 1989) [*CIC*]. Eng. trans. from *Code of Canon Law, Latin-English Edition: New English Translation* (Washington, DC: Canon Law Society of America, 2023). All English translations of canons from the 1983 code are taken from this source unless otherwise noted. When using charts to compare the changes in the canons, the Second Printing of the CIC by the CLSA in 2012 is used to view the canons before the revisions were made. The Fourth Printing of the CIC by the CLSA in 2023 is used for the canons as they exist in the current revision.

5 See Christina Hip-Flores, *Hermits and Consecrated Virgins, Ancient Vocations in the Contemporary Church* (Washington, DC: Fiat Press, 2018).

6 See Judith Stegman, *Mystically Espoused to Christ, the Son of God (c. 604 §1): The Basis for Proposing Juridic Principles to Guide the Development of Norms for the Ordo Virginum* (Washington, DC: Catholic University of America Press, 2019).

7 Canon 1192 §1 states: "A vow is *public* if a legitimate superior accepts it in the name of the Church; otherwise, it is *private*."

8 The code uses the term *religious institutes* to refer to both orders and religious congregations.

9 See the chart: "Significant Similarities and Differences" in Nancy Bauer, "Governance in General," Eileen Jaramillo and Donna Miller, eds., *Procedural Handbook for Institutes of Consecrated Life and Societies of Apostolic Life* (Washington, DC: Canon Law Society of America, 2021) [PH] 37-38.

10 Maria Casey, *Breaking from the Bud: New Forms of Consecrated Life* (Sydney, Australia: Sisters of St. Joseph, 2001).

11 *Annuario Pontificio,* "Altri Istitui di Vita Consecrata" (Rome, Italy: Libreria editrice Vaticana, 2019), 1642-1643. Seven ecclesial families are listed.

This seminar does not address all forms of consecrated life. It is limited to institutes and societies of apostolic life as well as associations of the faithful desiring to be established as an institute or society. Additionally, this seminar does not address the revised canons for cloistered institutes as seen in *Cor Orans*.[12] Occasionally this author refers to the changes in the Eastern Code of Canon Law.[13]

In this same apostolic letter, he then specifically challenges institutes and societies to analyze their fidelity to their charism and mission.[14] He says, "Are our ministries, our works, and our presence consonant with what the Spirit asked of our founders and foundresses? Are they suitable for carrying out today, in society and the Church, those same ministries and works"?[15] Francis gives more depth to such questions when he asks everyone in the Church to leave "our own comfort zone in order to reach all the peripheries in need of the light of the Gospel."[16]

In that same apostolic exhortation Francis says that this means entering a new era of evangelization that is marked by gospel joy. It is a missionary call that transforms the culture. It is a movement forward in a bold way because it reaches out to those who have fallen away or are standing at the crossroads. It is the liberation of injustices and the uplifting of the poor. It involves working with Christians from other denominations as well as other individuals who desire to encounter the suffering of women, men, and children.

---

12 See Congregation for Institutes of Consecrated Life and Societies of Apostolic Life [CICLSAL], *Cor Orans, Implementing Instruction of the Apostolic Constitution "Vultum Dei Quaerere: on Women's Contemplative Life,* April 1, 2018, https://www.vatican.va/roman_curia/congregations/ccscrlife/documents/rc_con_ccscrlife_doc_20180401_cor-orans_en.html (accessed on 7 Nov. 2023).

13 There are two codes of canon law: one for the Latin Church and another one for the Eastern Churches. This seminar concentrates on the Latin Church. The canons referenced in this seminar are taken from the Vatican website: https://www.vatican.va/archive/cod-iuris-canonici/cic_index_en.html. The seminar also provides a few references to the code for the Eastern Churches, *Codex Canonum Ecclesiarum Orientalium auctoritate Ioannis Pauli PP. II promulgatus* (Vatican City: Libreria Editrice Vaticana, 1990) [*CCEO*]. For changes in the *CCEO* see Francis, m.p. *Competentias quasdam decernere*, February 11, 2022: *AAS* 114 (2022) 290-295 [hereafter *CQD*].

14 CICLSAL, *The Gift of Fidelity The Joy of Perseverance,* 2020, http://www.xn--congregacinvidaconsagrada-zpc.va/content/dam/vitaconsacrata/LibriPPDF/Inglese/dono%20della%20fedelta_ING_testo_stampa.pdf. Canonist Marlene Weisenbeck stated, "The distinction between charism and mission or ministry is crucial. A ministry may be an expression of the charism but is not the charism itself." Marlene Weisenbeck, "Understanding Charism," *Health Progress* vol. 89, no. 6 (November-December 2008) 17.

15 ALCP I, 2; Eng. trans. at https://www.vatican.va/content/francesco/en/apost_letters/documents/papa-francesco_lettera-ap_20141121_lettera-consacrati.html (accessed on 7 Nov. 2023).

16 *EG* 20.

In keeping with this momentum, the universal law has moved forward in significant ways during the pontificate of Pope Frances. This author now turns to considering them.

The Apostolic Constitution *Praedicate Evangelium*

This evolution of the universal law is seen in our Holy Father's apostolic constitution on the reform of the Roman Curia *Praedicate evangelium.*[17] Remember this document reflects changes made to the apostolic constitution *Pastor bonus.*[18] The new constitution is a concrete way of living out the universal need for evangelization. Such a central thrust is the core reason why the major changes contained in that document emphasize preaching the gospel, synodality, decentralization, and a more significant lay involvement in the role of governance. This author believes that institutes and societies particularly see synodality in the process leading to the general chapter,[19] the experience of the general chapter and the implementation of its enactments.

Praedicate evangelium contains seven articles that point to how the newly named Dicastery for Institutes of Consecrated Life and Societies of Apostolic Life will be helpful to consecrated life regarding this evangelical direction. Article 121 in *Praedicate evangelium* is significant. When comparing it to its counterpart in article 105 of *Pastor bonus* it is evident that while both refer to the competency of the dicastery regarding the promotion of the practice of the evangelical counsels, there are differences. *Pastor bonus* speaks of *promoting* and *supervising* while *Praedicate evangelium* uses the term *regulate* and is more precise regarding approved forms and issues concerning societies. It says:

> The competence of the Dicastery is to promote, encourage and regulate the practice of the evangelical counsels, how they are lived out in the approved forms of consecrated life and all matters concerning the life and activity of Societies of Apostolic Life throughout the Latin Church.[20]

Paragraph one of article 122 indicates that the dicastery approves institutes of consecrated life and societies of apostolic life, erects them, and grants

---

17 See Francis, apostolic constitution *Praedicate evangelium,* March 19, 2022: *AAS* 114 (2022) 375-455 [*PE*].

18 See John Paul II, apostolic constitution *Pastor bonus*, June 28, 1988: *AAS* 80 (1988) 841-930.

19 See Eileen Jaramillo, "The Prophetic Role of the General Chapter" in *Review for Religious*, vol. 2 no. 2 (Washington, DC: *CUA Press*, 2022) 193-206.

20 *PE* art. 121; English text at https://press.vatican.va/content/salastampa/it/bollettino/pubblico/2022/ /03/19/0189/00404. html (accessed on 7 Nov. 2023) and in the CLSA's Fourth Printing of the *CIC* (2023) 577-615.

permission for the validity of the establishment of an institute or society of diocesan right on the part of the bishop. Its second paragraph indicates that mergers, unions and suppressions of such institutes or societies are also reserved to the dicastery. The third paragraph is new. It indicates that the dicastery is competent for approving and regulating new forms of consecrated life. The fourth paragraph addresses its competency to erect or suppress unions, confederations, and federations of institutes and societies.

Article 123 in *Praedicate evangelium* is similar to article 107 in *Pastor bonus*. Both refer to the charism of the founders and the tradition of each institute of consecrated life and society of apostolic life. However, *Praedicate evangelium* places a more concrete stress on Christ and the gospel when it says:

> The Dicastery works to ensure that Institutes of Consecrated Life and Societies of Apostolic Life make progress in following of Christ in conformity with the Gospel, according to their proper charism stemming from the spirit of the founder and sound traditions, that they faithfully pursue their own ends and contribute effectively to the building up of the Church and to its mission in the world.[21]

Article 124 is also significant because it provides a list of areas of competency of the dicastery, elaborating on the list that was already evident in article 108 §1 *Pastor bonus*. It now states:

> § 1. [T]he Dicastery deals with matters belonging to the competence of the Apostolic See regarding the activity of the Institutes of Consecrated Life and Societies of Apostolic Life, particularly with regard to:
>
> 1. the approval of Constitutions and their amendments;
> 2. ordinary government and discipline of members;
> 3. the incorporation and formation of members, including through specific norms and directives;
> 4. temporal goods and their administration;
> 5. the apostolate;
> 6. extraordinary measures of governance;
>
> § 2. The following belong to the competence of the Dicastery . . . :
>
> 1. the transfer of a member to another approved form of consecrated life;
> 2. the extension of absence and exclaustration beyond the term granted by the supreme Moderators;

21 *PE* art. 123.

3. the indult for members in perpetual vows to depart from Institutes of Consecrated Life or Societies of Apostolic Life of Pontifical right;
4. imposed exclaustration;
5. the examination of appeals against the decree of dismissal of members.[22]

There are three other articles. Article 125 concerns international conferences of major superiors. They can only be erected by the Dicastery for Institutes of Consecrated Life and Societies of Apostolic Life. The same dicastery is competent to approve their statutes and sees that their activities are ordered to their proper end. Article 126 §1 states that the eremitical life and the *Ordo Virginum* are subject to the dicastery because they are forms of consecrated life. Paragraph 2 speaks about establishing associations of consecrated virgins at the international level. Additionally, like article 111 of *Pastor bonus*, article 127 of *Preaedicate evangelium* has competency over third orders and those associations that are erected with a view to being established as an institute of consecrated life or a society of apostolic life.

With this foundation in mind, this author now turns to major changes made in some of the canons regarding institutes and societies.

Apostolic Letter *Communis vita*

This letter was issued motu proprio. This means that it is an apostolic letter from the Roman Pontiff. It is written on his own initiative and not at the request of another. When issued in this way it is designed to settle affairs that are significant but do not require a constitution. They are legislative in nature and directed to the Church at large. Thus, they modify existing legislation. They also provide assistance in understanding and interpreting the code.

Communis vita begins by stating that community life is "an essential element of religious life."[23] In accordance with canon 665 §1 religious are not to be absent from their house except with the permission of their superior. When someone is illegitimately absent canon 665 §2 requires the superior to seek out the person and help him/her return and persevere in his/her vocation.

There are times, however, when a superior is unable to locate the absent religious. After at least six months of illegitimate absence in accordance with canon 696 it is possible to begin the process of dismissal according to the

22 *PE* art. 124.

23 Francis, m.p. *Communis vita*, March 19, 2019: *AAS* 111 (2019) 483; Eng. trans. by the author.

established procedure in canon 697. However, when the residence of the illegitimately absent religious is unknown it becomes difficult to achieve a juridical certainty about the situation.

Therefore, as a way of helping institutes apply the necessary discipline as well as proceeding to the dismissal of the illegitimately absent religious, especially when his/her location is unknown, Pope Francis decided to add another reason to paragraph one of canon 694. Now there are more reasons for dismissal *ipso facto*. Paragraph three was also added. Hence, there is a need for confirmation in "order to produce juridical effects." This chart and the following ones on other canons compare the changes.

1983 Code of Canon Law	*Communis vita*
Can. 694 §1. A member must be held as *ipso facto* dismissed from an institute who: 1° has defected notoriously from the Catholic faith; 2° has contracted marriage or attempted it, even only civilly.	Can. 694 §1. A religious must be held as dismissed *ipso facto* from an institute who: 1° has defected notoriously from the Catholic faith; 2° has contracted marriage or attempted it, even only civilly; 3° has been illegitimately absent from the religious house, pursuant to can. 665 §2, for 12 consecutive months, taking into account that the location of the religious himself or herself may be unknown.
§2. In these cases, after the proofs have been collected, the major superior with the council is to issue without any delay a declaration of fact so that the dismissal is established juridically.	§2. In such cases the major superior, with his or her Council and without hesitation, having gathered the evidence, must issue the statement of the case so that the dismissal may be juridically constituted. §3. In the case envisaged by §1 n. 3, in order to be juridically constituted, this statement must be confirmed by the Holy See; for institutes of diocesan right the confirmation rests with the Bishop of the principal See.

Since the dismissal is *ipso facto* it is distinct from the specific procedures stated in canons 696 and 697 such as the provision that the cause be grave, external, imputable, and juridically proven as well as the various warnings, threats of dismissal, waiting a specific period of time before continuing, and full opportunity for self-defense.[24] Therefore, canon 694 does not require those same procedures. The second paragraph of this same canon simply directs the major superior to collaborate with the council to demonstrate the fact by gathering evidence and issuing a statement. The dismissal is accomplished by the fact itself. What about confirmation by the Holy See? As Father Michael Joyce, CM, says so clearly:

> The statement from the major superior and the council is sufficient, but the confirmation by the Holy See makes the process complete. The confirmation does not change the actual dismissal. It appears to be a kind of quality control, or it might serve as a data source.[25]

This canon binds religious institutes and societies of apostolic life. The reason is because canon 746, on the dismissal of a definitively incorporated member of a society of apostolic life, refers to canons 694-704.

At the same time, however, paragraph 1, number 3 has had conflicting interpretations of its application. Therefore, the then Congregation for Institutes of Consecrated Life (now known as the Dicastery for Institutes of Consecrated Life) issued a circular letter.[26] The general legislation of the Catholic Church does not provide for circular letters as an authentic source of law. Nevertheless, this form has been used more often in recent years to outline procedures or norms that are to be observed. Therefore, they appear to express the intentions and policies of a particular dicastery.

The letter says that "canon 694 §1, 3° applies exclusively to religious and members of a society of apostolic life, who are illegitimately absent and not able to be contacted."[27] The letter states that it does not apply to "religious who are legitimately absent but cannot be found; religious who are illegitimately absent but are able to be contacted."[28] It also states that a person is considered unable to be contacted if one knows *only* (my emphasis) "a telephone number, an email

---

24 For a good overview see Therese Guerin Sullivan, "Separation of Members from the Institute," in *PH*, 172-181.
25 Michael Joyce, "Missing in Action: Absent Members in Institutes of Consecrated Life and Societies of Apostolic Life," *CLSA Proceedings 82* (2020) 200-212.
26 See "Canon 694 §1, 3° Regarding the Application of *Ipso Facto* Dismissal of a Religious for Illegitimate Absence," Donna Miller, Michael Souckar, Patrick Cooney, eds., *Roman Replies and CLSA Advisory Opinions* (Washington, DC: Canon Law Society of America, 2020) 19-27, regarding the inquiry, the response from CICLSAL, the original Italian text of the circular letter, and the official English translation of that letter [hereafter CL refers to this circular letter].
27 CL, no. 2, 25.
28 CL, no. 2, 25.

address, a profile on social networks, a fictitious address."[29] Additionally, this new provision is not retroactive. It does not apply to cases prior to April 10, 2019.[30]

Communis vita also states that the new article added to §1 requires a modification to canon 729 with regard to secular institutes.

1983 Code of Canon Law	*Communis vita*
Can. 729 A member is dismissed from an institute according to the norm of cann. 694 and 695; moreover, the constitutions are to determine other causes for dismissal provided that they are proportionately grave, external, imputable, and juridically proven, and the method of proceeding established in cann. 697–700 is to be observed. The prescript of can. 701 applies to one dismissed.	Can. 729 Dismissal of a member of the institute proceeds pursuant to cann. 694 §1, 1 and 2; and 695. The constitutions may also define other causes for dismissal, provided that they be commensurately serious, external, attributable and juridically proven, and that the procedure established in cann. 697-700 also be observed. The provisions of can. 701 are applicable to the dismissed member.

The difference between the two is that the 1983 code text cites canon 694 in its entirety whereas *Communis vita* cites only the first two sections of the first paragraph of the new canon 694. Consequently, the causes for dismissal *ipso facto* in a secular institute remain notorious defection from the Catholic faith and either attempted or contracted marriage even only civilly.

Apostolic Letter *Recognitum Librum VI*[31]

With the Apostolic Constitution *Pacite gregem Dei,*[32] the new Book VI, *De sanctionibus poenalibus in Ecclesia,*[33] was promulgated. In Book VI some delicts have been typified differently. New ones have also been introduced and the succession of canons has also changed. This required modification to conform with the canons of other books of the code. The letter *Recognitum Librum VI* was

29 CL, no. 2, 25.

30 CL, no. 6, 26.

31 See Francis, m.p. *Recognitum Librum VI*, April 26, 2022: *AAS* 114 (2022) 551-552. English translations in the following chart are from https://www.vatican.va/content/francesco/la/motu_proprio/documents/20220426-motu-proprio-recognitum-librum-vi.html (accessed on 8 Nov. 2023).

32 See Francis, apostolic constitution *Pascite gregem Dei,* May 23, 2021: *AAS* 113 (2021) 534-537.

33 Francis, *De sanctionibus poenalibus in Ecclesia,* June 1, 2021: *AAS* 113 (2021) 537-555.

issued motu proprio. The changes affect canon 695. The basic purpose is so that this canon, which affects institutes and societies, coincides with the changes made to the canons in Book VI. Another difference is that the "major superior" now has the authority rather than simply the "superior." Numerous other special laws also have indirect consequences.[34]

1983 Code of Canon Law	*Recognitum Librum VI*
Can. 695 §1 A member must be dismissed for the delicts mentioned in cann. 1397, 1398, and 1395, unless in the delicts mentioned in can. 1395, §2, the superior decides that dismissal is not completely necessary and that correction of the member, restitution of justice, and reparation of scandal can be resolved sufficiently in another way.	Can. 695 §1 A member must be dismissed for the delicts mentioned in cann. 1395, 1397, and 1398 unless in the delicts mentioned in cann. 1395 §§2-3 and 1398 §1, the major superior decides that dismissal is not completely necessary and that correction of the member, restitution of justice, and reparation of scandal can be resolved sufficiently in another way.

This canon refers to the delicts mentioned in the three canons. Remember that a delict is a crime. It is an offense, and a canonical punishment has been established for it in canon law. Without going into the detail needed when dealing with crimes, this author will give a very brief overview of each canon. Canon 1395 refers to external sins against the sixth commandment of the Decalogue. Canon 1397 involves homicide, forcible or fraudulent kidnapping, grave wounding, detention, or mutilation of another as well as abortion. The first paragraph of canon 1398, speaks of punishments especially when a delict is committed against the sixth commandment of the Decalogue with a minor, or a person who habitually has the imperfect use of reason, or a person for whom the law recognizes equal protection. It includes recruitment or inducing such persons to show himself/herself pornographically or to participate in pornographic exhibitions as well as immorally acquiring, possessing or distributing pornographic images of such persons. This is known as grooming. Its second paragraph specifically refers to punishments for members of institutes and societies. Therefore, sexual abuse of minors by religious who are ordained or not ordained is a crime.

34 Two examples are Francis, m.p. *As a Loving Mother*, June 4, 2016: *AAS* 108 (2016) 715-717 and Francis, m.p. *Vos estis lux mundi,* May 7, 2019: *AAS* 111 (2019) 823-832.

Apostolic Letter *Competentias quasdam decernere*[35]

This motu proprio introduces changes not only in the 1983 code but also to the Eastern code. While there are numerous canons in this letter, this author is only dealing with the ones pertaining directly to institutes and societies in the Latin Church. This letter states that the changes are intended to foster "a healthy decentralization" in the way that is "without prejudice to its hierarchical dimension." Hence, areas of competence are changing in a way that safeguards the unity of discipline in the universal Church and executive power in the local Church and ecclesial institutions.

There are two canons on seminaries. Canon 237 §2 on the erection of an interdiocesan seminary and its statutes replaces the term "approval" with the term "confirmation." Canon 242 §1 concerns the program of priestly formation established by the episcopal conference. It replaces the term "approved" with the term "confirmed." It appears that using the word confirmed makes it firmer or strengthens it.

1983 Code of Canon Law	*Competentias quasdam decernere*
Can. 237 §2. An interdiocesan seminary is not to be erected unless the conference of bishops, if the seminary is for its entire territory, or the bishops involved have obtained the prior approval of the Apostolic See for both the erection of the seminary and its statutes.	Can. 237 §2. An interdiocesan seminary is not to be erected unless the conference of bishops, if the seminary is for its entire territory, or the bishops involved have obtained the prior confirmation of the Apostolic See for both the erection of the seminary and its statutes.
Can. 242 §1 Each nation is to have a program of priestly formation which is to be established by the conference of bishops, attentive to the norms issued by the supreme authority of the Church, and which is to be approved by the Holy See. This program is to be adapted to new circumstances, also with the approval of the Holy See, and is to define the main principles of the instruction to be given in the seminary and general norms adapted to the pastoral needs of each region or province.	Can. 242 §1 Each nation is to have a program of priestly formation which is to be established by the conference of bishops, attentive to the norms issued by the supreme authority of the Church, and which is to be confirmed by the Holy See. This program is to be adapted to new circumstances, also with the confirmation of the Holy See, and is to define the main principles of the instruction to be given in the seminary and general norms adapted to the pastoral needs of each region or province.

35 English translations of *CQD* are from https://www.vatican.va/content/francesco/en/motu_proprio/documents/20220211-motu-proprio-assegnare-alcune-competenze.html (accessed on 8 Nov. 2023).

Canon 265 is on incardination. It adds public associations of the faithful that have received that faculty from the Holy See to the structures that can incardinate. This addition is very significant. Those of us who assist such public associations know the problems that can occur when this faculty has not been given.

1983 Code of Canon Law	*Competentias quasdam decernere*
Can. 265 Every cleric must be incardinated either in a particular church or personal prelature, or in an institute of consecrated life or society endowed with this faculty, in such a way that unattached or transient clerics are not allowed at all.	Can. 265 Every cleric must be incardinated either in a particular church or personal prelature, or in an institute of consecrated life or society endowed with this faculty, or also in a public clerical association which has obtained that faculty from the Apostolic See, in such a way that unattached or transient clerics are not allowed at all.

Canon 686 §1 extends the time limit to five years for granting an indult of exclaustration. Recall that exclaustration means that a member is allowed to live outside of the religious institute for a period of time. The exclaustrated individual remains a member of the religious institute. However, there is a relaxation of some obligations. The key is the agreement entered into and understood by the exclaustrated person and the person granting the indult. If you are dealing with such a situation, this author encourages you to consult the chapter written by Therese Guerin Sullivan in the Procedural Handbook.[36] She gives an excellent overview of exclaustration and provides very practical samples of agreements and letters. After five years the competence for an extension is reserved to the Holy See or the diocesan bishop. In regard to societies of apostolic life, canon 742 indicates that the constitution governs this matter.

It is important to realize that this canon refers to voluntary exclaustration. It is also vital to remember that there are other types of exclaustration. One of them is involuntary or imposed exclaustation as described in canon 686 §3. The others are qualified exclaustration, *ad experimentum* exclaustration and exclaustration for as long as it is needed. The time periods for these other kinds of exclaustration vary according to the type of exclaustration. Once again, you can find more information in the Procedural Handbook.

36 For a detailed overview see T. Sullivan, in *PH*, 156-171.

1983 Code of Canon Law	*Competentias quasdam decernere*
Can. 686 §1. With the consent of the council, the supreme moderator for a grave cause can grant an indult of exclaustration to a member professed by perpetual vows, but not for more than three years, and if it concerns a cleric, with the prior consent of the ordinary of the place in which he must reside. To extend an indult or to grant it for more than three years is reserved to the Holy See, or to the diocesan bishop if it concerns institutes of diocesan right.	Can. 686 §1 With the consent of the council, the supreme moderator for a grave cause can grant an indult of exclaustration to a member professed by perpetual vows, but not for more than five years, and if it concerns a cleric, with the prior consent of the ordinary of the place in which he must reside. To extend an indult or to grant it for more than five years is reserved to the Holy See, or to the diocesan bishop if it concerns institutes of diocesan right.

Canon 688 §2 assigns the competence for the relevant indult to the supreme moderator with the consent of the council for individuals temporarily professed who ask, for a grave cause, to leave the institute. In accenting grave cause, the canon is clearly stating that profession is a serious commitment. This is a very significant accent. Therefore, the indult should not be granted unless the cause is grave. The gravity of the reason needs to be discerned with the individual, the formation director and the competent major superior. When there has been a very serious error regarding the vocation to religious life or when someone cannot observe the vows, it may be better for the individual and the community for this person to find another way of living the Christian life.

Based on numerous experiences this author welcomes this particular accent that is, once again reiterated in this canon. It appears to be a correction that crept into religious life sometime after Vatican II when temporary profession was incorrectly understood because the accent was based on temporary rather than profession. Indeed, there were some congregations that incorrectly thought that temporary profession was more similar to promises rather than vows.

This change applies to institutes of pontifical right, institutes of diocesan right and autonomous monasteries. Institutes of diocesan right no longer need to get the confirmation of the diocesan bishop. In regard to societies of apostolic life canon 742 indicates that the constitution governs departure of a member not yet definitively incorporated.

1983 Code of Canon Law	*Competentias quasdam decernere*
Can. 688 §2. During the time of temporary profession, a person who asks to leave the institute for a grave cause can obtain an indult of departure from the supreme moderator with the consent of the council in an institute of pontifical right. In institutes of diocesan right and in the monasteries mentioned in can. 615, however, the bishop of the house of assignment must confirm the indult for it to be valid.	Can. 688 §2 During the time of temporary profession, a person who asks to leave the institute for a grave cause can obtain an indult of departure from the supreme moderator with the consent of his or her council; in the case of an autonomous monastery, mentioned in can. 615, however, the bishop of the house of assignment must confirm the indult for it to be valid.

Canons 699 §2 and 700 indicates that the decree of dismissal from the institute, for a grave cause, of a temporarily or perpetually professed member takes effect from the time that the decree is issued by the supreme moderator with the consent of the council and communicated to that member who has the right to appeal.

1983 Code of Canon Law	*Competentias quasdam decernere*
Can. 699 §2. In the autonomous monasteries mentioned in can. 615, it belongs to the diocesan bishop, to whom the superior is to submit the acts examined by the council, to decide on dismissal.	Can. 699 §2 In the autonomous monasteries mentioned in can. 615, it belongs to the major superior, with the consent of his or her council, to decide on dismissal.
Can. 700 A decree of dismissal does not have effect unless it has been confirmed by the Holy See, to which the decree and all the acts must be transmitted; if it concerns an institute of diocesan right, confirmation belongs to the bishop of the diocese where the house to which the religious has been attached is situated. To be valid, however, the decree must indicate the right which the dismissed possesses to make recourse to the competent authority within ten days from receiving notification. The recourse has suspensive effect.	Can. 700 A decree of dismissal issued in the case of a professed member takes effect from the time that it is communicated to the member concerned. To be valid, however, the decree must indicate the right which the dismissed possesses to make recourse to the competent authority within ten days from receiving notification. The recourse has suspensive effect. [Note: see below for the motu proprio modifying the terms of recourse of a member given on April 2, 2023 and taking effect on May 7, 2023.]

Canon 1308 reduces the obligations of Masses and modifies competence.

1983 Code of Canon Law	*Competentias quasdam decernere*
Can. 1308 §1. A reduction of the obligations of Masses, to be made only for a just and necessary cause, is reserved to the Apostolic See, without prejudice to the following prescripts.	Can. 1308 §1 A reduction of the obligations of Masses, to be made only for a just and necessary cause, is reserved to the diocesan bishop and to the supreme moderator of a clerical institute of consecrated life or a society of apostolic life.
§2. If it is expressly provided for in the charters of the foundations, the ordinary is able to reduce the Mass obligations because of diminished revenues.	
§3. With regard to Masses independently founded in legacies or in any other way, the diocesan bishop has the power, because of diminished revenues and for as long as the cause exists, to reduce the obligations to the level of offering legitimately established in the diocese, provided that there is no one obliged to increase the offering who can effectively be made to do so.	§2 With regard to Masses independently founded in legacies, the diocesan bishop has the power, because of diminished revenues and for as long as the cause exists, to reduce the obligations to the level of offering legitimately established in the diocese, provided that there is no one obliged to increase the offering who can effectively be made to do so.
§4. The diocesan bishop also has the power to reduce the obligations or legacies of Masses binding an ecclesiastical institute if the revenue has become insufficient to pursue appropriately the proper purpose of the institute.	§3 The diocesan bishop also has the power to reduce the obligations or legacies of Masses binding an ecclesiastical institute if the revenue has become insufficient to pursue appropriately the proper purpose of the institute.
§5. The supreme moderator of a clerical religious institute of pontifical right possesses the same powers mentioned in §§3 and 4.	§4 The supreme moderator of a clerical institute of consecrated life or a society of apostolic life possesses the same powers mentioned in §§2 and 3.

Apostolic Letter Modifying the Terms of Recourse of Member Dismissed from Institute of Consecrated Life[37]

This letter issued motu proprio introduces changes the recently modified *Competentias quasdam decerne* not only for the Latin Code but also for the Eastern code. As indicated previously, this author is only addressing the Latin Church. The letter begins by quoting the sixth general principle that the Synod of Bishops in October 1967 approved for the revision of the Latin code: "[I]t is expedient that the rights of persons be properly defined and secured."[38] The safeguarding and protection of such rights holds a privileged place in the Church.

The letter continues by stating that the chronological time contained in canon 700 is not congruent with the protection of the rights of a person. A less restrictive modality of appealing would enable the person concerned to be better able to evaluate the situation and to use more appropriate modes of communication. The letter also believes that there could be a danger that the procedures envisaged in canons 697-699 might not always be correctly followed. There is a change from "ten days" to "thirty days" regarding the right of a dismissed religious to appeal to the competent authority without the need to request in writing the revocation or correction of the decree from its author (c. 1734 §1).

Competentias quasdam decernere	Apostolic Letter Modifying the Terms of Recourse of a Member Dismissed from an Institute of Consecrated Life
Can. 700 A decree of dismissal issued in the case of a professed member takes effect from the time that it is communicated to the member concerned. To be valid, however, the decree must indicate the right which the dismissed possesses to make recourse to the competent authority within ten days from receiving notification. The recourse has suspensive effect.	Can. 700 The decree of dismissal issued in the case of a professed member takes effect from the time that it is communicated to the member concerned. To be valid, however, the decree must indicate the right that the dismissed possesses to make recourse, without the petition mentioned in can. 1734 §1, to the competent authority within thirty days from receiving notification. The recourse has suspensive effect.

37 See Francis, m.p. *Modifying the Terms of Recourse of a Member Dismissed from an Institute of Consecrated Life*, April 2, 2023, https://press.vatican.va/content/salastampa/en/bollettino/pubblico/2023/04/03/230403e.html (accessed on 8 Nov. 2023).

38 ". . . expedit ut iura personarum apte definiantur atque in tuto ponantur." *Codex Iuris Canonici auctoritate Ioannis Pauli PP. II promulgatus*, *Praefatio*, January 25, 1983: *AAS* 75, Pars II (1983) xxii (principle 6). Eng. trans. in *Code of Canon Law. Latin-English Edition: New English Translation* (Washington, DC: CLSA, 2023) xli.

Rescriptum ex audientia SS.mi regarding Canon 588 §2

Canon 588 §2 states: "That institute is called clerical which, by reason of the purpose or design intended by the founder or by virtue of legitimate tradition, is under the direction of clerics, assumes the exercise of sacred orders, and is recognized as such by the authority of the Church."

At an audience on February 11, 2022, Pope Francis issued a rescript regarding this second paragraph.[39] Remember that in accordance with canon 59 a rescript is an administrative act given in writing by a competent executive authority by which there is granted to some person requesting it a privilege, a dispensation, or a favor. In this rescript Pope Frances granted to the Cardinal Prefect and the Archbishop Secretary of the now Dicastery for Institutes of Consecrated Life and Societies of Apostolic Life the faculty to authorize, at its discretion for individual cases, the conferral of the office of major superior to non-clerics in clerical institutes of pontifical right and in clerical societies of apostolic life in the Latin Church "without prejudice to canon 134 §1."[40] Recall that major superiors, along with their vicars, are those who govern an entire or a part of a clerical institute and are called to give themselves diligently to their office. Canon 134 §1 states that for their own members, major superiors of clerical religious institutes of pontifical right and of clerical societies of apostolic life of pontifical right who at least possess ordinary executive power are considered ordinaries.

The rescript provides for three separate cases: (1) the supreme moderator of an institute of consecrated life or society of apostolic life can appoint a non-cleric as a superior for a local community with the consent of his council; (2) likewise, the supreme moderator, acting with the consent of his council, can appoint a non-cleric as a major superior after having received written permission from the dicastery; and (3) a non-cleric can be elected as a supreme moderator or a major superior, in accordance with the law providing for such cases, but such an election must be confirmed in writing by the dicastery.

What is at the core of this rescript? A brief look at the past tells the story. Prior to this rescript the juridical norms prevented brothers of clerical institutes from participating fully in government. That distinction between "the brothers" and "the fathers" left its mark on the mentalities in institutes and societies, their way of life, and their ministries. Influenced by historical, social, and ecclesial circumstances from other eras, brothers were considered as a religious who, not having the intellectual preparation required for the exercise of priestly ministry,

---

39 See Francis, *Rescriptum ex audientia SS.mi*, May 18, 2022: *AAS* 114 (2022) 789-790.
40 Ibid., 789; Eng. trans. at https://press.vatican.va/content/salastampa/it/bollettino/pubblico/2022/05/18/0371/00782.html (accessed on 8 Nov. 2023).

concentrated on manual tasks. Far too often in the past brothers were appreciated only for their dedication and the usefulness of their work. They were not considered religious in the full sense of the word because they were not ordained.

Vatican II underlined that lay religious life "constitutes a state which of itself is one of total dedication to the profession of the evangelical counsels."[41] Even though it did not treat directly the question of the position of brothers in a clerical institute, Vatican II teaches that consecrated life draws its entire reality and meaning out of the practice of the vows and that priestly ordination does not complete it. Vatican II said, "To strengthen the bond of brotherhood between members of a community, those who are called lay brothers, assistants, or some similar name should be brought into the heart of its life and work."[42]

Therefore, it is the opinion of the author of this seminar that this rescript is a way of correcting the unhealthy distinction between "brothers" and "fathers" in clerical institutes and societies of apostolic life so that all of the members are viewed as "brothers" in a way that enhances their apostolate.

Rescriptum ex audientia SS.mi regarding Canon 579[43]

Canon 579 states, "Diocesan bishops, each in his own territory, can erect institutes of consecrated life by formal decree, provided that the Apostolic See has been consulted." The question that has been raised over the years is whether this consultation is for validity. The rescript that was issued on May 11, 2016, responds to this question.

The rescript indicates that every new institute that comes into existence is a gift for the entire Church. Therefore, there is a need to prevent new institutes from being established on the diocesan level that lack the proper discernment and to ascertain the true origin of each charism that defines the specific feature for consecration through profession of the evangelical counsels. Those are reasons for consulting with the Dicastery for Institutes of Consecrated Life and Societies of Apostolic Life before proceeding with the establishment of a new diocesan institute. The rescript goes on to say:

> Therefore, in accordance with the view of the Pontifical Council for Legislative Texts, the Holy Father Pope Francis at the Audience

41 Second Vatican Council, decree *Perfectae caritatis* 10, October 28, 1965: *AAS* 58 (1966) 706-707; Eng. trans. by the author.

42 *Perfectae caritatis*, 15; Eng. trans. by the author.

43 See Secretary of State, *Rescriptum ex audientia SS.mi pertinens ad canonem 579 Codicis Iuris Canonicis de Dioecesanis Institutis erigendis*, May 11, 2016: *AAS* 108 (2016) 696.

accorded to the undersigned Secretary of State on 4 April 2016, has set forth that prior consultation with the Holy See is to be understood as necessary *ad validitatem* before establishing a diocesan Institute of consecrated life, otherwise risking nullity of the decree of establishment of this said Institute.[44]

There is a lengthy list of requirements that must be sent to the Dicastery for Institutes of Consecrated Life and Societies of Apostolic Life. For a more thorough overview of the requirements and the various stages in the process the reader may want to consult the most recent seminar given on this topic by this author at the convention of the Canon Law Society of America in 2018.[45]

For those of us who work with these groups that hope to one day be erected as institutes of diocesan right, it has become apparent that something needs to be done prior to consulting with the dicastery regarding erection as a diocesan institute. Therefore, the next rescript is important.

Rescriptum ex audientia SS.mi regarding Public Associations of the Faithful

This rescript concerns groups that hope to one day be erected as an institute or society of diocesan right. Pope Francis, in an audience on February 7, 2022, in the presence of the Cardinal Prefect and Archbishop Secretary of the Dicastery for the Institutes of Consecrated Life and the Societies of Apostolic Life, specifically approved the following provision:

> The diocesan bishop, before erecting - by decree - a public association of the faithful with a view to becoming an Institute of Consecrated Life or a Society of Apostolic Life of diocesan right, must obtain the written permission of the Dicastery for Institutes of Consecrated Life and Societies of Apostolic Life.[46]

The rescript was promulgated on June 15, 2022, and became effective immediately. As a canonist who works with these groups regularly, this rescript comes as no surprise. Since Vatican II a number of bishops in the United States were already sending documents to the Holy See regarding groups that desired to be erected as a public association of the faithful. The comments from the Holy See were very helpful. The groups that had a solid beginning from the time of

---

44 *Rescript*, May 11, 2016; Eng. trans. at http://www.vatican.va/roman_curia/secretariat_state/parolin/2016/documents/rc_seg-st_20160511_parolin-rescritto-can579cdc_en.html (accessed on 7 Nov. 2023).

45 See Eileen Jaramillo, "Erection as an Institute of Consecrated Life or a Society of Apostolic Life: The Nuts and Bolts," in *CLSA Proceedings* 80 (2018) 153-173.

46 Francis, *Rescriptum ex audientia SS.mi Circa le associatzioni pubbliche di fideli "in itinere,"* June 15, 2022: *AAS* 114 (2022) 957; Eng. trans. at https://press.vatican.va/content/salastampa/en/bollettino/pubblico/2022/06/15/220615e.html (accessed on 8 Nov. 2023).

being erected as a public association are fruitful whereas other groups that did not have a solid foundation have caused all sorts of problems.

Conclusion

Pope Francis is a man of his word. For institutes and societies to continue the mission that has been entrusted to them by Christ and the Church, they need to be empowered so that they do not get sidetracked by certain kinds of situations. In addressing those situations Pope Francis is really asking elected and appointed leaders to accompany their members when certain circumstances occur.

Accompaniment has been a central theme of Pope Francis from the very beginning of his pontificate. Those elected or appointed leaders who accompany others must practice "prudence, understanding, patience and docility to the Spirit."[47] Accompaniment also requires tremendous faith and hope in a loving and merciful Christ-centered existence. It is a willingness to bear wrongs patiently and to forgive, since hurting people often hurt other people. Pope Francis continues his understanding of accompaniment when he says,

> Someone good at such accompaniment does not give in to frustrations or fears. He or she invites others to let themselves be healed, to take up their mat, embrace the cross, leave all behind and go forth ever anew to proclaim the Gospel.[48]

In the future there will be more changes in the law for institutes and societies. In fact, some canonists think that the entire section of the law on consecrated life will eventually be revised. The Synod on Synodality may very well offer some suggestions for such changes. This author encourages the reader to read *Instrumentum laboris*[49] because it contains many challenges and asks questions about what needs to change in canon law. In regard to institutes and societies it speaks about participative bodies such as the General Chapter. This author has been following it very closely and would like to be in Rome as one of the participants. Additionally, we await the revision of the document that addresses the relationship between bishops and religious. If even a few of the statements

---

47 *EG* 171.

48 *EG* 172.

49 "*Instrumentum laboris*" for the 16th Ordinary General Assembly of the Synod of Bishops, June 20, 2023, https://press.vatican.va/content/salastampa/en/bollettino/pubblico/2023/06/20/230620e.html (accessed on 8 Nov. 2023).

about the revision of *Mutuae relationes*[50] are true, it holds tremendous hope for improving relationships between bishops and institutes as well as societies.

It is also important to note that on Saturday, October 7, 2023, Pope Francis appointed Sister Simona Brambilla, an Italian-born Consolata Missionary as the Secretary of the Dicastery for Institutes of Consecrated Life and Societies of Apostolic Life.[51] She is now one of the highest-ranking women in the Roman Curia. Only one other woman holds the same position in another dicastery.

---

50 CICLSAL sent a letter dated May 2, 2016, to the presidents of conferences of major superiors. It requested contributions toward the revision of the 1978 document, *Mutuae Relationes.* In the letter a newly enunciated principle, "co-essentiality" of the hierarchical and charismatic gifts, was highlighted. See https://www.vatican.va/roman_curia/congregations/ccscrlife/documents/rc_con_ccscrlife_doc_14051978_mutuae-relationes_en.html (accessed on 7 Nov. 2023).

51 See, e.g., Vatican News, "Pope appoints religious sister as Secretary of Consecrated Life Dicastery," October 7, 2023, https://www.vaticannews.va/en/pope/news/2023-10/pope-francis-secretary-consecrated-life-dicastery-brambilla.html (accessed on 7 Nov. 2023).

CLSA PROCEEDINGS 85 (2023) 155-171

SEMINAR

UPDATES IN PENAL LAW: 2023

Reverend John Paul Kimes, JCOD

The first ten years of Pope Francis' pontificate have yielded an unprecedented amount of legislation. Following the complete overhaul of *Liber VI* of the 1983 code in 2021, in the spring of 2023, a revision of the penal norms of the Eastern code and a new version of *Vos estis lux mundi* were both promulgated. A few months later, a non-normative interpretation of *Liber VI* was issued by the Dicastery for Legislative Texts. This article will briefly address the new legislation and the non-normative interpretive guide, offer a few insights to some of the new crimes introduced in 2021, and offer a few thoughts about revitalizing particular law as a tool for addressing issues of local, or regional, concern.

New Texts

1. Revision of Title XXVII of the Eastern Code

Officially dated 20 March 2023 (but released on 5 April 2023), the motu proprio *Vocare peccatores* reformed twenty-two canons of Title XXVII of the Code of Canons of the Eastern Churches,[1] as well as canon 1152 therein. These changes were introduced "*itemque eadem ratione*" as those introduced two years prior in the motu proprio *Pascite gregem Dei*.[2] However, in a dissimilar manner,

---

1 See Francis, m.p. *Vocare peccatores*, March 20, 2023: *L'Osservatore Romano* (April 5, 2023) 10-11. The convention used on the Vatican website to distinguish the modified text of a canon of Title XXVII is to indicate it with closed quotation marks, such that canon 1453" refers to the text of the canon modified by the *motu proprio Vocare peccatores*. This convention will be adopted herein to prevent any confusion as to which version of the text is being indicated.

2 See Francis, apostolic constitution *Pascite gregem Dei*, May 23, 2021: *AAS* 113 (2021) 534–537; Vatican Eng. Trans. of the new Book Six/*Liber VI CIC* at https://www.vatican.va/archive/cod-iuris-canonicii/eng/documents/cic_lib6_en.pdf (accessed on 2 Jan. 2024).

Vocare peccatores is only available in Latin.[3] Not only are these changes introduced for similar reasons as those in *Liber VI*, for the most part they are exactly the same changes that were introduced in 2021, creating a sort of harmony between the two penal codes that previously did not exist. Nevertheless, some significant changes were not introduced into Title XXVII.

First and foremost, the "general norm" of canon 1399 of the 1983 code still has no parallel text in the Eastern code. While all other aspects of Title XXVII have been modified to conform to Book VI, this particular norm was not introduced into the Eastern penal discipline. Among the conformities introduced is the linguistic distinction between the "simulation" and the "attempted celebration" of a sacrament. Previously, the Eastern code used the older language of *simulatio* to refer to both *facti species*. The distinction was introduced in the 1983 code and then carried over into the original norms of *Sacramentorum sanctitatis tutela*.[4] With this revision of Title XXVII, this linguistic distinction has been imported into the Eastern code (see c. 1443" §1, 1-2°). Other changes include introducing the new delict found in canon 1392 of the 1983 code into the Eastern code, as well as importing the language regarding *delicta graviora* directly into the canons of Title XXVII.

While often overlooked, the two codes treat the question of imputability in different manners. Where the 1983 code treats imputability by reason of malice different than that due to negligence (c. 1321), canon 1414 of the Eastern code does not. This distinction is important in the consideration of the applicability of a penalty under the two distinct legislations and remains operative. It is also indicative of the larger understanding of penal law as exclusively medicinal in the Eastern code and as both expiatory and medicinal in the Latin code.

One inexplicable disparity is found in the revised text of canon 1453" of the Eastern code. In 2021, the text of canon 1395 §2 of the 1983 code was modified and transferred to canon 1398; these modifications included inserting into the code the text of article 6 of the *Normae de delictis Congregationi pro Doctrina*

---

3 As of December 2023, no other translation is available: https://www.vatican.va/content/francesco/la/motu_proprio/documents/20230320-motu-proprio-vocare-peccatores.html (accessed on 12 Feb. 2024). This stands in stark contrast to the revision of the *Liber VI CIC*. The motu proprio *Pascite gregem Dei* is available in an official Vatican translation in English, German, Italian, and Spanish (as well as the original Latin), and the canons modified therein are available in languages as varied as Belarusian, Italian, Portuguese, French, English, and Spanish. While no explanation is ever given for such a disparity, it mirrors the fact that, to date, the only version of the *CCEO* available on the Vatican website is the original Latin text.

4 See John Paul II, m.p. *Sacramentorum sanctitatis tutela*, April 30, 2001: *AAS* 93 (2001) 737-739.

Fidei riservata, on the violation of the sixth commandment of the Decalogue with minors (under the age of 18) and those who habitually have an imperfect use of reason. Also included in the revised text of canon 1398 of the 1983 code was the category of "vulnerable adult" as found in art. 1 of the original text of *Vos estis lux mundi*. As is widely known, this second category was not named directly, but rather with the indirect formula "[*persona*] *cui ius parem tutelam agnoscit*." Rather than copy the Latin text of canon 1398 of the 1983 code verbatim, the legislator chose to insert a new formula into the revised text of canon 1453 of the Eastern code which, at least on paper, introduces yet another new category of protected person. Rather than speak of one who habitually has an imperfect use of reason, a category introduced originally in the 2010 revision of the norms of *Sacramentorum sanctitatis tutela*, canon 1453" speaks of a person who habitually *lacks* the use of reason (*persona quae habitualiter usu rationis caret*). More will be said about this peculiarity later.

2. *Subsidium*[5]

While not released until August 2023, the Dicastery for Legislative Texts issued a document referred to as a "subsidium" to aid non-specialists in their reading of the revised norms of *Liber VI* that bears the date of 31 May 2023. Currently available in four languages,[6] the English version is entitled "Penal Sanctions in the Church: user guide for Book VI of the Code of Canon Law." The text's own introduction places it into its proper historical context and provides important information for potential readers. The text notes that, already during the redaction of the 1917 code, the *Coetus studii de iure penali* recognized the need for a sort of "penal directory" that would be of assistance to ordinaries in their application of penal norms. Obviously, this "directory" was never composed. Similarly, "[t]he same intention was shared by the commission that drafted the new Book VI, reserving to a later document the precise explanation of the norms and their correct application."[7] The *Subsidium* fills this need, but does so under particular conditions.

---

5 The official English title of the document is "Penal Sanctions in the Church: User Guide for Book VI of the Code of Canon Law." Hereafter, *Subsidium*.

6 All four versions (Italian, English, Spanish and French) are available on the website of the Dicastery for Legislative Texts: https://www.delegumtextibus.va/content/testilegislativi/it.html (accessed on 5 Jan. 2024).

7 *Subsidium*, p. 6; Eng. trans. at https://www.delegumtextibus.va/content/dam/testilegislativi/TESTI%20NORMATIVI/Testi%20Norm%20CIC/Libro%20VI/LibroVIsussidio/Penal%20sanctions%20User%20guide.pdf (accessed on 5 Jan. 2024). All subsequent translations of this text will be taken from this source, using "p." for page and "n." for paragraph number therein.

First, the document is not normative. While it offers instructive interpretations and presentation of the various revised canons, especially of the new delicts, none of the interpretations or insights can be taken as normative. This is important to keep in mind, as will be shown further on, when criticisms of the text are raised. Second, the document does not add any new legislation. Third, it is primarily designed as an aid to non-experts in law. This decision influences the discursive manner of the document which, at times, eschews technical terminology.

The discursive nature of the document is both a strength and a weakness. The strength is found in its ability, at times, to expound eloquently on certain aspects of the modifications to Book VI. At the same time, however, as the document was composed in a particularly Italianate style, this eloquence complicates the English translation, rendering it often significantly less clear than the original (when read by someone with a very high competence in Italian). Given that the document is designed for non-experts, the choice of language, at points, is perplexing, as it appears to place its own literary value above the simplicity and clarity one might expect in a text designed for an audience that is less familiar with the law of the Church.

For native English speakers, the document includes one very important clarification/reminder, which should significantly impact the practice of important aspects of penal law. The revised norms of Book VI, over and over, refer to the need to repair scandal. Rather than undertake an exhaustive study of the word, suffice it to say that for many in the English-speaking world, the canonical term "scandal" is often misinterpreted. "Scandal" is more often understood to refer to what would historically be described as *admiratio*—clamor, noise, media attention. The *Subsidium*, in number 80, speaks to just this point: "As has already been seen on several occasions, the revision of Book VI took particular account of the need to repair the scandal and any other damage caused by the delicts (on the notion of scandal, Cf. *Catechism of the Catholic Church* n. 2284)."[8] While some (like the author) would have preferred that the text dedicate more time to such an oft-misunderstood aspect of the law, at the very least it makes it clear that when the term *scandalum* is used in Book VI, it refers expressly to the understanding of "scandal" as defined in the *Catechism*: "*Scandalum* is an attitude or behavior which leads another to do evil. The person who gives scandal becomes his neighbor's tempter. He damages virtue and integrity; he may even draw his brother into spiritual death. Scandal is a grave offense if by deed or omission another is deliberately led into a grave offense" (n. 2284). While it is up to the

8 *Subsidium*, n. 80.

ordinary to determine the *scandalum* present in each case, the *Subsidium* makes it clear that what is to be evaluated is *scandalum* in the traditional, moral understanding, not in the secular understanding of the term.

Three caveats for the reader of the *Subsidium* are offered. The first refers directly to the language used in the text. As a discursive text for non-experts, it is common to find a certain lack of precision in the language. Again, this lack of technical precision should not present a problem, as the text is not normative. However, it is important to note such imprecision, especially where it can alter the meaning of the original text. For example, the standard which triggers an investigation in canon law is verisimilitude (cf. c. 1717 *CIC*-1983). [9] The determination of verisimilitude is an evaluation of the relationship between the information received and fact. However, in current usage, verisimilitude is replaced often with the term "credible." Without any polemical intent, it is well-known that many dioceses in the United States of America publish lists of priests who have been "credibly accused" of certain delicts. Credibility is a distinct kind of evaluation, different from that of verisimilitude; the two terms cannot be used interchangeably.

The *Subsidium* risks adding to the confusion by mimicking a standard first found in *Vos estis lux mundi*, [10] which lacks all canonical precision, but communicates to the non-expert: "sufficiently founded." In its discussion of the norm of canon 1341 of the 1983 code, the *Subsidium* speaks about the evaluation of "first information on (*sic*) the facts;" once this information is deemed as "sufficiently founded," the ordinary must begin a preliminary investigation (c. 1717 *CIC*-1983). Clearly, the expression "sufficiently founded" is descriptive, not normative. The caveat is raised just to call attention to the fact that any evaluation of evidence that leads to a penal process (c. 1341 *CIC*-1983) must meet the standards of the code, not the descriptive language of the *Subsidium*.

The second caveat regards the value of some of the interpretations made in the *Subsidium*. A specific example is found in the document's number 160. In a commentary on canon 1398 §1, 2° of the 1983 code, the *Subsidium* seeks to distinguish the responsible authority for the various crimes of "recruiting or

---

9 In its third section, which is a commentary on the proper execution of an extrajdudicial process *ex* c. 1720 *CIC*, the *Subsidium* uses the term verisimilitude almost exclusively, rather than the less technical terminology used elsewhere.

10 In the original version of *VELM*, art. 3 §1 speaks not only of "notice" of a delict, which is the traditional language of c. 1717 *CIC*-1983, but also of "well-founded motives to believe," thereby introducing an entirely new standard of proof.

inducing" certain protected categories of persons to participate in pornographic exhibitions. The *Subsidium* states that canon 1398 §1, 2° of the 1983 code

> punishes in concrete terms the delict of a cleric who recruits or induces a minor under the age of eighteen or a person who habitually has an imperfect use of reason or is otherwise 'vulnerable' (cf. n. 159) to perform or participate in exhibitions of a pornographic nature, real or simulated. . . . As in the previous case, the delict is reserved to the Dicastery for the Doctrine of the Faith if it concerns minors or persons who habitually have an imperfect use of reason (art. 6 §1 NSST). . . .[11]

However, article 6 of the norms on reserved delicts[12] does not make any mention of recruiting or inducing anyone into participating in a pornographic exhibition. This language originally came from *Vos estis lux mundi*-2019.[13] The language was then inserted into the revised text of canon 1398 in the 2021 revisions of Book VI. The 2021 revision of the *Normae de delictis Congregationi pro Doctrina Fidei reservata*, deliberately updated after the promulgation of the revised Book VI, avoids this terminology in its article 6.[14] The delicts related to pornography in article 6 are limited to "acquisition, possession, exhibition, or distribution" thereof.[15] No mention is made of recruiting or inducing anyone to participate in

---

11 *Subsidium*, n. 160.

12 See *Norms on the Delicts Reserved to the Congregation for the Doctrine of the Faith*, as amended by the *Rescriptum ex audientia SS.mi dell'*11 October 2021 (NSST-2021).

13 See *VELM* art. 1 §1, a, 3:

> §1. These norms apply to reports regarding clerics or members of Institutes of Consecrated Life or Societies of Apostolic Life and concerning: a) delicts against the sixth commandment of the Decalogue consisting of: iii. the production, exhibition, possession or distribution, including by electronic means, of child pornography, as well as by the recruitment of or inducement of a minor or a vulnerable person to participate in pornographic exhibitions.

Eng. trans. at https://www.vatican.va/content/francesco/en/motu_proprio/documents/papa-francesco-motu-proprio-20190507_vos-estis-lux-mundi.html (accessed on 5 Jan. 2024).

14 See NSST-2021 art. 6, 1°:

> The more grave delicts against morals which are reserved to the judgment of the Congregation for the Doctrine of the Faith are: 1° the delict against the sixth commandment of the Decalogue committed by a cleric with a minor below the age of eighteen years or with a person who habitually has the imperfect use of reason; ignorance or error on the part of the cleric regarding the age of the minor does not constitute an extenuating or exonerating circumstance; 2° the acquisition, possession, exhibition, or distribution, for purposes of sexual gratification or profit, of pornographic images of minors under the age of eighteen years, in any manner and by any means whatsoever, by a cleric.

Eng. trans. at https://www.vatican.va/roman_curia/congregations/cfaith/documents/rc_con_cfaith_doc_20211011_norme-delittiriservati-cfaith_en.html (accessed on 5 Jan. 2024).

15 NSST-2021 art. 6, 2°.

pornography. This leads to a broader discussion of the nature of the new crimes introduced in canon 1398, which go beyond this very preliminary examination of the *Subsidium*. Suffice to say that the *Subsidium*, here, offers an interpretation of the norms regarding reserved delicts that does not appear to correspond to the text of the norms on reserved delicts.

Finally, in a similar vein, the third caveat comes from this same text: *Subsidium* number 160. As quoted above, this text implies the delict recruiting or inducing certain categories of protected persons to participate in the production of pornographic images. Here, the text states clearly: "As in the previous case, the delict is reserved to the Dicastery for the Doctrine of the Faith if it concerns minors or persons who habitually have an imperfect use of reason (art. 6 §1 NSST)." Similarly, in number 161, the *Subsidium* refers to the crimes listed in canon 1398 §1, 3° of the 1983 code:

> The Code incorporates in can. 1398 §1, 3° the delict configured by art. 6, 2° NSST concerning the acquisition, possession, or distribution by a cleric, in whatever manner and by whatever technology, of pornographic images of minors or of persons who habitually have an imperfect use of reason.[16]

At no point, however, does article 6 of the 2021 amended norms on reserved delicts make mention of pornography and persons who habitually have an imperfect use of reason. While the norm regarding child pornography has been modified several times by interventions of Pope Francis,[17] at no point have the norms on reserved delicts been modified to reserve to the exclusive competence of the Dicastery for the Doctrine of the Faith any crime related to pornographic images of persons who habitually have an imperfect use of reason, with the notable exclusion of the production of such pornography, as the production of pornographic images has always been considered a violation of the sixth commandment of the Decalogue in the praxis of the Dicastery for the Doctrine of the Faith. In the revised version of the dicastery's "*Vademecum* on certain points of procedure in treating cases of sexual abuse of minors committed by clerics,

---

16 *Subsidium*, n. 161.

17 See, for example, *Rescriptum ex audientia SS.mi*, December 3, 2019: *AAS* 112 (2020) 70-71; Eng. trans. at https://www.vatican.va/roman_curia/secretariat_state/2019/documents/rc-seg-st-20191203_rescriptum_en.html (accessed on 5 Jan. 2024). Also, in the 2021 revision of NSST, the text of art. 6 includes, among the delictual actions regarding child pornography, "exhibition" of pornographic images, a crime initially introduced in *VELM*-2019 [art. 1 §1, a), iii.].

2.0,"[18] this specific topic is addressed: "Although the new canon 1398 §1, 2-3° CIC that entered into force on 8 December 2021 may have introduced a broader treatment of this matter, the competence of the DDF in this regard is still limited to those cases outlined in art. 6 SST."[19] Therefore, contrary to what the *Subsidium* would imply, the competence of the Dicastery for the Doctrine of the Faith in matters of pornography has not been expanded to include those categories found in canon 1398 § 1, 2-3° of the 1983 code that are not also contained in art. 6, 2° of the amended norms on reserved delicts.

3. *Vos estis lux mundi* – 2023

Given that the original norms of *Vos estis lux mundi* were promulgated in 2019 for an *ad experimentum* period of three years, close watchers expected that changes would be introduced by the expiration of that triennial period. Nevertheless, the "due date" of 31 May 2022 (three years after the effective date of 1 June 2019) passed with not so much as a mention of the expiration of the legislation. Rather than address this *lacuna*, like a lightning bolt out of a clear blue sky, on 25 March 2023, Pope Francis issued a revised version of *Vos estis*, this time in a definitive manner. On the topic of any possible *lacuna*, rather than specifically mention the expiration of the previous version of 31 May 2022, the new text simply stated:

> In this regard, I promulgated an Apostolic Letter issued *Motu Proprio* on 7 May 2019 containing norms *ad experimentum* for three years. Now that this period has passed, taking into consideration the observations of the Episcopal Conferences and the Dicasteries of the Roman Curia, having evaluated the experience of these past years, and in order to facilitate an improved application of what has been established, without prejudice to the penal and procedural provisions set forth in the Code of Canon Law and the Code of Canons of the Eastern Churches, I decree. . . .[20]

Without offering a detailed analysis of the text, it is important to note that its promulgation fills a serious *lacuna*—in the opinion of the author—created by

18 See DDF, *Vademecum* on certain points of procedure in treating cases of sexual abuse of minors committed by clerics, 2.0, June 6, 2022: *AAS* 114 (2022) 918-954. Hereafter, *Vademecum*.

19 *Vademecum*, 6; Eng. trans. at https://www.vatican.va/roman_curia/congregations/cfaith/ddf/rc_ddf_doc_20220605_vademecum-casi-abuso-2.0_en.html (accessed on 5 Jan. 2024).

20 Francis, m.p. *Vos estis lux mundi*, March 25, 2023: *L'Osservatore Romano* (March 25, 2023); Eng. trans. at https://www.vatican.va/content/francesco/en/motu_proprio/documents/20230325-motu-proprio-vos-estis-lux-mundi-aggiornato.html (accessed on 5 Jan. 2024).

the revision of Book VI. In an intentional decision to avoid the terminology of "vulnerable person" introduced in *Vos estis lux mundi*-2019,[21] the legislator added the phrase "person for whom the law recognizes equal protection"[22] to that offered to minors and to persons who habitually have an imperfect use of reason. The only place the law offers such a protection was found in *Vos estis lux mundi*-2019. With the technical expiration of *Vos estis* and the lack of renewed definition of the category of "vulnerable person," a *lacuna legis* existed.

While the definition of "vulnerability" is not altered in the 2023 version, *Vos estis lux mundi* now refers to "vulnerable adults" as opposed to "vulnerable persons," which would appear to be a distinction without a real difference. What is different, however, is that *Vos estis* has expanded the category of persons to which its norms are applicable to now include not only clerics and members of institutes of consecrated life or societies of apostolic life, but also "Moderators of international associations of the faithful recognized or erected by the Apostolic See."[23] A list of such organizations (while it is unknown how up to date it might be) can be found on the website of the now-rebranded Pontifical Council for the Laity.[24] This list includes 122 different organizations, ranging from the very well known (e.g., *Regnum Christi*, *Heralds of the Gospel*, and *Cooperators of Opus Dei*) to the less well known. All their supreme moderators, as of 30 April 2023, are now subject to the norms of *Vos estis*.

Another significant modification that has been made is the language of article 1. In 2019, article 1 of *Vos Estis* spoke of "delicts against the sixth commandment of the Decalogue" and then expressly limited them to specific categories:

> i. forcing someone, by violence or threat or through abuse of authority, to perform or submit to sexual acts; ii. performing sexual acts with a minor or a vulnerable person; iii. the production exhibition, possession

---

21 See *Subsidium*, n. 159:
> The Code has avoided using the expression "vulnerable subject" here, as it represents a notion that is not yet well-defined or doctrinally shared in the broad ambit in which canon law is in force. Therefore, the legislator prefers to use a formulation that was broad enough to include various forms of weakness and fragility of the victim.

22 *Codex Iuris Canonici auctoritate Ioannis Pauli PP. II promulgatus* (Vatican City: Libreria Editrice Vaticana, 1983); Eng. trans. in *Code of Canon Law, Latin-English Edition, New English Translation* (Washington, DC: Canon Law Society of America, 2023) c. 1398 §1, 1°. All subsequent English translations from this code will come from this source.

23 *VELM*-2023, art. 1, §1.

24 See Pontifical Council for the Laity, "International Associations of the Faithful: Directory," at https://www.vatican.va/roman_curia/pontifical_councils/laity/documents/rc_pc_laity_doc_20051114_associazioni_en.html (accessed on 5 Jan. 2024).

> or distribution, including by electronic means, of child pornography, as well as by the recruitment of or inducement of a minor or a vulnerable person to participate in pornographic exhibitions.[25]

This represented the first attempt to offer greater specificity to the category of "delict against the sixth commandment of the Decalogue." In fact, what this language did was create a division within the law such that the norms of *Vos estis* could have been interpreted as not incorporating all delicts against the sixth commandment of the Decalogue. This has been rectified in the revisions of 2023, such that article 1 speaks no longer of delicts against the sixth commandment of the Decalogue "consisting of" certain categories. While the language is still inconsistent with that found in other texts (specifically, c. 1398 and art. 6 NSST) the new version is more consistent with the canonical tradition than the initial text. An unexpected novelty is the fact that there is now a normative Latin version of the legislation.

The Concept of Vulnerability

The revisions introduced in the Eastern code and *Vos estis lux mundi*-2023 continue to raise questions about the governing law and the concept of "vulnerability." While the legislator avoided the use of the term in the revisions of Book VI and Title XXVII, the concept permeates both texts, perhaps leading to expectations that further clarity would have been introduced in a revised text of *Vos estis*. Rather than clarity, however, it appears that more confusion has been introduced.

As mentioned above, the revisions of Title XXVII particularly complicate the question. Before these revisions, the categories of persons to whom the law of the Church offered additional protection were minors, those who habitually have an imperfect use of reason, and "vulnerable persons/adults" as defined in *Vos estis*. Canon 1453" of the Eastern code, however, does not speak of any of these categories; rather, in what appears to be a genuine confusion of terminology, it echoes canon 909 §3 of the Eastern code and speaks of persons *usu rationis habitu caret*. The lack of the use of reason is clearly not the same as a habitual imperfect use of reason and should, in the opinion of the author, not be viewed as the intentional creation of a new category of vulnerability reserved to the Eastern Churches but, rather, as a simple mistake that, hopefully, will be clarified by the appropriate authority, in time. With this in mind, and given the recurrence of the topic, it is important to seek some greater clarity on the topic of "vulnerability."

---

25 *VELM*-2019, art. 1, §1, a, 1-3.

Setting aside the category of minor, which is clearly definable, both of the other categories of vulnerability defy easy definitions. Rather than definitions, the law offers descriptors that are indicative. There is less of an issue when it comes to the category of those who habitually have an imperfect use of reason. First, the category is limited to a single kind of vulnerability and one that can be measured in a concrete fashion. While the contours of the definition remain obscure, given that the category is subject to the exclusive competence of the Dicastery for the Doctrine of the Faith, there is also a final arbiter of what person falls into this category. The same cannot be said for that of the category of "vulnerable adult" created by *Vos estis*.

Again, it is helpful to consider the words of *Vos estis* art. 1 §2, b as descriptive rather than defining. What can be said about the form of vulnerability described in *Vos estis* is the following. First, it need only be temporary, not permanent, or even habitual. The peculiarity of this form of vulnerability is that it need only be present in the moment of a delict against the sixth commandment of the Decalogue against which *Vos estis* legislates. Second, because it is temporary, it can also be relational; this kind of vulnerability, in this person, can manifest itself only in relation to the perpetrator of the delict. Third, the vulnerability can be a physical or mental limitation; mental must be interpreted to include psychological conditions that go beyond those diagnosed as directly related to one's capacity to reason. Fourth, this condition must result in a deprivation of liberty. Again, given the Church's anthropology, liberty must be interpreted not only in the physical sense, but also as the freedom of conscience, such that psychological or spiritual pressure historically known as the manipulation of conscience, would create a kind of vulnerability in a person that would qualify under *Vos estis*. Finally, this deprivation of liberty, caused even only temporarily by a physical, mental, or psychological condition in relation to the perpetrator of a delict against the sixth commandment of the Decalogue must impact a person's ability to understand or resist a delict.[26]

A Look at Some of the Newer Delicts

Canon 1392 of the Latin Code; Canon 1446" §5 of the Eastern Code

The origin of this new delict is clearly the Special Faculties conceded to the then Congregation for the Clergy (and the Congregation for the Evangelization of

---

26 When *VELM* uses the expression "ability to understand or want or otherwise resist the offense," it is using a traditional category of moral and legal action: imputability. The "want" does not imply that the presumptive victim desired the sexual act, but rather the kind of volition that is necessary for one to commit a sin (or a crime).

the Peoples) by Pope Benedict XVI in 2009.[27] Unlike the Special Faculties, however, this new delict requires more than merely absence from an assignment. The unique formulation of the new crime includes a quasi-schismatic element: "the intent of withdrawing (himself) from the competent Church authority." Given that the unlawful absence need only be for six (6) months, and not the five (5) years foreseen in Special Faculties III, it is clear that there is an emphasis by the legislator on the other constitutive element of the delict. Therefore, it is imperative to have a clear understanding of what might demonstrate this "intent" in such a way as to allow a judge to arrive at moral certitude that this delict has been committed; similarly, a clear understanding will aid an ordinary in providing an appropriate warning to any cleric who might come into proximity of committing this delict (cf. c. 1339 *CIC*). In an effort to demonstrate what kinds of actions might indicate such an "intention," the following scenario is offered from a case of schism recently adjudicated by the Dicastery for the Doctrine of the Faith. While much of the information contained in the case is already within the public domain, no direct reference will be made to the persons and organizations involved in this case.

A priest offered a homily on a feast day that called into question certain aspects of the teaching of Vatican II. This homily was not only recorded and broadcast on electronic media, but the text was also later published in various on-line fora. Concerned that the criticisms of Vatican II in the homily constituted serious errors, the bishop approached the priest to discuss the matter. The bishop identified the particular error as schism, not heresy. The matter was examined by theologians and their point-by-point criticisms were shared with the priest. In an effort to reconcile the priest, the bishop asked him to sign a profession of faith. The priest did so, but then published a second work on the internet in which he reiterated all the problematic claims found in his original homily. The bishop sought advice from the then-Congregation for the Doctrine of the Faith, under the rubric of schism; the congregation authorized the bishop to adjudicate the matter by means of an extrajudicial process, given the lack of adequately trained canon lawyers in the diocese.

The priest was declared guilty in an extrajudicial decree against which recourse was then presented to the Dicastery for the Doctrine of the Faith. In responding to the arguments presented in recourse, the dicastery held the following. The statements of the cleric did, in fact, represent schism because they

---

27 See Sharon A. Euart and Siobhan M. Verbeek, eds., "Special Faculties for Congregation for Clergy: Administrative Procedures for the Laicization of Priests," *Roman Replies and CLSA Advisory Opinions 2009* (Washington, DC: Canon Law Society of America, 2009) 37-47.

were formulated to detract the speaker—and listeners and readers—from the authority of the Church. At a key point, the cleric posited that there are two groups within the Church: those who accept Vatican II as authoritative and, therefore, binding teaching; and those who, on the other hand, see the teachings of Vatican II as not binding, because they represent not pure, authentic Catholic teaching but rather a mix of authentic teaching and human speculation that leads to the reversal of certain elements of previously held Catholic doctrine. The key element in this decision is the intention of the cleric, demonstrated in public (a homily preached in an open church, later published on the internet),[28] to detract himself from the competent authority of the Church.

This specific case can provide some guidance in considering what kinds of actions might demonstrate a cleric's intention to withdraw himself from Church authority. Again, according to the foundational principles of penal law, the "intention" of the cleric must be demonstrable; that is, it must somehow be externalized in such a way that evidence can be entered into a canonical process which can then be used to support a juridical conclusion. To commit the crime found in canon 1392 of the Latin code and canon 1446" of the Eastern code it is not only necessary that a priest be unlawfully absent from his assignment for at least six months; the motive for this illegitimate absence must be related to a demonstrable intention to subtract himself from the competent ecclesiastical authority.

It could be based on public statements detracting from the authority of the cleric's own bishop. Similarly, it could be based on public statements that detract from the authority of the Roman Pontiff, or, as in the case above, the teaching authority of an ecumenical council. What must be attached in these public statements is the authority of the Church or of an office, not the character of the person in a role of authority. The canon is not designed to be used as a kind of litmus test for fealty; rather, it is designed to provide an innovative tool to help bishops respond to a new, and growing, phenomenon in a timely manner.

---

28 One question left unanswered in the DDF's rejection of the recourse was the question of how many such statements might be necessary to commit the delict of schism. The recourse posited that only one such statement was made; the dicastery responded that there were at least two separate publications repeating the same claims. Therefore, in this particular case, there is more than one example of the behavior in question.

Not New, but Helpful, Reminders

Penal Precept

Among the many tools at an ordinary's disposal, perhaps the most flexible is the penal precept (cf. c. 1319 *CIC*; c. 1406 *CCEO*). The purpose of a penal precept is to penalize a behavior that is not expressly covered in the penal norms of the code. It can mandate, or prohibit, certain actions. As such, it can be modified to meet the specific needs of a particular situation; it can be limited in duration; it can be as specific as necessary to respond to a legitimate concern of an ordinary. The precept must, however, clearly state the penalty to which an actor will be subject upon violation.

As such, the penalty must be guided by the principal of proportionality. The proportionality is not merely a balance between the gravity of the action prohibited or mandated and the severity of the penalty, but the penalty must proportionately correspond to the nature of the offense. Another question that must be considered, particularly when seeking to limit the exercise of priestly faculties, is the distinction between those faculties conceded by the bishop (i.e., for the hearing of confessions: cf. cc. 966-969 *CIC*) and those granted by the law itself. This is an issue that will require greater clarity, given the common use of a penal precept to prohibit all public sacramental ministry of clerics.

Particular Law

One of the most underused tools in penal law is particular law. Setting aside the most prominent example of a national particular law (the *Essential Norms*), on the local level, there are many issues that can, and should be, addressed through this mechanism. One such issue is the use of social media by clerics. While many dioceses have already formulated "policies" in this regard, it is important to consider the question of enforceability, which is inherent in the promulgation of penal law. To do so, the norms of canons 1315,[29] 1317,[30] and 1327[31] must be kept in mind.

It is estimated that only 10% of the American population over the age of twelve made use of social media in 2008. In 2021, that percentage was estimated at 82%, meaning that more than 230 million adults in the United States of America regularly use social media.[32] The various forms of social media range from the entirely innocuous, to those whose very purpose as stated by the creators runs contrary to Catholic moral teaching,[33] to morally ambiguous ones, designed to exchange thought or information, but not conceptualized as platforms for meeting new people.[34] Even those forms of social media not designed with a sexual end or intended to help people meet have come to be used to this end.[35] For questions of clerical continence and issues of scandal, perhaps the most problematic of the various forms of social media is the genre generally referred to as "dating apps."

Recent studies estimate the total revenue of the top ten "dating apps" at over $3 billion, with projected growth over the next few years to top $6 billion.[36] In

---

29 See c. 1315:
§1. One who has power to issue penal laws can also reinforce a divine law with an appropriate penalty. §2. A lower legislator, attentive to can. 1317, can also: 1° reinforce with an appropriate penalty a law issued by a higher authority observing the limits of his competence by reason of territory or of persons; 2° add other penalties to the penalties established by universal law for some delict; 3° make determinate or obligatory a penalty established by universal law as indeterminate or facultative.

30 See c. 1317: "Penalties are to be established only in so far as they are truly necessary to provide more suitable for ecclesiastical discipline. A lower legislator, however, cannot establish the penalty of Dismissal from the clerical state."

31 See c. 1327: "Particular law can establish other exempting, mitigating, or aggravating circumstances besides the cases mentioned in cann. 1323-1326, either by general norm or for individual delicts. Likewise, circumstances can be established in a precept that exempt from, mitigate, or increase a penalty established by the precept."

32 See Jay Baer, "Social Media Usage Statistics for 2021 Reveal Surprising Shifts," blog *Convince&Convert*, undated, at https://www.convinceandconvert.com/social-media-research/social-media-usage-statistics/ (accessed on 5 Jan. 2023).

33 *Grindr* and its notorious slogan, "Get on to get off" and *Down* with its "get down" button.

34 *Facebook* or *Instagram*, for example.

35 The use of *Twitter* or *Instagram* or *SnapChat* as "hook-up" apps has grown exponentially and is, likely, destined to continue to do so. See, e.g., Ginny Hogan, "How Twitter Accidentally became My Go-To Dating App," *The Bold Italic*, Feb. 10, 2020, at https://thebolditalic.com/how-twitter-accidentally-became-my-go-to-dating-app-7559054527e1 (accessed on 5 Jan. 2024).

36 See David Curry, "Dating App Revenue and Usage Statistics (2023), *Business of Apps*, May 2, 2023, at https://www.businessofapps.com/data/dating-app-market/ (accessed on 5 Jan. 2024).

the United States, alone, there are an estimated 13 million monthly active users on *Grindr*, 75 million for *Tinder*,[37] and over 30 million for *Tinder*'s rival, *Bumble*.[38] Interestingly, of the top eight apps in this classification, only *Grindr* and *Bumble* are not owned by IAC, Inc. (an American holding company specializing in media and internet companies). This is pertinent because it is related to the availability of tracking data generated by these apps, which are all geolocation based.

These apps pose a particular threat to prudence and clerical continence. The specific use of geolocation technology in these apps generates a "hook-up" mentality that leads to a greater risk to the health, safety, and reputation of clerics. Rather than a "wandering-eye," such apps are designed to facilitate the immediate meeting up of two-or-more persons; this immediacy leads to a greater risk of poor decisions than previously possible, without the immediate risk of exposure. However, such geolocation technology also facilitates the discovery of the identity of the persons using these apps by third parties who might obtain access to this data, some of which is commercially available.

Beyond the obvious risk of scandal, there is also a high risk to personal health (sexually transmitted diseases) and safety (risk of crime, extortion, etc.). In canonical terms, the use of these apps indicates a high degree of imputability, as they are expressly designed to facilitate violations of the sixth commandment of the Decalogue and it is difficult, if not impossible, to imagine any legitimate, moral usage thereof by a cleric.

In formulating any particular law in this regard, one important distinction to be remembered is that between sin and crime. In the Church's history, the topic of penal law has always been intimately connected with moral theology. The definition of sexual crimes in the Church always includes a reference to the sixth commandment of the Decalogue. The Church has never legislated against all violations of the sixth commandment of the Decalogue and the current draft intends to maintain the important distinction between sin and crime. A simple line could be drawn: accessing internet-based pornography could not be criminalized; the exchange of pornographic images with an adult, the use of sexualized language in virtual conversations with adults and any use of a "dating app," even inscription or creating a profile therein, is behavior that could be punished.

---

37 See Barry Elad, "Tinder Statistics – By Users, Demographic, Match Rate, Country, Usage and Social Media Traffic," *Enterprise Apps Today*, May 1, 2023, at https://www.enterpriseappstoday.com/stats/tinder-statistics.html (accessed on 5 Jan. 2024).

38 "Bumble Revenue and Usage Statistics 2023," *HelpLama*, last updated December 2023, at https://helplama.com/bumble-revenue-usage-statistics/ (accessed on 5 Jan. 2024).

Concluding Thoughts

The past few years have brought many dramatic changes to the penal law of the Church. Both codes have been revised; the norms of delicts reserved to the Dicastery for the Doctrine of the Faith have been updated; *Vos estis lux mundi* has been modified and promulgated in a definitive version. At the same time, the work of the Apostolic Signatura has continued to refine various administrative questions—which often mimic penal actions—through its jurisprudence. More recently, the Dicastery for the Clergy has also offered an interesting opinion or two that will require further study.[39] The constant change in law makes it even more necessary that different voices in the Church continue to raise questions and pose them to the appropriate authorities for the kinds of clarification necessary for the proper application of the law, an application that respects the legitimate rights of all parties involved. The ever-changing landscape of pastoral ministry in the 21st century also demands more efforts at developing particular law, responding to specific needs that arise in a diocese or region. Finally, as always, the more practitioners share their experiences, the better all can serve the needs of the Church.

39 The decisions of the dicastery referred to here have not yet been made public, but they deal with the interrelation between precautionary measures, penalties, and administrative restrictions imposed during recourse taken against an extrajudicial decree imposing a penalty.

CLSA PROCEEDINGS 85 (2023) 172-204

SEMINAR

UNASSIGNABLE PRIESTS: WHAT'S A BISHOP TO DO?

Reverend Monsignor Patrick R. Lagges. JCD

Six short scenarios, adapted from real life:

1. (Adapted from a question on the Canon Law Discussion Group) A priest has fathered a child, unbeknownst to his bishop. He is going in to confess to his bishop but wishes to remain in ministry. What's a bishop to do?

2. A pastor embezzles close to one million dollars over time. All of the money is found in a safety deposit box at a local bank. None has been spent. Civil authorities were notified, and the priest has served time in prison. Upon his release, he comes to see his bishop about a new assignment. What's a bishop to do?

3. A pastor embezzles several hundred thousand dollars and spends it at the track. After being caught, he says that he was just waiting for a big payday so that he could return all the money to the parish. Upon his release from prison, he comes to his bishop about a new assignment. What's a bishop to do?

4. In his first pastorate in a poor parish, a pastor buys things that the parish needs with his own money, and then pays himself back when the parish has the funds. There are no records kept, other than the checks to reimburse that pastor for the money he says he spent. The parish experiences more financial problems and eventually closes. The bishop decides that what the pastor needs is mentoring, so sends him to an established pastor as a parochial vicar. After six months, the bishop assigns the priest to a new pastorate, with the same results. The bishop removes him but the pastor seeks recourse. After the recourse fails, the priest comes to the bishop for a new assignment, telling the bishop, "I think I've got this figured out." What's a bishop to do?

5. A priest is accused of sexual misconduct with a minor. It is the only accusation and dates back more than thirty years. The Dicastery for the Doctrine of the Faith mandates a penal trial be conducted. The tribunal

reaches a decision of *non constat*. The priest comes to the bishop to see about future ministry. What's a bishop to do?

6. A young priest has had five assignments as parochial vicar in his first seven years after ordination. All of the assignments have ended because of his inability to work with the lay staff at the parish and with the parish deacons. His last request for a transfer was because "There is not sufficient distinction here between the ordained priesthood and the priesthood of the faithful." What's a bishop to do?

As Lawrence Dobkin solemnly intoned each week at the end of an episode of the TV detective program *Naked City*, "There are eight million stories in the Naked City. This has been one of them." For those of you who have dealt with the above such stories, you no doubt know several other ones.

The topic that I was given for this seminar was "unassignable priests." That implies that the priest is seeking an assignment. So, this seminar will not deal with the removal process for priests who are currently in an assignment,[1] nor any of the other processes described in the chapter on "Loss of Ecclesiastical Office" (cc. 184-196).[2] It will also not deal with the process of inflicting penalties[3] or the special faculties[4] that were granted to the Congregation for the Clergy in 2009 or the process for seeking a dispensation from the obligations of the clerical state.[5] (I will make reference to those processes but not describe them in depth.) Those are topics for other talks, hopefully given by someone else. I will also only be dealing with diocesan priests of the Western Church. The assignment of religious priests would be covered in their respective constitutions; and the Eastern code approaches the topic in a slightly different way.

---

1 See, e.g., cc. 1740-1747 for the removal of pastors.

2 See *Codex Iuris Canonici auctoritate Ioannis Pauli PP. II promulgatus* (Vatican City: Libreria Editrice Vaticana, 1983). Book I, Title IX, Chapter II lists five different ways of losing ecclesiastical office: lapse of time (c. 186), resignation (cc. 187-189), transfer (cc. 190-191), removal (cc. 192-195), and privation (c. 196). One might also add "death," although that is not mentioned in the Code.

3 The Dicastery for Legislative Texts released a "user's guide" for the infliction of penalties and the imposition of other disciplinary measures, such as warnings, precepts, penances, and decrees on 31 May 2023. See Dicastery for Legislative Texts, *Penal Sanctions in the Church: User Guide for Book VI of the Code of Canon Law* (Vatican City: Libreria Editrice Vaticana, 2023), available online at https://www.delegumtextibus.va/content/dam/testilegislativi/TESTI%20NORMATIVI/Testi%20Norm%20CIC/Libro%20VI/LibroVIsussidio/Penal%20sanctions%20User%20guide.pdf (accessed on 5 Feb. 2024).

4 Three special faculties were given to the Dicastery for the Clergy and announced in letters to all bishops and superiors on 18 April 2009 (PN 2009 0556) and 17 March 2010 (PN 2010 0823).

5 These can be found in the revised *Clergy Procedural Handbook,* which will be published by the Canon Law Society of America.

I highly recommend that you obtain the two volumes of *Ministerium Iustitiae* by Bill Daniel.[6] This is an invaluable collection of jurisprudence from the Apostolic Signatura on a wide variety of topics which heretofore we have not had access. The Signatura makes very careful distinctions regarding matters with which bishops and canonists must deal in these and other cases.

Having told you all the things that I will not talk about, it may leave you wondering what I *will* talk about.

My starting point will be canon 149, which says that to be appointed to an office in the Church, one must be "suitable." I'll then take a look at the canons on ordination regarding what qualities a candidate for ordination ought to have to be suitable for ministry. Briefly, I will talk about the distinction between "ministry" and "office" in the code, which will also lead to a discussion about "remuneration" and "sustenance." In addition to the canons on ordination, the Church has also recently promulgated a *Ratio fundamentalis*[7] regarding formation for priestly ministry, which has led to the United States Conference of Catholic Bishops issuing its sixth edition of the *Program of Priestly Formation in the United States of America*.[8] The latter document will be examined more closely to see how it envisions preparing suitable priests in the Church. Then various places in the code will be examined that might make a person "unsuitable" for office, and some remedies in the law, as well as some suggestions in the law that would help the bishop to find a person "suitable" or "unsuitable" for office. Finally, I will return to my original question, "What's a bishop to do?"

---

6 See William Daniel, translator and compiler, *Mimisterium Iustitiae: Jurisprudence of the Supreme Tribunal of the Apostolic Signatura, Official Latin with English Translation*, vol. I, Gratianus Series, (Montreal: Wilson & Lafleur Ltee, 2011), and William Daniel, translator and compiler, *Ministerium Iustitiae: The Lex propria and more recent contentious-administrative jurisprudence of the Supreme Tribunal of the Apostolic Signatura*, vol. II, Gratianus Series, (Montreal: Wilson & Lafleur Ltee, 2021) (hereinafter *Ministerium Iustitiae* vol. I and *Ministerium Iustitiae* vol II).

7 Congregation for the Clergy, *Ratio fundamentalis institutionis sacerdotalis,* December 8, 2016: https://www.vatican.va/roman_curia/congregations/cclergy/documents/rc_con_cclergy_doc_20161208_ratio-fundamentalis-institutionis-sacerdotalis_it.pdf (accessed on 5 Feb. 2024); Eng. trans. at: https://www.clerus.va/content/dam/clerus/Ratio%20Fundamentalis/The%20Gift%20of%20the%20Priestly%20Vocation.pdf (accessed on 5 Feb. 2024) (RFIS). See also the talk by Rev. Phil Brown, PSS, in this issue at: Phil Brown, "*Ratio Fundamentalis Institutionis Sacerdotalis*, PPF6. and the Code of Canon Law," *CLSA Proceedings 85* (2023) 46-67.

8 Committee on Clergy, Consecrated Life and Vocations of the United States Conference of Catholic Bishops, *Program of Priestly Formation*, sixth edition (Washington, DC: USCCB, 2022) (PPF).

Provision for Ecclesiastical Office

While the Code of Canon Law provides various ways of obtaining an ecclesiastical office,[9] the most common way is through free conferral.[10] While the canons provide various ways that presentation, election, and postulation might take place, canon 157 simply states that the diocesan bishop can provide for ecclesiastical office through free conferral. This does not necessarily mean that the diocesan bishop makes the decision completely by himself. For the assignment of priests, for example, many dioceses have a "priest placement board" or a "priest personnel board" or some other type of advisory group to assist him in doing this. Generally, these consultative bodies are made up exclusively of priests, but there is no reason why a bishop might not also have lay persons who assist him in making the free conferral.

There are some criteria in the law, however, that assist the bishop in providing for ecclesiastical offices in his diocese. The general requirement is found in canon 149 §1, which states that in order to obtain an ecclesiastical office, a person must be in the communion of the Church[11] and suitable, which the canon goes on to say means that they are "endowed with those qualities which are

---

9 Free conferral (c. 157), presentation (cc. 158-163), election (cc. 164-179), and postulation (cc. 180-183). Canon 149 §3 also mentions simony, but that is invalid by the law itself.

10 See c. 157: "Unless the law explicitly establishes otherwise, it is for the diocesan bishop to provide for ecclesiastical offices in his own particular church by free conferral." Eng. trans. from *Code of Canon Law: Latin–English Edition. New English Translation* (Washington, DC: CLSA, 2023). All English translations from this code will be taken from this source unless otherwise indicated. It should be noted that the canon does not specify the process a bishop might undertake to confer an office freely. As long as the bishop himself is making the determination, how he goes about it could be the subject of particular law. We might learn a lesson from the way that we applied canon 1717 after the Essential Norms. The bishop makes the decision, but he is assisted by his review board, which makes recommendations as to whether an accusation "at least seems to be true" and whether the matter ought to be further investigated and/or prosecuted.

11 Note that it does not say "in the full communion of the Church." Canon 204 states that the Christian faithful consists of those "who have been incorporated in Christ through baptism," with canon 205 specifying that the baptized are "fully in the communion of the Catholic Church on this earth who are joined with Christ in its visible structure by the bonds of profession of faith, the sacraments, and ecclesiastical governance."

required for that office by universal or particular law[12] or by the law of the foundation."[13]

A Presumption of Suitability?

In the question of suitability, we can first look at the canons that deal with the suitability for ordination. These canons give us an idea of how the person has been judged or how he's been found, leading up to his ordination. There are certain things that are specified in the law, and certain things that we find in the Program of Priestly Formation.

Canon 1025 §1 states that the candidate for ordination must have completed the period of probation that is specified in law (in this case, the Program of Priestly Formation), and "is endowed in the judgment of his own bishop or of the competent major superior with the necessary qualities, is prevented by no irregularity and no impediment, and has fulfilled the prerequisites according to the norm of cann. 1033-1039."[14] This same paragraph specifies that certain documents are to be obtained, according to a process established by the bishop or superior, according to canon 1051. These documents include "testimonial letters, public announcements, or other sources of information."[15] In 1997, the Congregation for Divine Worship and the Discipline of the Sacraments issued a

---

12 Bishops often look to universal law when making appointments to offices, but there is also ample room in this canon for a bishop to establish particular law for his diocese. This particular law could also specify what sort of things can be required of a person in a particular diocese. This would allow for regional specifications.

13 Canon 149 §2 provides for the situation where a person may not be "suitable" for an office when it states, "Provision of an ecclesiastical office to one who lacks the requisite qualities is invalid only if the qualities are expressly required for the validity of the provision by universal law or particular law or by the law of the foundation. Otherwise it is valid but can be rescinded by decree of competent authority or by sentence of an administrative tribunal."

14 Canon 1388 §2 provides that the voluntary concealment of an irregularity results in the person who has thus advanced to holy orders "is *ipso facto* suspended from the order received, in addition to what is established in can. 1044 §2, n. 1."

15 Canon 1051, 2°: "[I]n order to conduct the investigation properly, the diocesan bishop or major superior can employ other means which seem useful to him according to the circumstances of time and place, such as testimonial letters, public announcements, or other sources of information." Perhaps the "circumstances of time and place" that exist today are not the same ones that existed in the past. Most dioceses require some sort of periodic written evaluation of the seminarian. Perhaps there is room for some development in terms of what the seminarian is being evaluated on, and who is doing the evaluation.

circular letter which further explained to ordinaries what was to be included in a candidate's file.[16]

In addition, canon 1029 further specifies those other qualities of those to be promoted to ordination:

> Only those are to be promoted to orders who, in the prudent judgment of their own bishop or of the competent major superior, all things considered [*omnibus perpensis*] have integral faith, are moved by the right intention, have the requisite knowledge, possess a good reputation, and are endowed with integral morals and proven virtues and the other physical and psychic qualities in keeping with the order to be received.[17]

In addition, canon 1025 §2 says that the diocesan bishop or major superior must consider the candidate as "useful for the ministry of the Church."[18]

There also exists a kind of tension in the canons regarding orders. After maintaining that a candidate must possess "due freedom" to be ordained, canon 1026 states, "It is absolutely forbidden [*nefas est*] to force anyone in any way or for any reason to receive orders, or to deter one who is canonically suitable from receiving them." The other canons, as well as the documents from the Holy See, including the *Ratio fundamentalis* and its specification by the United States Conference of Catholic Bishops, state the other things that would make a candidate "canonically suitable." And canon 1030 establishes the presumption that someone who has been ordained to the diaconate will be ordained to the presbyterate, unless there is a canonical cause for not doing so.

But, even with that, canon 1052 provides one final possibility, when it states in paragraph 3: "If, all these notwithstanding, the bishop doubts for specific

---

16 See Congregation for Divine Worship the Discipline of the Sacraments, circular letter concerning Scrutinies regarding the Suitability of Candidates for Orders, November 10, 1997, https://www.usccb.org/resources/circular-letter-congregation-divine-worship-discipline-sacraments (accessed on 5 Feb. 2024).

17 Canon 1029.

18 As pointed out in the *Code of Canon Law Annotated,* 4th edition: "In the practice of the first centuries, ordinations were relative: a cleric was ordained to occupy a specific office. The number of clerics to be ordained and the degree of orders to which they were to be promoted was determined by the number and type of vacant offices." Juan I. Arrieta, ed., *Code of Canon Law Annotated*, 4th ed. (Montreal: Wilson & Lafleur, 2022) 780. As the concept of ordination developed and absolute ordinations occurred, there were requirements for a title (e.g., benefice). This disappeared in the 1983 code, where the concept of suitability was considered sufficient. In the 1917 code, this was referred to as being suitable for "service to the diocese." Ibid. The 1983 code expanded this to refer to beneficial to the ministry of the Church.

reasons whether a candidate is suitable to receive orders, he is not to promote him" (c. 1052 §3). Robert Geisinger, SJ, wrote:

> Ordinaries must be cautious indeed not to encourage persons whose ministerial fitness and utility are in doubt. One might hope that a man will develop positively, but if such growth is not likely, it is unjust to all parties concerned to encourage him. . . . In such situations, the faithful have had thrust upon them a sacred minister who might well be a burden—and even a source of damage or scandal—in their common and individual spiritual lives.[19]

Therefore, when someone is ordained to the ministry, there is a presumption that he has been found suitable for the ministry of the Church. As we know from canon 1584, a presumption is "a probable conjecture about an uncertain matter," which always yields to the truth. A bishop or superior cannot be absolutely certain that the candidate is "suitable." Likewise, just like no one comes to sacraments such as baptism or marriage fully formed, the priest will not be ordained fully formed in the priesthood. The sacrament of orders will be expected to develop and flourish under the grace of God, just as the sacraments of baptism and marriage are expected to do. The bishop will always ordain a "work in progress."

Suitability for What?

A distinction has to be made here between suitability for ordination and suitability for an office in the Church. As mentioned above, in the early Church, there was no such distinction: a person was ordained for a certain office in the Church. But with the development of the concept of "office," and with the number of different "offices" in the Church, the two concepts gradually moved apart. As mentioned above, we moved from ordination to a certain office, to the concept of absolute ordination, to the concept of ordination to a particular title, to the concept

---

19 Robert Geisinger, "Orders," in John Beal, James Coriden, and Thomas Green, eds, *New Commentary on the Code of Canon Law* (New York: Paulist Press, 2000) (CLSA Commentary) 1205.

of ordination to ministry in a particular church, to the present-day concept of ordination to ministry in the Church.[20]

However, a distinction still has to be made between suitability for ordination, and suitability for ecclesiastical office. The above-mentioned canons and the Program for Priestly Formation can give us the criteria for suitability for ordination. We have to look further to see what is meant by suitability for office.

The Code of Canon Law does not simply refer to a generic ordination. There are certain distinctions that are made in the law concerning what the person is ordained to. For example, someone ordained into a religious institute must be formed in the charism of that institute. Canon 646 states that during the novitiate, the novices "better understand their divine vocation, and indeed one which is proper to the institute, experience the manner of living of the institute, and form their mind and heart in its spirit . . . ." In this way, "their intention and suitability are tested."[21] Likewise, canon 659 states that after first profession formation should continue for members "so that they lead the proper life of the institute more fully and carry out its mission more suitably."[22] Thus, the suitability of the person for ordination is directed toward the life of the institute, and not simply some generic form of priestly life. It could very well be that someone is suitable for priesthood, but not suitable for priesthood in this institute. Their formation is directed toward a particular goal: the life of the institute. It is very focused.

For diocesan priests, the task is not so focused in the law. Benedict XVI, in an address to priests and religious in Warsaw on 25 May 2006 said: "The faithful expect only one thing from priests: that they be specialists in promoting the encounter between man and God. . . . [W]hat the faithful expect from him is that

---

20 This broadening of the ministry of priests comes from the Decree on the Ministry and Life of Priests: "The spiritual gift which priests receive at their ordination prepared them not for a sort of limited and narrow mission but for the widest possible and universal mission of salvation 'even to the ends of the earth' (Acts 1:8)." Paul VI, Decree on the Ministry and Life of Priests *Presbyterorum ordinis* 10, December 7, 1965: *AAS* 58 (1965) 1007; Eng. trans. at https://www.vatican.va/archive/hist_councils/ii_vatican_council/documents/vat-ii_decree_19651207_presbyterorum-ordinis_en.html (accessed on 22 Mar. 2024). The decree goes on to say that each priest must have a solicitude for all the churches (with which *Christus dominus* also tasks bishops) and that dioceses should freely allow priests to serve in other places where they are needed. There have been numerous documents to this effect subsequent to Vatican II, such that the "suitability" which is mentioned in the canons is broadened beyond the individual diocese.

21 Canon 646.

22 Canon 659 §1.

he be a witness to the eternal wisdom contained in the revealed word."[23] Quite the job description! However, just like with religious institutes, it might be possible that the ministry to which diocesan priests are ordained can be circumscribed by the particular church into which they are ordained, leaving room for the possibility of the just distribution of priests called for at Vatican II. There could be a list of more specific tasks that a candidate would be expected to accomplish in order for him to be deemed suitable for ordination into this particular church. Through ordination, a priest is incardinated into a specific particular church. His suitability needs to be determined in relation to the ministry he will be expected to do.[24]

Ministry vs. Office

There are a number of things mentioned in the code that a priest is expected to do. These might form the basis for evaluating his suitability for ministry prior to ordination, or his suitability for ecclesiastical office once he has been ordained. Some of these tasks are found in canons 273-289. For example, a priest is to show reverence and obedience to the Roman Pontiff and to his own ordinary (c. 273). Thus, his attitude toward authority is something which needs to be considered. If someone proves himself to be "a law unto himself," is he suitable for ministry in a church which is hierarchical? Priests are also expected to be united among themselves (c. 275 §1). In their preparation for ordination, the Program for Priestly Formation states, "Seminarians are to be fully committed to the life of the seminary community and are to learn how to contribute generously to it and to receive humbly from its resources" (n. 154). This should carry over into their lives as priests and their relationship to the presbyterate. How well the seminarian has accomplished this is part of his evaluation for suitability for ministry. It can also be considered in his evaluation for suitability for ecclesiastical office. Does he recognize himself as part of a presbyterate? Or does he see himself as a "Lone Ranger?"

The Code of Canon Law also specifies that the priest is to acknowledge and promote the mission of the laity (c. 275 §2); to pursue holiness (c. 276 §1); to act as a dispenser of the mysteries of God in the service of his people (c. 276 §1); to fulfill the duties of the pastoral ministry (c. 276 §2); and to nourish his spiritual life through the celebration of the eucharist, praying the liturgy of the hours, making time for mental prayer, and to make a spiritual retreat (c. 276). His

23 Benedict XVI, "Speech to Priests and Religious in the Cathedral of Warsaw," May 25, 2006; Eng. trans. at https://www.vatican.va/content/benedict-xvi/en/speeches/2006/may/documents/hf_ben-xvi_spe_20060525_poland-clergy.html (accessed on 5 Feb. 2024).

24 This could perhaps be accomplished through the handbook that each seminary is to have.

behavior is to promote perfect and perpetual continence (c. 277) and to refrain from things unbecoming or foreign to the clerical state (c. 285). In order to further his intellectual and spiritual life, he is to pursue sacred studies and studies in the other sciences (c. 279); to foster simplicity of life (c. 282); and to foster peace and harmony based on justice (c. 287).

All of these things form part of the person's formation for ordination as well. They are things that the seminarian will be evaluated on. They are also things that all priests are expected to do. They could also be used to evaluate how well the priest is suited for an ecclesiastical office. Has he been faithful to the specific things that are required of him as a priest?

Remuneration and Sustenance

There are also things to which canon 281 refers as deserving "remuneration which is consistent with their condition." This has been a much-debated topic with regard to priests who are not engaged in any ministry. Is the diocese still obligated to pay them?[25]

The Latin code is not entirely clear on the subject. It says that the priest deserves remuneration "which is consistent with their condition, taking into account the nature of their function and the conditions of places and times . . ." (c. 281). This seems to indicate that there could be different levels of compensation, depending on the condition of the priest, the nature of their function, and the conditions of places and times. But is that all considered *remuneration*, taking into account various aspects of the priest's life? Or do all priests have to receive the same amount of compensation? Some have argued that a priest removed from ministry, or a priest unable to engage in ministry should still receive the same compensation as every other priest of the diocese. Others have maintained that "the nature of their function and the conditions of places and times" would allow the diocese to reduce the compensation for priests not engaged in ministry. Others have maintained that if the priest is not ministering, he should not be paid.[26]

---

25 See, especially, Richard Bona, *The Right to Ministry, Remuneration, and Support of Unassignable Incardinated Presbyters: A Canonical Analysis* (Washington DC: The Catholic University of America, 2019) and M.J. Guevara, "Unassignable Priests and Their Remuneration," unpublished JCL thesis (Washington, DC: The Catholic University of America, 2015).

26 This clearly cannot be sustained. The Second Vatican Council clearly avoided using the term "salary" when referring to the compensation owed to priests. Subsequent documents have also warned against referring to priests' compensation as "salary," or viewing priests as "employees." The preferred terms are "sustenance" and "remuneration." The notion is delineated more in the Eastern code.

The Code of Canons of the Eastern Churches does not contain such ambiguities. Canon 390 §1 of the Eastern code states, "Clerics have the right to suitable support [*sustentationem*] and to receive a just remuneration [*remunerationem*] for carrying out the office or function committed to them."[27] Thus it refers to both "remuneration" and "support," with "support" indicating what all priests receive, and "remuneration" indicating compensation for the ministry performed. The Eastern code also refers to this as a "right," a term which is not used in the Latin code. As W. Becket Soule has described it:

> The Eastern code also distinguishes between *sustenance* and *remuneration*: the first is associated with a man being a cleric, and the second is associated with an office or function. Sustenance would mean that a cleric is given sufficient resources to live on (such as a place to live and provision for necessities of life); remuneration, however, extends beyond what is necessary to meet basic needs, and it would cover continuing education, a vacation, hospitality, charitable giving, and the ability to maintain a reasonable standard of living.[28]

Soule further opines, "In the case of a cleric who is not involved in active ministry, such as one who is sick, disabled, retired, or unable to be assigned, the canon appears to state that he is due sustenance, even where he is not to receive remuneration."[29]

This can also be seen in a more careful reading of Latin canon 281. The canon starts out by stating, "Since clerics dedicate themselves to ecclesiastical ministry [*cum minsterio ecclesiastico se dedicant]. . . .*" This refers to what they did at their ordination; they dedicated themselves, not to their own benefit, but to the ministry of the Church. Because of this dedication, they are owed "remuneration" (which involves, in the Latin code, "taking into account the nature

---

27 *Codex Canonum Ecclesiarum Orientalium auctoritate Ioannis Pauli PP. II promulgatus* (Vatican City: Libreria Editrice Vaticana, 1990) (*CCEO*) c. 27. Eng. trans. from *Code of Canons of the Eastern Churches, Latin-English Edition* (Washington, DC: CLSA, 1992). All subsequent English translations from this code are taken from this source unless otherwise indicated.

28 W. Becket Soule, "Clerics," in John D. Faris, and Jobe Abbass, eds., *A Practical Commentary to the Code of Canons of the Eastern Churches* (Montreal: Wilson & Lafleur, 2019) (Faris Commentary) 801-802.

29 Ibid. In a footnote, Soule states, "The canon clearly states that the obligation to provide sustenance lasts as long as the person is a cleric, even though he would not be receiving remuneration because of an office or function." He states that the provision is left to particular law, but, "The adoption of differing, and conflicting, provisions in particular law, and the inconsistent application of dismissal from the clerical state, has made this question even more difficult to follow or resolve" (fn. 229).

of their function and the conditions of places and times") or "sustenance" (in the Eastern code, to which "remuneration" can be added for the ministry performed).

The Latin code makes provision in canon 1350 for cases involving a penalty, but not for cases involving other conditions that would make a priest unable to exercise ministry. Canon 1350 §1 states, "Unless it concerns dismissal from the clerical state, when penalties are imposed on a cleric, provision must always be made so that he does not lack those things necessary for his decent support." This seems to correspond to the *sustentatio* which is found in the Eastern code. This distinction between *remuneratio* and *sustentatio* can be found in two decisions of the Apostolic Signatura.[30] However, canon 1350 only applies to penal cases. Its application to other types of cases where a priest is found unable to exercise ministry could be made *mutatis mutandis*, but it would be preferable if the distinction could be found in the law, as in the Eastern code.

However, even though there is no clear distinction in the universal law between remuneration and sustenance, there is nothing preventing particular law for a diocese from making that distinction. Particular law could distinguish between what is owed to the priest as "sustenance" and what is owed to him as "remuneration." It could also take into account what is meant by the priest's condition, the nature of his function, and the conditions of places and times.[31] This is all in keeping with the bishop's responsibility as given in canon 384.[32] This will avoid a certain arbitrariness in a bishop's decision.

Unsuited for Exercising Ministry vs. Unsuitable for Office

There are two distinctions that are made in the Code of Canon Law with regard to priestly ministry: being unsuited for exercising any ministry in the Church and being unsuited for being appointed to an ecclesiastical office.

---

30 See "Prohibition to Exercise Ministry and Denial of Sustenance after Alleged Commission of Delicts with a Minor and a Sentence of Acquittal Issued by the CDF," in *Ministerium Iustitiae,* vol. II, 143-178 (especially 174-176), and "Refusal of Remuneration for a Suspended Priest," in *Ministerium Iustitiae,* vol. II , 223-226 (also published in *Ius Ecclesiae* 27 [2015] 114-117).

31 See c. 281§1. "Conditions of places and times," for example, could take into account things such as the "cost of living" adjustment set by the government each year.

32 With special solicitude, a diocesan bishop is to attend to presbyters and listen to them as assistants and counsellors. He is to protect their rights and take care that they correctly fulfill the obligations proper to their state and that the means and institutions which they need to foster spiritual and intellectual life are available to them. *He also is to take care that provision is made for their decent support* [*honestae sustentationi*] *and social assistance according to the norm of law.*

Canon 384 (emphasis added).

Unsuited for Ministry: Irregularities and Impediments

There are certain things which prevent a priest from being ordained or from exercising ministry. These are known as irregularities or impediments. An irregularity, according to canon 1040, is a perpetual impediment; an impediment that is not perpetual is simply referred to as an impediment and is presumed to be temporary. Irregularities for receiving orders are specified in canon 1041: a person who is affected by a psychic illness, such that, after experts have been consulted, he is judged to be "unqualified to fulfill the ministry properly;" a person who has committed the delict of apostasy, heresy, or schism;[33] a person who has attempted marriage, even only civilly, "while either impeded personally from entering marriage by a matrimonial bond, sacred orders, or a public perpetual vow of chastity, or with a woman bound by a valid marriage or restricted by the same type of vow;" a person who has either committed or positively cooperated in a voluntary homicide or a completed abortion; a person who has mutilated himself or another "gravely and maliciously" or has attempted suicide; or a person who has placed an act of orders while lacking that order or prohibited from its exercise.[34]

While these are irregularities for receiving orders, canon 1044 also lists those who are irregular for the exercise of orders once received: a person who illegitimately received orders while bound by an irregularity to receive orders; a person who has publicly committed the delict of apostasy, heresy, or schism; a person who committed the delict of attempted marriage, committed homicide or a completed abortion or positive cooperated in either; a person who has mutilated himself or another "gravely and maliciously" or attempted suicide; a person who has placed an act of orders when they are either lacking that order or prohibited from exercising it.[35]

Canon 1044 also lists those who are simply impeded from exercising orders once received: a person who has illegitimately received an order while impeded from receiving them;[36] and "a person who is affected by amentia or some other

---

33 See c. 751.

34 See c. 1041. Some of these irregularities are straightforward, but others deserve further study and explication. For example, with the prevalence of suicide attempts in the United States, there might be more candidates presenting themselves for ordination who have made some sort of suicide gesture or attempt in the past.

35 See c. 1044 §1. These include the list of irregularities for reception of orders listed in c. 1041, 2° (if the delict is public), 3°, 4°, 5°, and 6°.

36 See c. 1042.

psychic illness mentioned in canon 1041, 1° until the ordinary, after consulting an expert, permits the exercise of the order."[37]

Canons 1041–1044 refer to those who are unqualified (*inhabilies*) for receiving orders or for exercising orders. Obviously, those who are unqualified for receiving or exercising orders would also be unsuitable for any ecclesiastical office that involves holy orders. But it is a broad category, since it refers to ministry in general. The person is unqualified for any ministry.

At times, these canons can be used when faced with someone who is simply unassignable if the reason for his inability to be assigned stems from a psychological disorder. The issue might be larger than just canon 149. He might be unqualified for any ministry. In some cases, this is for the reason specified in canon 1041, 1° or canon 1044 §2, 2°; that is, he is afflicted by some sort of psychic illness which makes him unqualified to fulfill the ministry properly. As we know from canon 1095, 3°, though, how we determine "causes of a psychic nature" can be rather difficult.

One of the difficulties with the use of canons 1041 and 1044 is that there is no process specified for determining how a cleric might be found unqualified for ministry. More specifically, there is nothing in the law that provides for the protection of his rights. But it would be possible for a diocese to specify a procedure through particular law. There are a number of concerns that could be addressed through such a process.

Canon 1041 says that the priest must be found "unqualified to fulfill the ministry properly." This is confirmed "after experts have been consulted." The canon does not specify that psychological experts must be consulted, although that might be assumed since the canon deals with a "psychic illness." But, as we have seen with marriage nullity cases, simply having an expert in the psychological sciences is not sufficient for judging whether a person is capable of assuming the essential obligations of marriage. The canon does not specify that the expert has to personally evaluate the priest, or whether he just reads the priest's file. Just like we do not want our court experts to be making judgments about marriage nullity, so we also wouldn't want the psychological experts to make judgments about fitness for ministry.

---

37 In order to be judged "unqualified to fulfill the ministry properly" (c. 1041, 1°), more than one expert must be consulted (*consultis peritis)*; in order to be declared qualified for exercising ministry (c. 1044 §2, 2°), the bishop only has to consult one expert (*consulto perito)*.

The canon specifies that the bishop is the one who is to make the decision. But it states that he is to consult "experts." Thus, more than one. Particular law can specify how the consultation is to be done.

Just like in our marriage nullity cases, it must be determined that there are psychic issues that render the person unqualified to fulfill the ministry of the Church, and not just characteristics that make his fulfillment of ministry difficult. When a priest has experienced difficulty in his ministry, and when his bishop believes that there may be a psychological issue at its root, it is obvious that his ministry has become difficult. The canon states that the psychic illness must make the priest unqualified (*inhabiles*) for ministry, not just that his psychological condition has made his ministry difficult or has caused difficulties in his assignments. Moreover, just like not every psychological problem makes a person incapable of assuming the obligations of marriage, so not every psychological problem would make a person incapable of fulfilling ministry properly. The psychological problem has to be in some way related to the fulfillment of ministry. Just like in marriage nullity cases, the judge must show how the "causes of a psychic nature" relate to the assumption of the specific obligations of marriage, so in canon 1044 cases, the bishop must show how the priest's psychological problem makes the priest unable to fulfill ministry properly.

It would also be helpful if the people who are assisting the bishop in this matter are also experts in ministry, and not just experts in psychology. It is the priest's ability to exercise ministry that is in question, not merely his psychological well-being, so experts in ministry might also be consulted when the bishop makes this decision. Unlike the canons on the removal of pastors, which require consultation with two pastors chosen by a group proposed by the presbyteral council (and thus have some expertise in being a pastor), canon 1044 does not specify the number of experts that must be consulted, or what field they must be expert in. Particular law could make this more specific and might perhaps use the canons on the removal of pastors as a model.

And finally, there are issues regarding the priest's right of defense that have to be taken into consideration. Does he have a right to know why his psychological abilities are being called into question? Does he have a right to suggest psychological and pastoral experts? Does he have a right to an advocate or canonical counsel? Does he have a right to see whatever material the bishop will be using to make a decision? Are his rights concerning recourse clearly spelled out for him?

These are some of the issues that need to be specified in particular law, lest the decisions of bishops appear arbitrary, or vary from person to person. The fact here is that there will not be a lot of situations dealt with under this canon. But when one arises, it is good to have a road map for dealing with it.

Unsuited for Ecclesiastical Office

There are a number of things that might make a person unsuitable for ecclesiastical office. They may not possess the requirements specified in the Code of Canon Law. They may labor under an ecclesiastical penalty. They may not be able to fulfill the office physically because of things like the effects of a stroke or other condition which makes them unable to physically fulfill the demands of an office,[38] the results of an accident, some sort of paralysis. They may not be able to fulfill the office because of advanced age, or the effects of Alzheimer's disease or dementia. Or they may not be suitable for certain ecclesiastical offices because they are not competent administrators or have engaged in administrative practices which were contrary to civil or canon law and cannot be trusted with the administration of goods.[39]

So the question becomes: How do you determine whether a priest is suitable for an ecclesiastical office? For some offices in the Church, the law specifies some of the requisites. There are requirements for the suitability of bishops themselves (c. 378), as well as requirements for a vicar general and episcopal vicar (c. 478); for a chancellor and notaries (c. 483 §2); for the finance officer (c. 494); for the judicial vicar and adjutant judicial vicar (c. 1420 §4); for judges (c. 1421); auditors (1428 §2); for advocates (c. 1483); and for the promoter of justice and defender of the bond (c. 1435).

But suitability can also be determined by the nature of the office the person is assuming; they have to be able to do the tasks of the office they are assuming. Thus, a bishop is expected to do the things specified in canons 381-400, in the Decree on the Pastoral Office of Bishops in the Church (*Christus dominus*), in the Directory on the Pastoral Ministry of Bishops, and in other documents that refer to the duties of a bishop. The Church also has a separate instrument for determining suitability for the episcopate, usually administered through the papal legate.

With regard to pastors, canons 528–529 specify the functions of a pastor, and hence the qualities that should be looked for in determining suitability for the

---

38 Those who have worked in administration know that it is important in job descriptions to list any Americans with Disabilities Act requirements for the job. Failure to do so, and terminating an employee because of a physical disability, can result in serious lawsuits.

39 The new Book VI of the Code of Canon Law makes provision for this as a delict. See canon 1376, especially §3.

pastorate.[40] Moreover, canon 521 says that he must be "in the sacred order of the presbyterate."[41] He is also "to be outstanding in sound doctrine and integrity of morals and endowed with zeal for souls and other virtues." The same canon also notes that other qualities can be specified by universal or particular law for the parish in question.[42] Canon 521 also refers to suitability for office when it states in paragraph 3, "For the office of pastor to be conferred on someone, his suitability must be clearly evident by some means determined by the diocesan bishop, even by means of an examination." For those old enough to remember the "junior clergy exams," this might engender some fear and trepidation, or concern that we are going back in time to a former era. But "examination" does not necessarily mean a multiple choice or true/false written or oral exam. It doesn't even imply a written examination at all. There are many ways that a person can be "examined," similar to the ways a job applicant might be "examined" in the secular world. These usually include a number of interviews by a variety of people, and even might include meeting with a board of people to determine suitability for a given job. This "board" might also include lay ministers, and other laity, with whom the priest would be expected to work.

In all of this it must be kept in mind that it is bishop who appoints to offices in his diocese. Others can make recommendations, but, with whatever process you use, it must be clear that the bishop is making the appointment.

Determining Suitability for Office

Since we don't have time to examine all the various offices in the Church, and since some of them have criteria for appointment listed in the universal law,

---

40 While not specifically addressing the office of pastor, we can also look to canons 618–619 in religious law to see the qualities for leadership in the religious community. Canon 618 begins by reminding leaders that they are to exercise their office "in a spirit of service." They are "to govern their subjects as sons or daughters of God . . . . and, with reverence for the human person, they are to listen to them willingly and foster their common endeavor. . . ." Canon 619 lists specific duties of the leader: to strive to build a community . . . in which God is sought and loved before all things." They are to:

> nourish the members regularly with the food of the word of God and are to draw them to the celebration of the sacred liturgy. They are to be an example to them in cultivating virtues and in the observance of the laws and traditions of their own institute; they are to meet the personal needs of the members appropriately, solicitously to care for and visit the sick, to correct the restless, to console the faint of heart, and to be patient toward all.

41 Since the Latin code does not use the more inclusive term *Sacerdos*, it is at least debatable whether a bishop could be the pastor of a parish.

42 It is interesting to note that the canon specifically states that there could be particular law "for the parish in question." This seems to imply that there could be something else required than just for a "parish in general."

I will concentrate on the office of pastor, since this is the most common appointment that a bishop makes. Determining what makes someone suitable for an office can also help us to understand what makes a person unsuitable for an office.

After the general requirements that we've already seen in canon 521, it is possible to discern suitability for office by examining what a pastor is expected to do. This will help to determine whether a person is apt for the office of pastor.

Canons 528–529 provide four major areas that the pastor is to be proficient at: a) proclamation of the Word of God;[43] b) making the Eucharist the center of the parish assembly;[44] c) knowing the faithful entrusted to his care[45]; and d) promoting the proper role of that lay members of the parish have and ensuring that they have concern for parochial communion as part of the diocese and the universal Church.[46]

To this might be added a fifth area, that of administering the temporal goods of the parish, which canon 1284 says that he should do "with the diligence of a good householder."[47]

---

43 See c. 528 §1, as well as Book III, Title I: The Ministry of the Divine Word (cc. 756–780), and Title III: Catholic Education (cc. 793-806). This paragraph includes instructing the laity through the homily and catechetical instruction; fostering works that promote the spirit of the gospel, especially social justice; caring for the Catholic education of children and youth; and, with the help of the laity, ensuring that the gospel message comes to those who have ceased the practice of religion or do not profess the Catholic faith.

44 See c. 528 §2, as well as Book IV, Title III: The Most Holy Eucharist (cc. 897–958). This paragraph includes a devout celebration of the sacraments, leading people to practice family prayer, and to participate consciously and actively in the liturgy.

45 See c. 529 §1: the pastor is to strive to know the faithful entrusted to his care; visit families; help the sick; seek out the poor, the afflicted, the lonely, those exiled from their country, and those weighed down with special difficulties. He is also to work so that spouses and parents are supported in fulfilling their proper duties and to foster the growth of Christian life in the family.

46 See c. 529 §2. The proper role of the laity would also include their participation in things such as the parish pastoral council and parish finance council. This would also indicate how well the priest collaborates with others in the fulfillment of his ministry.

47 See c. 1284. The second paragraph details nine particular responsibilities for administrators: to exercise vigilance to protect the goods entrusted to them; to take care that the goods are protected by civilly valid methods; to ensure that both canon law and civil law are followed so that no damage comes to the Church through the non-observance of civil laws; to collect the return of goods and income and protect what is collected according to the intention of the donor; to pay interest due on a loan or mortgage and to repay debts in a timely manner; invest surplus funds with the consent of the ordinary; to keep well-organized books; to draw up a yearly report; and to maintain archives.

In looking at these responsibilities, it should be possible to design a system for evaluating a person's abilities in each of these areas, and help to assess their suitability for an ecclesiastical office, particularly the office of pastor. These can also be combined with those things that are mentioned in "The Obligations and Rights of Clerics."[48] These obligations and rights might give some indication of who would be suitable for an office in the Church. Those who seriously neglect or ignore these responsibilities might not be suitable for serving in an ecclesiastical office. Not fulfilling the obligations specified in these canons, while not delictual, can be used in assessing a person's suitability for office. These things, again, can be specified in the particular law of a diocese.

In addition to the law itself, there are other documents that might assist a bishop in assessing suitability for office: the apostolic exhortation *Pastores dabo vobis*,[49] which is cited extensively in the Program of Priestly Formation in the United States of America, the *Ratio fundmentalis institutionis sacerdotalis* (upon which the Program for Priestly Formation is based), and the Basic Plan for the Ongoing Formation of Priests.[50] One might also consider the body of the Holy Thursday letters to priests, which Pope John Paul II wrote, and which contain other qualities of the priest that could be considered in determining the suitability both for ordination and for assignment.

In particular, though, the current Program for Priestly Formation in the United States provides what it calls the essential elements for pastoral ministry.[51] These might provide tools for assessment of whether someone is suitable for assignment to a particular office.

While the Program for Priestly Formation is mainly concerned with seminary formation, it briefly also speaks of "The Ongoing Formation of Priests" (nn. 399-405).[52] As we have seen Pope Francis do in proposing a catechumenal approach to marriage, the Program for Priestly Formation compares priestly

---

48 See Book II, Part I, Title III, Chapter III (cc. 273–289).

49 See John Paul II, post-synodal apostolic exhortation *Pastores dabo vobis*, March 25, 1992: *AAS* 84 (1992) 657-804.

50 See USCCB, *The Basic Plan for the Ongoing Formation of Priests*, 2001, https://www.usccb.org/beliefs-and-teachings/vocations/priesthood/priestly-life-and-ministry/national-plan-for-the-ongoing-formation-of-priests (accessed on 5 February 2024).

51 PPF n. 370 a-o: Proclamation of the Word, the sacramental dimension, ecclesial formation, the community dimension, collaboration with others, Catholic education, a personal synthesis for practical use, an initiation to various practical, pastoral experiences, especially in parishes, cultural sensitivity, religious pluralism, the poor, ministry to all walks of life, leadership development, professional standards, and the cultivation of personal qualities. PPF 370, 145–151.

52 The USCCB published a "Basic Plan for the Ongoing Formation of Priests" in 2001, which probably needs to be updated in light of more recent documents.

formation to initiation into the sacramental life of the Church, "not unlike the process envisioned in the Order of Christian Initiation of Adults." It goes on to say, "Just as the catechumen is introduced into a lifetime relationship of missionary discipleship with Jesus Christ, so too—for he one being formed for a lifetime of priestly service in the Church—the term 'ongoing formation' is a reminder that the one experience of discipleship of those called to priesthood is never interrupted."[53]

Unfortunately, the Program for Priestly Formation leaves out laity in this ongoing formation. It states, "In the process of beginning priestly ministry and life, significant formational roles are played by the diocesan bishop, the director of ongoing formation of priests, and the entire presbyterate" (n. 405). There is no specific mention of the laity in the ongoing formation process. Perhaps building on the image of sacramental initiation, a diocese might have a team approach to ongoing formation of priests, one that would include lay persons.

Finally, there are a number of assessment tools available which might assist a bishop in making assignments to suitable candidates. One that appears to be popular is from the Catholic Leadership Institute, which has partnered with over 100 dioceses in the U.S. to design what they call "Pastoral Leadership 360 for Priests." They describe this as "a valid and reliable indication of leadership performance and effectiveness, grounded in Catholic instruction for the ongoing formation of priests."[54] There are obviously a lot of other types of instruments out there that measure a person's aptitude for certain tasks, or their competencies in certain areas. Many of these come from a business model, and so they need to be coordinated with Catholic Church documents so that we don't just use a business model for our assessments.

The Goal: Not Having Unassignable Priests

So far we have talked about preparing suitable priests for ecclesial ministry or ecclesiastical office, and assessing priests to see whether they are suitable for ecclesiastical office. The hope is that with proper preparation and assessment, including concrete goals that are to be accomplished, there will be fewer priests who are found to be unassignable. However, as we know from marriage preparation, even with the best preparation, and even if a couple seeks counseling when difficulties arise, we still end up with cases of failed marriages that come before our tribunals. Just like with marriage, the commitment to the priesthood is a commitment to the future. It is unrealistic to expect that bishops, or seminary

---

53 See PPF n. 399, quoting the *Ratio fundamentalis,* n. 80.
54 See www.catholicleaders.org (accessed on 5 Feb. 2024).

formators, be clairvoyant. Sometimes the decision that is made at one stage of a person's life does not bear fruit in subsequent stages. Sometimes people fail, and sometimes they fail miserably.

The law also provides some remedies for that. Hence the final section of this presentation.

What's a Bishop to Do?

In this final section, I am going to offer ten possibilities for dealing with the problem of unassignable priests. Five of them will be proactive; five will be reactive.

First, be careful who you ordain. As I pointed out in a previous talk a few years ago, in Tom Stoppard's play, "Rosencrantz and Guildenstern are Dead," as the two characters are facing their demise, the one says to the other, "There must have been a time, at the beginning, when we could have said 'No.'" Sometimes the problem of unassignable priests can be alleviated if the often difficult decisions are made early in their training. As Robert Geisinger has pointed out in commenting on canon 1025 §2, "For cases in which probable or at least potential, fitness and long-term utility are not clear, an aspirant should be dismissed from formation early if there is moral certitude that he is not a risk worth taking."[55] Geisinger goes on to say:

> Ordinaries must be cautious indeed not to encourage persons whose ministerial fitness and utility are in doubt. One might hope that a man might develop positively, but if such growth is not likely, it is unjust to all parties concerned to encourage him. If he later must be dismissed from formation because of problems which were known earlier and not considered remediable, then he has been treated unjustly if he has not been advised to pursue another vocation. If after ordination it becomes clear in practice that a man is ministerially inept, as earlier suspected, then he has been unjustly encouraged by superiors to believe that he might be something he cannot be.[56]

The latest version of the Program for Priestly Formation is somewhat helpful and somewhat not helpful in this regard. It is helpful that there are yearly evaluations that must take place regarding the seminarian's suitability for

55 See Geisinger, CLSA Commentary, 1204.
56 Ibid.

ministry, and that there are definite benchmarks for that evaluation.[57] It is also helpful that the Program for Priestly Formation states, "It is essential that a seminarian's formation be truly ecclesial through the formal participation of lay members of the seminary community. The laity, particularly women, offer insightful recommendation, opinions and points of view to the rector and community of formators."[58] What is not helpful is that, although the Program for Priestly Formation speaks of the "formal participation of lay members of the seminary community," and in particular calls attention to the value of lay women in this process, it is only the lay members of the seminary community who are mentioned. Moreover, the final evaluations must always be made by priests, and the only observation of the seminarian in a parish setting is after he has been ordained a deacon. The Program for Priestly Formation refers to this final stage (called the Vocational Synthesis Stage) as "a time of integration and transition (n. 137), not a time of evaluation."[59] Canon 1030, as seen above, creates the presumption that someone ordained to the diaconate will be ordained to the priesthood. It is a weakness of the Program for Priestly Formation that the first time the seminarian is introduced to parish life is after he has been ordained a deacon, where the canonical presumption is that he will be ordained a priest.

Second, be careful of who you incardinate or allow to minister in your diocese. The code contains a process for incardination.[60] There needs to be further development of that process at the diocesan level, through some sort of particular law. At times, particularly in large, urban dioceses, priests "drift in," perhaps to attend a university, or to work in a hospital, perhaps to take care of a family member or just visit a relative. Sometimes what was envisioned as a short stay has become much longer. In these cases, a bishop needs to be attentive to the provisions of canon 268 §1 which states, "A cleric who has legitimately moved from his own particular church to another is incardinated in the latter particular church by the law itself after five years if he has made such a desire known in

57 PPF n. 59 also states, "In forming a prudent judgment about the suitability of an applicant for priestly formation, the principle of gradualism should be used. According to the principle of gradualism, progressively higher levels of expectations should be sought as an individual advances to progressively higher levels of preparation."

58 PPF n. 113.

59 PPF n. 138.

60 See canons 267-272, which also includes the process for permitting a priest to minister outside his diocese. This was called for at the Second Vatican Council (PO, n. 10), and is mentioned in a number of documents since, including a document from the USCCB, "Guidelines for Receiving Pastoral Ministers in the United States," https://www.usccb.org/sites/default/files/flipbooks/cclv-guidelines/cclv-guidelines/assets/basic-html/ (accessed on 22 Mar. 2024).

writing both to the diocesan bishop of his host church and to his own diocesan bishop and neither of them has expressed opposition in writing to him within four months of receiving the letter." (In my own experience, sometimes these things are not entirely clear. What the priest claims is his expression of desire to remain in a diocese is not always perceived as such by the diocesan bishop.) A diocese should establish some process by which a person who wants to incardinate or wants to minister in your diocese is found to be suitable for ecclesiastical office. For those seeking incardination, it is important to know why someone wants to come to you, and the reason why they want to leave their own diocese or order. Sometimes the problems which they experienced in their former place are the problems that you will soon be dealing with. There should always be personal contact between the diocesan bishops, and not just the acceptance of a dog-eared letter that Father X has permission to minister in your diocese. And, of course, all the provisions of the Charter for the Protecting of Minors and Young People need to be observed, as well as any pertinent civil laws, if the person is coming from outside the United States.[61]

Third, find ways to require ongoing formation and ministerial assessment. Both the Program for Priestly Formation (nn. 399-405) and the Basic Plan for the Ongoing Formation of Priests suggest plans for an ongoing formation for priests; particular law can specify it or make it mandatory. Various forms of ministerial assessment mentioned above can also be re-enforced through local legislation. A priest's participation in ongoing formation and his periodic assessment can also be used to establish suitability or unsuitability for office.

Fourth, establish clear expectations for suitability for the office. It has been said in the past that priests ultimately take on the pastoral style of their first pastor. Is that sufficient in today's Church? Those who have worked in diocesan administration are familiar with writing job descriptions that indicate what skills are necessary for the job, what the duties will be, etc. There is a need to do that for other pastoral offices in the diocese. For example, if the parish has a school attached to it, there should be a clear statement that anyone chosen as pastor has to be responsible for the school. Sometimes presumptions are made—"You know how to do this"—that may or may not be true. Assigning another priest as mentor can be helpful, but this leaves out the majority of the people with whom the priest will be expected to work, thus leaving out a necessary perspective.

---

61 It is important that a diocese keeps up to date on immigration laws, especially regarding work permits. These laws are constantly changing, and what was permissible at one time is no longer permissible at another time.

Fifth, use particular law creatively. There are a number of places in the code that refer to particular law. Many dioceses have established certain policies or procedures or guidelines for the activities that take place within the diocese. Sometimes it's just necessary to gather all these together in one place. The bishop can use his executive authority to issue a general executory decree (c. 31), "which more precisely determines the methods to be observed in applying the law or which urge the observance of laws." Thus a diocese could have particular law that determines how the bishop will determine suitability for office, perhaps requiring a yearly evaluation or assessment that we typically require of our lay employees. Particular law could also establish the consequences of not following something established in the universal law of the Church. As mentioned above, the canons on the rights and obligations of clerics (cc. 273-289) specify in a general way what a priest is obliged to do. Particular law can specify what the consequences would be of not doing those things.[62]

These are the five proactive things that a bishop could do in his diocese that would perhaps make it less likely that a priest would be unassignable. There are also five reactive things that a bishop could do if it appears that one of his priests is truly unassignable.

The first is a process that we have already seen: *declaring a priest impeded from the exercise of orders because of psychic issues*, according to canon 1044 §2, 2°. It would be important that a diocese would establish some sort of process for doing this, as noted above.

Second, an unassignable priest could be encouraged to seek *voluntary dispensation from the obligations of the clerical state, including the obligation of celibacy.*[63] While it is not likely that the priest would do this, since most of the time he will be looking to return to ministry, it is still a requirement if later on a

---

62 There are a number of new realities that could suggest the need for particular laws in a diocese. At the 2022 CLSA convention, Jay Conzemius gave a presentation on new sacramental record realities. Also at the 2022 convention, Diane Barr presented on the topic of whether diocesan policies were changing with regard to outdoor weddings. The Diocese of Cleveland has established some well thought-out policies regarding gender issues. And several years ago, Vincent Gardiner gave a presentation on requests for canonical separations, which have been appearing with more frequency in some dioceses.

63 It is important that "including the obligation of celibacy" always be included when the case is sent to the Holy See. Even if the priest does not have any plans to marry, the Dicastery for the Clergy will often send the case back to the diocesan bishop, reminding him that the full title is "a dispensation from the obligations of the clerical state, including the obligation of celibacy." There have been exceptions to this, but to avoid any delays, it is best to include the full title.

bishop wishes to use the next possibility: the use of the Special Faculties of the Dicastery for the Clergy.

A third possibility for dealing with priests who are unassignable is the use of the so-called Special Faculties. These originated in a letter of 18 April 2009 from the Congregation for the Clergy (P.N. 2009 0556). This was followed by a subsequent letter of 17 March 2010 which described the process for handling such cases (P.N. 2010 0823). These can be found in the Canon Law Society of America database. After an excellent introduction in which the late Cardinal Hummes discusses the ministerial priesthood, the theological reasoning behind priestly celibacy, the responsibility of bishops toward his priests, and criteria bishops should keep in mind in exercising his judicial function, the document details three special faculties conceded to the congregation by Benedict XVI. The congregation's letter directs that in all three cases, the cases ought to be instructed according to the administrative process, and refers to canons 35–58, 1342, and 1720. It is important that the diocese pays close attention to these canons and makes reference to them in describing the actions that it has taken.

Special Faculty I referred to the dismissal from the clerical state *in poenam* for those clerics who have attempted marriage and, after being admonished, "persist in an irregular and scandalous life (c. 1394), and of clerics guilty of grave sins against the Sixth Commandment (c. 1395.1-2)." The matter is presented to the Holy Father for his approval *in forma specifica*.

It is interesting to see how the dicastery approaches this. First, Special Faculty I refers to the commission of a delict ("lives in concubinage and commits other grave delicts"[64]). The letter states, "Often in such cases, the penalty of 'suspension' and of irregularity. . . . have not been demonstrated to be sufficiently effective or suitable to repair the scandal caused, to restore justice, and to reform the offender."[65] This implies that other attempts have been made to regularize the priest's situation. The Holy See does not look kindly on the use of these Special Faculties as a "one-off" attempt. It wants to see what other steps the bishop has taken in the process. The letter also accepts the possibility that the cleric, "having been legitimately cited, has neglected to make himself available." Sometimes the

64 This would not refer to the *graviora delicta* of *Sacramentorum sanctitatis tutela*, since those cases would have to be referred to the Dicastery for the Doctrine of the Faith.

65 Note that the revised Book VI has changed the order of c. 1341 to read, "restore justice, reform the offender, and to repair the scandal." This is a subtle change, but may reflect the fact that in the past too much emphasis was placed upon not wanting to cause scandal. This resulted in actions being concealed, lest the faithful be scandalized.

priest is simply uncooperative. He could then be declared absent from the process, and the case could continue.[66]

Special Faculty II permits the dicastery to intervene itself, or to confirm the decision of an ordinary, in accord with canon 1399, and, at the ordinary's request, for actions which involve "the special gravity of the violation of law and the need or urgency to avoid an objective scandal." This derogates from the prescription of then-canons 1317, 1319, 1342 §2, and 1349. The matter is presented to the Holy Father for his approval *in forma specifica* and his decision. A perpetual penalty can be imposed by decree, contrary to the normal prescripts in the law which prohibit perpetual penalties by decree. The letter reminds the bishop that this is to be used in those cases where every pastoral and canonical approach has been tried but has been unsuccessful, as quoted above.

Note that the letter does not mention that there must be evidence of a delict having been committed. The priest's actions are "damaging the common good of the Church and Her spiritual mission." Thus it is a matter of Church discipline having been gravely breached by the cleric. This can relate back to the canons on "The Obligations and Rights of Clerics" (cc. 273-289).

Moreover, the use of Special Faculty II does not necessarily have to seek dismissal from the clerical state. In referencing canon 1399, the letter states that the request of the ordinary can be "to apply a just penalty or penance for an external violation of divine or canon law." Nevertheless, it maintains that "in truly exceptional and urgent cases, when the offender has no intention to amend his ways, sometimes even perpetual penalties may be imposed."

Special Faculty III allows the dicastery to handle cases of clerics who have abandoned priestly ministry for a period of more than five consecutive years[67] and who "persists in such freely chosen and illicit absence" and to declare them dismissed from the clerical state.[68] Its purpose is "to guarantee order in the

---

66 This could be helpful in those cases where the priest simply won't talk to you.

67 See also canon 1392, which permits the penalty of suspension for a cleric "who voluntarily and illegitimately abandons the sacred ministry for six continuous months with the intention of withdrawing himself from the competent authority of the Church…." This is consistent with the application of penalties in Book VI, which allow for a gradual increasing of penalties, culminating in the dismissal from the clerical state. Special Faculty III allows for the dismissal from the clerical state if the abandonment lasts more than five years. It might be assumed that, in the period between six months and five years the bishop has made attempts to get the cleric to return to the ministry or has increased the penalties which have been imposed on him. These should be documented in the priest's file and sent to the Dicastery as proof that the bishop has attempted to get the priest to return to ministry.

68 On the CLSA Research Database, there is a 64-page *vademecum* that was prepared and presented at a CLSA convention by Daniel Smilanic, Dan Welter, and Frank Dolan.

ecclesiastical society" and "preserve the faithful from falling into *error communis* (c. 144) regarding the validity of the Sacraments."

This is the only Special Faculty that has its own process described in the law,[69] but it includes the proviso: "After the dismissal from the clerical state, in exceptional cases, a cleric who might wish to seek rehabilitation must present that request to the Apostolic See through a benevolent bishop."

A fourth way to deal with unassignable priests is through the application of penalties, either in universal or in particular law. As noted above, the Dicastery for the Clergy requires that these be tried before seeking to use any of the Special Faculties. As seen in the Special Faculties, as well as a number of penal canons, penalties can be gradually increased or added to; and, for continued violation of the penalty, can lead to dismissal from the clerical state.

Universal Penal Law

The revised Book VI of the Code of Canon Law contains a number of actions which might be helpful in the case of unassignable priests.[70] Like the 1983 code, the revised Book VI divides penalties into two categories, medicinal and expiatory, with the main change being that the medicinal penalty of suspension is no longer limited to clerics.

The revised canon 1336 deserves closer study, since it more clearly delineates the types of expiatory penalties that could be incurred and is often referred to in the canons elaborating expiatory penalties.[71] It lists four types of expiatory penalties: an *order* (to reside in a certain place or territory, which the former law also did; but also "to pay a fine or sum of money for the purposes of the Church, according to the regulations defined by the conference of bishops"); a *prohibition* (against residing in a certain place or territory, "against exercising all or some offices, tasks, ministries or functions, or only some activities attached to offices or tasks, either everywhere or in a certain place or territory, or outside them;" against placing all or some acts of the power of orders or the power of governance; against exercising some right or privilege or using an insignia or title; against possessing active or passive voice in elections; against voting participating

---

69 See especially the previously-mentioned 64-page *vademecum* in the Research Database on the CLSA website.

70 I will not attempt to go into a detailed discussion of the changes in Book VI, which would be beyond the scope of this talk. However, in general, there are places in the code which might prohibit a priest from acting and others that would make him unsuitable for any office.

71 The aforementioned "User's Guide" from the Dicastery for Legislative Texts is particularly helpful in this regard.

in ecclesial councils or colleges; and—in an issue which has come up in sexual abuse cases—against wearing ecclesiastical or religious attire). An expiatory penalty could also be a *privation* (of all or some offices, tasks, ministries, or functions; or of only some activity attached to offices or tasks; of the faculty of hearing confessions or of preaching;[72] of the delegated power of governance;[73] of some right or privilege, or insignia, or title; and, added in the revision, "of total or partial ecclesiastical remuneration, according to the regulations of the conference of bishops, without prejudice to the prescript of canon 1350 §1"[74]). Finally, an expiatory penalty, according to canon 1336, could entail *dismissal from the clerical state.*[75]

In addition to the new wording of canon 1336, there are also five canons in the revised Book VI that touch on our subject.

Canon 1392, which is related somewhat to Special Faculty III which was discussed above, refers to clerics who have abandoned their ministry for six consecutive months "with the intention of withdrawing himself from the competent authority of the Church."[76] Such clerics can be punished by a suspension, or by one of the penalties mentioned in canon 1336 §§2–4, or, in more grave cases, dismissed from the clerical state.[77]

Canon 1393 envisions two possibilities. First a cleric who exercises trade or business contrary to the prescripts of the canon (see e.g., c. 286), can be punished

---

72 This was also at issue with regard to clerical sexual abuse of minors.

73 It could not affect the ordinary power of governance, unless the person were at the same time removed from the office that entailed that governance.

74 This would hint at the difference between remuneration and sustenance, as discussed above. The penalty could remove remuneration but not sustenance, which is why it is important for a diocese to distinguish between these two things.

75 Canon 1342 §2 contains the reminder that "perpetual penalties cannot be imposed or declared by decree," although as we have seen, the Special Faculties allow for that in certain cases.

76 The inclusion of the phrase, "with the intention of withdrawing himself from the competent authority of the Church," complicates the matter. It must be proven not only that the priest has abandoned for six months, but that he has done do with the intention of withdrawing himself from the competent authority of the Church. Intention implies some sort of act of the will. It should be something more than just "drifting away from ministry." Sometimes the last thing a diocese has in a priest's file is his last assignment. There has been no further correspondence with him since then, and thus no way of being able to state with any certainty what his intention was.

77 Special Faculty III refers to clerics who have left ministry for more than five years. This is also similar to the newly added c. 694 §1, 3° which states that a religious is "*ipso facto* dismissed from an institute who . . . has been illegitimately absent from the religious house, pursuant to c. 665 §2, for twelve consecutive months."

by penalties established in canon 1336 §§2-4; and second, "a cleric or religious who commits a delict involving finances or who gravely violates the prescriptions listed in canon 285 §4, is to be punished with the penalties mentioned in canon 1336 §§2-4, without prejudice to the obligation to repair harm." Note that this does not include reference to dismissal from the clerical state.

Canon 1394 refers to clerics or religious who marry, even civilly, and who therefore incur a *latae sententiae* suspension. The canon states, "but if he does not repent after being warned and continues to give scandal, he must be punished gradually by privation or even by dismissal from the clerical state. This is similar to Special Faculty I, but prescribes gradually adding penalties to the original offense, with the final penalty being dismissal from the clerical state.

Canon 1395 also provides for the gradual addition of penalties, including dismissal from the clerical state for: a) clerics who live in concubinage; b) clerics who persist with scandal in some other sin against the sixth commandment of the Decalogue, who are to be punished with a suspension. Clerics who otherwise commit a delict against the sixth commandment publicly are to be punished with just penalties; and clerics who "by force, threats, or abuse of his authority commits a delict against the sixth commandment of the Decalogue, or who compels someone to perform or submit to a sexual act" can also be punished by just penalties. In each of these cases, the penalty of dismissal from the clerical state can be imposed.

Finally, canon 1396 provides that someone who "gravely violates the obligation of residence that binds by reason of ecclesiastical office is to be punished by a just penalty, not excluding, after a warning, privation from office." It should be noted that canon 1395 contains exceptions to the fact that expiatory penalties do not generally require a prior warning, as do medicinal penalties.

Particular Penal Law

With regard to sanctions, canon 1317 states that "penalties are to be established only insofar as they are truly necessary to provide more suitably for ecclesiastical discipline." But canon 1316 urges bishops to make sure that "penal laws are uniform in the same city or region."

With regard to what might be the subject of sanctions, canon 1315 allows the bishop, as a lower legislator, the power to "reinforce divine law with an appropriate penalty;" to "add other penalties to the penalties established by universal law for some delict;" and, if the universal law is indeterminate or facultative, to make a penalty determinate or obligatory. And, while canons 1322 through 1326 list exempting, mitigating, and aggravating factors in the law, canon

1327 states, "Particular law can establish other exempting, mitigating, or aggravating circumstances . . . either by general norm or for individual delicts." This same canon also allows for exempting, mitigating, or aggravating circumstances to be established in a penal precept. Furthermore, canon 1399 allows for penalties "when the special gravity of the violation (in cases mentioned in the canons of Book VI or in other laws) demands punishment and there is an urgent need to prevent or repair scandals."

In addition to the expiatory penalties that are mentioned in the canons, canons 1339–1340 also provide for the possibility of imposing penal remedies and penances. The revision of Book VI greatly expanded this notion, offering more examples of what actions might be possible. By and large, these were taken from the 1917 code, but, once again, there is no process described for the imposition of these remedies and penances, and what right of defense might be involved.[78]

According to canon 1339 §1, as a penal remedy an ordinary or his delegate can *warn someone* "who is in the proximate occasion of committing a delict." He can also carry out an investigation,[79] and issue a warning to a person upon whom "falls grave suspicion of a delict having been committed."

If an act has already been committed, again as a penal remedy, the ordinary "can *rebuke* one whose behavior causes scandal or a grave disturbance of order, in a manner accommodated to the particular conditions of the person and the facts" (c. 1339 §2), with the provision that both the warning and the rebuke are to be given in writing and kept in the secret archive of the curia (c. 1339 §3).

The legislator must have been aware that these warnings or rebukes may not have their intended effect, since canon 1339 §4 allows for the possibility of the issuance of a *penal precept* "if once or several times warnings or rebukes have been given to one without effect, or if an effect cannot be expected from them." The precept should follow the canons in general norms on "Singular Decrees and Precepts" (cc. 48-58),[80] particularly canon 50 which states "before issuing a singular decree, an authority is to seek out the necessary information and proofs, and, insofar as possible, to hear those whose rights can be injured." It should be

78 The User's Guide from the Dicastery for Legislative Texts describes these as disciplinary and not penal. This is an important distinction.

79 There is no indication about how this investigation is to be done, who is to do it, whether the person being investigated has the right to know about it, participate in it personally, or know the results. This might be specified in particular law.

80 Canon 49 states, "A singular precept is a decree which directly and legitimately enjoins a specific person or persons to do or omit something, especially in order to urge the observance of law."

issued in writing and should be reasonable ("with the reasons at least summarily expressed"). Since no process is described in the law, particular law could establish such a process, once again guaranteeing the right of defense.[81]

Finally, canon 1339 §5 provides an additional possibility for a *penal remedy*, in addition to a penal warning, rebuke, and decree. The canon states, "If the gravity of the case warrants it, and especially if one is in danger of relapsing into a delict,[82] the ordinary is to submit the person to vigilance in a manner determined by a singular precept, even beyond the penalties imposed or declared by a sentence or decree according to the norm of law."[83]

In addition to penal remedies, the code also allows the bishop to impose a *penance,* according to canon 1340. A penance is "the performance of some work of religion, piety, or charity" and can be added to penal warnings and rebukes (c. 1340 §3).

It must always be kept in mind, though, that penalties are always seen as a last resort. However, the revised Book VI is a bit stronger than the 1983 code about the use of penalties. Canon 1341 in the 1983 code stated, "An ordinary is to take care to initiate a judicial or administrative process to impose or declare penalties only after he has ascertained the fraternal correction or rebuke or other means of pastoral solicitude cannot sufficiently repair the scandal, restore justice, reform the offender." The revised canon 1341 makes the ordinary's action more obligatory: "An ordinary must initiate a judicial or administrative procedure to impose or declare penalties, when he has ascertained that neither means of pastoral solicitude, especially fraternal correction, nor a warning or rebuke can sufficiently restore justice, reform the offender, repair the scandal." Thus, the canon makes the ordinary's action obligatory, and suggests that it follows upon fraternal correction, and the above figures of penal warning, rebuke, and precept. That seems to suggest that the ordinary has tried other methods, and that they have failed.

The fifth process established in the code that could be used when dealing with unassignable priests is *declaring the nullity of orders* (cc. 1708–1712). These canons are seldom, if ever, used. I mention these canons here simply because this

---

81 Some sort of process is suggested by c. 1353, which refers to an appeal or recourse from a judicial sentence or from a decree having suspensive effect.

82 This would seem to indicate that a delict has already been committed, but it doesn't require that a second already be committed. The person's actions would just have to be a danger of relapsing into the delict they have committed.

83 This is somewhat similar to what some dioceses have established as "monitoring protocols" for clerics accused of sexual abuse of a minor.

is another process in the code that could deal with an unassignable priest. Canon 1708 gives the cleric himself, his ordinary, or the ordaining ordinary the right to petition to have the validity of a priest's ordination overturned. The *libellus* must be sent to the proper dicastery, which will decide whether the dicastery itself or a designated tribunal will hear the case (c. 1709). The case proceeds according to the ordinary contentious process, and the case must be appealed to a second tribunal (c. 1712).

One Last Attempt

Canon 1284 says that the pastor must fulfill his administrative functions "with the diligence of a good householder." Canon 1741, 5° allows for the removal of a pastor for "poor administration of temporal affairs with grave damage to the Church," but then it tempers that by saying, "whenever another remedy to the harm cannot be found."

Perhaps particular law might be able to find "another remedy" to taking some sort of action against the priest whose suitability for an assignment is being called into question. There are three places in the code where some alternative is suggested in order to resolve issues. The first was already discussed in canon 1341: fraternal correction, penal warnings, and penal rebukes.

The second suggestion is found in canon 1446 §1, which states the general principle: "All the faithful and especially bishops, are to strive diligently to avoid litigation among the people of God as much as possible, without prejudice to justice, and to resolve litigation peacefully as soon as possible." Canon 1446 §2 goes on to suggest that a judge encourage and suggest collaboration among the disputing parties, even including mediation.

Finally, Book VII, Part III, Title III contains suggestions for "Methods for Avoiding Trials" (cc. 1713-1714), as well as Part V, Section I, "Recourse Against Administrative Decrees" (cc. 1732-1739). Canon 1713 suggests that, in order to avoid judicial contention, "an agreement or reconciliation is employed usefully, or the controversy can be committed to the judgment of one or more arbitrators." Canon 1733 provides that "whenever a person considers himself or herself aggrieved by a decree, it is particularly desirable that the person and the author of the decree avoid any contention and to take care to seek an equitable solution by common counsel, possibly using the mediation and effort of wise persons to avoid or settle controversy in a suitable way," and suggests that the bishop can establish a council for this in his diocese.

In the revision of the code, there was a section proposed on administrative tribunals. Toward the end of the revision process, these canons were dropped from the code. The United States Conference of Catholic Bishops had a committee "On Due Process," which produced a document of that name. However, any attempts to achieve this on the level of the conference of bishops ultimately failed.[84] However, there is nothing preventing a bishop from establishing such an office or such a process on his own. This again could be done through particular law.

Conclusion

In this paper I have tried to show the many places in the Code of Canon Law that can assist a bishop in dealing with unassignable priests. There are some processes that are proactive, and some that are reactive. The proactive processes deal with being careful about who is ordained and who is incardinated or permitted to minister in your diocese. They also deal with finding ways to do ministerial assessment and continuing education, and having clear expectations of the various offices that priests can be appointed to. It is hoped that by using these processes there will be fewer priests who are deemed "unassignable." The reactive processes deal with declaring a priest psychologically incapable of ministering, requesting his voluntary dispensation from the obligations of the clerical state including the obligation of celibacy, using the Special Faculties of the Dicastery for the Clergy, using the penal canons, particularly on penal remedies and penances, establishing particular penal law, or declaring the nullity of orders. These processes can be used in those cases where none of the proactive processes have worked. I have also suggested that some of these issues can be avoided, or at least dealt with in a less contentious manner, by employing mediation, arbitration, or conciliation, and establishing a council or office to deal with those cases.

In all of this, the Code of Canon Law reminds us that what we are searching for is a just solution to the problem, keeping before our eyes the salvation of souls, which, canon 1752 reminds us, must always be the supreme law of the Church.

---

84 Kurt Martens wrote two articles in *The Jurist* detailing the development and the demise of these canons. He provides an in-depth description of the process that took place during the revision of the code. See Kurt Martens, "The Law That Never Was: the *motu proprio Administrativae potestatis* on Administrative Procedures," *The Jurist* 68 (2008) 178-222; and Kurt Martens, "Protection of Rights: Experiences with Hierarchical Recourse and Possibilities for the Future," *The Jurist* 69 (2009) 646-702.

CLSA PROCEEDINGS 85 (2023) 205-224

Seminar

Not a Ground: The Case against Determining Error

Dr. Felix Menendez JCD, STL

EDITOR'S NOTE: *A summary outline of this seminar talk is included at the end of the article.*[1]

Introduction

What I am about to say in this seminar directly contradicts what wiser and more experienced canonists have taught in past national conventions.[2] In a spirit of humility, I present the following ideas for the sake of scientific progress and to promote cooperation among scholars.

So here is my thesis: Canon 1099 states that the error regarding unity, indissolubility, and sacramentality of marriage does not invalidate consent *dummodo non determinet voluntatem* (unless it determines the will). I believe that these four words contradict both logic and canonical tradition and should be

1 This summary outline serves to help the reader understand the main ideas of the article. Prior to the 2023 Convention, the following video was provided as auxiliary material on the grounds of error: https://youtu.be/KHfx4AYUWdc. It can also be accessed by scanning this QR code:

2 The content of this seminar is based on the research of my doctoral dissertation, *Dummodo non determinet voluntatem. Análisis histórico-jurídico de la cláusula del c. 1099,* Dissertationes Canonicae (Madrid: Ediciones Universidad San Dámaso 2014). I refer to it for the historical sources behind this seminar. More recently, I have published a summary of the dissertation in English: "Error Determinans. A Ground of Nullity? The Perspective of the Tradition," *The Jurist* 77 (2021) 103-124, where I included most of the relevant sources. Given the nature of this seminar, I excuse myself from including here all the bibliographical references, which can be found in these two publications.

erased from the Code of Canon Law. It's a bold statement, I know. So please, let me try to convince you.

Structure of Marriage

In order to do so, we need to go back to the fundamental structure of marriage. Let's begin with the essence. If we want to know the essence of marriage, we need to know the definition of marriage. Where can we find the definition of marriage in the Code of Canon Law? A rookie mistake would be to answer canon 1055. Canon 1055 is not a definition of marriage. It is a description of the sacrament of marriage.

A proper definition includes *proximum genus* and *differentia specifica*. All the members of the group fall within the definition and none of them are left outside. The essential definition of marriage is in canon 1096: "Marriage is a permanent partnership between a man and a woman ordered to the procreation of offspring by means of some sexual cooperation."[3] The *genus* is "partnership." Marriage is a partnership. And what is the *differentia specifica*? What makes marriage different to other partnerships? Canon 1096 gives us four notes.

First, marriage is permanent. Unlike other sexual partnerships, like prostitution or concubinage, which are merely temporary, marriage is permanent. Notice, however, that the code says "permanent" and not "indissoluble." Permanence means that the marriage lasts indefinitely. Indissoluble means that only death can dissolve it, with no exceptions at all.[4]

---

3 See *Codex Iuris Canonici auctoritate Ioannis Pauli PP. II promulgatus* (Vatican City: Libreria Editrice Vaticana, 1983) (*CIC*83) c. 1055:

> §1. The matrimonial covenant, by which a man and a woman establish between themselves a partnership of the whole of life and which is ordered by its nature to the good of the spouses and the procreation and education of offspring, has been raised by Christ the Lord to the dignity of a sacrament between the baptized. §2. For this reason, a valid matrimonial contract cannot exist between the baptized without it being by that fact a sacrament.

Eng. trans. in *Code of Canon Law, Latin-English Edition, New English Translation* (Washington, DC: Canon Law Society of America, 2023). All subsequent English translations from this code are from this source unless otherwise indicated.

4 Tomás Sánchez was decisive in the distinction between the tendency to perseverance, which belongs to the essence of marriage, and indissolubility *sensu stricto*, which is the essential property. Cf. Humberto Domine, *L'errore semplice intorno alle proprietà essenziali del matrimonio ed il suo influsso sulla validità del medesimo. Dissertatio ad lauream in Facultate iuris canonici Pontificiae Universitatis Gregorianae* (Parma 1966) 18; Tomás Sánchez, *De sancto matrimonii sacramento disputationum* I, lib. 2, disp. 1, n. 8 (Lyon 1739) 119.

So, marriage is a partnership with four characteristics: it is permanent, between a man and a woman, open to procreation, and through sexual intercourse. The right to have sexual intercourse or *jus coeundi* is the formal object of the contract of marriage.

If this is the essence of marriage, everything else is accidental. Typical examples of accidental elements of marriage are the adoption of the husband's surname, or to live under the same roof. Many spouses don't do these things, and they are validly married.

So, what about the essential properties? Unity and indissolubility do not appear in canon 1096, so they must not be essential. But they are so important for us Christians. How can they not be essential? Remember Jesus' words on divorce? How can indissolubility be accidental? And what about the equal dignity of spouses? Polygamy is unacceptable to us. It cannot be merely accidental, can it? But unity and indissolubility are not featured in canon 1096. So, are they essential or not?

If we consider the matter carefully, it is impossible that they are essential, because in that case most marriages celebrated throughout history would be invalid. And this is simply absurd. The Catholic Church did not invent marriage. People were getting married thousands of years before Jesus established his Church. We cannot deny the legitimacy of all the marriages that have existed throughout history. Our forefathers were perfectly aware of this. So, they concluded: unity and indissolubility must be very important, but they cannot be essential.[5] Hence the peculiar name: "essential properties." They follow the essence and they pertain to every marriage, but they do not belong to that minimum that you need to know if you want to marry.

And what about the sacramentality? It is not a property. It is marriage itself when celebrated between two baptized. However, when it comes to error and exclusion, it assimilates to the properties. It is not a property, but it functions as a property.[6]

---

5 One insight that appears very clearly from the historical research of my dissertation is that the Church did not deduce the essential properties from a preconceived schema, in a deductive manner. On the contrary, the distinction between essence and essential properties is the result of an inductive process. It represents the best explanation of the data at hand, in a similar way as how the Christological-Trinitarian dogma was developed throughout the first centuries of the history of the Church.

6 Hence its mention in c. 1099 *CIC*83 and c. 1084 *CIC*17.

Error and Exclusion

These so far are the fundamental elements of the structure of marriage: essence, accidents, and essential properties. Now let's see the effects of error and exclusion on each of them.

Whenever we speak of error, we always bring up the adagio *nihil volitum nisi praecognitum*. In English: "Nothing is wanted if not known beforehand," or simply put "we cannot want what we don't know." Indeed, we only want what we know. If we don't know something, we cannot want it. But this is only true for the essence of thing,; not for the accidents. When we want the essence of something we want the accidents as well, even if we are unaware of them.

For instance, when you agreed (when you gave your consent) to attend this seminar, you didn't know the color of the chairs, or what my exact words would be. These elements are accidental and were implied in your consent.

This is why Francisco Suárez says, "*voluntas intrat ubi intellectus foris stat.*"[7] That is, "the will goes inside where the intellect remains outside" or, more freely translated, "the will reaches further than the intellect."

Simply put, essential error invalidates consent, accidental error does not. Exclusion, on the other hand, is different. When it comes to exclusion, what matters is not so much the object, but the intensity of the act of the will. It is a matter of prevalence. In cases of exclusion, we have two wills: the will to marry and the will to exclude. If the will to exclude is stronger, there is no consent. If the will to marry is stronger, the exclusion is irrelevant. What really matters is the strength of the will to exclude, and not so much what was excluded.

And what about the error in quality of canon 1097 §2?[8] That is an accidental error that makes the marriage invalid. And indeed, it seems like an exception. But it is not. In fact, this is not a ground of error, but a ground of condition. The key here is the phrase *directly and principally intended.* What makes the marriage invalid is the implicit, but prevalent, intention to have that quality. The error about that quality does not make the marriage invalid. The quality is just a circumstance or an accident of the implicit exclusion.

---

7 Francisco Suárez, "Commentaria in secundam secundæ divi Thomæ," tract. 6, lib. 1, cap. 3, n. 9, in: Id., *Opera omnia* XIV, ed. C. Berton (Paris 1859) 765: ". . . ut philosophi dicunt, voluntas fertur in rem prout est in se, et hoc satis est ut implicite quis velit quod ignorat; sic enim dicitur etiam a Theologis, quod voluntas intrat ubi intellectus foris stat."

8 See c. 1097 §2: "Error concerning a quality of the person does not render a marriage invalid even if it is the cause for the contract, unless this quality is directly and principally intended."

History

This so far is an extremely brief summary of the doctrine on marriage treasured and developed by the Catholic Church throughout the centuries. Particularly relevant for us is Cardinal Pietro Gasparri, who offered in his famous *Tractatus Canonicus de Matrimonio* one of the most accomplished syntheses of this Catholic doctrine on marriage.

Gasparri is relevant to us because his language, his expressions, were adopted by the first Code of Canon Law. Not in vain, he was the editor of the 1917 code. This adoption is particularly evident when it comes to substantial marriage law.

And so, we read in canon 1084 of the 1917 code that a simple error about the properties or the sacramentality does not make the marriage invalid, even if it was the reason for the marriage.[9] In other words, the error about the properties is not diriment in any case, including the error *dans causam* or error that motivates the marriage.

A typical example of error *dans causam* is the *error fortunae* or error about the wealth. For instance, a man who marries a woman because she is rich, while in fact she is poor. As long as this man does not attach an implicit and prevalent condition, his consent is naturally sufficient to marry. He is choosing to establish a permanent partnership open to procreation through sexual congress with this poor woman, whom he believes to be rich. He is mistaken about a quality, about an accident, not about the essence or identity of the woman.

Therefore, according to canon 1084 of the first code, the error about the properties and the sacramentality is an accidental error and, therefore, it does not make consent invalid, even if it is the very reason for the marriage. Remember: error *causam dans* is not diriment.

Now, the code says that "simple" error does not vitiate consent. Why simple? What does this *simplex* mean? *Simplex* means just the error and nothing else—error exclusion. This is evident to anyone who is familiar with Gasparri's *Tractatus,* not only because he uses the adjective *simplex* in this way again and

9 See *Codex Iuris Canonici Pii X Pontificis Maximi iussu digestus Benedicti Papae XV auctoritate promulgatus* (Rome: Typis Polyglottis Vaticanis, 1917) c. 1084: "Simplex error circa matrimonii unitatem vel indissolubilitatem aut sacramentalem dignitatem, etsi det causam contractui, non vitiat consensum matrimonialem."

again, but also because of Gasparri's very explanation of this particular type of error.[10]

However, canonists started early on to attempt to discover a hidden meaning behind this *simplex*. And very soon a tiny stream of doctrine began to distinguish between this error, which is simple, and another one, which is complex or *qualificatus*. Soon other words appear to refer to this error, like error *radicatus*, error *pervicax*, or error *inveteratus*, to name just a few.

Ultimately, these theories imply that canon 1084 does not mean that error about the properties is irrelevant. It would mean that this particular type of error is irrelevant, but other types of error about the properties are diriment. Notice the radical change in meaning. Based on the flawed analysis of one word, the original and traditional meaning of the canon has been overturned.

This radical interpretation of the old canon 1084 was never broadly accepted, but the distinction between *error simplex* and *error pervicax* became relatively popular. It was even mentioned in seven Rotal sentences.[11]

To be sure, never has a Rotal sentence declared a marriage invalid because of an error about the properties. Not even the handful of affirmative sentences on determining error issued after the promulgation of the new code in 1983. These more recent sentences declare the marriage invalid because of the act of the will, and the error itself is the occasion or the motive for the act of the will.[12]

However, even though there was no record of a diriment error about the properties, during the revision of the code, the members of the *Coetus de Matrimonio* mysteriously decided to include a reference to this new trend in canon

---

10 Pietro Gasparri, *Tractatus Canonicus de Matrimonio* n. 902 (Paris 19043) II/24: Jam vero hoc in casu certum est haberi consensum matrimonialem, ideoque matrimonium per se valere cum simplici errore juris, etiam dante causam contractui, nempe si contrahens, qui in eo errore versatur, modo vult inire matrimonium verum, prout a Deo institutum est, etc., et positive voluntatis actu non excludit proprietatem matrimonio essentialem, licet excluderet, si de ea cogitaret. Nam si res bene perpendatur, in casu est unicus voluntatis actus in matrimonium verum, juxta divinam institutionem, etc., qui sufficit pro consensu matrimoniali et matrimonii valore.

11 Cf. SRR Decisio coram Felici, 13 iul. 1954; SRR Decisio coram Felici, 17 dec. 1957; SRR Decisio coram Filipiak, 23 mar. 1956; SRR Decisio coram Sabattani, 12 nov. 1964; SRR Decisio coram Ewers, 24 feb. 1968; SRR Decisio coram Ewers, 16 maii 1968; SRR Decisio coram Anne, 11 mar. 1975.

12 Compare the recent study of the Rotal jurisprudence on c. 1099 by William Daniel, "Error Determining the Will (c. 1099) as an Autonomous *Caput Nullitatis* in Rotal Jurisprudence," *The Jurist* 77 (2021) 407-463.

1099. Why they chose this language is unknown. In fact, the act of the meeting is very obscure.[13]

Some fathers proposed keeping the mention of the error *causam dans* as in the old code; others proposed the phrase *dummodo non excludat voluntatem*; and others (we do not know how many) *dummodo non determinet voluntatem*. And then, after a brief discussion (*post brevem discussionem*), just like that, they chose the last one.

Interpretations

And this is the new canon 1099 that they gave us: "Error concerning the unity or indissolubility or sacramental dignity of marriage does not vitiate matrimonial consent provided that it does not determine the will." But what is this determination? Our errors always determine our will in some sense. Is this a special kind of determination? It's not clear. What are we talking about?

The best proof that determining error is a bad ground is what its defenders say about it. Stankiewicz, the main proponent of the new ground, literally says that determining error is "easier to intuit than to understand"[14] and recognizes that it is a *crux interpretum* (a cross for the interpreters).[15]

Determining error is such a bad ground because there is no consensus about its very nature. With other grounds, we may disagree on the nuances, but we all agree on what the ground is. For instance, exclusion of children makes a marriage invalid because the right to procreate is not exchanged. We may disagree on the

---

13 See *Communicationes* 9/2 (1977) 373:
Can. 301 (CIC 1084). Error circa matrimonii unitatem vel indissolubilitatem, dummodo non afficiat voluntatem, non vitiat consensum matrimonialem.
Circa hunc canonem sequentes praecipuae animadversiones factae sunt:
a) aliqui (paucissimi tamen) negant substantiam huius canonis et petunt ut statuatur norma contraria, scilicet si habeatur error circa unitatem vel indissolubilitatem, praesumitur vitiatum fuisse consensum matrimonialem. Consultores autem tenent doctrinam traditionalem in qua fundatur hic canon, scilicet de compossibilitate erroris simplicis in mente, qui non determinet voluntatem, quia in casu voluntas versatur circa matrimonium prout communiter habetur, id est unum et indissolubile. b) Aliqui dixerunt verba CIC « etsi det causam contractui » esse clariora, alii proposuerunt « dummodo non excludat voluntatem », alii « dummodo non determinet voluntatem ». Post brevem discussionem, Consultores eligunt verba « dummodo non determinet voluntatem ».

14 Antoni Stankiewicz, "L'errore di diritto nel consenso matrimoniale e la sua autonomia giuridica," *Periodica* 83 (1994) 651. This is a quote from Villeggiante.

15 Ibid. This is a quote from V. De Paolis.

precise content of the right, or on the ways to prove the exclusion. But the general dynamic of the nullity, the nature of the ground, is peacefully accepted by all.

Of course, determining error is a *crux interpretum*! The law itself is unclear. There are even different schools of thought on the meaning of this clause. I am going to describe the main theories dividing them into three clusters.[16]

The first ones are the irenics. According to them, *dummodo non determinet voluntatem* is just a remission to the exclusions of canon 1101. No error on the properties can make a marriage invalid, but it can be the basis or the motive for an exclusion. This seems the most reasonable interpretation. It agrees with canonical tradition and with the statement of the fathers of the *coetus,* who clearly established that they did not have the intention to change the traditional doctrine.

On the opposite side, we have the revolutionaries. They claim that the essential properties are now essential to marriage. Therefore, the wrong conceptions about unity, indissolubility, or sacramentality are now essential errors. This error, by itself, makes the marriage invalid when it is your only notion of marriage.

These authors do not seem to understand the consequences of their hypothesis. If the essential properties are essential knowledge required for marriage, then the absolute majority of marriages would be invalid.

This argument alone is more than enough to cast this thesis aside. But in addition, this theory contradicts two millennia of canonical tradition, which means that the Church would have been gravely mistaken on a matter *de fide et moribus* for centuries and centuries. Countless judicial sentences, administrative decisions, and magisterial teachings would have been dead wrong.

The third group of authors are the innovators, who try to identify a new and autonomous ground without distorting our canonical tradition. The main proponent is Monsignor Stankiewicz, the late dean of the Roman Rota.

Stankiewicz affirms, and reasonably so, that the word *dummodo*, according to legislative technique, implies the existence of a new ground of nullity. Trying to be obedient to the apparent innovation, while at the same time respectful of tradition, Stankiewicz proposed that there must be a new ground, different from diriment exclusion and from irrelevant error. He defends that a deeply rooted error

---

16 This distribution in three groups of theories is, like all generalizations, unable to convey the many nuances of the proposals of each author. However, I consider it to be a fair description of the *status quaestionis* and I refer, once again, to my doctoral dissertation for the full investigation of the theories on the meaning of determining error. In the fifth chapter, I explain the main interpretations of c. 1099 in a nuanced way.

about the properties is able to determine the will to choose a marriage deprived of the properties:

> Therefore, it seems to us that the canonical notion of the juridically relevant and efficacious error, alongside the erroneous judgment on the object defined by canon 1099, must also encompass the act of will that determines the concrete choice of the object defined by the error, that is, entirely contrary to what the canonical law establishes as the object of matrimonial consent. Thus, in the sense of such an error, is the emphasis not only on the transition of error from the intellect to the will through the determination of the "real and true content of the consenting party's intent," which is not in accordance with canonical matrimonial norms, but also on the act of will of the erring party. This act of the will, influenced profoundly by that error, aims for a marriage that is positively and voluntarily devoid of unity, indissolubility, or sacramentality. In this specific case, therefore, the error becomes "determining for the act of will," and consequently, the object of the will, that is, the consent specified by the error, cannot be "qualifiable as matrimonial."[17]

Why not? If this is not an exclusion, why is the error able to make the marriage invalid? And also, if this is not an exclusion, why do we need to consider the act of the will? Otherwise, if the act of the will is so important, how is this different from a traditional exclusion? I must confess that whenever I read Stankiewicz's ideas on determining error I am always left with so many questions. As much as I admire the canonical genius of the former dean of the Roman Rota, in all fairness, his production on determining error labors from an evident lack of clarity. Moreover, his position contradicts two millennia of canonical tradition,

---

17 Stankiewicz, "L'errore di diritto," 665:
Ci sembra, quindi, che l'accezione canonica dell'errore giuridicamente rilevante ed efficace, accanto al giudizio erroneo sull'oggetto definito dal c. 1099, debba comprendere anche l'atto di volontà che determina la scelta concreta dell'oggetto definito dall'errore, cioè del tutto contrario a quello stabilito dalla legge canonica come oggetto del consenso matrimoniale. Pertanto nell'accezione di siffatto errore è necesaria non solo l'accentuazione del passaggio dell'errore all'intelletto alla volontà attraverso la determinazione «del contenuto reale e vero del consenso del contraente», non conforme all'ordinamento matrimoniale canonico, ma anche l'accentuazione dell'atto di volontà dell'errante, «il quale, per l'influsso radicale di quell'errore, vuole un matrimonio privo positivamente e volontariamente di unità, d'indissolubilità o di sacramentalità». In questa fattispecie, quindi, l'errore diventa «determinante per l'atto di volontà» e di conseguenza l'oggetto di volere, ossia del consenso specificato dall'errore, non può essere «qualificabile come matrimoniale».

which has never known an error concerning the properties that invalidates consent.

The other great proponent of an explanation of the meaning of determining error is cardinal Urbano Navarrete, the late rector of the Gregorian University. Like Stankiewicz, Navarrete presumed the existence of a new ground and, like many other canonists tried to find a place for it among the grounds of nullity. And he proposed an elegant solution. His starting point is the error *recidens* of canon 126, according to which, "an act placed . . . out of error . . . which amounts to a condition *sine qua non* is invalid."

Let me give you an example of error *recidens.* Let us say that I want to get an electric car, a Tesla. So, I go online, find a nice Tesla, and buy it. But when the car arrives, oh surprise, it runs on gas! What have I done? I didn't even know that Tesla made gas cars (they do not, by the way; this is just a thought experiment). I got a Tesla precisely because I wanted an electric car, and the Tesla that I got has a gasoline engine. When I bought it, I was in error, assuming that all Teslas are electric. My error amounts to a prevalent condition that was not fulfilled. This type of error is called *error recidens* because it amounts to a diriment condition, a condition that renders consent invalid: I want a Tesla because I do not want to have a gasoline engine.

Secondly, Navarrete considered the distinction between error of fact and error of law. Error of fact is the error about the other spouse and their qualities. Error of law is the error about the legal institute, the matrimonial contract itself. In our example with the Tesla, the error was an error of fact: whether the car is electric or not. An error of law would be, for instance, whether I'm buying or leasing the car.

Considering this distinction, Navarrete proposed that the error in quality of canon 1097 is the *error recidens* applied to the error of fact, and determining error is the *error recidens* applied to the error of law.[18] It was a beautiful and elegant solution.

The Second Navarrete

However, with time, Navarrete changed his mind. Twenty years ago, in 2003, at the Ecclesiastical University of San Dámaso, in Madrid, he gave a conference where he explained his new thoughts on the matter:

> . . . psychologically, a state of error about the essential properties seems incompatible . . . with the fact that the same person can determine his or her will to not want, in the concrete case of their marriage, one of the properties or the sacramentality; and the motive is precisely because the person is certain, even if based on the error, that these properties do not belong to the structure of marriage. If they are certain that these properties do not belong to marriage, how could they determine their will to not want them for their marriage . . . ?[19]

And indeed, error of law and error of fact are very different from each other. For instance, there is an infinite diversity of people's characteristics: there are tall people, short people, fat, thin, rich, poor, smart, foolish, fun, boring... We are so diverse that when we get married, we are always in error about certain qualities

---

18 Urbano Navarrete, "De sensu clausulae 'Dummodo non determinet voluntatem' can. 1099," *Periodica* 81 (1992) 490:

> Meo iudicio, in c. 1099 habetur alius casus applicationis principii generalis enuntiati in c. 126. Acceptato enim ordine systematico, quem Legislator indicat, quoad nullitates actus iuridici ex errore positi, concludendum videtur clausulam 'dummodo non determinet voluntatem' c. 1099 aequivalere clausulae 'ex errore, qui . . . recidit in condicionem sine qua non' c. 126. Aliis verbis: in c. 1099 habetur applicatio principii generalis enuntiati in c. 126 ad errorem circa matrimonii unitatem vel indissolubilitatem aut sacramentalem dignitatem, aliis tamen verbis propositi; haud secus ac accidit in c. 1097 & 2 quoad errorem in qualitate personae si 'qualitas directe et principaliter intendatur.'

19 Urbano Navarrete, "El matrimonio canónico a la luz del concilio Vaticano II: cuestiones fundamentales y desarrollos doctrinales," in Urbano Navarrete, *Derecho matrimonial canónico. Evolución a la luz del Concilio Vaticano II* (Madrid: Biblioteca de Autores Cristianos 2007) 1187-1188:

> . . . psicológicamente parece ser incompatible un estado de error acerca de las propiedades esenciales . . . con el hecho de que la misma persona pueda determinar su voluntad a no querer, en el caso concreto de su matrimonio, una de las propiedades o la sacramentalidad; y el motivo es precisamente porque la persona está cierta, aunque fundada en el error, de que esas propiedades no pertenecen a la estructura del matrimonio. Si está cierta de que dichas propiedades no pertenecen al matrimonio no se ve cómo puede eficazmente determinar su voluntad a no quererlas en su matrimonio o a querer que no se den en su matrimonio.

of our spouses. But legal institutions are not like people. There is only one true marriage, and the differences between the different existing conceptions of marriage are pretty narrow.

In this sense, the error about a quality of the other spouse does not work in the same way as the error about a quality of the matrimonial contract. Someone who is completely oblivious to the essential properties of marriage (someone with a *pervicax* or deep-seated error) cannot make implicit conditions against them, because they are simply unaware of their existence.

For instance, consider a Muslim man who marries a woman that he doesn't really love because he believes that he can have another marriage if he finds someone better later on, or a Jewish man who marries in the same situation because he thinks that he can repudiate the first one if he finds another woman that he likes better. These men only know marriage deprived of unity and indissolubility, respectively. Their error is so deep-seated that they believe God himself has made marriage like this. And precisely because this is the only concept of marriage that they know, it is impossible for them to include an implicit condition against the properties. Their errors are *dans causam*; they marry because of their errors. They both think, "I marry you because I can marry another one," or "because I can repudiate you." But they cannot think, "and if I cannot, then I don't want to marry you." And they cannot do it precisely because they are ignorant that marriage is exclusive and until death.

Ecumenical Concerns

So far, I have proposed two arguments of authority: the canonical tradition and the teachings of Navarrete. I have given as well an argument of reason: it is metaphysically impossible to refuse with prevalent will something that you do not know. Allow me to give you one more argument: a practical one with ecumenical implications.

The following are some of the first results we obtain if we make a simple Google search of the words, "canon 1099 Catholic tribunal." I have concealed the names of the tribunals out of respect and discretion.[20] But please keep in mind that all this is public information. Anyone can find this easily with a quick search on their phones or computers.

---

20 Indeed, tribunals are not scholars and the content in their websites is merely informational. I have no doubt that they all act with the best intentions, trying to do what they can with a difficult legislation that has been handed down to them. The Google search was performed in September 2023 and the six websites quoted in this article were featured within the first ten results.

1. The first one is not from America. It comes from an inter-diocesan tribunal overseas. They say, "This ground of nullity means that only if someone actually chooses to marry because he/she did not have to be faithful, or because he/she believed in divorce, can the marriage be considered as null. In other words, if the error about marriage is the reason why someone chooses to marry, it is null." This is a direct contradiction of the traditional teaching on error *dans causam*, which according to this website, is now a diriment error.

2. The second example is from a parish in Texas. On their website, we find a short version of the most radical interpretation of canon 1099. They propose three grounds of nullity on determining error: "Error regarding marital unity that determined the will (1099). You or your spouse married believing that marriage was not necessarily an exclusive relationship." In other words, the millions of marriages in cultures that accept polygamy are now invalid marriages. Second ground: "Error regarding marital indissolubility that determined the will (Canon 1099). You or your spouse married believing that civil law had the power to dissolve marriage and that remarriage was acceptable after civil divorce." This means that virtually everyone in the world, with the exception of a few devout Catholics who refuse divorce, is incapable of a valid marriage. Third ground: "Error regarding marital sacramental dignity that determined the will (Canon 1099). You and your spouse married believing that marriage is not a religious or sacred relationship but merely a civil contract or arrangement." This is literally the case for millions of Protestants all over the world.

3. The third website is from a diocese in California, and this is how they explain determining error: "You or your spouse did not know or understand the Church's teaching on indissolubility, fidelity or sacramentality, and you chose a marriage that you could end at will, or in which you could be unfaithful, or that was not a sacrament." This is another version of the most radical interpretations of canon 1099 that we have seen before.

4. Another American tribunal also proposes three grounds. "Error about fidelity;" "perpetuity;" and "sacramental dignity." And when is this error diriment? Here they try to propose Stankiewicz's doctrine: ". . . to the degree that the party only understood marriage with that error." Once again, most marriages fall under these three grounds, because most grooms and brides throughout history and also today only understand marriage with at least one of these errors.

5. Here is another American tribunal: "A person entered marriage in error concerning the unity or indissolubility or sacramental dignity of marriage. They held very deep and pervasive beliefs that are in error concerning marriage, so much so, that they could not and did not marry according to the

Church's understanding of marriage." Here we get some echoes from Stankiewicz's teachings. Somehow, the pervasive beliefs are "so much so" rooted that they make marriage impossible. Once again, with this criterion, most marriages celebrated ever would be invalid.

6. Let us see one more from a diocese in the northern U.S.: "A person must know that the Church teaches that marriage is permanent, requires fidelity and openness to children." This is an unfortunate expression. For a person to get married, they don't need to know anything about what the Church teaches. People were getting married millennia before the Church was founded by Christ. What they need to know is the essence of marriage, not that the Church understands marriage correctly.

   It goes on: " . . . as well as the fact that it is an equal partnership between spouses." Equality is certainly a positive thing but does not pertain to the essence of marriage either. "Evidence of this ground: If an error about the Church's teachings determines one's will to enter the marriage, the consent was invalid. . . . If a person leaves the marriage upon this occurring, this error regarding the permanent nature of marriage can be said to have determined their will." This is new: determination of the will as being consistent. To determine means to act, after the exchange of consents, probably years after, according to your erroneous understanding of indissolubility. "The error must determine one's action. Simply having an erroneous belief about marriage and not acting on it is not enough."

We could go on and on for hours reading remarks like these. It is very concerning. But it is not their fault. They are trying to do their best with what has been given to them. What we are witnessing here is what happens when the Legislator promulgates laws that are difficult to understand. We scholars make beautiful books and articles, but what trickles down to tribunals is not so pretty; let alone what reaches the average petitioner.

Please consider carefully the implications of these statements. We are openly and carelessly saying that the marriages of Protestants, Jews, Atheists, Orthodox, Buddhists, Anglicans, and basically everyone who is not a devout Catholic are invalid or presumed invalid. This is not what the Church teaches. It represents an insult to the absolute majority of humanity, and it is certainly detrimental to our institutional relations with other confessions, Christian and non-Christian alike. If other confessions understood the implications of these affirmations, we would be flooded with formal protests. And rightfully so.

Conclusion

In conclusion,

since determining error has no root in our canonical tradition;

since after 40 years, there is no consensus about the very nature of this ground;

since it appears to be a metaphysically impossible error;

since it keeps generating confusion in the practices of local tribunals worldwide;

since it risks having negative ecumenical implications;

based on the authority of Cardinal Navarrete; and

with all due respect to the Legislator;

I defend that the words *dummodo non determinet voluntatem*

should be removed from canon 1099 of the Code of Canon Law.

PRACTICAL EXERCISE

Now, since this is a seminar, I would like for us to do a practical exercise. I am going to propose some cases of apparent determining error, and then I will open the floor for proposals of authentic diriment determining errors.

1. The first example is from the Gospel: In that time, Jesus said to his disciples, "Now I tell you that whoever divorces his wife and marries another woman, commits adultery." His disciples said to him, "If this is the case between a man and his wife, it is better not to marry." And Jesus replied, "Amen, amen, I tell you, fear not little flock, for all your marriages are invalid due to a determining error about indissolubility."

Please forgive the joke. But I think that this *reductio ad absurdum* is the best evidence against determining error. Indeed, it is difficult to find a more deep-seated error than that of the Jews, who believe that God himself has given us the right to divorce. Moses himself, the Prophet, the mouth of God, came down the sacred mountain and told us that repudiation was acceptable. Can there be a more inveterate error than that?

2. And our second case is similar: St. Joseph. He had a deep-seated error against indissolubility, to the point that he attempted to repudiate the Virgin Mary. Let's scrap the endless debates among theologians and canonists about this marriage because it was virginal. Nonsense. It was invalid due to a determining error.

Here are some more examples of deeply-seated errors that the Catholic Church has constantly considered irrelevant throughout the centuries, as is evident in magisterial teachings, the praxis of the Roman Curia, and the jurisprudence of the Supreme Tribunals:

3. Islam gives the husband the right to marry up to four wives.

4. Polygamist societies encountered by the missionaries in sub-Saharan Africa.

5. Orthodox, Protestants, Jews, Muslims, Buddhists, many Catholics, and virtually everyone in the world today and throughout history accepts some form of divorce.

6. Protestants consider marriage a rite, not a sacrament.

Now, if you want to, please try to come up with a true case of determining error. It must be an invalid marriage, and the case should not be already covered by one of the traditional grounds of error or exclusion. I would love to learn that there is some basis for this ground, but I remain skeptical. Otherwise, you are welcome to propose questions or comments.

Thank you very much.

ARTICLE OUTLINE

I. THESIS

1. Canon 1099 says: error about unity, indissolubility, and sacramentality
    1. does not make the marriage invalid
    2. unless it determines the will.
2. This last clause
    1. does not make sense
    2. and should be erased from the Code.

II. FUNDAMENTALS

A. Marriage

a. Essence

1. Canon 1096 defines the ESSENCE of marriage:
    1. A permanent partnership
    2. between a man and a woman
    3. ordered to procreation
    4. through sexual intercourse.
2. Christ made this contract a SACRAMENT.
    1. He didn't invent a new marriage.
    2. He raised the pre-existing contract to the dignity of a sacrament.

b. Properties

1. If canon 1096 defines the essence,
    1. everything else is non-essential;
    2. all other elements are ACCIDENTS.
2. So, what about unity and indissolubility?
    1. They are paramount to our Christian understanding of marriage.
    2. But they cannot be essential:
        1. Because most humans ignore them and have ignored them throughout history.
        2. So almost all marriages would be invalid, which is absurd.
        3. They are special; hence the peculiar name ESSENTIAL PROPERTIES.

c. Sacramentality

1. It is not an element within this structure.
2. It is marriage itself when celebrated among two baptized.
3. For error and exclusion, it assimilates to the properties.

B. Error and Exclusion

a. Error

1. When it comes to error, we typically quote the axiom
    1. *nihil volitum nisi praecognitum*
    2. (we cannot want what we ignore).
2. This is true for the essence of things, not for the accidents.
    1. When we want the essence, we want the accidents, even if we ignore them.
    2. Suárez: *Voluntas intrat ubi intellectus foris stat.*
    3. (the will reaches deeper than the intellect).
3. In sum:
    1. Essential error invalidates consent.
    2. Accidental error does not.

b. Exclusion

1. Exclusion is a matter of prevalence.
    1. If the will to exclude is stronger, there is no consent.
    2. If the will to marry is stronger, there is no diriment exclusion.
2. So what about the error in quality of canon 1097?
    1. Seems to be an exception:
        1. A diriment error,
        2. about a non-essential element.
    2. But, in fact,
        1. it is a ground of condition: *directe et principaliter intendatur.*
        2. The nullity comes from the intentional exclusion.

III. DETERMINING ERROR

A. History

a. *CIC*17

1. Canon 1084:
    1. *Simplex error non vitiat consensum.*
    2. *Simplex* means only error, and no exclusion.
2. Canonists try to give meaning to the word *simplex*:
    1. A simple error as opposed to an error *pervicax, veteratus…*
    2. Even some Rotal decisions mention this.

b. *CIC*83

1. Canon 1099: *error non vitiat consensum.*
2. But then it adds *dummodo non determinet voluntatem.*

B. Interpretations

1. There is no agreement on the precise nature of *error determinans*

2. Even its proponents acknowledge that it is a *crux interpretum.*

a. Three main clusters

1. The irenics:
    1. Thesis: Remission to canon 1101.
        1. The error is not diriment.
        2. But it can be the base for an exclusion.
    2. Seems the most reasonable interpretation.
        1. It agrees with canonical tradition.
        2. It agrees with the *coetus*, who refused will to innovate.
2. The revolutionaries:
    1. Thesis: Essential properties are now essential.
        1. The Church has changed the essence of marriage.
        2. Determining error is an essential error.
    2. Refutation:
        1. Contradicts canonical tradition.
        2. Means that the Church has been wrong *de fide et moribus* for centuries.
        3. Means that barely any marriages are valid.
    3. The innovators:
        1. Thesis: A new autonomous ground.
            1. *Dummodo* implies a different ground.
            2. Different from diriment exclusion and irrelevant error.
            3. The error determines the will to choose marriage without properties.
        2. Refutation:
            1. Lacks clarity: "easier to intuit than to understand."
            2. Contradicts canonical tradition.
            3. If the error is so deep, how can the will be so determined to refuse what is ignored?

b. The first Navarrete

1. *Error recidens* of canon 126:
    1. An accidental error does not make an act invalid,
    2. unless it amounts to a condition *sine qua non.*
2. Two types of error:
    1. *Error facti*, about the other spouse.
    2. *Error juris*, about marriage itself.

3. Navarrete proposed that:

    1. *Error in qualitate* is the *error recidens* applied to the *error facti*.
    2. *Error determinans* is the *error recidens* applied to the *error juris*.

c. The second Navarrete

1. *Error juris* does not operate like *error facti*.
    1. There is an infinite diversity of people's characteristics.
    2. It is common to err about the qualities of the other spouse.
    3. It is possible to attach to them an implicit condition.
2. But legal institutions are different.
    1. Someone who is wrong about the essential properties
    2. cannot make an implicit condition against them.

d. The praxis of local tribunals

1. The ground is a source of confusion.
2. A simple internet search shows the negative effects of this obscure ground.
3. It even has negative ecumenical implications.

IV. CONCLUSION

1. Therefore, since *error determinans*
    1. has no root in canonical tradition,
    2. has not generated a consensus in 40 years about its very nature,
    3. seems to be a metaphysically impossible error,
    4. still generates confusion in the praxis of local tribunals around the world, and
    5. risks having negative ecumenical implications;
2. based on the authority of Card. Navarrete; and
3. with all due respect to the Legislator;
4. I defend that
    1. the clause *dummodo non determinet voluntatem*
    2. should be erased from canon 1099 of the Code of Canon Law.

SEMINAR

INVESTIGATIONS TODAY

Mr. Timothy O'Malley, JD

Editor's Note: The speaker did not provide a written text for Proceedings. *This summary was supplied instead.*

This summary reflects the structure of the presentation and sets forth the investigative topics discussed. I spoke mostly from a similar outline and do not have a verbatim version of my comments.

The introduction portion set the stage for clarifying the roles played during the investigative process and the influence that process has on both the individual case at hand and the broader, longer-term good of our Church. Within the Fairness, Accountability and Transparency portions, key investigative factors were identified. During the presentation, these factors were discussed in the context of the objectives set out in the introduction. Then, their practical applications were emphasized through real-life stories. Some of my comments and stories were responsive to reactions of the attendees. Those stories and responsive interactions do not lend themselves to a written summary. The same holds true for exchanges during the question-and-answer portion that covered about the last twenty-five minutes of the session.

I believe that for those who attended the Investigative Process session, the summary will serve as a solid reminder of what was covered. For those who did not attend, it will highlight important guiding principles and provide key factors for them to consider when commencing an investigation.

CLSA PROCEEDINGS 85 (2023) 226-255

SEMINAR

NOW AND AT THE HOUR OF OUR DEBT: CATHOLIC DIOCESES IN BANKRUPTCY

Professor Marie T. Reilly, Esq.

I. Introduction

The child sexual abuse crisis is a multifaceted challenge for the Church. The scandal has significantly and negatively affected the Church's moral authority.[1] It has alienated Catholics. In a 2019 Pew Research Center study, Catholics in the United States said they have cut back on Mass attendance (27%) and reduced contributions to their parishes (26%) in response to reports of Catholic clergy sexual abuse.[2] The

---

1 See Paul Elie, "The Reinvention of the Catholic Church," *The Atlantic*, Dec. 11, 2022 (review of John T. McGreevy, *Catholicism: A Global History from the French Revolution to Pope Francis* (2022) noting that the sex abuse scandal left bishops "stripped of moral authority"), https://www.theatlantic.com/magazine/archive/2023/01/catholic-church-changes-roe-v-wade-pope-francis/672235/ (accessed on 17 Nov. 2023). The president of the United States Conference of Catholic Bishops (USCCB) described the abuse accusations against Archbishop Theodore McCarrick as "reveal[ing] a grievous moral failure within the Church." USCCB, press release "President of U.S. Bishops Conference Issues Statement on Course of Action Responding to Moral Failures on Part of Church Leaders," Aug. 1, 2018, https://www.usccb.org/news/2018/president-us-bishops-conference-issues-statement-course-action-responding-moral-failures (accessed on 17 Nov. 2023).

2 See Pew Research Center, "Americans See Catholic Clergy Sex Abuse as an Ongoing Problem," June 11, 2019, 9, https://www.pewresearch.org/religion/wp-content/uploads/sites/7/2019/06/Pew-Resarch-Center-Sex-Abuse-Full-Report-06.11.19.pdf (accessed on 28 Nov. 2023). Among Catholics who attend Mass regularly, only 39% think that U.S. Catholic bishops have done a good job responding to reports of abuse. Ibid. at 9. The percentage of U.S. Catholics who say they belong to a parish declined 18% between 1998 and 2020. See Jeffrey M. Jones, "U.S. Church Membership Down Sharply in Past Two Decades," Gallup News, Apr. 18, 2019, https://news.gallup.com/poll/248837/church-membership-down-sharply-past-two-decades.aspx (accessed on 28 Nov. 2023). See also Kathy Frankovic, "How the Child Sex Abuse Scandal Impacts the Catholic Church and Catholics," YouGov, Feb. 28, 2019, https://today.yougov.com/topics/politics/articles-reports/2019/02/28/how-sex-abuse-scandal-impacts-catholic-church (accessed on 17 Nov. 2023) (noting a 2019 poll showing 50% of the public and 30% of Catholics view the Church unfavorably); James Martin, "The Virtues of Catholic Anger," *The New York Times* (op. ed.), Aug. 15, 2018, https://www.nytimes.com/2018/08/15/opinion/the-virtues-of-catholic-anger.html (accessed on 17 Nov. 2023, subscription required) (observing the anger of Catholic faithful and clergy against church leaders and encouraging a response of constructive action).

financial impact of liability for child sexual abuse is massive, although it is hard to estimate accurately. Based on data provided to the United States Conference of Catholic Bishops by Catholic organizations, amounts paid as settlements to victims and attorneys' fees were $157 million for 2022, and $4 billion from 2004 through 2022.[3]

Intense media coverage of the Catholic sex abuse story for the last two decades has fueled sustained public outrage against Catholic organizations for their failure to protect children from known abusers and their cover up of the abuse.[4] Since 2002, Catholic organizations have been the subject of at least twenty-one state and local governmental investigations.[5] The media coverage of the Pennsylvania Attorney General's investigative grand jury report in 2018 was particularly vitriolic.[6]

Sexual abuse litigation is big business. Private equity funds finance the cost of litigating sexual abuse claims in exchange for a share of the payment lawyers

---

3 See USCCB Secretariat of Child and Youth Protection, "2022 Annual Report on the Implementation of the Charter for the Protection of Children and Young People" July 2023, 31, https://www.usccb.org/resources/2022-annual-report-implementation-charter-protecti on-children-and-young-people (accessed on 28 Nov. 2023); hereafter "USCCB 2023 Implementation Report."

4 See *The New York Times* ran 225 articles on Catholic clergy sexual abuse over the course of 100 days in 2002, including 26 days on the front page. J. A. Nelson, "Sex Abuse in the American Catholic Church, and the Attempt at Redemption," *J. Comm. and Theater Ass'n. of Minn. J.* 36 (2009) 37, 38.

5 See BishopAccountability.org, "Reports of Attorneys General, Grand Juries, Individuals, Commissions, and Organizations," https://www.bishop-accountanility.org/At AGlance/reports.htm (accessed on 17 Nov. 2023).

6 Pennsylvania Attorney General, "Pennsylvania Diocese Victims Report" (2018), downloadable from https://www.attorneygeneral.gov/wp-content/uploads/2023/05/INVES TIGATING-GRAND-JURY-REPORT-NO.-1_FINAL_May-2023_Redacted.pdf (accessed on 17 Nov. 2023). In the wake of that report, an op ed writer concluded that "[t]he Catholic church is a pedophile ring." Anthea Butler, "The grand jury report about Catholic priest abuse in Pennsylvania shows the church is a criminal syndicate," *Think*, NBC News, Aug. 15, 2018, https://www.nbcnews.com/think/opinion/grand-jury-report-about-catholic-priest-abuse-pennsylvania-shows-church-ncna900906 (accessed on 28 Nov. 2023).

ultimately obtain from defendants.[7] Litigation funders take an estimated 57% of the payments that lawyers obtain on the claims in which they have invested.[8]

Almost all tort claims for child sexual abuse against Catholic organizations allege abuse that occurred decades ago. The generally applicable limitations period to bring a civil action for compensation has long expired.[9] Statutory and common law reforms regarding the limitations defense to tort claims for child sexual abuse opened the way for plaintiffs to recover damages for abuse that they claim occurred decades earlier.[10] Twenty-five states, the District of Columbia, and three U.S. territories have enacted laws that invalidate the statute of limitations defense for lawsuits by adults seeking compensation for sexual abuse they allegedly experienced as children. The legislation, known as claim revival laws or lookback window laws eliminate the statute of limitations defense against claims

---

7 See Samir D. Parikh, "Opaque Capital and Mass Tort Financing," *Yale L. Forum*, Oct. 31, 2023, https://www.yalelawjournal.org/forum/opaque-capital-and-mass-tort-financing (accessed on 28 Nov. 2023); Matthew Goldstein and Jessica Silver-Greenberg, "Hedge Funds Look to Profit from Personal-Injury Suits," *The New York Times*, June 25, 2018, https://www.nytimes.com/2018/06/25/business/hedge-funds-mass-torts-litigation-finance.html_(accessed on 29 Nov. 2023, subscription required); "What is Litigation Funding & How Does it Work for Attorneys in 2023," *Attorney at Law Magazine*, March 21, 2023, https://attorneyatlawmagazine.com/legal-vendors/litigation-funding/what-is-litigation-funding (accessed on 28 Nov. 2023). Litigation funding has raised ethical concerns about the lawyer's fidelity to the client and control over the case. See Maya Steinitz, "The Litigation Finance Contract," *Wm. & Mary L. Rev.* 54 (2012) 455, 457 (the big concern is control—that funders are looking over lawyers' shoulders providing input that the lawyers don't necessarily welcome or agree with—interfering with how lawyers are doing their jobs).

8 See Thomas Holzheu, et al, "U.S. litigation funding and social inflation: The rising costs of legal liability," Swiss Re Institute (Dec. 9, 2021) 13, https://www.swissre.com/institute/research/topics-and-risk-dialogues/casualty-risk/us-litigation-funding-social-inflation.html (accessed on 29 Nov. 2023).

9 See Timothy D. Lytton, *Holding Bishops Accountable: How Lawsuits Helped the Catholic Church Confront Clergy Sexual Abuse* (Cambridge, MA: Harvard University Press, 2008) 185 (estimating that between 80-90% of child sexual abuse claims filed in the U.S. are time barred under the statutory limitations periods that generally apply to tort claims).

10 See generally Marie T. Reilly, "Retribution Against Catholic Dioceses by Revival: The Evolution and Legacy of the New York Child Victims Act," *Alb. L. Rev.* 84 (2022) 735.

for child sexual abuse filed within a certain time period following enactment.[11] This legislative development has resulted in a flood of claims against Catholic organizations. When nine states enacted claim revival legislation in 2019, the average annual number of sexual abuse claims against Catholic dioceses tripled relative to the annual average over the prior five years.[12] New York enacted claim revival legislation in 2019, and subsequently six of the eight dioceses in New York filed for bankruptcy.[13] On April 11, 2023, Maryland enacted the Maryland Child Victims Act, which revives time-barred child sexual abuse claims with a damage cap of $1.5 million per claim against a private organization and $800,000 per claim against a local government.[14] The Archdiocese of Baltimore filed for bankruptcy on September 29, 2023, two days before the Maryland legislation

---

11 See Child USA, "The Relative Success of Civil SOL Window and Revival Statutes State-by-State," June 2017, https://childusa.org/wpcontent/uploads/2020/03/child_relative success_june2017_final.pdf [https://perma.cc/HM76972J] (accessed on 29 Nov. 2023) (reporting the number of lawsuits filed after revival window legislation opened in six states and Guam before nine states enacted revival window legislation in 2019); Associated Press, "New Wave of sexual-abuse lawsuits could cost Catholic Church more than $4 billion," MarketWatch, Dec. 2, 2019, https://www.marketwatch.com/story/new-wave-of-sexual-abuse-lawsuits-could-cost-catholicchurch-over-4-billion-2019-12-02 [https://perma.cc/W3JV-EYRM] (accessed on 29 Nov. 2023) (estimating more than 5,000 new sexual abuse lawsuits cases in response to extension or suspension of statute of limitations); Associated Press, "Clergy sex abuse allegations triple, U.S. Catholic bishops report," *Los Angeles Times*, June 26, 2020, https://www.latimes.com/world-nation/story/2020-06-25/clergy-sex-abuse-allegations-tripleus-roman-catholic-bishops-report [https://perma.cc/XV6U-3RG9] (accessed on 29 Nov. 2023) (reporting that in the 2018-2019 audit year there were 4,434 sex abuse allegations against clergy).

12 Arizona, Arkansas, California (twice), Colorado, Connecticut, Delaware, Georgia, Hawaii, Kansas, Kentucky, Louisiana, Maine, Maryland, Massachusetts, Michigan, Minnesota, Montana, Nevada, New Jersey, New York, North Carolina, Oregon, Rhode Island, Vermont, West Virginia, District of Columbia, Northern Mariana Islands, Guam. Child USA, *Statutes of Limitation by Jurisdiction*, https://childusa.org/2023sol/ (accessed on 29 Nov. 2023). U.S. Catholic organizations have lobbied in opposition to limitations reform. See Scott Malone, "The Catholic Church is fighting to block bills that would extend the statute of limitations for reporting sex abuse," *Business Insider*, Sept. 10, 2015, https://www.businessinsider.com/r-as-pope-visit-nears-us-sex-victims-say-church-remains-obstacle-to-justice-2015-9 (accessed on 29 Nov. 2023); George Joseph, "U.S. Catholic Church has spent millions fighting clergy sex abuse accountability," *The Guardian*, May 12, 2016, https://www.theguardian.com/us-news/2016/may/12/catholic-church-fights-clergy-child-sex-abuse-measures (accessed on 29 Nov. 2023).

13 See Marie T. Reilly, "B: Outcomes of Cases," in "Catholic Dioceses in Bankruptcy," *Penn State Law* eLibrary, June 3, 2019, appendix B, https://elibrary.law.psu.edu/bankruptcy/36/ (accessed on 29 Nov. 2023).

14 See S.B. 686, Gen. Assemb., Reg. Sess. (Md. 2023).

became effective.[15] Since 2004, in response to mission-threatening tort liability to child sexual abuse claimants, thirty-seven U.S. Catholic religious organizations have filed for relief in bankruptcy court. Twenty-four cases have concluded. Thirteen cases are pending.[16] More cases are likely.

Catholic organizations' use of bankruptcy to manage potential liability to thousands of plaintiffs for child sexual abuse has revealed the profound impact of bankruptcy law on the life of the Church. Canon law governs the relationships *among* juridic persons[17] and their respective responsibilities within the Church hierarchy. Secular tort law establishes Catholic organizations' *external* duty of care and liability to persons who claim to have been sexually abused as children. Secular law governing creditors and debtors frames this liability unemotionally as debt and recognizes abused persons as creditors. The President of the United States Conference of Catholic Bishops recently stated that U.S. bishops have endeavored to "do what is right—be accountable for the hurt and pain caused by the abuse, make amends so that abuse would not happen again, and strive to make for right relationships by publicly offering statements of sorrow and responsibility for allowing such horror to happen in the first place."[18] Notwithstanding the benevolent sentiment expressed in this statement, a debtor obtains "accountability and amends" for its liability to creditors by payment in exchange for a release of liability.

This presentation explains the law that governs a Catholic organization's liability to a person who was sexually abused as a child by an actor within that organization's control. It explains how sexual abuse claimants become creditors with enforcement rights against the organization and its property. When the number of claimants exceeds the organization's practical and financial capacity to manage on a case-by-case basis—the so-called "mass tort" problem—the potential liability puts the organization's mission and existence in peril. Bankruptcy is an attractive option through which to negotiate a comprehensive and final resolution of that liability while preserving sufficient resources to survive.

---

15 See Ruth Graham, "Baltimore Archdiocese, Bracing for More Abuse Claims, Files for Bankruptcy," *The New York Times*, Sept. 29, 2023, https://www.nytimes.com/2023/09/29/us/baltimore-archdiocese-sex-abuse-bankruptcy.html (accessed on 29 Nov. 2023, subscription required).

16 See Marie T. Reilly, "Catholic Dioceses in Bankruptcy," *Penn State Law* e-Library, https://elibrary.law.psu.edu/bankruptcy/105 (accessed on 29 Nov. 2023) (compiling information about the cases).

17 See 1983 Code of Canon Law c. 116 § 1 (aggregates of persons or things established by competent ecclesiastical authority to act in the name of the Church and in accordance with law to fulfill their assigned task for the public good).

18 USCCB 2023 Implementation Report, Preface by Archbishop Timothy P. Broglio, at v.

II. Child Sexual Abuse as Debt Problem

A. Liability and Persons Liable

Sexual abuse of a child is particularly horrifying because of the unique confluence of the taboo nature of the abuse, the debilitating shame it can cause the victim, and the victim's status as a vulnerable child.[19] It is even more egregious when the abuser is a Catholic cleric who abuses clerical status to gain access to a vulnerable child, and the Catholic organization responsible for the abuser fails to protect the children in its care.

Legal culpability for harm caused by sexual abuse of child falls into two categories: criminal and civil. Criminal acts are offenses against the state which the state prosecutes through the criminal justice system. Adjudicated criminal culpability is called "guilt." In contrast, harm causing conduct may give rise to civil liability. The civil liability litigation system recognizes an injured person's private entitlement to compensation from persons whose behavior was at least a proximate cause of their injury. Law defines and distinguishes among types of legally culpable wrongdoing based on the wrongdoer's state of mind—negligent, reckless, or intentional.[20] To establish liability and a right to compensation, a plaintiff must establish that the wrongdoer a) failed to exercise reasonable care; b) in breach of a duty of care to the person seeking compensation; c) that proximately results in injury to that person.[21]

Multiple persons can contribute to an injury, and more than one person can be liable. In the case of sexual abuse of a child, obviously the perpetrator of abuse is the direct cause of the injury. Sexual abuse of a child is both a crime and the basis for a civil action against the perpetrator for intentional wrongdoing. Even if the plaintiff can establish the abuser's liability, the perpetrator likely cannot discharge that liability by payment of damages because intentional wrongdoers tend to be "judgment proof," meaning they tend to be uninsured and impecunious.

The injured person's strategy in a situation like this is to try to establish the liability of another actor as a contributing cause of his injury, ideally one who has

---

19 See Korinna McRobert, "Childhood Sexual Abuse (CSA): moving past the taboo and into the postcolonial," *Society Register* vol. 6, no. 2 (Mar. 15, 2022), https://pressto.amu.edu.pl/index.php/sr/article/view/29275 (accessed on 29 Nov. 2023).

20 See generally Richard A. Epstein, "Intentional Harms," *J. Leg. Stud.* 4 (1975) 391, 391 (noting that throughout legal history intentional wrongdoing is distinct from unintentional wrongdoing). In some circumstances a defendant is "strictly" liable without regard to its state of mind. See *Restatement (Third) Torts*: Products Liability §§ 1, 2 (Am. L. Inst. 1998).

21 See, e.g., H. Gerald Chapin, *Handbook on the Law of Torts* § 105, at 501 (1917).

insurance or other assets to pay damages. Persons who claim to have been sexually abused as children typically seek to establish liability and recover damages against an organization, like a Catholic diocese or religious order, who they claim is culpable along with the perpetrator for their injury.

One strategy to establish the co-liability of an organization for the intentional wrongdoing of another is by doctrine that recognizes the "vicarious" liability of a principal for torts committed by an agent. An employer is vicariously liable for harm its employee causes while acting as an agent on behalf of the employer within the scope of employment. This vicarious liability arises due to the employment relationship and without regard to the culpability of the employer's conduct.[22] The scope of employment is an important limit on the employer's vicarious liability. Catholic employers have generally escaped vicarious liability for harm caused by an employee who sexually abuses a child on grounds that sexual abuse of children is outside the employee's scope of employment.[23]

Sexual abuse plaintiffs have successfully advanced an alternative theory of liability against Catholic organizations based on their own negligence. An actor is co-liable for harm a third party causes to persons to whom the actor owes a duty of care when the actor was on notice of the risk of that harm and failed to use reasonable care to prevent it.[24]

In general, a Catholic organization has a duty to protect persons from abuse based on its legal authority over the abuser, or its legal authority over an

---

22 See *Restatement (Third) of Agency* § 7.07 (Am. L. Inst. 2006). An employee's conduct is within the scope of employment if it is the kind the employee is employed to perform, occurs within the authorized time and space limits of employment, and furthers the employer's business, even if the employer has expressly prohibited it. E.g., Baker ex re. Hall Brake Supply, Inc. v. Stewart Title & Tr. of Phoenix, Inc., 5 P. 3d 249 (Ariz. App. 2000).

23 See, e.g., Doe v. Liberatore, 478 F. Supp. 2d 742 (M.D. Pa. 2007) (diocese was not vicariously liable for priest's abuse of child because "the acts of sexual abuse perpetrated by [the priest] were both outrageous and certainly not actuated by any purpose of serving the [diocese]"); Doe v. Roman Catholic Church of Diocese of Phoenix, 2023 Ariz. App. Unpub. LEXIS 275 (June 29, 2023) (holding that a diocese is not vicariously liable for a priest employee's sexual abuse of a child because that conduct is outside the scope of a priest's employment); Bernie v. Catholic Diocese of Sioux Falls, 2012 S.D. LEXIS 103 at *9-10 (same). But see Fearing v. Bucher, 328 Ore. 367 (Or. 1999) (holding that a diocese could be vicariously liable for a priest's sexual abuse of a child if acts within the priest's scope of employment "resulted in" the acts which led to the injury).

24 See *Restatement (Third) of Torts*: Liability for Physical and Emotional Harm § 19 (Am. L. Inst. 2010). E.g., Doe v. Diocese of Rockville Ctr., 2020 N.Y. Misc. LEXIS 1964 at *21 (Nassau Cty. Sup. Ct. May 11, 2020).

organization that in turn had legal authority over the abuser.[25] The requisite legal authority arises from the organization's actual control via an employment or other agency relationship.[26] Once the plaintiff establishes the organization's duty of care to him, the plaintiff must show that the organization breached that duty by its negligence.[27] An organization is negligent if it placed its employee or agent in a position to cause *foreseeable* harm to the plaintiff that it likely could have prevented.[28]

To establish a Catholic diocese's negligence in connection with an employee's sexual abuse of a child generally requires evidence that the diocese knew or should have known *before* the abuse to the plaintiff occurred that its employee had a propensity to sexually abuse children.[29] The evidence must show that the diocese had advance notice of the employee's propensity for sexual abuse of children. Notice after the alleged abuse occurred, or notice before the abuse of an employee's propensity for other misconduct, for example sexual misconduct with adults, is not sufficient.[30] Moreover, another party's notice of the abuser's propensity for child sexual abuse does not establish the diocese's notice unless the

---

25 See, e.g., In re Roman Cath. Diocese of Rockville Ctr., 651 B.R. 399, 414 (Bankr. S.D. N.Y. 2023) (terming the two bases of duty the "abuser control theory" and the "institution control theory"). See generally *Restatement (Third) of Torts*: Phys. and Emot. Harm § 7a, b (Am. L. Inst. 2010) (stating that, subject to exceptions, "an actor has a duty to exercise reasonable care when the actor's conduct creates a risk of physical harm").

26 See, e.g., In re Roman Cath. Diocese of Rockville Ctr., 651 B.R. at 414.

27 See *Restatement (Third) of Torts*: Phys. & Emot. Harm § 3 (Am. L. Inst. 2023) ("A person acts negligently if the person does not exercise reasonable care under all the circumstances.").

28 See, e.g., Detone v. Bullit Courier Serv., Inc., 140 A.D. 2d 278, 279 (N.Y. Sup. Ct. App. Div. 1988).

29 See, e.g., Doe v. Alsaud, 12 F. Supp. 3d 674, 680 (S.D. N.Y. 2014) ("New York courts have held in employee sexual misconduct cases that an employer is only liable for negligent supervision or retention if it is aware of specific prior acts or allegations against the employee"): In re Roman Catholic Diocese of Rockville Ctr., 2023 Bankr. LEXIS 1799 (Bankr. S. D. N.Y. July 19, 2023); Doe v. Roman Catholic Church of the Diocese of Phoenix, 2023 Ariz. App. LEXIS 275 at *10-12 (June 29, 2023); Murray v. Nazareth Reg'l High Sch., 2022 U. S. Dist. LEXIS 139708 at *9 (E. D. N.Y. Aug. 5, 2022); Kenneth R. v. Roman Catholic Diocese of Brooklyn, 229 A.D. 2d 159, 161 (N.Y. App. 1997). See generally *Restatement (Third) of Torts*: Liability for Physical and Emotional Harm § 302B19 (Am. L. Inst. 2010) (an actor is liable for negligent supervision" where the actor has brought into contact or association with the other a person whom the actor knows or should know to be peculiarly likely to commit intentional misconduct, under circumstances which afford a peculiar opportunity or temptation for such misconduct. The conduct of a defendant can lack reasonable care insofar as it *foreseeably* combines with or permits the improper conduct of the plaintiff or a third party.") (Italics supplied).

30 Doe v. Alsaud, 12 F. Supp. 3d at 681.

party with notice is the diocese's agent.[31] That a diocese had notice of sexual abuse of children by clerics in general, or of sexual abuse of children by an employee or agent other than the particular employee the plaintiff names as his abuser, is not sufficient.[32] There is no independent tort of "covering up" a diocese's general knowledge of the potential risk of harm to children by sexually abusive employees.[33]

The evidentiary burden on a plaintiff to show a diocese's negligence for sexual abuse of a child committed by an employee is high. Claims revival legislation removes only the organization's statute of limitations defense. It does not change the plaintiff's burden to prove the elements of liability or affect any other defenses to liability.[34]

On the other hand, a diocese has no special status to protect it from liability for its negligence. It cannot assert its status as a religious organization as a defense.[35] The First Amendment prevents a court from applying religious doctrine to resolve an essentially religious dispute.[36] For at least the last two decades, courts have declined to recognize a First Amendment defense for religious organizations in negligence actions based on employee wrongdoing. Whether a

---

31 Jonathan A. v. Board of Educ. of City of N.Y., 779 N.Y.S. 2d 3, 5-6 (N.Y. Sup. Ct. App. Div. 2004).

32 See, e.g., In re Roman Catholic Diocese of Rockville Ctr., 651 B.R. 146, 167 (Bankr. S. D. N.Y. 2023); Murray v. Nazareth Reg'l High Sch., 579 F. Supp. 3d, 390 (E. D. N.Y. 2021) (dismissing complaint because allegations that the abuser had been transferred and the diocese was on notice that bishops used transfers to cover up clergy sexual abuse was insufficient to plead notice to the diocese of the employee's propensity for sexual abuse of children).

33 See, e.g., Murray v. Nazareth Reg'l High Sch. 579 F. Supp. 383, 389 (E.D. N.Y. 2021) (generalized allegations of the Church's "scandalous history of covering up sexual abuse" is insufficient to show a diocese's negligent supervision of a priest).

34 See generally Marie T. Reilly, "Retribution Against Catholic Dioceses by Revival: The Evolution and Legacy of the New York Child Victims Act Claims Revival Window," *Alb. L. Rev.* 84 (2022) 735 (discussing the statute of limitations defense in child sexual abuse cases).

35 The church autonomy doctrine derives from the First Amendment prohibition against "law respecting an establishment of religion or free exercise thereof….." U.S. Const. amend. I. See Malicki v. Doe, 814 So. 2d 347, 353 (Fla. 2002) (recognizing church autonomy doctrine as a corollary application of the First Amendment). The doctrine has also been called the "religious autonomy" doctrine" and the "ecclesiastical abstention doctrine." See Archdiocese of Miami, Inc. v Mangorri, 954 So. 2d 640, 641 (Fla. 3d DCA 2007).

36 See Serbian E. Orth. Diocese v. Milivojevich, 426 U. S. 696, 708-09 (1976). See generally Scott C. Idleman, "Tort Liability, Religious Entities, and the Decline of Constitutional Protection," *Ind. L.J.* 75 (2000) 291, 225.

religious organization failed to act with reasonable care to those to whom it owed a duty of care is unrelated to religious doctrine.[37]

B. Creditors' Rights Against the Debtor and Its Property

To understand what happens to the debtor and its creditors in a bankruptcy case, consider creditors' rights outside of bankruptcy in the civil liability litigation system. Plaintiffs assert claims as lawsuits. Courts determine whether the alleged wrongdoers are liable and if so the compensation to which the plaintiff is entitled by trial of the evidence. The plaintiff bears the burden of proof of all the elements of his claim by a preponderance of the evidence (more likely than not). If the plaintiff carries this burden, the court enters a judgment in his favor. The judgment establishes the defendant's liability and states the damages the defendant owes. After all appeals are exhausted, if the defendant does not pay the judgment voluntarily, the plaintiff can execute the judgment by recourse to the debtor's property.[38]

Procedural law governing execution of a judgment against the debtor's property varies among the states. Generally, the plaintiff obtains an order authorizing the sheriff or other executive branch officer to locate the debtor's property and seize it. The next step is a public auction sale to the highest bidder and application of the proceeds to pay the executing creditor's judgment.[39] A creditor may execute a judgment only against *the debtor's* interests in property. When a Catholic organization faces massive liability and the accompanying threat

---

37 See Malicki v. Doe, 814 So. 2d at 347-59 (discussing split of authority as to whether the doctrine bars a tort claim against a religious institution and joining the majority in declining to do so in a suit against a church for injury caused by sexual assault based on the church's alleged negligent hiring and supervision of a cleric); but see, Doe v. Marianist Province of the United States, 620 S.W. 3d 73, 77 (Mo. 2021) (holding that the question of a church's negligence in ordaining, hiring, assigning, supervising a priest involves interpretation of religious doctrine and constitutes impermissible entanglement between church and state under the First Amendment); Kenneth R. v. Roman Catholic Diocese of Brooklyn, 229 A.D. 2d 159, 165 (N.Y. App. Div. 1997).

38 See, e.g., *Fed. R. Civ. P.* 69(a) (describing process for execution of a judgment of a federal court for the payment of money to be by writ of execution).

39 See, e.g., N.Y. State Unified Courts System, "How Do I Collect on a Judgment?" https://ww2.nycourts.gov/courts/6jd/tompkins/ithaca/webpageJudgement.shtml (accessed on 30 Nov. 2023).

of loss of property to sexual abuse creditors, exactly who "the debtor" is and what that debtor's property interests are becomes critically important.[40]

Catholic archdioceses and dioceses in the United States are not organized identically. They have chosen their respective organizational forms among those available under secular law of their state. These forms include corporation sole, religious non-profit corporation, general non-profit corporation, charitable trust, or unincorporated association.[41]

In a diocese organized as corporation sole, the person holding the office of bishop is the exclusive legal agent for the corporation sole.[42] The corporation sole form centralizes both title and control over property in the bishop.[43] It is consistent with canon law that reposes supervisory authority over property (direct and indirect) in the bishop. It is, however, inconsistent with canon law that recognizes parishes and other entities as juridical persons capable of acquiring and holding their own property distinct from the diocese.[44] Juridical persons affiliated with a corporation sole diocese typically are not incorporated under secular law, and do not hold legal title to the property that canon law attributes to them as juridical persons.[45]

---

40 See, e.g., Tort Claimants Comm. v. Roman Catholic Archbishop, 335 B.R. 842, 861 (Bankr. D. Or. 2005) (holding that treating as property formally titled in the diocese as corporation sole as property of the debtor notwithstanding that canon law attributed it to parishes within the diocese would not violate the First Amendment because secular law governing corporate form and attribution of title to property does not impose a substantial burden on exercise of religion).

41 See generally Patty Gerstenblith, "Associational Structures of Religious Organizations," *BYU L. Rev.* (1995) 439.

42 See Gerstenblith, 454 (noting that as of 1995, twenty-six states permitted a religious organization to incorporate as a corporation sole). State corporation sole laws generally require that the sole agent of the corporation sole must be duly chosen and must act according to the rules of the religious organization. See Adam J. Maida and Nicholas P. Cafardi, *Church Property, Church Finances, and Church-Related Corporations: A Canon Law Handbook* (St. Louis, MO: Catholic Health Association of the United States, 1983) 128.

43 Centralized control of property in the bishop may have a political purpose. See Baxter v. McDonnell, 49 N.E. 667, 668 (N.Y. Ct. App. 1898) (finding that the purpose of corporation sole is "to exclude the laity from that power of interference which they would have were the title vested in a [parish] corporation").

44 See 1983 Code of Canon Law cc. 1255-1256; John Beal, James Coriden & Thomas Green (eds.), *New Commentary on the Code of Canon Law* (New York/Mahwah, NJ: Paulist Press, 2000) 164.

45 *New Commentary*, note 44 at 1457 (noting that "internal ecclesiastical disputes" between bishops administrators of other juridic persons within a diocese arise "when the civil law structure, of a diocese does not mirror . . . the canonical structure, resulting in divergent views of the ownership of church-related property and the appropriate persons to administer and alienate that property").

In contrast, a diocese that is organized as a corporation typically holds legal title only to property attributed to the diocese as a canonical juridic person. Parishes and other entities affiliated with the diocese are separately incorporated and each holds title to its own property.[46] In contrast with the corporation sole organizational form, separate incorporation of diocese and parishes aligns their secular forms with the canonical distinctions among juridic persons. The problem is that separate incorporation of the diocese and the parishes under secular law presumes and requires their independence and compliance with legal formalities that do not easily accommodate the bishop's supervisory authority over pastors and parish property under canon law.

The organizational form of the debtor under secular law answers the question of who the debtor is for purposes of a creditor's right to enforce a judgment against the debtor's property. The next question is what the debtor's interests in property are under secular law. Secular law governing property interests fixates on the state of the debtor's "title" based on formal and public documentation of transfers of interests in an item of property through history, ending with the transfer of the interest to the debtor (the "chain of title").[47] It provides a complex array of rules and exceptions that rank the priority of the debtor's interest relative to that of other parties who claim a competing interest in the same item of property.[48] For example if the debtor owns a parcel of real property subject to a mortgage in favor of a lender, both the debtor and the lender hold an interest in that parcel. The law governing mortgages provides rules that govern the priority of the mortgagee's interest relative to the debtor's interest. Moreover, the debtor's ability to use the parcel may be regulated by zoning laws. Or, it may be restricted by donor-imposed covenants or historical preservation laws.

The importance of a debtor's secular organizational form and interests in property when creditors seek to enforce their judgments invites asset protection strategy by debtors to shield property from creditors. A debtor faced with impending creditor collection action has an incentive to hide it, or as a more sophisticated move, to transfer it to a cooperative, but legally distinct entity. For

---

46 See Marie T. Reilly, *Catholic Dioceses in Bankruptcy*, 49 Seton Hall L. Rev. 871, 886-890 (2019) (discussing organizational forms of Catholic dioceses that have filed for bankruptcy).

47 See generally Harold Demsetz, *Toward a Theory of Property Rights*, 57 Amer. Econ. Rev. 347 (1967) (describing the common law of property rights and proposing an economic theory of property rights); Carol M. Rose, "Possession as the Origin of Property," *U. Chi. L. Rev.* 52 (1985) 73 (exploring the origin or "first link" in the chain of title).

48 See, e.g., Paul Wangerin, "The Hierarchy of Property," *J. Bus., Entr. & the Law* 9 (2015) 153 (describing the priority rules in Article 9 of the Uniform Commercial Code).

centuries, debtors have engaged in these asset protection strategies. Since the 1500s, fraudulent transfer law has recognized creditors' right to undo or "avoid' "ertain illegitimate property transfers that deplete the debtor's property that would, but for the transfer, be available to satisfy their claims.[49] Fraudulent transfer law is more complex than this brief explanation because it is not easy to draw the line between legitimate and illegitimate transfers.

III. The Bankruptcy Option

A. The Purpose of Bankruptcy

The word "bankruptcy" as used in ordinary conversation has a connotation of insolvency and failure. Surprisingly, perhaps, federal bankruptcy law has a non-depressing purpose: 1) to provide an efficient alternative to the individual creditor litigation and collection action, and 2) to provide a procedure for debtors to obtain a "fresh start" through comprehensive and final forgiveness (discharge) of debt.[50]

Bankruptcy offers a solution to the inefficiency of uncoordinated individual creditor collection action.[51] In the litigation system outside of bankruptcy, the first claimant to obtain a judgment against the debtor can execute that judgment against the debtor's property. These first judgments are likely to be large reflecting the jury's outrage and desire to punish the defendant. This is the so-called "lottery effect." The entry of the first colossal judgment against the debtor will likely cause other creditors to rush in with litigation and collection, triggering a panic cascade that destroys the debtor as a going concern and reduces the assets available to pay all creditors.

---

49 See, e.g., Twyne's Case, 3 Coke 806, 76 Eng. Rep. 809 (Star Chamber, 1601) (invalidating a fraudulent gift of goods under 13 Eliz. cap. 5).

50 See Thomas H. Jackson, "Bankruptcy, Non-Bankruptcy Entitlements, and the Creditors' Bargain," *Yale L. J.* 91 (1982) 857, 860-868 (arguing that bankruptcy law tends to reflect the bargain creditors would make with debtor ex ante [the "creditors' bargain"] to provide for a collective solution that reduces costs, preserves value, and improves creditors' collective recovery relative to the individualistic creditors' remedy system outside of bankruptcy); Local Loan Co. v. Hunt, 292 U.S. 234, 244 (1934) (noting that bankruptcy law "gives to the honest but unfortunate debtor… a new opportunity in life and a clear field for future effort, unhampered by the pressure and discouragement of preexisting debt").

51 See Charles Mooney, "A Normative Theory of Bankruptcy Law," *Wash. & Lee L. Rev.* 61 (2004) 931, 934 (describing and defending a normative theory of bankruptcy law as a procedure for maximizing the recovery of those with legal entitlements against the debtor under non-bankruptcy law). This theory posits that bankruptcy procedure ought to provide a solution to the 'tragedy of the commons' created by individual creditor actions that tend to externalize loss to other creditors against the same commons. See Garrett Hardin, *The Tragedy of the Commons*, 162 Science 1243 (1968) (coining the term "tragedy of the commons").

Bankruptcy imposes a collective claim resolution process on all creditors no matter where they may be in the process of asserting their claims. The norm in bankruptcy is equality of treatment among creditors with similar types of claims. Unsecured creditors such as sexual abuse claimants can expect a *pro rata* share in the debtor's assets in the bankruptcy case. Creditors negotiate a settlement of their claims collectively, without regard to how much they may have invested in pursuing their cases, or how close they may have been to obtaining a judgment outside of bankruptcy.[52] This equality norm contrasts sharply with the winner-take-all tournament of speed in the tort litigation system outside of bankruptcy.

Coordinated resolution of all liability in bankruptcy occurs under the supervision of a bankruptcy court with jurisdiction over all creditors and all the debtor's property. Bankruptcy law sublimates individual creditors' entitlements under non-bankruptcy law to protect the value of the debtor's property, preserve the debtor as a going concern, and maximize payment to creditors collectively. In theory, the total costs of incurred by all parties in a bankruptcy case are lower than the costs the parties would incur in individual litigation and judgment enforcement outside of bankruptcy.

Catholic bishops that have resorted to bankruptcy have noted the collective, egalitarian, and value-preserving features of bankruptcy to explain their decisions to use it to resolve sexual abuse claims. For example, in a letter to the faithful announcing the Archdiocese of San Francisco's bankruptcy case, Archbishop Salvatore Cordileone wrote: "We believe the bankruptcy process is the best way to provide a compassionate and equitable solution for survivors of abuse while ensuring that we continue the vital ministries to the faithful and to the communities that rely on our services and charity."[53] The Archbishop of Baltimore, in a letter to the faithful announcing that he was considering a bankruptcy filing to respond to sexual abuse claims, wrote that litigating claims outside of bankruptcy would:

> potentially lead to some very high damage awards for a very small number of victim-survivors while leaving almost nothing for the vast majority of them. The archdiocese simply does not have unlimited resources to satisfy such claims; its assets are indeed finite. . . . [In a chapter 11 bankruptcy case] the archdiocese would be required to

---

52 See 11 U.S.C. § 1123(a)(4) (requiring that a plan of reorganization must "provide the same treatment for each claim . . . of a particular class . . . unless the holder of a particular claim . . . agrees to a less favorable treatment. . . .").

53 Salvatore J. Cordileone, Archbishop, "Letter to the Faithful," August 21, 2023, https://sfarchdiocese.org/letter-to-the-faithful-from-archbishop-salvatore-j-cordileone-on-the-archdiocese-of-san-franciscos-filing-for-chapter-11-bankruptcy-to-facilitate-settlements-with-abuse-survivors/ (accessed on 30 Nov. 2023).

provide resources which would be used to compensate victim-survivors while at the same time ensuring our mission can continue.[54]

B. Types of Bankruptcy

Bankruptcy law offers a debtor a choice among several types of bankruptcy proceedings. In a case filed under chapter 7 of the Bankruptcy Code, the debtor's property passes by operation of law to a bankruptcy trustee. The trustee is responsible for collecting the debtor's property, selling it, and using the proceeds to pay creditors claims.[55]

In contrast, a debtor who wants to resolve its debts *without* relinquishing control of its property can choose a chapter 11 case. In this type of bankruptcy case, the debtor seeks to "reorganize" by agreeing with its creditors on a plan to pay claims while the debtor retains control of the business and retains enough property to survive. If a debtor tries but fails to confirm a plan, the case may be converted to a liquidation case under chapter 7. Alternatively, the bankruptcy court may dismiss the chapter 11 case whereupon creditors may resume pursuit of their claims in the litigation system.

C. The Estate, the Debtor in Possession, and the Creditors' Committee

At the moment a debtor begins a bankruptcy case (the petition date), all civil actions, including lawsuits for sexual abuse, that were or could have been filed against the debtor as of the petition date are enjoined by a statutory provision known as the "automatic stay."[56] The debtor's interests in property "wherever located and by whomever held" transfer automatically into an "estate."[57] At the same moment, the debtor transforms into a legally distinct entity known as the "debtor in possession."[58] The debtor in possession looks just like the debtor. Its property, managers, employees, and operations are the same as before the bankruptcy case. Unlike the debtor, which operates to maximize return on investment for its equity shareholders, or, in the case of a non-profit corporation,

---

54 William E. Lori, Archbishop, "A Message from Archbishop Lori: Healing and Ministry in the Archdiocese of Baltimore," Sept. 5, 2023, https://www.archbalt.org/a-message-from-archbishop-lori-healing-and-ministry-in-the-archdiocese-of-baltimore/) (accessed on 30 Nov. 2023).

55 See 11 U.S.C. § 704 (describing the duties of the trustee).

56 11 U.S.C. § 362(a)(1) (with certain exceptions, a bankruptcy petition once filed "operates as a stay applicable to all entities" against "the commencement or continuation…[an] action or proceeding against the debtor that could have been commenced before the commencement of the case under this title . . . .").

57 11 U.S.C. § 541(a)(1) (the commencement of a bankruptcy case creates "an estate" consisting, with some exceptions and including certain other property interests, of "all the debtor's legal and equitable interests in property as of the commencement of the case").

58 11 U.S.C. § 1101(1).

for advancement of its mission, the debtor in possession is a fiduciary for creditors.[59] The debtor in possession may use or sell property and operate during the bankruptcy case, but the Bankruptcy Code limits its freedom considerably. For example, to use or dispose of property other than in the ordinary course of business, the debtor in possession must either obtain creditors' prior consent or court approval after a hearing at which creditors may object.[60]

Unsecured creditors are represented collectively in a chapter 11 case by a committee typically known as the Official Creditors' Committee.[61] In diocesan bankruptcy cases, sexual abuse claimants dominate the diocese's unsecured creditors by both number of claims and amount and typically these claimants comprise the committee. Lawyers who represent groups of sexual abuse claimants vie to have their clients appointed to the committee, and committee members' lawyers vie among themselves for leadership of the committee. The committee represents all sexual abuse creditors. It hires its own lawyers and other professionals.[62] The debtor in possession pays the fees of the committee's professionals, subject to bankruptcy court review.[63] The responsibility of the debtor to pay the committee's professional fees amplifies the already powerful incentive of the debtor to streamline negotiation with the committee and to provide it with the information it needs to evaluate the debtor's financial situation and reach agreement on the terms of a plan support the debtor's proposed plan expeditiously.

D. Property Issues in Bankruptcy

Bankruptcy law permits creditors to challenge the debtor's assertion as to what is or is not the debtor's property. It also provides creditors with the power to avoid as so-called fraudulent transfers otherwise valid pre-bankruptcy, outbound transfers of the debtor's property to third parties that, but for the transfer, would have been available to pay creditors.

Creditors in Catholic diocesan bankruptcy cases have challenged the diocese's attribution of property among the diocese and its parishes, cemeteries, schools, foundations and other affiliate entities within the diocese. They have also

---

59 See 11 U.S.C. § 1107(a); see, e.g., Commodity Futures Trading Comm'n v. Weintraub, 471 U. S. 343, 355 (1985) (debtor in possession owes the same fiduciary duty to creditors as a trustee in a chapter 7 case). The debtor in possession has the same statutory powers and responsibilities to creditors as a trustee does in a chapter 7 liquidation case. 11 U.S.C. § 323(a).

60 See, e.g., 11 U.S.C. § 363(a)-(p).

61 See 11 U.S.C. §§ 1102, 1103(a).

62 See 11 U.S.C. § 1103(a).

63 See 11 U.S.C. § 328(a).

challenged pre-bankruptcy transfers of diocesan property by asserting transfer avoiding powers in bankruptcy to recover property from affiliates who received it.

For example, in the Archdiocese of Milwaukee case, the Official Creditors' Committee challenged the archdiocese's pre-petition transfer of $55 million to an entity known as the Cemetery Trust whose purpose was to provide for maintenance of archdiocesan cemetery property. The committee contended that the transfer was avoidable under bankruptcy law and that the Cemetery Trust should return the $55 million to the debtor's estate. [64] The archbishop responded that the committee's exercise of the avoiding power infringed on the archbishop's First Amendment right to free exercise of religion, namely, the archbishop's canonical obligation to maintain the cemetery as a consecrated Catholic burial place.[65]

The Seventh Circuit rejected the archdiocese's religious liberty argument. The archdiocese appealed to the Supreme Court, but before the Court could hear the case, the committee and the debtor agreed to a joint plan of reorganization in the bankruptcy case and the archdiocese withdrew its appeal. The committee's challenge to the Cemetery Trust transfer was successful as a strategy to leverage a more favorable payout for sexual abuse creditors. The plan the debtor offered the committee after the committee's victory in the Seventh Circuit paid creditors five times more than the previous plan.[66]

In the Archdiocese of Santa Fe case, the committee similarly challenged certain of the archdiocese's pre-petition property transfers and objected to the debtor's assertion that it held title to certain property subject to a trust in favor of parishes.[67] The bankruptcy court held that the challenge did not implicate the archdiocese's right to free expression of religion and was not the type of intra-church dispute that implicates the church autonomy doctrine.[68] It allowed the

---

64 See Listecki v. Official Comm. of Unsecured Creditors, 780 F. 3d 731, 895-96 (7th Cir. 2015).

65 Listecki v. Official Comm. of Unsecured Creditors, 895-96. See also 1983 Code of Canon Law c. 1267 §3 (offerings given by the faithful for a particular purpose may be applied only for that purpose).

66 See Annysa Johnson, "Archdiocese of Milwaukee Settles Sexual Abuse Claims for $21 Million," *J. Sentinel*, August 4, 2015, https://archive.jsonline.com/news/religion/archdiocese-settles-sexual-abuse-claims-for-21-million-b99542352z1-320651132.html/) (accessed on 30 Nov. 2023).

67 In re Roman Catholic Church of the Archdiocese of Santa Fe, 621 B. R. 502, 504 (Bankr. N.M. 2020). At about the same time, the archdiocese created a similar trust structure to hold title to financial assets and transferred about $25 million into it. Id. On the petition date, the corpus of the financial assets trust was $36.7 million. Id.

68 See ibid. at 509-12.

committee to proceed with its challenges, noting that the litigation over the archdiocese's property "will be very expensive and time consuming."[69] It cautioned both parties that, unless settled, litigation would consume millions of dollars for fees and costs, money that "could have paid valid abuse claims."[70] The archdiocese settled with the committee and confirmed a plan in 2022 without a litigated resolution of the property disputes.

In the St. Paul and Minneapolis case, the committee contended that although the archdiocese and parishes were separately incorporated under Minnesota law with title to their own property, parishes property should be treated in the bankruptcy case as though it were the archdiocese's. The committee argued that the archbishop's canonical supervisory authority over parishes justified disregard of the secular legal distinction between the archdiocese and parishes.[71] The bankruptcy court and the 8th Circuit on appeal rejected the committee's argument on grounds that disregard of the legal separateness of the parishes and the archdiocese would in effect force the parishes involuntarily into bankruptcy, a result that the Bankruptcy Code expressly prohibits.[72] The 8th Circuit held that the committee's allegations that the archbishop dominated the parishes via his canonical supervisory authority was insufficient to invalidate the legal distinction between the archdiocese and the parishes as distinct corporate entities under Minnesota law.[73]

In the Archdiocese of Portland case, the debtor, a corporation sole under Oregon law, asserted that its formal title to certain property was subject to a trust for the benefit of unincorporated parishes who acquired it and to whom it belonged under canon law.[74] The committee sought a determination that all property titled in the Archbishop as corporation sole under was the debtor's property without regard to canon law that attributes some of that property to parishes.[75] The archdiocese argued that the bankruptcy court lacked subject matter jurisdiction over the issue under the First Amendment.[76] The court disagreed,

---

69 In re Roman Catholic Church of the Archdiocese of Santa Fe, at 513.

70 Ibid. at 513-14.

71 See In re Archdiocese of St. Paul and Minneapolis, 888 F.3d 944, 949-50 (8th Cir. 2018).

72 See 888 F.3d at 953. See 11 U.S.C. § 303(a).

73 See 888 F.3d at 953 ("The isolated incidents of lack of corporate formality and commingling of assets fall far short of the requirement for alter ego status under Minnesota law.").

74 See Tort Claimants Comm. v. Roman Catholic Archbishop, 334 B. R. 842, 848-49 (Bankr. D. Or. 2005).

75 See 1983 Code of Canon Law c. 1256 (". . . ownership of goods belongs to that juridic person which has acquired them legitimately").

76 See 334 B.R. at 849.

holding that the issue of title to property is a question of purely secular law.[77] It noted that the archdiocese "is free to organize its internal affairs in accordance with its internal church law" and judicial enforcement "of the consequences of those choices . . . neither rearranges the church's polity in violation of the First Amendment nor interferes with the church's right to make those choices."[78] The archdiocese was able to confirm a plan with the support of sexual abuse claimants without litigating the validity of the asserted trust in which it claimed hold property for the benefit of parishes.

E. Sexual Abuse Claims

Under bankruptcy law, a person who holds any right to payment from the debtor has a "claim," even if that right is disputed, unliquidated, unmatured, or contingent.[79] The time to test for whether a person has a "claim" and therefore is a "creditor" is on the date the debtor files for bankruptcy.[80] A person has a claim and is a creditor if the events that resulted in his injury and cause of action against the debtor occurred before the bankruptcy filing date even if he has not filed a lawsuit or made a demand for compensation from the debtor.[81]

A person who is a creditor must file in the bankruptcy court a short statement of the nature and amount of their claim known as a "proof of claim form"[82] In sex abuse bankruptcy cases, the court approves a form that elicits basic information about the person claiming to have been abused and facts regarding the alleged abuse.[83] Although proof of claim forms are ordinarily part of the public docket in

---

77 334 B.R at 853.

78 Ibid.

79 See 11 U.S.C. § 101(5)(A) (defining "claim" as a "right to payment, whether or not such right is reduced to judgment, liquidated, unliquidated, fixed, contingent, matured, unmatured, disputed, undisputed").

80 See 11 U.S.C. § 101(10) (defining "creditor" as an "entity that has a claim against the debtor that arose at the time of or before [the petition date]").

81 See, O'Loughlin v. County of Orange, 229 F.3d 871, 874 (9th Cir. 2000) (noting that a "claim" arises at the time of the events giving rise to the claim, not at the time the plaintiff is first able to file suit on the claim").

82 See United States Courts, Services and Forms, "Proof of Claim" Official Form 410, downloadable at https://www.uscourts.gov/forms/bankruptcy-forms/proof-claim-0 (accessed on 30 Nov. 2023). See also Fed. Bankr. R. 3001-08 (explaining how to complete and file a proof of claim form).

83 See In re Roman Catholic Diocese of Rockville Ctr., 651 B. R. 146, 177 (Bankr. S. D. NY 2023) (noting that the proof of claim form required only general information about the alleged abuse and did not require claimants to state facts showing all the elements of a claim against the debtor that would be required for a complaint in state court litigation).

a bankruptcy case, sexual abuse proofs of claim are protected from public disclosure and do not become part of the public docket.[84]

The proof of claim form can be completed without the assistance of a lawyer. Lawyers represent sexual abuse claimants on a contingency fee basis under which the lawyer is entitled to a percentage of the payment the clients receive. In the Diocese of Camden case, the bankruptcy court denied confirmation of a plan proposed jointly by the debtor and the committee among other grounds because it allowed some claimants' attorneys to receive fees greater than those permitted by New Jersey lawyer ethics laws.[85] The court noted that "[t]he survivor proof of claim form contains nine pages of questions, many of which require the claimant or attorney to check a box."[86] It opined that a contingency fee of 40% of what a client recovers from the settlement trust may be unreasonably large (and therefore unethical) for work consisting solely of filing a claim form on behalf a client.[87]

To achieve a *comprehensive* resolution of claims against the debtor, bankruptcy law makes creditor participation *compulsory*. If a person is a creditor on the day the debtor files for bankruptcy, the person must timely file a proof of claim form to participate in the case and receive payment under a confirmed plan. Shortly after the bankruptcy case begins, the bankruptcy court sets a deadline for filing a proof of claim form known as the "bar date." Unfiled or late filed claims, unless the court excuses the failure, are disallowed, not entitled to payout under a confirmed plan, but are subject to the channeling injunction that blocks the claimant from suing the debtor after it emerges from a successful bankruptcy.[88] A creditor that misses the bar date can try to persuade the bankruptcy court that the bar should not apply to him because he did not have constructive notice or actual knowledge of the case in time to comply with the bar date.[89] Typically, the debtor negotiates, and the court approves, an advertising program designed to inform

84 Recent settlement approved between creditors and claims agent that accidentally published sexual abuse creditor identifying information.

85 See *Memorandum Decision Denying Confirmation of Eighth Amended Plan*, Poslusny, Jr., J. Case 20-21257, doc. 3336 at 68, Sept. 29, 2003.

86 Ibid. at 68-69.

87 Ibid.

88 See, e.g., Brogdon v. Roman Catholic Archbishop of L.A., 2021 U.S. Dist. LEXIS 237762 at *25 (D. Ariz. 2021) (holding that civil actions against the Diocese of Tucson for child sexual abuse were discharged by confirmation of its plan of reorganization).

89 See 11 U.S.C. §§ 501(b)(9), 726(a)(2)(C)(i).

claimants about the debtor's bankruptcy case and how to file a proof of claim form to maximize the number of claims resolved through the case.[90]

Some advocates for sexual abuse claimants contend that bishops use the bar date in diocesan bankruptcy cases as a ploy to undermine claims revival legislation that provides a longer window to commence a lawsuit free of a limitations defense, or otherwise to discourage claimants from coming forward with their claims.[91] To the contrary, the debtor's incentive in a chapter 11 case is to provide the widest possible notice to all creditors of their right to participate in the bankruptcy case to minimize exceptions to the bar date.

The bankruptcy process flips the burden of proof as to the validity of claims relative to the litigation system. To obtain a judgment against an organization for injuries caused by an individual perpetrator of sexual abuse outside of bankruptcy, a sexual abuse claimant must prove each element of his cause of action to a preponderance of the evidence (more likely than not). In contrast, the Bankruptcy Code provides that all claims for which a proof of claim has been timely filed are "deemed allowed," unless the debtor or another party objects. This means a timely filed claim is presumptively valid as to liability and damages unless the debtor or another party objects to the claim and prevails in bankruptcy court.[92]

Advocates for sexual abuse creditors have criticized Catholic organizations' resorting to bankruptcy as a ploy to bar access to diocesan records that might

---

90 See In re Roman Catholic Diocese of Rockville Ctr., 651 B. R. 146, 177 (Bankr. S. D. NY 2023) (noting that the debtor provided a list of clergy for whom the diocese may have had notice of a propensity for abuse as part of the materials made available to prospective claimants and notes that the materials clarified that the absence of a person's name on this list "does not mean that you should not file a Sexual Abuse Proof of Claim" and instructed prospective claimants to file a proof of claim even if the claimant "did not report your sexual abuse to the Diocese or to anyone else").

91 See, e.g., Jeff Anderson & Assoc. P.A., *The Impact of California Diocese Bankruptcies on Survivors*, April 4, 2023, https://tinyurl.com/rc4jb2wv (accessed on 30 Nov. 2023) ("Bishops want to stall the justice process, keep evidence and information hidden, discourage other survivors from coming forward, and continue "business as usual.")

92 11 U.S.C. § 502(a) ("a claim, proof of which is filed under section 501 . . . , is deemed allowed, unless a party in interest . . . objects."); 11 U.S.C. § 502(b)(1) (providing that a claim shall be allowed except to the extent that "such claim is unenforceable against the debtor . . . under . . . applicable law").

"reveal the scope of previous and present cover-ups."[93] In bankruptcy, creditors do not need this discovery because their claims are deemed valid.

To negotiate a plan, the debtor and the committee must estimate the value of the pool of sexual abuse claims asserted against the debtor taking possible defenses to liability into account. They must also estimate the debtor's ability to pay claims and retain resources sufficient to survive. This requires estimation of the value of the debtor's property and projected income. The committee is entitled to information relevant to these issues via bankruptcy court supervised discovery.[94] Catholic dioceses in bankruptcy have produced clergy personnel files and other information potentially relevant to the validity and value of sexual abuse claims under court orders that protect the confidentiality of the information and limits the committee's use of it to purposes relevant to the committee's responsibilities in the bankruptcy case. The confidentiality order typically does not permit disclosure to lawyers for individual sexual abuse creditors, or to the public.[95]

Until relatively recently, Catholic organizations in bankruptcy have refrained from objecting to sexual abuse creditors' claims. This strategy makes sense because objections to sexual abuse claims tend to undermine, or at least distract from, settlement negotiations. During the summer of 2023, the Diocese of Rockville Centre objected successfully to the allowance of certain sexual abuse claims. The bankruptcy court, applying federal pleading standards,[96] held that the claimants' conclusory allegations that the diocese "knew or should have known

---

93 SNAP Press Release, March 14, 2023, https://www.snapnetwork.org/diocese_of_santa_rosa_files_for_bankruptcy_snap_responds (accessed on 30 Nov. 2023) (noting that the Diocese of Santa Rosa's bankruptcy filing would unfairly deprive sexual abuse claimants of access to these records and that other Catholic dioceses have similarly abused the bankruptcy system to deprive claimants of information); Jeff Anderson & Assoc. P.A., *The Impact of California Diocese Bankruptcies on Survivors* (asserting that the "core reason" Catholic dioceses use bankruptcy is "to hinder the public from learning of the magnitude of clergy sex abuse and the cover-up of the crimes committed").

94 See 11 U.S.C. § 1103(c) (the committee may "investigate the acts, conduct, assets, liabilities, and financial condition of the debtor, the operation of the debtor's business and the desirability of the continuance of such business, and any other matter relevant to the formulation of a plan").

95 See, e.g., In re Roman Catholic Diocese of Rockville Ctr, 651 B. R. 146, 178 (Bankr. S.D. NY 2023) (noting that the debtor had produced its confidential clergy personnel files to lawyers who represent members of the Official Creditors' Committee but that the Committee had not produced those files to counsel for claimants).

96 Federal court pleading standards require allegation of specific facts in contrast to the more lenient N.Y. court pleading standards. In re Roman Catholic Diocese of Rockville Ctr, 651 B. R. at 166 (citing In re Residential Cap., LLC, 531 B.R. 1, 12 [Bankr. S. D. N.Y. 2015]).

of the abuse" were not adequate to plead the particular advance notice required to show the diocese's negligence in connection with the alleged abuse.[97] The bankruptcy court granted the creditors leave to amend their proofs of claim, but it denied their demand that the diocese produce clergy personnel files with the hope of discovering evidence of advance notice.[98]

The Diocese of Rockville Centre objected to other claims on grounds that the claimants did not allege facts that showed the diocese had a duty of care to the claimant to prevent the abuse the plaintiff alleged. Claimants named the diocese as a co-defendant along with a school operated by a religious institute within the geographic diocese that employed the perpetrator and that the claimant attended at the time of the alleged abuse. They contended that their abuser, a member of the religious order that owned and operated the school, was an employee of both the institute and the diocese, and that the school was an agent of the diocese.[99] The claimants offered affidavit testimony of Thomas Doyle as an expert on canon law and sex abuse liability. Doyle testified that a diocesan bishop has canonical authority and control over "pastoral ministerial activities" of all religious institute schools and all clerics within the diocese.[100] The bankruptcy court held that the bishop's canonical authority over religious institute schools and clerics within the geographic diocese was not sufficient to show the requisite legal agency between the diocese and the religious institute who employed the alleged abuser.[101] In 2012, the South Dakota Supreme Court similarly held that the Diocese of Sioux Falls did not "control" the religious institutes that operated schools within the geographic diocese in which plaintiffs claimed to have been abused.[102]

F. The Plan of Reorganization

1. The Settlement Trust

In the late 1980s Johns-Manville Corporation chose bankruptcy to resolve potential liability for an overwhelming number of claims for injuries from past

---

97 See In re Roman Cath. Diocese of Rockville Ctr., 651 B.R. 146, 170, 171-72 (Bankr. S. D. N.Y. 2023).

98 Ibid. at 178. Instead, the court scheduled a hearing "to discuss documents in the possession of the Diocese that should be produced to counsel for the Claimants before they must file their amended claims." Id.

99 Ibid. at 413.

100 651 B.R. at 422.

101 Ibid. (holding that claimants must "prove the existence of such relationships based on underlying secular facts"). The bankruptcy court had earlier held that allegations that a diocese controlled religious orders or clerics operating *outside* the geographic diocese were not plausible. In re Roman Cath. Diocese of Rockville Ctr., 2023 Bankr. LEXIS 1055 at *9-10 (Bankr. S. D. NY April 19, 2023).

102 See, e.g., Bernie v. Catholic Diocese of Sioux Falls, 2012 S.D. 103 at *17 (Sept. 5, 2012).

exposure to its asbestos products.[103] It filed for chapter 11 and proposed a plan that created and funded an independent entity (a settlement trust) to value and pay asbestos claims. The plan channeled all claims that were or could have been filed in its bankruptcy case against the settlement trust and permanently enjoined those claimants from thereafter suing Johns-Manville. The legally independent settlement trust would validate and pay asbestos claims according to the terms agreed upon in the plan. Johns-Manville would emerge from bankruptcy free from the value-destructive shadow of long-tail liability for injury caused by pre-petition exposure to its asbestos products.[104]

Plans in the Catholic bankruptcy cases so far use the basic structure of the plan in the Johns-Manville case. They provide for the creation and funding of a settlement trust, an entity legally independent from the debtor. The debtor, diocesan parishes, schools, and other affiliated entities, and their insurers agree to contribute cash and other assets to the trust. The plan channels all claims for pre-petition sexual abuse to the trust and enjoins creditors from suing the debtor and the non-debtor entities that contribute to the trust.

The negotiation over the amount each of these parties must contribute to the trust is complicated for several reasons. The value of the pool of sexual abuse claims is unknown and not easily estimated based on similar claims settlement history outside of bankruptcy. Unlike claims for injury due to asbestos exposure, claims for injury from child sexual abuse are not readily comparable. Rather, they are highly idiosyncratic. The nature, circumstances, and impact of child sexual abuse varies from claimant to claimant.

One technique used in mass tort bankruptcy cases to estimate the value of claims is to extrapolate the value of the claims in the aggregate based on jury verdicts in "comparable" cases in the litigation system. This technique is controversial.[105] It is especially so applied to child sexual abuse claims because

---

103 See In re Johns-Manville, 68 B.R. 618, 635 (Bankr. S.D. NY 1986) (confirmation of a plan that created a trust to satisfy the claims of all present and future asbestos injury claimants). See Craig Calhoun & Henry K. Hiller, "Coping with Insidious Injuries: The Case of Johns-Manville Corporation and Asbestos Exposure," Social Probs. 35 (1988) 162 (describing the Johns-Manville's chapter 11 case and arguing that it balanced the interests of known claimants and future claimants).

104 See Samuel Issacharoff and John Fabian Witt, "The Inevitability of Aggregate Settlement: An Institutional Account of American Tort Law," *Vand. L. Rev.* 57 (2004) 1571; Michelle J. White, "Why the Asbestos Genie Won't Stay in the Bankruptcy Bottle," *U. Cin. L. Rev.* 70 (2002) 1319.

105 See e.g., In re Eagle-Picher Indus. Inc., 189 B.R. 681, 690-91 (Bankr. S.D. Ohio 1995) (stating "qualitative considerations" for use of values of comparable claims to estimate claims filed in a bankruptcy case).

only a small number of child sexual abuse claims have ended in jury verdicts. In the litigation system, lawyers select for trial those cases with the highest potential expected verdicts. The only screen for claims in a bankruptcy case is the "deemed valid" proof of claim form. Thus, "comparable" jury verdict data is likely to overestimate the value of claims filed in bankruptcy cases.[106]

Uncertainty about what property is legally attributable to the debtor and what the value of the debtor's property is further complicates settlement in a chapter 11 case. Catholic organizations differ in many ways, including organizational form, the extent and nature of their interests in property, and the wealth of their donor constituents. The property holdings or ability of one Catholic organization to pay have no bearing on the financial circumstances of another.

Insurance issues also complicate the plan negotiation process. Insurers in several recent Catholic organization bankruptcy cases have asserted defenses to coverage. For example, the Diocese of Rochester sued its insurers as part of its bankruptcy case to resolve dispute over their coverage obligations [107] The bankruptcy court had enjoined the litigation so the parties could negotiate a settlement on the coverage issues as part of the plan negotiation process. After years of mediation in the bankruptcy case in which the parties failed to reach a settlement, the bankruptcy court lifted the injunction on the coverage litigation.[108] The diocese and its insurers agreed to a settlement of coverage liability for $148 million. The committee objected to the settlement and the debtor withdrew it before the court could approve it.[109]

Without a comprehensive settlement with all insurers, the debtor and the committee proposed a joint plan that included a cash contribution from the debtor, parishes, and certain insurers. The plan proposed that the debtor would assign to the settlement trust its rights to coverage against the non-settling insurers and provided the settlement trustee with the right to assert the debtor's rights through

---

106 See e.g., Paul Hinton, David McKnight & Pietro Grandi, "The Verdict Valuation Paradox: Implications for Mass Torts," *ABI Journal*, April 2023 (describing "selection bias" in using jury verdicts as comparable values of mass tort claims in bankruptcy). See generally Press Release, "Justice Department Files Statement of Interest Urging Transparency in the Compensation of Asbestos Claims," December 28, 2020 (explaining the U.S. Department of Justice's concern that claims filed in Bestwall, LLC's bankruptcy case may be duplicative, based on inaccurate information, or fraudulent and that "the lack of transparency in the compensation of asbestos claims [in bankruptcy cases] has been a significant problem"), https://www.justice.gov/opa/pr/justice-department-files-statement-interest-urging-transparency-compensation-asbestos-claims (accessed on 30 Nov. 2023).

107 See The Diocese of Rochester v. The Continental Insurance Co., 2023 Bankr. LEXIS 1114 (Bankr. W. D. NY April 25, 2023).

108 Ibid.

109 Ibid. at *6.

what promised to be years of coverage litigation.[110] Two insurers subsequently agreed to settle, bringing the total cash to be contributed to the settlement trust to $126.75 million. One of the diocese's insurers that had not settled stated its intention to file a competing plan of reorganization which will complicate the confirmation process for the diocese on the joint plan.[111]

The Diocese of Camden reached a similar impasse with insurers and the committee. To obtain the support of the committee for its plan, the debtor abandoned a settlement it had reached with certain insurers and agreed to contribute the debtor's rights against those insurers to the settlement trust The insurers objected to the plan on grounds the plan unfairly compromises the insurers' rights under the insurance policies.[112]

In Catholic organization bankruptcy cases filed since the wave of sexual abuse claims revival legislation in 2019, insurers have taken a more aggressive position in negotiations over coverage liability. This development appears to have made the path to confirmation of a plan longer and more expensive for debtors.[113]

2. The Confirmation Requirements: Protections for Creditors

The Bankruptcy Code requires that a plan must comply with certain statutory protections for creditors before the bankruptcy court may confirm it.[114] Creditors are entitled to vote on whether they accept the plan.[115] The plan organizes similar creditors into classes (for example, a class of "sexual abuse survivor" claims). A

---

110 Explaining its decision to lift the injunction, the bankruptcy court noted that the harm to the insurers from enjoining the coverage litigation "now substantially and manifestly outweighs any harm to the diocese or the abuse victims who, through their attorneys, have announced their intention to accept the considerable risks of litigation." Ibid. at *10.

111 See Dietrich Knauth, "Rochester Diocese receives insurer's competing $201 million bankruptcy plan," September 5, 2023, Reuters, https://www.reuters.com/legal/litigation/rochester-diocese-receives-insurers-competing-201-mln-bankruptcy-plan-2023-09-01/ (accessed on 30 Nov. 2023).

112 See *Memorandum Decision Denying Confirmation of Eighth Amended Plan*, Poslusny, Jr., J. Case 20-21257, doc. 3336 at 68, Sept. 29, 2003.

113 See Jay Tokasz, "Insurers in Buffalo Diocese bankruptcy put on notice by Rochester abuse settlement plan," *The Buffalo News*, November 16, 2022, updated September 13, 2023, https://tinyurl.com/ywdrknny (accessed on 30 Nov. 2023, subscription required) (explaining how the plan structure in the Rochester case may affect negotiations in the Diocese of Buffalo case); Soma Biswas, "Catholic Diocese Bankruptcy Drag On as Insurers Fight Rising Costs of Sex-Abuse Claims," *Wall Street Journal,* August 4, 2022, https://www.wsj.com/articles/catholic-diocese-bankruptcies-drag-on-as-insurers-fight-rising-costs-of-sex-abuse-claims-11659605402 (accessed on 30 Nov. 2023).

114 See 11 U.S.C. § 1129(a)(1).

115 See 11 U.S.C. § 1126(a). The plan proponent must provide a disclosure statement along with the plan which provides "adequate information" for creditors to decide whether to vote in favor of the plan. 11 U.S.C. § 1125(a).

class of creditors votes to approve the plan if at least two thirds in amount and more than half in number vote in favor of the plan.[116] The easiest pathway to plan confirmation depends on unanimous support by all classes of creditors entitled to vote on the plan.[117] If one of the classes entitled to vote does not vote to accept the plan, the plan proponent can still obtain confirmation (known as "cramdown"), but only if the court concludes that the plan "does not discriminate unfairly" and is "fair and equitable" to each dissenting class.[118]

The Bankruptcy Code provides protections for dissenting creditors even when their class votes to approve the plan. A plan may not be confirmed over the objection of a creditor unless the court determines that the payment the creditor is to receive under the plan is in the creditor's "best interest," that is, the payment the creditor will receive under the plan is at least as much as the amount that creditor would receive if the debtor (hypothetically) liquidated in a chapter 7 bankruptcy case.[119] This protection ties confirmation of a plan to the value of the debtor's property. The bigger the hypothetical liquidation value of the debtor's property, the more the plan must propose to pay a recalcitrant creditor to satisfy the best interest test.

The best interest test compares the payment the creditor will receive under the plan with liquidation in a chapter 7 bankruptcy case, which usually is the creditor's best option if the debtor cannot confirm a plan. Under the Bankruptcy Code, creditors cannot force a non-profit organization into a bankruptcy liquidation (involuntary bankruptcy).[120] Thus, for creditors of a Catholic diocese in a chapter 11 case, the only *actual* alternative to a chapter 11 plan is dismissal of the case, and individual creditor litigation and judgment enforcement outside of bankruptcy, without the cost savings of liquidation coordinated by the bankruptcy court and bankruptcy trustee for the benefit of all creditors.

The best interest test, with its hypothetical chapter 7 liquidation analysis, seems complicated. In practice, however, the payout under Catholic organizations' plans have been typically better for all creditors than the alternative. For example, as part of a confirmation hearing in the Diocese of Camden case, the debtor's expert testified that taking all creditors' claims into account and assuming payment of those claims in a hypothetical chapter 7 case sexual abuse claimants would receive, at best, about three cents per dollar for their

---

116 See 11 U.S.C. § 1126(c).
117 See 11 U.S.C. § 1129(a).
118 1129(b)(1).
119 See 11 U. S.C. § 1129(a)(7).
120 The Bankruptcy Code protects religious organizations from involuntary bankruptcy initiated by its creditors. 11 U.S.C. § 303(a).

claims.[121] Under the proposed plan, accepting the highest estimated value of sexual abuse claims at $785.1 million, the $87.5 million in cash the plan proposed to transfer to the settlement trust alone would yield an average payout of over 11%, which clearly satisfied the best interest test.[122] In the Catholic diocesan bankruptcy cases so far, the plans have easily satisfied the best interest test because the settlement trust fund included contributions from parishes, affiliates and insurers, whereas the pool of assets available in a hypothetical liquidation payout includes only on the net liquidation value of the debtor's property.

3. Non-Debtor Releases

Insurers with potential coverage liability to the debtor and/or parishes and other diocesan affiliates are willing to contribute to the settlement trust in exchange for a release of liability based on claims that were or could have been asserted against them at the time the debtor filed the petition. A common plan feature in Catholic organization bankruptcy cases so far is the inclusion of so-called "non-debtor releases" by sexual abuse creditors in favor of these parties.

The Bankruptcy Code clearly provides for release of *the debtor's* pre-petition liability via a confirmed plan. It is also clear that a bankruptcy court can confirm a plan that includes non-debtor releases by unanimous consent of all creditors whose claims are released. It is not clear whether a bankruptcy court has statutory authority to confirm a plan that extinguishes the liability of a non-debtor if a creditor affected by the release objects.

The Second Circuit Court of Appeals recently held that a bankruptcy court has this authority in *In re Purdue Pharma L.P.*[123] The plan confirmed in Purdue Pharma's bankruptcy case to resolve its liability for injury caused by its opioid drugs included a contribution from and release of Purdue Pharma's shareholders, members of the Sackler family. The Supreme Court has accepted the appeal and will resolve the question.[124] The outcome will affect the utility of reorganization in bankruptcy for all debtors facing all types of mass tort liability.

4. The Claims Payment Protocol

---

121 See *Memorandum Decision Denying Confirmation of Eighth Amended Plan*, Poslusny, Jr., J. Case 20-21257, doc. 3336 at 34, Sept. 29, 2003.

122 Ibid.

123 See Purdue Pharma, L.P. v. City of Grande Prairie (In re Pharma L.P.), 69 F. 4th 45 (2d Cir. 2023).

124 See Abbie VanSickle & Jan Hoffman, "What the Supreme Court's Decision to Hear the Purdue Pharma Case Means," *The New York Times*, Aug. 11, 2023, https://www.nytimes.com/2023/08/11/us/supreme-court-purdue-case.html (accessed on 30 Nov. 2023, subscription required).

After the parties reach agreement on the amount to be contributed to the settlement trust, sexual abuse claimants negotiate the claims validation and payment protocol largely among themselves. So-called "trust distribution procedures" differ from case to case. In the St. Paul and Minneapolis case, for example, the procedures required the trustee to review the proof of claim to determine whether "the Tort Claimant proved his or her claim by a preponderance of the evidence."[125] For claims that pass this initial screen, the trustee shall assign a designated number of points for various "plus" factors, for example fifteen points if the abuser is on the Archdiocese's "credibly accused" list, ten points if the abuser is on any Catholic organization's "credibly accused" list, five points if the abuser was accused by other claimants but is not on any organization's list.[126] The trustee may assign from zero to forty points based on considerations such as the duration and frequency of the alleged abuse, the type of abuse, and circumstances of the abuse (grooming, coercion or threat, relationship of trust or respect between the claimant to the perpetrator, multiple perpetrators, and the location of the abuse (isolated location, church, rectory, etc.). The trustee also has discretion to assign between zero and forty points based on the alleged impact of the abuse on the claimant, for example, the mental health consequences, physical health effects and negative impact on "spiritual wellbeing."[127] The trustee can award from zero to five points to reward those claimants who have "previously asserted claims against the Archdiocese and have participated in the legal and factual development of claims against the Archdiocese."[128] If the claimant had filed a lawsuit against the Archdiocese before the bankruptcy case, the trustee awards thirty points.[129] The trustee has no discretion to subtract points because the allegations do not state a claim for liability of the diocese because the diocese had no duty to the claimant. Rather, the trustee "shall reduce" the claimant's payment by 33% "[if] the [claimant's] abuser belonged to a religious order."[130] To induce the support of the committee for the plan, the procedures provided that every claimant shall receive a minimum distribution of $50,000 "unless the Claim is disallowed in its entirety."[131]

Until recently trust distribution procedures were not the subject of on-the-record objections in Catholic organization bankruptcy cases. As discussed above,

125 In re Archdiocese of St. Paul and Minneapolis, Third Amended Plan, doc. 1262, Exhibit D Trust and Trust Distribution Procedures at 93 (filed September 19, 2018).
126 Ibid. at p. 94.
127 Ibid. at 96.
128 Ibid.
129 Ibid.
130 Ibid. at 97.
131 Ibid.

beginning in the New York and New Jersey Catholic organization bankruptcy cases following enactment of claims revival legislation in those states in 2019, insurers who did not settle coverage liability on terms acceptable to the committee began to object to confirmation of the plans proposed by the debtor and supported by the committee. They argued, among other things, that the trust distribution procedures failed to winnow out fraudulent or facially invalid claims, inflated the value of claims, and deprived the insurers of defenses to coverage.[132] Insurers have managed to prevent or at least delay confirmation of plans that do not include settlement and release of their liability, increasing insurers' settlement negotiating leverage, and complicating the pathway to plan confirmation for Catholic organization debtors.

IV. Conclusion

In the last two decades, thirty-seven Catholic organizations have sought relief in bankruptcy to resolve hundreds of claims of decades-old child sexual abuse. Retroactive repeal of statutes of limitations on sexual abuse claims will no doubt yield more claims and more bankruptcy cases. Although bankruptcy cases have become common, the bankruptcy process—and Catholic organizations' resort to it—has been unfairly maligned by advocates for sexual abuse claimants in media coverage. Catholic organizations in bankruptcy have remained silent. They are, understandably, focused on the work of reaching a settlement with sexual abuse creditors in the bankruptcy case and rehabilitating their credibility and reputation. For the Catholic faithful and other observers, the use of bankruptcy proceedings by Catholic organizations thus remains mysterious or misunderstood. The legal nuances of bankruptcy as a procedural and substantive response to mass tort liability are no match for the morally and emotionally compelling narrative of sexual perversion, child suffering, and failure of trusted religious leaders to stop it. Nonetheless, bankruptcy law and process is an essential part of the sexual abuse crisis story. Canon lawyers can serve an important role in clarifying how bankruptcy offers hope for a mutually beneficial, comprehensive, and final resolution of sexual abuse claims.

---

132 See James Nani and Alex Wolf, "Bankrupt Catholic Dioceses' Victim Payout Deals Spurn Insurers," *Bloomberg Law*, November 17, 2022, https://news.bloomberglaw.com/bankruptcy-law/bankrupt-catholic-dioceses-victim-payout-deals-spurn-insurers (accessed on 30 Nov. 2023, subscription required).

CLSA PROCEEDINGS 85 (2023) 256-285

SEMINAR

PARISH FINANCE COUNCILS: GUIDING PRINCIPLES, LEGALITIES, PRACTICALITIES, AND BEST PRACTICES

Reverend Monsignor John Renken, STD, JCD
Mr. Gary M. Ruesch, JD

Seminar Description

Just like society, the Church has seen an "epochal change!" She is guided by the Holy Spirit toward better recognizing the contribution of the Christian faithful through new evangelization and synodality. This renewed ecclesial framework impacts especially the parish and its financial management. Priests, administrators, and parishioners are called to work together on finance councils or similar committees to develop economic support for parish programs and services. After highlighting some guiding principles for the administration of ecclesiastical goods, this presentation will address the civil and canonical legal parameters and rules that govern parish financial decision-making. Some best practices for their operation and methods to address ethical and practical controversies will also be suggested.

Introduction

The Synodality of the Evangelizing Church

"The Church of God is convoked in Synod."[1] The Synod on Synodality (2021-2024) is underway throughout the universal Church. This synod in which we are all active participants, a synod such as has never before been celebrated in the Church, continues for another year. It is impossible to know the conclusions of the unique worldwide synodal event, but we certainly do know 1) that the

---

1 Synod of Bishops, *The Preparatory Document: For a Synodal Church: Communion, Participation, and Mission* (Vatican City State: Libreria Editrice Vaticana, 2021) 1. See the several special studies on synodality produced by the members of the research project of the Peter and Paul Seminar in *Studia canonica* 56 (2022) 369-707.

Synod awakens the awareness of the synodality of the Church everywhere, and 2) that this refreshed awareness is not going away. Synodality is an ancient concept that has become very prominent during the pontificate of Pope Francis.

As we know, "synodality" finds its root in two Greek terms: συν (with) and ὁδός (path, road). In the ecclesiastical context, the term connotes that the People of God accompany each other on a common journey in this life that leads to the eternal Presence. In brief, synodality means that we accompany each other on this path to heaven together, led by the Spirit of God.

Many reflections by pastors, theologians, and canonists enrich our faith-filled understanding of this journey. To be sure, more such reflections are expected and will be shared. Fundamental to any such reflections, though, are two foundational texts with which we are wise to be familiar: the speech of Pope Francis on the occasion of the 50th anniversary of the institution of the Synod of Bishops (October 17, 2015);[2] and the study on synodality issued by the International Theological Commission titled *Synodality in the Life and Mission of the Church* (March 2, 2018).[3]

In his 2015 speech, Pope Francis describes synodality as a "constitutive dimension" of the Church. He insists: "We must continue along this path. The world in which we live, and which we are called to love and serve, even with its contradictions, demands that the Church strengthen cooperation in all areas of her mission. It is precisely this path of *synodality* which God expects of the Church of the third millennium."

The 2018 study of the International Theological Commission explains that synodality:

> indicates the path along which the People of God walk together. Equally, it refers to the Lord Jesus, who presents Himself as "the way, the truth, and the life," and to the fact that Christians, His followers, were originally called "followers of the Way." [Synodality] expresses

2 Pope Francis, "Ceremony Commemorating the 50th Anniversary of the Institution of the Synod of Bishops, Address of Pope Francis," October 17, 2015: *AAS* 107 (2015) 1138-1144, https://www.vatican.va/content/francesco/en/speeches/2015/october/documents/papa-francesco_20151017_50-anniversario-sinodo.html (accessed on 19 Dec. 2023) (hereafter Pope Francis, Jubilee Address).

3 International Theological Commission, *Synodality in the Life and Mission of the Church*, March 2, 2018, https://www.vatican.va/roman_curia/congregations/cfaith/cti_documents/rc_cti_20180302_sinodalita_en.html (accessed on 19 Dec. 2023) (hereafter ITC, *Synodality*).

how the disciples of Jesus were called together as an assembly and in some cases it is a synonym for the ecclesial community.[4]

Rightly, we say synodality is the "hermeneutic" whereby we interpret all aspects of Church life. It is the Spirit-given "light" that guides everything that the Church is and does.

In light of various reflections, we reasonably and responsibly can distinguish two "manifestations" of synodality: "affective synodality" and "effective synodality."[5]

"Affective synodality" identifies the common and daily "life-style" of missionary disciples. It explains how we live our lives as we accompany each other on our journey to the fullness of the Kingdom. It identifies our constant *modus vivendi et operandi* as the pilgrim People of God.[6]

"Effective synodality" describes the synodal interaction of missionary disciples (who are already living "affective synodality") in institutional structures and synodal processes in various ways—at all local, regional, and universal levels of the Church.[7] Effective synodality requires a refreshed commitment to the

---

4 ITC, *Synodality*, no. 3 (internal citations omitted).

5 Pope Francis mentions "effective synodality" in the apostolic constitution on the organization of the vicariate of Rome, *In Ecclesiarum communione*, January 6, 2023, tit. I, art. 4, https://www.vatican.va/content/francesco/it/apost_constitutions/documents/20230106-in-ecclesiarum-communione.html (accessed on 19 Dec. 2023):

> The individual offices, while responding to peculiar purposes, while respecting the competencies of each, will have among them unity and close coordination of directions, choices, and activities, in order to achieve an effective synodality, for an organic and fruitful pastoral action, according to the diocesan orientations, which must always be the fruit of listening and co-responsibility of the baptized.

Author's translation. See also art. 17 therein.

6 ITC, *Synodality*, no. 70.

7 Ibid., no. 70b.

inestimable role of consultation in the life of the Church,[8] and a commitment to the rich complementarity of *decision-making* (within organs of synodality in the community) and *decision-taking* (by leaders of the community).[9] Within the synodal Church, all the missionary disciples participate and have co-responsibility:

> A synodal Church is a Church of participation and co-responsibility. In exercising synodality she is called to give expression to the participation of all, according to each one's calling, with the authority conferred by Christ on the college of bishops headed by the Pope. Participation is based on the fact that all the faithful are qualified and called to serve each other through the gifts they have all received from the Holy Spirit.[10]

The Spirit of God blesses and enriches every parish through the synodal living of the parishioners—both their "affective synodality" and their "effective synodality." Pope Francis invites all parishes to engage in an "ecclesial renewal

---

8 ITC, *Synodality*, no. 68. Later, the document continues:

> Consulting [the lay faithful] is thus indispensable for initiating processes of discernment in the framework of synodal structures. We must, therefore, overcome the obstacles created by the lack of formation and recognised spaces in which the lay faithful can express themselves and act, and by a clerical mindset which runs the risk of keeping them on the edges of ecclesial life. This requires a priority commitment in the task of forming a mature ecclesial sense, which, at the institutional level, needs to be transformed into a regular synodal process.

Ibid., no. 73 (internal citations omitted). See also International Theological Commission, *Sensus fidei in the Life of the Church*, no. 126 (2014), https://www.vatican.va/roman_curia/congregations/cfaith/cti_documents/rc_cti_20140610_sensus-fidei_en.html (accessed on 19 Dec. 2023):

> Structures of consultation such as those mentioned above can be greatly beneficial to the Church, but only if pastors and lay people are mutually respectful of one another's charisms and if they carefully and continually listen to one another's experiences and concerns. Humble listening at all levels and proper consultation of those concerned are integral aspects of a living and lively Church.

9 ITC, *Synodality*, no. 69:

> The synodal process must take place at the heart of a hierarchically structured community. In a diocese, for example, it is necessary to distinguish between the process of *decision-making* through a joint exercise of discernment, consultation, and co-operation, and *decision-taking*, which is within the competence of the bishop, the guarantor of apostolicity and Catholicity. Working things out is a synodal task; decision is a ministerial responsibility. A correct exercise of synodality must contribute to a better articulation of the ministry of the personal and collegial exercise of apostolic authority with the synodal exercise of discernment on the part of the community.

10 Ibid., no. 67.

which cannot be deferred."[11] Such parish renewal has one primary goal: to encourage and train parishioners to be evangelizers. Pope Francis expresses his prophetic and pastoral vision of parish renewal to promote evangelization in his great apostolic exhortation, *Evangelii gaudium*:

> I dream of a "missionary option," that is, a missionary impulse capable of transforming everything, so that the Church's customs, ways of doing things, times and schedules, language and structures can be suitably channeled for the evangelization of today's world rather than for her self-preservation. The renewal of structures demanded by pastoral conversion can only be understood in this light: as part of an effort to make them more mission-oriented, to make ordinary pastoral activity on every level more inclusive and open, to inspire in pastoral workers a constant desire to go forth and in this way to elicit a positive response from all those whom Jesus summons to friendship with himself. As John Paul II once said to the Bishops of Oceania: "All renewal in the Church must have mission as its goal if it is not to fall prey to a kind of ecclesial introversion."
>
> The parish is not an outdated institution; precisely because it possesses great flexibility, it can assume quite different contours depending on the openness and missionary creativity of the pastor and the community. While certainly not the only institution which evangelizes, if the parish proves capable of self-renewal and constant adaptivity, it continues to be "the Church living in the midst of the homes of her sons and daughters." This presumes that it really is in contact with the homes and the lives of its people and does not become a useless structure out of touch with people or a self-absorbed group made up of a chosen few. The parish is the presence of the Church in a given territory, an environment for hearing God's word, for growth in the Christian life, for dialogue, proclamation, charitable outreach, worship, and celebration. In all its activities the parish encourages and trains its members to be evangelizers. It is a community of communities, a sanctuary where the thirsty come to drink in the midst of their journey, and a centre of constant missionary outreach. We must admit, though, that the call to review and renew our parishes has not yet sufficed to bring them nearer to people, to make them environments of living

---

11 Francis, apostolic exhortation *Evangelii gaudium* 27-33, November 24, 2013: *AAS* 105 (2013) (hereafter *EG*) 1019-1137; Eng. trans. https://www.vatican.va/content/francesco/en/apost_exhortations/documents/papa-francesco_esortazione-ap_20131124_evangelii-gaudium.html (accessed on 19 Dec. 2023).

communion and participation, and to make them completely mission-oriented.[12]

This seminar offers reflections on the parish finance council mandated universally in the Latin Church by the Code of Canon Law.[13] These councils (as well as the parish pastoral councils)[14] are "organs of synodality" within every parish where "effective synodality" reveals the gifts of the Holy Spirit for the life

---

12 *EG* 27-28 (internal citations omitted).

13 In this seminar presentation, the following primary resources are used:

- *Codex Iuris Canonici auctoritate Ioannis Pauli PP. II promulgatus* (Vatican City: Libreria Editrice Vaticana, 1983); Eng. trans. from *Code of Canon Law. Latin-English Edition: New English Translation*, 4th printing (Washington, DC: CLSA, 2023).
- *Codex Canonum Ecclesiarum Orientalium auctoritate Ioannis Pauli PP. II promulgatus* (Vatican City: Libreria Editrice Vaticana, 1990); Eng. trans. from *Code of Canons of the Eastern Churches. Latin-English Edition* (Washington, DC: CLSA, 2001).
- Pontifical Commission for the Revision of the Code of Canon Law, *Relatio complectens synthesim animadversionum ab Em.mis atque Exc.mis Patribus Commissionis ad novissimum schema Codicis Iuris Canonici exhibitarum, cum responsionibus a Secretaria et Consultoribus datis* (Vatican City: Typis Polyglottis Vaticanis, 1981) (hereafter *Relatio*).
- Pontifical Commission for the Revision of the Code of Canon Law, *Schema Canonum Libri II. De Populo Dei* (Vatican City: Typis polyglottiss vaticanis, 1977) (hereafter 1977 *Schema*).
- Pontifical Commission for the Revision of the Code of Canon Law, *Schema Codicis Iuris Canonici iuxta animadversiones S.R.E. Cardinalium, Episcoporum Conferentiarum, Dicasteriorum Curiae Romanae, Universitatum Facultatumque ecclesiasticarum necnon Superiorum Institutorum vitae consecratae recognitum* (Vatican City: Libreria Editrice Vaticana, 1980) (hereafter 1980 *Schema*).

14 Canon 536 provides legislation for the parish pastoral council. The diocesan bishop can mandate its establishment in every parish of the diocese, but the *parochus* may establish one even if it is not mandated by particular law. Canon 536 states:

> §1. If the diocesan bishop judges it opportune after he has heard the presbyteral council, a pastoral council is to be established in each parish, over which the pastor presides and in which the Christian faithful, together with those who share in pastoral care by virtue of their office in the parish, assist in fostering pastoral activity. §2. A pastoral council possesses a consultative vote only and is governed by the norms established by the diocesan bishop.

The parish pastoral council exists to address parish pastoral planning, in a manner analogous to the diocesan pastoral council (cc. 511-514). During the review of the 1980 *Schema* of the proposed revised *Code*, Franz Cardinal König had suggested that it may be opportune to provide for some connection or relationship between the parish pastoral council and the parish finance council. The Secretariat explained that no connection is foreseen because these organs are diverse. *Communicationes* 14 (1982) 226; *Relatio* 127.

of the community. All these gifts, all organs of synodality,[15] have one fundamental purpose: the new evangelization of the world by every missionary disciple. Any such reflections, both in canon law and in civil law, would advance that ecclesial renewal that cannot be deferred.

PART ONE:

CANON LAW CONSIDERATIONS ABOUT PARISH FINANCE COUNCILS

Reverend Monsignor John A. Renken

Any informed conversation concerning parish finance councils expects prior recollection of the *Code*'s description of the parish and its presentation of the role of its *parochus* in caring for parish property.[16] All this leads to a consideration of proposed "best practices" for the parish finance council as an "organ of synodality" in service to the life of the parish and its mission of evangelization.

---

15 The Code of Canon Law does not offer a single "collective" term to identify groups (whether deliberative, consent-giving, counsel-giving, or "mixed") at various levels of the Church. In his apostolic exhortation *Evangelii gaudium*, no. 31, Pope Francis referred to such bodies as "means of participation" that further the missionary aspiration of reaching everyone. In his Jubilee Address on October 17, 2015, he referred to them as "organs of communion" in the particular Church. In *Synodality in the Life and Mission of the Church*, the International Theological Commission refers to them as "synodal structures which serve mission," "structures at the service of synodal life in the particular Church," and parochial "structures that have a synodal character" (nos. 77-84, *passim*). Earlier this year, in his apostolic constitution on the organization of the vicariate of Rome, *In Ecclesiarum communione*, January 6, 2023 (nn. 21-24), Pope Francis referred to these bodies as "organs of synodality in service to the mission" of the Diocese of Rome. Given the current ecclesial context, it seems most appropriate to adopt this "collective" terminology to identify those diocesan and parochial bodies that exercise effective synodality. Put succinctly, the "mission" of the Church (and all its parts and members) is evangelization: "Evangelization is the task of the Church. The Church, as the agent of evangelization, is more than an organic and hierarchical institution; she is first and foremost a people advancing on its pilgrim way towards God." Pope Francis, *Evangelii Gaudium*, no. 111; see Pope Paul VI, apostolic exhortation on evangelization in the modern world *Evangelii nuntiandi* 14, December 8, 1975: *AAS* 68 (1976) 5-76, https://www.vatican.va/content/paul-vi/en/apost_exhortations/documents/hf_p-vi_exh_19751208_evangelii-nuntiandi.html (accessed on 19 Dec. 2023).

16 See the helpful analysis of: Lawrence Rasaian, *The Collaboration of the* Parochus *and the Parish Finance Council in the Protection of Parish Property: Practical Reflections on the Relation between Canons 532 and 537 of the 1983 Code of Canon Law*, JCD Thesis, Faculty of Canon Law (Ottawa, ON: Saint Paul University, 2014).

> Can. 515 §1. A parish is a certain community of the Christian faithful stably constituted in a particular Church, whose pastoral care is entrusted to a pastor *(parochus)* as its proper pastor *(pastor)* under the authority of the diocesan bishop.
>
> §2. It is only for the diocesan bishop to erect, suppress, or alter parishes. He is neither to erect, suppress, nor alter notably parishes, unless he has heard the presbyteral council.
>
> §3. A legitimately erected parish possesses juridic personality by the law itself.

Canon 515 offers a two-fold description of the parish. From one perspective, the parish is a stable community of Christian faithful: "a certain community of the Christian faithful stably constituted in a particular Church, whose pastoral care is entrusted to a pastor (*parochus*) as its proper pastor (*pastor*) under the authority of the diocesan bishop" (c. 515 §1).[17] From a complementary perspective, it is *ipso iure* a non-collegial public juridic person, a *universitas personarum* (c. 515 §3).[18]

The parish is a stable community of the Christian faithful. It is a group of missionary disciples who, led and fortified by the Spirit of God, accompany each other on a pilgrim journey on earth to the fullness of life in heaven. Within the parish community, they are enriched by the word of God, enlivened by the sacraments, strengthened by effective and life-transforming pastoral care (cc. 528, 529 §1). *Inter alia*, the *parochus* promotes synodality, both affective and effective, when he performs his duty to "recognize and promote the proper part which the lay members of the Christian faithful have in the mission of the Church" and to "work so that the faithful have concern for parochial communion, consider themselves members of the diocese and of the universal Church, and participate in and sustain efforts to promote this same communion" (c. 529 §2).

The parish is also *ipso iure* a non-collegial public juridic person, a *universitas personarum*. Parishes are the most numerous juridic persons in the Church. As a person in the Church, the parish is the subject of obligations and rights corresponding to its nature (c. 129 §1).[19] It is an aggregate of persons

---

17 The parish *pastoral* council serves to enhance the pastoral effectiveness of the parish as a community in the midst of the neighborhood. It promotes the mission of the parish.

18 The parish *finance* council serves to maintain the presence of the parish as a public juridic person ministering *nomine Ecclesiae* in the midst of the neighborhood. It maintains the presence of the parish.

19 See James A. Coriden, *The Parish in Catholic Theology: History, Theology, and Canon Law* (New York: Paulist Press, 1997) 72-79.

(*universitas personarum*) ordered for a purpose that is in keeping with the mission of the Church (i.e., works of piety, the apostolate, and charity—both spiritual and temporal) and that transcends the purpose of the individual physical persons (c. 114 §§1-2). It functions in a non-collegial fashion since its members do not collectively render binding decisions on its behalf (c. 115 §1). It is a public juridic person that fulfills its proper function in the name of the Church in view of the public good (c. 116 §1). While parish statutes are very beneficial, the parish does not need to have statutes approved before or after it is established (see c. 117) because, by the law itself (*ipso iure*), it is a juridic person the moment it is established (cc. 116 §1; 515 §3). Its legal representative (who acts in its name) is its *parochus* (c. 118; see cc. 515 §1; 519; 532; 1279 §1). It is perpetual by nature (c. 120 §1), but it can be modified by unification with another parish (c. 121) or by division (c. 122), or it can be extinguished (c. 123).

The Role of the *Parochus* as the Administrator ("Manager") of Parish Property

> Can. 532 In all juridic affairs the pastor represents the parish according to the norm of law. He is to take care that the goods of the parish are administered according to the norm of cann. 1281-1288.[20]

Canon 532 explains that the *parochus* represents the parish according to the norm of the law (*ad normam iuris*) (see c. 118).[21] In a related vein, he also is the administrator ("manager") of parochial property inasmuch as he governs the parish (c. 1279 §1) that has been entrusted to his care under the authority of the

---

20 Canon 366 of the 1977 *Schema* had stated: "In omnibus negotiis iuridicis parochus personam gerit paroeciae, ad normam iuris; curet ut bona paroeciae administrentur ad normam cann. (*De iure Ecclesiae patrimoniali*, cann. 25-33)." When the consultors reviewed the observations made about the 1977 Schema on May 9, 1980, they approved the text as it has been composed and they rejected a recommendation from a consultative body that particular law could remove from the *parochus* his juridic representation of the parish. *Communicationes* 13 (1981) 284. When the secretariat reviewed recommendations on the 1980 *Schema*, it rejected a proposal made Cardinal Franz König of Vienna and Cardinal Johannes Willebrands of Utrecht that the proposed canon add the words "et ad normam iuris particularis." The secretariat said that this addition is unnecessary for two reasons: (1) the *normam iuris* in the canon can also be *ius particulare*; and (2) the canons on temporal goods often mention *ius particulare*. *Communicationes* 14 (1982) 225; *Relatio* 127. Accordingly, the promulgated canon 532 is the same as initially proposed in the 1977 *Schema* (with the specific identifications of canons 1281-1288). Thereafter, this canon was unchanged during the remainder of the process drafting the revised code: it became promulgated canon 532.

21 The code provides that every parish always have a "priest-leader:" the *parochus* (c. 519); the "*co-parochi*" and their moderator (c. 517 §1; see cc. 542-544); the priest-director (c. 517 §2); the parochial administrator (cc. 539-540); and, in the case of a vacant parish or an impeded *parochus*, the (senior) parochial vicar or, if there is no vicar, a *parochus* determined by particular law (c. 541).

diocesan bishop (cc. 515 §1; 519). Accordingly, canon 532 adds that the *parochus* is to take care that parish property is administered according to the norm of canons 1281-1288.[22]

Book V of the code provides universal legislation governing the temporal goods of the Church. It states in its first canon:

> Canon 1254 §1. To pursue its proper purposes, the Catholic Church by innate right is able to acquire, retain, administer, and alienate temporal goods independently from civil power.
>
> §2. The proper purposes are principally: to order divine worship, to care for the decent support of the clergy and other ministers, and to exercise works of the sacred apostolate and of charity, especially toward the needy.

This canon identifies a four-fold relationship between the "Church"[23] and temporal goods: acquisition, retention, administration, and alienation. The *parochus* is the only competent agent of the parish to perform, on its behalf, specific acts in his "management" of parish property: 1) acts of acquisition, whereby temporal goods are acquired, and after which these temporal goods are called "ecclesiastical goods;"[24] 2) acts of retention, whereby ecclesiastical goods are preserved and possessed securely; 3) acts of administration, whereby ecclesiastical goods are used for their proper purposes and made to bear fruit; and 4) acts of alienation, whereby ownership of ecclesiastical goods is lost.[25] Most of these four-fold acts are "ordinary" or "routine," but they are "extraordinary"

---

22 See Gianfranco Ghirlanda, *Chiesa universale e Chiesa particolare* (Rome: Gregorian and Biblical Press, 2023) 965-967.

23 In Book V, "church" is a "technical term" that identifies the universal Church, the Apostolic See, and "also any public juridic person in the Church unless it is otherwise apparent from the context or the nature of the matter" (c. 1258).

24 In Book V, "ecclesiastical goods" is a "technical term" that identifies the temporal goods that belong to the universal Church, the Apostolic See, and other public juridic persons in the Church (c. 1257 §1). Therefore, it is correct to state that "ecclesiastical goods" are *never* the property of private juridic persons or physical persons.

25 See Velasio De Paolis, *De bonis Ecclesiae temporalibus. Adnotationes in Codicem: Liber V* (Rome: Pontifical Gregorian University, Faculty of Canon Law, 1986) 26; Anthony O. Ekpo, "The Retention of Ecclesiastical Goods in Book V of the 1983 Code: A Merely Notional Concept?" *The Canonist*, 12 (2021) 22-54; John A. Renken, *Church Property: A Commentary on Canon Law Governing Temporal Goods in the United States and Canada* (Staten Island: Alba House, 2009) 17-18.

whenever the *parochus* requires the involvement of others before he is able to perform them.[26]

In light of the four "acts" that the *parochus* performs on behalf of the parish as the administrator ("manager") of its property, it is obvious that the reference to only canons 1281-1288 in canon 532 is inadequate.[27] Indeed, Cardinal Francesco Coccopalmerio suggested that canon 532 would more properly refer to the *parochus* as the sole agent responsible for performing all four acts of management (acquisition, retention, administration, and alienation—i.e., all the acts mentioned in Book V et al.) on behalf of the parish.[28] It is noteworthy that canon 290 §1 of the Eastern code, which corresponds to Latin canon 532, states simply: "The pastor represents the parish in all juridic affairs." It does not make specific mention of his role of performing acts of administration (*only*) of the ecclesiastical goods owned by the parish.

The *parochus* is the sole agent to perform acts of management for the parish, the goods, but he manages are owned by the parish (not by him). Canon 1256 explains: "Under the supreme authority of the Roman Pontiff, ownership of goods belongs to that [public or private] juridic person that has acquired them legitimately."[29]

The Parish Finance Council in the Code

> Can. 537 In each parish there is to be a finance council which is governed, in addition to universal law, by norms issued by the diocesan

---

26 See John A. Renken, "Acts of the Church in Relation to Temporal Goods: The Ordinary and the Extraordinary," *Studia canonica* 50 (2016) 519-530. See also John P. Beal, "Ordinary, Extraordinary, and Something in Between: Administration of the Temporal Goods of Dioceses and Parishes," *The Jurist* 72 (2012) 109-129.

27 Care must be taken to distinguish four canonical terms with the same root: "*administrare*" (= *ad* [to] + *ministrare* [to assist, to serve, to wait upon]): 1) An *administrator* is a physical person who governs a juridic person (c. 1279 §1). 2) *Administration*, which refers to acts of governance [e.g., administrative acts] that are functions proper to ecclesiastical governance, as distinct from legislative and judicial functions (Pontifical Council for Legislative Texts, "*Nota* La funzione dell'autorità sui beni ecclesiastici, February 12, 2004, *Communicationes* 36 [2004] 26). 3) An *act of administration* is one of the four-fold responsibilities of an administrator in caring for temporal goods of a juridic person; the other three responsibilities are "acquisition," "retention," and "alienation" (cc. 1254 §1; 1255). (4) A singular *administrative* act is "a decree, a precept, or a rescript … issued by one who possesses executive power within the limits of that person's competence" (c. 35; see c. 76 §1).

28 Francesco Coccopalmerio, *De paroecia* (Rome: Editrice Pontificia Università Gregoriana, 1991) 204. The same observation is made in Velasio De Paolis, "Il consiglio per gli affairi economici ed i beni patrimoniali della parrocchia," in *La Parrocchia*, Studi Giuridici 43 (Vatican City: Libreria Editrice Vaticana, 1997) 285-286.

29 On the legitimate acquisition of goods, see canons 1259-1272; 1299-1310 *passim*.

> bishop and in which the Christian faithful, selected according to these same norms, are to assist the pastor in the administration of the goods of the parish, without prejudice to the prescript of can. 532.[30]

Codified legislation on parish finance councils is an innovation in the 1983 code:[31] no corresponding legislation had existed in the 1917 code.[32] Further, in the 1990 code, canon 295 requires each Church *sui iuris* to develop particular law for mandated "appropriate councils dealing with pastoral and financial matters." Accordingly, the specific norms for parish finance councils will be promulgated by the competent legislative authorities of the several Eastern Catholic Churches.

Canon 537 mandates a finance council for every parish, just as canon 492 mandates a finance council for every diocese. Canon 1280 says: "Each juridic person is to have its own finance council or at least two counselors who, according to the norm of the statutes [of the juridic person], are to assist the administrator in fulfilling his function." Canon 537 (and canon 492) do not give the parish (or the diocese) the "option" of "at least two counselors" to replace the finance council.

Canon 537 requires that every diocesan bishop establish, by particular law, norms that govern the functioning of parish finance councils. These norms are not to contradict universal law (concerning the juridical structure of a parish, the role of the *parochus*, the laws governing temporal/ecclesiastical goods, etc.). The

---

30 The 1977 *Schema* made no reference to parish finance councils. When the consultors reviewed the observations made about the 1977 *Schema* on May 14, 1980, a consultor proposed that the future code would provide for a parish finance council "where circumstances suggested it." The secretary of the Pontifical Commission, Archbishop Rosalio José Castillo Lara, opined that such a council is not strictly necessary because of the general norm of *De munere patrimoniali* already proposes that all juridic persons have a council of administration. But, if the Pontifical Commission chooses to retain legislation for the parish finance council, Castillo Lara (together with Monsignor Willie Onclin, relator) proposed that the canon read thus:

> In unaquaque parochia habeatur concilium a rebus oeconomicis, quod, praeterquam iure universali, regituir normis ab Episcopo dioecesano latis et in quo christifideles, secundum easdem normas selecti, parocho in administratione bonorum parochiae adiutorio sint, firmo praescripto can. 477.

(indicating that the *parochus* represents the parish in all juridic affairs, which became promulgated as canon 532.) The proposed canon on parish finance councils was accepted by all members of the Pontifical Commission present at the meeting. *Communicationes* 13 (1981) 307-308; *Relatio* 127-128. Thereafter, this canon remained unchanged during the remainder of the process drafting the revised code: it became promulgated canon 537.

31 See De Paolis, "Il consiglio per gli affairi economici ed i beni patrimoniali della parrocchia," 267-288.

32 Similarly, codified legislation on parish pastoral councils is an innovation in the 1983 code, canon 536: no corresponding legislation had existed in the 1917 *Code*. And *CCEO* canon 295 provides for the establishment of parish pastoral councils through legislation established by the competent authorities in each Eastern Catholic Church.

norms are to indicate how the councilors of the parish finance council, who are to be members of the Christian faithful, are selected. The norms must explain that the councilors "assist the *parochus* in the administration of the goods of the parish" but "without prejudice to the prescript of canon 532." Canon 532, as we have seen already, requires that the *parochus* represent the parish in all juridic affairs in accord with the norm of law; it adds that he "is to take care that the goods of the parish are administered according to the norm of cann. 1281-1288." And, also as already mentioned, inasmuch as Cardinal Francesco Coccopalmerio suggests that canon 532 would more property refer to the *parochus* as the sole agent responsible for performing all four acts (acquisition, retention, administration, and alienation—i.e., all the acts mentioned in Book V et al.) on behalf of the parish, it follows that the parish finance council would assist him in all aspects of "managing" parish property.

It is worthy of observation that canon 537 does not state that the parish finance council performs its *munus* in a consultative manner, just as canon 492 does not say that the diocesan finance council serves in a consultative manner.[33] Indeed, there are many instances when the diocesan finance council must offer its counsel or even give its consent to the diocesan bishop before he is able to act.[34]

---

33 The law does, however, explain that the diocesan pastoral council (c. 514) and the parish pastoral council (c. 536 §2) each "has only a consultative vote (*voto gaudet tantum consultativo*).

34 The code requires the diocesan bishop to receive the *consent* of the diocesan finance council: (1) to place acts of extraordinary diocesan administration as defined by the conference of bishops (c. 1277: the college of consultors must also give its consent); (2) to give permission to alienate goods of public juridic persons subject to his authority, and to alienate diocesan goods, which belong to stable patrimony and whose value is beyond the minimum amount established by the conference of bishops (c. 1292 §2: the college of consultors and "those concerned" must also give their consent); and (3) to give permission to administrators to perform any contractual transaction that can worsen the patrimonial condition of a public juridic person subject to his authority, or to perform the transaction himself if it involves diocesan goods (c. 1295: the college of consultors and "those concerned" must also give their consent; see c. 1292 §2). The code requires the diocesan bishop to receive the *counsel* of the diocesan finance council before he performs the following eight acts: (1) to appoint the diocesan finance officer (c. 494 §1: the college of consultors must also give its counsel); (2) to remove the diocesan finance officer (c. 494 §2: the college of consultors must also give its counsel); (3) to impose a moderate tax upon public juridic persons subject to his authority (c. 1263: the presbyteral council must also give its counsel); (4) to impose an extraordinary tax upon other juridic persons and upon physical persons subject to his authority (c. 1263: the presbyteral council must also give its counsel); (5) to place "non-routine" acts of ordinary diocesan administration that are more important in light of the economic condition of the diocese (c. 1277: the college of consultors must also give its counsel); (6) to determine acts of extraordinary administration placed by public juridic persons subject to him (c. 1281 §1); (7) to make a prudent judgment

In fact, if the diocesan finance officer is elected diocesan administrator *sede vacante*, the diocesan finance council issues a deliberative vote by electing a new diocesan finance officer *pro tempore* (c. 423 §2): in this situation, a group (which may be composed entirely of lay persons) is required by the code to confer an ecclesiastical office (temporarily). The law does, however, explain that the diocesan pastoral council (c. 514) and the parish pastoral council (c. 536 §2) each "has only a consultative vote" (*voto gaudet tantum consultativo*).

The Parish Finance Council in the 2020 Instruction of the Congregation for the Clergy

On 29 June 2020, the Congregation for the Clergy issued its instruction[35] titled "The Pastoral Conversion of the Parish Community in the Service of the Evangelising Mission of the Church."[36] *Inter multa alia*, this instruction offers guidance on the parish finance council (arts. 101-107) and the parish pastoral council (arts. 108-114), identified as "Organs of Ecclesial Co-responsibility" (*Gli organismi di corresponsabilità ecclesiale*).[37] We now consider its reflections on the parish finance council.

The instruction explains that the management (*la gestione*) of parochial property is an important area of evangelization and that the *parochus* must be

---

on the investment of money and movable goods assigned to an endowment for the benefit of a foundation (c. 1305); and (8) to reduce, moderate, or commute the wills of the faithful for pious causes, only for a just and necessary cause, with the intention of the founder preserved as much as possible (c. 1310 §1: "those concerned" must also give their consultative vote). See John A. Renken, *Church Property: A Commentary on Canon Law Governing Temporal Goods in the United States and Canada*, 103-104.

35 Canon 34 explains instructions: "§1. Instructions clarify the prescripts of laws and elaborate on and determine the methods to be observed in fulfilling them. They are given for the use of those whose duty it is to see that laws are executed and oblige them in the execution of the laws. Those who possess executive power legitimately issue such instructions within the limits of their competence. §2. The ordinances of instructions do not derogate from laws. If these ordinances cannot be reconciled with the prescripts of laws, they lack all force. §3. Instructions cease to have force not only by explicit or implicit revocation of the competent authority who issued them or of the superior of that authority but also by the cessation of the law for whose clarification or execution they were given."

36 Congregation for the Clergy, instruction *The Pastoral Conversion of the Parish Community in the Service of the Evangelising Mission of the Church*, June 29, 2020, (hereafter Congregation for the Clergy, *Pastoral Conversion*) https://press.vatican.va/content/salastampa/it/bollettino/pubblico/2020/07/20/0391/00886.html#ing (accessed on 19 Dec. 2023); See Andrea Ripa, "Presentation of the Instruction *The Pastoral Conversion of the Parish Community in the Service of the Evangelising Mission of the Church*," July 8, 2020, https://www.clerus.va/content/dam/clerus/ Dox/Istruzione2020Presentation_EN.pdf (accessed on 19 Dec. 2023).

37 Congregation for the Clergy, *Pastoral Conversion*, tit. X.

assisted in the care of parish property by collaborators who have evangelizing zeal and a missionary spirit:

> The management [*la gestione*] of goods which every parish has to some extent is an important area of evangelization and evangelical witness, both in the Church and in civil society, since "all the goods that we have, the Lord gives them to go to the world, to go to humanity, to help others." The [*parochus*], therefore, cannot and must not remain only at this task, so it is necessary that he be assisted by collaborators to administer [*amministrare*] the goods of the Church above all with evangelizing zeal and a missionary spirit [in conformity with *CIC* c. 532, the *parochus* is responsible for the goods of the parish, even if in administering them, he must avail himself of the collaboration of lay experts].[38]

The instruction presents the following specific elements about the parish finance council:

- Mandated for Each Parish. Every parish must have its own parish finance council, because each parish retains its own "juridic personality and capacity"—even if the diocesan bishop permits the establishment of a pastoral council serving more than one parish in a "grouping of parishes" such as a vicariate forane or a "pastoral unit."[39]
- Consultative Nature. The parish finance council is constituted as a consultative body (*organismo consultivo*) in the parish.
- President (Non-Member). Its president is the *parochus* who is not counted among its members: he presides over it.[40]
- Minimum Number of Councilors. It must be composed of at least three members in order to be considered "collegial" (see c. 115 §2 and, by analogy, c. 492 §1).[41]
- Number and Selection of Councilors. Norms governing membership can be established by the diocesan bishop. Absent such particular legislation, the *parochus* will determine: (1) the number of councilors, taking into account the size of the parish; and (2) their manner of selection (e.g., appointment by the *parochus* or election in some fashion by the parish community).[42] The norms issued by the diocesan bishop must take into account the specific

---

38 Congregation for the Clergy, *Pastoral Conversion*, no. 101 (Eng. trans. by the author; some internal citations omitted).
39 Ibid., no. 59; see nn. 52-53 on the "vicariate forane" and nn. 54-60 on "pastoral units."
40 Ibid., no. 102.
41 Ibid., no. 102.
42 Ibid., no. 103.

situation of parishes—e.g., those of particularly modest means, those in a "pastoral unit" (see cc. 517, 526).[43]

- Qualifications of Councilors. Parish finance councilors must be of proven good reputation and expert in financial and legal questions (c. 537; Congregation for Bishops, *Apostolorum successores*, no. 210). These qualifications will enable them to render effective and competent service, thereby demonstrating that the parish finance council is not "a mere formality."[44]
- Parish Membership Not Required to Be a Councilor. Councilors need not "necessarily" belong to the parish itself.[45] "Unless the diocesan Bishop has decided otherwise, observing the necessary prudence and any pertinent norms of civil law, nothing prevents the same person from being a member of the finance council of multiple parishes, whenever circumstances require."[46] This displays that the finance council is a "council of the parish"—not necessarily a "council of parishioners."
- Promotion of a Culture of Co-Responsibility, Administrative Transparency, Service to Church Needs. "The finance council fulfils a role of particular importance in the growth, at the level of the parish community, of a culture of co-responsibility, of administrative transparency, and of service to the needs of the Church."[47]
- Transparency: *Modus agendi.*

  In a particular way, transparency should not be understood as a mere formal presentation of statistics, but more as information that is the community's due, and an advantageous opportunity for its formative involvement. Transparency refers to a *modus agendi*, indispensable for the credibility of the Church, especially where there are significant goods to administer.[48]
- Transparency: Goal.

  Ordinarily, the goal of transparency may be attained by publishing the annual financial report that must first be presented to the local ordinary [c. 1287 §1], with detailed indications of income and expenditure. From the annual report, the community as a whole may be aware that these goods belong to the parish, not the *parochus*; that he is the administrator [*amministratore*] of them; how they are administered;

43 Congregation for the Clergy, *Pastoral Conversion*, no. 105; see nn. 54-60 on "pastoral units."
44 Ibid., no. 103.
45 Ibid., no. 103.
46 Ibid., no. 104.
47 Ibid., no. 106.
48 Ibid., no. 106.

what the financial situation of the parish is; and what resources are effectively at its disposal.[49]

Best Practices for the Effective Synodality of the Parish Finance Council

The code provides legislation for several "organs of synodality" that safeguard church property.[50] Inasmuch as parishes are the most numerous public juridic persons in the Church, and inasmuch as each parish must have its own parish finance council, it follows that parish finance councils are the most numerous organs of synodality in the Church. In light of the preceding considerations, the following are suggested as best practices that would enable these tens of thousands of finance councils to offer the finest "effective synodality" in the parishes.

Commitment to Effective Synodality.

Inasmuch as the parish finance council is a mandated "organ of synodality" in the parish, councilors will be formed in the art and practice of synodality, both affective and effective. This demands attentive listening (which is more than "simply hearing"), as Pope Francis explained:

> A synodal Church is a Church which listens, which realizes that listening 'is more than simply hearing.' It is a mutual listening in which everyone has something to learn. The faithful people, the college of bishops, the Bishop of Rome: all listening to each other, and all listening to the Holy Spirit, the 'Spirit of truth' (*Jn* 14:17), in order to know what he 'says to the Churches' (*Rev* 2:7).[51]

The councilors will also recall the insistence of Pope Francis that the entire Church persevere in synodal life:

> We must continue along this path. The world in which we live, and which we are called to love and serve, even with its contradictions, demands that the Church strengthen cooperation in all areas of her mission. It is precisely this path of synodality which God expects of the Church of the third millennium.[52]

---

49 Congregation for the Clergy, *Pastoral Conversion*, nn. 106-107. The English translation of no. 107 on clerus.va translates the Italian *amministratore* into English as "steward." This is incorrect.

50 See John A. Renken, "Organs of Synodality and the Revised Penal Law: Effective Means to Safeguard Church Property," CLSGBI, *Annual Conference*, May 1-5, 2023, Galway Bay, Ireland, 33-65.

51 Pope Francis, Jubilee Address (internal citation omitted).

52 Ibid.

Admittedly, clericalism can often block synodal practice in the Church.

> Clericalism is the maintaining or increasing of the power of clergy rooted in an unfounded sense of power and entitlement. It is a false and fabricated superiority, often reflective of a vane and base ambition, by which some clergy presume to dominate over and/or to feed off the faithful entrusted to their care. Clericalism does not give life but, like a slow-growing cancer, brings forth increasing pain and hurt, decay and death. It is *always* destructive. … Clericalism denies that the Spirit also bestows manifold gifts upon lay persons, who constitute the majority of the Church. In *Evangelii gaudium*, 102, Pope Francis states that excessive clericalism can exclude lay persons from the Church.[53]

Ongoing Formation of Councilors

The parish finance councilors, certainly enjoying a good reputation, must have expertise in finances, civil law, and canon law. The Church will take care to provide them with ongoing formation especially in canonical legislation governing all aspects of the management of parish property. his formation will include the legislation contained in the code and elsewhere, including especially particular laws. Councilors will also understand the "special instructions"[54] issued by the ordinary as he exercises careful vigilance over the management of parish property (c. 1276 §1).

Regular and Open Rapport with the Parish Pastoral Council

The code mandates that every parish have its own parish finance council (c. 537), but it allows that the diocesan bishop, after he hears the presbyteral council, mandate every parish to have its own parish pastoral council (c. 536). Even if parish pastoral councils are not mandated in a diocese, nothing prevents their establishment, as Pope Francis urges: "How necessary pastoral councils are! A bishop cannot guide a diocese without pastoral councils. A *parochus* cannot guide without pastoral councils."[55]

---

53 John A. Renken, "Synodality: A Constitutive Element of the Church. Reflections on Pope Francis and Synodality," *Studia canonica* 52 (2018) 41.

54 The subjects that may be addressed in "special instructions" are identified in John A. Renken, "Canonical Challenges in Caring for Church Property," *Studies in Church Law* 9 (2013) 143-146.

55 Francis, "Pastoral Visit to Assisi: Meeting with the Clergy, Consecrated People, and Members of Diocesan Pastoral Councils," October 4, 2013, https://www.vatican.va/content/francesco/en/speeches/2013/october/documents/papa-francesco_20131004_clero-assisi.html (accessed on 19 Dec. 2023). Quoted in Congregation for the Clergy, *Pastoral Conversion of the Parish Community*, no. 108.

The parish finance council and the parish pastoral council have distinct roles of service in the parish, but they cannot be radically separated because they serve the same parochial community and because oftentimes the decision of one council has an impact on the other.[56]

The parish pastoral council exists to address parish pastoral planning, in a manner analogous to the diocesan pastoral council (cc. 511-514). In order to plan parish programs in an effective fashion, the parish pastoral council will need to ensure sufficient funding. In a corresponding way, in order to prepare a realistic parish budget (see c. 1284 §3), the parish finance council will need to be aware of proposed parish initiatives. Accordingly, there must be regular and open rapport between the two parish councils in order to serve the parish community and to enable its evangelizing mission. Indeed, nothing prevents an individual from being a member of both parish councils.[57]

Transparency and Full Disclosure

Parish finance councils promote a culture of transparency in the parish, as explained by the Congregation for the Clergy in its instruction on the pastoral conversion of the parish community, mentioned above.[58] The instruction invites parish finance councils to make transparency its "*modus agendi*, indispensable for the credibility of the Church, especially where there are significant goods to administer." It says that transparency is seen in publishing the annual financial report of income and expenditures (see c. 1287, which requires particular law to determine how "administrators are to render an account to the faithful concerning the goods offered by the faithful to the Church.") The instruction says that the published annual financial report results in "community awareness" in five ways: the community understands 1) that the goods are property of the parish, not the *parochus*; 2) that the *parochus* is the administrator of parish property; 3) the manner in which parish property is administered; 4) the financial situation of the parish; and 5) resources effectively at the disposal of the parish.

In addition to the above, the parish finance council will promote transparency in the regular and complete disclosure of its operations (e.g., its deliberations, its recommendations, its development and on-going monitoring of the annual budget, etc.) Such disclosure will be seen in detailed, complete, and

---

56 Ghirlanda, *Chiesa universale e Chiesa particolare*, 988-989; see Coccopalmerio, *De paroecia*, 177.
57 See Ghirlanda, *Chiesa universal e Chiesa particolare*, 989.
58 See Chad J. Glendinning, "Structures of Accountability in the Parish and Diocese: Lessons Learned in North America and Possibilities of Reform," *Studia canonica* 56 (2002) 656.

timely publication of the agenda and minutes of council meetings, using the available means of dissemination of information (e.g., parish bulletin, website, email, etc.).

The parish finance council is called to promote a culture of transparency. To do this effectively and successfully, the councilors must be treated with the exemplary transparency. *All* matters dealing with parish finances must be fully disclosed to them: they are to be "thoroughly informed . . . of the economic state" of the parish (see c. 1292 §4). Not divulging the complete picture of parish income and expenditures to the parish finance council makes its service to be an absurd misrepresentation, an abusive mockery. Indeed, if the *parochus* refuses full disclosure, his malevolent behavior appears to reflect clericalism: parish property is the possession of the parish, not its *parochus*.

Diocesan Particular Law on Rights and Obligations of the Parish Finance Council

Canon 537, which mandates a finance council for every parish, requires the diocesan bishop to issue norms identifying how the councilors will assist the *parochus* in his management of parish property.[59] In an effort to promote the effective synodality of the parish finance council, these norms may assign the following specific rights and obligations to the councilors.[60]

A. Rights to Receive Full and Transparent Information

1) the right to receive regular and complete accountings of all financial transactions (e.g., monthly reports of income and expenditures);
2) the right to be informed of the fulfilment of any obligations arising from an accepted gift with an attached condition or modal obligation (c. 1267 §2; see c. 1284 §2, 3°); debt reduction; (c. 1284 §2, 5°); non-autonomous pious foundations (c. 1303 §1, 2°); etc.;
3) the right to regular and open access to all parish financial records (c. 1284 §2, 8°) and parish legal documents (c. 1284 §2, 2°, 9°), in complete format and without any alterations; this includes, but is not limited to, the right to access to all parochial financial documents,

59 Norms governing the operation of the parish finance council may be included in the statutes (c. 94) of the parish. Note: As mentioned earlier, statutes, approved in advance by the competent ecclesiastical authority, are required only before the establishment of juridic persons erected *ab homine* (c. 177); accordingly, statutes are *not* required for parishes since they are erected *ipso iure* (c. 515 §3).

60 The following can also be found in Renken, "Canonical Challenges in Caring for Church Property," 137-138.

reports, audits, etc.—whether these pertain in the civil forum, the canonical forum, or both;

4) the right to receive from the *parochus* full and complete disclosure, transparently and regularly, of all aspects of the management of parish property;

B. Rights and Obligation to Give Informed Counsel

5) the right and the obligation to offer counsel concerning any proposed "non-routine" acts of the management of temporal/ecclesiastical goods: acts of extraordinary acquisition; acts of extraordinary retention; acts of extraordinary administration; and acts of extraordinary alienation. The norms may require the *parochus* to present written indication of the counsel of the councilors in these matters to the diocesan bishop, inasmuch as he is required to give the *parochus* the power or consent to perform the proposed act;

6) the right and the obligation to offer counsel in the development of, to review, and, as an assurance of accuracy, to affix the their signatures to: the annual parish administration report (c. 1284 §2, 8°); the annual financial report (c. 1287 §1); the regularly updated inventory (c. 1283, 2°-3°); the annual budget (if mandated by particular law: c. 1284 §3);

7) the right and the obligation to offer prior counsel on contracts binding the parish (see cc. 1290; 22): e.g., insurance contracts (c. 1284 §2, 1°); loan contracts (see c. 1284 §2, 5°); investment contracts (c. 1284 §2, 6°); employment contracts (see c. 1286); lease contracts (c. 1297), etc.;

C. Obligations toward Others

8) the obligation to inform the diocesan bishop, at least annually, in a written document to which are affixed the councilors' signatures, that the finance council has met regularly (indicating the dates of the meetings) and has performed the multiple roles assigned to it by universal and particular law;

9) the obligation to make certain that the agenda and minutes of parish finance council meetings are published to the parishioners in a timely fashion, using effective means of dissemination;

10) the obligation to approach the diocesan bishop (or another competent diocesan official) whenever suspicious financial activity surfaces (establishing delicts of financial malfeasance are cc. 1376; 1377 §1; 1377 §2; 1380; 1383; 1393 §2);

11) the obligation to ensure that all aspects of the management of parish property conform completely to the obligations of civil law and canon law (see c. 1284 §2, 2°), including particular law and special instructions (see c. 1276 §2) in particular, to ensure that the canon laws concerning property management are equally operative in binding parallel civil documents (especially regarding "acts of the extraordinary" identified in canon law that are identical in "powers reserved to competent ecclesiastical authority" established in civil law);

12) the obligation to inform the *parochus* (and perhaps another competent authority) of their resignation as a councilor, lest harm come to the parish by arbitrarily withdrawing from their *munus* (see c. 1289).[61]

In some of these examples, particular law may require the parish finance council provide counsel before the *parochus* is able to perform certain acts validly (see c. 127 §1). This is in keeping with its consultative nature.[62]

PART TWO:

CIVIL LAW CONSIDERATIONS ABOUT PARISH FINANCE COUNCILS

Mr. Gary M. Ruesch, J.D.

Introduction

To understand the civil structure of the parish finance council, one must address the overall leadership components of the parish. These have been addressed previously, but we have to remember them as they fit in the civil law structure. These civil officers may include the diocesan bishop, parishioners, the parish clergy—which would include permanent deacons, priests, and the pastor—and lay employees.

It is also important to remember that lay employees go beyond what we would normally think of as immediately involved in the administration of the parish, such as a parish secretary, a finance administrator, finance manager, an adult education person, etc. Lay employees also include school principals,

---

61 Velasio De Paolis suggests notes that canon 1282 refers to "all clerics and lay persons who take part in the administration of ecclesiastical goods by a legitimate title." His reflections prompt the consideration that perhaps canon 1282 also refers to members of the parish finance council. De Paolis urges that proper law regulate all this better and more precisely. "Il consiglio per gli affairi economici ed i beni patrimoniali della parrocchia," 286.

62 Ghirlanda, *Chiesa universale e Chiesa particolare*, 988.

custodians, teachers, and development directors. A lot of people involved are lay employees who work in the parish that are not always considered when we analyze the structure that is set up.

Other individuals that are important to consider in the administration of a parish are the local community, neighbors, and other people that are involved in the parish that aren't necessarily those that we might consider formally as a leadership component, but ought to be included in the analysis.

Parish structures typically include, among others, these several components:

- parish pastoral council;
- parish finance council;
- parish corporation board or other legal structure governing the affairs of the legal entity;
- school board or advisory committee; and
- athletic association.

These components are all relevant to finance. Some of the most exasperating issues related to parish finance can relate to clubs or athletic associations that have their own checking accounts, savings accounts, fundraising, etc. These are often where we run into civil law issues relating to management and safety of funds. Most parish administrators would agree that schools can often be the largest organization as far as parish expenditures go.

Corporation Sole

Structural basics of parishes within a diocese include two types of state laws that affect how parishes are organized from a civil law standpoint. The centralized or corporation sole model is the model that has traditionally been most universally applied. This type of corporate model arose, in part, from some historical attempts to divide the church and its clergy from the corporate entity of a parish.

The corporation sole model is designed with the diocesan bishop at the top as the legal center; parishes do not exist as a separate legal entity under this model but are created as part of diocesan policies and canon law. This model treats all diocesan entities as one civil legal structure that is administered at the diocesan level. However, much of that authority is, was, and can be delegated into other mechanisms within the parish through canon and civil law.

As more and more bankruptcies are administered in the United States, a singular issue that emerges is the question of who is liable for the conduct of whom. In answering this question, the civil structure can play a crucial role.

Decentralized Structure

The alternative to corporation sole is a decentralized model wherein parishes are their own civil corporations. They are separate but connected to the diocese by canon law and by the civil statutes that create them. These civil statutes are dependent on state law and may allow for differences on a parish-by-parish basis. In a decentralized system, parish property is usually owned by the parish corporation, but not always. There are checks and balances built into the structure. The details of the civil corporation are established in state law, but diocesan policy develops the specifics of who does what and how everything is administrated.

The Board of Directors

In parishes that are part of a decentralized structure, there is a civil board of directors that govern financial matters and more. This board can cover things such as human resource issues, liability issues, the filing of lawsuits, etc. This board of directors is what we refer to when discussing the civil management of the parish and is separate from the canonically required finance council. The term "board of directors" can be ambiguous, but it accurately summarizes this civil corporate board. When discussing the board of directors and the members of the board of directors, as it relates to the finance council, we are talking about a body that has broader areas of responsibility.

This board of directors will have different members based on the state civil statutes but they are often similar. Both Connecticut[63] and Wisconsin[64], for example, mandate that the board should include the diocesan bishop, the vicar general or other appointee of the bishop, the pastor of the parish, and two lay appointees:

> The bishop and vicar-general shall be and remain members of the corporation as long as they shall be and remain respectively bishop and vicar-general of the diocese; and the pastor shall be and remain a member of the corporation so long as the pastor shall be pastor of the congregation; . . . The bishop and vicar-general or either of them may be represented at any meeting of the congregation or at any meeting of the directors by proxy with like effect as if personally present. The 2 laypersons shall be and remain members of the corporation for the term of 2 years. . . .[65]

63 CT Gen. Stat. Section 33-279.
64 WI State Stat. Section 187.19(3).
65 See WI State Stat. Section 187.19(3); see also CT Gen. Stat. Section 33-279.

It is important to note the balance between the clerical and lay members of the board, in most cases the automatically appointed clerical members of the board will make up three-fifths of it.

The term trustee or trustee treasure or trustee secretary typically reference the lay people on the board of directors that is established by state law. A trustee manual is prepared by many dioceses to introduce these lay members of the parish to the civil governance of the parish. A good example of a well-constructed manual is available from the Archdiocese of Milwaukee,[66] and a good example of a corporate overview is available from the Diocese of Madison.[67] These trustee manuals typically give an overview of parish structural basics, the board of directors, parish schools, parish cemeteries, trustee endowment funds, legal disputes and lawsuits, and the incorporation of canon law requirements.

State statutes also lay out the roles that each member of the board undertakes. In the relevant Wisconsin statute, the president of the board is the diocesan bishop, the vice president is the pastor, the treasurer is one of the lay trustees, and the secretary is the other lay trustee:

> The bishop, a successor or administrator or other person appointed according to the rules of the Roman Catholic Church, or administrator for the time being, shall be president; the pastor shall be vice president, and the treasurer and secretary shall be selected or chosen from among the laypersons as provided by the bylaws.[68]

However, it should be noted that the board of directors often meets without the presence of the diocesan bishop, and his second appointee that is listed in the statutory provision. In mandating the exact role of the members of the board, civil law is trying—to the best extent it can—give guidance on how canon law is best implemented within the civil structure. The legislatures will attempt to implement that which the church recommends:

> The directors, by unanimous vote, may adopt such bylaws, not contrary to the constitution and laws of this state, the statutes of the diocese and the discipline of the Roman Catholic Church, as may be deemed necessary for the proper government of such corporation and the management and business thereof or the temporal affairs of such

---

66 "Parish Trustee Manual," August 15, 2014, https://www.archmil.org/ArchMil/Resources/ParCnl1/Manuals-for-Parishes/ParishTrusteeManual_v2.pdf (accessed on 19 Dec. 2023).

67 "Parish Corporations - Diocese of Madison - Madison, WI," Catholic Diocese of Madison, https://madisondiocese.org/parish-corporations (accessed on 19 Dec. 2023).

68 WI State Stat. Section 187.79(4).

> congregation which may become connected therewith or attached thereto.[69]
>
> Subject to laws of church, such corporation shall at all times be subject to the general laws and discipline of the Roman Catholic Church, and shall receive and enjoy its franchises as a body politic, solely for the purposes mentioned in section 33-280; and, upon the violation or surrender of its charter, its property, real and personal, shall vest in the archbishop or bishop of the archdiocese or diocese and his successors, in trust for such congregation and for the uses and purposes above named.[70]

And this is not limited to the Roman Catholic Church. There are often equivalent state statutes for Episcopal churches, Presbyterian churches, etc.[71] Each will have a statutory provision that relates to its organization, and they are different. The reason for this is an interpretation of the free exercise clause and the freedom of religion component of the First Amendment. Churches have to be free to operate consistent with their tenants and organizational requirements within the civil structure and that is what's trying to be achieved here.

Duties and Responsibilities

Beyond laying out the requirements for the civil board, state statutes typically lay out certain duties and responsibilities for the board of directors:

> Such corporation shall assume an appropriate name in its articles of incorporation and may purchase, accept, own and hold property, real and personal, and sell, convey and otherwise dispose of the same and contract debts, all of which shall be done subject to the bylaws and the restrictions hereinafter provided. Such corporation may sue and be sued, have a common seal, which may be changed at pleasure, and do all things necessary for the proper transaction of its business and duties and all things needful in the management of the temporal affairs of the Roman Catholic church of such congregation, and for the benefit thereof and of such members as may become attached and belong to said church in conformity with such rules and regulations as may be established by its bylaws; and also to purchase, own, hold, regulate, control, manage or dispose of any eleemosynary, educational, cemetery, religious or other property which it may acquire in

---

69 WI State Stat. Section 187.79(6).

70 CT Gen. Stat. Section 33-281; see also WI State Stat. Section 187(6).

71 See, e.g., WI State Stat. Section 187.04.

connection with said church and the congregation thereof or be assigned to it by the bishop or other person or persons.[72]

These civil requirements may align with canonical requirements or may be separate. In addition, not all state statutes require non-profits or religious organizations to have annual corporate meetings, but dioceses often do. The term may not be corporate meeting, but it may be called an annual parish meeting or something similar.

As discussed previously, state statutes often have a clause that notes that the board of directors of a parish are subject to the general laws and discipline of the Church.[73] And there is an emphasis on the purpose and the requirements. The duties and purposes of the board of directors mirror what is necessary to run a parish. These duties and responsibilities go beyond the finance council.

The civil authority of the parish board of directors includes, interestingly, that such corporation may receive and hold all property conveyed to it for the purposes of maintaining religious worship according to doctrine, discipline, and ritual of the Roman Catholic Church, etc.: "Such corporation may receive and hold all property conveyed to it for the purpose of maintaining religious worship according to the doctrine, discipline and ritual of the Roman Catholic Church, and for the support of the educational or charitable institutions of that church."[74]

Corporation Sole vs. Decentralized Structure.

After analyzing both methods of parish structures, it is apparent that the basic system can be accomplished with either organization. The distinction comes in from where the actual legal authority flows from in each. In the sole model, the legal authority is seen in:

- a singular corporate structure
- parishes operate as unincorporated associations
- the diocese develops policies, rules, guidelines, etc., to manage parish operations
- parishes may have their own bank accounts, pay operational and maintenance expenses, etc.

72 WI State Stat. Section 187.19(2).

73 Cf. CT Gen. Stat. Section 33-281; see also WI State Stat. Section 187(6).

74 CT Gen. Stat. Section 33-280.

- other corporations may be established by the diocese to support certain assets, properties, and missions.[75]

The corporation sole model stands in opposition to the decentralized structure, wherein the individual corporations are governed by the policies of the diocese and the requirements of canon law.

Under both models the civil structure is likely, and by definition separate from the structure anticipated by canon law.

However, this can lead to a board of directors making decisions outside of the policies of the diocese, not properly consulting with bodies such as the finance council. This can be avoided by integrating members of the corporate board and finance council by having civil board members:

- assist the finance council in understanding and developing parish financial undertakings, budget, and holdings;
- attend meetings of the finance council;
- review and aides in the disbursement of parish funds, as needed;
- assist in the preparation of reports and documents for the diocese and parish; and
- ensure appropriate communication of financial and budget issues through the organization and operation of the corporate (parish) annual meeting.[76]

The Church as an Employer

One of the biggest struggles in the Church as an employer is how to address issues relating to Catholic moral teaching within civil laws, such as non-discrimination statutes. For example, when can a Catholic school terminate a teacher for having children outside of a valid marriage? These types of questions are not unique to Catholic churches. There are also other denominations in which employees are ministers of the church and engage in conduct inconsistent with the teachings and requirements of that church. The law takes into account the free

---

75 See, e.g., The Roman Catholic Archbishop of San Francisco, United States Bankruptcy Court, Northen District of California, Case No. 23-30564 (2023); see also Douglas Champagne and Steven Gallant, et al, v. The Roman Catholic Episcopal Corporation of Halifax, The Roman Catholic Episcopal Corporation of Yarmouth, The Archbishop of Halifax, Supreme Court of Nova Scotia (Sep 19, 2019, Halifax, N.S).
76 See, e.g., "Parish Corporations - Diocese of Madison."

exercise clause as it relates to these other statutes. These laws are being applied to lay people, not only clerics.[77]

Corporate bylaws are established within the confines and the requirements set up by the diocese and developed on a parish-by-parish basis consistent with state and federal law, and canon law. For example, the Wisconsin state statute says that the bylaws cannot be contrary to the constitution laws of the state, the statutes of the diocese and the discipline of the Roman Catholic Church as it may be deemed necessary for the proper government of such corporations.[78] This is a common inclusion in state statutes and is important for the Church and its existence in the civil sphere.

PART THREE:

BEST PRACTICE FOR EFFECTIVE SYNODALITY WITHIN THE CIVIL CORPORATE STRUCTURE

Given the statutory structural impediments to having a unified civil law and canon law structure, practices, traditions and training must be applied to encourage the appropriate symmetry between the two. These should include:

- the parish corporate board should attend training and understand the requirements of state law as it relates to corporate governance;
- the parish corporate board should attend training and understand their role, with the pastor, finance council, and parish council in the financial management of the parish;
- the parish corporate board should understand and effectively administer matters affected by civil law, including leasing of property, investment management, execution of certain contracts, use of funds, etc.;
- the board treasurer should understand and be trained in their role in financial management, including, fund disbursements, budget development, financial reports, parish finance council responsibilities, and parish council responsibilities, etc.;
- the board secretary should understand and be trained in their role as to corporate meetings, minutes, annual parish and diocesan reports, record keeping, parish finance council and parish council responsibilities, etc.;

---

77 See, for example, Our Lady of Guadalupe School v. Morrissey-Berru, 140 S. Ct. 2049 (2020).

78 Cf. WI State Stat. Section 187.79(6).

- the board should understand and be trained as to the limits and role of their position in relation to the diocesan bishop, pastor, parish council, parish finance council, etc., according to canon law;
- the board should cooperate as a part of the parish administration, while understanding the need for effective communication, partnership, and trust in effectively accomplishing the mission of the Church and local parish;[79]
- Other

In addition, on the diocesan level, consideration should be given to establishing a process by which the diocese could monitor, evaluate, and assist parishes in harmonizing the requirements of parish governance so as to best implement the synodality of the Catholic Church within the bounds of civil law.

Conclusion

Parishes are *the most numerous public juridic persons* that exist in the entire Church. Each parish is mandated to have a parish finance council, that is, an "organ of synodality" that sustains the presence of the parish in the neighborhood in its life-giving mission of evangelization, near and far. Parish finance councils are *the most numerous organs of synodality* that exist in the entire Church. This seminar has intended to offer insights to enhance the effectiveness of the mission of parish pastoral councils by promoting accountability, transparency, and collaboration—in the Church that, by the divine design, is a synodal gathering of richly gifted missionary disciples who accompany each other in a common journey to a more abundant life in Jesus, here and forever.

79 See, e.g., a parish trustee manual.

CLSA PROCEEDINGS 85 (2023) 286-304

"VALIDATION" OR RADICAL SANATION OF MARRIAGE: WHY CHOOSE ONE OVER THE OTHER?

Dr. Lynda Robitaille, JCD

Consent makes marriage, as highlighted by Canon 1057: "§1. The *consent* of the parties, *legitimately manifested* between persons *qualified by law*, makes marriage; no human power is able to supply this consent."[1] In today's presentation we will focus on consent given in a civil ceremony, and then consider what happens later in a Catholic context: consent can be given again, or that first consent can be recognized by the Church. Why proceed one way or the other?

Quoting the *Relatio Finalis* of the 2015 Synod, Francis sets the context for today's presentation:

> When a couple in an irregular union attains a noteworthy stability through a public bond—and is characterized by deep affection, responsibility towards the children and the ability to overcome trials—this can be seen as an opportunity, where possible, to lead them to celebrate the sacrament of Matrimony.[2]

How can the Church accompany Catholics who choose or have chosen to marry outside canonical form? In this presentation we will explore marriage ("validation") and radical sanation as pastoral means to walk with the faithful who choose to celebrate marriage in the Church. We will also consider pastoral means of avoiding this "catch up" situation entirely by ensuring that the wedding the parties choose to enter at the beginning is one that can be recognized in the Church, whether celebrated within the canonical form of marriage or with a

1 *Codex Iuris Canonici auctoritate Ioannis Pauli PP. II promulgatus* (Vatican City: Libreria Editrice Vaticana, 1983) c. 1057 §1; Eng. trans. in *Code of Canon Law. Latin-English Edition: New English Translation* (Washington, DC: CLSA, 2012). All subsequent translations from this code will be taken from this source unless otherwise indicated.

2 Francis, apostolic exhortation *Amoris laetitia* 78, March 19, 2016: *AAS* 108 (2016) (hereafter *AL*) 343, citing the *Relatio Finalis* 2015, nos. 53-54; Eng. trans. on pages 61-62 at https://www.vatican.va/content/dam/francesco/pdf/apost_exhortations/documents/papa-francesco_esortazione-ap_20160319_amoris-laetitia_en.pdf (accessed on 8 Nov. 2023). All subsequent translations from this apostolic exhortation will be taken from this source.

dispensation from form. Finally, we will reflect on the requirement of canonical form and what it means for our pastoral practice.

In 2019 Sean Bransfield spoke at the Canon Law Society of America convention on the subject of Catholics choosing to marry in a non-religious venue. He began by asking rhetorical questions:

> To what extent are Catholics still getting married today in the Church? Is the observance of canonical form still considered as important today by the average Catholic as it was in the past? If these numbers are changing, what can local churches do to help address these changing practices? Is it best to double down on catechizing the faithful as to why more traditional marriage policies are the best way of proceeding, or is it better to accommodate and modify more traditional policies so as to perhaps more effectively meet the people where they are. There are no simple answers to these questions . . . .[3]

Bransfield cited different statistics outlining the decline in the number of Catholics in the U.S. practicing their faith, having their children baptized, and marrying in the Church.[4] As the literature makes clear, at least in North America, fewer and fewer Catholics are choosing Church weddings. In *Amoris laetitia* Francis cites the *Relatio Finalis* of the 2015 Synod when reflecting on a couple's decision to marry outside the Church, noting: "The choice of a civil marriage or, in many cases, of simple cohabitation, is often not motivated by prejudice or resistance to a sacramental union, but by cultural or contingent situations."[5] It seems more precise to say that they do not know why the Church would care where they marry. Francis recalls the essential point when considering people's choice to marry in a non-Catholic ceremony:

> In the Church's Latin tradition, the ministers of the sacrament of marriage are the man and the woman who marry; by manifesting their consent and expressing it physically, they receive a great gift. Their consent and their bodily union are the divinely appointed means whereby they become "one flesh." . . . The Church can require that the wedding be celebrated publicly, with the presence of witnesses and other conditions that have varied over the course of time, but this does not detract from the fact that the couple who marry are the ministers of the sacrament. Nor does it affect the centrality of the consent given by

3 Sean Bransfield, "Canonical Norms Regarding Place of Marriage: Both a Challenge and an Opportunity," in *CLSA Proceedings* 81 (2019) 85.

4 Ibid., 85-87.

5 *AL* 292.

the man and the woman, which of itself establishes the sacramental bond.[6]

Thus, we the pastoral ministers of the Church are faced with Catholic couples who come to the Church either wanting to marry in a non-Catholic venue, or having married in a non-Catholic venue, they now want the Church to recognize their unions. What are the solutions that the Church offers? There are two solutions that take place after consent: marriage in the Church and radical sanation; and two solutions that can take place before consent: permission to marry in a non-Catholic setting and dispensation from canonical form.

Marriage in the Church / "Validation"

Boccafola clarifies terminology:

> Whenever consent is required to be and is actually manifested by the use of canonical form, as in the ceremony that rectified a merely *civil union,* it is inappropriate to describe or characterize such an act as simply the validation of a prior consent because it is also the manifestation of at least outward actual consent present and exchanged in the liturgical ceremony.[7]

We must distinguish a *new marriage* from *simple validation.* Simple validation is not used in the case of a Catholic bound to canonical form who "married" in a non-Catholic ceremony and who now wishes the Church to recognize that marriage. The Signatura has been very clear about this, both in its decree of November 23, 2005,[8] and then in a private response sent to a number of dioceses on December 17, 2007, in regard to canon 1160 on simple validations. Catholics who marry in a non-Catholic ceremony have merely "attempted marriage." In such a situation, should this couple wish to have the Church recognize their union, they must go through "a celebration in the canonical form."[9] In other words, they must undertake the obligations of marriage as though for the first time.

---

6 *AL* 75, citing Pius XII, encyclical *Mystici Corporis Christi,* June 29, 1943: *AAS* 35 (1943) 202.

7 Kenneth Boccafola, "Invalid Convalidation: A Legitimate Autonomous Ground of Marriage Nullity?" *The Jurist* 74 (2014) 197.

8 See Supremum Signaturae Apostolicae Tribunal, Decretum, 23 November 2005, *Periodica* 96 (2007) 285-288.

9 Supreme Tribunal of the Apostolic Signatura, letter of December 19, 2007, in Joseph Koury and Siobhan Verbeek, eds., *Roman Replies and CLSA Advisory Opinions* (Washington, DC: CLSA, 2008) 55, #2.

Reflecting on the December 2007 letter of the Apostolic Signatura on convalidation, John Foster summarizes the important conclusion: "Catholics married outside canonical form who approach the Church to regularize their union do not convalidate their marriage (in the sense of canon 1160) but contract marriage."[10] The focus of the Signatura's clarification was to highlight the misuse of the term *convalidation* in pastoral and canonical practice. Thus, applying canons 1157 and 1160, which speak of a renewal of consent in cases of convalidation in the case of an impediment or a defect of form, is inappropriate. Rather, the parties who were bound by canonical form and did not follow it need to marry in the Church for the first time.

While in many ways this is clear, difficulties in interpretation arise when it comes to understanding what comes into being when a Catholic gives consent in a non-Catholic ceremony. As Foster notes: "canonical tradition has held that a simple convalidation is the act of making an invalid marriage valid. The problem comes, however, when one concludes that if a marriage is not valid, then it is invalid."[11] Invalid unions are either null or inexistent, and there is no clear consensus on this.[12] Emmanuel Petit echoes this: "[T]he question of the canonical status of civil marriages of those who were bound to canonical form is far from being resolved. This question arises most often in debate about the matter of convalidation."[13] Petit explains: "The present jurisprudence of the Rota prefers to speak of inexistent marriage when speaking of the civil marriage of those who are bound to canonical form, thereby underlining that this can neither benefit from the status of a putative marriage, nor can it be convalidated."[14]

---

10 John Foster, "Sacramental Law: Selected Developments in Twenty-Five Years of Praxis," *The Jurist* 69 (2009) 488.

11 Ibid., 479.

12 For summaries of the different viewpoints, see: Emmanuel Petit, *Consentement matrimonial et fiction du droit*, in series Tesi Gregoriana (Rome: Editrice Pontificia Università Gregoriana, 2010); W. J. Swengros, *Simple Convalidation According to the 1983 Code of Canon Law*, Dissertatio ad lauream (Rome: Pontifical University of St. Thomas, 2001); Foster, "Sacramental Law," 480-490; D. Witham, *Inexistent Juridic Acts*, JCL thesis, CUA, unpublished (2023) 56-64.

13 Petit, *Consentement matrimonial et fiction du droit*, 293-294. Over pages 294-298, Petit summarizes arguments regarding whether a civil marriage of Catholics could be convalidated through a simple convalidation. This debate was ended by the Signatura in a letter of December 17, 2007, on defective convalidation (see below).

14 Petit, *Consentement matrimonial et fiction du droit.*, 292. In footnote 162, he cites a decision *c.* Boccafola of March 12, 1998, #10.

Null vs. Inexistent (Non-existent)

The July 19, 2007, decision, *coram* Yaacoub, makes the following distinction between null and inexistent (non-existent) marriages:

> If a Catholic party attempts marriage before a civil authority or a minister of another religion (i.e., without dispensation from the canonical form), such a celebration obviously lacks all elements of the canonical form and it is rightly described as an 'inexistent marriage,' because it does not have any semblance or figure of marriage.
>
> In the case of a civil marriage of those baptized in the Catholic Church or received into it . . . the marriage is certainly null and it is clear that the nullity depends on the defect of due form; but many experts in canon law prefer rather to speak of an inexistent marriage in the case.[15]

In 2009 Augustine Mendonça explained the distinction between null and inexistent:

> [T]he controversy over the juridic status of a marriage contracted by Catholics before a civil official or a non-Catholic minister is still raging both in doctrine and jurisprudence. Some authors maintain that a marriage celebrated before a civil official or a non-Catholic minister by Catholics is non-existent, and therefore, it cannot be convalidated through the application of simple convalidation. The only way those who wish to have such a union regularized before the Church is by marrying fresh in the canonical form. Others argue that even in such a marriage there exists an ontological reality and a juridically inefficacious consent on the part of both parties. Therefore, it can be convalidated following the norms provided in the Code for simple convalidation. Because such a marriage can be radically sanated, these authors do not see why it cannot be convalidated using the institute of simple convalidation.[16]

John Foster cites Bill Swengros's explanation of the distinction between a null and a non-existent (inexistent) union and how a Catholic marrying outside the Church fits into this framework:

> [A]ccording to natural law, consent is the sole efficient cause of marriage. While positive law has determined that the absence of diriment impediments and the observance of canonical form are essential for the efficacy of the consent,

---

15 Tribunal of the Roman Rota, decree *c.* Yaacoub, July 19, 2007, Prot. No. 19.685, in *RRAO* (2008) 28, #8.

16 Augustine Mendonça, "Defective Consent in the Convalidation of a Marriage Null due to Lack of Canonical Form," in *Studies in Church Law* 5 (2009) 360.

> they do not constitute marriage. For this reason, a marriage which lacks canonical form is simply invalid, not non-existent.

Thus, when a Catholic marries outside canonical form, the consent exchanged by the parties, while juridically inefficacious, gives rise to a *matrimonium nullum* and not a *matrimonium inexistens*.[17]

Pastoral Implications of Requiring a Wedding in the Church

The civilly married Catholic couple who approach the Church to have their situation regularized need to understand that the Church considers their previous attempted marriage as nothing more than marriage preparation. With the wedding in the Church, this couple is starting a brand new marital relationship. These are the words that do not describe this ceremony: *convalidation, validation, blessing, regularization*. Rather, this is a wedding, a marriage. Does this reflect these people's reality? Is this what the parties request of the Church?

In requiring a new wedding, is the Church reacting pastorally to their reality? Or is the Church asking them to jump through hoops that they struggle to understand? Is the non-Catholic marriage truly non-existent in the lives of these couples?

Is That First Attempted Non-Catholic Marriage Non-Existent in the Lives of the People?

In reality, these unions do not appear inexistent. Couples have been together, sometimes for years, had children, created a home, a life together, etc. When they are required to consent as though they are creating a new bond, how does that reflect their reality? They are being asked to promise—as though for the first time—to be faithful, open to children, lifelong, and a partnership. They are not being asked to consent to build on or continue what they already have; they are being asked to create a new union, as though what was there before was nothing—inexistent. If they marry in the Church as though for the first time, their consent brings a marriage into being at that time. Everything that happened before the Church wedding—the living together, the home, the children—happened when the parties were not married. Does this describe their reality?

In fact, the Church is recognizing in reality that these unions are something. John Paul II and Francis have both highlighted the positive realities of stable civil unions. As John Paul II noted: "There are increasing cases of Catholics who for

17 Foster, "Sacramental Law," 482, where in footnote 33 he cites William Swengros, *Simple Convalidation According to the 1983 Code of Canon Law*, Dissertatio ad lauream (Rome: Pontifical University of St. Thomas, 2001) 87.

ideological or practical reasons, prefer to contract a merely civil marriage, and who reject or at least defer religious marriage. . . . [T]here is at least a certain commitment to a properly-defined and probably stable state of life . . . ."[18] After reviewing this, Swengros stated that John Paul II:

> clearly refutes the idea that a civil marriage involving a Catholic bound to canonical form without a dispensation is merely concubinage or a "non-existent" marriage. Matrimonial consent was manifested even though it was not efficacious. While the consent may or may not have been defective, there was an intent to contract marriage and exchange the corresponding rights and duties.[19]

In *Amoris laetitia* Francis spoke similarly where he reflected on the discussions at the Synod:

> The Fathers also considered the specific situation of a merely civil marriage or, with due distinction, even simple cohabitation, noting that "when such unions attain a particular stability, legally recognized, are characterized by deep affection and responsibility for their offspring, and demonstrate an ability to overcome trials they can provide occasions for pastoral care with a view to the eventual celebration of the sacrament of marriage."[20]

In both these papal statements we see a recognition of the fact that the parties have attempted a union together; they have made promises, embraced rights and duties, lived together. It may not be perfect, but is it really inexistent? Perhaps it is better understood as invalid, null.

Would It Make a Difference If the Civil Marriage Were Considered Null, Not Inexistent?

This is a question that cannot be easily addressed in the present law. In the present law, canons 1156-1159 speak of marriages that are null by reason of a diriment impediment or a defect of consent. Canon 1160 requires a new celebration in the canonical form in order for the marriage to "become valid" (*ut validum fiat*). Authors speak of the renewal of consent as required by canon 1157

---

18 John Paul II, apostolic exhortation *Familiaris consortio* 82, November 22, 1981: *AAS* 74 (1981) 183; Eng. trans. at https://www.vatican.va/content/john-paul-ii/en/apost_exhortations/documents/hf_jp-ii_exh_19811122_familiaris-consortio.html (accessed on 9 Nov. 2023).

19 Swengros, *Simple Convalidation,* 195, as cited in Foster, "Sacramental Law," 484, note 40, where Foster also states: "Lynda Robitaille agrees with this assessment ('Defective Validations of Marriages Lacking Canonical Form: An Interpretation of Total Simulation,' *The Jurist* 66 [2006] 448)."

20 *AL* 293, citing the *Relatio finalis* 2015, #71.

as a requirement of the positive law.[21] Whether it is or not is not our question today. Rather, the point is: because of the requirement of the new consent, the marriage will come into being only at the time of this consent. In other words, even if the civil marriage were considered null, at this point in the law of the Church, the couple would be required to begin their marriage at the time of that second consent. The possibility that the civil union of Catholics is, in fact, a null marriage (not inexistent) makes a difference when it comes to understanding the radical sanation of such a union.

Radical Sanation

In 2010 John Renken recalled that: "simple convalidation is the *ordinary* means to convalidate an *invalid* marriage, radical sanation is the *extraordinary* means."[22] Renken distinguished two important points: "The radical sanation . . . entails *ipso facto* a dispensation from the factor(s) invalidating the marriage—i.e., . . . the defect (or lack) of required canonical form. . . . Unlike simple convalidation, it does not require that the partners elicit a new act of consent."[23] At the time of the sanation, the consent originally given is recognized and a dispensation from canonical form takes place by the law itself. In other words, there is an acceptance of the power of that consent, a consent that was prevented from bringing about the marriage by the positive law requirement of the form of marriage.

Renken makes some distinctions:

> Traditionally authors have distinguished two basic categories: *total/perfect* or *partial/imperfect* sanations, and *properly so-called* and *improperly so-called* sanations.
>
> A *total/perfect* radical sanation includes: (1) the convalidation of the invalid marriage; (2) the dispensation from the invalidating factors; (3) no required renewal of consent; and (4) retroactivity of canonical effects. A *partial/imperfect* sanation lacks at least one of these elements. . . . A radical sanation *properly so-called* involves the convalidation of the invalid marriage. A radical sanation *improperly*

21 See Foster, "Sacramental Law," 477, citing Urbano Navarrete, "A Proposito del Decreto del S.T. della Segnatura Apostolica del 23 novembre 2005," *Periodica* 96 (2007) 333: ". . . la legge ecclesiastica sull'obbligo di rinnovare il consenso per la validità della convalidazione semplice, si limita soltanto al caso di nullità 'ob impedimentum dirimens.'"
22 John Renken, "Extraordinary Convalidation: the Radical Sanation of an Invalid Marriage," in *Periodica* 99 (2010) 462.
23 Ibid., 501.

> *so-called* does not convalidate the marriage but bestows the retroactivity of canonical effects.[24]

Renken raises distinctions here that affect the pastoral concerns highlighted above. If civilly married Catholics request a radical sanation, would it be a total/perfect radical sanation (properly so-called) because that civil union is an invalid (null) union? Or would it be an imperfect radical sanation (improperly so-called) of a civil marriage of Catholics, which would result only in the retroactivity of the canonical effects? In other words, would the marriage come into being at the time the sanation is granted? Or would the sanation grant the retroactive dispensation from form which then permits the consent to retroactively take effect at the moment it was given?

This is an area where there are differing opinions. Emmanuel Petit addressed this question in his doctoral dissertation in 2010, asking whether the retroactivity touched only the effects of marriage, or did it also make the validity of the marriage retroactive.[25] For Renken, the marriage would only come into being at the moment of the sanation, with no retroactive validity:

> Both simple convalidation and radical sanation result in the validity of a hitherto invalid marriage (*ex nunc*). Radical sanation *does not* retroactively validate an invalid marriage …; it *does*, however, unlike simple convalidation, bestow the retroactivity of the canonical effect of the legitimation of any children born to the invalid marriage.[26]

John Beal understands it differently, explaining that radical sanation "is an intervention of church authority that gives naturally sufficient and still perduring consent retroactive validity. … the effect of radical sanation is to render a marriage valid from the moment the original, naturally sufficient consent was exchanged."[27] He explains further:

> A radical sanation is a fiction of law by which competent ecclesiastical authority renders retroactively valid a marriage which was invalid from its origin without the renewal of consent by either party. An essential

---

24 Ibid., 462-463, fn 6, where he is summarizing information from: Th.Ch. Ryan, *The Juridical Effects of the Sanatio in Radice: A Historical Synopsis and a Commentary*, Canon Law Studies 135 (Washington, The Catholic University of America Press, 1955) 4; A Bernárdez Cantón, "Commentary on Canons 1161-1165," in *Exegetical Commentary on the Code of Canon Law*, ed. Ernest Caparros, et al. (Montreal: Wilson & Lafleur/Chicago: Midwest Theological Forum, 2004) 3/2:1615.

25 Petit, *Consentement matrimonial et fiction du droit,* 199ff.

26 Renken, "Extraordinary Convalidation," 501.

27 John Beal, "The Convalidation of Marriage," in *New Commentary on the Code of Canon Law*, ed. John Beal et al. (New York: Paulist Press, 2000) 1379.

> precondition for a radical sanation is that both parties gave naturally sufficient but juridically inefficacious consent to marriage in the past and that this consent continues into the present. … The effect of a radical sanation is to render a marriage valid not only from the moment the sanation is granted but from the moment naturally sufficient consent was initially given.[28]

Petit cites authors like Wernz and Vidal, Cappello, and Navarrete who hold the view that not only does radical sanation render the children legitimate, it also renders the spouses retroactively legitimate.[29]

When Is the Marriage Validated—At the Moment of Consent or the Moment of Sanation?

Why would authors understand that sanation only renders the marriage valid from the moment of the sanation? Renken explains:

> Logic reveals that the legitimacy of offspring is the sole canonical effect achieved by radical sanation. Inasmuch as radical sanation establishes the validity of a marriage at the moment the favor is granted (*ex nunc*), and inasmuch as the other canonical effects identified in the code concern only the marriage itself and the consequent rights/obligations of the spouses, these other canonical effects logically cannot be retroactively established since no marriage exists to which they would pertain. The historical fact of the past invalidity of the bond itself cannot be undone. Therefore, the sole retroactive canonical effect achieved by a radical sanation is the legitimacy of offspring.[30]

Örsy seems to agree with this interpretation: "Although this type of validation is called *sanatio in radice*, the 'healing of the marriage in its root,' strictly speaking no retroactive healing takes place because the fact of past invalidity cannot be changed ever, not even by God. The healing regards the future; the past receives a new standing in law."[31] This interpretation seems to arise from an understanding of the consent of Catholics to a civil marriage as

---

28 Beal, "The Convalidation of Marriage," 1388. Here Beal is highlighting "naturally sufficient" consent which comes from canon 1139 §1 of the 1917 code. Consent can only create the marriage bond if it is naturally sufficient. Even if the words of canon 1139 are not explicit in the 1983 code, the requirement that the consent must be naturally sufficient continues. For more on this see Urbano Navarrete, "'Consensus naturaliter sufficiens, sed iuridice inefficax' Limiti alla sovranità del consenso matrimoniale," *Periodica* 88 (1999) 361-389.

29 Petit, *Consentement matrimonial et fiction du droit.*, 221, notes 200, 201, 202.

30 Renken, "Extraordinary Convalidation," 497.

31 Ladislas Örsy, *Marriage in Canon Law* (Wilmington: Michael Glazier, 1986) 252, as cited by Renken, "Extraordinary Convalidation," 495.

inexistent. If the marriage were inexistent, Renken's interpretation would be logical: there is no bond to validate. However, if the consent is recognized as being naturally sufficient and only prevented from bringing about a marriage bond by reason of the positive law of canonical form, and if the union were considered null (not inexistent), then Beal's understanding makes sense.

Or perhaps there is a middle ground. Emmanuel Petit explains why radical sanation is possible in cases of Catholics in a civil union when simple validation is not possible:

> The *convalidatio in radice* recognizes the value of the consent exchanged. In other words, it accepts that consent exchanged civilly by those bound to canonical form can have the value of a true consent from a natural point of view. It is thus possible to convalidate the consent and to make it produce a true marriage. On the contrary, simple convalidation is based on the form of marriage. The form or appearance of marriage must exist, which is what canon law has constantly denied to the civil marriage of those bound to canonical form. Thus, one can say that the civil marriage of Catholics is non-existent canonically and thus impossible to convalidate in a simple way, but the consent which exists can be convalidated *in radice*.[32]

Pastoral Implications of Validity of Sanation Reverting to the Original Exchange of Consent

A radical sanation granted to Catholic couples who married outside the Church respects their original consent; it respects the lives they have built together and does not require them to start a new "marriage." This is especially true if we understand the radical sanation as sanating the validity of the marriage retroactively to the moment of consent. Both Popes John Paul II and Francis have recognized that there are those whose previous unions demonstrate stability and an undertaking of the responsibilities of marriage. Let the Church recognize that. To my mind, radical sanation that recognizes the efficacy of that original consent is preferable to requiring a new consent in the Church that ignores what has come before.

How Can the Church Avoid These Situations?

Encourage Catholics to marry according to the rules of the Church

What can ministers in the Church do to encourage Catholics to marry in a Catholic ceremony? Of course, they can encourage Catholics to marry in a religious ceremony in a Catholic church. However, there are many people who

32 Petit, *Consentement matrimonial et fiction du droit,* 297.

choose to marry in a non-religious setting, or even in a non-religious ceremony. Do ministers in the Church encourage people to apply for a dispensation from form or a permission to celebrate the wedding outside the Church?

Permission to marry in a non-Catholic setting

For the requirement of place of marriage, there are different requirements if the marriage will be sacramental or not (cf. canon 1118 §3 and the 1990 Rite of Marriage, #105). Bransfield asks the question: "How is the Church to respond when people with good intentions, if not fully informed of the Church's reasons for preferring marriage to take place in the Church, approach the Church to have these non-traditional marriages take place and have them sanctioned by the Church?"[33] In 2022, Diane Barr wrote on outdoor weddings. She reflected:

> In the mid to late 1980s, concerns arose that the faithful were not well prepared to enter the sacrament of marriage because of the perceived large increase in the number of decrees of nullity being issued by diocesan tribunals and the influence of a "divorce mentality" in the secular culture . . . .
>
> This perception of ill preparedness led many bishops in the United States to implement a variety of changes in the requirements for marriage preparation and the granting of permissions for weddings outside Catholic Church as well as the availability of validations after a civil union. . . . some dioceses prohibited any weddings for two Catholics outside of a Catholic Church. Many also placed limitations on what other secular or religious sites were permitted to host weddings witnessed by Catholic clergy . . . .[34]

Barr noted that as a result of this "rule enforcement approach," "the number who sought to be married in the Church has continued to decease. These restrictions have come to be viewed by many as 'unjust' by Catholics who see a Catholic marrying an unbaptized person at a hotel or in a garden."[35] Barr notes that more recently, "dioceses have again begun revisiting this permission. . . . The major reason for reconsidering the manner in which this permission is applied is the realization that the Church is missing out on an opportunity to evangelize already baptized Catholics who want the Church to recognize their union."[36]

33 Bransfield, "Canonical Norms Regarding Place," 88.
34 Diane Barr, "Outdoor Weddings: Are Policies Changing?" in *CLSA Proceedings* 84 (2022) 81.
35 Barr, "Outdoor Weddings," 81.
36 Ibid., 82.

In 2019, Bransfield conducted a survey in the United States to which seventy-six dioceses responded.[37] Let us consider this statement regarding place of the celebration of marriage: "One diocese noted that its territory is a destination wedding locale, and so its policy has been very careful to make it clear what it will allow or not allow, so as to protect the sanctity of marriage."[38] How does the place of marriage protect the sanctity of marriage? These people have all come to the Church looking for permission to marry in the eyes of the Church. Why is the Church not bending over backwards to make that happen? Bransfield continued:

> One diocese noted that its previous bishop was much more permissive in his place of marriage policies, seeing a greater allowance for weddings in non-traditional venues as being a tool for greater evangelization, but the new / current bishop does not share that same philosophy and so the diocesan policies have been made more strict.[39]

Further from the survey:

> One responder spoke at length about the bishop's decision to allow newer, more permissive policies in the past few years. Recognizing that making this decision creates positive and negative consequences, the responder nevertheless focused on the positive reasons that motivated the bishop's decision to change his diocese's policy. It was first noted that allowing Catholics to marry in non-traditional venues allows their marriages to be valid from the very beginning of their marital unions. Secondly, it allows for more couples to be evangelized through diocesan pre-Cana programs. Thirdly, these more permissive policies allow for a Catholic cleric (priest or deacon) to be personally involved in the wedding liturgy, as opposed to rent-a-clerics being hired to officiate. Having clergy in good standing involved in the liturgy helps ensure that the Catholic Rite of Marriage is celebrated with Scripture and a homily, along with Catholic prayers. When all of these elements are present, it helps to reinforce to all attending the wedding the realities of the presence of God, the sacramentality and the goods of marriage. All of this makes good catechesis possible, with the liturgy itself being a powerful teaching tool.[40]

Bransfield noted: "for many couples, the wedding venue is one of their most important considerations in planning their wedding. When the Church says No to their proposed venue, the Church loses the opportunity to catechize, and, most

37 Bransfield, "Canonical Norms Regarding Place," 89.
38 Ibid., 96.
39 Ibid.
40 Ibid., 97.

likely, that couple's (and their future family's) future relationship with the Church will be adversely affected."[41]

Bransfield reflects on place of wedding policies:

> It is important to remember, at least in terms of marriages employing canonical form, that what is being talked about here is a permission and not a dispensation. Have we made permissions more difficult to obtain than dispensations? If we as local churches routinely grant disparity of worship dispensations, for example, which bear on validity, but are much stricter in the granting of permissions, which oftentimes bear on liceity, is this not something that should be a significant point of reflection as we continue to evaluate what our place of marriage policies should be?[42]

Dispensation from form

Daly explains the dispensation from form: "A dispensation from Canonical form enables someone other than a cleric or officially designated Catholic minister to officiate and it usually involves a wedding taking place outside a Catholic church or oratory."[43] While this is something that takes place regularly, it is not possible when the two parties involved are Catholic. Daly speaks of the dispensation from form for two Catholics:

> The law does not provide for a diocesan bishop to dispense from form when two Catholics are marrying. Such an event is considered to be truly extraordinary or applies in a situation of danger of death. The Congregation for the Doctrine of the Faith will grant dispensations from form in special circumstances, such as when a spouse is a convert or when the father of a bride refuses to attend the wedding in a Catholic Church.[44]

41 Bransfield, "Canonical Norms Regarding Place," 97.

42 Ibid., 100-101.

43 Brendan Daly, "Form for Marriage: Technicality or Protecting a Sacrament?" in *Australasian Catholic Record*, 82 (2005) 173.

44 Ibid., 174, citing the August 1, 1985, response of the Pontifical Council for the Interpretation of Legislative Texts.

What kinds of reasons would be considered "serious difficulties"[45] to grant the dispensation from form as required by canon 1127 §2? Daly cites #154 of the 1993 Directory on Ecumenism, which gives examples of possible reasons.

What about the radical sanation of a civil union of two Catholics? Renken addresses this in light of the 1985 authentic interpretation which stated that "the diocesan bishop cannot dispense two Catholics from the canonical form of marriage. Some canonists hold, therefore, that the diocesan bishop cannot grant the radical sanation of an invalid marriage involving two Catholics."[46] Renken goes on to distinguish between ordinary and extraordinary circumstances and also recalls that granting a radical sanation is not the granting of a dispensation, but rather the dispensation is granted by the law itself as part of the sanation.[47]

Is Canonical Form Still Relevant?

Regarding having a liturgical celebration and the sacrament of marriage, Daly notes:

> It could be argued that the *Tametsi* decree was the first step towards uniting the celebration of the sacrament of marriage to a liturgical celebration because the presence of a priest was now required for the validity of the celebration. With a priest present there could be a liturgical celebration. When sacraments are celebrated they are acts of worship and they are effective celebrations of God's saving presence amongst us. So, it is appropriate that there be a liturgical celebration.[48]

The Catechism of the Catholic Church reminds us that the spouses themselves are the "ministers of Christ's grace, [who] mutually confer upon each other the sacrament of Matrimony by expressing their consent before the Church."[49] Navarrete summarizes the implications of this for canonical form: "In the Latin Church, it is the spouses and only the spouses who put into action the essential rite (ritual) of the sacrament, given that the Church has added nothing to that established by Christ. Thus, the ministers of the sacrament are the spouses

---

45 Daly, "Form for Marriage," 173, citing #154 of the Directory on Ecumenism: "Among these reasons for dispensation may be considered the maintaining of family harmony, obtaining parental consent to the marriage, the recognition of the particular religious commitment of the non-Catholic partner or his/her blood relationship with the minister of another Church or ecclesial Community."

46 Renken, "Extraordinary Convalidation," 492; see footnote 54, referencing Chiapetta, A. Bernárdez Cantón, and Ghirlanda.

47 Renken, "Extraordinary Convalidation," 493.

48 Daly, "Form for Marriage," 167.

49 John Paul II, *Catechism of the Catholic Church* (Rome: Libreria Editrice Vaticana, 1994) no. 1623; Eng. trans. taken from https://www.vatican.va/archive/ENG0015/P52.HTM (accessed on 27 Aug. 2023).

and only the spouses."[50] Thus, the essential rite consists only of the expression of the juridically efficacious consent of the two spouses.[51]

Petit concludes: "Nothing would prevent canon law from seeing the status of the civil marriage of Catholics differently and accepting the civil form as the juridic form for a putative marriage."[52] Navarrete states clearly: "in the Latin Code, the 'sacred ritual' (*ritus sacer*) is not required for validity; nevertheless, when marriage is celebrated using the ordinary (canonical) form, it is celebrated with a liturgical ritual."[53] He notes that this is different from the Eastern practice and he reminds the reader that this difference is important because it is based on different ecclesial and cultural perspectives.[54]

Distinct from the exchange of consent is the blessing of the priest.[55] Navarrete summarizes the roles of canonical form and of the priestly blessing:

> Role of canonical form: to reliably attest to the celebration of the marriage. That is the main role of the priest or official witness for canonical form.
>
> Role of the 'sacred ritual': to express the sacred meaning of the event and to sanctify the spouses and their union.[56]

Ortiz speaks of how for many people, those situations of civil marriages declared non-existent (*inesistenti*) after a long common life, and with the ease of being able to marry in the Church once this union is recognized as non-binding, is often a source of scandal.[57] Ortiz asks the question whether it might better serve the purpose of protecting the *ius connubii* of the parties to require the canonical form of marriage only for liceity. Then, those who do not marry according to canonical form can have their choice to marry recognized by the community, even the ecclesial community. Ortiz recommends that we avoid a "pessimistic presumption of nullity" toward those who have abandoned the faith or are far from

---

50 Urbano Navarrete, "Questioni sulla forma canonica ordinaria nei codici latino e orientale," *Periodica* 85 (1996) 497.
51 Ibid.
52 Petit, *Consentement matrimonial et fiction du droit*, 297-298.
53 Navarrete, "Questioni sulla forma canonica ordinaria nei codici latino e orientale," 490.
54 Ibid.
55 For a short history of the priestly blessing in the East and in the West, see: Navarrete, "Questioni sulla forma canonica ordinaria nei codici latino e orientale," 490-492. There is a long history of requiring the priestly blessing in the East; at 492, Navarrete notes that in the West, it is only since the decree *Ne temere* of August 2, 1907, that the priestly blessing was required as an element for validity.
56 Ibid., 492-493.
57 See Miguel A. Ortiz, "La forma canonica quale garanzia della verità del matrimonio," *Ius Ecclesiae* 15 (2003) 391.

the Church and have chosen a civil union. Ortiz reminds us that this "pessimistic presumption" contrasts with Pope John Paul II's statement in #68 of *Familiaris consortio* of the matrimonial intent of many people, even those of seemingly little faith.[58] Ortiz notes that the Tridentine canonical form has served the Church well as a guarantor of the fact of a marriage, particularly in times of uncertainty and lack of ability to disseminate information, of the defense of the fact that the Church has jurisdiction over marriage. Certainly today, civil jurisdictions can fulfill the role of guarantor of the fact of a marriage. Today the role of defending the Church's jurisdiction over marriage does not need to be accomplished only through canonical form.[59] Thus, Ortiz asks the question: does the canonical form of marriage need to remain for validity, or can it be required for liceity? Matrimonial consent creates marriage. That will not change. For validity, the parties will still exchange the same promises: partnership, fidelity, lifelong, openness to children; the union will still be a sacrament between the baptized.

Ortiz concludes: the most important function of the canonical form of marriage is to recognize and protect the truth / fact of consent; if the canonical form of marriage were to be required for liceity, the Christian faithful could report their marriages to the Church.[60]

Why Move Away from Canonical Form?

Wrenn reminds us of our history:

> From its earliest days ... the Church has always urged Christians to marry in the context of a Christian celebration, and as the centuries passed, a marriage of Christians contracted without the presence of a priest came to be strictly forbidden and was viewed as gravely illicit.[61]

Nevertheless, for many centuries illicit clandestine marriages continued to take place. Wrenn speaks of the Council of Trent:

> [T]he Church had gone for more than fifteen centuries without requiring for validity that consent be exchanged before a priest, and the Fathers were not at all sure that the Church even had the power to do that since it seemed to many that the sacrament of matrimony, as

---

58 Ortiz, "La forma canonica," 392-393. He cites *Familiaris consortio* 68, on the fact that even those of little or no faith can marry.

59 Ibid., 393-394.

60 Ibid., 397.

61 Lawrence Wrenn, "Requesting and Receiving Marital Consent: A Chronology," in *The Jurist* 59 (1999) 39; a more recent article outlining the history of canonical form is: Philippe Hallein, "Le *motu proprio Omnium in mentem* et les consequences canoniques des modifications," in *Studia canonica* 45 (2011) 411-441.

> instituted by Christ, was effected by the consent of the parties alone and that it was not therefore within the competence of the Church to demand more than that.[62]

In 2005 Brendan Daly addressed the question of canonical form highlighting: "a number of people argue that the Catholic Church should do away with the requirement of Canonical form when Catholics marry."[63] Daly states: "Many argue that abolishing the requirement of Canonical form for marriage would actually increase respect for and the dignity of marriage. All marriages would be regarded as valid no matter which church, garden or registry office they took place in."[64] Daly further notes:

> The Church has struggled to give coherent reasons for the requirement of form apart from the practical safeguards that the requirement of form provides. In particular, it has prevented secret, unprovable marriages taking place. The motive of the requirement of form was to preserve the validity of marriages as far as possible, and the requirement was not just a technicality.[65]

Roland Jacques adds to this:

> The long and convoluted history of the canonical form shows clearly that it is not an absolute. It did, and does, render Christ's faithful eminent services. There is no doubt, however, that it is revisable, just as it was radically revised in 1563. Instead of focussing on the letter of an ecclesiastical law, pastors and canon lawyers should consider what values are at stake.[66]

Jacques notes that even if the Church were to give up demanding canonical form, that does not mean the Church needs to give up important values like marriage preparation, the liturgical celebration of marriages, etc.[67]

---

62 Wrenn, "Requesting and Receiving Marital Consent," 41.

63 Daly, "Form for Marriage," 163.

64 Ibid., 164.

65 Ibid., 167.

66 Roland Jacques, "The Canonical Form of Marriage Revisited: Did the Decree *Ne Temere* Outlast Its Usefulness?" in V.G. D'Souza, ed., *In the Service of Truth and Justice* (Bangalore: St Peter's Pontifical Institute, 2008) 359.

67 Ibid., 361. At 364, Jacques proposes an alternate canonical form that comprises these different steps: "Preparatory steps (enquiry on the freedom, catechetical instruction. . .) described in the Code, cc. 1063-1072 . . . Exchange of consent outside the church, *without* the presence of the assistant mentioned in c. 1108 . . . . Blessing by the priest or deacon in church, within a liturgical celebration . . . . Special records could be kept . . . ."

Conclusion

To summarize, we have reviewed different approaches to recognizing the consent of Catholic parties who choose to marry in a non-Catholic ceremony. In all approaches, the pastoral care of the Church needs to accompany the people and recognize their needs.

CLSA PROCEEDINGS 85 (2023) 305-355

SEMINAR

CATECHUMENAL PATHWAYS FOR MARRIAGE AND THE RELEVANCE OF CANON LAW

Ms. Adrienne A. Yates, JCL, MS, MA

Introduction

> [A]ware that the well-being of society and her own good are intimately tied to the good of the family, the Church perceives in a more urgent and compelling way her mission of proclaiming to all people the plan of God for marriage and the family, ensuring their full vitality and human and Christian development, and thus contributing to the renewal of society and of the people of God.
>
> \- *Familiaris consortio, no. 3*[1]

Heeding the above exhortation of Pope Saint John Paul II and recognizing that "marriage preparation must be set within the urgent need to evangelize culture," the Pontifical Council for the Family issued the 1996 guideline document, Preparation for the Sacrament of Marriage.[2] "Marriage preparation constitutes a providential and favorable period for those oriented toward this Christian sacrament, and a *Kayrós,* i.e., a period in which God calls upon the engaged and helps them to discern the vocation to marriage and family life."[3] Pope Francis found that "the couple is particularly amenable to listen to the

---

1 John Paul II, apostolic exhortation *Familiaris consortio* 3, November 22, 1981: *AAS* 74 (1982) (hereafter *FC*) 84; Eng. trans. in *On the Family, Apostolic Exhortation* Familiaris consortio (Washington, DC: United States Conference of Catholic Bishops, 2001) 2 (hereafter *OTF*).

2 Pontifical Council for the Family, guidelines *Preparazione al Sacramento del Matrimonio* 20, May 13, 1996 (hereafter *PSM*).

3 Ibid., 2. All English translations of this document are from http://www.vatican.va/roman_curia/pontifical_councils/family/documents/rc_pc_family_doc_13051996_preparation-for-marriage_en.html (accessed on 9 Nov. 2023).

Gospel and to accept Jesus as Teacher of life."[4] In other words, marriage preparation is a period that is ripe for God's purpose of re-evangelizing the couple engaged to be married, precisely that they might embrace the divine plan for life and love within their marital vocation.

In view of the personalist understanding of marriage present in the 1983 Code of Canon Law, Book IV emphasizes not only the freedom to marry and the valid exchange of consent but also marriage preparation that disposes the spouses to a fruitful reception of the holiness and duties of enduring married life.

At the dawn of the new millennium, Hartmann urged, "preparation for marriage is no longer understood as merely a pre-marital investigation where the goal is to ensure the freedom of the parties to enter marriage. Included now is a far more encompassing notion of catechesis" in keeping with the life-long process as defined in the General Directory for Catechesis.[5] The Congregation for the Clergy in the same directory hailed the baptismal catechumenate, The Rite of Christian Initiation of Adults,[6] as the inspiration and paradigm for adult catechesis in the Church.[7] Although the structure of the Rite of Christian Initiation of Adults is not to be "slavishly imitated," the elements of a gradual progression through definite stages,[8] and the connection with the community of faith, with its meaningful rites, symbols, and liturgical and biblical signs characterize the

---

4 Francis, Address to Participants at the Formation Course Promoted by the Tribunal of the Roman Rota at the Basilica of Saint John Lateran, September 27, 2018 (hereafter Roman Rota Formation Course 2018); Eng. trans. at https://www.vatican.va/content/francesco/en/speeches/2018/september/documents/papa-francesco_20180927_corso-rotoromana.html (accessed on 11 Nov. 2023).

5 Paul Hartmann, "Marriage and Future Practice of the Faith," in *Roman Replies and CLSA Advisory Opinions 2001*, eds. Stephen Pedone and John Donlon (Washington, DC: CLSA, 2001) 124.

6 *Ordo initiationis christianæ adultorum, editio typica* (Vatican City: Typis polyglottis Vaticanis, 1972), (hereafter *OICA*); adapted English version *Rite of Christian Initiation of Adults* (Collegeville, MN: Liturgy Training Publications, 1988) (hereafter *RCIA*).

7 See Congregation for the Clergy, *General Directory for Catechesis* 90, August 11, 1997; Eng. trans. in *General Directory for Catechesis* (Washington, DC: United States Catholic Conference, 1998) (hereafter *GDC*) 82.

8 See Appendix I for a convergence of the four periods of RCIA with those of a catechumenal pathway for marriage. The definite stages of the RCIA are marked by the four periods: 1) evangelization and pre-catechumenate, 2) catechumenate, 3) purification and enlightenment and 4) *mystagogia*. These correspond respectively to actions of 1) initial inquiry and conversion, 2) catechesis, 3) continued spiritual conversion, growth and discernment, and 4) on-going lived reception and reflection of the mysteries of faith. See Thomas H. Morris, *The RCIA: Transforming the Church: A Resource for Pastoral Implementation,* (New York/ Mahwah, NJ: Paulist Press, 1997) 81-222.

comprehensiveness and integrity of this process of formation and make it a "preparatory school for Christian life."[9]

Over forty years ago Pope Saint John Paul II emphasized the need for a preparative journey for marriage in his apostolic exhortation on the Christian Family in the Modern World, *Familiaris consortio*:

> Among the elements to be instilled in this journey of faith, which is similar to the catechumenate, there must also be a deeper knowledge of the mystery of Christ and the Church, of the meaning of grace and of the responsibility of Christian marriage, as well as preparation for taking an active and conscious part in the rites of the marriage liturgy.[10]

This pastoral concern for a comprehensive preparation for marriage and family life is reflected in canon 1063.[11] The code points to an on-going formation process for marriage involving human, spiritual, intellectual, and pastoral dimensions[12] within the context of the ecclesiastical community (c. 774 §1) that ultimately leads to a manifest living and active faith (c. 773). Although not specifically denoted by name, the formation or "assistance" indicated in this canon also spans the three principal periods of marriage preparation as called for by Pope Saint John Paul II —remote, proximate, and immediate[13]—as well as the period of post-sacramental

---

9 *GDC* 83-84.

10 *FC* 161; *OTF* 63.

11 For an in-depth study of this canon see Fintan Gavin, *Pastoral Care in Marriage Preparation (Can. 1063): History, Analysis of the Norm and Its Implementation by Some Particular Churches* (Rome: Gregorian University Press, 2004).

12 The dimensions referred to here are known as the pillars of formation commonly used in vocational formation processes. As regards priestly formation, see John Paul II, post-synodal apostolic exhortation *Pastores dabo vobis* 42, 71, March 25, 1992: *AAS* 84 (1992) 731, 783; Eng. trans. *I Will Give You Shepherds, Pastores Dabo Vobis: Post-synodal Apostolic Exhortation* (Washington, DC: United States Catholic Conference, 1992) 83, 135. As regards diaconal formation, see Congregation for Catholic Education and Congregation for The Clergy, *Basic Norms for the Formation of Permanent Deacons, Directory for the Ministry and Life of Permanent Deacons,* 66-88 (Washington, DC: USCCB, 2002) 58-69. As regards formation of lay ecclesial ministers see United States Catholic Bishops, *Co-Workers in the Vineyard of the Lord: A Resource for Guiding the Development of Lay Ecclesial Ministry* (Washington, DC: USCCB, 2005) 34-50. For formation of RCIA candidates and catechumens see Morris, 45, referring to the components of catechesis, community, liturgy, and service described in *OICA* 75; *RCIA* 37, which align with the dimensions of formation. While the pillars are not mentioned specifically in the *PSM*, the dimensions are referred to throughout the document, e.g., *PSM,* 22, 23, 35, 36, 38, 41.

13 See *FC* 66. Cf. *PSM* 22-59.

assistance, *mystagogia*, in view of the perpetual conjugal covenant.[14] Each period of marriage preparation is relatively distinct according to the objective and action appropriate to it.[15]

Pope Francis "reaffirms the need for a *permanent catechumenate* for the Sacrament of Matrimony, which concerns its preparation, celebration and the initial years that follow. It is a journey to be shared with priests, pastoral workers and Christian spouses."[16] In response to this urgent need, the 2022 document titled *Catechetical Pathways for Married Life, pastoral guidelines for local Churches*[17] was prepared by the Dicastery for the Laity, the Family and Life as a pastoral tool to assist in the implementation of a catechumenal pathway for married life at local levels. The following study of the canonical, theological, and doctrinal basis relevant to these periods of marriage preparation supports the alignment of preparation envisioned by the Code of Canon Law with preparation for marriage according to a catechumenal pathway.

1. Remote Preparation - Evangelization

According to the guidelines *Preparation for the Sacrament of Marriage*, remote preparation includes infancy through late adolescence and occurs primarily within the family, assisted by the parish, the school, and other means.[18] Remote preparation is akin to the evangelization and pre-catechumenate period of the Rite of Christian Initiation of Adults.[19]

---

14 Cf. Ignatius Gramunt, Javier Hervada and Leroy Wauck, *Canons and Commentaries on Marriage* (Collegeville, MN: The Liturgical Press, 1987) 10, to compare the stages of c. 1063 with the four stages in *FC* 66.

15 Some pedagogical methods employed may differ by period and others may be the same throughout the process of preparation and beyond, such as those mentioned in c. 1063, 1°. Cf. Gavin, *Pastoral Care in Marriage Preparation (Can. 1063)* 70.

16 Francis, Roman Rota Formation Course 2018; cf., Francis, Address on the occasion of the Inauguration of the Judicial Year of the Tribunal of the Roman Rota, 29 January 2018: *AAS* 110 (2018) 1440; Eng. trans. at https://www.vatican.va/content/francesco/en/speeches/2018/january/documents/papa-francesco_20180129_annogiudiziario-rotaromana.html (accessed on 11 Nov. 2023).

17 Dicastery for the Laity, the Family and Life, *Catechumenal Pathways for Married Life, pastoral guidelines for local Churches,* October 4, 2022 (Vatican City: Libreria editrice Vaticana, 2022) (hereafter *CPML*); Eng. trans. at http://www.laityfamilylife.va/content/dam/laityfamilylife/amoris-laetitia/OrientamentiCatecumenatomatrimoniale/Catechumenal%20Pathways_ENG.pdf (accessed on 17 Nov. 2023).

18 *PSM* 22.

19 On November 17, 2021, the USCCB approved a revised English edition of the *Order of Christian Initiation of Adults*. At the time of writing of this article a subsequent confirmation and recognition by the Vatican Congregation for Divine Worship is awaited.

1.1 Canonical Considerations of Remote Preparation

The preparation during this period involves the norms of those canons, which regard early Christian education and canon 1063, 1°:

> Pastors of souls are obliged to take care that their ecclesial community offers the Christian faithful the assistance by which the matrimonial state is preserved in a Christian spirit and advances in perfection. This assistance must be offered especially by: preaching, catechesis adapted to minors, youth, and adults, and even the use of instruments of social communication, by which the Christian faithful are instructed about the meaning of Christian marriage and about the function of Christian spouses and parents.[20]

Canons 762-772 specifically regard preaching, one of the principle means of both proclaiming the good news of the Gospel *(kerygma)* and relating the Christian doctrine *(didache)*. Social communications as a tool at the service of the ministries of the word is considered in this section in the context of preaching according to canon 772. The norms for catechesis, the other vital form of ministry of the divine word, are found in canons 773-780.

1.1.1 Preaching

The fundamental activity of the Church is evangelization through the ministry of the Word.[21] This building up of the people of God through the Word is constituent to the domestic Church, the institutional Church, and all of the Christian faithful. The import of preaching relates directly to the lived discipleship of the faithful and the salvation of humanity (c. 768).

During the period of remote preparation, at a minimum, children and adolescents are to benefit from the rich preaching offered at the Sunday celebration of Eucharist. Consonant with the doctrine of the magisterium (c. 760), preaching is to inspire, inform, and support the domestic Church in teaching Christian anthropology and a healthy ecclesiology directed toward a universal

---

20 *Codex Iuris Canonici auctoritate Ioannis Pauli PP. II promulgatus* (Vatican City: Libreria Editrice Vaticana, 1983) c. 1063, 1°; Eng. trans. *Code of Canon Law. Latin-English Edition, New English Translation* (Washington, DC: Canon Law Society of America, 2023). All subsequent English translations from this code will be taken from this source unless otherwise indicated.

21 See Michael A. Nobel, unpublished commentary *CIC* Canons 747-833: Faithful, Magisterium, Church and Civil Society: Part b, Magisterium, 40. See also John M. Huels, *The Teaching Office of the Catholic Church. A Commentary on Book III of the Code of Canon Law* (Ottawa: Faculty of Canon Law Saint Paul University, 2017) 70-71, for a discussion of c. 762 and the right of the faithful to receive preaching and the obligation of preachers to preach rightly.

communion, in addition to upholding the unity and constancy of the family as a sign and role model of Christian *communio*. The liturgical homily[22] serves to undergird the strength and wellness of the family through relating the Christian vision, as well as the requisites and obligations toward living as disciples. Canon 770 envisions and even exhorts more direct addresses according to special needs or circumstances: "At certain times according to the prescripts of the diocesan bishop, pastors are to arrange for those types of preaching which are called spiritual exercises and sacred missions or for other forms of preaching adapted to needs."[23] Various types of non-liturgical sacred preaching[24] such as at spiritual retreats, missions, and other devotionals can provide for the spiritual needs of the faithful and can be formative when preaching is directed toward a select purpose or group, e.g., marriage and the family. Yet even the most pointed and powerful message can be effective only if there are properly disposed families present to hear it. Canon 835 §4 states the proper role of the Christian faithful and especially parents in accomplishing the work of liturgy.[25]

Apart from those who fail to make attendance a priority or those who have willingly turned away from the Church, there are those who are disenfranchised beyond the exercise of their will, due to their situation in life. The code calls the pastor of souls to a special solicitude for those who lack this ordinary care of preaching ministry (c. 771).

Regarding those who may lack ordinary pastoral care, Huels suggested the example of migrants, itinerant workers, military personnel, homebound, prisoners, hospital patients, and others.[26] Moreover the exhortation to provide care extends to those who are non-believers within the territory. Among the former and the latter may be families whose children[27] would benefit from the remote preparation for marriage that preaching might offer. While canon 771 calls for the spread of the Gospel to non-believers and those who lack pastoral care, it

---

22 See James H. Provost, "Brought Together by the Word of the Living God: Canons 762-772," *Studia canonica* 23 (1989) 359-365, regarding the constitutive nature of c. 767 in determining the legal elements of the homily, and Huels, *The Teaching Office,* 86, regarding a discussion of c. 760.

23 Canon 770.

24 Regarding particular cases in which the diocesan bishop can admit lay faithful to preach including spiritual conferences or instructions, see USCCB, decree, Complementary Norm for Canon 766: Lay Preaching, December 13, 2001, https://www.usccb.org/beliefs-and-teachings/what-we-believe/canon-law/complementary-norms/canon-766-lay-preaching (accessed on 13 Nov. 2023).

25 Canon 835 §4.

26 See Huels, *The Teaching Office*, 98-99.

27 Children as minors remain subject to the authority of their parents unless canon law provides otherwise (c. 98 §2). See c. 105 §1.

specifies neither the nature nor method of "provision" but allows for regional adaptation.[28]

1.1.2 Social Media

In addition to books and printed materials intended for public distribution (see cc. 822-832), the current variety of social media offers unprecedented immediate accessibility to a plurality of people. Since the code was written prior to the advent of the technology in the new millennium, particular legislation attempts to keep pace with these ever-developing technological means of communication as regards Catholic religious instruction and education.[29] Special training is urged by the Canadian Conference of Catholic Bishops to facilitate the proper and effective proclamation of the Gospel via such communication methods. The United States Conference of Catholic Bishops left the requirements and approval to the diocesan bishop or competent superior.[30]

The task of ensuring the proper use of the tools of social media cannot be underestimated, nor its value in building up the faith.[31] The internet offers the opportunity to livestream or upload video recorded Masses, podcasts, lectures, papal announcements, marriage preparation courses as well as to host web pages with doctrinal and spiritual content or blogs regarding marriage and family. The possibilities for sharing the ministry of preaching and catechesis for faithful of all ages by these means of communication have not yet been exhausted.[32]

---

28 For a discussion of the implications of preaching and catechizing via the online environment in these circumstances, see Michael A. Nobel, "To Proclaim the Gospel Online–Challenges and Difficulties: Towards a Possible Diocesan Protocol for Ministers of the Divine Word in the Online Environment," *The Canonist* 10/1 (2019) 101-102.

29 Canon 772 calls for norms of the diocesan bishop regarding preaching and the competency of the episcopal conferences in establishing precepts regarding radio and television talks. See Nobel, "To Proclaim the Gospel Online," 95-96, 98, for comments on cc. 822 and 823 §1 that basically negate the need for these additional precepts. For a discussion of the sole competence of the diocesan bishop to issue norms in accord with cc. 763-766, regarding *sermons* given via the Internet see: Huels, *The Teaching Office,* 101-102. Note the suggested meaning of *sermo,* which in this norm refers only to one offered by those who are approved to preach according to cc. 763-766.

30 See Huels, *The Teaching Office,* 101-102.

31 See cc. 822 and 823 regarding the exercise of the bishops' *munus docendi* through instruments of mass media and the due cooperation of the faithful.

32 Cf. Pontifical Council on Social Communications, *The Church and the Internet* 9, February 22, 2002, http://www.vatican.va/roman_curia/pontifical_councils/pccs/documents/rc_pc_pccs_doc_20020228_church-internet_en.html (accessed on 13 Nov. 2023).

1.1.3 Catechesis

"The [Second Vatican] Council taught that both the institution of marriage and the marital love of spouses 'are ordained for the procreation and education of children, and find in them their ultimate crown.'"[33] This responsibility is assumed during the Rite of Marriage as the couple answers positively to the question "Are you prepared to accept children lovingly from God and to bring them up according to Christ and his Church?"[34] They also give consent to marriage, which by canonical definition includes the procreation and education of children as a marital end (c. 1055).[35]

Book IV, Chapter VIII of the 1983 code upholds this right-duty of parents: "Parents have the most grave duty and the primary right to take care as best they can for the physical, social, cultural, moral, and religious education of their offspring" (c. 1136).

Nobel noted the use of four Latin terms employed in the canons regarding Catholic education: *educatio*, *formatio*, *institution*, and *instructio*. He found that although there is no absolute consistency in usage of these terms, generally *educatio* "is mostly used in the Code of Canon Law in the context of parents who have the right to educate their children, indicating an overall education of the entire human person, including religious education."[36]

Canon 774 §2 articulates the parents' duty of formation in the faith: "Parents above others are obliged to form [*efformandi*] their children by word and example

---

33 Michael Lawler, *Marriage and Sacrament: A Theology of Christian Marriage* (Collegeville, MN: The Liturgical Press, 1993) 11-12. Cf. Second Vatican Council, pastoral constitution *Gaudium et spes*, 48, December 7, 1965: *AAS* 58 (1966) (hereafter *GS*) 1068; Eng. trans. in Austin Flannery, gen. ed., *Vatican Council II: The Conciliar and Post-Conciliar Documents*, vol. 1, new rev. ed. (Collegeville, MN: Liturgical Press, 2014) (hereafter *Flannery1*) 950.

34 *Ordo celebrandi Matrimonium,* editio typica altera, (Vatican City: Typis polyglottis Vaticanis, 1991) 60, 94, 125; adapted English version *The Order of Celebrating Matrimony*, new rev. 2nd ed. (Washington, DC: United States Conference of Catholic Bishops 2016) 19, 34, 125 (hereafter *OCM*).

35 For the implicit acceptance of the ends of marriage within consent and of *educatio prolis* as it pertains to the validity of marriage see Tribunal of the Roman Rota, *coram* Alwan, Prot. N. 18.640, July 9, 2010 (Lebanon), no. 7; as cited in Augustine Mendonça, unpublished commentary Substantive Jurisprudence on Defects of Consent, 440. See also Antoni Stankiewicz, "L'esclusione della procreazione ed educazione della prole," in La simulazione del consenso matrimoniale canonico, ed. Piero A. Bonnet (Libreria editrice Vaticana, 1990) 165-168. For further consideration, Schmidt, K., "*Educatio prolis* and the Validity of Marriage," *The Jurist* 55 (1995) 243-280.

36 Michael A. Nobel, "Catholic Education and Formation with Regard to Selected Issues of Book III of the Code of Canon Law," *Philippine Canonical Forum* 20 (2018) 231.

in faith and in the practice of Christian life; sponsors and those who take the place of parents are bound by an equal obligation." During remote preparation parents have the responsibility of advancing the sacramental life of their children with the assistance of the pastor, friends, and other members of the community.[37] Concomitantly, outside of death, children of the age of reason have the responsibility to manifest the intention to receive a sacrament, to have been carefully prepared, sufficiently instructed, properly disposed, and to have contrition for their sins.[38]

According to canon 793 §1, parents or those who take their place *in iure* or *de facto,* have the strict obligation to provide suitably for their Catholic education in the free exercise of their right to choose the appropriate school and means of education.[39] Care must be taken with children who attend a school of another confessional, that they are properly educated in the Catholic religion.

Canon 794 states, the duty of assistance in providing a Catholic education to all the faithful belongs to the Church under the administration of the pastor of souls (cf. cc. 773 and 776-780). The pastor of souls must arrange everything necessary to assist the parents in fulfilling their obligation "with a proper application of the principle of subsidiarity."[40]

Parents and teachers are to cooperate synergistically in fostering a full Catholic education that is faithful to Catholic teaching and tradition (c. 796 §2). Canon 795 describes these goals:

> Since true education [*educatio*] must strive for complete formation [*formatio*] of the human person that looks to his or her final end as well as to the common good of societies, children and youth are to be nurtured in such a way that they are able to develop their physical, moral, and intellectual talents harmoniously, acquire a more perfect

---

37 See *Ordo Baptismi parvulorum,* editio typica altera, August 29, 1973 (Vatican City: Typis polyglottis Vaticanis, 1973), Introduction, no. 5.5; adapted English version *The Order of Baptism of Children* (Collegeville, MN: Liturgical Press, 2020). See also ibid., nos. 56 and 93: "For your part, you must strive to bring them/him/her up in the faith, so that this divine life may be preserved from the contagion of sin, and may grow in them/him/her day by day."

38 See the following norms: baptism—cc. 865 §1, 867 §1 and 868 §1; confirmation—cc. 889 §2 and 890; Eucharist—cc. 913 §1, 914, and 920; and penance—c. 988 and 989.

39 See cc. 793 §2 and 798 for the parents' right to assistance from civil society and the right to choose a private school if this obligation for Catholic education must be filled outside of Catholic school.

40 John Paul II, Letter to the Families *Gratissimam sane* 16, February 2, 1994: *AAS* 86 (1994) 901 (hereafter *GmS*); Eng. trans. at https://www.vatican.va/content/john-paul-ii/en/letters/1994/documents/hf_jp-ii_let_02021994_families.html (accessed on 14 Nov. 2023).

> sense of responsibility and right use of freedom, and are formed [*conformetur*] to participate actively in social life.[41]

Nobel agreed with Huels' understanding of the meaning of *educatio* in this parental context as "upbringing," indicating "to bring their children up in the Catholic religion and provide for their religious formation."[42] The term *formatio* is mostly used in the context of a specific formation, e.g. a priestly formation (c. 249). Nobel considers *formatio* to be a subset of *educatio*.[43]

The goal of remote preparation is evangelization, through which is fostered the overall maturation and development of the human person on the physical, moral, spiritual, intellectual, and interpersonal levels (c. 795). Based on Nobel's explanation of the use of the terms *educatio* and *formatio* in the Code of Canon Law, it can be concluded that the period of remote preparation is largely concerned with *educatio*, the upbringing necessary to reach the fullness of Christian life. In contrast, the proximal and immediate periods are more focused on *formatio*, the specific formation for Christian marriage. However, *formatio* remains rooted in *educatio*.

1.2 Theological and Doctrinal Considerations of Remote Preparation

Pope Saint John Paul II described remote preparation, the initial stage of a gradual and continuous marriage preparation process, as:

> . . . that wise family training which leads children to discover themselves as being endowed with a rich and complex psychology and with a particular personality with its own strengths and weaknesses. It is the period when esteem for all authentic human values is instilled, both in interpersonal and in social relationships, with all that this signifies for the formation of character, for the control and right use of one's inclinations, for the manner of regarding and meeting people of the opposite sex, and so on. Also necessary, especially for Christians, is solid spiritual and catechetical formation that will show that marriage is a true vocation and mission, without excluding the possibility of the total gift of self to God in the vocation to the priestly or religious life.[44]

---

41 Canon 795.

42 Huels, The Teaching Office of the Catholic Church, 178.

43 See Nobel, "Catholic Education and Formation with Regard to Selected Issues of Book III," 233.

44 *FC* 66; *OTF* 62.

Pope Benedict XVI aptly summarized, "[Children] are taught to understand life as the vocation to love, which is subsequently specified in the form of marriage or virginity for the Kingdom of Heaven, but is always a vocation to love."[45]

1.2.1 Evangelization

As in the pre-catechumenate period of the baptismal catechumenate, the beginning of the journey of formation for the vocation of marriage focuses on the evangelical elements of *kerygma* and *metanoia.*[46] The Council Fathers defined catechesis as a "ministry of the word."[47] Preaching and catechesis together assist in the process of evangelization through Christian maturation, that is, from proclamation to praise.[48] According to Pope Saint John Paul II, "Catechesis thus prepares for the important Christian commitments of adult life . . . . From infancy until the threshold of maturity, catechesis is thus a permanent school of the faith."[49]

Ideally, children benefit from the word of God lived and shared within the context of the domestic church and the wider ecclesial community, including the ecumenical community for those born of mixed marriages. In the process of evangelizing their children, these parents have the duty of creating a common unity within their family that respects the beliefs and practices of each spouse while upholding the promise made to bring up their children as Christians.[50] This instills a spirit of synodality during the remote period that will later serve those Catholics who seek interfaith or mixed marriages.

1.2.2 Proclamation

Lumen gentium 11, which undergirds canon 774 §2, designated parents as the first preachers of the Gospel to their children by word and example. As

---

45 Benedict XVI, address to the participants in the Plenary Assembly of the Pontifical Council for the Family, February 8, 2010; Eng. trans. in Pontifical Council for the Family, *Compendium on the Family and Human Life* (Vatican City: Libreria editrice Vaticana 2015) 150 (hereafter *CFHL*). Cf. Second Vatican Council, dogmatic constitution *Lumen gentium* 11, November 21, 1964: *AAS* 57 (1965) 16.

46 See *OICA* 36-37, *RCIA* 15.

47 Second Vatican Council, dogmatic constitution *Dei verbum* 24, November 18, 1965: *AAS* 58 (1966) 828-829; Eng. trans. in *Flannery1* 763–764.

48 For an explanation see: John Paul II, apostolic exhortation *Catechesi tradendae* 25, October 16, 1979: *AAS* 71 (1979), 1297-1298.

49 *Catechesi tradendae* 39; Eng. trans. in Austin Flannery, gen. ed., *Vatican Council II: More Post Conciliar Documents*, vol. 2, new rev. ed. (Northport, NY: Costello Publishing Co., 1998) (hereafter *Flannery2*) 786-787.

50 Canon 1125 regards the sincere promise required by the Catholic to do all in his or her power to baptize and bring up offspring in the Catholic faith and the requirement of informing the non-Catholic party of this promise and obligation made by the Catholic party.

children hear the truths of sacred scripture, from the advent of humankind (Gen 1 and 2)[51] through the fulfillment of Jesus as the *new Adam*[52] (Rom 5:12-21), they learn the foundational teachings of Christian anthropology. They come to know themselves to be created in God's own image and likeness, as adopted sons and daughters of God through baptism and as stewards of God's creation who are guided by the natural law written on their hearts. It is by means of this original moral sense that they are enabled to freely discern by reason good and evil.[53]

Children must be introduced by parents, assisted by ecclesial ministers, to the mystery of the incarnation through the proclamation of the infancy narratives. They are to learn of the Triune God, as a relationship of the love of Father, Son, and Holy Spirit.[54] In the Gospel stories of Jesus' earthly ministry, they encounter God's abiding love shared with humankind through his Son. Participating in the love of God through the Spirit within the family enkindles in the children the desire to care justly for others with mercy, respect, and loving-kindness. Hearing the resurrection narratives, they observe the full circle of Christ's fulfillment of the *exitus-reditus,* his emanation from and return to the Father. In adolescence they begin to understand the depth of this redemptive love of Jesus as savior, who giving up his life opened the way to heaven for all. As stewards of the Catholic faith, parents, pastors, and ecclesial ministers must teach the children to respond to these mysteries with an obedience of faith, a heart of gratitude and the gift of praise.[55] This discovery of the Christian mystery forms the basis for the *formatio* of Christian marriage.

1.2.3 Witness and Conversion

Parents must "create a family atmosphere inspired by love and devotion to God and fellow-men, which will promote an integrated, personal and social education of children."[56] Through the witness of love and care, married parents sow the seeds for their children's future mature and healthy relationships. Pope Francis used feminine imagery to describe the interpersonal relationships of the family: "It is in the very womb of the family that education draws in a substantial

51 All references to sacred scripture are from *The Holy Bible*, Revised Standard Version, New York, Thomas Nelson and Sons, 1952.

52 See Walter Bruggeman, "Genesis," in *Interpretation: A Bible Commentary for Teaching and Preaching,* ed. Paul J. Achtemeier and Patrick D. Miller (Atlanta: John Knox Press, 1982) 1:11-54.

53 See *CCC* 1954.

54 See *PSM*, no. 25.

55 Cf. Benedict XVI, homily at Mass in Valencia, Spain, July 9, 2006; Eng. trans. in *CFHL*, 128-131.

56 Second Vatican Council, declaration *Gravissimum educationis* 3, October 28, 1965: *AAS* 58 (1966) 728-739; Eng. trans. in *Flannery1* 728.

manner from relations of solidarity. The 'womb' of the family provides a nurturing environment for development and maturation of faith, wisdom and understanding."[57]

Parents have the arduous task of urging children from the comfort of their self-interest to a life that conforms to Christ. Catechesis is to be "permeated by *the mystery of Christ's Passover.*"[58] Marriage preparation in all periods should no less reveal the paschal nature of marriage.[59] Ideally, children learn in large and small ways from the conjugal life of their parents that "no one has greater love than this, to lay down one's life for one's friends" (Jn 15:13; Eph 5:25-26).[60] Consequently, proper remote preparation prepares children and adolescents not only for the eventual discernment of the vocation but in a real way to live as a sacrament at the service of communion in the world.

1.3 Suggestions for the Pastoral Implementation of Remote Preparation

During remote preparation, parents are called to awaken an initial faith in their children in light of God's word proclaimed through the Gospel of the Family (see Appendix II for suggested doctrinal topics), such that their baptismal faith will grow and mature.[61] Children's progress in *educatio,* and its lived expression is dependent on the influence of their parents, extended family, friends and their catechists.[62] The national pastoral framework for marriage and family life ministry, *Called to the Joy of Love,* envisioned a robust age-appropriate curricula

---

57 Francis, Message to the Participants in the General Assembly of the Pontifical Academy for Life, February 19, 2014; Eng. trans. by Zenit, https://zenit.org/articles/pope-francis-message-to-the-general-assembly-of-the-pontifical-academy-for-life/ (accessed on 14 Nov. 2023). Cf. Francis, message for the 49th World Communications Day *Communicating the Family: A Privileged Place of Encounter with the Gift of Love;* Eng. trans. at http://w2.vatican.va/content/francesco/en/messages/communications/documents/papa-francesco_20150123_messaggio-comunicazioni-sociali.html (accessed on 14 Nov. 2023): "Even after we have come into the world, in some sense we are still in a 'womb', which is the family. A womb made up of various interrelated persons: the family is 'where we learn to live with others despite our differences.'"

58 *GDC* 90-91.

59 From the earliest memory children should witness the dying to self of one parent-spouse for the other, and the rising of as a new creation of the two-in-one of the married couple *in Christ* as sacrament. This *kenosis* (self-emptying) of Christ continually *eventing* within the spouses as self-less love, gives Christian marriage its paschal character. Cf. Ladislas Örsy, *Marriage in Canon Law, Texts and Comments Reflections and Questions* (Wilmington, DE: Michael Glazier Inc., 1988) 271-272.

60 See also *GmS* 16: *AAS* 86 (1994) 899-903; Eng. trans. at https://www.vatican.va/content/john-paul-ii/en/letters/1994/documents/hf_jp-ii_let_02021994_families.html (accessed on 14 Nov. 2023). Cf. *PSM* 26.

61 John Paul II, *Catechesi tradendae* 20: *AAS* 71 (1979) 1294; Eng. trans. in *Flannery2* 774.

62 Cf., *OICA* 254; *RCIA* 155.

in Catholic schools, faith formation classes, and programs in youth ministry facilitated by ministers trained in the art of accompaniment.[63] In addition to sacred scripture study and rich liturgical preaching, the complementary instruments of the Catechism of the Catholic Church and the General Directory for Catechesis may be used.[64] Family faith experiences are needed at local ecclesial levels to provide positive role modelling of the transmission of the faith within families. Family movements, apostolates and associations are also instrumental in assisting to strengthen the solidarity of the family. They share in religious values and virtues, such as "respect, justice and forgiveness in personal and collective relations,"[65] as well as collaborate in building a spiritual life of prayer and worship as a community of families.[66] The Church must actively accompany the family in creating and nurturing the domestic Church, since the future of evangelization depends on it.[67]

2. Proximate Preparation - Catechesis

This period can be likened to the *RCIA* period of the catechumenate. From a fitting age, proximate preparation builds on the foundations of remote preparation through ongoing catechesis and personal preparation for the holiness and duties of marriage.

2.1 Canonical Considerations of Proximate Preparation

Canon 1063, 2° describes a personal *formatio* for marriage that intentionally involves personal growth and development:

> Pastors of souls are obliged to take care that their ecclesial community offers the Christian faithful the assistance by which the matrimonial state is preserved in a Christian spirit and advances in perfection. This assistance must be offered especially by:

---

63 United States Conference of Catholic Bishops, *Called to the Joy of Love: National Pastoral Framework for Marriage and Family Life Ministry,* June 2021 (Washington DC: United States Conference of Catholic Bishops 2021) 19-20. Regarding training objectives for ministers including mutual complementarity, ecclesial co-responsibility, see Francis, post-synodal apostolic exhortation *Amoris lætitia* 203, March 19, 2016: *AAS* 108 (2016) (hereafter *AL*) 392. See also *CPML* 20: Those who accompany engaged and married couples should possess a formation and style of accompaniment suited to the catechumenal journey. They should be formed in evangelizing young adults, in order to facilitate an encounter with the Gospel through listening, witnessing, guiding, and assisting.

64 *CPML* 28. See ibid., 49, for scriptural suggestions: e.g., Genesis, the Prophets, and the Song of Songs.

65 *PSM* 20.

66 See *EV* 93: *AAS* 87 (1995) 507-508. See also *FC* 66, 69.

67 See *FC* 65.

2° personal preparation to enter marriage, which disposes the spouses to the holiness and duties of their new state."[68]

Although pastors of souls, *pastores animarum*, refers to those who are ultimately entrusted with the pastoral care of the faithful, either bishops in their diocese or pastors in their parish, it is the ecclesial community *in solidum* with the pastors of souls that has the responsibility of offering the assistance needed.[69]

In organizing the marriage preparation process, the local ordinary may confer with men and women who have expertise in the area, presumably those who are married as well as experts in medicine, psychology, relational therapists and others who can assist in providing the appropriate personal care of couples, according to canon 1064.[70] Ideally a catechumenal pathway for married life is structured such that there includes a personal mentoring of the engaged couple by a married mentor/sponsor couple during the proximate, immediate and *mystagogia* periods.[71] Mentoring not only provides the personal preparation of the parties but also the ecclesial nature of preparation that is inherent to the sacrament.[72]

2.1.1 Determining Canonical Readiness

Accorded by human nature, the right to marry is a fundamental right of all persons, albeit not totally unrestricted in view of the greater good (cf. c. 843).[73]

---

68 Canon 1063, 2°.

69 See Fintan Gavin, "Canon 1063: Marriage Preparation as a Lifetime Journey," *StC,* 39 (2005), 186. See also ibid., 182-184 for a summary of the drafting of c. 1063 and the debate within the *coetus* regarding the *right* to marriage preparation.

70 "It is for the local ordinary to take care that such assistance is organized fittingly, after he has also heard men and women proven by their experience and expertise if it seems opportune" (c. 1064).

71 Numerous marriage formational programs in the United States call for the use of mentor or sponsor couples. See also USCCB, "An Analysis of Diocesan Marriage Preparation Policies: Formational Programs, 8," http://www.usccb.org/issues-and-action/marriage-and-family/marriage/marriage-preparation/mpanalysis.cfm (accessed on 14 Nov. 2023). Regarding the "guidance of a few exemplary couples of Christian spouses, dialog with future spouses individually and as a group" occurs in addition to clergy and experts during proximate preparation, see also Benedict XVI, Address to the Participants in the Plenary Assembly of the Pontifical Council for the Family, February 8, 2010; *CFHL,* 150-151. See also Gavin, *Pastoral Care in Marriage Preparation (Can. 1063),* 98-99.

72 The faithful may also be involved as qualified catechists in preparing Catholics who have not yet received the sacrament of confirmation, to receive it prior to marriage, as called for in c. 1065 §1.

73 "The right to marry is not absolute... It depends on the capacity to exercise the right. Capacity is determined by certain factors or standards which derive from natural law itself or from ecclesiastical (and civil) legislation" (Thomas Doyle, "The Individual's Right to Marry in the Context of the Common Good," in *StC*, 13 (1979), 266.

In fact, although framed in a positive statement: "All persons who are not prohibited by law can contract marriage," canon 1058 emphasizes that the right to marry "is subject to limitations of divine and ecclesial law." Canon 1059 further states that a marriage with at least one Catholic party is governed by divine law and canon law without prejudice to the competence of civil authority regarding the civil effects of the same marriage. "Before a marriage is celebrated, it must be evident that nothing stands in the way of its valid and licit celebration" (c. 1066). Positive proof of canonical readiness to marry must be ascertained. Furthermore, the person responsible for preparation must be morally certain about the freedom of the parties to marry.[74] The faithful are active in advising the pastor or local ordinary of any known impediments to the marriage of a given couple (cc. 1069 and 1070),[75] for example in response to marriage banns (c. 1067).[76]

The required prenuptial investigations and other evaluative tools are useful in assisting ministers to discover possible impediments and deficiencies, as administered according to the norms established by the conference of bishops. To provide for the spectrum of diversity concerning culture and marital customs around the world, legislative action by the conference of bishops is permitted according to the norm of canon 1067:

> The conference of bishops is to establish norms about the examination of spouses and about the marriage banns or other opportune means to accomplish the investigations necessary before marriage. After these norms have been diligently observed, the pastor can proceed to assist at the marriage.[77]

---

74 See Donal Kelly, "Part I: The Sacraments; Title VII: Marriage," in Gerard Sheehy et al. (eds.), *The Canon Law: Letter & Spirit, A Practical Guide to the Code of Canon Law* (Collegeville, MN: The Liturgical Press, 1995) 581.

75 "All the faithful are obliged to reveal any impediments they know about to the pastor or local ordinary before the celebration of marriage" (c.1069). "If someone other than the pastor who is to assist at a marriage has conducted the investigations, the person is to notify the pastor about the results as soon as possible through an authentic document" (c. 1070).

76 For an exception to positive proof required and the assistance of the community in the danger of death, see c. 1068. See also c. 1077 for another special case in which the local ordinary can prohibit marriage for a grave cause for as long as the cause continues.

77 Canon 1067.

To accommodate regional circumstances as per canon 1067, the National Conference of Catholic Bishops issued complementary legislation that became effective on December 1, 2000.[78]

This legislation further gives general directives and requirements applicable to all dioceses to provide for a large degree of uniformity and consistency in marriage preparation. However, it also grants discretion to the diocesan bishop in approving the type of education and pastoral preparation such that the program or process can be adapted to local needs and circumstances. This is consonant with a marriage catechumenal pathway.

2.1.2 Catechetical Topics

In order to deepen the conversion that was begun in the remote period through an appropriation of the doctrine of the faith, the importance of canon 1063, 1° with regard to preaching, social communication, and catechesis is evident in this period. In particular, instruments such as books, videos, podcasts, and websites are utilized in both proximate and immediate preparation in accordance with canons 822-831.

Furthermore, guided by the norm of canon 1063, 2° the proximate period provides time to verify and promote the maturation of human values pertaining to the relationships, including the chaste friendship that characterizes engagement[79] and the interpersonal relationship of spouses that is rooted in the matrimonial covenant. A mature understanding of Christian marriage as a covenantal partnership of the whole of life, *totius vitae consortium* is to be ensured,[80] inclusive of those canons relevant to the following: marital covenant in comparison with marital contract, free consent, consummation, marital ends, essential properties, and sacramentality of marriage.[81]

---

78 See National Conference of Catholic Bishops (NCCB), decree, Complementary Norm for Canon 1067: The Investigation of the Freedom to Marry, October 20, 2000: http://www.usccb.org/beliefs-and-teachings/what-we-believe/canon-law/complementary-norms/canon-1067-the-investigation-of-freedom-to-marry.cfm (accessed on 14 Nov. 2023). For example, due to the transient nature of many faithful in the United States, the norm does not mention marriage banns but allows for additional documentation such as affidavits to attest to the Catholic party's freedom to marry.

79 See *PSM,* no. 32.

80 Cf. *FC* 66.

81 See Lynda Robitaille, "Pastoral Care and Those Things Which Must Precede the Celebration of Marriage: [cc. 1063-1075]," in John Beal et al., eds., *New Commentary on the Code of Canon Law* (New York/Mahwah, NJ: Paulist Press, 2000) 1263. Cf. *PSM* 35.

Canon 1055 defines marriage using theologico-juridical language:

> The matrimonial covenant, by which a man and a woman establish between themselves a partnership of the whole of life, [*totius vitae consortium*], and which is ordered by its nature to the good of the spouses, [*bonum coniugum*], and the procreation and education of offspring, has been raised by Christ the Lord to the dignity of a sacrament between the baptized.[82]

The current canonical terminology on marriage is influenced by the Second Vatican Council's vision of the "*intima communitas vitae et amoris coniugalis*"[83] that flows directly from the marriage covenant. While marriage is a divine institution, Lawler notes that the Church instituted the *sacrament* of marriage and its institutional forms.[84] As such, marriage establishes a new juridical reality in the Church with essential rights and obligations[85] that involve the *bonum sacramenti,* the *bonum fidei,* and the *bonum prolis.*[86]

The 1917 code described the marriage contract in terms of the hierarchical ends of the object of consent: primarily, the procreation and education of children and secondarily, mutual assistance and the remedy for concupiscence (*CIC/17*, c. 1013 §1) through the "perpetual and exclusive rights to the body, for those actions that are themselves suitable for the generation of children" (*CIC/17*, c. 1081 §2).[87] In contrast to this rather utilitarian description of marriage, the revised code typically views *matrimonium in fieri* as "the matrimonial covenant" and

---

82 Canon 1055.

83 Translations of *GS* 4 vary in English for the original Latin: *DE,* 1100: "the intimate sharing of married life and love;" *Flannery1* 950: "the intimate partnership of life and the love;" Walter M. Abbott, *The Documents of Vatican II* (NY: Guild Press, 1966) 250: "the intimate partnership of married life and love."

84 See Michael Lawler, "Blessed Are Spouses Who Love, for Their Marriages Will Be Permanent: A Theology of the Bonds in Marriage," *The Jurist,* 55 (1995) 220.

85 See c. 1151 for the positive formulation of the mutual duty and right of spouses to sustain conjugal living; see also cc. 1134-1140 which define: effects of the perpetual and exclusive bond of marriage (c. 1134); the equal duty regarding marital obligations and rights (c. 1135); the duty and right of spouses to care for their offspring (c. 1136); and the canonical legitimacy of children (cc. 1137-1140).

86 For a discussion of St. Augustine's *tri bona* (*bonum fidei, bonum prolis,* and *bonum sacramenti)*, see Patrick Connolly, The Nature of Marriage as Proposed in the *Codex Iuris Canonici* and in the *Codex Canonum Ecclesiarum Orientalium*, JCD thesis, Ottawa, Saint Paul University, 1995, 18. Compare St. Augustine, *De genesi ad litteram,* liber 9, cap. 7, no. 12, in J. Migne, ed., *Patrologia latina*, vol. 34 (Paris: Migne, 1845) col. 397.

87 *Codex iuris canonici Pii X Pontificis Maximi iussu digestu, Benedicti Papæ XV auctoritate promulgates* (Rome: Typis polyglottis Vaticanis, 1917). Eng. trans. in Edward N. Peters, *The 1917 Pio-Benedictine Code of Canon Law in English Translation with Extensive Scholarly Apparatus* (San Francisco: Ignatius Press, 2001) 372.

matrimonium in facto esse as the "partnership of the whole of life."[88] This "working definition" has its roots in the theology of the Second Vatican Council principally found in the *Pastoral Constitution on the Church in the Modern World, Gaudium et spes* and reflects a personalist approach not found in any of the canons on marriage of the earlier code.[89]

The word *covenant*,[90] which is used to translate the Latin word *foedus* in canon 1055 of the revised code, has a theologically rich meaning rooted in the covenant that God established with his chosen people (Jer 31:33) and in the sacred reality of the Church as the spouse of Christ according to Pauline understanding (Eph 5:32).

The marital covenant is established through legitimately manifested consent between persons qualified by law (cc. 1057 §1; 1058 and 1059; *CCC* 1626), who possess the necessary capacity and are free of impediments rooted in divine or ecclesial law (c. 1073 and 1075; cf. cc. 1083-1094). No human power can supply for this private juridic act of consent[91] (c. 1057 §1), neither relatives nor legal or ecclesial entities. Moreover, canon 1057 §2 qualifies consent: "Matrimonial consent is an act of the will by which a man and a woman mutually give and accept each other through an irrevocable covenant in order to establish marriage." This canon presumes that the will has been determined by the knowledge of marriage as defined by the Church in canons 1055 §1 and 1056. Fittingly, valid consent must be free of defects of intellect and will, and devoid of human incapacity (cc. 1095-1103).

A valid marriage is consummated through the conjugal act of the bride and groom who become one flesh in a human fashion and in a manner that is suitable in itself for the procreation of offspring (c. 1061 §1). In light of the widespread use of contraception in the Western world, some forms of which affect the

---

88 See John Beal, "Title VII: Marriage: [cc. 1055-1165]," in *CLSA Comm*, 1240-1241. To distinguish between "marriage in the act of being constituted" and "marriage in the act of being lived out" canonists have long spoken of *matrimonium in fieri* and *matrimonium in facto esse,* respectively. The commentators of the 1917 code referred to *matrimonium in fieri* as the contract and *matrimonium in facto esse* as the sacred bond, with the emphasis markedly on the former.

89 See Ladislas Örsy, "Christian Marriage: Doctrine and Law *Glossae* on Canons 1012-1015," *The Jurist* 40 (1980) 302-306.

90 See John Beal, "Title VII: Marriage" in *CLSA Comm*, 1241, who noted the Revision Commission of the 1983 code used the terms *contract* and *covenant* interchangeably. See also Ladislas Örsy, "Marriage in the Code of Canon Law," in *Law and Justice* 88 (1986) 12, who suggests that within the term *covenant* is the notion of *contract* accompanied by enriched meaning. For an in-depth treatment of covenant versus contract see Connolly, 89-94.

91 See John Huels, "Acts with a Juridic Effect in the Canons on Marriage," in *Studia Canonica* 49 (2015) 314.

physical act itself, valid consummation may be delayed accordingly.[92] The Second Vatican Council recognized that conjugal communion is a physical, spiritual, and social reality that is intended to signify the mutual life-giving indissoluble union of two baptized spouses, created through the shared covenantal love of God that redounds to the well-being of society.[93]

Following this important understanding, canon 1096 §1 requires for validity that:

> For matrimonial consent to exist, the contracting parties must be at least not ignorant that marriage is a permanent partnership between a man and a woman ordered to the procreation of offspring by means of some sexual cooperation.

"At least not ignorant" indicates the minimal knowledge of the object of consent required for validity in order for the object to be willed.[94] Regarding the ends of marriage as reflected in the revised code, the good of the spouses and the procreation and education of children are equally important (c. 1055).[95]

Arising from the irrevocable personal consent is the unbreakable bond, "*vinculum sacrum*" which by its nature is perpetual and exclusive (c. 1134). Furthermore, it takes on a juridic dimension evidenced in canon 1056, which states, "The essential properties of marriage are unity and indissolubility, which

---

92 Cf. c. 1142: Until consummation occurs, the valid marriage between baptized is termed *ratum et non consummatum* and can be dissolved by the Roman Pontiff for a just cause according to the prescripts of law. Under certain circumstances even a new marriage can then be contracted (cc. 1142-1147; 1697-1706). Once consummated however, the marriage is termed *ratum et consummatum* and cannot be dissolved by human power (c. 1141). Thus, the delay of consummation has juridic significance.

93 See Barnard Häring, "Fostering the Nobility of Marriage and the Family," in *Commentary on the Documents of Vatican II*, ed. Herbert Vorgrimler (Montreal: Palm Publishers, 1969) 5: 233. Cf. Connolly, 91-92.

94 "From an analysis of the principles of Thomistic rational psychology illustrated in Rotal jurisprudence we know that an act of matrimonial consent placed with sufficient general knowledge of what marriage naturally consists of—even though this knowledge might be somewhat vague and incomplete—and placed with free consent of the will, is all that is necessary to create the natural marital pact, which in the baptized is *eo ipso, ex opere operato*, elevated to the Sacrament of Marriage." Kenneth Boccafola, "Lack of Faith and Its Effect on the Validity of the Matrimonial Consent of the Baptized," *The Jurist* 74 (2014) 65. See also Gramunt et. al., *Canons and Commentaries on Marriage*, 40-41.

95 "No longer, therefore, is the act of consent to be viewed juridically as primarily the exchange of the '*ius in corpus*'; rather the rights exchanged, the essential duties and obligations, must be fully human and truly interpersonal" (Brian G. O'Loughlin, *Marriage, A Covenant and Consortium Totius Vitae: Scriptural Basis, Conciliar Teaching and The Revised Code of Canon Law*, JCD thesis, Ottawa, Saint Paul University, 1985, xiv).

in Christian marriage obtain a special firmness by reason of the sacrament."[96] While unity and indissolubility are the essential properties of all true marriages, sacramental marriages enjoy a special measure of firmness. Sacramentality is intrinsic to the nature of the marriage bond between the baptized (c. 1055 §2).

As an action of Christ and the Church, sacraments are "signs and means which express and strengthen the faith, render worship to God, and effect the sanctification of humanity and thus contribute in the greatest way to establish, strengthen, and manifest ecclesiastical communion" (c. 840). There has been much debate regarding the efficacy and even validity of the sacrament of marriage among those baptized who possess weak or little faith. Boccafola stated of those baptized, "As long as a one freely seeks to enter a real, true natural nuptial pact, such consent is sufficient to enter a valid contract. Nothing more specific needs to be included in that consent" precisely because the sacrament is not extrinsic to the contract. Furthermore, in willing the marriage contract one implicitly wills that which is inseparably connected, the sacrament. [97] Moreover, this circumstance is an evangelization opportunity for which the marriage catechumenate is well-suited.

2.2 Theological and Doctrinal Considerations of Proximate Preparation

The General Directory for Catechesis rightly identified that those who are preparing for marriage "are more disposed than ever to seek out the true meaning of life."[98] Proximate preparation offers the opportunity of specific formation for married life through a gradual process of appropriation and assimilation involving a deeper integration of religious catechesis with interpersonal elements of the marriage. Accordingly, beginning with the discernment of an intended spouse through the engagement period, proximate preparation must include the elements of intellectual, human, spiritual, and pastoral dimensions in order to properly dispose future spouses for the holiness and duties intrinsic to the vocation of matrimony.

2.2.1. Readiness for Marriage

At this time pastoral care should initially include the determination of the physical, psychological, pedagogical, moral and legal readiness for marriage and family life. Wherever lacking, pastoral care should assist the party in becoming

---

96 On the inviolable stability see Pius XI, Encyclical Letter on Christian Marriage *Casti connubii* 34, December 31, 1930: *AAS* 22 (1930) 551; Eng. trans. in Claudia Carlen, ed., *The Papal Encyclicals 1903-1939* (Wilmington, NC: McGrath Publishing Co., 1981) 396.
97 Boccafola, 68. Cf., *CPML* 44-45.
98 *GDC* 176.

ready to the extent that is possible.[99] In some cases this may also involve preparation for the celebration of the initiation sacraments of confirmation and the Most Holy Eucharist through which the baptized will be "more perfectly bound to the Church," be endowed special spiritual strength and will "manifest in a concrete way that unity of the People of God" as true witnesses of Christ.[100]

The Pontifical Council for the Family rightly recognized that this stage must involve personal, familial, and ecclesial dimensions.[101] The social and familial milieu in which the vocation of marriage was discerned during remote preparation will positively or negatively impact the relationships to be formed in the new nuclear family.[102] For example, issues of prolonged adolescence and delayed emergence from the family home can have an effect on maturity, selflessness, and the ability to make commitments.[103] The formation of this proximate period should reinforce any positive social sense engendered in the parties' families of origin and also positively orient them toward their own future families. In addition to an understanding of healthy relationships, the United States Conference of Catholic Bishops recommended formation regarding sexuality, the virtue of chastity, and responsible parenthood.[104]

Pastoral care aimed at readiness for marriage must be directed at fostering the awareness of the communal nature of humanity, as a reflection of and a participation in the likeness of the one Triune God. God as a God of relationship is the origin of any union based on committed self-gifting love. "God is love" (Jn 4:16) and is the giver of all good gifts (Jas 1:17). The right understanding of the stewardship of these gifts (Gn 2:15) includes knowing oneself in relationship to God and freely making the proper moral choices in managing the gifts of relationships, temporal and spiritual goods, and even one's own body. It requires of the steward a unity of body and soul in addition to the self-knowledge that

99 Cf. *PSM* 35.

100 *LG* 11; *Flannery1*, 361-362.

101 See *PSM* 32. Note: The Pontifical Council for the Family [PCF] preceded the Dicastery of Laity, Family and Life.

102 Cf. Synod of Bishops, III Extraordinary General Assembly, *The Pastoral Challenges of the Family in the Context of Evangelization* Instrumentum Laboris, June 24, 2014, 43-45; Eng. trans. at: https://www.vatican.va/roman_curia/synod/documents/rc_synod_doc_20140626_instrumentum-laboris-familia_en.html (accessed on 14 Nov. 2023).

103 See ibid., 80. See also *PSM* 33.

104 See USCCB, *Marriage: Love and Life in the Divine Plan* (Washington DC: United States Conference of Catholic Bishops, 2009) 44. Cf. *PSM* 35, which adds the conjugal act with its requirements.

although a creature, one is a sharer "in the light of the divine mind."[105] The stewardship of gifts is a communal project guided by divine wisdom.

Reflecting on Genesis 1, the Fathers of Vatican II emphasized that men and women are created for communion: "This partnership of man and woman constitutes the first form of communion between people. For by their most innermost nature men and women are social beings; and if they do not enter into relationships with others they can neither live nor develop their gifts."[106] The "reciprocal giving of self reveals the spousal nature of love"[107] from which flows the mission of the family "to guard, reveal and communicate love"[108] in the world. Readiness for marriage means readiness to fully embrace God's loving design for marriage and family.

2.2.2. Catechetical Topics

The goal of the proximate period is to engender a clear understanding of essential characteristics of Christian marriage, which the PCF summarized as:

> . . . unity, fidelity, indissolubility, fruitfulness; the conscience of faith regarding the priority of the sacramental Grace which associates the spouses, as subjects and ministers of the sacrament to the love of Christ, the Bridegroom of the Church; the willingness to carry out the mission proper to families in the educational, social and ecclesial areas.[109]

In order to accomplish this end, engaged couples will need to be taught that the freedom of consent required by law has its origin in God, "as its author, its primary witness, and its guarantor"[110] whose love is freely given without coercion, force or fear. Consent is "the indispensable element that makes marriage" (*CCC* 1626), by establishing the perpetual coinherence of the spouses.[111] The immediate object is the mutual giving and accepting of the spouses to create the covenantal union encompassing the whole of married life, which "includes the procreative dimension."[112]

---

105 *GS* 15; *Flannery1*, 915.
106 *GS* 12; *Flannery1*, 175.
107 *PSM* 40.
108 *PSM* 4.
109 *PSM* 45.
110 M. Lawler, "Marriage as Covenant in the Catholic Tradition" in E. Ellison, and J. Witte JR., eds., *Covenant Marriage in Comparative Perspective* (Grand Rapids, MI /Cambridge, UK: William B. Eerdmans Publishing Company, 2005) 87. Cf. *GS* 48 and *CCC* 1603.
111 See Lawler, "Blessed Are Spouses," 221; Cf. *CCC* 1627 and c. 1057 §2.
112 Kelly, "Part I: The Sacraments; Title VII: Marriage," 575.

Especially for those engaged couples actively cohabitating, consummation of the marriage may not have its due import. With regard to the personalist understanding of the marriage covenant, Himes and Coriden tested the present canonical understanding of consummation in consideration of the nature of *ratum*:

> In the traditional view consummation was attained by the first act of coitus following the exchange of consent. The logic was clear, if marriage is a contract involving the spouses' exchange of rights to their bodies then the deal was sealed upon the first exercise of the right. However, if marriage is a covenant of love between two persons involving the creation of a consortium of intimacy it is less clear that one act of sexual intercourse is an appropriate symbol of consummation.[113]

Looking deeper into the sign of the conjugal act reveals a transcendence that can perhaps make sense of the traditional view of consummation. The communion of the bodies in this perspective is a sign and pledge of the "happy covenanting" of the couple with God in marriage (Gen 2:18-25).[114] The Council Fathers spoke of the interrelationship of human and divine love:

> Authentic married love is caught up into divine love and is directed and enriched by the redemptive power of Christ and the salvific action of the Church, with the result that the spouses are effectively led to God and are helped and strengthened in their lofty role as fathers and mothers.[115]

Engaged couples must come to appreciate that participation in the divine love is a participation in a redemptive and creative love. Moreover, divine love is fruitful.

The Council Fathers understood, "Children are the supreme gift of marriage and contribute to the greatest extent to the good of the parents themselves."[116] Pope Saint John Paul's theology of the body espoused that fertility is a divine gift. The stewardship of that gift through natural family planning (NFP) methods creates intimacy in the married couple, as it requires continual sensitivity, communication, commitment and cooperation.

The marital ends of the good of the spouses and the procreation of children are mutually beneficial and are fundamental to role that God intends for those

---

113 K. Himes and J.A. Coriden, "Indissolubility", in *Theological Studies*, 65 (2004), 483-484. For more on these complexities of consummation see Lawler, "Blessed Are Spouses," 232-237.

114 Bruggeman, 53. Cf. *FC* 25.

115 *GS* 48; *Flannery1*, 951.

116 *GS* 50; *Flannery1*, 953.

called to the vocation of married life. However, "Even in cases where despite the intense desire of the spouses there are no children, marriage still retains its character of being a whole manner and communion of life and preserves its value and indissolubility."[117]

The good of the spouses (*bonum coniugum*) arises from the human and supernatural growth in holiness and perfection mutually gained throughout the covenantal life. Husband and wife "help and serve each other by their marriage partnership; they become conscious of their unity and experience it more deeply from day to day . . . fulfilling their conjugal and family role . . . they increasingly further their own perfection and their mutual sanctification, and together they render glory to God."[118] According to Burke, the *bonum coniugum* is a finality gained through the interior transformation that ensues from faithfully sharing daily life.[119]

Engaged couples should come to fully comprehend that marriage in the divine plan is seen as the vocation of a communion of love. The image of God revealed through marriage is a personal loving communion of persons, which is unitive, generative, and perpetual.[120] The etiological statement of marriage in Genesis 2:24, "Therefore a man leaves his father and his mother and cleaves to his wife, and they become one flesh," speaks to the intended unity of marriage. In the Gospel of Matthew, Jesus appended, "So they are no longer two but one flesh. What therefore God has joined together, let not man put asunder" (Mt 19:6). Haring holds that "the stability of the covenant is explained by the 'divine ordination,' which is more than a factual arrangement. Its counterpart is the divinely-willed stability and irrevocability of the consent."[121] The very Word of God makes the essential properties of unity and indissolubility normative.[122]

---

117 *GS* 50; *Flannery1*, 954.

118 *GS* 48; *Flannery1*, 950-951.

119 See Cormac Burke, "The *Bonum Coniugum* and the *Bonum Prolis*, Ends or Properties of Marriage?" *The Jurist* 49 (1989) 706-708.

120 Compare from *Familiaris consortio*:

> God created man in his own image and likeness calling him to existence through love, he called him at the same time for love. God is love and in himself he lives a mystery of personal loving communion. Creating the human race in his own image and continually keeping it in being, God inscribed in the humanity of man and woman the vocation, and thus the capacity and responsibility, of love and communion. Love is therefore the fundamental and innate vocation of every human being.

FC 11; *OTF* 9.

121 Haring, "Fostering the Nobility of Marriage and the Family," 233.

122 See John Paul II, *TOB* 26.

The exclusive relationship between one man and one woman is inherent to the institution of marriage. "This is a moral unity, conditioned and constituted by love. Love not only unites the two subjects, but allows them to be interpenetrated, spiritually belonging to one another."[123] Cleaving of the man to the woman in the marital covenant involves more than a mere physical unity. The moral unity is a unity of personhood without confusion.

The Council Fathers spoke of the penetration of the spirit of Christ in the spouses as the agency of the sacramental strengthening in marriages between the baptized: "Spouses, therefore, are fortified and, as it were, consecrated for the duties and dignity of their state by a special sacrament; . . . spouses are penetrated with the spirit of Christ and their whole life is suffused by faith, hope and charity; . . . and together they render glory to God."[124] A Christian marriage "that both reflects and shares in the divine love" is an efficacious sign (*CCC* 1613) of God's covenant with humanity and a true manifestation of Christ's love for the Church.[125]

2.3 Suggestions for Pastoral Implementation of Intermediate and Proximate Preparation

To date, only the pastoral guidelines *Catechumenal Pathways for Married Life* inserted an intermediate phase between the remote period and the proximate period of marriage preparation beginning about twelve to fourteen months prior to marriage. Accordingly, the intermediate phase is a time of discernment and reception into the catechumenate phase, which is comprised of three stages: proximate, immediate, and first years' accompaniment. This phase can be provided whenever couples join later in the process.[126] The length of the intermediate phase is determined according to the formation of the couple, from a few weeks to a few months in order to deepen their baptismal identity. This is a time of discernment led by a married couple, joined by a priest, when possible,

---

123 John Paul II, *TOB* 320.

124 *GS* 4; *Flannery1* 951.

125 Cf. Michael Smith Foster, *Annulment, The Wedding that Was: How the Church Can Declare a Marriage Null* (New York, Mahwah: Paulist Press, 1999) 43-44. Cf. John Paul II, *TOB*, 347: "As a sacrament born of the mystery of redemption and reborn in a certain sense, in the spousal love of Christ and of the Church, marriage is an efficacious expression of the saving power of God."

126 *CPML* 31. Cf. *PSM* 51:

> [This preparation] can be dispensed with only for proportionally serious reasons . . . the parish priest and his co-workers will have the responsibility of offering them some occasions to make up an adequate knowledge of the doctrinal, moral and sacramental aspects set out in the proximate preparation for marriage and finally include them in the phase of immediate preparation.

who discuss the motives for marriage preparation and marriage in the Church.[127] They assist the engaged couple in considering their subjective and objective ease or difficulty in understanding and living a Christian marriage in the Church, including the essential properties of indissolubility, fidelity, and the ordering of marriage to the good of the spouses and the good of offspring. It is a time of introspection and reflection on their readiness to embark upon a journey of faith conversion in the marriage catechumenate. The intermediate phase concludes with a simple ritual entry into the marriage catechumenate that can be celebrated with the ecclesial community or within the catechumenal group as circumstances necessitate. Special attention should be given regarding how this and other rituals are culturally perceived. Entrusting couples with a Bible is a fitting symbol at this time.[128]

The Pontifical Council for the Family stated that "proximate preparation takes place during the period of engagement and generally coincides with the period of youth,"[129] whereas the United States Conference of Catholic Bishops included the time from puberty through formal engagement.[130] The Dicastery for the Laity, the Family and Life indicated that this period ideally begins approximately one year prior to the wedding date.[131] The prescribed canonical investigation/ examination ought to be accomplished at this time or later as necessitated by pastoral circumstances.[132] Sessions with the catechumenal team, experts, and clergy can be arranged based on subject matter and availability of pastoral resources. For example, couples may be introduced to Church-approved methods of Natural Family Planning and infertility treatment, such as NaPro

---

127 *CPML* 41.

128 *CPML* 23, 26, 37, 41-43.

129 *PSM* 32-33.

130 Cf. USCCB, *Marriage: Love and Life in the Divine Plan,* 44. For the care required in choosing a partner, which belongs to proximate preparation see *Casti Conubii*, no. 115, in *AAS* 22 (1930) 585-586, Eng. trans. in Carlen, *The Papal Encyclicals*, 410.

131 For alternate views regarding the betrothal period in a catechumenal model see Michael Lawler, "A Marital Catechumenate, A Proposal" in *INTAMS review, Journal for Marriage & Spirituality,* 13/2 (2007) 161-177.

132 See *CPML* 65 regarding "canonical talks;" Benedict XVI, Address on the occasion of the Inauguration of the Judicial Year of the Tribunal of the Roman Rota, January 22, 2011. Pope Benedict XVI stated of the canonical examination:

> This examination has a mainly juridical purpose: to ascertain that which impedes the valid and licit celebration of the wedding. However juridical does not mean formal, as though it were a bureaucratic step, like filling up a form based on set questions. Instead it is a unique pastoral opportunity in which, through a dialogue full of respect and cordiality, the pastor seeks to help the person to face seriously the truth about himself or herself and about his or her own human and Christian vocation for marriage.

technology by experts in the field.[133] Personalized sessions with mentor/sponsor couples can follow group session topics to deepen understanding and encourage practical assimilation of the teaching. The latter sessions are usually held at the home of the mentor/sponsor couple in order to give witness of the domestic Church.[134] The number of group and mentor/sponsor couple sessions may be increased or decreased according to the particular needs of the engaged couple, (e.g., their faith foundation and psycho-social disposition). There are several published works designed for personal preparation that may be used during this time and may be adapted to the group or mentor/sponsor couple format. Suggested catechetical topics are listed in Appendix II, but may vary by the resource selected.[135]

During the period of proximate preparation, a praxis nuptial liturgy or a "wedding workshop" may be offered for engaged couples at which the pastor or another clergy member first demythologizes secular wedding practices and explains the Catholic nuptial rite with its meaningful signs and symbols. Mentor/sponsor couples may then assist him in role-modeling a modified praxis nuptial liturgy, which can be helpful for those engaged parties with limited liturgical experience.[136]

---

133 See John Paul II, *The Theology of the Body, Human Love in the Divine Plan* (Boston, MA: Pauline Books and Media, 1997) 349, 437-438 (hereafter *TOB*). Cf. Paul VI, encyclical letter *Humanae Vitae* 16: *AAS* 60 (1968) 491-492. Eng. trans. in *Flannery2*, 405-406. For an in-depth study of infertility and approved treatment, see Sebastian Tumuslime, *The Church's Response to Childless Couples: Canonical and Pastoral Considerations on Sterility in the Ugandan Context (c. 1084 §3),* JCD thesis (Ottawa: Saint Paul University, 2017).

134 *PSM* 37 which infers the accompaniment of married couples, "During this stage of preparation, frequent meetings will be necessary in an atmosphere of dialogue, friendship and prayer, with the participation of pastors and catechists. […] Christian married couples who are apostolically committed, in a vision of sound Christian optimism, can contribute to shedding greater light on Christian life in the context of the vocation to marriage […]."

135 "*Required* topics are: Communication (includes conflict resolution, problem solving); Sacramental Marriage (a permanent, covenantal, exclusive, unconditional, life giving, commitment that unites the couple as a sign of Christ's love); Sexuality (includes Natural Family Planning, intimacy); and Spirituality (includes faith, moral decision making, values, prayer). *Recommended* topics are: Self-Awareness (includes personality inventories, roles); Parenthood (includes family of origin and extended family issues); and Finances (includes stewardship, lifestyle, and career issues)" as found in USCCB, "An Analysis of Diocesan Marriage Preparation Policies," 8."

136 This was a practice in the Diocese of Cleveland, Ohio, under the direction of Rev. Daniel Schlegel. Music ministers were also present to make suggestions for proper liturgical music and provide accompaniment during the praxis liturgy. The engaged couples and family members gained an understanding of the *OCM* and of their roles and deepened their appreciation for the liturgy as it points to married life.

Since the Pontifical Council for the Family recommended that the depth of the engagement be recognized as a significant sign of the initial commitment toward marriage, the blessing of the engaged couple or rite of betrothal[137] can serve as a liturgical marker for the end of the period of proximate preparation.[138] A blessing of the engagement rings may be included in places where this custom is commonplace. As a caution the Dicastery for Laity, Family and Life stated, "The celebration of the rite should in no way be confused with marriage. For this reason, neither the promise of marriage nor the special blessing of the engaged couple should ever be performed during the celebration of Mass."[139]

3. Immediate Preparation - Purification and Enlightenment

The period of immediate preparation should take place in the months and weeks before the celebration of the marriage.[140] The parallel period in the baptismal catechumenate is the period of purification and enlightenment, which similarly focuses on prayerful recollection of all that has been learned as well as continued spiritual growth, founded in liturgy.[141] The preparative liturgical catechesis that is specifically called for in the code is directed toward the meaning of marital rite with its implications for the spouses' mission in the Church and the holiness due marriage.[142]

3.1 Canonical Considerations of Immediate Preparation

Canon 1063, 3° urges the pastor of souls to take care that their ecclesiastical community offers assistance to ensure that there is "a fruitful liturgical celebration of marriage which is to show that the spouses signify and share in the mystery of

---

137 See *PSM* 17. Cf. *De Benedictionibus*, edito typica, 31 May 1984, nos. 195-214, Typis polyglottis Vaticanis, 1984, 79-84, adapted English version, Book of Blessings, The Roman Ritual, Approved for Use in the Dioceses of the United States of America by the National Conference of Catholic Bishops and Confirmed by the Apostolic See, prepared by ICEL, New York, Catholic Book Publishing Co. 1989, nos. 195-214. See Robert Ruhnke, *For Better and Forever: A Resource for Couples Preparing for Christian Marriage*, rev. ed. (San Antonio, TX: Litho Press, 2012) 167-169. See also *CPML*, nos. 59-62. See canon 1062 regarding the provision for betrothal/promise to marry and the intention of the NCCB to issue no complementary norm, https://www.usccb.org/comm ittees/canonical-affairs-church-governance/complementary-norms#tab--canon-1062-§1-engagement (accessed on 8 Nov. 2023).

138 This presupposes that the engaged couple has already met with the priest or deacon and has completed all that is required for the prenuptial investigation and their freedom to marry has been determined.

139 *CPML*, 61. Cf., Book of Blessings, 198.

140 See *FC* 66.

141 See Morris, 166. Cf. Robitaille, 1263.

142 Cf. *PSM* 55-57.

the unity and fruitful love between Christ and the Church."[143] Hartmann suggested that this canon does not intend to narrowly focus on the liturgical celebration alone, but also on the "inherent connection between the wedding liturgy and a consistent sacramental life."[144] Pope Benedict XVI affirmed that the aim of this catechesis is to ensure that "the vocation of the spouses becomes an enrichment for the whole Christian community and especially in today's context a missionary and prophetic witness."[145] The Code of Canon Law supports the understanding of the nuptial liturgy as a celebration that both forms and informs the bride and groom, who administer the sacrament to one another in the Latin Church (cc. 836 and 837 §1; *CCC* 1623).[146] It duly recognizes that the formation in this mystery is a lifelong process.

3.1.1 The Liturgical Celebration

Liturgy is never a private work (c. 837); marriage itself is a public institution of social and ecclesial import and consequence. Kelly stated that "In addition to its sanctifying role, the liturgy also has a valuable teaching function for the spouses" and the entire gathered assembly.[147] Whether the nuptial liturgy[148] takes place within a celebration of the Most Holy Eucharist or outside of Mass, it is a formative experience. Liturgical preparation of the engaged couple is instrumental in aiding this outcome.

The Pontifical Council for the Family envisioned canonical talks with the parish priest[149] that will reinforce the obligations of Catholics to marry according to canonical form for the validity of the marriage (c. 1117). Accordingly, canon 1108 requires that marriage be contracted before a local ordinary, priest, deacon

---

143 *LG* 41; *Flannery1*, 399. For a contrasting view regarding the application of St. Paul's use of *mystery* in Ephesians see Kenneth Himes and James A. Coriden, "Indissolubility," *Theological Studies* 65 (2004) 493.
144 Hartmann, "Marriage and Future Practice of the Faith" 124.
145 Benedict XVI, Address to the Participants in the Plenary Assembly of the Pontifical Council for the Family, *CFHL*, 151.
146 See canon 1108 §3. "Only a priest validly assists at a marriage between Eastern parties, or between a Latin party and an Eastern party, whether Catholic or non-Catholic." See Francis, Apostolic Letter *motu proprio, De concordia inter Codices,* art. 6: *AAS* 108 (2016) 605.
147 Kelly, "Part I: The Sacraments; Title VII: Marriage," 580.
148 See c. 1120 regarding the faculty of the Conference of Bishops to draft its own rite of marriage "in keeping with the usages of place and people which accord the Christian spirit," which is to be approved by a general decree of the conference as per cc. 455 and 838 §3 and reviewed by the Holy See. Cf. Huels, "Acts with a Juridic Effect in the Canons on Marriage," 318.
149 *CPML* 65: If these talks mentioned in the *PSM* 50, were already incorporated into the proximate period, the content may be reviewed in the immediate period.

(c. 1111), or, if necessary (c. 1112), a lay person, who assists by asking for and receiving the manifestation of the consent of the parties before two witnesses.[150] Ordinary or extraordinary canonical form can be dispensed under certain circumstances (c. 1127 §2).

While outdoor weddings are popular in civil society, canon 1118 requires that a marriage between a Catholic and a baptized party take place in a parish church or with permission of the local ordinary or pastor in another church or oratory (§1), or with permission of the local ordinary some other suitable place (§2). The United States Conference of Catholic Bishops addresses the appropriateness of the celebration within a church setting:

> As a vocation, or call from God, marriage has a public and ecclesial status within the Church. Catholic spouses ordinarily exchange marital consent within a church setting, before a priest or deacon. The living-out of marriage takes place within the whole Body of Christ, which it serves and in which it finds nourishment.[151]

In contrast to the trend of destination weddings, an engaged couple recognizing the importance of the ecclesial status of marriage, may choose a parish church according to the norms of canon 1115, which is meaningful to the sacramental life of one or both of the parties. Marriage between a Catholic and a non-baptized party may be celebrated in a church. Another suitable place is possible for the celebration of a natural marriage (c. 1118). Ideally, the parties know the ecclesiastical minister.[152]

The Order of Celebrating Matrimony is to be observed faithfully without unsanctioned alterations, additions or omissions (c. 846),[153] keeping in mind the

---

150 Eastern Churches differ in that *CCEO,* c. 828 stipulates marriage is to be celebrated by a sacred rite, before a local hierarch, local pastor, or a priest (not a deacon or lay person) for validity. However, *CCEO,* c. 832 provides that a marriage can be validly and licitly celebrated in the presence of only the two witnesses if no priest, even a non-Catholic priest [Orthodox] can be approached, in the danger of death or if the state affairs continues for a month. The couple is to seek the nuptial blessing from a priest as soon as possible. In the Latin code the extraordinary form has no such provision for the latter blessing (cf. c. 1116). See also J. Abbass, *Two Codes in Comparison*, Rome: *Pontificio Instituto Orientale,* 2007, 18: "It is generally agreed that, because marriages involving Eastern Catholics must be celebrated with a sacred rite (*CCEO*, c. 828 §1), lay persons cannot be delegated to assist at interecclesial marriages or marriages of Eastern Catholics entrusted to the care of a Latin bishop."

151 USCCB, *Marriage: Love and Life in the Divine Plan*, 45. Cf. c. 1108 and *CCEO*, c. 828.

152 See Huels, "Acts with a Juridic Effect in the Canons on Marriage," 314, who finds that the act of the *assistens* isthe most important non-jurisdictional juridic act in marriage. See also c. 124.

153 See *Ordo celebrandi Matrimonium*, editio typica altera, nos. 33-38, *OCM*, 7-8.

right of the faithful "to worship God according to the prescripts of their own rite approved by the legitimate pastors of the Church" (c. 214). Instruction regarding optional regional adaptations prescribed for the marriage rite is to be given when needed.

3.1.2 Liturgy as a Participation in the Mystery of Unity and Fruitful Love

The Pontifical Council for the Family urged that the immediate period of formation should include a suitable liturgical preparation, which envisions the active informed participation of the engaged, in addition to special attention given to reconciliation.[154] Bearing this in mind, canon 1065 §2 states, "To receive the sacrament of marriage fruitfully spouses are urged especially to approach the sacraments of penance and of the Most Holy Eucharist." Though not an absolute obligation, the sacrament of penance provides an entry point for continuing evangelization and conversion, as the penitent encounters and experiences the divine mercy through forgiveness of sins (cc. 959-960) and actualizes a proper disposition for the celebration of matrimony.

Due to the connection that all sacraments have with the paschal mystery of Christ, it is especially fitting that two Catholics celebrate the sacrament of matrimony in the context of Eucharistic liturgy (*CCC* 1621).[155] Canon 834 §1 speaks to participation in the sanctifying action of the Church through liturgy:

> The Church fulfills its sanctifying function in a particular way through the sacred liturgy, which is an exercise of the priestly function of Jesus Christ. In the sacred liturgy, the sanctification of humanity is signified through sensible signs and effected in a manner proper to each sign. In the sacred liturgy, the whole public worship of God is carried out by the Head and the members of the mystical Body of Jesus Christ.[156]

In the nuptial liturgy the groom and the bride themselves are a sensible sign of the coming of the Kingdom.[157] As Breck observed, "The nuptial relationship achieves its true purpose and attains its true fullness insofar as it is based upon an eternal

---

154 See *PSM* 50, 52-53.

155 See ibid., 53.

156 Second Vatican Council, Constitution *Sacrosanctum Concilium* 7, December 4, 1963: *AAS* 56 (1964) 100-101(hereafter *SC*); Eng. trans. in *Flannery1,* 4-5.

157 "The spouses, by committing themselves mutually to each other, give a new orientation to their own life. They choose the values that marriage represents and they make their decisions and direct their actions accordingly. [...] When this new orientation is sealed by God's grace, it belongs to the saving events of the Kingdom" (Örsy, *Marriage in Canon Law,* 203).

covenantal commitment."[158] The liturgical preparation for the sacrament of marriage should assist the Catholic parties in understanding that "according to their own vocation, those who live in the marital state are bound by a special duty to work through marriage and the family to build up the people of God" (c. 226 §1).[159]

3.2 Theological and Doctrinal Considerations of Immediate Preparation

As the final period of preparation for marriage, immediate preparation calls for enlightenment and growth in the spiritual and personal readiness necessary to successfully undertake the rights and obligations of marriage. The United States Conference of Catholic Bishops summarizes these aspects and the involvement of wise mentors:[160]

> By the time of *immediate* preparation, the couple has developed a conviction that God is calling them to marriage with a particular person. Prayer, especially for the guidance of the Holy Spirit, and the help of wise mentors are crucial in this discernment process. Discernment also involves an honest assessment of qualities that are foundational for the marriage. These include an ability to make and keep a commitment, the desire for a lifelong, faithful relationship, and openness to children. The couple will also want to reflect on the values they share, their ability to communicate, and agreement on significant issues.[161]

This period is more characterized by intense spiritual preparation and interior reflection than by the catechesis of the earlier periods of preparation.[162] Roman suggested utilizing the Order Celebrating Marriage as the primary source of the experience of introspective prayer in addition to theological and scriptural reflection, which includes *lectio divina*. He asserted that prayer and liturgy are essential "to the continued conversion process of adults as they seek to live a new

---

158 J. Breck, *The Sacred Gift of Life: Orthodox Christianity and Bioethics*, Crestwood, NY, St. Vladimir's Seminary Press, 1998, 63.

159 See *Ordo celebrandi Matrimonium, editio typica altera,* 19 March 1990, no. 21, *OCM,* 5, for the circumstance in which a couple rejects what the Church intends in Marriage. See also cc. 843, 1101 §2 and 1071 §1, 4°. Cf. *FC* 56 and D. Nakameti, *Preparation for Marriage and Proof for Nullity,* JCD thesis, Roma, Pontificia Universitas Lateranensis, 2006, 64-65.

160 For requirements of pastoral workers and leaders in the field see *PSM,* no. 43.

161 USCCB, *Marriage: Love and Life in the Divine Plan*, 44-45.

162 See *OICA,* no. 139, *RCIA,* 77. See also M. Roman, *Nurturing a Living, Explicit, and Fruitful Profession of Faith: The Baptismal Catechumenate as a Comprehensive Christian Formation,* PhD thesis, New York, Fordham University, 2009, 218.

vocation, both in their own, individual, spiritual lives and in their parish community life."[163]

3.2.1 The Liturgical Celebration

With guidance, engaged couples should come to appreciate in liturgy that interaction with liturgical symbols is evocative on several levels of experience: human, biblical, ecclesial, and liturgical.[164] In addition, the discipleship experience accounts for the direct active response elicited through the encounter with symbol.[165] "For in the liturgy God speaks to his people, Christ is still proclaiming his Gospel, and the people respond both in song and in prayer."[166]

3.2.2 Liturgy as a Participation in the Mystery of Unity and Fruitful Love

"In the earthly liturgy we take part in a foretaste of the heavenly liturgy."[167] The Mass is a present spiritual participation in the eternal wedding feast of the Lamb (cf. Mt 22:2; cf. Rev 19:7) and an encounter with the mystery of unity and fruitful love that is Christ Jesus. By virtue of their royal priesthood, the newlyweds join in the offering of the Most Holy Eucharist.[168] "In this sacrifice of the New and Eternal Covenant, Christian spouses encounter the source from which their own marriage covenant flows, is interiorly structured and continuously renewed."[169] "Receiving the Eucharist as their 'first meal' together is a beautiful expression of the newlyweds' reliance on God to sustain and strengthen them throughout their lives."[170] The Catechism of the Catholic Church finds it "fitting that the spouses should seal their consent to give themselves to each other through the offering of their own lives by uniting it to the offering of Christ for his Church made present in the Eucharistic sacrifice" (*CCC* 1621).

---

163 Ibid., 226-227.

164 The response to symbols is related to human experiences both personally and culturally, e.g. the entrance procession of the bride and groom with their parents echoes a lifetime of familial support. Sacred scripture gives context to the experience of symbols, e.g. from the biblical accounts of God's covenantal relationship with his people, the couple recognizes that "through the sacrament God covenants with them and promises to sustain them" (See Örsy, *Marriage in Canon Law,* 272). The ecclesial experience regards the missionary nature of liturgical action, e.g., the call to service, to care for children and to provide hospitality via the domestic church. Dialog between the symbol and the lived experience provides the liturgical experience, e.g. "take this ring as a sign of my love and fidelity. . . ." elicits memory and future intention of the meaning attached to the words spoken.

165 See Morris, 133-134.

166 *SC* 33; *Flannery1* 11-12.

167 *SC* 8; *Flannery1* 5.

168 See *LG* 10.

169 *FC* 57; *OTF* 53.

170 USCCB, "The Order for Celebrating Matrimony within Mass," https://www.foryourmarriage.org/rite-for-celebrating-marriage-within-mass/ (accessed on 19 Nov. 2019).

3.3 Suggestions for Pastoral Implementation of Immediate Preparation

The Dicastery for the Laity, Family and Life suggested that a retreat to be offered at the beginning and at the ending of this final period of preparation.[171] Given the brevity of immediate preparation and proximity to the nuptial liturgy, two retreats may not be possible. Alternatively, at the first group gathering the betrothed or engaged couples may be presented with a symbolic object, such as a blessed votive candle inscribed with a prayer for discernment and participation in the spousal love of Christ for the Church. The witness of newly married couples regarding the "spiritual dynamic of Christian life that forms the basis of marriage"[172] may be incorporated. Follow up mentor/sponsor couple sessions are useful in assisting the betrothed or engaged couples in continued personal discernment and appropriation of the Christian vision of marriage.

In addition to a review of the main content of the journey, The Order of Celebrating Matrimony may be utilized the as the primary source of liturgical catechesis.[173] Accomplished in either a group or personalized setting, this catechesis and introspective prayer is to focus on the understanding of the bride and groom as ministers of the sacrament, the symbols and the ritual texts of the nuptial liturgy in addition to the lived implications of the celebration (see Appendix III).[174]

The prayer support of the community should be actively encouraged.[175] The betrothed or engaged are also to be introduced by the catechumenal team and/or the ecclesial community to "works of penance and charity, which help to root and strengthen the kingdom of Christ in souls" (c. 839). Finally, a retreat in which couples are able to celebrate the sacraments of penance and Eucharist would be ideal to help properly dispose the engaged couple for their nuptial celebration.[176]

4. Enrichment for Marriage - *Mystagogia*

The final period of a catechumenal pathway is the post-sacramental period, which in the Rite of Christian Initiation of Adults is known as *mystagogia.* For

---

171 See Section 3.1 and *CPML* 64.

172 See *CPML* 66.

173 Ordo celebrandi Matrimonium, editio typica altera 17; OCM, 4. See CPML 65 regarding discernment of the object.

174 *CPML* 68-69 elaborates on the "pedagogical approach" of the liturgical rite by which the "Christian spouses are called to become 'living icons' of Christ the Bridegroom".

175 If permitted, the engaged couples may have their pictures with brief biographies on display in the parish or on prayer cards. Cf. *PSM* 50, "Experiences of prayer (retreats, spiritual exercises for the engaged) in which the encounter with the Lord can make them discover the depth and beauty of the supernatural life."

176 *CPML* 65, 71.

both neophytes and newlyweds, *mystagogical* catechesis embraces a deeper understanding of the Christian experience, perpetual reflection on the sacrament(s) celebrated and a full integration into the community of faith within one's new state.[177] In both cases there is a need for pastoral accompaniment.

4.1 Canonical Considerations of *Mystagogia*

According to canon 1063, 4°, pastors of souls supported by their faith communities are required to provide assistance to all Christian faithful such that "the matrimonial state is preserved in a Christian spirit and advances in perfection," especially by "help offered to those who are married, so that faithfully preserving and protecting the conjugal covenant, they daily come to lead holier and fuller lives in their family" (c. 1063, 4°). This canon sets an expectation that must be fulfilled in the future as an on-going dimension of formation by the ecclesial community.[178] "Such support will be of special importance in the early years of marriage, particularly in the case of those whose faith is weak or who have difficulty in adjusting to their new state."[179] Likewise, ongoing pastoral care for mixed marriages is specifically required by canon 1128, while canon 1129 regards the pastoral care of marriages with disparity of cult.

What is the nature of the ongoing assistance to preserve and protect the conjugal covenant, which allows it to flourish according to canon 1063, 4°? The code does not provide detail regarding the means by which this lofty goal will be accomplished, however it is to be a concerted effort guided by the bishop and pastors. In general, as members of the Christian Faithful, canon 213 ensures the right to receive assistance from the sacred pastors out of the spiritual goods of the Church and canon 217 grants the right to a Christian education by which they are to strive for the maturity of the human person and know and live the mystery of salvation.

Accordingly, the Pontifical Council for the Family envisioned that this protective and supportive function of lifelong formation will occur in "post-

---

177 See Morris, 215.

178 For an interesting discussion regarding this requirement and those couples who intend to attend a "compromise church" such that the Catholic Church is hindered in providing post-sacramental care, see Hartmann, "Marriage and Future Practice of the Faith," 121-124.

179 Kelly, "Part I: The Sacraments; Title VII: Marriage," 580. Cf. Synod of Bishops, III Extraordinary General Assembly of the Synod of Bishops, *The Pastoral Challenges of the Family in the Context of Evangelization* Relatio Synodi, 19 October 2014, no. 40, Eng. trans. at http://www.vatican.va/roman_curia/synod/ documents/rc_synod_doc_2014 1018_relatio-synodi-familia_en.html#Accompanying_the_Married_Couple_in_the_Initial_ Years_of_Marriage (accessed on 16 Nov. 2023).

marriage courses to take place in parishes or deaneries" in accordance with the guidelines of the episcopal conferences.[180] The United States Conference of Catholic Bishops listed other means of support such as retreats, anniversary Masses, marriage conferences and workshops, "general intercessions, bulletin inserts, and homilies; diocesan or parish support programs specifically directed to couples in the first five years of marriage."[181]

4.1.1 Preserving and Protecting the Conjugal Covenant

Preserving implies nourishing and sustaining the conjugal covenant, while *protecting* indicates guarding from unwanted diversions or temptations that lead to the "the erosion of marital and family life."[182] Pope Francis observed that as a result of a secularized society "the Catholic faithful struggle to bear witness to a lifestyle that is consistent with the Gospel, including with regard to the Sacrament of Marriage."[183] Some of the areas to be safeguarded are found in the code: sacramental dignity (c. 1056), the nature of the bond (c. 1134), the rights and obligations of the spouses (cc. 1135-1136) and the definition of marriage itself including its ends (c. 1055). However, the fulfillment of this safeguarding belongs to the ongoing pastoral care[184] that is required in canons 1063, 4° and 1064. Furthermore, a charter of family rights to be defended by the Church was provided in *Familiaris consortio*.[185]

4.1.2 Leading Holier and Fuller Lives

Christian married couples share in the common apostolate through baptism and confirmation and so possess the right to join in associations in order to form and strengthen Gospel living in marriage and family life (cf. cc. 204, 216, and 225). Those who live in the marital state are "bound by a special duty to work through marriage and the family to build up the people of God" (c. 226 §1). Their actions are to be imbued with the spirit of the Gospel and consonant with the teaching of the magisterium (cc. 211, 227 and 759) providing an example of

---

180 See *PSM* 73.

181 USCCB, "An Analysis of Diocesan Marriage Preparation Policies: Support After Marriage," 11.

182 Kelly, "Part I: The Sacraments; Title VII: Marriage," 580.

183 Francis, Address to the Officials of the Tribunal of the Roman Rota for the Inauguration of the Judicial Year, 29 January 2019, Eng. trans. at: http://www.vatican.va/content/francesco/en/speeches/2019/january/documents/papa-francesco_20190129_rota-romana.html (accessed on 25 Jan. 2024).

184 Paul VI urgently implored marriage ministers to work zealously in "safeguarding the holiness of marriage, in order to guide married life to its full human and Christian perfection." Paul VI, encyclical *Humanae vitae* 30: *AAS* 60 (1968) 502; Eng. trans. in *Flannery2*, 413-414.

185 See *FC* 46.

Christian life for all persons, especially their children (cc. 226 §2 and 774 §2). Many of the canons involved in the *educatio* of children, previously treated in remote preparation in view of the child, can be applied in this period of *mystagogia* from the perspective of the party who is now a parent or a parental figure.

As participants in the Church's sanctifying function, spouses are to actively partake in and to be bolstered by a life of prayer, including Eucharistic celebrations (c. 835 §4), pious practices, and sacred exercises in addition to works of penance and charity (c. 839). As a living sacrament *in Christ*, "they are a sign and means that express and strengthen the faith, render worship to God, and effect the sanctification of humanity and thus in the greatest way to establish, strengthen and manifest ecclesiastical communion" (c. 840).

4.2 Theological and Doctrinal Considerations of *Mystagogia*

"*Mystagogical* catechesis weds truth and experience," according to Birmingham. Such an agenda respects the condition and situation of the participants' lives [186] and leads to theological reflection. This pondering and assimilation of the meaning of the sacramental mysteries educes the subsequent discernment of a transformed life. [187]

"To discover and live their new vocation and mission," Pope Saint John Paul II directed that the local ecclesial community should train newlyweds in their responsibilities as they face new problems in the context of new values that makes them vulnerable. [188] According to Pope Francis, pastoral care is most effectively realized where the accompaniment "doesn't end with the wedding, but 'escorts' at least the first years of conjugal life [...] through a path of growth in the faith of the couples themselves." [189]

During the period of *mystagogia* in the Rite of Christian Initiation of Adults, godparents have ongoing responsibility of assisting "neophytes to remain faithful to their baptismal promises" and "to become included into the life of the

---

186 Their strengths, challenges, spiritual and cultural resources, and other differences are considered. See *GDC* 173-174, 167. Cf. *CPML* 77.

187 See Mary Birmingham, *Year-Round Catechumentate* (Chicago, IL: Liturgical Training Publications, 2002) 125, 127. See also Peter Murphy, *From Rite to Mystagogy: An Online Blog on the Sacrament of Marriage,* DMin thesis, The Catholic University of America, Washington, D.C., 2012, 25. Murphy finds that an integration of catechesis, mystagogy, and blogging using a process of theological reflection "allows spouses to reflect on their marriage, their covenant bond, the meaning and implications of their professed vows and their impact on daily experiences in married life."

188 See *FC* 69; *OTF* 67.

189 Francis, Roman Rota Formation Course 2018. Cf., *CPML,* nos. 74-75.

community."[190] Analogously in the marriage catechumenate, mentor/sponsor couples and all married couples within the community of faith are called to the same role of witness, invitation, and support. Accompaniment assists the newly married in the synthesis of doctrinal mysteries with their lived experience.

4.2.1 Preserving and Protecting the Conjugal Covenant

"All families should, above all, be treated with respect and love and accompanied on their journey as Christ accompanied the disciples on the road to Emmaus." Carefully discerned "pastoral work of charity and mercy"[191] must help them to recover and restore relationships within marriage and the family to the extent possible.[192] Recent synods on the family universally revealed circumstances of marriage and family life that can affect a stable faith practice and inhibit the opportunity to receive care.[193] In safeguarding the conjugal covenant, practical and accessible assistance is to be offered to help married persons live marital unity through humility, sacrificial love, fidelity, chastity, and fruitfulness within their present complex social environment.[194]

Pope Francis taught that this permanent period of marital assistance should:

> . . . cover the various phases of married life, presenting them in a serious and structural way, by means of a thorough formation aimed at increasing the spouses' awareness of the precise values and commitments inherent in their vocation. . . .
>
> To fulfill the Church's steady and permanent pastoral care for the good of marriage and of the family, various pastoral tools are required: drawing close to the Word of God, especially through the *lectio divina*, catechetical encounters, involvement in the celebration of the Sacraments, especially the Eucharist; spiritual dialogue and direction.

---

190 John Huels, *The Catechumenate and the Law: A Pastoral and Canonical Commentary for the Church in the United States* (Chicago: Liturgy Training Publications, 2003) 44-45.

191 See Pontifical Council for the Family, "Family, Marriage and '*De Facto*' Unions," 21 November 2000, in *OssRomEng*, 33 (2000), i-xii; Eng. trans. in *CLD* vol. 14, 1020: Ultimately "Christians must understand the personal, social, cultural, and ideological reasons for the spread of *de facto* unions" and other pastoral challenges when providing care and catechesis for those who seek assistance from the Church."

192 See Synod of Bishops, *The Pastoral Challenges of the Family* Relatio Synodi, 44-46.

193 See ibid., for the example of couples experiencing critical challenges to their married life as well as those that are separated, civilly divorced, or abandoned by spouses. Furthermore, there are couples that live together *ad experimentum*, marriages celebrated in stages, and other *de facto* unions. See also PCF, "Family, Marriage and '*De Facto*' Unions," *CLD* 14:980-1021, for a thorough discussion of *de facto* unions and pastoral care.

194 This pastoral care presupposes a persistent and stable involvement in the Church yet this is not always the case. Cf. Hartmann, "Marriage and Future Practice of the Faith," 125.

Informal groups and charitable services can be organized to promote exchanges with other families and openness to the needs of the most disadvantaged.[195]

Pope Francis upholds "unity and fidelity as indispensable and fundamental marital values" in becoming a stable *consortium totius vitae* (c. 1135).[196] Unity and fidelity are "the very essence of Christ's Church." Pope Francis added, "spouses who live in unity and fidelity are a good reflection of the image and likeness of God. This is the good news: that fidelity is possible, because it is a gift in spouses and in priests."[197] According to Pope Saint John Paul II, the witness of the fidelity of priests in living their celibacy should also strengthen the fidelity of Christian couples.[198] "Marriage and family, wife and husband in and through their children, are at the heart of her [the Church's] existence and mission," thus the pastoral care of marriage "cannot become one concern in the midst of others."[199]

4.2.2 Leading Holier and Fuller Lives in the Domestic Church

'"Become what you are!" might be a great exhortation to newly married couples as the "real work of marriage begins" according to the U.S. Catholic bishops; that is "to grow through grace into an image of Christ's love for his

---

195 Francis, Address to the Officials of the Tribunal of the Roman Rota, January 29, 2019: *AAS* 111 (2019) 156; Eng. trans. at https://www.vatican.va/content/francesco/en/speeches/2019/january/documents/papa-francesco_20190129_rota-romana.html (accessed on 24 Jan. 2024). See also *Gaudium et spes*: "The word of God regularly invites engaged and married couples to nourish and cherish their betrothal with chaste love and their marriage with undivided love." *GS* 49; *Flannery1*, 221.

196 Compare the Catechism of the Catholic Church:

> By its very nature conjugal love requires the inviolable fidelity of the spouses. This is the consequence of the gift of themselves which they make to each other. Love seeks to be definitive; it cannot be an arrangement "until further notice." The "intimate union of marriage, as a mutual giving of two persons, and the good of the children, demand total fidelity from the spouses and require an unbreakable union between them."

CCC 1646.

197 Francis, Address to the Officials of the Tribunal of the Roman Rota, January 29, 2019: *AAS* 111 (2019) 157; Eng. trans. at https://www.vatican.va/content/francesco/en/speeches/2019/january/documents/papa-francesco_20190129_rota-romana.html (accessed on 13 Feb. 2024).

198 See *FC 16*: "Marriage and virginity or celibacy are two ways of expressing and living the one mystery of the covenant of God with His people." See also *OTF* 13.

199 F. Meroni, "Pastoral Care of Marriage: Affirming the Unity of Mercy and Truth," in *Communio, International Catholic Review,* 41 (2014), 441. Cf. *FC* 73; *OTF* 71, for the solicitude within the diocese due the family in "personal interest, care, time, personnel and resources" and the importance of the pastoral care of the family revealed in setting up the Pontifical Council of the Family.

Church."[200] Growth happens in response to prayer according to the Council Fathers:

> The Lord, wishing to bestow special gifts of grace and divine love on it, has restored, perfected, and elevated it. A love like that, bringing together the human and the divine, leads the partners to a free and mutual giving of self, experienced in tenderness and action, and permeates their whole lives; besides, this love is actually developed and increased by the exercise of it.[201]

With maturation spouses will learn, "It is the nature of love to overflow, to be life-giving. Thus, it is no surprise that marriage is ordained not only to growing in love but to transmitting life."[202] In this ongoing period of *mystagogia*, giving witness to this mystery of unity rightly bears hope to all who strive to create communion in their lives.[203] There are many ways in which married couples are fruitful within the Church and society. Pope Saint John Paul II affirmed that marital unions themselves are the fruit and sign of a universal human need:

> This conjugal communion sinks its roots in the natural complementarity that exists between man and woman and is nurtured through the personal willingness of the spouses to share their entire life project, what they have and what they are: For this reason such communion is the fruit and the sign of a profoundly human need. But in the Lord Christ God takes up this human need, confirms it, purifies it and elevates it, leading it to perfection through the Sacrament of Matrimony: the Holy Spirit who is poured out in the sacramental celebration offers Christian couples the gift of a new communion of love that is the living and real image of that unique unity which makes of the Church the indivisible mystical body of the Lord Jesus.[204]

The nourishment of word and sacrament is needed to live this mystery fully.[205] *Mystagogical* catechesis should foster a more profound understanding of

---

200 USCCB, *Marriage: Love and Life in the Divine Plan,* 45. Cf. *FC* 17; also cf. *LG* 11.
201 *GS* 49; *Flannery1*, 952.
202 USCCB, *Marriage: Love and Life in the Divine Plan,* 13.
203 Cf. *Ordo celebrandi Matrimonium, editio typica altera,* 11; *OCM,* 3: "Those who marry in Christ are able, with faith in the Word of God, to celebrate fruitfully the mystery of the union of Christ and the Church, to live it rightly, and to bear witness to it publically before all."
204 *FC* 19; *OTF* 16.
205 Cf. *Ordo celebrandi Matrimonium, editio typica altera,* no. 6, *OCM,* 2: "By his presence, Christ brought blessing and joy to the wedding at Cana, where he changed water into wine and is foreshadowed the hour of the new and eternal covenant of love and fidelity, so now the Savior of the human race offers himself to the Church as Spouse, fulfilling his covenant with her in his Paschal Mystery."

the Eucharistic celebration as an encounter with "the love that animates and sustains them, Christ's love for the Church." Spouses participate in that unifying love that immerses them into the heart of the community "of which they are a living part."[206] Joining in the offering of Eucharist, through prayer and thanksgiving, they are able to offer themselves for others as a "spiritual sacrifice" sharing in the common mission of the Christ. "As a representation of Christ's sacrifice of love for the Church the Eucharist is the fountain of charity."[207] Inherently, the Eucharist "commits us to the poor" (*CCC* 1397). Consequently in Eucharistic sharing, the hospitality of Christian marriage is transformed and magnified as a commitment to the "preferential option for the poor."[208] In fact, "In the Eucharistic gift of charity the Christian family finds the foundation and soul of its 'communion' and its 'mission.'"[209] Through their acts of hospitality and charity, the spouses bear witness to Christ's love in the world and the authentic nature of the Church.[210] Fortified by Eucharist as their source and summit, they may truly become the domestic Church.

The practical guidance of one family to another should aid spouses in learning their role as Christian parents and help them to embrace their responsibilities and duties.[211] They must learn how to create "an atmosphere of faith within the home" in which they can teach their children how to pray thereby introducing them "to the gradual discovery of the mystery of God and personal dialogue with God.[212] In doing so they will find and fulfill their shared mission within the family "to learn to cooperate actively in building up the Church and its work of evangelization." It is this service of true *communio* in Christ that furthers the *oikonomia*, the economy of salvation. For these reasons, Pope Saint John Paul II proclaimed, that the family is the "heart of a civilization of love."[213]

---

206 USCCB, *Marriage: Love and Life in the Divine Plan*, 53.
207 *FC* 57; *OTF* 53.
208 *FC* 47, 64; *OTF* 45, 59.
209 *FC* 57; *OTF* 53.
210 See USCCB, *Marriage: Love and Life in the Divine Plan*, 54. Cf. *GS* 48; *Flannery1* 951.
211 Compare *Gaudium et spes*: "Families will generously share their spiritual treasures with other families." *GS* 48; *Flannery1* 951. See also *Familiaris consortio*: "Thus young families will not limit themselves merely to receiving, but in their turn, having been helped in this way, will become a source of enrichment for other longer established families, through their witness of life and practical contribution." *FC* 69; *OTF* 67.
212 *PSM* 56; Such that "In the joys of their love and family life he gives them here on earth a foretaste of the wedding feast of the Lamb" (*CCC* 1642).
213 *GmS*, no. 13, in *AAS* 86 (1994), 891, Eng. trans. at: http://www.vatican.va/content/john-paul-ii/en/letters/1994/documents/hf_jp-ii_let_02021994_families.html (accessed on Jan. 2020).

4.3 Suggestions for Pastoral Implementation of *Mystagogia*

During *mystagogia*, the ongoing pastoral accompaniment takes on many forms across the stages of marriage and family life and should involve the ecclesial community, clergy, pastoral leaders, mentor/sponsor couples, family apostolates, movements, and associations. "Through conversations with the individual couple and moments in community, young spouses can be helped to acquire the instruments and the support for living their vocation." The parish should provide the opportunity for spiritual direction, "meaningful liturgies, devotional practices, the Eucharist celebrated for families," and opportunities for apostolic service, which are "vital factors in fostering evangelization through the family."[214] Enrichment activities, conferences, courses, lectures, retreats, and similar offerings regarding realistically building a mature marital union may be organized at the either the parish, deanery, diocesan, or universal levels. A cooperative climate for ministry is thus created between the parishes, so that all parishes have access to good, on-going formation. Other marriage and family-centered associations, ecclesial movements and small communities should be available that inculcate within marriage and families the "true experience of participation in ecclesial life and thoroughly treat the various aspects of family life."[215]

The United States Conference of Catholic Bishops has recommended national and international movements or programs that may be implemented at the diocesan or parish level,[216] or as online enrichment.[217] "Regarding those spouses who experience serious problems in their relationship and who find themselves in a situation of crisis, it is important to help them revive their faith and rediscover the grace of the Sacrament."[218] Through programs such as

---

214 Synod of Bishops, *The Pastoral Challenges of the Family* Relatio Synodi, no. 40.

215 Ibid., no. 39. Cf. *AL,* 202, 218.

216 See USCCB, "An Analysis of Diocesan Marriage Preparation Policies," 11. See also: World Wide Marriage Encounter at http://www.wwme.org (accessed on 24 Jan. 2024): Structured as a retreat weekend with follow up mentor sessions that is based on inter-sacramentality as the priests are integral to the movement as members of an ecclesial team; see also The Third Option at http://thethirdoption.com/mentor-couples/ (accessed on 24 Jan. 2024): A peer program with trained local mentor couples who aid in strengthening good marriages and supporting challenged marriages through role-modeling and pastoral accompaniment.

217 See the USCCB-sponsored website that hosts content for all periods of the marriage catechumenate called "For Your Marriage" at https://www.foryourmarriage.org/married-life/enriching-your-marriage/ (accessed on 24 Jan. 2024).

218 Francis, Roman Rota Formation Course 2018: *AAS* 110 (2018) 1440; Eng. trans. at https://www.vatican.va/content/francesco/en/speeches/2023/february/documents/20230218-operatori-didiritto.html (accessed on 24 Jan. 2024). Cf., CPML, no. 81.

Retrouvaille International[219] married couples can accompany spouses in crisis and help them to restore and rebuild their marital relationship. As spouses deepen their marital identity and their sense of mission through the early years of marriage, their catechumenal pathway naturally segues into the family ministry within their parish.

Conclusion

Having considered the importance of marriage in building Church and society and the concurrent need to evangelize or re-evangelize many who seek marriage in the Church, it is clear that preparation primarily consisting of a pre-Cana workshop or retreat weekend is profoundly inadequate. Other vocations in the Church require far more formation, and yet marriage is primarily the font from which these vocations flow. A catechumenal pathway for married life respects the need for gradual and comprehensive preparation for marriage.

The pathway truly begins with remote preparation in the domestic Church and continues to offer the fullness of a journey in which to build upon this foundation.[220] A marriage catechumenate therefore can effectively "fill in the gaps" of education and formation as needed. According to Pope Francis, "The deeper and longer the preparatory path is, the more young people will learn to correspond to God's grace and strength, and will develop the 'antibodies' to face the inevitable moments of difficulty and struggle in conjugal and family life."[221]

A catechumenal pathway for married life can help marriages and families thrive, not merely survive. The pastoral practice aims to personally meet the pastoral need inside the family, so that its members may become "active agents of the family apostolate."[222] In *Amoris lætitia* Pope Francis summarized, "Only on the basis of this experience will the Church's pastoral care for families enable

---

219 See Retrouvaille International, at https://www.helpourmarriage.org/ (3 Feb. 2020).

220 "For it cannot be denied that the basis of a happy wedlock, and the ruin of an unhappy one, is prepared and set in the souls of boys and girls during the period of childhood and adolescence." Pius XI, encyclical letter *Casti Connubii*, December 31, 1930: *AAS* 22 (1930) 584; Eng. trans. at https://www.vatican.va/content/pius-xi/en/encyclicals/documents/hf_p-xi_enc_19301231_casti-connubii.html (accessed on 24 Jan. 2024).

221 Francis, Roman Rota Formation Course 2018. The Pope spoke of "the gaps that are so widespread today: be it the lack of catechetical formation or the absence of filial sentiment towards the Church, which nevertheless is part of the foundations of Christian marriage." Eng. trans. at https://www.vatican.va/content/francesco/en/speeches/2018/september/documents/papa-francesco_20180927_corso-rotaromana.html (accessed on 24 Jan. 2024).

222 *AL*, 200; Eng. trans. at https://www.vatican.va/content/dam/francesco/pdf/apost_exhortations/documents/papa-francesco_esortazione-ap_20160319_amoris-laetitia_en.pdf (accessed on 24 Jan. 2024).

them to be both domestic churches and a leaven of evangelization in society."[223] The Code of Canon Law and magisterial teaching are consonant with and highly relevant to this pathway of preparation for married life.

223 *AL*, 290.

APPENDIX I

Marriage Preparation in the Code and Catechumenal Pathways for Marriage

Canon 1063

Pastors of souls are obliged to take care that their ecclesiastical community offers the Christian faithful the assistance by which the matrimonial state is preserved in a Christian spirit and advances in perfection. This assistance must be offered especially by

1° preaching, catechesis adapted to minors, youth, and adults, and even the use of instruments of social communication, by which the Christian faithful are instructed about the meaning of Christian marriage and about the function of Christian spouses and parents;

2° personal preparation to enter marriage, which disposes the spouses to the holiness and duties of their new state;

3° a fruitful liturgical celebration of marriage which is to show that the spouses signify and share in the mystery of the unity and fruitful love between Christ and the Church;

4° help offered to those who are married, so that faithfully preserving and protecting the conjugal covenant, they daily come to lead holier and fuller lives in their family.

See "Table 1: Convergence" on the next page.

TABLE 1: CONVERGENCE

1. RCIA/OCIA 4 PERIODS	2. MARRIAGE CATECHUMENATE 4 PERIODS	3. CORRESPONDING ACTIONS	4. CONTENT OF MARRIAGE CAT. (Cf. *FC, PSM, OCM, CPML, CJL, CCC, GDC, GE, GS, HV, LG, TOB & CLSA & CLSGBI COMM*)	5.CANON 1063	6. RELATED CANONS	7. MINISTERS, WITNESSES & EXPERTS
Evangelization and Pre-Catechumenate	Remote [Early childhood-adolescence/ youth]	Initial inquiry and conversion; Evangelization and Re-evangelization	1) Relationships 2) Values 3) Character formation- learning to control one's inclinations, TOB 4) A sense of marriage as a vocation 5) Spiritual/Catechetical education	1° General preaching, catechesis, social communication/instruction about marriage adapted for minors	cc. 762-772: Preaching cc. 822-832: Social media cc. 773-780; 793-795: Catechesis c .1136: Parental right-duty	Parents, Guardians, Pastor, Other Clergy, Catechists, and Ecclesial Community
Catechumenate	Proximate [19-39 y.o.]-*CJL* [Engagement Period]- *PSM* [14 -12 months prior to Marriage]-*CPML*	Catechesis/ Personal Preparation	1) The interpersonal relationship of man and woman 2) Conjugal sexuality 3) Responsible parenthood 4) Essential biological knowledge 5) Domestic economy, duties, career and finance, etc. 6) Education of children 7) Membership and involvement in the family apostolate of the Church	1° (adapted for youth and adults) 2° Specialized personal preparation/formation prior to marriage	cc. 1064-1070: Readiness for marriage Canonical talks: cc. 1055-1062: Marriage cc. 1073-1075;1083-1094: Impediments cc. 1095-1103: Consent cc. 1134-1136: Effects c. 840: Sacrament	Pastor, Other Clergy, Mentor/Sponsor Couples, Experts, Catechist and Ecclesial Community
Purification and Enlightenment	Immediate/Final [Weeks/Months prior to M]-*FC* [2-3 Months prior to Marriage]-*CPML*	Continued spiritual conversion, growth in holiness and discernment	1) Liturgical catechesis using the *OCM*, scripture, signs, symbols and the actual sharing in the mysteries 2) Spiritual preparation toward a proper disposition for the celebration of marriage	1° (adapted for adults) 3° Formative liturgical celebration of marriage [Also see c. 1065: the reception of sacraments of P, E and C]	cc. 226, 834-837; 846: Sanctifying function and liturgical actions cc. 1108-1123: Celebration of marriage: canonical form and ministers	Pastor, Other Clergy, Mentor/Sponsor Couples, Catechist and Ecclesial Community
Mystagogia	*Mystagogia*-Enrichment/ Support [2-3 years]- *CPML* [1-5 years]- *PSM* [Ongoing]- MLLDP	On-going lived reception and reflection on the mysteries of faith and sacramental support	Retreats, anniversary Masses, days of reflection, marriage conferences and workshops, general intercessions, bulletin inserts, and homilies; diocesan or parish enrichment and support programs specifically directed to couples in the first five years of marriage; family movements	1° General preaching, catechesis, social communication/instruction about marriage adapted for minors 4° Continuing support after marriage, growth in holiness and vocation	cc. 1128-1129: Ongoing care for mixed marriages and those with disparity of cult cc. 204, 216 and 225: Apostolic mission and associations cc. 226; 774: Build Church and witness cc. 835; 839: Sanctifying function, Eucharist, charity and piety	Pastor, Other Clergy, Mentor/Sponsor Couples, Experts, and Ecclesial Community

Abbreviations: *RCIA-Rite of Christian Initiation of Adults*, 1988; *FC-Familiaris consortio*, 1981; *PSM-Preparation for the Sacrament of Marriage*, 1996; OCM *The Order of Celebrating Matrimony*, *GDC-General Directory for Catechesis*, 1998; *Catechism of the Catholic Church*, 2000; *GS- Gaudium et spes*, 1966; *LG- Lumen gentium*, 1964; *GE- Gravissimum educationis*, 1965; *HV- Humanae vitae*, 1968; *TOB- The Theology of the Body*, 1997; MLLDP- *Marriage Life and Love in the Divine Plan* (2009); *CJL- Called to the Joy of Love* (2021); *CPML-Catechumenal Pathways for Married Life* (2022).

APPENDIX II

Some Recommended Catechetical Topics

1.1 Remote Preparation of Early Childhood and Adolescence

- 1.1.1 God is a Relationship of Love as the Trinity
  - 1.1.1.1 Respect for Yourself and Others: Introduction to Basic Christian Anthropology; Divine Origins and Human Dignity
  - 1.1.1.2 Complementarity: The Uniqueness and Goodness of the Male and Female; Theology of the Body
  - 1.1.1.3 Relationships: Friendship, Marriage, Chastity and Fidelity
- 1.1.2 Living as a Child of God
  - 1.1.2.1 Sharing in Your Catholic Identity
  - 1.1.2.2 Sharing in the Love and Mercy of God
  - 1.1.2.3 Sharing in Christ's Humble Care and Service of Others
- 1.1.3 Trusting in God in Good Times and in Bad
  - 1.1.3.1 Seeing God's Presence: A Grace-filled World
  - 1.1.3.2 Taking Responsibility: Personal and Communal Sin, Developing Discretionary Judgment
  - 1.1.3.3 Experiencing Transformation: Christ as Savior

2.1 Proximate Preparation, Proximal to and During the Period of Engagement

- 2.1.1 Self-Understanding
  - 2.1.1.1 Family of Origin and Family Values
  - 2.1.1.2 Discernment of Vocation
  - 2.1.1.3 Prenuptial Investigation and Marriage Preparation Evaluative Tool
- 2.1.2 Spousal (Trinitarian) Spirituality in Marriage
  - 2.1.2.1 Prayer and Sacraments
  - 2.1.2.2 Personal and Shared *Charisms*; Mutual Self-sacrifice and Self-gifting
  - 2.1.2.3 Path of Holiness as Spouses
- 2.1.3 Marriage as Vocation and Indissoluble Covenant within the Sacramentality of the Church and the Secularity of Society
  - 2.1.3.1 Partnership of the Whole of Life, *totius vitae consortium*
  - 2.1.3.2 *Tri Bona* of Marriage - *sacramenti, fidei, et prolis*
  - 2.1.3.3 The Good of Spouses, *bonum coniugum*

2.1.4 Stewardship in Marriage

2.1.4.1 Stewardship of Gifts: Freedom, Possessions, Careers, Finances, and Talents

2.1.4.2 Stewardship of Relationships: Communication, Conflict Resolution, Christian Parenting and Education of Children

2.1.4.3 Stewardship of the Body: Self-care, Chaste Engagement Period, Exclusive Conjugal Sexuality, The Inviolable Gift of Life, Natural Family Planning, Infertility, and Fidelity

3.1 Immediate Preparation During the Last Meetings Prior to Marrying

3.1.1 Spouses as Living Liturgists

3.1.1.1 Experience of Prayer, Reflection, Spiritual Exercises or Retreat

3.1.1.2 Reception of the Sacraments as prescribed by Canon Law

3.1.2 Liturgical Celebration of Marriage

3.1.2.1 Texts of the Rite: Consent, Vows, Promise of Fidelity and Nuptial Blessing

3.1.2.2 Symbols of the Rite: Ring, Lasso, and *Arras*

3.1.2.3 Sign of the Union: Icon of Christ's Love for His Bride, the Church; Consummation

4.1 *Mystagogia,* Accompaniment During the First Years of Married Life

4.1.1 Review of Topics from Earlier Periods from a *Mystagogical* Perspective

4.1.2 Marriage as a Sacrament at the Service of Communion: Eucharist, Unity and Mission

4.1.2.1 Intentional Discipleship

4.1.2.2 Domestic Church

4.1.2.3 Apostolic and Missionary Spirit

APPENDIX III

The Rite: Readings, Signs, Symbols, and Prayers

Suggested Elements of Liturgical Catechesis

The liturgy uses visible signs and symbols to signify invisible reality. The minds of those who participate fully, actively and consciously in worship through prayer, sacred hymns, and reverent action ". . . are raised to God so that they may offer him their spiritual homage and receive his grace more abundantly."[224] For this reason Fagerberg sees the creation of man and woman as "rational liturgists of the material world…in order to transform the praise of mute matter into speech and symbol."[225] The notion of the bride and groom as liturgists is clearly evidenced throughout their nuptial liturgy and is the beginning of a life of liturgical ministry within the domestic church.

The Liturgy of the Word expresses the importance of Christian marriage throughout salvation history, in addition to the duties, responsibilities, and love that are shared for their sanctification and that of their children (*OCM*, 34-35). The questions asked of the bride and groom by the person assisting regard constituent elements of marriage: the freedom of will to give valid consent, the love that leads to unity and fidelity, and the intention of permanence and openness to procreation and Christian *educatio* of children. Especially when exchanged unprompted, the words of consent are poignant, mutually professing perpetual unconditional faithfulness, love, and honor. These words connote a power of humble acceptance of the divinely given gift of marriage. "The consent by which the spouses mutually give and receive one another is sealed by God himself" (*CCC* 1639). Furthermore, it should be explained to the witnesses that they are not only the guarantors of a juridical act, but also representatives of the Christian community which, through them, participates in a sacramental act relevant to it, because a new family is a cell of the Church.[226]

An alternate form of the blessing of the wedding rings calls on the Lord to grant fidelity, peace and a life of mutual charity lived according to the will of God. As unending circles, the blessed rings given are both a sign and a remembrance of the love and fidelity vowed in the exchanged consent that establishes the indissoluble covenant with each other and with God. Where certain customs are practiced, the blessing and giving of *arras*, the gold coins, signifies the abundance

---

224 *SC* 33: *AAS* 56 (1964) 108; *Flannery1*, 12.

225 David Fagerberg, *Theologia Prima, What is Liturgical Theology?* (Mundelein, IL: Hillenbrand Books, 2004) 8.

226 *PSM* 55.

of God's blessings and gifts showered upon the couple. The blessing and placing of the *lazo*, the wedding garland, or veil over the bride and groom also symbolizes their indissoluble union. Clearly these cultural additions to the liturgy "harmonize with its true and authentic spirit."[227]

The Universal Prayer in part witnesses to the role of the couple in the sanctification of the world by praying for and creating communion. The collects of the Eucharistic Prayer challenge the bride and groom to a mutuality and fruitfulness in living out their vocation of marriage as a holy covenant. Furthermore, the prefaces speak to the divine design of marriage:

> For you willed that the human race created by the gift of your goodness should be raised to such a high dignity that in the union of husband and wife you might bestow a true image of your love. For those you created out of charity you call to the law of charity without ceasing and grant them a share in your eternal charity. And so, the Sacrament of holy Matrimony, as the abiding sign of your own love, consecrates the love of man and woman through Christ our Lord.[228]

Following Eucharist, the priest—or if not within Mass the deacon—invites the assembled community to pray for God's blessing and help to be upon the bride and groom, indicating the ongoing role of the community in supporting them in their vocation.

The nuptial blessing reveals, "The purpose of marriage between a man and a woman is to create between them a bond of covenant responsibility and faithfulness that represents and re-actualizes the eternal bond established by God with his chosen people."[229] This blessing upon the wife and husband, as servants and witnesses of Christ, is a petition for strength, fidelity, fruitfulness, and the fullness of years until they make at last, heaven their home. Örsy summarizes, "The two Christians are part of a new creation, clothed with eternal life. Their promises take place within the Kingdom that is now at hand. Through the sacrament God himself covenants with them and promises to sustain them in their weakness."[230]

227 *SC* 37: *AAS* 56 (1964)110; *Flannery1*, 13.
228 *OCM*, 201.
229 Lawler, "Marriage as Covenant," 84. Cf. J. BRECK, *Sacred Gift of Life*, 62.
230 Örsy, *Marriage in Canon Law*, 272.

Officers' Reports

Report of the President

Reverend John P. Donovan, JCL

Welcome to Milwaukee! It is my first time here and I am hoping to have a few minutes here and there to enjoy the attractions. When I think of Milwaukee, three "Bs" come to mind: Brewers, Bucks, and beer! However, I have quickly learned there is something even greater, and that is hospitality of the staff of the Archdiocese. Thank you for all your assistance and graciousness.

Although there were 365 days in the year, they seem to have gone by in half the time. The hours and days spent preparing for Rome seem long past. Angst for publications and eleventh-hour changes of the Code when it was set to go to print have winnowed away. Copyright issues and the new commentary move forward. Now, I think I have the hang of it.

As we left last year's convention, filling committees and seating chairs were a priority. We were purposeful in wanting a mix of those with experience and those who may offer fresh perspectives. We will be making committee appointments for the 2023-2024 year right after this convention, and we will be reviewing online profiles of those who have indicated an interest. If you haven't indicated your interest, please be sure your profile on the CLSA website is thorough and up to date! I hope you have registered to participate in the Listening Lunch on Tuesday, as the same holds true; experience and fresh perspective is the only way we can move forward to meet the needs in an ever-changing culture of what it means to work in the Church!

We had two virtual orientation sessions this past year. In January, we had an orientation for new committee chairs, addressing questions, concerns, and expectations. In February, we had a new-member orientation, welcoming them to the CLSA and sharing with them the many resources available. The greatest resource of course is the members! I made a video for first-time attendees reminding them of just that and encouraging them to ask questions. For the members who have attended five, ten, or thirty-five times, I encourage you to reach out to our first-time attendees and newer members and make them feel welcome.

The Canon Law Society of America Report to the Membership of the Rome Visit is online and included in *Roman Replies*. I simply do not have enough adjectives to describe the whole experience. I will start with how humbling it was;

thank you for entrusting me with such a responsibility. I hope you find the report informative and helpful in addressing the questions. The biggest takeaway is do not wait for these visits, contact the dicasteries with questions when they arise; they are willing to help from the beginning!

There have been several notable publications achievements this year. The Fourth Edition of the Code was released in May, and it is selling well. Of course, there are already changes that will need to be made in the next edition. There are several other projects in the work that Donna Miller will highlight and some proposed at this convention.

Work is continuing on the commentary. We have made some changes in the editors, as their other commitments took precedence. I'm very grateful to the four content editors who are working diligently with our staff to move this project through the editorial and production process. Thank you to Rev. Brian Austin, FSSP; Sr. Nancy Bauer, OSB; Chorbishop John Faris; Dr. Siobhan Verbeek, and all those who have contributed their scholarship to the project. This is a mammoth undertaking as you might expect, so I do not expect the book to be ready until 2025.

The BOG met in person in July in San Antonio, Texas with our usual full agenda. We accomplished our tasks, but we also spent time purposefully reflecting on our common mission as elected representatives. We assessed the importance we place on our responsibilities and actions and developed recommendations for how we can be even more effective for the Society. At this convention, expect to be approached by BOG members who want to hear about your work and the value you place on CLSA membership and service to you. We especially want to hear if you have an interest in serving on committees or on the Board.

As I conclude my term, there are things I wish had done differently; communication is always at the core of that. I have been honored to serve the Society as President this year, and I look forward to assuming the role of Past President. I thank all the BOG members, especially those who terms are ending: Dr. Lynda Robitaille, Past President; Rev. Greg Luyet, Secretary; and Dr. Siobhan Verbeek and Rev. Luke Millette, Consultors. These have been some of my favorite people before we served together, they now also have my utmost respect and gratitude for their commitment and insight for the CLSA.

CLSA has a small staff, and they accomplish a tremendous amount work with professionalism and good humor. I extend personal thanks to Mark Francisco, Donna Miller, and Kathleen Butler. I have enjoyed working with them immensely, and they have my heartfelt admiration.

Enjoy Milwaukee! To all the staff and volunteers from the Archdiocese of Milwaukee, thank you.

Report of the Treasurer

Very Reverend Jamin Scott David, JCL

Canonists who are "in the trenches" know that no matter the particular church in which we minister, 2022/2023 represents a period of significant fiscal challenge. Despite the source—be it geopolitical tension or post-pandemic recovery—economic uncertainty, higher energy and fuel prices, market volatility, and mounting inflation have all left an impact on nearly every fabric of society.

Yet, despite this ever-changing financial landscape, the Canon Law Society of America's finances remain strong. Our success can be credited to the wise stewardship of our office staff and the predecessors in the Treasurer's seat, especially Father Kevin Niehoff, OP, the immediate past Treasurer. However, other factors including increased membership, more participation in the Society's annual convention, and sales of publications have all served as contributing factors of success in adversity.

Clearly, charting a path forward that includes financial discipline, investment in development, and strategizing for the future will help the CLSA weather any future challenges that may arise. Helpful in this resolve is the Society's continuity in engaging Walsh Accounting. The work of Michaela Allen, our primary accountant at Walsh, combined with the organization of Kathleen Butler—our General Secretary—provide necessary professionalism during these fiscal headwinds.

A path forward also includes every member of the CLSA! Allow me to thank our membership for increased giving to the JCL and JCD Scholarship funds. As far back as the Chicago Convention of October 1981, the CLSA publicly resolved that one of its highest priorities is the canonical education of membership and the people of God. Prior to the current fiscal year during which many of you gave $85 or more to the appeal as the Society celebrates 85 years, only 70 members and five organizations donated to our scholarship funds in 2022/2023. Proudly, during the past months, the Society has now achieved 100% giving to the scholarship fund from the Board of Governors.

Everything we have is truly a gift from God, and the Lord encourages us to generously share those blessings with others. When we do, we accumulate lasting treasure. Because we define giving as an act of love, and because we measure it against the great gift of God's Son, then giving generously and sacrificially is exactly the point. Giving is planned, proportionate, sacrificial, born of free expression, and prayerful. Can we rely upon you to consider generously giving to show that canonical education is of highest import?

The Society this year engaged in a full audit with an outside firm per the dictates of our financial policy. No anomalies were found in this review, and cash flow is sufficient to maintain our obligations in the short term. The report of the auditor is contained in these convention proceedings.

To ensure that good stewardship is forefront in the mind of our leadership, the Board of Governors considered and approved several policies to ensure funds are protected, accounting standards are reviewed and observed, and there is uniformity in practice regarding operations. Simply stated, these policies will continue to lay a sure foundation for fiscal responsibility.

As Treasurer, I am committed to reducing costs as realistically feasible to ensure good stewardship! However, I firmly believe that strategically, the Society will have to continue to evolve to reach a larger audience by investing in electronic communications, and such investment will not be without cost. Part of good stewardship is to remain realistic regarding the actual cost of business. Did you know, for example, that registration fees do not cover the full cost of convention attendance per participant? The CLSA regularly subsidizes more than $100 per convention participant per year. Finding more creative ways to generate revenue will be necessary, especially in an environment of increasing costs.

Yet, there is good news despite the turbulence! Losses in the 2022/2023 fiscal year primarily due to market performance, have been reversed, and as you may observe in attached reports, a positive gain in our bottom line has been achieved again this fiscal year. This is a tangible demonstration that there is prudence in our stewardship!

Our fiscal performance is shown in the following reports which show how the society has grown in successful recruiting and wise spending; please peruse them at your leisure. Other reports will give you more specifics about business details and growth plans moving forward. While economic conditions might not be most favorable, continue to be a champion of the work of the Society, especially its potential to bring canonists together and to engender positive change in the Church. The Canon Law Society of America is fiscally healthy, and the foundation of our success rests with your work and diligence. Challenges will continue to be encountered, but I know that the next decades of our ministry and work will be feasible and fulfilling if we "stay the course."

LSWG

CERTIFIED PUBLIC ACCOUNTANTS
& BUSINESS ADVISORS

September 6, 2023

To the Board of Governors and Management of
Canon Law Society of America
415 Michigan Avenue NE Suite 101
Washington, DC 20017

We have audited the financial statements of Canon Law Society of America for the year ended June 30, 2023, and we will issue our report thereon dated September 6, 2023. Professional standards require that we provide you with information about our responsibilities under generally accepted auditing standards, as well as certain information related to the planned scope and timing of our audit. We have communicated such information in our letter to you dated June 20, 2023. Professional standards also require that we communicate to you the following information related to our audit.

Significant Audit Matters

Qualitative Aspects of Accounting Practices

Management is responsible for the selection and use of appropriate accounting policies. The significant accounting policies used by Canon Law Society of America are described in Note 2 to the financial statements. The Organization implemented Accounting Standards Codification Topic 842, *Leases*. We noted no transactions entered into by the Organization during the year for which there is a lack of authoritative guidance or consensus. All significant transactions have been recognized in the financial statements in the proper period.

Accounting estimates are an integral part of the financial statements prepared by management and are based on management's knowledge and experience about past and current events and assumptions about future events. Certain accounting estimates are particularly sensitive because of their significance to the financial statements and because of the possibility that future events affecting them may differ significantly from those expected. The most sensitive estimate affecting the financial statements was:

> Management's allocation of the time spent by category (program and supporting services) is based on an estimate. We evaluated the methods, assumptions, and data used to develop the estimate in determining that it is reasonable in relation to the financial statements taken as a whole.

The financial statement disclosures are neutral, consistent, and clear.

Difficulties Encountered in Performing the Audit

We encountered no significant difficulties in dealing with management in performing and completing our audit.

201 Thomas Johnson Drive
Frederick, Maryland 21702-5166

301.662.9200
www.LSWG.cpa

1801 Research Boulevard, Suite 320
Rockville, Maryland 20850-3184

Corrected and Uncorrected Misstatements

Professional standards require us to accumulate all misstatements identified during the audit, other than those that are clearly trivial, and communicate them to the appropriate level of management. Management has corrected all such misstatements. In addition, none of the misstatements detected as a result of audit procedures and corrected by management were material, either individually or in the aggregate, to the financial statements taken as a whole.

Disagreements with Management

For purposes of this letter, a disagreement with management is a disagreement on a financial accounting, reporting, or auditing matter, whether or not resolved to our satisfaction, that could be significant to the financial statements or the auditor's report. We are pleased to report that no such disagreements arose during the course of our audit.

Management Representations

We have requested certain representations from management that are included in the management representation letter dated September 6, 2023.

Management Consultations with Other Independent Accountants

In some cases, management may decide to consult with other accountants about auditing and accounting matters, similar to obtaining a "second opinion" on certain situations. If a consultation involves application of an accounting principle to the Organization's financial statements or a determination of the type of auditor's opinion that may be expressed on those statements, our professional standards require the consulting accountant to check with us to determine that the consultant has all the relevant facts. To our knowledge, there were no such consultations with other accountants.

Other Audit Findings or Issues

We generally discuss a variety of matters, including the application of accounting principles and auditing standards, with management each year prior to retention as the Organization's auditors. However, these discussions occurred in the normal course of our professional relationship and our responses were not a condition to our retention.

Other Matters

FDIC Coverage - The Organization has approximately $145,000 of funds in excess of FDIC coverage at June 30, 2023 at TD Bank which is a risk. We recommend that the Organization evaluate its cash needs and determine if these excess funds can be placed in another bank or in the investment account.

Investments – It was noted during the year under audit that there were 3 transfers from the CBIS investment account into the TD Bank account. We noted that it was discussed at a Board meeting but there did not seem to be formal approval of these transfers before they occurred. There also did not seem to be any documentation about whether these funds needed to be returned to the investment account or not. We recommend that the Organization evaluate whether a policy could be adopted to outline when transfers can take place, how much can be taken out in any given year, whether it is a permanent withdrawal or a short-term "loan", etc. You may consider working with an investment manager to assist in creating additional investment policies.

LSWG
CERTIFIED PUBLIC ACCOUNTANTS
& BUSINESS ADVISORS

This information is intended solely for the use of the Board of Governors and management of Canon Law Society of America and is not intended to be, and should not be, used by anyone other than these specified parties.

Very truly yours,

LSWG, P.A.

LSWG
CERTIFIED PUBLIC ACCOUNTANTS
& BUSINESS ADVISORS

CANON LAW SOCIETY OF AMERICA

Financial Statements and Independent Auditor's Report

For the Year Ended June 30, 2023

LSWG

CERTIFIED PUBLIC ACCOUNTANTS
& BUSINESS ADVISORS

LSWG
CERTIFIED PUBLIC ACCOUNTANTS
& BUSINESS ADVISORS

INDEPENDENT AUDITOR'S REPORT

To the Board of Governors of
Canon Law Society of America

Opinion

We have audited the accompanying financial statements of Canon Law Society of America (a nonprofit organization), which comprise the statement of financial position as of June 30, 2023, and the related statements of activities and changes in net assets, functional expenses and cash flows for the year then ended, and the related notes to the financial statements.

In our opinion, the financial statements referred to above present fairly, in all material respects, the financial position of Canon Law Society of America as of June 30, 2023, and the changes in its net assets and its cash flows for the year then ended in accordance with accounting principles generally accepted in the United States of America.

Basis for Opinion

We conducted our audit in accordance with auditing standards generally accepted in the United States of America. Our responsibilities under those standards are further described in the Auditor's Responsibilities for the Audit of the Financial Statements section of our report. We are required to be independent of Canon Law Society of America and to meet our other ethical responsibilities in accordance with the relevant ethical requirements relating to our audit. We believe that the audit evidence we have obtained is sufficient and appropriate to provide a basis for our audit opinion.

Responsibilities of Management for the Financial Statements

Management is responsible for the preparation and fair presentation of the financial statements in accordance with accounting principles generally accepted in the United States of America, and for the design, implementation, and maintenance of internal control relevant to the preparation and fair presentation of financial statements that are free from material misstatement, whether due to fraud or error.

In preparing the financial statements, management is required to evaluate whether there are conditions or events, considered in the aggregate, that raise substantial doubt about Canon Law Society of America's ability to continue as a going concern within one year after the date that the financial statements are available to be issued.

Auditor's Responsibilities for the Audit of the Financial Statements

Our objectives are to obtain reasonable assurance about whether the financial statements as a whole are free from material misstatement, whether due to fraud or error, and to issue an auditor's report that includes our opinion. Reasonable assurance is a high level of assurance but is not absolute assurance and therefore is not a guarantee that an audit conducted in accordance with generally accepted auditing standards will always detect a material misstatement when it exists. The risk of not detecting a material misstatement resulting from fraud is higher than for one resulting from error, as fraud may involve collusion, forgery, intentional omissions, misrepresentations, or the override of internal control.

201 Thomas Johnson Drive
Frederick, Maryland 21702-5166

301.662.9200
www.LSWG.cpa

1801 Research Boulevard, Suite 320
Rockville, Maryland 20850-3184

Misstatements are considered material if there is a substantial likelihood that, individually or in the aggregate, they would influence the judgment made by a reasonable user based on the financial statements.

In performing an audit in accordance with generally accepted auditing standards, we:

- Exercise professional judgment and maintain professional skepticism throughout the audit.
- Identify and assess the risks of material misstatement of the financial statements, whether due to fraud or error, and design and perform audit procedures responsive to those risks. Such procedures include examining, on a test basis, evidence regarding the amounts and disclosures in the financial statements.
- Obtain an understanding of internal control relevant to the audit in order to design audit procedures that are appropriate in the circumstances, but not for the purpose of expressing an opinion on the effectiveness of Canon Law Society of America's internal control. Accordingly, no such opinion is expressed.
- Evaluate the appropriateness of accounting policies used and the reasonableness of significant accounting estimates made by management, as well as evaluate the overall presentation of the financial statements.
- Conclude whether, in our judgment, there are conditions or events, considered in the aggregate, that raise substantial doubt about Canon Law Society of America's ability to continue as a going concern for a reasonable period of time.

We are required to communicate with those charged with governance regarding, among other matters, the planned scope and timing of the audit, significant audit findings, and certain internal control related matters that we identified during the audit.

LSWG, P.A.

Rockville, Maryland
September 6, 2023

LSWG
CERTIFIED PUBLIC ACCOUNTANTS
& BUSINESS ADVISORS

CANON LAW SOCIETY OF AMERICA
Statement of Financial Position
June 30, 2023

	Assets	
Current Assets		
Cash and cash equivalents	$	313,690
Accounts receivable		3,353
Inventory		73,536
Prepaid expenses		60,155
Total Current Assets		450,734
Furniture and Equipment - at cost		
Furniture and equipment		37,071
Less: accumulated depreciation		(27,189)
Furniture and Equipment, Net		9,882
Other Assets		
Security deposit		2,094
Investments		831,804
Investments - scholarship funds		1,233,606
Right of use operating lease assets		75,422
Total Other Assets		2,142,926
Total Assets	$	2,603,542
	Liabilities and Net Assets	
Current Liabilities		
Accounts payable and accrued expenses	$	106,820
Accrued vacation		4,914
Deferred revenue		338,412
Operating lease liability - current portion		30,647
Total Current Liabilities		480,793
Long-Term Liabilities		
Operating lease liability - net of current portion		45,862
Total Long-Term Liabilities		45,862
Total Liabilities		526,655
Net Assets		
Without donor restrictions		
Undesignated		1,056,329
Board designated - publications		(117,397)
Total Unrestricted		938,932
With donor restrictions		1,137,955
Total Net Assets		2,076,887
Total Liabilities and Net Assets	$	2,603,542

The accompanying notes are an integral part of this statement.

3

CANON LAW SOCIETY OF AMERICA
Statement of Activities and Changes in Net Assets
For the Year Ended June 30, 2023

	Without Donor Restriction				
	Undesignated	Publications	Total	With Donor Restrictions	Total
Revenue					
Membership dues	$ 279,537	$ -	$ 279,537	$ -	$ 279,537
Convention revenue	223,006	-	223,006	-	223,006
Sale of publications	-	135,442	135,442	-	135,442
Contributions	1,838	-	1,838	17,260	19,098
Interest and dividends	11,832	-	11,832	17,265	29,097
Royalties	-	3,959	3,959	-	3,959
Unrealized and realized gains on investments	69,076	-	69,076	99,816	168,892
Net assets released from restrictions	35,026	-	35,026	(35,026)	-
Total Revenue	620,315	139,401	759,716	99,315	859,031
Expenses					
Program Services					
Publications	-	135,060	135,060	-	135,060
Convention and workshops	302,737	-	302,737	-	302,737
Membership outreach	45,474	-	45,474	-	45,474
Scholarship fund	35,027	-	35,027	-	35,027
Total Program Services	383,238	135,060	518,298	-	518,298
Supporting Services	272,704	-	272,704	-	272,704
Total Expenses	655,942	135,060	791,002	-	791,002
Changes in Net Assets	(35,627)	4,341	(31,286)	99,315	68,029
Net Assets - Beginning of Year	1,091,956	(121,738)	970,218	1,038,640	2,008,858
Net Assets - End of Year	$ 1,056,329	$ (117,397)	$ 938,932	$ 1,137,955	$ 2,076,887

The accompanying notes are an integral part of this statement.

4

CANON LAW SOCIETY OF AMERICA
Statement of Functional Expenses
For the Year Ended June 30, 2023

	Program				Supporting	
	Publications	Convention and Workshops	Member Services	Scholarship Fund	General and Administrative	Total
Administrative office						
Salaries and benefits	$ 61,792	$ 34,893	$ 27,007	$ 3,696	$ 86,117	$ 213,505
Operating lease expense	-	-	-	-	32,525	32,525
Professional fees	25,630	-	-	-	83,736	109,366
Other	854	355	20	-	7,411	8,640
Bank, financial and payroll fees	-	-	-	-	22,080	22,080
Telecommunications	-	-	-	-	4,846	4,846
Website and information technology	-	-	4,340	-	4,557	8,897
Depreciation expense	-	-	-	-	4,014	4,014
Convention	-	242,746	-	-	2,357	245,103
Board of Governors	-	20,117	-	-	9,994	30,111
Membership outreach	-	1,047	14,107	-	1,548	16,702
Outsourced publications and resources	13,663	-	-	-	-	13,663
Cost of publications sold	19,754	-	-	-	-	19,754
Publication and resource	887	-	-	-	-	887
Royalty expense	4,648	-	-	-	-	4,648
Scholarships	-	-	-	31,331	-	31,331
Committees	6,287	3,579	-	-	3,356	13,222
Product partnerships	1,545	-	-	-	-	1,545
Professional development	-	-	-	-	10,163	10,163
	$ 135,060	$ 302,737	$ 45,474	$ 35,027	$ 272,704	$ 791,002

The accompanying notes are an integral part of this statement.

CANON LAW SOCIETY OF AMERICA
Statement of Cash Flows
For the Year Ended June 30, 2023

Increase (Decrease) in Cash and Cash Equivalents		
Cash Flows From Operating Activities		
Changes in net assets	$	68,029
Adjustments to reconcile changes in net assets to net cash provided by (used in) operating activities:		
Depreciation		4,014
Amortization of right of use operating lease assets		32,526
Unrealized and realized gains on investments		(168,892)
Changes in assets and liabilities:		
Accounts receivable		2,845
Inventory		(43,727)
Prepaid expenses		(41,756)
Accounts payable and accrued expenses		34,979
Accrued vacation		(4,185)
Deferred revenue		98,062
Operating lease liability		(31,438)
Net Cash Provided by (Used in) Operating Activities		(49,543)
Cash Flows From Investing Activities		
Purchase of investments		(148,020)
Proceeds from sale of investments		300,000
Net Cash Provided by (Used in) Investing Activities		151,980
Increase (Decrease) in Cash and Cash Equivalents		102,437
Cash and Cash Equivalents - Beginning of Year		211,253
Cash and Cash Equivalents - End of Year	$	313,690
Supplemental Disclosures:		
Income taxes paid	$	-
Interest paid	$	-
Supplemental Disclosure of Non-Cash Investing and Financing Activity:		
Operating lease liabilities arising from new right of use operating lease assets	$	105,393

The accompanying notes are an integral part of this statement.

Canon Law Society of America
Notes to Financial Statements
For the Year Ended June 30, 2023

1. Nature of Activities

The Canon Law Society of America (CLSA) is a national, not-for-profit corporation, established in November 1939 in Washington DC to promote canonical and pastoral approaches to significant issues within the Roman Catholic Church. In addition to a publication service, CLSA conducts an annual convention and other symposia to promote a better understanding of church law and its pastoral applications. Major sources of revenue include: membership dues, sales of publications and annual convention and workshops.

2. Summary of Significant Accounting Policies

The accompanying financial statements are presented on the accrual basis of accounting, whereby revenue is recognized when earned and expenses when they are incurred.

Cash and Cash Equivalents – For purposes of the statement of cash flows, CLSA considers all cash accounts and all highly liquid debt instruments purchased with an initial maturity of three months or less to be cash and cash equivalents.

Investments - Investments in marketable securities with readily determinable fair values are reported at their fair values in the statement of financial position. Investment income or loss (including gains and losses on investments, interest and dividends) is included in the statement of activities and changes in net assets as an increase or decrease in net assets without donor restrictions unless the income or loss is restricted by donor or law. Investments consist principally of two mutual funds. Fair value of investments in securities is based on the latest reported sales price at June 30, 2023.

Accounts Receivable - Accounts receivable are stated at the amount management expects to collect from outstanding balances. The provision for uncollectible accounts is based on management's evaluation of the collectability of accounts receivable. CLSA considers accounts receivable to be fully collectible; accordingly, no provision for doubtful accounts is required. Books and publication receivables are considered uncollectible if not collected within 90 days after the sale.

Inventory – The inventory of books and publications is stated at the lower of cost or net realizable value by the first-in, first-out method.

Furniture and Equipment - Purchases of furniture and equipment are recorded at cost. CLSA's policy is to capitalize expenditures for equipment purchased in the amount of $1,000 or more. Depreciation is calculated over an estimated useful life of five to ten years using the straight-line method. Depreciation for the year ended June 30, 2023 totaled $4,014.

2. Summary of Significant Accounting Policies (continued)

Net Assets - CLSA adopted Financial Accounting Standards Board (FASB) Codification Standards. Under the Codification Standards, the Organization is required to report information regarding its financial position and activities according to two classes of net assets:

> Net Assets Without Donor Restrictions – Net assets that are not subject to or are no longer subject to donor-imposed stipulations.
>
> Net Assets with Donor Restrictions – Net assets whose use is limited by donor-imposed time and/or purpose restrictions.

Revenues are reported as increases in net assets without donor restrictions unless use of the related assets is limited by donor-imposed restrictions. Expenses are reported as decreases in net assets without donor restriction. Gains and losses on investments and other asset or liabilities are reported as increases or decreases in net assets without donor restrictions unless their use is restricted by explicit donor stipulation or by law. Expirations of donor restrictions on the net assets (i.e. the donor-stipulated purpose has been fulfilled and/or the stipulated time period has elapsed) are reported as reclassifications between the applicable classes of net assets.

Tax Status - CLSA is exempt from federal income tax under Section 501(c)(3) of the Internal Revenue Code. CLSA has not been classified by the Internal Revenue Service as a private foundation. Income which is not related to the exempt purpose, less applicable deductions, is subject to Federal and state corporate income tax. CLSA is covered under a group religious exemption and is not required to file the IRS Form 990.

Estimates - In preparing financial statements in conformity with U.S. generally accepted accounting principles, management is required to make estimates and assumptions that affect the reported amounts of assets and liabilities, the disclosure of contingent assets and liabilities at the date of the financial statements, and the reported amounts of revenues and expenses during the reporting period. Actual results could differ from those estimates.

Financial Instruments – CLSA's financial instruments consist of investments, accounts receivable, accounts payable and accrued expenses. It is management's opinion the CLSA is not exposed to significant interest rate or credit risk arising from these instruments. Unless otherwise noted, the fair values of these financial instruments are market values of these financial instruments, and approximate their carrying values.

Revenue Recognition – Revenues from membership dues, which are non-refundable, are recognized pro-rata (on a straight-line basis) over the membership period, which corresponds with CLSA's fiscal year-end. Convention and workshop registration fees are recognized as revenue without donor restrictions at the point in time the meeting or program is held. Publication revenues are recorded at the point in time the revenue is collected.

2. **Summary of Significant Accounting Policies (continued)**

Membership dues, convention and workshop revenues received in advance are deferred and recognized as revenue in the subsequent year.

CLSA recognizes contributions as revenue when cash, securities or other assets, an unconditional promise to give or a notification of a beneficial interest is received. Conditional promises to give – that is, those with a measurable performance of other barrier and a right of return – are not recognized until the conditions on which they depend have been met.

Adoption of New Accounting Standard – In February 2016, the Financial Accounting Standards Board (FASB) established Topic 842, *Leases*, by issuing Accounting Standards Update (ASU) No. 2016-02, which requires lessees to recognize leases on the Statement of Financial Position and disclose key information about leasing arrangements. Topic 842 has been subsequently amended by various ASU's to allow for practical expedients and targeted improvements. The new leasing standard establishes a right-of-use (ROU) model that requires a lessee to recognize a ROU asset and lease liability on the Statement of Financial Position for all leases with a term longer than 12 months. Leases will be classified as finance or operating leases, with the classification affecting the pattern and classification of expense recognition in the statement of activities and changes in net assets.

The new standard is effective for non-public entities as of July 1, 2022. The modified retrospective approach was used upon adoption to apply the standard to all leases that existed at the date of initial application. Because this approach was selected, Topic 842 was not applied to periods prior to adoption and did not have an impact on previously reported results. The adoption did have a material effect on the statement of financial position, with a July 1, 2022 ROU asset of $105,393 recorded and a July 1, 2022 lease liability of $105,393 recorded. There was no material cumulative effect adjustment required to net assets on July 1, 2022. There was no material effect on the statement of cash flows. CLSA has chosen to separate lease and non-lease components in determining the ROU asset and lease liability; therefore, charges for common area maintenance (CAM) have not been included with the ROU asset and lease liability on the statement of financial position.

In addition, CLSA has applied the practical expedient which allows the use of a risk-free rate to determine the present value of the lease liability. CLSA has also chosen not to reassess any expired or existing contracts for leases. Lastly, CLSA has chosen not to apply Topic 842 to low value assets. Additional information regarding leasing is included in Note 11.

3. **Functional Allocation of Expenses**

Directly identifiable expenses are charged to programs and supporting services. Salaries and benefits have been allocated among the programs and supporting services benefited based on estimated time and effort.

4. Fair Value Measurement and Investments

FASB Codification Standards defines fair value, establishes a framework for measuring fair value, and expands disclosures about fair value measurements and establishes a hierarchy for valuation inputs.

Fair value is the price that would be received to sell an asset or paid to transfer a liability in an orderly transaction between market participants at the measurement date. A fair value measurement assumes that the transaction to sell the asset or transfer the liability occurs in the principal market for the asset or liability or, in the absence of a principal market, the most advantageous market. Valuation techniques that are consistent with the market, income or cost approach are used to measure fair value.

The fair value hierarchy prioritizes the inputs to valuation techniques used to measure fair value into three broad levels:

- Level 1 - inputs are based upon unadjusted quoted prices for identical instruments traded in active markets.
- Level 2 - inputs are based upon quoted prices for similar instruments in active markets, quoted prices for identical or similar instruments in markets that are not active, and model-based valuation techniques for which all significant assumptions are observable in the market or can be corroborated by observable market data for substantially the full term of the assets or liabilities.
- Level 3 - inputs are generally unobservable and typically reflect management's estimates of assumptions that market participants would use in pricing the asset or liability. The fair values are therefore determined using model-based techniques that include option pricing models, discounted cash flow models, and similar techniques.

Investments in mutual funds at June 30, 2023, which are all considered level 2, consist of the following:

	Cost	Market
CRI Magnus 60/40 Alpha Plus Fund	$ 2,248,952	$ 2,065,410

By fund type at June 30, 2023:

	Cost	Market
Without donor restrictions	$ 923,557	$ 831,804
With donor restrictions	1,325,395	1,233,606
Total Investments	$ 2,248,952	$ 2,065,410

4. Fair Value Measurement and Investments (continued)

CLSA invests in a professionally managed portfolio that contains mutual funds. Such investments are exposed to various risks such as interest rates, market and credit. Due to the level of risk associated with such investments and the level of uncertainty related to changes in the value of such investments, it is at least reasonably possible that changes in risks in the near term would materially affect investment balances and the amounts reported in the financial statements.

5. Concentration of Credit Risk

CLSA maintains its cash and cash equivalents in bank deposit accounts, which at times, may exceed federally insured limits. CLSA has not experienced any losses in such accounts and believes it is not exposed to any significant financial risk on cash and cash equivalents.

6. Board Designated Funds

The Board has designated that net income from the sale of publications and books be set aside for use only in the publication activities. As reported on the statement of activities and changes in net assets, the net assets from publications increased in fiscal year 2023 by $4,341 to ($117,397).

7. Net Assets with Donor Restrictions

The activity in net assets with donor restrictions for fiscal year 2023 is as follows:

	Scholarship Fund	Doctoral Scholarship	Total
Balance June 30, 2022	$ 945,725	$ 92,915	$ 1,038,640
Income	27,939	6,586	34,525
Unrealized gain on investments	91,916	7,900	99,816
Expenses	(34,702)	(324)	(35,026)
Balance June 30, 2023	$ 1,030,878	$ 107,077	$ 1,137,955

8. Revenues from Contracts with Customers

The following table provides information about significant changes in deferred revenue for the year ended June 30, 2023:

Membership Dues	
Deferred revenue, beginning of year	$ 217,125
Revenue recognized that was included in deferred revenue at the beginning of year	(217,125)
Increase in deferred revenue due to cash received during the year	301,437
Deferred revenue, end of year	$ 301,437

Convention Revenue	
Deferred revenue, beginning of year	$ 23,225
Revenue recognized that was included in deferred revenue at the beginning of year	(208,275)
Increase in deferred revenue due to cash received during the year	222,025
Deferred revenue, end of year	$ 36,975

9. Annual Meeting Site Reservation Agreements

CLSA has reserved hotel space for future conventions. The terms of these reservation agreements provide that a fee will be assessed to CSLA if the reservation is canceled due to site change, within a specified period prior to the meeting dates.

10. Retirement Plan

CLSA has a 403(b) Retirement Savings Plan. Eligible employees must meet certain hours and age requirements. Under the plan participants may elect but are not required to defer a portion of their salary up to a maximum allowed by law. The employer contributes 3% of the participant's compensation if the employee participates in the plan. Retirement expense for the year ended June 30, 2023 was $6,177.

11. Commitments

Office Lease - In December 2015, CLSA entered into a ten-year lease for office space. Monthly rent payments are $2,501 currently and increase 3% annually.

Equipment Lease - In January 2021, CLSA entered into a fifty-one month lease for a postage machine. Payments of $226 are billed quarterly.

11. Commitments (continued)

For the year ended June 30, 2023, these leases have been accounted for under ASC Topic 842. The operating lease liability as of June 30, 2023 consists of the following:

Current portion of operating lease liability	$ 30,647
Long-term portion of operating lease liability	45,862
Total operating lease liability	$ 76,509

Future annual minimum lease payments under the leases for the next five years are as follows at June 30:

2024	$	32,354
2025		33,072
2026		13,663
2027		-
2028		-
Total undiscounted cash flows		79,089
Less: present value discount		(2,580)
Total lease liabilities	$	76,509

Lease expense under these leases was $32,525 for the year ended June 30, 2023 which is included as components of "operating lease expense" on the statement of functional expense.

Additional information regarding these leases is summarized below:

Weighted-average remaining lease term	2.40
Weighted-average discount rate	2.85%

12. Liquidity and Availability of Financial Assets

The following table reflects the CLSA's financial assets as of June 30, 2023, reduced by amounts not available for general expenditures within one year.

Financial assets:		
Cash and cash equivalents	$	313,690
Accounts receivable		3,353
Investments		831,804
Investments - scholarship fund		1,233,606
Financial assets, at year-end:		2,382,453
Less those unavailable for general expenditure within one year, due to:		
Donor restrictions		1,137,955
Financial assets available to meet cash needs for general expenses within one year	$	1,244,498

CLSA has a policy to structure its financial assets to be available as its general expenditures, liabilities and other obligations come due. The Organization can authorize the transfer of funds from the investment accounts to the operating bank accounts to assist in cash flow needs. Transfers of $300,000 were made in fiscal year 2023.

13. Subsequent Events

Management has evaluated subsequent events through September 6, 2023, the date that the financial statements were available to be issued. There were no significant events to report.

Canon Law Society of America

Balance Sheet

As of June 30, 2023

	TOTAL
ASSETS	
Current Assets	
Bank Accounts	
1010 TD Operating Account - 9622	277,170.81
1011 TD Money Market Account - 9630	36,543.76
1050 Cash Box	325.30
Total Bank Accounts	$314,039.87
Accounts Receivable	
Accounts Receivable (A/R)	3,353.33
Total Accounts Receivable	$3,353.33
Other Current Assets	
1400 Prepaid Expenses	0.00
1410 Prepaid/Rent Insurance	624.75
1420 Other Prepaid Expenses	5,302.85
1421 Other Prepaid Exp (Publications	1,500.00
1422 Other Prepaid Ex (Convention)	52,726.98
Total 1400 Prepaid Expenses	60,154.58
1500 Inventory Asset	
1510 Inventory - Books & CDs (Pub)	29,035.84
1520 Commentary	44,500.00
Total 1500 Inventory Asset	73,535.84
Undeposited Funds	-350.00
Total Other Current Assets	$133,340.42
Total Current Assets	$450,733.62
Fixed Assets	
1700 Fixed Assets	
1710 Furniture and Equipment (Ops)	31,471.00
1720 Technology Equipment	5,600.00
1790 Accumulated Depreciation(contra	-27,188.70
Total 1700 Fixed Assets	9,882.30
Total Fixed Assets	$9,882.30
Other Assets	
1230 Security Deposit (Ops)	2,094.40
1600 Investment	
1612 CUIT Magnus-Ops (Ending 2001)	831,804.07
Total 1600 Investment	831,804.07
1650 Investment - Scholarship Fund	
1622 CUIT Magnus-Licentiate (..2002)	1,132,156.66
1623 CUIT Magnus-Doctoral (...2003)	101,448.74
Total 1650 Investment - Scholarship Fund	1,233,605.40
1800 Finance Right of Use (net)	75,421.84
Total Other Assets	$2,142,925.71

Canon Law Society of America

Balance Sheet

As of June 30, 2023

	TOTAL
TOTAL ASSETS	$2,603,541.63
LIABILITIES AND EQUITY	
Liabilities	
Current Liabilities	
Accounts Payable	
Accounts Payable (A/P)	19,775.62
Total Accounts Payable	$19,775.62
Credit Cards	
2160 Bank of America - 7812	5,024.99
Total Credit Cards	$5,024.99
Other Current Liabilities	
2115 Accrued Scholarships Licentiate	38,250.01
2120 Accrued Expenses - Royalties	
2121 AccruedExp-Holy See CCEO (8%)	88.40
2123 Accrued Exp-Holy See Dignit(6%)	27.00
2124 AccruedExp(CMSM/NCVR/LCWR/SI60%	31.44
2126 QUOQEU, Code - 4th Edition	3,780.00
Total 2120 Accrued Expenses - Royalties	3,926.84
2130 Accrued Payroll	
2131 Accrued Wages	4,914.19
Total 2130 Accrued Payroll	4,914.19
2135 Accrued Expenses	5,343.17
2136 Accrued Commentary Contributors	34,500.00
2150 Short Term Lease Liability	30,647.32
2200 Deferred Revenue	
2201 Deferred Revenue (Conv. Reg.)	36,975.00
2204 Deferred Rev - Membership Dues	301,437.50
Total 2200 Deferred Revenue	338,412.50
Total Other Current Liabilities	$455,994.03
Total Current Liabilities	$480,794.64
Long-Term Liabilities	
2700 Long Term Lease Liability	45,862.18
Total Long-Term Liabilities	$45,862.18
Total Liabilities	$526,656.82
Equity	
3101 Unrestricted	0.00
3102 Undesignated	897,022.34
3103 Board designated - Publications	-133,999.60
Total 3101 Unrestricted	763,022.74
3120 Temporarily restricted	1,138,987.95
3126 Unrestricted Retained Earn-Scho	106,839.15
Net Income	68,034.97

Canon Law Society of America

Balance Sheet

As of June 30, 2023

	TOTAL
Total Equity	$2,076,884.81
TOTAL LIABILITIES AND EQUITY	$2,603,541.63

Note
FY2023 Investment Account Transfers to be Replenished:
General Investment Fund
Withdrawals $(300,000.00)
Replenishment $101,838.50
Remaining to replenish $(198,161.50)

For Management Purposes Only
These financial statements are the property and responsibility of the management of Canon Law Society of America. The Fiscal Year 2021-2022 financial statements have not been audited or reviewed and accordingly no opinion or any other form of assurance is expressed on them.

Canon Law Society of America

Budget Overview: FY 2024

July 2023 - June 2024

	TOTAL
Income	
4100 Stewardship	
4110 Membership Dues	
4111 New Member Dues	20,000.00
4112 Annual Dues Renewal	330,000.00
Total 4110 Membership Dues	**350,000.00**
4130 Scholarship Contributions	
4131 Licentiate Scholarship	15,000.00
4132 Doctoral Scholarship	3,000.00
Total 4130 Scholarship Contributions	**18,000.00**
4140 Investment Income	
4141 Interest & Dividend-Operations	11,000.00
4142 Interest & Dividend-Licentiate	15,000.00
4143 Interest & Dividend - Doctoral	1,300.00
4160 Unreal. Gains/Loss - Gen Ops (001)	42,000.00
4161 Unreal Gains/Loss-Licentiate Sch (002)	45,000.00
4162 Unreal Gains/Loss-Doctoral Sch (003)	1,950.00
Total 4140 Investment Income	**116,250.00**
Total 4100 Stewardship	**484,250.00**
4300 Membership Development	
4310 Annual Convention-Members Mtg	
4311 Exhibitors/Sponsorships	6,200.00
4312 Banquet Fees (Additional)	800.00
4313 Convention Registration	181,750.00
4314 Pre-Convention Fees	16,250.00
4315 W2. Pre-Convention Fees	7,500.00
4316 One Day Registration	125.00
4318 Contract Commission	12,000.00
Total 4310 Annual Convention-Members Mtg	**224,625.00**
Total 4300 Membership Development	**224,625.00**
4400 Product Development	
4410 Publication and Resources	
4411 Publications Sales	87,000.00
4413 Product Partnership Royalties	3,500.00
4417 Sales - Digital, Electronic Media	1,200.00
4420 Publications - Amazon sales	6,000.00
Total 4410 Publication and Resources	**97,700.00**
Total 4400 Product Development	**97,700.00**
Total Income	**$806,575.00**
GROSS PROFIT	**$806,575.00**
Expenses	
5100 Stewardship Expense	
5120 Scholarships	

Canon Law Society of America

Budget Overview: FY24

July 2023 - June 2024

	TOTAL
5121 Licentiate Scholarship Awards	26,500.00
5123 Other Scholarship Expenses	4,000.00
Total 5120 Scholarships	**30,500.00**
Total 5100 Stewardship Expense	**30,500.00**
5200 Professional Developmnt	
5223 Networking	13,500.00
Total 5200 Professional Developmnt	**13,500.00**
5300 Convention and workshops (Membership Dev)	
5310 Membership Outreach	3,000.00
5320 Annual Convention - Members Mtg	
5321 Convention Exhibit/Advertising	200.00
5322 Convention Hotel, Food Events	95,000.00
5323 Convention Audio Visual Contractor	45,000.00
5324 Convention Supplies	3,000.00
5325 Convention Travel	6,000.00
5327 Convention Postage/Shipping	1,500.00
5328 Convention Printing/Copying	6,500.00
5329 Promotion; Program Materials/Banner	5,500.00
5330 Liturgy & Environment	3,500.00
5331 Speaker Honoraria/ Stipends	19,000.00
5332 Speaker/Travel	5,000.00
5333 Convention Lodging/Meals	10,000.00
5334 Convention Planner	57,000.00
Total 5320 Annual Convention - Members Mtg	**257,200.00**
5340 Board of Governors	
5345 BOG Travel	10,400.00
5346 BOG Lodging/Meals	26,000.00
5347 Officers' Expenses	3,000.00
5348 President Discretionary Fund	2,000.00
Total 5340 Board of Governors	**41,400.00**
Total 5300 Convention and workshops (Membership Dev)	**301,600.00**
5350 Committees	
5351 Constitutional Committees	3,000.00
5352 Standing Committees	6,500.00
5353 Convention Planning Committee	6,500.00
5355 Strategic Visioning	30,000.00
5356 Publication Advisory Board Comm	12,000.00
Total 5350 Committees	**58,000.00**
5400 Product Dvelopment	
5410 COGS - Publication & Resources	
5411 Cost of Goods Sold	27,300.00
Total 5410 COGS - Publication & Resources	**27,300.00**
5420 Expenses-Publication & Resource	

Canon Law Society of America

Budget Overview: FY24

July 2023 - June 2024

	TOTAL
5423 Books/Media/Materials	140,000.00
5424 Membership Dues/Subscription/Licensing	1,000.00
5427 Publications Postage/Shipping	1,000.00
5428 Supplies	500.00
Total 5420 Expenses-Publication & Resource	**142,500.00**
5430 Logistech-Outsourcing Pub & Res	
5433 Project Management Fees	200.00
5434 Rent-Storage Space (Pallet/Quic	1,000.00
5435 Ordering Processing	4,000.00
5436 Website, IT Services	5,000.00
5437 Printing/Copying Reports	2,000.00
5438 Prof Services (Projects/Warehouse Support)	300.00
5440 Postage/Shipping	13,000.00
Total 5430 Logistech-Outsourcing Pub & Res	**25,500.00**
5450 Expenses-Royalties Pub & Resour	
5451 Royalties for CCEO (8% of NR)	150.00
5452 Royalties for CIC (8% of NR)	2,700.00
5453 Royalties for Dignitas Connubbii (6% of NR)	150.00
Total 5450 Expenses-Royalties Pub & Resour	**3,000.00**
5460 Product Partnerships	
5461 CLSA Research Database Hosting	1,600.00
Total 5460 Product Partnerships	**1,600.00**
Total 5400 Product Dvelopment	**199,900.00**
6100 Canon Law Society Operating Exp	
6110 Salaries and Benefits	
6111 Salaries	200,000.00
6112 Employer Payroll Taxes	14,780.00
6113 Professional Development (Staff	1,000.00
6114 Employee Health Benefit Plan	26,000.00
6115 Pension Plan Administration	220.00
6116 403b Obligations	6,000.00
Total 6110 Salaries and Benefits	**248,000.00**
6120 Operating Expenses	
6121 Publication/Media Materials	15,000.00
6127 Rent	32,000.00
6132 Professional Services (Contract	10,000.00
6134 Accounting/Audit Fees	65,000.00
6135 Legal Fees	15,000.00
Total 6132 Professional Services (Contract	**90,000.00**
6133 Bank/Financial Fees/PayrollFees	25,000.00
6145 Other Business Expenses	
6122 Software/Subscription/Licenses	3,000.00
6123 Advertising/Marketing/Graphic Design	100.00

Canon Law Society of America

Budget Overview: FY24

July 2023 - June 2024

	TOTAL
6124 Awards/Gifts	1,000.00
6125 Equipment Lease/Purchase/Maint	2,000.00
6126 Business Insurance	1,200.00
6128 Telecommunications	6,000.00
6129 Postage/Shipping	1,500.00
6131 Supplies	4,000.00
6136 Executive Coordinator/Travel	2,000.00
6137 Lodging/Meals	1,000.00
6140 Depreciation Expense	4,000.00
Total 6145 Other Business Expenses	25,800.00
Total 6120 Operating Expenses	187,800.00
Total 6100 Canon Law Society Operating Exp	435,800.00
Total Expenses	$1,039,300.00
NET OPERATING INCOME	$ -232,725.00
NET INCOME	$ -232,725.00

Canon Law Society of America

Budget vs. Actuals: FY23

July 2022 - June 2023

	TOTAL		
	ACTUAL	BUDGET	REMAINING
Income			
4100 Stewardship			
4110 Membership Dues	0.00		0.00
4111 New Member Dues	20,687.50	12,500.00	-8,187.50
4112 Annual Dues Renewal	258,850.00	250,000.00	-8,850.00
Total 4110 Membership Dues	279,537.50	262,500.00	-17,037.50
4120 Donations			
4122 General Donations	1,838.50		-1,838.50
Total 4120 Donations	1,838.50		-1,838.50
4130 Scholarship Contributions	0.00		0.00
4131 Licentiate Scholarship	12,057.48	7,500.00	-4,557.48
4132 Doctoral Scholarship	5,202.52	3,500.00	-1,702.52
Total 4130 Scholarship Contributions	17,260.00	11,000.00	-6,260.00
4140 Investment Income			
4141 Interest & Dividend-Operations	11,832.33		-11,832.33
4142 Interest & Dividend-Licentiate	15,882.28		-15,882.28
4143 Interest & Dividend - Doctoral	1,365.13		-1,365.13
4144 Int & Div - Scholarship (TD Bank)	17.93		-17.93
4150 Realized Gains/Loss	-4,750.19		4,750.19
4160 Unreal. Gains/Loss - Gen Ops (001)	73,825.78	25,000.00	-48,825.78
4161 Unreal Gains/Loss-Licentiate Sch (002)	91,916.06	25,000.00	-66,916.06
4162 Unreal Gains/Loss-Doctoral Sch (003)	7,900.46	2,000.00	-5,900.46
Total 4140 Investment Income	197,989.78	52,000.00	-145,989.78
Total 4100 Stewardship	496,625.78	325,500.00	-171,125.78
4300 Membership Development			
4310 Annual Convention-Members Mtg			
4311 Exhibitors/Sponsorships	2,675.00	1,500.00	-1,175.00
4312 Banquet Fees (Additional)	800.00	300.00	-500.00
4313 Convention Registration	202,450.00	165,000.00	-37,450.00
4314 Pre-Convention Fees		16,500.00	16,500.00
4315 W2. Pre-Convention Fees		7,500.00	7,500.00
4317 Sponsorship Donations	3,400.00		-3,400.00
4318 Contract Commission	13,681.29		-13,681.29
Total 4310 Annual Convention-Members Mtg	223,006.29	190,800.00	-32,206.29
Total 4300 Membership Development	223,006.29	190,800.00	-32,206.29
4400 Product Development			
4410 Publication and Resources			
4411 Publications Sales	114,030.48	70,000.00	-44,030.48
4413 Product Partnership Royalties	3,958.92	2,500.00	-1,458.92
4417 Sales - Digital, Electronic Media		1,200.00	1,200.00
4420 Publications - Amazon sales	5,528.36	10,000.00	4,471.64
4430 Publication shipping income	15,536.53		-15,536.53

Canon Law Society of America

Budget vs. Actuals: FY 23

July 2022 - June 2023

	TOTAL		
	ACTUAL	BUDGET	REMAINING
Total 4410 Publication and Resources	139,054.29	83,700.00	-55,354.29
Total 4400 Product Development	139,054.29	83,700.00	-55,354.29
Uncategorized Income	346.87		-346.87
Total Income	$859,033.23	$600,000.00	$ -259,033.23
GROSS PROFIT	$859,033.23	$600,000.00	$ -259,033.23
Expenses			
5100 Stewardship Expense			
5120 Scholarships	-1.99		1.99
5121 Licentiate Scholarship Awards	31,333.34	15,000.00	-16,333.34
5122 Doctoral Scholarship Awards		2,200.00	2,200.00
5123 Other Scholarship Expenses		1,500.00	1,500.00
Total 5120 Scholarships	31,331.35	18,700.00	-12,631.35
Total 5100 Stewardship Expense	31,331.35	18,700.00	-12,631.35
5200 Professional Developmnt			
5220 Partnerships	35.00		-35.00
5223 Networking	10,127.62		-10,127.62
Total 5200 Professional Developmnt	10,162.62		-10,162.62
5300 Convention and workshops (Membership Dev)			
5310 Membership Outreach	2,675.19	5,000.00	2,324.81
5313 Membership Expenses	14,026.36		-14,026.36
Total 5310 Membership Outreach	16,701.55	5,000.00	-11,701.55
5320 Annual Convention - Members Mtg			
5322 Convention Hotel, Food Events	89,465.97	90,000.00	534.03
5323 Convention Audio Visual Contractor	48,082.44	40,000.00	-8,082.44
5324 Convention Supplies	2,556.39	5,000.00	2,443.61
5325 Convention Travel	2,642.76	4,750.00	2,107.24
5327 Convention Postage/Shipping	1,323.01	2,500.00	1,176.99
5328 Convention Printing/Copying	6,576.89	3,500.00	-3,076.89
5329 Promotion; Program Materials/Banner	5,203.97	5,500.00	296.03
5330 Liturgy & Environment	3,638.09	3,000.00	-638.09
5331 Speaker Honoraria/ Stipends	15,932.25	18,600.00	2,667.75
5332 Speaker/Travel	6,338.88	5,000.00	-1,338.88
5333 Convention Lodging/Meals	7,929.56	20,000.00	12,070.44
5334 Convention Planner	55,414.04	53,000.00	-2,414.04
Total 5320 Annual Convention - Members Mtg	245,104.25	250,850.00	5,745.75
5340 Board of Governors	60.00		-60.00
5341 BOG Telecommunications	1,443.75	150.00	-1,293.75
5342 BOG Postage/Shipping		100.00	100.00
5343 BOG Printing/Copying	34.26	150.00	115.74
5345 BOG Travel	5,493.27	9,000.00	3,506.73
5346 BOG Lodging/Meals	21,388.68	22,000.00	611.32
5347 Officers' Expenses	1,690.80	4,500.00	2,809.20

Canon Law Society of America

Budget vs. Actuals: FY23

July 2022 - June 2023

	TOTAL		
	ACTUAL	BUDGET	REMAINING
5348 President Discretionary Fund		2,000.00	2,000.00
Total 5340 Board of Governors	30,110.76	37,900.00	7,789.24
Total 5300 Convention and workshops (Membership Dev)	291,916.56	293,750.00	1,833.44
5350 Committees			
5351 Constitutional Committees	2,564.31	10,000.00	7,435.69
5352 Standing Committees	896.71	5,000.00	4,103.29
5353 Convention Planning Committee	2,065.86		-2,065.86
5355 Strategic Visioning	468.00	15,000.00	14,532.00
5356 Publication Advisory Board Comm	7,226.07		-7,226.07
Total 5350 Committees	13,220.95	30,000.00	16,779.05
5400 Product Dvelopment			
5410 COGS - Publication & Resources			
5411 Cost of Goods Sold	19,753.97	14,000.00	-5,753.97
Total 5410 COGS - Publication & Resources	19,753.97	14,000.00	-5,753.97
5420 Expenses-Publication & Resource		700.00	700.00
5421 Administrative Expenses		150.00	150.00
5423 Books/Media/Materials	0.00		0.00
5425 Advertising/Public Relations		500.00	500.00
5427 Publications Postage/Shipping	887.12	500.00	-387.12
Total 5420 Expenses-Publication & Resource	887.12	1,850.00	962.88
5430 Logistech-Outsourcing Pub & Res			
5433 Project Management Fees		200.00	200.00
5434 Rent-Storage Space (Pallet/Quic	694.92	1,000.00	305.08
5435 Ordering Processing	2,631.75	2,500.00	-131.75
5438 Prof Services (Projects/Warehouse Support)	102.61	100.00	-2.61
5440 Postage/Shipping	10,233.66	10,000.00	-233.66
Total 5430 Logistech-Outsourcing Pub & Res	13,662.94	13,800.00	137.06
5450 Expenses-Royalties Pub & Resour			
5451 Royalties for CCEO (8% of NR)	218.40	250.00	31.60
5452 Royalties for CIC (8% of NR)	556.80	2,000.00	1,443.20
5453 Royalties for Dignitas Connubbii (6% of NR)	42.00	250.00	208.00
5454 Royalties for Selected Issues (60% of NR)	50.88	150.00	99.12
5456 QUQQEI, Code - 4th Edition	3,780.00		-3,780.00
Total 5450 Expenses-Royalties Pub & Resour	4,648.08	2,650.00	-1,998.08
5460 Product Partnerships			
5461 CLSA Research Database Hosting	1,544.75	1,600.00	55.25
Total 5460 Product Partnerships	1,544.75	1,600.00	55.25
Total 5400 Product Dvelopment	40,496.86	33,900.00	-6,596.86
6100 Canon Law Society Operating Exp			
6110 Salaries and Benefits			
6111 Salaries	176,006.64	167,000.00	-9,006.64
6112 Employer Payroll Taxes	13,336.65	13,000.00	-336.65

Canon Law Society of America

Budget vs. Actuals: Y23

July 2022 - June 2023

	TOTAL		
	ACTUAL	BUDGET	REMAINING
6113 Professional Development (Staff	75.00		-75.00
6114 Employee Health Benefit Plan	17,707.44	15,000.00	-2,707.44
6115 Pension Plan Administration	202.50	150.00	-52.50
6116 403b Obligations	6,176.69	3,800.00	-2,376.69
Total 6110 Salaries and Benefits	213,504.92	198,950.00	-14,554.92
6120 Operating Expenses			
6121 Publication/Media Materials	110.00	11,000.00	10,890.00
6127 Rent	75.02	30,000.00	29,924.98
6130 Printing/Copying	358.28	1,200.00	841.72
6132 Professional Services (Contract	11,822.50	25,000.00	13,177.50
6134 Accounting/Audit Fees	71,913.58	45,000.00	-26,913.58
6135 Legal Fees	25,629.66	1,000.00	-24,629.66
Total 6132 Professional Services (Contract	109,365.74	71,000.00	-38,365.74
6133 Bank/Financial Fees/PayrollFees	22,080.43	24,000.00	1,919.57
6138 CMS and Website Licensing	4,339.37	5,000.00	660.63
6144 Operating Lease Expense	32,525.52		-32,525.52
6145 Other Business Expenses			
6122 Software/Subscription/Licenses	4,556.51	3,000.00	-1,556.51
6123 Advertising/Marketing/Graphic Design	299.00	1,000.00	701.00
6124 Awards/Gifts	162.36		-162.36
6125 Equipment Lease/Purchase/Maint	731.25	1,500.00	768.75
6126 Business Insurance	1,148.25	1,200.00	51.75
6128 Telecommunications	4,845.96	4,000.00	-845.96
6129 Postage/Shipping	451.46	1,600.00	1,148.54
6131 Supplies	1,966.67	2,000.00	33.33
6136 Executive Coordinator/Travel	2,039.94	5,000.00	2,960.06
6137 Lodging/Meals	789.02	1,500.00	710.98
6139 Bad Debt/Write-Offs	81.70		-81.70
6140 Depreciation Expense	4,013.52	2,500.00	-1,513.52
Total 6145 Other Business Expenses	21,085.64	23,300.00	2,214.36
6150 Miscellaneous Expenses	425.00		-425.00
Total 6120 Operating Expenses	190,365.00	165,500.00	-24,865.00
Total 6100 Canon Law Society Operating Exp	403,869.92	364,450.00	-39,419.92
Total Expenses	$790,998.26	$740,800.00	$ -50,198.26
NET OPERATING INCOME	$68,034.97	$ -140,800.00	$ -208,834.97
NET INCOME	$68,034.97	$ -140,800.00	$ -208,834.97

Note
Unaudited: For Management Purposes Only
These financial statements are the property and responsibility of the management of Canon Law Society of America. These financial statements have not been audited or reviewed and accordingly no opinion or any other form of assurance is expressed on them.

Canon Law Society of America

Profit and Loss Comparison

FY 23 and FY 22

	TOTAL	
	JUL 2022 - JUN 2023	JUL 2021 - JUN 2022 (PY)
Income		
4100 Stewardship		
4110 Membership Dues	0.00	
4111 New Member Dues	20,687.50	14,687.50
4112 Annual Dues Renewal	258,850.00	254,977.33
Total 4110 Membership Dues	279,537.50	269,664.83
4120 Donations		
4122 General Donations	1,838.50	647.59
Total 4120 Donations	1,838.50	647.59
4130 Scholarship Contributions	0.00	605.00
4131 Licentiate Scholarship	12,057.48	9,700.00
4132 Doctoral Scholarship	5,202.52	2,550.00
Total 4130 Scholarship Contributions	17,260.00	12,855.00
4140 Investment Income		
4141 Interest & Dividend-Operations	11,832.33	
4142 Interest & Dividend-Licentiate	15,882.28	
4143 Interest & Dividend - Doctoral	1,365.13	
4144 Int & Div - Scholarship (TD Bank)	17.93	14.60
4150 Realized Gains/Loss	-4,750.19	
4160 Unreal. Gains/Loss - Gen Ops (001)	73,825.78	-152,200.76
4161 Unreal Gains/Loss-Licentiate Sch (002)	91,916.06	-167,226.82
4162 Unreal Gains/Loss-Doctoral Sch (003)	7,900.46	-14,382.39
Total 4140 Investment Income	197,989.78	-333,795.37
Total 4100 Stewardship	496,625.78	-50,627.95
4300 Membership Development		
4310 Annual Convention-Members Mtg		
4311 Exhibitors/Sponsorships	2,675.00	800.00
4312 Banquet Fees (Additional)	800.00	120.00
4313 Convention Registration	202,450.00	154,200.06
4314 Pre-Convention Fees		16,500.00
4315 W2. Pre-Convention Fees		6,925.00
4317 Sponsorship Donations	3,400.00	2,000.00
4318 Contract Commission	13,681.29	23,182.92
4350 Discounts/Refunds Given		-25.00
Total 4310 Annual Convention-Members Mtg	223,006.29	203,702.98
4320 Events		
4321 Miscellaneous income		27,980.00
Total 4320 Events		27,980.00
Total 4300 Membership Development	223,006.29	231,682.98
4400 Product Development		
4410 Publication and Resources		
4411 Publications Sales	114,030.48	63,547.07

1/5

Canon Law Society of America

Profit and Loss Comparison

FY 23 and FY 22

	TOTAL	
	JUL 2022 - JUN 2023	JUL 2021 - JUN 2022 (PY)
4413 Product Partnership Royalties	3,958.92	3,866.43
4417 Sales - Digital, Electronic Media		582.00
4420 Publications - Amazon sales	5,528.36	9,737.76
4430 Publication shipping income	15,536.53	901.70
Total 4410 Publication and Resources	139,054.29	78,634.96
Total 4400 Product Development	139,054.29	78,634.96
Uncategorized Income	346.87	137.84
Total Income	$859,033.23	$259,827.83
GROSS PROFIT	$859,033.23	$259,827.83
Expenses		
5100 Stewardship Expense		
5120 Scholarships	-1.99	
5121 Licentiate Scholarship Awards	31,333.34	2,014.08
5122 Doctoral Scholarship Awards		1,500.00
5123 Other Scholarship Expenses		1,415.40
Total 5120 Scholarships	31,331.35	4,929.48
Total 5100 Stewardship Expense	31,331.35	4,929.48
5200 Professional Developmnt		
5220 Partnerships	35.00	
5223 Networking	10,127.62	193.48
Total 5200 Professional Developmnt	10,162.62	193.48
5300 Convention and workshops (Membership Dev)		
5310 Membership Outreach	2,675.19	27,201.05
5313 Membership Expenses	14,026.36	
Total 5310 Membership Outreach	16,701.55	27,201.05
5320 Annual Convention - Members Mtg		
5322 Convention Hotel, Food Events	89,465.97	87,523.39
5323 Convention Audio Visual Contractor	48,082.44	40,865.00
5324 Convention Supplies	2,556.39	4,743.19
5325 Convention Travel	2,642.76	5,155.98
5326 Convention Telecommunications		50.00
5327 Convention Postage/Shipping	1,323.01	2,834.89
5328 Convention Printing/Copying	6,576.89	2,629.00
5329 Promotion; Program Materials/Banner	5,203.97	2,513.00
5330 Liturgy & Environment	3,638.09	3,016.43
5331 Speaker Honoraria/ Stipends	15,932.25	14,260.96
5332 Speaker/Travel	6,338.88	1,933.90
5333 Convention Lodging/Meals	7,929.56	20,551.32
5334 Convention Planner	55,414.04	52,526.27
Total 5320 Annual Convention - Members Mtg	245,104.25	238,603.33
5340 Board of Governors	60.00	
5341 BOG Telecommunications	1,443.75	135.00

2/5

Canon Law Society of America

Profit and Loss Comparison

FY 23 and FY 22

	TOTAL	
	JUL 2022 - JUN 2023	JUL 2021 - JUN 2022 (PY)
5342 BOG Postage/Shipping		579.58
5343 BOG Printing/Copying	34.26	427.31
5345 BOG Travel	5,493.27	402.60
5346 BOG Lodging/Meals	21,388.68	12,849.29
5347 Officers' Expenses	1,690.80	1,111.30
Total 5340 Board of Governors	30,110.76	15,505.08
Total 5300 Convention and workshops (Membership Dev)	291,916.56	281,309.46
5350 Committees		
5351 Constitutional Committees	2,564.31	3,801.07
5352 Standing Committees	896.71	723.28
5353 Convention Planning Committee	2,065.86	
5355 Strategic Visioning	468.00	
5356 Publication Advisory Board Comm	7,226.07	7,203.06
Total 5350 Committees	13,220.95	11,727.41
5400 Product Dvelopment		
5410 COGS - Publication & Resources		
5411 Cost of Goods Sold	19,753.97	12,664.57
Total 5410 COGS - Publication & Resources	19,753.97	12,664.57
5420 Expenses-Publication & Resource		430.00
5421 Administrative Expenses		105.85
5425 Advertising/Public Relations		160.00
5427 Publications Postage/Shipping	887.12	466.10
7500 Obsolete Inventory		336.00
Total 5420 Expenses-Publication & Resource	887.12	1,497.95
5430 Logistech-Outsourcing Pub & Res		
5433 Project Management Fees		57.50
5434 Rent-Storage Space (Pallet/Quic	694.92	544.94
5435 Ordering Processing	2,631.75	2,535.58
5438 Prof Services (Projects/Warehouse Support)	102.61	50.85
5440 Postage/Shipping	10,233.66	9,183.32
Total 5430 Logistech-Outsourcing Pub & Res	13,662.94	12,372.19
5450 Expenses-Royalties Pub & Resour		-29.52
5451 Royalties for CCEO (8% of NR)	218.40	222.00
5452 Royalties for CIC (8% of NR)	556.80	2,090.40
5453 Royalties for Dignitas Connubbii (6% of NR)	42.00	127.20
5454 Royalties for Selected Issues (60% of NR)	50.88	172.80
5456 QUOQEI, Code - 4th Edition	3,780.00	
Total 5450 Expenses-Royalties Pub & Resour	4,648.08	2,582.88
5460 Product Partnerships		
5461 CLSA Research Database Hosting	1,544.75	1,535.22
Total 5460 Product Partnerships	1,544.75	1,535.22
Total 5400 Product Dvelopment	40,496.86	30,652.81

Canon Law Society of America

Profit and Loss Comparison

FY 23 and FY 22

	TOTAL	
	JUL 2022 - JUN 2023	JUL 2021 - JUN 2022 (PY)
6100 Canon Law Society Operating Exp		
6110 Salaries and Benefits		
6111 Salaries	176,006.64	161,281.43
6112 Employer Payroll Taxes	13,336.65	12,225.85
6113 Professional Development (Staff	75.00	
6114 Employee Health Benefit Plan	17,707.44	12,068.12
6115 Pension Plan Administration	202.50	144.00
6116 403b Obligations	6,176.69	4,119.77
Total 6110 Salaries and Benefits	213,504.92	189,839.17
6120 Operating Expenses		
6121 Publication/Media Materials	110.00	21,962.57
6127 Rent	75.02	29,968.70
6130 Printing/Copying	358.28	2,087.26
6132 Professional Services (Contract	11,822.50	12,125.87
6134 Accounting/Audit Fees	71,913.58	55,500.22
6135 Legal Fees	25,629.66	
Total 6132 Professional Services (Contract	109,365.74	67,626.09
6133 Bank/Financial Fees/PayrollFees	22,080.43	20,022.49
6138 CMS and Website Licensing	4,339.37	4,070.15
6144 Operating Lease Expense	32,525.52	
6145 Other Business Expenses		
6122 Software/Subscription/Licenses	4,556.51	3,815.70
6123 Advertising/Marketing/Graphic Design	299.00	
6124 Awards/Gifts	162.36	579.53
6125 Equipment Lease/Purchase/Maint	731.25	1,214.64
6126 Business Insurance	1,148.25	1,115.06
6128 Telecommunications	4,845.96	4,254.37
6129 Postage/Shipping	451.46	1,848.88
6131 Supplies	1,966.67	1,739.61
6136 Executive Coordinator/Travel	2,039.94	8.26
6137 Lodging/Meals	789.02	547.79
6139 Bad Debt/Write-Offs	81.70	
6140 Depreciation Expense	4,013.52	4,013.18
Total 6145 Other Business Expenses	21,085.64	19,137.02
6150 Miscellaneous Expenses	425.00	
Total 6120 Operating Expenses	190,365.00	164,874.28
Total 6100 Canon Law Society Operating Exp	403,869.92	354,713.45
Total Expenses	$790,998.26	$683,526.09
NET OPERATING INCOME	$68,034.97	$ -423,698.26
Other Income		
7100 Other Miscellaneous Income		39,330.00
Total Other Income	$0.00	$39,330.00

Canon Law Society of America

Profit and Loss Comparison

FY 23 and FY 22

	TOTAL	
	JUL 2022 - JUN 2023	JUL 2021 - JUN 2022 (PY)
NET OTHER INCOME	$0.00	$39,330.00
NET INCOME	$68,034.97	$ -384,368.26

Note
For Management Purposes Only
These financial statements are the property and responsibility of the management of Canon Law Society of America. These financial statements have not been audited or reviewed and accordingly no opinion or any other form of assurance is expressed on them.

Canon Law Society of America

Profit and Loss by Class - FY 23

July 2022 - June 2023

	CONVENTIONS AND WORKSHOPS	GENERAL AND ADMINISTRATIVE	MEMBER SERVICES	PUBLICATIONS	SCHOLARSHIP FUND	TOTAL
Income						
4100 Stewardship						$0.00
4110 Membership Dues			0.00			$0.00
4111 New Member Dues			20,687.50			$20,687.50
4112 Annual Dues Renewal			258,850.00			$258,850.00
Total 4110 Membership Dues			**279,537.50**			**$279,537.50**
4120 Donations						$0.00
4122 General Donations		1,838.50				$1,838.50
Total 4120 Donations		**1,838.50**				**$1,838.50**
4130 Scholarship Contributions					0.00	$0.00
4131 Licentiate Scholarship					12,057.48	$12,057.48
4132 Doctoral Scholarship					5,202.52	$5,202.52
Total 4130 Scholarship Contributions					**17,260.00**	**$17,260.00**
4140 Investment Income						$0.00
4141 Interest & Dividend-Operations		11,832.33				$11,832.33
4142 Interest & Dividend-Licentiate					15,882.28	$15,882.28
4143 Interest & Dividend - Doctoral					1,365.13	$1,365.13
4144 Int & Div - Scholarship (TD Bank)		3.05			14.88	$17.93
4150 Realized Gains/Loss		-4,750.19				$ -4,750.19
4160 Unreal. Gains/Loss - Gen Ops (001)		73,825.78				$73,825.78
4161 Unreal Gains/Loss-Licentiate Sch (002)					91,916.06	$91,916.06
4162 Unreal Gains/Loss-Doctoral Sch (003)					7,900.46	$7,900.46
Total 4140 Investment Income		**80,910.97**			**117,078.81**	**$197,989.78**
Total 4100 Stewardship		**82,749.47**	**279,537.50**		**134,338.81**	**$496,625.78**
4300 Membership Development						$0.00
4310 Annual Convention-Members Mtg						$0.00
4311 Exhibitors/Sponsorships	2,675.00					$2,675.00
4312 Banquet Fees (Additional)	800.00					$800.00
4313 Convention Registration	202,450.00		0.00			$202,450.00
4317 Sponsorship Donations	3,400.00					$3,400.00
4318 Contract Commission	13,681.29					$13,681.29
Total 4310 Annual Convention-Members Mtg	**223,006.29**		**0.00**			**$223,006.29**
Total 4300 Membership Development	**223,006.29**		**0.00**			**$223,006.29**
4400 Product Development						$0.00
4410 Publication and Resources						$0.00
4411 Publications Sales			12,262.00	101,768.48		$114,030.48
4413 Product Partnership Royalties				3,958.92		$3,958.92
4420 Publications - Amazon sales				5,528.36		$5,528.36
4430 Publication shipping income			29.12	15,507.41		$15,536.53
Total 4410 Publication and Resources			**12,291.12**	**126,763.17**		**$139,054.29**
Total 4400 Product Development			**12,291.12**	**126,763.17**		**$139,054.29**
Uncategorized Income	0.00	346.87				$346.87
Total Income	**$223,006.29**	**$83,096.34**	**$291,828.62**	**$126,763.17**	**$134,338.81**	**$859,033.23**
GROSS PROFIT	$223,006.29	$83,096.34	$291,828.62	$126,763.17	$134,338.81	$859,033.23
Expenses						
5100 Stewardship Expense						$0.00
5120 Scholarships					-1.99	$ -1.99
5121 Licentiate Scholarship Awards					31,333.34	$31,333.34
Total 5120 Scholarships					**31,331.35**	**$31,331.35**
Total 5100 Stewardship Expense					**31,331.35**	**$31,331.35**
5200 Professional Developmnt						$0.00
5220 Partnerships		35.00				$35.00
5223 Networking		10,127.62				$10,127.62
Total 5200 Professional Developmnt		**10,162.62**				**$10,162.62**

	CONVENTIONS AND WORKSHOPS	GENERAL AND ADMINISTRATIVE	MEMBER SERVICES	PUBLICATIONS	SCHOLARSHIP FUND	TOTAL
5300 Convention and workshops (Membership Dev)						$0.00
5310 Membership Outreach	1,046.51	1,547.55	81.13			$2,675.19
5313 Membership Expenses			14,026.36			$14,026.36
Total 5310 Membership Outreach	**1,046.51**	**1,547.55**	**14,107.49**			**$16,701.55**
5320 Annual Convention - Members Mtg						$0.00
5322 Convention Hotel, Food Events	89,465.97					$89,465.97
5323 Convention Audio Visual Contractor	48,082.44					$48,082.44
5324 Convention Supplies	2,556.39					$2,556.39
5325 Convention Travel	2,642.76					$2,642.76
5327 Convention Postage/Shipping	1,323.01					$1,323.01
5328 Convention Printing/Copying	6,576.89					$6,576.89
5329 Promotion; Program Materials/Banner	5,036.47	167.50				$5,203.97
5330 Liturgy & Environment	1,448.58	2,189.51				$3,638.09
5331 Speaker Honoraria/ Stipends	15,932.25					$15,932.25
5332 Speaker/Travel	6,338.88					$6,338.88
5333 Convention Lodging/Meals	7,929.56					$7,929.56
5334 Convention Planner	55,414.04					$55,414.04
Total 5320 Annual Convention - Members Mtg	**242,747.24**	**2,357.01**				**$245,104.25**
5340 Board of Governors		60.00				$60.00
5341 BOG Telecommunications	1,383.75	60.00				$1,443.75
5343 BOG Printing/Copying		34.26				$34.26
5345 BOG Travel	337.86	5,155.41				$5,493.27
5346 BOG Lodging/Meals	18,395.35	2,993.33				$21,388.68
5347 Officers' Expenses		1,690.80				$1,690.80
Total 5340 Board of Governors	**20,116.96**	**9,993.80**				**$30,110.76**
Total 5300 Convention and workshops (Membership Dev)	**263,910.71**	**13,898.36**	**14,107.49**			**$291,916.56**
5350 Committees						$0.00
5351 Constitutional Committees	516.33	2,047.98				$2,564.31
5352 Standing Committees	158.39	738.32				$896.71
5353 Convention Planning Committee	2,065.86					$2,065.86
5355 Strategic Visioning	468.00					$468.00
5356 Publication Advisory Board Comm	370.10	569.41		6,286.56		$7,226.07
Total 5350 Committees	**3,578.68**	**3,355.71**		**6,286.56**		**$13,220.95**
5400 Product Dvelopment						$0.00
5410 COGS - Publication & Resources						$0.00
5411 Cost of Goods Sold				19,753.97		$19,753.97
Total 5410 COGS - Publication & Resources				**19,753.97**		**$19,753.97**
5420 Expenses-Publication & Resource						$0.00
5427 Publications Postage/Shipping				887.12		$887.12
Total 5420 Expenses-Publication & Resource				**887.12**		**$887.12**
5430 Logistech-Outsourcing Pub & Res						$0.00
5434 Rent-Storage Space (Pallet/Quic				694.92		$694.92
5435 Ordering Processing				2,631.75		$2,631.75
5438 Prof Services (Projects/Warehouse Support)				102.61		$102.61
5440 Postage/Shipping				10,233.66		$10,233.66
Total 5430 Logistech-Outsourcing Pub & Res				**13,662.94**		**$13,662.94**
5450 Expenses-Royalties Pub & Resour						$0.00
5451 Royalties for CCEO (8% of NR)				218.40		$218.40
5452 Royalties for CIC (8% of NR)				556.80		$556.80
5453 Royalties for Dignitas Connubbii (6% of NR)				42.00		$42.00
5454 Royalties for Selected Issues (60% of NR)				50.88		$50.88
5456 QUOQEI, Code - 4th Edition				3,780.00		$3,780.00
Total 5450 Expenses-Royalties Pub & Resour				**4,648.08**		**$4,648.08**
5460 Product Partnerships						$0.00
5461 CLSA Research Database Hosting				1,544.75		$1,544.75
Total 5460 Product Partnerships				**1,544.75**		**$1,544.75**

2/3

	CONVENTIONS AND WORKSHOPS	GENERAL AND ADMINISTRATIVE	MEMBER SERVICES	PUBLICATIONS	SCHOLARSHIP FUND	TOTAL
Total 5400 Product Dvelopment				40,496.86		$40,496.86
6100 Canon Law Society Operating Exp						$0.00
6110 Salaries and Benefits						$0.00
6111 Salaries	29,226.01	70,783.66	22,085.02	50,965.68	2,946.27	$176,006.64
6112 Employer Payroll Taxes	2,179.75	5,489.90	1,646.39	3,795.94	224.67	$13,336.65
6113 Professional Development (Staff		75.00				$75.00
6114 Employee Health Benefit Plan	2,199.91	7,653.02	2,352.61	5,105.67	396.23	$17,707.44
6115 Pension Plan Administration		202.50				$202.50
6116 403b Obligations	1,287.39	1,912.94	923.10	1,925.15	128.11	$6,176.69
Total 6110 Salaries and Benefits	34,893.06	86,117.02	27,007.12	61,792.44	3,695.28	$213,504.92
6120 Operating Expenses						$0.00
6121 Publication/Media Materials		110.00				$110.00
6127 Rent		75.02				$75.02
6130 Printing/Copying		358.28				$358.28
6132 Professional Services (Contract		11,822.50				$11,822.50
6134 Accounting/Audit Fees		71,913.58				$71,913.58
6135 Legal Fees				25,629.66		$25,629.66
Total 6132 Professional Services (Contract		83,736.08		25,629.66		$109,365.74
6133 Bank/Financial Fees/PayrollFees		22,080.43				$22,080.43
6138 CMS and Website Licensing			4,339.37			$4,339.37
6144 Operating Lease Expense		32,525.52				$32,525.52
6145 Other Business Expenses						$0.00
6122 Software/Subscription/Licenses		4,556.51				$4,556.51
6123 Advertising/Marketing/Graphic Design		299.00				$299.00
6124 Awards/Gifts		162.36				$162.36
6125 Equipment Lease/Purchase/Maint		731.25				$731.25
6126 Business Insurance		1,148.25				$1,148.25
6128 Telecommunications		4,845.96				$4,845.96
6129 Postage/Shipping		451.46				$451.46
6131 Supplies		1,193.87		772.80		$1,966.67
6136 Executive Coordinator/Travel		2,020.04	19.90			$2,039.94
6137 Lodging/Meals		789.02				$789.02
6139 Bad Debt/Write-Offs				81.70		$81.70
6140 Depreciation Expense		4,013.52				$4,013.52
Total 6145 Other Business Expenses		20,211.24	19.90	854.50		$21,085.64
6150 Miscellaneous Expenses	355.00	70.00				$425.00
Total 6120 Operating Expenses	355.00	159,166.57	4,359.27	26,484.16		$190,365.00
Total 6100 Canon Law Society Operating Exp	35,248.06	245,283.59	31,366.39	88,276.60	3,695.28	$403,869.92
Total Expenses	$302,737.45	$272,700.28	$45,473.86	$135,060.02	$35,026.63	$790,998.26
NET OPERATING INCOME	$ -79,731.16	$ -189,603.94	$246,354.74	$ -8,296.85	$99,312.18	$68,034.97
NET INCOME	$ -79,731.16	$ -189,603.94	$246,354.74	$ -8,296.85	$99,312.18	$68,034.97

Note
Unaudited: For Management Purposes Only
These financial statements are the property and responsibility of the management of Canon Law Society of America. These financial statements have not been audited or reviewed and accordingly no opinion or any other form of assurance is expressed on them.

Staff Reports

Report of the Executive Coordinator

Donna Miller, JD, JCL

Welcome to Milwaukee and the Society's 85th Annual Convention. Over thirty-five years ago I spent a year living here in "Cream City" while I was in formation with the Sisters of the Divine Savior. During most of that year, I lived at Divine-Savior Holy Angels High School on the northwest side and taught sixth grade at St. Anthony Catholic School on the southside. Although I did not continue in formation with that religious institute, I came to appreciate Milwaukee for its friendly people, the ease of access in getting around (through gridded streets and flat walking paths), and the lakeshore's activities and expansive views. I will always have fond memories of Milwaukee from the late 1980s; being back here thirty-five years later for our convention is sure to foster more happy memories for me.

All that aside, let me jump right in and tell you about what has been going on with the Society's publications since we last gathered in Cleveland a year ago.

New Commentary Project

As I write this report, we are making changes to the editorial personnel for the new commentary. Right after the convention last year, Chorbishop John Faris came aboard as an editor to replace Professor Bill Daniel. Sister Nancy Bauer, OSB, remains as an editor, but Father John Beal has resigned from the project. We have secured two new content editors to assist with the editing duties, and those plans are being finalized as I write. Most of the authors who are creating new content for this endeavor have completed and submitted their contributions. Another complicating factor is that new law has been promulgated by the Holy Father several times in the past two years, so content that was already submitted by several authors has had to be updated to account for these changes. Busy schedules and commitments have delayed some authors, but we hope to get all of the content in by the end of this year.

As I noted last year, this commentary is a massive undertaking; for that reason, we have hired a company called TextFormations as Managing Editor to do the copyediting and other production tasks. They will oversee upcoming stages of the production process for the commentary, in consultation with the content editors and our administrative staff. We are still more than two years out from completion of this project, but we continue to maintain hope and belief that this important project will come to fruition and be a substantial contribution in the world of canonical research and dialogue.

Fourth Printing of the Code of Canon Law

After significant dialogue and perseverance, we were able to agree on a new license agreement with the USCCB in October of last year, the week before our convention was held. In January of this year, we were notified that our changes to the fontes were approved by the USCCB. That was the last hurdle, and we finally were able to assemble the entire publication into its final format—even incorporating "last-minute" changes to the code by Pope Francis in April. We went to the printer in May. Based largely on the voluminous amount of work that went into production of the code, we set the price at $125 for non-members and $85 for members.

As I write this report, we have sold well over 1300 copies of the fourth printing, which is tremendously satisfying given the fact that we had been without a code to sell for over eight months. We have not yet put this edition of the code on Amazon for sale, but we plan to do so in the not-too-distant future. The orders that are made through Amazon have to be fulfilled through our office, so we need to wait until the staff has time to absorb the extra workload that such orders will create.

Not surprisingly, the code has been altered again by the Holy Father with changes that he made to two canons on personal prelatures (cc. 295-296) in early August of this year. We have been able to add these updates to the version of the code that is in our website's Research Database, and we will save the changes for the next (fifth) printing of the code, which will not happen for several years!

Revised English Translation of the Code of Canons of the Eastern Churches

The Holy Father fulfilled predictions earlier this year when he promulgated *Vocare peccatores* and the updates to the penal law of the Eastern code (Title 27), comparable to the Latin code's new Book VI. Our English translation of the CCEO has not been updated since 2001, so we are working with our formatter to access the old, outdated files that stored the electronic version of the code. There are also a lot of changes to the supplemental materials—including the index, tables, and fontes—that have to be incorporated as well. Moreover, we must secure approval of all new translations (back to 2015 and *Mitis et Misericors Iesus*) and secure the necessary permissions from the Holy See to print a new version of the code. We will keep you posted on the status of the second printing of the Eastern code through our website, social media postings, and emails.

Proceedings 2022

With the help of our full-time administrative staff—Kathleen Butler and Mark Francisco—we were able to get the *Proceedings* from the 2022 convention ready for mailing in early June. As Kathleen mentions in her General Secretary's report herein, we implemented a new process for ordering and fulfilling orders this year; just over half of our membership adapted and responded favorably to the change. We appreciate all of you who were patient and cooperative with this new process. As we suspected, over 25% of our members did not order a free copy, so in the future we will be able to save significantly on printing costs without having to print hundreds of unwanted copies of *Proceedings*. Watch for emails in the new year when we begin to take pre-orders for our 2023 *Proceedings*.

Roman Replies and CLSA Advisory Opinions 2023

Those attending this convention received their complimentary copy of the 2023 edition of *Roman Replies and CLSA Advisory Opinions*. Thanks go out once again to the editors for advisory opinions, Monsignor Michael Souckar and Father Patrick Cooney, OSB, who have been providing this valuable service for many years. Please take time to read the issue and keep it handy for consultation purposes. We are grateful to the members who submitted advisory opinions, some of which this year presented us with an opportunity for reflection and adaptation. I invite you to read the issue and see what changes have been implemented; whether these changes are only temporary or become permanent will depend on the feedback that we receive.

Only three members contributed Roman replies that were able to be published this year, and that was two fewer than last year. In my 2022 convention report, I indicated the concern that has grown in recent years over the (un)necessity of this annual publication. I invited you to share your thoughts and ideas with me about whether we should continue to publish RRAO. No one reached out with any thoughts on the publication. However, I was surprised at the support that we received from several dicasteries in Rome when we visited in April. They actually were happy to see that their decrees, rescripts, sentences, etc., were being shared. They reminded us that we have to make sure that identifiable information is redacted and that the person who submits the reply needs to ask permission of the issuing dicastery or tribunal first. But they do appreciate that there is interest in the decrees, rescripts, sentences, etc.

Last year I also told our members that we had received approval from the Roman Rota to translate into English the *Excerpta Argumentorum* from *Decisiones seu Sententiae.* I arranged with a number of translators in early 2022 to translate the 2014 *excerpta,* and we submitted them to the Rota in late July of 2022 for approval. We were under the impression that this would be a "a quick review before publication." Unfortunately, we did not get approval of the translations from the Rota until December of 2022, which was far beyond the deadline to publish the excerpta in RRAO 2022. This year, we started a month earlier with the translations for the 2015 *excerpta,* and we sent them over six weeks earlier to the Rota to request approval. Once again, despite multiple inquiries and in-person intervention by a member to try to move along the approval process, we did not hear anything from the Rota before our publication deadline. So, we published only the 2014 *Excerpta Argumentorum* this year in RRAO.

I am grateful to all of these translators who worked on the 2015 translations earlier this year, and I regret that the necessary approval did not come before our publication deadline. If you open your RRAO 2023, you will see a section containing the *Excerpta Argumentorum* translations from *Decisiones seu Sententiae* vol. 106. The translators' names in the 2022 endeavor are included in the introduction to the section.

Whether we continue to do these translations remains to be seen since it is very frustrating for those who put in a lot of time working on the translations are not seeing their work published for over eighteen months. Still, if you are interested in helping with this translation project in the future, please contact me and let me know whether you are interested in being a translator or if you wish to help coordinate the project as an editor.

Clergy Procedural Handbook

Father Peter Mottola and Tim Olson continue to work on the revision of this important publication. We have peer reviewers lined up, and a projected release date is planned in the Spring of 2024. This publication will be a huge help to non-canonists and canonists alike.

History Project

Father Michael Joyce, CM, has been diligently working on a new publication that will document and narrate the history of the CLSA since its inception in 1939. He has conducted dozens of Zoom call interviews with previous presidents and executive coordinators of the society to gather the information he needs for this endeavor. We owe Father Joyce our collective support and gratitude for taking the initiative to help enhance the society's institutional memory through this historic undertaking. Thank you, Father Joyce!

Tribunal Handbook

Sister Victoria Vondenberger, RSM, and Father Dan Smilanic have been busy working on an update to this publication that was originally published in the early 2000s. Both *Dignitas connubii* and *Mitis Iudex Dominus Iesus* have affected tribunal practices in the last two decades, so we are very much looking forward to this publication being updated and released—hopefully before we meet in Albuquerque in October of 2024.

Married Priests

The pre-convention workshop on this topic in October of 2022 in Cleveland provided the majority of the material that is being used to compile this publication. Dr. Margaret Chalmers and Chorbishop John Faris are spearheading the project. We look forward to a 2024 release date as their work progresses.

Rome Trip 2023

In April of this year, I was privileged to accompany Father John Donovan (President) and Father Ken Riley (Vice President) on a visit to Rome. This was the first such trip since 2017. The absence of an Executive Director (Oct. 2018-May 2019) and the onset of COVID-19 (2020-2022) combined to create a six-year hiatus from what was normally a biennial trip. We all felt the trip was very productive and worthwhile. The weather cooperated and we got plenty of exercise walking to and from meetings. The three of us who made the trip have written a report that is available to members on our CLSA website, in the Documents and Downloads section. It is also published in this year's edition of *Roman Replies and CLSA Advisory Opinions 2023*.

Webinars

After nearly a year with no new webinars, several CLSA members stepped forward and volunteered to share their expertise through the webinar platform. In order to facilitate the sharing of canonical resources, we made all of these webinars available for free to anyone on the date of broadcast. The recorded sessions are reserved to CLSA members as a benefit of membership. Following are the sessions that have been presented so far this year:

April 4, 2023	Rev. George Mukuka, JCD Candidate "Where There Is No Accuser There Is No Accused: A Comparative Study of VELM and the 1917 Code"

May 25, 2023	Rev. Giorgio Giovanelli "The Penal Trial in the Canonical System: Part 1 – The Crime"
June 22, 2023	Dr. J. Michael Ritty "An Advocate's Practical Guide for Penal Cases: Initial Contact to Review Board"
July 20, 2023	Rev. Giorgio Giovanelli "The Penal Trial in the Canonical System: Part 2 – The *Investigatio Praevia* (Part 1)"

In late September, we will host another webinar by Dr. J. Michael Ritty. It will be a sequel to his first webinar in the practical guide series for advocates in penal cases and will be titled: "An Advocate's Practical Guide for Penal Cases: Walking Through the Preliminary Investigation."

All of our 2023 webinars have been very successful and well-received, with over 100 registrants for each one. One individual session even attracted 360+ registrations, and over half actually participated on the day of broadcast. We are incredibly grateful to all three of the presenters who have spent time preparing for and presenting these important sessions. We need more of our canonist members to come forward to share their knowledge! Contact me at ExecutiveCoordinator@clsa.org to volunteer!

Conclusion

Thank you for letting me serve another year as the Executive Coordinator of the CLSA. Amid the intensity of the work that kept me occupied day after day, I was able to take a couple of days to travel "north" from Florida and meet my new granddaughter. "Nora Rae" was born on July 18 in central Ohio, and she and her proud mom and dad are thriving and loving life. This precious, innocent new life filled my heart with love beyond measure, and her presence gave me a new perspective. I am grateful to God for the many blessings in my life, and I count all of you in the Society among those blessings. Until next year, may God bless us all!

Report of the General Secretary

Kathleen Butler

"It's a rebuilding year." I say this often about my beloved and beleaguered Washington Nationals baseball team. We're not where we want to be, but we're making progress. The Nats' manager is fond of saying "bumpy roads lead to beautiful places."

Administratively, I can say the same thing about CLSA. We've spent the last year rebuilding some of our processes and procedures while documenting them extensively, so that we know we're consistent and at the same time, agile. Every time we finish a project, we step back and assess where the process can be more efficient in terms of financial or staff resources.

For example, last year we changed how we distribute *Proceedings*. For years, we simply mailed the books to everyone in our system. We never knew if people wanted—or used—the book at all (and there are some who don't). Often, addresses were out of date, and books were returned to us. In some cases, the post office charged us $10 to get a book back when the address was bad. When we could, we would research where the people had moved to and attempt to contact them for an updated address. This is an inefficient use of time and dollars, given our very small staff and our very robust online database system. We asked members this year to request a free copy of *Proceedings* through their online profile by a set deadline.

The new initiative was not without some bumpy roads, and we have assessed what we can do differently to make it easier for the coming year. 57% of members requested a copy of the 2022 *Proceedings*. Having these pre-order numbers enabled us to make more cost-effective purchasing decisions. Last year's edition came out a bit later than usual because we were working on the code. The silver lining was that because dues invoices had gone out, many people had already updated their mailing addresses by the time we mailed *Proceedings,* so we had greater confidence in our mailing list. An additional benefit was that many people called us to help them access their profile, so we were able to show them all the resources the website offers to members.

As we assessed, we took a hard look at the effort and dollars that went into this project and the data that came out of it to consider if this was the right distribution method for CLSA members. The Board concluded that this "free *Proceedings* by request" should be continued. We hope that some of the bumps we all encountered will be smoothed out this year. We will publish the promo code in the e-newsletters, and you can use it to order your *Proceedings* from this convention. If you are among the 19% of our members who skip opening those e-newsletters, I encourage you to open them up when the email notice comes in. If you miss one, the current issue is always linked on the "News and Events" page of the website, and back issues are available in your Member Center under "Newsletter Archive."

Since I mentioned dues, let me talk for a moment about some trends. For the last couple years, we have seen a small decrease in the numbers of Active members. For this fiscal year (FY 24), we mailed dues invoices on April 20, and 79% of our members renewed their membership by the June 30 deadline; thank you! As you know, there is a grace period through the month of July, and of the 274 remaining, 174 renewed before their account was made inactive. We contacted the remaining 100 with a reminder, and we received a disappointing 10% response. This means that for the fourth consecutive year, we have seen a decrease in Active members. The good news is that we continue to see Student members increase; in fact, Student membership has increased nearly 30% in the last three years. Thank you to those students who recognize the value CLSA offers and to all the deans and professors who are sharing our story with their students. A long-term strategic concern will be how to attract new Active members and how to convert Student members to Active members when they complete their studies.

This long-term forecasting leads me to finances. There were a few lean months this year when we did not have code income. We rely on publications income and dues for our operating expenses, so as Fr. John Donovan has noted, the uptick in sales has had a positive effect on our day-to-day operations. Fr. Jamin David likewise has a comprehensive Treasurer's report. On the expense side, we continue to refine our reporting. All of the staff now allocate their time to program areas, which enables us to calculate a more realistic cost of what we offer. This is one of those "bumpy roads" where we need the day-to-day income to offset actual costs so that we don't have to ask members to pay for the entire cost of the convention, for instance.

A quick note about our scholarship appeal. Thank you to everyone who contributed, especially those who contributed to our "$85 for our 85th year" appeal. Your generosity is at work right now helping ten aspiring canonists, three of whom began their JCL just this fall. It's important to remember that scholarship contributions do not benefit individuals only. Recipients, in turn, continue the efforts and traditions of the Society by their service to the Church and their activity within the Society.

Allow me to be pragmatic though. This year, we saw a 2% increase in the number of donors, and it's wonderful to see an upward trend. The eighty-five individuals who donated comprise just 6.65% of our FY23 membership. This data is important for potential grant-funders we might seek out. There is a great deal of competition for faith-based grants, and we need to distinguish ourselves through our mission and our members' vigorous support of it. With such a low percentage of our members supporting our fundraising, our ability to secure grants for new initiatives and projects may be limited, at best. We need to demonstrate a greater percentage of our members donating to the educational aspect of our mission to better position ourselves in the crowded grant market. The donation amount is less important than the number of donors at this point. If you are able to contribute at any point during the year, we would be grateful.

The Find a Canon Lawyer feature on our website finally hit my stretch goal this year. We have 124 Active members on that registry, which meets (and actually exceeds a tiny bit) my 10% goal. If you want to be listed, all you have to do is log into your profile and change the No to a Yes in the field that says, "I would like to be listed in CLSA's Find a Canon Lawyer listing." The directory pulls limited information from your online profile, which you can update any time. If you decide you no longer want to be on the listing, you can go back into your profile, and change the answer back to No.

Finally, let me offer my grateful thanks to my extraordinary colleagues, Mark Francisco and Donna Miller. Over my last three years, there have been some bumpy places, but their spirit of teamwork, generosity and good humor genuinely make for a beautiful place to work.

COMMITTEE REPORTS

CONSTITUTIONAL COMMITTEES

Committee: Nominations

Constituted: Constitutional Committee

Mandate: Articles IX and X of the Constitution

1. To submit to the active members, at least one month prior to the date of election, the names of nominees as provided for in Article IX of the Constitution
2. To formulate and recommend to the Board of Governors plans for maintaining and increasing membership in the Society. And, in accord with Article X, revise all proposals so that the meaning of each is clear.

Members: Mr. Christopher Siuzdak, chair, Portland, ME
Dr. Susan Mulheron, St. Paul, MN
Dr. Siobhan Verbeek, Washington, DC

BOG Liaison: Dr. Lynda Robitaille

REPORT

The Nominations Committee convened on January 19, 2023, at the CLSA offices in Washington, DC to fulfill its central task of identifying and securing a pair of nominees for the position of: vice president/president-elect, secretary, and two consultors. Additional meetings took place virtually and via text messaging so that a particular role, which had been turned down by numerous potential candidates, could be filled successfully. Shortly before the meeting of January 19, Rev. Joseph Newton of Indianapolis stepped down from the Committee, and thanks to the prompt response of the CLSA leaders, Dr. Siobhan Verbeek was named to the committee so that a quorum could be achieved. The chair wishes to gratefully acknowledge Rev. Joseph Newton's prior service on the committee and Dr. Siobhan Verbeek's willingness to serve on the committee on short notice.

In keeping with prior custom, the deliberations gave due consideration to the issues of gender, cultural diversity, geographic location, status of person in the Church, and service to the society in order to ensure that the leadership of the society reflects the diversity of the society's broad membership. The committee also maintained the custom that no speaker at the upcoming convention could be a nominee for any of the positions open for election at the same convention.

After careful consideration, the committee presented the following nominees for election at the 85th Annual Meeting of the Canon Law Society of America:

Office of Vice President/President-Elect
Dr. Margaret Chalmers
Rev. Patrick Cooney, OSB

Office of Secretary
Mr. Stephen Garbitelli
Sr. Rose Marie Timmer, RSM

Office of Consultor (2)
Sr. Nancy Bauer, OSB
Deacon Gerald Jorgensen
Dr. Jeannine Marino
Rev. Msgr. Robert Oliver

When contacting potential nominees, the designated committee member verbally explains the duties of the office, the number of board meetings involved each year, and the practical tasks required as part of the election process (e.g., preparing a video and introducing speakers at the upcoming convention). An improvement for the future would be to develop a comprehensive job description for each elected position so that the multifaceted expectations of each office are clear and evident from the outset. Such a shareable document would aid potential nominees as they discern whether to accept the nomination for a given office. It is not uncommon for a significant number of potential nominees decline standing for election because of pre-existing, time-intensive commitments.

Lastly, the committee wishes to share how helpful it was to meet in person to deliberate over potential candidates. Having experienced candidate selection in both virtual, hybrid, and in-person formats over the past several years, the organic dynamic of an in-person meeting seems the most beneficial. Both virtual and in-person formats have allowed for the successful completion of the central task; however, the consensus was that the budget for future years should plan for travel expenses (i.e., one in-person meeting) for this small but vitally important committee. The Chair of the Committee on Nominations recommends to the Board of Governors that they maintain the budgeted amount for the 2023-2024 meetings of the Committee.

Submitted By: Mr. Christopher Siuzdak

Committee: Resolutions

Constituted: Constitution, Article X 2009

Mandate: The mandate of the Committee on Resolutions is as follows:

1. To solicit, develop and draft proposed resolutions which will express the concerns of the Canon Law Society of America;
2. To consult with the membership at large and, in particular with the Board of Governors, the standing and *ad hoc* committees of the Society, and the organizers of the annual convention;
3. To formulate proposed resolutions on given points in response to requests of the members of the Society;
4. To compose differences in the formulation of similar proposals and to revise all proposals so that the meaning of each is clear; (and)
5. To encourage resolutions which authentically express in a positive way the activities and concerns of the Society.

Members: Dr. Linda Budney, Chair, Bethesda, MD
Mrs. Anne Ameno Gunner, Buffalo, NY
Rev. William (Liam) Quinlan, Darien, CT
Ms. Amy Tadlock, St. Paul, MN

BOG Liaison: Rev. Greg Luyet

REPORT

The committee met on August 3, 2023 to review the single proposed resolution received. Editorial changes were suggested to the committee submitting the proposal and accepted. The General Secretary was invited to the meeting to review the reasonableness of the estimated cost to the society.

During the coming year, the committee plans to discuss the format to be used when submitting proposed resolutions to determine if additional information should be included. The committee will continue to consider how it might encourage the membership and committees to submit proposed resolutions that address the concerns of the society and its members.

Submitted By: Linda Budney
August 17, 2023

Committee: Resource and Asset Management

Constituted: Constitutional (See Article X)

Mandate: It is the function of the Committee on Resource & Asset Management to:

1. Develop a comprehensive budget for all the activities of the Society and report on the funding available for projects;
2. To submit the proposed budget for the coming fiscal year to the Board of Governors for approval at its spring meeting;
3. To conserve, invest, and disperse the monies of the Scholarship Fund in accord with the criteria established by the Society; (and)
4. To advise the Treasurer on all matters pertaining to the Society's investments (Article X, 7).

Members: Very Rev. Jamin Scott David, *chair*, Albany, LA (2025)
Rev. Thomas Cronkleton, Jr., Cheyenne, WY (2025)
Rev. Chris Palladino, West Roxbury, MA (2025)
Very Rev. Luke Millette, Houston, TX (2023) (*ex officio*)
Rev. Ken Riley, Kansas City, MO (2023) (*ex officio*)
Rev. Kevin Niehoff, OP (2023) (*Past Treasurer, ex officio*)

REPORT

The Committee on Resource and Asset Management met on 31 March 2023 virtually via the Go To Webinar platform. The meeting began at 10:02AM CST. Present were Fathers Jamin David, Chris Palladino, Thomas Cronkleton, and Kevin Niehoff, and Ms. Kathleen Butler. Due to other commitments, Fathers Riley and Millette were unable to be present for the meeting.

After leading the group in an opening prayer, since this was the first meeting of the group since Father David's election as Treasurer in October 2022, he asked members to introduce themselves. He also gave a quick review of the functions of the Committee on Resource and Asset Management as defined by the CLSA, namely to:

1. Develop a comprehensive budget for all the activities of the Society and report on the funding available for projects;
2. To submit the proposed budget for the coming fiscal year to the Board of Governors for approval at its spring meeting;
3. To conserve, invest, and disperse the monies of the Scholarship Fund in accord with the criteria established by the Society; (and)
4. To advise the Treasurer on all matters pertaining to the Society's investments (Article X, 7).

Father David then presented to the group a financial review including a balance sheet and profit and loss statement as of 28 February 2023. Total assets of the Society, including cash assets in operating accounts, accounts receivable, prepaid expenses, inventory assets, fixed assets, and investment accounts totaled $2,116,238.01 as compared to assets in July 2022 that totaled $2,478,244.09. Liabilities and equity including accounts payable, credit card balances, accrued royalty expenses, accrued payroll expenses, and deferred revenue totaled $59,24406 as compared to liabilities in July 2022 totaling $128,366.56.

The Profit and Loss statement, as presented, shows a total income of $610,767.51 for the period July 2022 through February 2023. Expenses totaled $562,623.40 for the same period. Thus, net income for the period totaled $48,144.11. Detailed statements were presented to committee members for review. Father David noted that market volatility was a major concern for the Society at the end of Father Niehoff's tenure and at the beginning of his tenure as Treasurer.

Father David then presented a proposed budget for the 2023/2024 fiscal year. The proposed budget would include $939,075 in revenue, primarily generated from membership dues, investment income, conference fees, and publication sales. Anticipated expenses would total $1,039,300 which would primarily include expenses related to the annual convention, Board of Governors and committee work, publication expenses including storage and shipping, salaries, and operating expenses, resulting in a $100,225 deficit. This does not include repayment to investment accounts of monies used to cover operating expenses in this fiscal year. After some discussion, a motion was made by Father Niehoff and seconded by Father Cronkleton that the proposed budget, as presented, be forwarded to the Board of Governors for consideration and approval. There were no objections to this motion, and it passed unanimously.

Father David then updated the committee regarding the CLSA Scholarship Funds. Over time, the amount of money contributed to the funds has remained stagnant or has decreased. In the 2022 fiscal year, 72 persons contributed approximately $15,000. So far in the 2023, fiscal year, 84 contributors have contributed. At the President and Treasurer's insistence, every member of the Board of Governors has contributed in 2023 to the Scholarship Fund. Discussion continued about ways to bolster contributions.

Father David, with the assistance of Ms. Butler, noted that in the past, the BOG inadvertently abrogated a standing policy which allowed investment interest from the scholarship funds to be used for scholarship administration (printing, advertising, etc.). Father Palladino motioned that investment interest from the scholarship fund be used for scholarship administration according to the same measures provided before the "rule" was abrogated; this motion was seconded by Father Cronkleton and passed with unanimous consent.

Finally, Father David asked the committee members their opinion regarding the potential of hiring an investment manager. Currently, the society only has a customer service manager. Father David admitted that there would be costs involved with this strategy. Several potential investment managers were mentioned by name by committee members. Father Niehoff suggested that a request for proposal be created as a first step forward. During the discussion, Father Palladino suggested that given current bank failures in the United States, there may be an opportunity to diversify to ensure cash assets are safe.

Father David also suggested to the group that they meet more frequently than has been done traditionally (perhaps quarterly) to discuss ideas for cost savings, investment strategies, and to review current finances.

With no other business, the meeting adjourned at 11:44AM CST after the *Glory Be* was led by Father Niehoff.

Submitted By: Very Reverend Jamin Scott David, JCL

Committee: Professional Responsibility

Constituted: Constitution, Article X (as last amended in 1995)

Mandate: The mandate of the committee is as follows:

1. Regarding complaints:
   a. To receive complaints of any party aggrieved with respect to provisions of the Code of Professional Responsibility of the CLSA;
   b. To make an initial finding that the complaint is not frivolous but is serious in character;
   c. By majority vote, to refer the matter to one of the Hearing Officers;
2. To issue advisory opinions and decisions on the application of the Code of Professional Responsibility; (and)
3. To advise on all other questions concerning the professional responsibility of canonists.

Members: Dr. Siobhan Verbeek, chair, Washington, DC (2023)
Dr. David Castronovo, Beaumont, TX (2023) (*ex officio*)
Very Rev. Luke Millette, Houston, TX (2023) (*ex officio*)
Mr. Michael Dunnigan, Hearing Officer, St. Meinrad, IN (2025)
Dr. Lynda Robitaille, Hearing Officer, North Vancouver, BC (2023)

REPORT

Since the Professional Responsibility Committee's last annual report, no complaints were received related to provisions of the Society's Code of Professional Responsibility. As a result, it was unnecessary to initiate any formal processes.

Over the past year, Committee members were made aware of ongoing discussions within the Society underscoring the importance of maintaining academic honesty when making presentations to the membership, and in the development of materials intended for Society publications. Attentiveness to contemporary concerns related to the increased availability of artificially generated content was also considered. Likewise, the committee was apprised of continuing considerations that are being given by the Board of Governors leading to the possible development of processes for the suspension or dismissal of Society members, for a sufficiently grave cause.

Submitted By: Dr. Siobhan Verbeek
August 18, 2023

ONGOING COMMITTEES

Committee: Clergy

Constituted: 2009

Mandate: The mandate of the committee is as follows:

1. To initiate as needed any projects pertinent to the study of canon law pertaining to the life and ministry of bishops, priests and deacons or the implementation thereof, including, but not limited to, the following:
   a. canonical issues related to the sexual abuse of minors;
   b. clergy personnel issues and resources;
   c. advocacy for clergy in penal cases;
2. To oversee projects referred to the committee by the BOG;
3. To oversee its subcommittees working on projects concerning clergy; and
4. To collaborate with national organization and other groups dealing with clergy issues

Members: Most Rev. Edward Lohse, chair, Kalamazoo, MI (2023)
Rev. James Bradley; Washington, DC (2024)
Rev. Ernie Carpio, Beaumont, TX (2025)
Rev. Msgr. Stephen Doktorczyk; Orange, CA (2023)
Deacon Michael Forbes; Austin, TX (2024)
Rev. Robert Hyde, Jr.; Syracuse, NY (2025)
Mr. Tim Olson; Fargo, ND (2023)
Rev. Pius Pietrzyk, OP; Rome, Italy (2024)

BOG Liaison: Very Rev. Luke Millette

REPORT

Since the last report, the Clergy Committee has not met. Work does continue, however, behind the scenes on the committee's project of producing a new updated and revised version of the *Clergy Procedural Handbook*. As of this report, some of the submitted chapters have been edited and returned to the authors, and work to edit the remaining submissions is ongoing. Once the chapters have received final formatting, they will be sent for peer review, after which any remaining edits will be suggested to the authors and the material will be made ready for publication. The editors have set September 1 as the goal for completing all their edits and November 1 for completing all the formatting.

Members of the committee have also been finalizing the draft of a document entitled *Circular Letter to the Members of the CLSA Concerning the Rights of Clerical Recurrents in Hierarchical Recourse*. A first draft was reviewed by members of the BOG. The draft was returned with some suggested edits and a request for a conclusion. As noted in the last report, Msgr. Fred Easton (no longer a committee member but still working with us on the *Circular Letter* project) sent word to all of the members that he has offered a suggested conclusion to the draft but doesn't think that it has been approved yet.

There has been initial conversation of considering drafting a handbook or commentary regarding ecclesiastical law surrounding seminary formation, including things such as seminary structure, juridic personhood, process of formation, c. 220 rights, and the revised *Program for Priestly Formation*, but nothing has happened in that regard beyond an initial suggestion of the possibility.

There is one remaining scheduled meeting, slated for September 11, 2023. As of right now, it's not clear if there will be anything on the agenda for that meeting, since wrapping up two major projects has taken most of the committee's attention.

Submitted By: Most Rev. Edward M. Lohse
August 16, 2023

Committee: Convention Planning

Constituted: 1971

Mandate: It is the function of the Committee on Convention Planning:

1. To receive from the Board of Governors the approved general theme of the next convention as well as any suggestions from the Committee on Research & Discussion for the development of the theme;
2. To recommend to the BOG, in accord with the general theme, topics for major addresses, seminars or other presentations at future convention, as well as a list of potential speakers and the honoraria for such speakers;
3. Following BOG approval, to arrange for the speakers, addresses and seminars for the annual convention;
4. To oversee the planning of all convention liturgies and prayer services in cooperation with its subcommittee for Convention Liturgies; (and)
5. To review the evaluations of the most recent Convention and assist the Convention Chairperson in planning future arrangements, as needed.

Members: Dr. Chad Glendinning, chair, Ottawa, ON (2023)
Mr. Jay Conzemius, Bethel Park, PA (2024)
Dr. Felix Menendez, Smyrna, GA (2025)
Mrs. Adrienne Yates, Chapel Hill, NC (2025)
Dr. Lynda Robitaille, North Vancouver, BC (*ex officio*, Past President)
Mrs. Donna Miller (*ex officio*, Executive Coordinator)
Ms. Kathleen Butler (*ex officio*, General Secretary)

BOG Liaison: Very. Rev. Ken Riley

REPORT

1. **Committee Meetings:** Since the last convention, the Convention Planning Committee met virtually on December 15, 2022, and June 23, 2023. The committee also met in person on March 20, 2023 in Orlando, FL. The purpose of the meeting was to develop and propose a speaker slate for the 2024 convention, which will be held on the theme of "Ministry of Justice in the 21st Century."

2. **Change of Committee Membership:** The committee welcomed two new members in Fall, 2022: Dr. Felix Menendez and Ms. Adrienne Yates. The committee was notified that Ms. Rebecca Ruesch had resigned from the committee. Mr. Jay Conzemius has been appointed to serve the remainder of her term of office. We thank Rebecca for her contribution to the committee.

3. **2023 Convention:** The following slate of speakers has been confirmed for the 2023 convention.

Theme: Role of Law in the Life of the Church: Is it Relevant Now?

Location: Hyatt Regency, Milwaukee, WI

Preconvention Workshops

The Art of Dissolving Marriages
Rev. Alexander Laschuk

Best Practices for Locally Training Procurators/Advocates
Ms. Anna Marie Chamblee
Sr. Victoria Vondenberger, RSM

Keynote and Major Addresses

Meandering in the Thickets of the Law: The Code that Was, That Is, and That Still Might Come
Rev. John Beal

The Current Application and Development of Canon Law
Most Rev. Juan Ignacio Arrieta

Update from the Dicastery for the Doctrine of the Faith
Rev. Msgr. John Kennedy

Seminars

Recent Updates in Penal Law
Rev. John Paul Kimes

Now and at the Hour of our Debt: Catholic Organizations in Bankruptcy
Prof. Marie T. Reilly

'Validation' or Radical Sanation of Marriage: Why Choose One Over the Other?
Dr. Lynda Robitaille

Investigations Today
Mr. Timothy J. O'Malley

Unassignable Priests
Rev. Msgr. Patrick R. Lagges

Catechumenal Pathways for Marriage and the Relevance of Canon Law
Mrs. Adrienne Yates

Not a Ground. The Case Against Determining Error
Dr. Felix Menendez

Restructuring Canonical Governance in Religious Institutes in Fidelity to the Journey
Sr. Sharon A. Euart

Parish Finance Councils: Guiding Principles, Legalities, Practicalities, and Best Practices
Rev. John Renken
Mr. Gary M. Ruesch

Traditiones Custodes
Dr. Chad Glendinning
Rev. Peter Mottola

Pope Francis Empowers Institutes and Societies: Ten Years of Revised Canons
Dr. Eileen Jaramillo

Sacred Stories and Those Who Tell Them: Trauma-Informed Ministerial Principles for Responding to Survivors of Clergy Sexual Abuse and Other Forms of Trauma
Dr. Heather T. Banis, Ph.D.

Canon Law and Seminary Administration: The New Ratio, PP46, and the Code of Canon Law
Very Rev. Phillip J. Brown, PSS

The Experience of Synodality in the Eastern Churches
Chorbishop John Faris

4. **2024 Convention:** The committee has worked diligently in preparing a program for 2024 and contacting proposed speakers. Although not all speakers and topic are confirmed, the proposed slate of speakers and topics is as follows:

Theme: Ministry of Justice in the 21st Century

Location: The Clyde Hotel, Albuquerque, NM

Preconvention Workshop

Gathering Testimony and Evaluating Proofs for Marriage and Penal Causes
To be confirmed

Keynote and Major Addresses

To be confirmed

Seminars

Dignitas Connubii at 20: Unresolved Procedural Questions
To be confirmed

Use of Social Media by Bishops and Priests: Upsides and Downsides for Evangelization
Mr. Ben Nguyen

Reconfiguration of Religious Life
Sr. Bonnie MacLellan

Pope Francis and the Advancement of Lay Persons
Dr. Zabrina Decker

Financial Crimes
Rev. Valère Nkouaya Mbandji, SJ

Sacramental Issues Concerning Transgender Persons: Sponsors and Candidates for Sacraments
To be confirmed

Governance in a Synodal Church Society of St. Pius X: Current Status and Pastoral Challenges
Rev. John Lessard-Thibodeau

Ongoing Formation of Clerics
Rev. Emmett Hall

Influence of Civil Law on Canon Law: Historical Perspectives
Rev. Brian Austin, FSSP

Jurisprudence on the *Bonum Prolis*
Mr. Thomas Sundaram

Organization of Churches *sui iuris* in Canada and the United States
Rev. Alexander Laschuk

Common Psychological Issues in Marriage Cases
Dr. Anne Greif Howe, Ph.D.

Dismissal of Diocesan and Religious Clerics
To be confirmed

5. **2025 Convention:** Work will begin on preparing the convention program for the 2025 convention, to be held in Orlando, FL, in Fall, 2023. It is anticipated that this will be a joint convention with the Canadian Canon Law Society.

6. **Convention Evaluation Forms.** The committee has worked with the General Secretary to review and revise the evaluation forms used at the convention. A new version of the evaluation form will be utilized at the 2023 convention.

Submitted By: Chad Glendinning
August 17, 2023

Committee: Eastern Churches

Constituted: January 2018

Mandate: The mandate of the committee is as follows:

1. To foster the study of the law of the Eastern Catholic and Eastern non-Catholic Churches through seminars at CLSA conventions and symposia and in publications and translations.
2. To serve as a resource to respond to inquiries regarding pastoral questions involving Eastern Christians.
3. To serve as a resource to other CLSA Committees when initiatives call for consideration of Eastern Catholic issues.
4. To promote the involvement of canonists proficient in Eastern canon law in the Society.
5. To promote the unity of Churches in all publications and discussions.

Members: Chorbishop John D. Faris, chair, Glen Allen, VA (2023)
Dr. Margaret Chalmers, Birmingham, AL (2024)
Dr. Sean Doyle, North Wales, PA (2025)
Rev. Alexander Laschuk, Toronto, ON (2023)
Rev. George Oonnoonny, Buchanan, NY (2024)
Rev. Ed Shestak, Old Forge, PA (2025)

BOG Liason: Msgr. Stephen Doktorczyk

REPORT

The committee has been working on two projects.

Code of Canons of the Eastern Churches, Revised English Translation. This will be the third English translation that the Canon Law Society has produced since the promulgation of the Eastern code in 1990. The body of the text and fontes are complete. We are reviewing the analytical index to be sure that all changes have been taken into account.

After the successful pre-convention workshop on best practices regarding Catholic priests who are married, the committee is preparing a publication of the presentations as a resource. Dr. Margaret Chalmers and Dr. Sean Doyle are the editors. We anticipate that the work will be published in a year.

Submitted by: Chorbishop John D. Faris
August 10, 2023

Committee: Institutes of Consecrated Life and Societies of Apostolic Life

Constituted: 2009 (Revised Mandate 2019)

Mandate: It is the function of the Committee on Institutes of Consecrated Life and Societies of Apostolic Life:

1. To initiate as needed any projects pertinent to the study of canon law pertaining to the life and ministry of Institutes of Consecrated Life and Societies of Apostolic Life or the implementation thereof, including, but not limited to, the following:
    a. Sponsorship;
    b. Mergers and restructuring of institutes;
    c. Governance;
    d. Membership;
    e. New forms of consecrated life;
    f. The process for private and public associations to be established as Institutes of Consecrated Life or Societies of Apostolic Life.
2. To initiate as needed any projects pertinent to the study of canon law pertaining to the life and ministry of solitary forms of consecrated life, including but not limited to, the following:
    a. Eremitic or anchoritic life;
    b. Hermits;
    c. Consecrated virgins;
    d. Widows.
3. To oversee projects referred to the committee by the BOG.
4. To oversee its subcommittees working on projects concerning any form of religious life listed in 1 or 2 above.
5. To collaborate with national organizations and other groups dealing with issues of any form of religious life listed in 1 or 2 above.

Members: Rev. John Chrysostom Kozlowski, OP, chair, New York, NY (2024)
Dr. Christina Hip-Flores, Brentwood, MD (2024)
Sister Mariette Moan, ASCJ, New Britain, CT (2025)
Sister Margaret Sullivan, CSJ, Braintree, MA (2023)
Sister Marlene Weisenbeck,FSPA, La Crosse, WI (2023)

BOG Liaison: Sister Tracey Sharp, SCRH

REPORT

SUBJECT: Recommendations for Convention Presentations

1. That CLSA purchase a booth at the LCWR Assembly in August as well as the CMSWR annual Assembly, staff it with a CLSA representative and sell the book at half price, or simply gift the book to any Major Superior who may desire to have it.

Rationale: There is a lot of canonical consultation being done among religious institutes as related to the demographic decline in religious life. Much has been offered by RCRI, LCWR, and CHAUSA. These organizations frequently/annually attend the conferences of women religious and offer advice and assistance. They have provided a wealth of publications pertaining to matters related to consecrated life. The recently revised CLSA procedural handbook is little known among religious institutes. It gets no publicity in the arenas of religious conferences, except by canonists who might be consulting with individual major superiors.

2. Possible topics for a convention seminar:

a. Canon 603 on eremitic life.

Rationale: Canonists and Vicars for Religious have received increasing requests for resources related to the vocation of eremitic life in the past few years Is this an indication about the resurgence of eremitic life in the 21st century?

b. Primer on the multiple changes to the law pertaining to consecrated life

Rationale: During the last ten years many changes in the area of religious law have been promulgated (e.g. *Vultum Dei quaerere*, multiple motu proprios, and changes to penal law which affect those in consecrated life and local ordinaries). The session could survey the various emendations to the law and discuss practical implications, especially in dealing with accused religious clerics/brothers/ women.

c. Autonomous Monasteries and Their Unique Needs

Rationale: This never ceases to be a sticky area of the law for diocesan Ordinaries. What are the bishop's responsibilities and best practices in dealing with the questions? Moreover, some monasteries could benefit from a canonical presentation about the need for record keeping and archival preservation for the sake of preserving the cultural heritage of the contemplative life. Perhaps the latter could be offered as an online seminar to autonomous monasteries so their unique concerns may be addressed internally in this matter.

d. Gender questions as related to our ministries in education but also regarding who will be accepted into our congregations in the future.

Rationale: Guidance is needed since the law of our land looks toward welcoming all kinds of changes, how will we be able to navigate all these without being constantly in the courts?

3. A manual for clergy and parish administrators entitled, "So a Sister/Brother shows up at the Parish and . . ."

Rationale: The Dicastery on Institutes of Consecrated Life and Societies of Apostolic Life is emphasizing the importance of educating bishops and other clergy about the role of consecrated life in the Church, and how their presence is integrated into the life of the local church. In addition, information might be gathered for topics such as forming new communities, communication with the Chancery before getting too far into the process when hiring someone, knowing diocesan agreements with religious (if there are any), recourse if there are issues, collection policies of the diocese for charities, etc.

The Committee on Consecrated Life should be apprised of the themes of the upcoming convention(s), so that it can brainstorm topics that dovetail with those themes.

Submitted By: Reverend John Chrysostom Kozlowski
May 31, 2023

Committee: Laity

Constituted: 2009

Mandate: The mandate of the committee is as follows:

1. To initiate as needed any projects pertinent to the study of canon law pertaining to the life and ministry of lay persons or the implementation thereof, including, but not limited to, the following:
   a. Lay ecclesial ministry;
   b. Collaboration with clergy;
   c. Rights of the lay faithful;
2. To oversee projects referred to the committee by the BOG;
3. To oversee its subcommittees working on projects concerning the laity, (and)
4. To collaborate with national organizations and other groups dealing with the role of the laity in the Church.

Members:
Dr. Andrea Ponzone, chair, Braintree, MA (2023)
Mrs. Anne Ameno, Buffalo, NY (2023)
Ms. Mary Gen Blittschau, Evansville, IN (2024)
Mr. Gregory Caridi, Dallas, TX (2025)
Rev. Anthony Dill, Harrisburg, PA (2023)
Mrs. Shannon Fossett, Saco, ME (2024)
Ms. Lori Peery, San Antonio, TX (2024)

BOG Liaison: Dr. David Castronovo

REPORT

We had regular Zoom meetings during the year, where we discussed the following projects:

1) Data Gathering of Lay People Holding Canonical and Semi-Canonical Offices in Arch/Dioceses

We have developed a survey to gather information about lay people holding canonical and semi-canonical offices in U.S. Arch/Dioceses. In the questionnaire, specific information is asked about the role of lay chancellors and what they can do within their Arch/Diocese, particularly regarding the granting of dispensations and permissions. We have submitted the questionnaire to the BOG.

2) Newly Instituted Stable Lay Ministries

As a result of both *motu proprio Spiritus Domini* and *Antiquum ministerium*, Pope Francis has given women access to the stable lay ministries of the lectorate and acolyte and has instituted the stable lay ministry of catechist for lay people, male and female, who have a particular call to serve the Catholic Church as teachers of the faith.

Following our expression of interest in providing assistance to the USCCB on this issue, Dr. Siobhan Verbeek contacted us, and we held a Zoom meeting with her to share some initial insights on how to implement both *motu proprio* in the United States.

3) New Penal Law – Impact of New Canons on Lay People

Due to the new book VI promulgated in 2021, actions that were previously considered "only" sinful behavior by lay people might now be interpreted as canonical delicts. Since those delicts might now be grounds for loss of job, loss of ministry in the parish or diocese, separation from or isolation in the faith community, this committee considers it necessary to study some of those new canons that may affect the life of lay people employed by Arch/Dioceses and Institutes of Consecrated Life and Societies of Apostolic Life.

Specifically, three groups of canonical delicts are to be considered:

- delicts related to public speech (cc. 1368, 1373)
- financial delicts (cc. 1376–1377)
- delicts against the Sixth Commandment of the Decalogue (cc. 1395 §3, 1398 §2)

In order to contribute to the study of those canons, this committee proposes writing CLSA advisory opinions on them.

Submitted By: Andrea Ponzone
August 17, 2023

CLSA Laity Committee (Arch) Diocesan Survey

This survey is being conducted to show different ways laity are serving in (arch) diocesan offices. No particular dioceses will be named.

1. Are any departments in your (arch) diocesan offices led by lay people (education, evangelization, finance, etc.)?
2. Does a lay person help draft canonical decrees? If yes, what position does that person hold?
3. Does a lay person have access to priest personnel files? Is this *ad hoc* or generally? If yes, what position does that lay person hold?
4. Has a non-cleric ever been delegated to sign dispensations and permissions for marriage files? If yes, what position does that person hold?

5. Has your (arch) diocese ever had a non-cleric as chancellor?
6. Please check all that apply, your (arch) diocesan chancellor:
    a. Notarizes documents
    b. Maintains the diocesan files excluding priest files
    c. Maintains the diocesan files including priest files
    d. Drafts decrees
    e. Does HR work for the (arch) diocesan offices
    f. Functions as a Chief Operating Officer for the Diocese
    g. Functions as a Safe Environment coordinator
    h. Signs dispensations
    i. Is a cleric
    j. Is a lay person
    k. Works in the tribunal
    l. Works as a canonical consultant
    m. Other notable duties (please specify):
7. Please check the qualifications that apply to your current chancellor:
    a. Undergraduate degree
    b. Degree in library or information sciences
    c. Certification in archiving or information sciences
    d. Graduate degree in theology
    e. JCD
    f. JCL
    g. STL
    h. PHD
    i. JD / Civil Attorney
    j. Certification in financial accounting
    k. Certification in Human Resources
    l. Work experience in archiving
    m. Work experience in HR
    n. Work experience in finance
    o. Other qualifications (please specify):
8. Please check yes or no for the following statements:
    a. There are lay people on our seminary acceptance board
    b. There are lay people on our priest personnel board
    c. There are lay people who mentor young priests/pastors
    d. There are lay people who mentor vicars forane
9. Please write any other comments you wish to share regarding laity in your (arch) diocesan offices.

Committee: Publications Advisory Board

Constituted: Board of Governors (2007)

Mandate: It is the function of the Committee on the Publications Advisory Board:

1. To advise the BOG about all aspects of current, periodic and proposed CLSA publication projects, including financial, literary, educational and marketing issues;
2. To monitor the progress of all CLSA publication projects;
3. To implement the procedures for peer review of CLSA publications;
4. To make the final recommendation to the Board of Governors regarding specific publications.
5. To review the coordination and management of the CLSA's publications activity on the part of the Office of the Executive Coordinator; (and)
6. To provide a written report to the CLSA membership at the annual convention.

Members:
Msgr. Michael Souckar, chair, Coral Springs, FL (2025)
Fr. Christopher Brashears, Guymon, OK (2025)
Fr. Phillip Brown, P.S.S., Baltimore, MD (2024)
Fr. Patrick Cooney, O.S.B., Owensboro, KY (2024)
Msgr. Jason Gray, Peoria Heights, IL (2025)
Msgr. Patrick Lagges, Merrilville, IN (2024)
Fr. John Paul Kimes, South Bend, IN (*ex officio*)
Mrs. Donna Miller, The Villages, FL (*ex officio*)
Ms. Kathleen Butler, Washington, DC (*ex officio*)

BOG Liaison: Mr. Benedict Nguyen

REPORT

Since last year's convention report, the Publications Advisory Board (PAB) has met three times—twice in person and once on-line.

1. The fourth printing of the *Code of Canon Law*, including *fontes*, was published this Spring. The canons from this printing will be available electronically at the CLSA Research Database.

2. The PAB is monitoring the progress on the following future publications:
   - *Code of Canons of the Eastern Churches* (Second Printing): Work continues on this publication, despite a delay caused by the revision of Title XXVII on penal law.
   - *New CLSA Code Commentary*: A significant majority of the contributors have submitted their work and the project is now into the editing phase.

- *Clergy Procedural Handbook*: This revised text should be ready for publication by the Spring of 2024.
- *Tribunal Procedural Handbook*: Work continues on this revision project that will include procedural norms for marriage nullity cases promulgated since the last edition of this text.
- This year's *Roman Replies and CLSA Advisory Opinions* includes the inaugural publication of English translations of *Excerpta Argumentorum* from *Decisiones seu Sententiae* (Vol. 106).
- The presenters of the 2022 pre-Convention seminar "Best Practices Regarding Married Priests" are working on a publication on the same topic.
- Work continues on *A Future Full of Hope*, a history of the CLSA (1939-2019), including interviews of Past-Presidents and Executive Coordinators, and researching the CLSA Archives held at the University of Notre Dame.

3. *Roman Replies and CLSA Advisory Opinions* is at something of a crossroads. In recent years, there has been a significant dearth of materials. The PAB is considering the possible evolution of this publication, while maintaining its unique role and purpose. CLSA members are encouraged to consider writing an "advisory opinion" of suitable length on topics of interest and of benefit to their canon law colleagues. The Executive Coordinator is available for helpful guidance.

4. The PAB is proposing a resolution at this year's convention for the establishment of a Task Force on Church Finances. The results of that one-year project will guide future CLSA publications, workshops, and/or other educational initiatives on the best practices in the area of Church finances, a topic of perceived great interest and need.

5. The PAB supports pursuing an offer from Hein Online to make certain CLSA publications available online. The recommendation is to begin with *Proceedings* and to observe a one-year embargo from the publication date.

6. CLSA webinars and podcasts continue to be popular. CLSA members are especially encouraged to consider offering a webinar. In addition, suggestions for topics and/or presenters are welcome.

The PAB will meet next during the convention in Milwaukee.

Submitted by: Msgr. Michael Souckar
August 17, 2023

Committee: Research and Development

Constituted: 2008

Mandate: It is the function of the Committee on Research and Development:

1. To initiate or cooperate in all CLSA research projects such as seminars, symposia and special studies;
2. To design and implement Think Tanks that will allow for diverse views on issues of ecclesial life having canonical implications;
3. To develop and recommend themes for the annual Conventions for submission to the Board of Governors for approval and subsequent referral to the Convention Planning Committee for implementation;
4. To maintain close communication with all the committees of the Society in order to facilitate needed research and discussion;
5. To interact with the Publications Advisory Board in order to assess the current and contemplated publications of the CLSA and offer suggestions and guidance for publication planning.

Members:
Rev. John Paul Kimes, chair, Notre Dame, IN (2023)
Rev. Brian Austin, FSSP, Mableton, GA (2025)
Very Rev. John Foster, Stockon, CA (2025)
Mr. Vincent Gardiner, Cleveland, OH (2024)
Dr. Sofia Markovich, Washington, DC (2024)
Rev. Msgr. Bruce Miller, Covington, LA (2025)
Dr. Sara Paglialunga, Fort Worth, TX (2024)

BOG Liaison: Very Rev. Ken Riley

REPORT

The Research and Development Committee discussed topics for conventions, potential speakers and other opportunities to promote both the practical exercise and the intellectual study of canon law. Some of the proposals the Committee has forwarded to the BOG include:

1. Recognizing that the Society typically focuses on providing guidance to practitioners, in an effort to stimulate also a more reflective/intellectual examination of the law, we proposed that there be a seminar to discuss the works of Msgr. Joaquín Llobel, exposing those unfamiliar with his nearly fifty years of work to his more important publications.
2. The R&D committee suggests exploring (again) the idea of organizing a trip for practitioners to the Roman Dicasteries, on the lines of those visits that are arranged for students of canon law by various faculties.

3. The R&D committee proposes to the BOG to formulate a proposal to the Dicastery for the Doctrine of the Faith for a collaborative effort to make more guidance (so as to not call it jurisprudence) available in matters of *delicta graviora*. The idea would be to propose a list of canonists to the DDF, to allow them to choose/approve and then to allow the DDF to select a certain number of decrees/sentences/correspondence which the CLSA would then translate and publish. The model would be similar to the new arrangement between CUA and the Rota and the work Msgr. Jenkins is doing to make more Rotal jurisprudence available to English speaking canonists.

In regard to upcoming conventions, the committee made the following recommendations:

Doctrine and Law – celebrating the 1700th Anniversary of the Council of Nicea

Focusing on *CIC* Book III (*CCEO* Titles XIV and XV) and contemporary reflections on the relationship between law and doctrine

The Role of Particular and Proper Law

Focusing on possibilities for national, diocesan, and proper religious law; the relationship between synodality and particular law; the role of subsidiarity in law

Renovation of the Law – law in the 21st century

Ten years of *Mitis Iudex*

Select speakers from among the contributors to the new CLSA commentary to provide a general update in light of all the recent legislation

Administration, Finances and Responsibility

Focusing on questions of proper administration and new financial responsibilities, in light of the continued legislative focus on the concept of "responsibility"

Understanding the Holy See – Theology and Practice

Major Addresses:

- *Pastor Bonus* and the new document delineating the powers of the organs of the Roman Curia – A Shift In Theological Focus Or A New Vision?
- The Relationship Governance Between Congregations and Dioceses – What Needs To Change?

- Understanding The Organs Of The Curia – How Do They Interact Together?

Seminars could include:

- The role or specific practices of specific groups such as DDF, the Rota, the Signatura, Dicastery for Clergy, Dicastery for Religious, Dicastery for Bishops or some aspect related to the authority of each one individually
- Appeals To The Rota: What To Know And How To Do It
- Petrine Privilege Cases – What To Do and When
- *Vos Estis* The Roman Curia – Questions and Practice
- Canonical Discipline For Bishops – What Is Possible And How Should It Work?
- The Role of CICLSAL and Sponsored Works – Oversight Or Window Dressing?
- Understanding The New Book VI – What Now?
- What, When, Where? Financial Issues Invoke Something About The Holy See?
- Implications Of The Resignation Of Pope Benedict XVI
- Lessons for Dioceses from the Financial Problems of the Holy See
- Making Saints: The Practical Aspects of the Sainthood Process
- Remnants of the McCarrick Report – Overseeing Gifts for Church Officials – Practical Options

At the conclusion of the year, the chairman of the Research and Development Committee submitted his resignation from that role to the President of the CLSA.

Submitted By: Fr. John Paul Kimes
August 22, 2023.

Committee: Sacramental Law

Constituted: 2009

Mandate: The mandate of the committee is as follows:

1. To initiate as needed any projects pertinent to the study of canon law pertaining the sacramental life of the Church or the implementation thereof;
2. To oversee projects referred to the committee by the BOG;
3. To oversee its subcommittees working on projects concerning the sacramental life of the Church;
4. To offer suggestions to the BOG for marriage topics for pre-convention workshops; (and)
5. To collaborate with national organizations and other groups dealing with the sacramental life of the Church.

Members:
Ms. Cecilia Brennan, chair, Monterey, CA (2023)
Ms. Anne Bryant, Houston, TX (2025)
Rev. Gerardo Galaviz, Los Angeles, CA (2025)
Rev. Tim Hedrick, New Orleans, LA (2025)
Dr. Sofia Markovich, Washington, DC (2023)
Mr. James Salamy, Syracuse, NY (2025)
Rev. Leo Walsh, Anchorage-Juneau, AK (2025)

BOG Liaison: Dr. Siobhan Verbeek

REPORT

The Sacramental Law Committee met at the CLSA Convention in Cleveland, OH, in October 2022. Outgoing chair Rev. Jamin David acknowledged the resignation of two members and the expiration of the terms of others resulting in all positions being vacant except the BOG liaison and Mrs. Cecilia Brennan who was subsequently appointed Committee Chair. Dr. Sofia Markovich was appointed to complete the term of one member and five new members representing various demographics/regions were appointed for a three-year term.

The Sacramental Law Committee met via Zoom five times this year. We discussed the role of the committee and reviewed the committee's work in previous years to guide the future. We agreed to pursue the issue of valid/invalid baptisms and the proliferation of the "Valid Baptism Lists." We will consider the increasing modification of the formula within an ecumenical context based on a presentation to this committee by Rev. Walter F. Kedjierski, Executive Director of the USCCB's Secretariat of Ecumenical and Interreligious Affairs, last year. This uncertainty regarding proper form led to discussing the possible need to return to conditional baptisms to ensure validity. We are developing a list of criteria for a valid baptism to be made available on the CLSA website as a canonical resource to parishes and tribunals. To augment that, we will draw up a sample of special situations that provide a unique pastoral challenge as examples for how to determine baptismal status and include suggestions of how to prove the validity of a baptism. We will include a section on a range of LGBT and gender identity issues including sacramental record keeping, RCIA, godparents and admissibility to baptism. This section will also include scenarios to guide those responsible for these decisions.

We will consider any information that has been published by the Holy See and do an informal survey of dioceses to glean current practices. We will meet in person in Milwaukee to continue the discussion.

Submitted By: Ms. Cecilia Brennan

AD HOC COMMITTEES

Committee: Strategic Visioning Task Force

Constituted: CLSA Resolution - 84th Annual Convention, Cleveland, OH - October 12, 2022

Mandate: The mandate of the Task Force is as follows:

1. As a result of the audit by done in 2022 by John Schlageter (of the JKT Group) and the Future Initiative Project completed in 2007, the Task Force is to undertake a strategic planning process to understand how the Board of Governors, committees, and staff function today in their present roles, and to recommend ways forward to prepare to meet future needs and challenges. This will begin after the 2022 Convention and end with a report and recommendations presented to the membership at the 2024 Convention.
2. Because the mandate of the Task Force will focus on the work of the Board and staff, and how they interact with committees of the Society, most members of the Task Force should have prior experience on the Board of Governors.
3. The *ad hoc* Task Force will study the Constitution and Bylaws of the CLSA, the Future Initiatives Project, and John Schlageter's audit report. In addition, the Task Force will conduct listening sessions at the 2023 Convention, in virtual meetings, and at other gatherings, as possible.

Members:
Very Rev. Paul D. Counce, co-chair, Baton Rouge, LA (2024)
Dr. Lynda Robitaille, co-chair, Vancouver, BC (2024)
Ms. Barbara A. Bettwy, Harrisburg, PA (2024)
Ms. Mary Gen Blittschau, secretary, Evansville, IN (2024)
Rev. Anthony R. Dill, Harrisburg, PA (2024)
Deacon Matthew A. Glover, Little Rock, AR (2024)
Msgr. D. Bruce Miller, Covington, LA (2024)
Very Rev. Kevin Niehoff, OP, Grand Rapids, MI (2024)

BOG Liaisons:
Rev. John P. Donovan
Very Rev. Jamin S. David

REPORT

The Strategic Visioning Task Force held seven online meetings on January 27, February 3, March 24, April 21, May 19, June 2, and August 4. It will meet again online as needed and in person before, during and after the 2023 convention in Milwaukee, Wisconsin.

CLSA President John Donovan asked Immediate Past President Lynda Robitaille to serve as co-chair of the task force. Mary Gen Blittschau serves as recording secretary, keeping wonderful minutes of the discussions.

At its first two meetings, the task force principally tried to familiarize itself with its mandate and what had led up to it. Discussions on what seemed to be important things upon which to focus took place (for example, problematic aspects of the society's structures and operations). Task force members began to brainstorm how it would function, and in the end narrowed this into two things in particular: preparing to host listening sessions both at the 2023 convention and in other venues and ways, and how to solicit advance input using the resource of an internet survey.

Regarding the first, mindful of the opportunities and limitations of consultation during our convention, assisted by the more immediate convention-planners, preparations began to be made to host listening lunches at the convention on Tuesday, October 10. Members of the task force and of the BOG will serve as facilitators and recorders at these. The task force will remain after the convention's close for a Thursday afternoon in-person meeting.

Regarding the second, in March, April and May much attention was focused on developing the internet survey which was then publicized and until the end of July 2023 open to not only to CLSA membership but to any who were interested in canon law. The findings of this survey are still being read and understood, and will be organized and compiled in a helpful way, but already there have been some surprises regarding what the respondents were interested in. For example, responses regarding the society's structure as adequate or not was hardly mentioned, and almost a third of those responding do not use or really much support increasing use of digital publishing and the like. To no one's surprise, responders seem dissatisfied with the costs of CLSA membership in general, and many lamented the difficulty in enabling younger members to become active in the projects and works—especially on committees—of the society. A summary of these and other significant findings of the internet survey will be prepared as a handout for attendees at the listening lunches.

Submitted By: Very Rev. Paul Counce
August 18, 2023

Committee: Canonist Wellness

Constituted: 2021

Mandate: As a response to the presentation by Susan Mulheron and Rev. Daniel Griffin on Restorative Justice at the 2021 Convention in San Diego, the question arose:

How can those canonists who work with traumatizing material care for their own spiritual and mental health?

The Wellness Committee is to develop resources to foster the ongoing human and spiritual formation of canonists, particularly those who work with traumatizing material that may include but not be limited to: Days of Recollection, Retreats, Webinars, Convention Seminars.

Membership: Very Rev. Peter Mottola, chair, Rochester, NY (2023)
Dr. Marie Hilliard, Washington, DC (2023)
Mr. Tim Olson, Fargo, ND (2023)
Ms. Amy Tadlock, St. Paul, MN (2023)

BOG Liaison: Sr. Tracey Sharp, SCRH

REPORT

The Wellness Committee has discussed ways to identify the challenges to wellness for canonists and potential resources that promote the integration of spiritual, psychological, emotional, and physical health, particularly as it relates to a canonist's relationships and responsibilities. A survey is being developed by the committee. The distribution of the survey will raise awareness and encourage discussion of wellness issues, and the responses to the survey will aid in the planning of future days of recollection, retreats, webinars, and convention seminars.

Submitted By: Fr. Peter Mottola, Chairperson
August 18, 2023

VARIA

Canon Law Society of America Eighty-Fifth Annual Business Meeting Milwaukee, Wisconsin October 11, 2023

MINUTES

CALL TO ORDER AND OPENING PRAYER

Reverend John Donovan, President, called to order the Eighty-Fifth Annual Business Meeting of the Canon Law Society of America (CLSA) on October 11, 2023 at the Hyatt Regency Milwaukee at 11:15 a.m. He presided over the meeting as Chair.

The Chair led the assembly in an opening prayer. He announced that the parliamentarian for the meeting would be Mr. Aldean Hendrickson and that *Robert's Rules of Order* would be used in matters not included in the CLSA *Constitution* or *Bylaws*.

The Chair entertained a motion that Associate Members present at the meeting would have the opportunity to address the assembly as called for in Article 5.3 of the *CLSA Constitution.* The motion was made and seconded and passed by the assembly.

REVIEW OF MINUTES

The Chair invited the Secretary, Reverend Gregory Luyet, to read the minutes of the Eighty-Fourth Annual Business Meeting of the CLSA found on pages 509-518 of the 2022 *Proceedings.* The Chair entertained a motion to dispense with reading the minutes. A motion was made and seconded and passed by the assembly. The Chair called for any corrections to the minutes as submitted; none were proposed. The Chair heard a motion to approve the minutes, which was seconded and passed unanimously. The Chair announced the minutes of the Eighty-Fourth Annual Business Meeting were approved.

ELECTION OF OFFICERS AND CONSULTORS

The Chair called Mr. Christopher Siuzdak, Chair of the Nominations Committee, to present the slate of nominees for officers and consultors. The Chair asked if there were any nominations from the floor. There were none.

The Chair then read the provisions of the CLSA's *Bylaws* regarding elections. Following the reading of the election procedures, he invited the members to cast their ballots.

For the Office of Vice President/President-Elect

236 valid ballots were cast; 119 were needed for election. There were 0 invalid ballots and 1 abstention. The votes cast were as follows:

Dr. Margaret Chalmers received 116
Reverend Patrick Cooney, OSB, received 119

The Chair declared an election with Reverend Patrick Cooney, OSB, elected as Vice President/President-Elect.

For the Office of Secretary

237 valid ballots were cast; 120 were needed for election. There were 0 invalid ballots and 1 abstention. The votes cast were as follows:

Mr. Stephen V. Garbitelli received 103
Sr. Rose Marie Timmer, RSM, received 132

The Chair declared an election with Sr. Rose Marie Timmer, RSM, elected as Secretary.

For the Office of Consultor

On the first ballot, 236 valid ballots were cast; 119 votes were needed for election. There were 0 invalid ballots and 0 abstentions. The Reverend Monsignor Robert Oliver received an absolute majority of 160 votes and was elected on the first ballot. None of the other candidates received an absolute majority, requiring a runoff election.

The President invited those members eligible to vote to use the ballot provided to write the name of the preferred candidate between top two candidates who did not receive an absolute majority. 222 ballots were received with 0 invalid ballots or abstentions. In the runoff election, the absolute majority needed for election was 112. The votes cast were as follows:

Sr. Nancy Bauer, OSB, received 96
Deacon Gerald T. Jorgenson received 108

Dr. Jeannine Marino received 113
Reverend Monsignor Robert Oliver received 160

The Chair declared an election with Dr. Jeannine Marino and Reverend Monsignor Robert Oliver, elected as consultors.

REPORTS

PRESIDENT'S REPORT

The Chair referred the assembly to the complete text of the presidential report in the *85th Annual Reports* booklet found on pages 19-20. He announced the CLSA Board of Governors approved policies and an application for the Fr. Frank Morrissey Memorial Membership established by a resolution presented at the 2020 Convention. Details will be forthcoming in the December newsletter.

TREASURER'S REPORT

The Chair invited CLSA Treasurer, the Very Reverend Jamin David to present the Treasurer's report. Fr. David referred to the written version of his report in the convention booklet on pages 21-56. He reviewed the line items in the budget and balance sheet and explained the CLSA's accrual accounting method (rather than a cash-based accounting method). The budget for FY 2024 includes a deficit. He explained that the deficit is projected because the Society will need to borrow from the investment accounts to pay upfront costs for the new commentary project. Though the budget reveals a deficit, the investment account will be replenished from the sales of CLSA publications. As the COVID-19 restrictions have disappeared, committees are beginning to meet, and some committees need to gather in person, which comes with associated costs. He mentioned the office and BOG are cutting costs as much as possible. He announced that all the members of the BOG contributed to the scholarship fund, as well as other members gave generously to the $85 campaign for the 85th anniversary of CLSA.

Fr. David directed the assembly's attention to the auditor's report and their recommendations, which the Board has either already completed since the audit was finished or are researching now. He took questions from members regarding the budget deficit and its relationship to CLSA's accrual accounting method.

EXECUTIVE COORDINATOR'S REPORT

The chair invited Mrs. Donna Miller, the Executive Coordinator of the CLSA, to deliver her report to the members. Mrs. Miller highlighted items from her report which is found on pages 57-62 of the convention booklet. She reported on the robust sales of the 4th edition of the Code. She announced changes are being made to the composition of the editorial board of the new commentary which will be announced in the December newsletter. She thanked all who have contributed in any way to the CLSA publications and thanked those who have been supportive and encouraging. She invited members to contact her with any questions or concerns.

GENERAL SECRETARY'S REPORT

The chair invited Ms. Kathleen Butler, the General Secretary, to give her report. She thanked Mr. Mark Francisco, CLSA Membership Coordinator, for his work. She noted the increased number of attendees who were using the Guidebook app. She demonstrated how a member can use the CLSA website to access account information, the groups, forums, member directory, and other useful information. She reminded members that they will need to request their free copy of *Proceedings* in the spring just as they did last year.

A member asked if the details of the schedules of the regional meetings of canonists be placed on the CLSA website to assist members decision making about which regional meetings to attend. Ms. Butler encouraged those involved in the planning to send the information to her to be added to the Society's website.

RESOLUTIONS

Fr. Donovan read the applicable CLSA *Bylaws* that govern the proposal of resolutions from the floor and asked if there were any such resolutions to be presented. None were brought forward. He called Mrs. Amy Tadlock of the Resolutions Committee, to present the resolution.

RESOLUTION #1

PROPOSED BY: PUBLICATIONS ADVISORY BOARD

TITLE: Working Group on Publications, Workshops, and Other Initiatives on Church Finance

STATEMENT OF RATIONALE:

WHEREAS, Book V of the Code of Canon Law includes general provisions regulating the acquisition, administration, and alienation of temporal goods by juridic persons;

WHEREAS, the most current CLSA's *Church Finance Handbook*, published in 1999 and now out of print, is outdated due to the many changes in civil laws that relate to charitable corporations and foundations in the United States;

WHEREAS, most, if not all, Church institutions have been given juridic personality in civil law as non-profit corporations and are subject to strict laws, regulations, and policies regarding their financial affairs with which they must comply to preserve their tax-exempt status.

WHEREAS, in recent years, efforts have been undertaken in the Church to review, revise and safeguard financial practices that are in accord with canon law and civil law; and further it is desired that financial best practices derived from the principles of public accounting in the civil realm be employed by Church entities in the management of their financial affairs;

WHEREAS, any failure to fulfill recognized moral, canonical, and fiduciary duties in financial matters can lead to serious adverse consequences, including canonical, civil law, and criminal liabilities, as well as grave scandal among the Christian faithful and society in general;

BE IT RESOLVED that the Board of Governors of the Canon Law Society of America constitute from the membership of the society a task force to conduct a survey for the purpose of compiling a list of topics to be covered in 1) new publications, 2) workshops, and/or 3) other initiatives to provide educational and practical resources concerning best practices around Church finance.

IMPLEMENTATION BY MEANS OF: The Task Force will report to and receive guidance from the Publications Advisory Board. The Task Force will determine the scope of the survey (in terms of the parties to be surveyed and questions to be asked); select the survey methodology (online, paper); distribute the survey; and analyze responses. The Task Force is to prepare a report on its findings and offer recommendations for new or updated publications and initiatives to the Publications Advisory Board. The report is to be submitted to the Publications Advisory Board no later than May 31, 2024.

ANTICIPATED COST: The cost of implementing this Resolution shall not exceed $5,000 without prior approval of the Board of Governors.

After reading the resolution, Mrs. Tadlock announced that the Resolutions Committee moved the resolution. She invited Reverend Monsignor Michael Souckar, Chair of the Publications Advisory Board, to come forward to present the resolution. Hearing no further discussion, the Convention Chair called for the vote. The assembly passed the resolution.

OLD BUSINESS

The Chair opened the floor to discuss any Old Business of interest to the assembly; there was none.

NEW BUSINESS

The Chair opened the floor to discuss any New Business of interest to the assembly; there was none.

VARIA

President Reverend John Donovan welcomed the representatives of the sister canon law societies to come forward and address the assembly.

Father Frank Bradley of the Canon Law Society of Great Britain and Ireland thanked the CLSA for its hospitality and invited members to attend the Canon Law Society of Great Britain and Ireland. He advised the members of that the CLSGBI has launched a new website and made available many of its resources available through electronic means. He invited the members of CLSA to access their website at www.canonlawsociety.org.

They have revised their Society's constitution. He extended an invitation for members of CLSA to join the CLSGBI and to attend their upcoming conference in Krakow, Poland.

Father Ken Cafe, OFM, of the Canon Law Society of Australia and New Zealand. He extended greetings from his Society to the CLSA. He welcomed members of the CLSA to join the Canon Law Society of Australia and New Zealand and to access their website to consult copies of the proceedings of their conferences and their publication, *The Canonist.* He also mentioned that Monsignor Brendan Daly has published a book on penal law.

Dr. Chad Glendinning represented the Canadian Canon Law Society (CCLS) on behalf of their president Father Michael Fahlman. He reported that the Canadian Canon Law Society revised their bylaws. He announced that the 2023 convention will be in Edmonton, Alberta next week and the 2024 Convention will be held in Quebec City, Quebec. In 2025, the CLSA and CCLS are in the process of planning a joint convention in Orlando, Florida. Additionally, he invited CLSA members to avail themselves of the webinars produced in cooperation between the CCLS and St. Paul University covering various themes. The webinars are advertised on the canon law listserv, the CLSA website, and other places. The webinars are free however, attendees are requested to register.

ADJOURNMENT

The Chair entertained a motion to adjourn. The motion was seconded and approved by the assembly. The Eighty-Fifth Annual Business Meeting adjourned at 12:40 p.m.

Respectfully submitted,
Reverend Gregory Thomas Luyet
Secretary

VARIA

Role of Law Citation

The Reverend John Donovan, JCL
CLSA President

Each year the Canon Law Society of America presents its distinguished Role of Law Award to an individual considered to be outstanding in the field of canonical science. The Bylaws of the Society directs the Board of Governors to select a person who demonstrates in his or her life and legal practice the following characteristics:

- Embodiment of pastoral attitude
- Commitment to research and study
- Participation in the development of law
- Response to needs or practical assistance
- Facilitation of dialogue and the interchange of ideas within the Society and with other groups.

These qualifications are a concise restatement of the constitutionally expressed purposes of the society.

The person to whom this award is given is viewed by us as one who embodies all that we, as members of the society hold dear, as one to whom we can look for guidance and inspiration. Such an official statement alone is perhaps the greatest honor that can be bestowed on anyone—to to be selected by one's friends and peers as outstanding among them.

This year's recipient of the Role of Law grew up on a farm, the youngest of four, in a small town known for their food and the Mud Hens. As the youngest child, our recipient was subjected to several head injuries with a fall of a bale of hay, and a sister with a sledgehammer, and later a baseball bat! They learned to drive a tractor before a car.

An appreciation of creation and outdoor activities came naturally, inspired by seasonal extremes, wildlife and the delicate nature of butterflies and wildflowers. Our recipient's knowledge of racoons, foxes, and hawks, well, is frightening.

This year's Role of Law recipient is stealth-like, often not noticed in the crowd, but relied upon to depict a clear vision. The viewpoint offered often sheds new light on what is not noticed by most. The person has been called upon by several groups, including the CLSA, on numerous occasions to capture for history, moments of change.

There is a true love of learning, with collections of the complete works of Walt Whitman, Emily Dickinson, and Robert Frost. Our recipient has worked as an author, editor, recordkeeper, an academic, superior and in their undergraduate field, as photojournalist.

Having made a final profession on the founders' feast in 1981, she states:

> I love being in the Oratory of our monastery, praying the Liturgy of the Hours with my Benedictine sisters. I love all of the sacred moments in our community life together and all of the funny moments. We bring Christ to each other, and we bring each other to Christ. Her motto is: "I live in hope."

I think I've probably given it away by now.

Our honoree enjoys doing research and writing on canonical and monastic topics. At Catholic University of America, where our recipient obtained a JCL and JCD, she taught Consecrated Life, Rights of the Lay Faith, Introduction and Marriage to Seminarians, and the History of Canon Law.

She has been a member of the CLSA since 2014 and has served the society as member of the Convention Planning Committee and contributed to the Procedural Handbook for Institutes of Consecrated Life and Societies of Apostolic Life in 2021. She is a three-time presenter at conventions. She is often consulted by a vast range of members of the society regarding the unique perspective, knowledge and experience she offers. Her responses are given joyfully with thorough, factual information and a kind and gentle way to implement the law, recognizing that lives of people will be affected. She truly appreciates that law is about people's rights and order.

It is my pleasure to announce the 2023 Role of Law recipient is Minnesota's own, Benedictine Sister Nancy Bauer, OSB. Please join me in congratulating Sister Nancy.

VARIA

ROLE OF LAW AWARD RESPONSE

Sister Nancy Bauer, OSB, JCD

My parents got my name, Nancy, from a comic strip, so sometimes it is difficult for me to take things seriously. Thus, when Father John Donovan called me many months ago to inform me that the CLSA Board of Governors selected me for this year's Role of Law Award, I listened to him politely and then, when the call ended, I thought something like, "Uh huh. And tomorrow I'm going to receive the Nobel Peace Prize." But I kept getting emails from Kathleen Butler with instructions for receiving this award. And now, here I am, standing before you, my colleagues, with the Role of Law Award in my possession. I have become a believer. I am grateful for this affirmation of my canonical work, meager as it is compared to that of so many of you. Thank you, John, and members of the BOG.

People ask me how I got into canon law. It happened at 70 miles per hour on Interstate Highway 94 between my monastery in Minnesota and Annunciation Monastery in Bismarck, ND. We were on our way to our general chapter. I was driving. My then-prioress was in the passenger seat and a sister from Taiwan was asleep in the back seat. She had given up on looking for bison ,which she had heard wandered around freely in the Dakotas. I took the opportunity to say to my prioress that I had been working at our diocesan newspaper for nearly twenty years and I was ready for a change and, in particular, I would like to go back to school. She said, "You wouldn't be interested in canon law, would you?" I said, "I could be." And that, dear friends, is how the vow of obedience works.

As I continued discerning the possibility of studying canon law, I called a Benedictine sister who was a canonist—Sister Lynn McKenzie, a member of Sacred Heart Monastery in Cullman, Alabama. I asked her one question: "What does canon law have to do with Jesus Christ?" That was important to me because the Rule of St. Benedict says more than once, "Prefer nothing whatever to Christ." If canon law had nothing to do with Christ, I would have nothing to do with canon law. Sister Lynn's response was, "You'd be surprised how much canon law has to do with Jesus Christ." That settled it. This Minnesota farm girl flew off to Washington, DC, and studied at the School of Canon Law at The Catholic University of America. Later, I had the privilege of joining this marvelous canon law faculty.

Frequently I wonder if there is a specifically Benedictine approach to canon law. Or, more precisely, does the Rule of Benedict say anything that might shape how we canonists practice our craft.

The ancient monastic rules were among the earliest forms of legislation within the Church and the Rule of Benedict is among the few still in use today. The Rule is a hybrid sort of document. It is a spiritual text. It is wisdom literature. It contains a liturgical ordo. But it is also a code, a book of rules or regulations to order a community toward its proper end. It even contains a so-called "penal code," just as our *Codex Iuris Canonici* has its Book VI on Penal Sanctions in the Church. As someone who has lived according to this Rule for more than 40 years, I am convinced it does have something significant to contribute to our understanding and practice of church law.

The first contribution of the Rule that I want to identify is its admonition that we recognize Christ in everyone we encounter. Benedict says that we must see Christ especially in the poor and in the sick. In other words, we must see Christ in those who are suffering, who are sad, vulnerable, hopeless, angry, cynical, and resistant. Thus, Christ comes to us as canonists in the person of a spouse petitioning for a declaration of nullity of her marriage, in the respondent who is angry at the petitioner, in the religious who is threatened with dismissal from his religious institute, in the pastor who is removed from his parish and does not understand why, in the religious superior who is removed from her office because of mental illness, and in the lay person whose right to a sacrament has been denied.

Secondly, I believe Benedict can teach us something about handling cases of potential dismissal from a religious institute and even about handling delicts. The Rule actually has a form of excommunication, although it is not the ecclesiastical excommunication described in the Code of Canon Law; rather, it is separation from the common prayer and common table for offenses against the community. Benedict's approach is one of concern for the wayward monastic. The abbot is to imitate the loving example of the Good Shepherd and go in search of the sheep who has strayed and, with compassion, place it on his shoulders and carry it back to the flock. This is reflected in canon 665 §2 of the code: a religious who is illegitimately absent "is to be sought out solicitously by the superior and is to be helped to return to and persevere in his or her vocation."

Benedict advocates other acts of solicitude. The abbot secretly sends in *senpectae*, wise old monastics to console the offender—that's right, console the offender—and pray for him "lest he be overwhelmed by excessive sorrow." (RB 27). Quoting 2 Corinthians 2:8, Benedict writes of the troublesome monk, "Let love for him be reaffirmed." Every effort must be made to heal the sick brother.

Although, for the good of the community, dismissal of an unrepentant offender is a possible outcome, it is a last resort. I am concerned that the revision of canon 700, eliminating the necessity of confirmation by ecclesiastical authority of a decree of dismissal of a religious, will result in superiors acting too quickly and without the necessary procedures to "get rid of" religious they consider irksome. I have already heard of a superior who has advised other superiors that they can now "more easily" dismiss members. I also have some fear that, still stinging from criticism over how bishops mishandled—or failed to handle—cases of sexual abuse, the Church will become overly punitive in response to delicts. I recall Msgr. Tom Green's class on Book VI and his fondness for the Church's more merciful approach to delicts and penalties following Vatican II. As canonists, we must insist on reform of the offender, restoration justice, and repair of scandal, but we must also insist that these do not devolve into destroying an offender's hope of redemption as a means of appeasing anger and outrage.

The Rule of Benedict insists that we must always let mercy triumph over judgment (RB 64). During the Church's Year of Mercy, some people warned against an overemphasis on mercy at the expense of justice. Dear colleagues, justice is indeed essential, but I say it is not possible to be too merciful while it is possible to be too harsh. I am speaking from experience. I have yet to witness a positive effect from breaking bruised reeds, but I have seen the power of mercy.

I could say much more about adapting the wisdom of the Rule of Benedict to our canonical practice, but I will be merciful to you and wrap this up. I will end at the beginning of the Rule, with the first word in the Rule – *audire*. Listen. Listen carefully. Listen with the ear of your heart. Listen for the voice of Christ in the voice of petitioners, respondents, witnesses, and clients. Listen for the voice of Christ in all those who call on you for canonical assistance.

Thank you for listening to me. And again in the words of St. Benedict, Let us prefer nothing whatever to the love and Christ and may he bring us all together to everlasting life. And in the words of Nancy of comic book fame, "I'll have the super-large jumbo ice cream cone."

Varia

Board of Governors 2022-2023

The Reverend John Donovan, JCL
President

The Very Reverend Kenneth Riley, JCL
Vice President/President-Elect

The Very Reverend Jamin David, JCL
Treasurer

Dr. David Castronovo, JCD
Consultor

The Reverend Monsignor Stephen Doktorczyk, JCD
Consultor

The Reverend Gregory Luyet, JCL
Secretary

The Very Reverend Luke Millette, JCL
Consultor

Mr. Benedict T. Nguyen, JCL
Consultor

Sr. Tracey Sharp, SCRH, JCL
Consultor

Dr. Siobhan Verbeek, JCD
Consultor

Administrative Staff

Donna Miller, JD, JCL
Executive Coordinator

Kathleen Butler
General Secretary

Mark Francisco
Membership Coordinator

VARIA

Convention Contributors

The Most Reverend Juan Ignacio Arrieta, JCD, Secretary of the Dicastery for Legislative Texts

Dr. Heather Banis, PhD, Victims Assistance Coordinator, Archdiocese of Los Angeles

The Very Reverend Phillip J. Brown, PSS, JD, JCD, President and Rector, St. Mary's Seminary and University, Baltimore, MD

Ms. Anna Marie Chamblee, JCL, Judge, Metropolitan Tribunal, Archdiocese of Milwaukee

Sister Sharon A. Euart, RSM, JCD, Executive Director, Resource Center for Religious Institutes

Chorbishop John Faris, JCOD, Assistant Professor, The Catholic University of America

Dr. Chad Glendinning, JCD, Dean, Faculty of Canon Law, St. Paul University, Ottawa

Dr. Eileen Jaramillo, DMin, JCL, Adjunct Faculty for various universities; Canonical Consultant to Bishops and Religious, USA and other countries

The Reverend Monsignor John J. Kennedy, JCD, Secretary for the Discipline Section of the Dicastery for the Doctrine of the Faith

The Reverend John Paul Kimes, JCOD, Associate Professor of the Practice, Notre Dame University

The Reverend Monsignor Patrick Lagges, JCD, Retired Presbyter, Archdiocese of Chicago

The Reverend Alexander Laschuk, JCD, PhD, Judicial Vicar, Archdiocese of Toronto

Dr. Felix Menendez, JCD, STL, Tribunal Director, Metropolitan Tribunal of Atlanta

The Reverend Peter Mottola, JCL, Judicial Vicar, Rochester, NY

Mr. Timothy O'Malley, JD, Director of Ministerial Standards and Safe Environment, Archdiocese of St. Paul & Minneapolis

Professor Marie T. Reilly, JD, Professor of Law, Pennsylvania State University

Dr. Lynda Robitaille, JCD, Dean of Theology, St. Mark's College, Vancouver, BC

Mr. Gary M. Ruesch, JD, Of Counsel Attorney, Buelow Vetter Buikema Olson & Vliet, LLC

Dr. Brandon Vaidynathan, Associate Professor and Chair, Department of Sociology, The Catholic University of America

Sister Victoria Vondenberger, RSM, JCL, Defender of the Bond, Promoter of Justice and Canonical Advisor, Archdiocese of Cincinnati

Mrs. Adrienne Yates, JCL, MS, MA, Defender of the Bond, Archdiocese of Military Services and the Diocese of Cleveland

VARIA

List of Participants

Joseph Abraham
Reno, NV

Peter Akpoghiran
New Orleans, LA

Ben Altenhofen
Shoreline, WA

John R. Amos
Traverse City, MI

Diana Anderson
Orlando, FL

Arthur Anderson
Gary, IN

Daniel Andree
Chicago, IL

Michael Andrews
Lansing, MI

Bruce Ansems
Kansas City, KS

William Anton
Lubbock, TX

Joseph Arsenault
Kansas City, KS

Francis Asagba
Oakland Gardens, NY

Mark Augustine
Chicago, IL

Joseph Augustine
Wheeling, WV

Leo Awojinrin
Salzano-Robegano, Italy

Kevin L. Badeaux
Beaumont, TX

Chrysostom Baer
Silverado, CA

Diane Barr
Baltimore, MD

Mark Bartchak
Altoona, PA

Ronald Barusefski
Harrisburg, PA

Nancy Bauer
St. Joseph, MN

Anthony Bawyn
Seattle, WA

R. Paul Beach
Louisville, KY

Katherine Beall
Madison, WI

John Bell
Plano, TX

Joseph Bellerive
Orlando, FL

Iden Bello
Laredo, TX

Mary Gen Blittschau
Evansville, IN

Nathan Bockrath
Kalida, OH

Mary Boda
Ferdinand, IN

Phillip Bogacki
Wauwatosa, WI

Kevin Bordelon
Lafayette, LA

Francis Bradley
Buncrana, Ireland

James Bradley
Washington, DC

Michael Bradley
Chicago, IL

Sean Bransfield
Philadelphia, PA

Christopher Brashears
Guymon, OK

Douglas Braun
Harrison Twp, MI

Claire Breaux
Baton Rouge, LA

Cecilia Brennan
Monterey, CA

Phillip J. Brown
Baltimore, MD

Samuel Brown
Santa Rosa, CA

Anne Bryant
Pasadena, TX

Michael Burbeck
Raleigh, NC

Kurt Burnette
Woodland Park, NJ

Jeffrey Cabral
Fall River, MA

Ken Cafe, OFM
Sydney, Australia

Marjorie Campbell
Park City, UT

Luis Capacetti
Raleigh, NC

Brian Caperton
Cincinnati, OH

Giovanni Capucci
Denver, CO

Gregory Caridi
Dallas, TX

John Caronan
San Pedro, CA

Ernie Jun Karol Carpio
Bridge City, TX

David Castronovo
Beaumont, TX

Timothy Cavanaugh
Madison, WI

Anthony Celino
El Paso, TX

Martin Celuch
Youngstown, OH

Krikor Chahin
San Antonio, TX

Jorge Chalaco
Los Angeles, CA

Margaret Chalmers
Birmingham, AL

Anna Marie Chamblee
Smyrna, GA

Peter Chineke
Decatur, IL

Jean Chrostoski
Cheyenne, WY

James Clark
Memphis, TN

George Cobb
Gastonia, NC

Oscar Coelho
Albuquerque, NM

Daniel Condon
Rochester, NY

James Conn
Leominster, MA

Jay Conzemius
Bethel Park, PA

Patrick Cooney
Owensboro, KY

August Cordova
Loveland, CO

Paul Counce
Baton Rouge, LA

Michael Courtney
Salt Lake City, UT

Matthew Crane
Saint Augusta, MN

Amanda Crawford
North Little Rock, AR

Philip Creurer
Edmonton, Canada

Thomas Cronkleton
Cheyenne, WY

Eric Culler
Swanton, OH

Barbara Anne Cusack
Greenfield, WI

Emily Danchisin
Owensboro, KY

William Daniel
Washington, DC

Jamin David
Morganza, LA

Andreas Davison
Milton, MA

Zabrina Decker
Milwaukee, WI

David Deibel
Indian River, MI

Jesus del Angel
Fresno, CA

Frank Del Prete
Newark, NJ

Nicole Delaney
Phoenix, AZ

Brian Dellaert
Dubuque, IA

David Demirbilek
Milwaukee, WI

John Dermond
Lawrenceville, NJ

Joseph Di Loreto
Hamilton, ON

John Dickinson
Scarborough, ME

Anthony Dill
Harrisburg, PA

Lien Do
Washington, DC

John Doherty
Riverwood, Australia

Stephen Doktorczyk
Yorba Linda, CA

Francis Dolan
Chicago, IL

Carlos Donato da Silva
Memphis, TN

John Donovan
Hamilton, NY

Theodore Dudzinski
Lafayette, IN

Beverly Dunn
Seattle, WA

Frederick Easton
Bloomington, IN

Juan Echavarria
Boylston, MA

Heather Eichholz
Grand Island, NE

Peter Eke
Prudenville, MI

Chidi Ekpendu
Los Angeles, CA

Martins Emeh
Houston, TX

Scott Emerson
Madison, WI

Charles English
Louisville, KY

Simon Peter Engurait
Houma-Thibodaux, LA

Philip Erickson
Louisville, KY

David Esquiliano
Sioux City, IA

Sharon Euart
Silver Spring, MD

Ramil Fajardo
Chicago, IL

John Faris
Glen Allen, VA

Jean Felicien
Princeton, NJ

Karla Felix-Rivera
Citrus Heights, CA

Victor Finelli
Allentown, PA

Ryan Fitzgerald
Sugar Land, TX

Anna Flanigan
West Peoria, IL

David Fons
Lansing, MI

Robert Forlenza
Loveland, CO

Shannon Fossett
Saco, ME

John Foster
Stockton, CA

Matthew Furgiuele
Gaylord, MI

Christopher Fusco
Metuchen, NJ

Ricardo Gaiotti Silva
Orlando, FL

Gerardo Galaviz
Inglewood, CA

Stefania Galka
Chicago, IL

Engelbaro Gammad
Mountain View, CA

Mark Gantley
Honolulu, HI

Stephen Garbitelli
Oregon City, OR

Jose Garcia
Houston, TX

Chris Garcia
Castro Valley, CA

Vincent Gardiner
Mentor, OH

Paul Garner
Irondale, AL

Joseph Gehret
Indianapolis, IN

John Giel
Orlando, FL

Chad Glendinning
Ottawa, Canada

Matthew Glover
Little Rock, AR

Justin Golna
Wellsburg, WV

Jesus Hernandez Gonzalez
Washington, DC

Felipe Gonzalez
St. Petersburg, FL

Heidi Gonzales
Flushing, MI

John-Paul Gonzalez
West Hollywood, CA

James Goodwin
Fargo, ND

Jason Gray
Peoria Heights, IL

Kevin Grimditch
Phoenix, AZ

Jeffrey Grob
Elmwood Park, IL

Janice Grochowsky
Dodge City, KS

Ralph Gross
Greenfield, WI

Alan Guanella
La Crosse, WI

Michael Hack
Bridgman, MI

James Hagel
Chestermere, Canada

Emmett Hall
Coppell, TX

John Hammond
Nashville, TN

Fredrik Hansen
Baltimore, MD

William Harkins
Mobile, AL

Paul Hartmann
Washington, DC

Andrew Haskins
Halfmoon, NY

Timothy Hedrick
Metairie, LA

Aldean Hendrickson
New Ulm, MN

Marie Hilliard
Washington, DC

Christina Hip-Flores
Brentwood, MD

Thuan Hoang
San Francisco, CA

Richard Hobbs
Cincinnati, OH

George Ryan Holly
Pembroke, Canada

Christopher House
Springfield, IL

Jimmy Hsu
Washington, DC

Kathryn Hubbard
Indianapolis, IN

Dustin Hungerford
Louisville, KY

Robert Hyde
Camillus, NY

Francisca Igweilo
Englewood, CO

Hilary Ike
Columbus, OH

Fernanda Jaimes
Austin, TX

Eileen Jaramillo
Lansing, MI

Douglas Jeffers
Austin, TX

Ronny Jenkins
Washington, DC

Bryan Jerabek
Birmingham, AL

Diana Jimenez
Lake Mary, FL

Lawrence John
Dalhart, TX

Johnson John
Beltsville, MD

Gerald Jorgensen
Dubuque, IA

Michael Joyce
St. Louis, MO

Elizabeth Kabacinski
Chicago, IL

Victoria Kaczmarek
Lansdale, PA

Thomas Kadera
Ham Lake, MN

David Keene
Chicago, IL

Adela Maria Kim
Peoria, IL

John Paul Kimes
Notre Dame, IN

William King
Emmitsburg, MD

Robert Kitsmiller
Columbus, OH

Daniela Knepper
Muskego, WI

Jose Kochuparambil
Lubbock, TX

Pierre Konja
West Bloomfield, MI

Joshua Korf
Sylvania, OH

Barbara Kosinska
Chicago, IL

Douglas Krebs
Bismarck, ND

Alexander Kreidler
Kansas City, MO

Matthew Kuettel
Saint Paul, MN

Mollie Kulig
Coventry Twp, OH

Bartosz Kunat
Biloxi, MS

Patrick Lagges
Merrillville, IN

Julio Lara
Kansas City, MO

Alexander Laschuk
Toronto, Canada

Adam Laski
Rice Lake, WI

Sarah Lauhead
Cheyenne, WY

Daniel Laurita
Athens, AL

Fiona Laverty
Jefferson City, MO

Matthew Lee
Madison, WI

John Lessard-Thibodeau
Chicopee, MA

Eric Leyble
Schriever, LA

John List
Lexington, KY

Kelly Littleton
Happy Valley, OR

Beatriz Livingston
Kansas City, MO

John LoCoco
St. Francis, WI

Douglas Loecke
Dubuque, IA

Edward Lohse
Kalamazoo, MI

Gabriel Lopez-Betanzos
Madison, WI

Elias Lorenzo
Summit, NJ

Douglas Lucia
Syracuse, NY

Paul Luniw
Terryville, CT

Gregory Luyet
Little Rock, AR

Elyn Macek
Atlanta, GA

Paul Madrid
Labadie, MO

John Maksym
Mt. Clemens, MI

W. Curtis Mallet
Lafayette, LA

Jeannine Marino
Chillum, MD

Sofia Markovich
Washington, DC

Juliette Marsh
Glendora, CA

Kurt Martens
Washington, DC

Augustine Laiju Mathew
Grants, NM

Reynaldo Matunog
Los Angeles, CA

Alberto Maullon
Houston, TX

Michael Mazza
Box Elder, SD

Valere Nkouaya Mbandji
Ottawa, Canada

Kevin W. McAuliffe
Las Vegas, NV

Joseph McCabe
Maryknoll, NY

Micheal McGavigan
Feeny, Ireland

Joseph McQuaide
Wilmington, DE

Lester Mendonsa
Calgary, Canada

Felix Menendez, STL
Smyrna, GA

George Michalek
Lansing, MI

Donna Miller
The Villages, FL

Bruce Miller
Covington, LA

Pamela Miller
Carpenter, WY

Richard Millette
Houston, TX

Edith Miranda
Oklahoma City, OK

Mariette Moan, ASCJ
New Britain, CT

Daniel Moll
Marquette, MI

Christopher Moore
Parkville, MD

Peter Mottola
Rochester, NY

Colin Mulhall
Grandville, MI

Susan Mulheron
St. Paul, MN

Patrick Mullins
Brisbane, Australia

Philip Najim
El Cajon, CA

Sateesh Narisetti
Wheeling, WV

Joseph Newton
Indianapolis, IN

Truc Nguyen
Cypress, CA

Bao Nguyen
Camarillo, CA

Benedict Nguyen
Sugar Land, TX

Kevin Niehoff
Grand Rapids, MI

Robin Nordyke
Kansas City, MO

Matthew Northenscold
St. Paul, MN

Andrew Obel
Crookston, MN

Martin Obeng
Dubuque, IA

Mary Judith O'Brien
Saginaw, MI

Kelly O'Donnell
Bakersfield, CA

Peter O'Donnell
Salina, KS

Hamilton Okeke
Ellicott City, MD

Robert Oliver
Braintree, MA

Kathryn Olsen
OK City, OK

Timothy Olson
Fargo, ND

George Oonnoonny
Buchanan, NY

Jose Opalda
Baltimore, MD

Michael Padazinski
San Francisco, CA

Roch Pagé
Ottawa, Canada

Sara Paglialunga
Fort Worth, TX

William Palladino
West Roxbury, MA

Raju Panackal
Welsh, LA

Thomas Paprocki
Springfield, IL

Vincent Parsons
Grand Island, NE

John Payne
Waddell, AZ

Mark Payne
Milwaukee, WI

F. Stephen Pedone
Worcester, MA

Lori Peery
Bigfoot, TX

Pius Pietrzyk, OP
Rome, Italy

Anthony Pileggi
Kansas City, MO

Kyle Poje
Bethesda, MD

Andrea Ponzone
Weymouth, MA

Rothell Price
Shreveport, LA

Linda Price
Scranton, PA

Frank Pugliese
Oceanside, CA

Daniel Quinan
Saint Paul, MN

Gerry Quinn
Saint Louis, MO

Francisco Quiroz
Laredo, TX

Lawrence Rasaian
Tyler, TX

Michael Ravenkamp
San Diego, CA

Thomas Reitmeyer
Austin, TX

Charles Renati
San Francisco, CA

John Renken
Ottawa, Canada

Nancy Reynolds
Louisville, KY

Michael Richard
Lafayette, LA

Mark Richards
Sacramento, CA

Kenneth Riley
Kansas City, MO

Natasha Rios
San Antonio, TX

Michael Ritty
Feura Bush, NY

Matthew Robinson
Oklahoma City, OK

Lynda Robitaille
North Vancouver, BC

Robert Rodgers
Worland, WY

Giselle Rodriguez
Orlando, FL

Francisco Rodriguez
Lodi, NJ

Zack Rodriguez
Austin, TX

Margaret Romano-Hogan
Frisco, TX

Ana Romero
Oklahoma City, OK

Benjamin Roodhouse
Jefferson City, MO

Eloise Rosenblatt, RSM
Saratoga, CA

Steve Rosera
Albuquerque, NM

Daniel Ross
Indianapolis, IN

James Rowland
Flint, TX

Rebecca Ruesch
St. Francis, WI

Mark Rutherford
Washington, DC

Anthony Saiki
Kansas City, KS

David Salvato
Crest Hill, IL

Luis Sanchez
Brownsville, TX

M. Casey Sanders
Louisville, KY

Peter Santandreu
Buffalo, NY

Noel Sanvicente
San Jose, CA

Cheryl Sarkisian
Fresno, CA

Edward Schaefer
St. Rose, IL

Mary Schaumber
DeWitt, MI

Tait Schroeder
Madison, WI

Christopher Seibt
Syracuse, NY

Eric Seitz
West Fargo, ND

J. Sessions
Chelsea, AL

Dany Shaba
El Cajon, CA

Tracey Sharp
Rancho Palos Verdes, CA

Peter Shaw
Bryson City, NC

Eduard Shestak
Old Forge, PA

Gaurav Shroff
Duluth, GA

Langes James Silva
Salt Lake City, UT

Robert Sinatra
Vineland, NJ

Christopher Singer
Erie, PA

Christopher Siuzdak
Dudley, MA

Jaroslaw Skrzypek
Honolulu, HI

Daniel Smilanic
Chicago, IL

Rosemary Smith
Jersey City, NJ

Nathaniel Sokol
Lansing, MI

Jonathan Sorensen
Grand Island, NE

Michael A. Souckar
Coral Springs, FL

Anthony Spellacy
Manor, TX

Anthony St. Louis-Sanchez
Denver, CO

Susan Stankis
Orange, CA

Richard Stansberry
Oklahoma City, OK

Anne Stephens
Fort Wayne, IN

Adam Storey
Des Moines, IA

Erin Stracener
Brentwood, TN

Mary Kay Summers
Indianapolis, IN

Marea Suozzi
Orange County, CA

John Sweeney, LC
Potomac, MD

Krzysztof Swierczynski
Forest Park, IL

David Szatkowski
Southaven, MS

Amy Tadlock
St. Paul, MN

Jobin Thomas
Elmont, NY

William Thompson
Owensboro, KY

D. Thompson
Lake Charles, LA

William Thompson
Winona, MN

Rose Marie Timmer
Toledo, OH

Myviet Tran
Carthage, MO

Gregory Trawick
Cadiz, KY

Mark Tucker
Washington, DC

Jeffrey Tudgay
Scranton, PA

Elisa Ugarte
Richmond, VA

Daniel Ulishney
North Huntingdon, PA

Rodrigo Valdivia
San Diego, CA

Lou Vallone
McKees Rocks, PA

Guadalupe Vargas
Hanford, CA

Alberto Vargas
Saginaw, MI

Paul Velazquez
Los Angeles, CA

Siobhan Verbeek
Washington, DC

Manuel Viera
Tucson, AZ

Ruben Villarreal
Lake Charles, LA

Ann Vincent
Lake Charles, LA

Victoria Vondenberger
Cincinnati, OH

Richard Wahl, CSB
Houston, TX

DeAnn Walker
Austin, TX

Marlene Weisenbeck
La Crosse, WI

Adam Westphal
Indianola, IA

Reginald Whitt
Baltimore, MD

Paul Wienhoff
Shiloh, IL

Thomas Wisniewski
Darby, PA

Daniel Witham
Seattle, WA

Geri Woodward
New Orleans, LA

Timothy Wyciskalla
Indianapolis, IN

Adrienne Yates
Chapel Hill, NC

Jose Ricardo Zanetti
Amarillo, TX

V. Ellie Zeitzmann
Houston, TX

Carter Zielinski
Emporia, KS

Made in the USA
Monee, IL
05 November 2026

67811162R00262